UNDERSTANDING CONFLICT AND WAR

VOLUME 4

WAR, POWER, PEACE

UNDERSTANDING CONFLICT AND WAR

VOLUME 4

WAR, POWER, PEACE

R. J. Rummel
University of Hawaii

SAGE PUBLICATIONS   Beverly Hills/London

For information address:

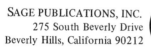
SAGE PUBLICATIONS, INC.
275 South Beverly Drive
Beverly Hills, California 90212

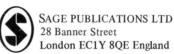
SAGE PUBLICATIONS LTD
28 Banner Street
London EC1Y 8QE England

Printed in the United States of America

Library of Congress Cataloging in Publication Data (Revised)

Rummel, Rudolph J
    Understanding conflict and war.

    Includes bibliographical references and indexes.
    CONTENTS: v. 1. The dynamic psychological field.--
v. 2. The conflict helix.--v. 3. Conflict in
perspective.--v. 4. War, power, peace.
    1. International relations--Research. I. Title,
JX1291.R8   327   74-78565
ISBN 0-470-74501-0 (v. 1)

FIRST PRINTING

CONTENTS

[5]

Contents [7]

LIST OF TABLES

LIST OF FIGURES

To freedom and dignity,
with peace.

ACKNOWLEDGEMENTS

This volume is the consummation of theoretical and empirical research that began in the late 1950s. Many people therefore have contributed in diverse ways to this product since then. Where this help has been direct I have indicated this in my preliminary and foundation publications and reports. Moreover, both the National Science Foundation and the Advanced Research Projects Agency of the Department of Defense have supported much of the basic research on which this volume is based, and have been previously acknowledged by grant and contract number in the appropriate work. However, research specific to this volume, its preparation and writing were unfunded.

Now, I simply want to express here my debt to those whose scholarly and scientific works have had the most intellectual influence on this volume and the effort underlying it: Alfred Adler, Yrjö Ahmavaara, Raymond Cattell, Ralf Dahrendorf, Bertrand de Jouvenel, Will Durant, F. A. Hayek, Immanuel Kant, Ludwig von Mises, Karl Popper, Pitirim Sorokin, Paul Ushenko, and Quincy Wright.

Finally, I wish to thank the Department of Political Science, University of Hawaii, particularly Betty M. Strom, for typing this manuscript and its many tables. And, as for my previous publications, I continue to be indebted to my wife Grace for her careful editing, demands for clarity, and help in overcoming scientific pretensions.

Chapter 1

PERSPECTIVE AND SUMMARY

Now tell us about the war,
And what they fought each other for.
                    Robert Southey, The Battle of Blenheim

1.1. UNDERSTANDING WAR

There have been about 350 wars of all kinds since the Battle of Waterloo in 1815, which once and for all defeated Napoleon's lust for power. If this number fairly well represents the frequency of war in history, there have been nearly 13,600 wars since 3,600 B.C.[1]

The toll of human misery measures around 30,000,000 direct battle deaths since Waterloo and 1,000,000,000 since 3,600 B.C. Then there are the uncountable deaths, the broken bodies and lives from the ravages and effects of these wars.

Nor has war abated. Not with civilization. Not with education and literacy. Not with burgeoning international organizations and communications. Not with the swelling library of peace plans and antiwar literature. Not with the mushrooming antiwar movements and demonstrations. In the 25 years after World War II, for so many the war to create and insure peace for generations, some 97 internal and international wars have occurred. Total deaths about equal those killed in World War II. On any single day during these 25 years slightly more than 10 internal or international wars were being fought somewhere.

Nor is war increasing. Although there are ups and downs in the intensity and scope of warfare, the historical trend is level: a little more than six major international wars per decade and 2,000,000 battle deaths. Around this trend there are at least three cycles of warfare, showing different peaks around every 10, 25, and 50 years.[2]

As I write there are wars between Ethiopia and Somalia, Vietnam and Cambodia, and Rhodesia and her Black African neighbors. Major internal wars fought with international involvement in the Western Sahara, Ethiopia, Lebanon,

Laos, Angola, Zaire, and Chad. Guerrilla and civil wars with international support and aid in Laos, Philippines, Thailand, Burma, Namibia. And major wars may again erupt in Korea and in the Middle East; and Africa is becoming another arena for a new and dangerous U.S.-Soviet confrontation.

All these data and forecasts do not aid our understanding of such international violence, of course. They are simply interesting or depressing, like information in the Guinness *Book of World Records*. Understanding requires digging beneath the numbers to the how and why of each war: the personality and perceptions of leaders, the decision-making process, the environmental and cultural limits and forces, the political and social context, and the historical grievances.

But seeking such understanding is most difficult. Certainly, bias and personal judgment color one's view of a war. But so can the images and models of war we carry around in our head. Any grasp of a specific war, say the Korean War in 1950-1953, is a melding of two sources of understanding. One is an intimate knowledge and feel for the peculiarities of the war. The second is an image of war's general nature, causes, and conditions.

But to apply such a general image one must ask what in the specific war was *common* to other wars. Was it the military superiority of the aggressor? Was it an expressed, initial lack of interest in defending the victim by the status-quo Big Power? Was it an aggressive ideology? or Common borders? or Sociocultural disparity? or Personality?

But any general image of war begs the question. Is not war unique? Perhaps war is a peculiar conjunction of events and forces within a particular situation? Possibly insight into a war comes only from a deep, historical familiarity.

After all, it is through an intimate, personal experience with our close friends and relatives, with all their virtues and vices, that enables us to see them as individuals and develop reliable expectations (predictions) of their behavior. But yet, we also find that for an understanding of those close to us we must push toward common elements. Certain common needs (hunger, sex), certain common interests (status, love), certain common psychological mechanisms (frustration, ego), certain social and cultural factors (peer-group pressure, cultural norms). Even in our closest relationships, understanding seems to presuppose a mixture of intimate personal knowledge and an insight into common causes, conditions, explanations, and so on.

Similarly with war. To understand a war or a situation in which war is likely is *partly* to know the war or situation intimately, of course. As historians, journalists, and diplomats do. But to understand also requires knowing what this war or situation has in common with other such wars or situations.

But like Chinese puzzle boxes, each contained in another, an analysis of wars' commonness includes problem upon problem nested inside. How do we define commonness? How do we determine such commonness beyond subjective impression and bias? Of what—wars, international conflict, all conflict—are we determining commonness? Indeed, how do we commonly define wars?—a legal condition, level of casualties, or size of armies involved?

These problems are just beginning. Is answering the above a matter of philosophy, history, or science? Is an empirical (operational) definition of commonness sufficient, or must we seek some essential commonness? Is it necessary also to seek a commonness in man, his relations, and his society?

The problems get deeper. What indeed is an empirical approach and how valid is it? Where do values come into the study? What do we mean by a common cause or condition? Actually, what is the ontological reality of this commonness we seek? And so on. This small list of problems could be extended easily to fill a volume.

My professional career has been involved in working through these problems. My academic search for the causes of war began as a university undergraduate in the late 1950s and continued through my MA thesis, Ph.D. dissertation, and academic career.[3]

I first assumed that all these problems could be resolved within a philosophy of science or by scientific methods and theory, particularly through an empirically tested mathematical theory of war. This, it seemed, would precisely define what was common to war, enable exact comparison and tests, and particularly permit sound predictions. And all the philosophical—the ontological, epistemological and ethical—questions were answered, I thought, by analytic philosophy, particularly logical positivism. My equation was simple: understanding war = explaining war = predicting war = scientific prediction = well-tested mathematical theory.

Problems and solutions, however, get their meaning and substance within a perspective.[4] I first approached the problems of understanding war as a theoretical (mathematical) scientist and logical positivist because my frame of reference had always been science. It was my religion. But our experience widens and deepens, our consciousness expands, and we change. Our perspective becomes uncomfortable, out of alignment with our mentality, and subsequently "clicks" into a new, more satisfactory view.

Thus, my search for an understanding of war began within a scientific perspective. But after many years this perspective simply did not provide the insight and understanding I sought, and eventually underwent several shifts. My view is now that this understanding of war requires the merging of three ways of defining truth.

One is that of "metaphysics," more correctly in this context, of metasociology. This is the understanding of the social philosopher. It is intuitive, insightful, imaginative, and of course, speculative.[5] It is concerned with essence, with definition, with being, with concepts and categories. It is Aristotlian, Hegalian, and Kantian. And it gets to the core problems of war and peace.

However, while philosophy may provide a fundamental insight into war, how do we know this insight is really significant or correct? How do we discriminate between any man's opinion, a philosopher's bias, an apologist's ideology, and truth? We cannot. Not by intuition alone. Insight must be joined with a second way of understanding.

This is with experience. Quite simply, profound insights on war and peace must stand the test of history and events. Philosophic insight must be disciplined by facts. Speculations must be tested in real life.

To be sure, facts and experience cannot replace philosophy. Facts, events, history must be interpreted. We see reality through a framework—a paradigm— which gives identity and meaning to experience. A fact in one view may not be so in another. Simply consider what are social and historical facts to a Catholic, Marxist and Liberal. Thus, facts require a philosophy. And philosophy requires facts. They are synergistic.

But, then, the history and events of war mix two kinds of experience. One is of the unique aspects of a war. The other is of those aspects common to all wars. Then, again, how do we define what is common? What is unique? This is where I admit empirical science. Quantitative methodologies in science have been devised to uncover commonalities in reality, to reduce bias and subjectivity, and to test speculations and insight. Scientific methods order our experience in a way to carve away mistaken insights and establish an empirically sound understanding of war and peace.

Or so it would seem. But there are profound epistemological problems for both the philosophical and empirical partners in this marriage. Social philosophy is seldom precise enough to provide direction to scientific methods. Intuitive insight can state profundities like (imagine this delivered with Henry Kissinger's style and intonation): "War is fundamentally caused by misperception," or "Peace is a balance of power; war, its absence." And convey meaning and cause heads to nod. But empirically, how is perception defined? Or power, or balance? Or war or peace, for that matter? And what is the proof for these insights?

Moreover, and this may be less obvious, social philosophy is mainly concerned with categories and essence. These are often untestable by empirical *science.* They constitute the givens, the assumptions. They carve out the reality in which the empirical methods provide comparison and tests. If social philosophy asserts, for example, that "conflict is a balancing of vectors of power," there is no way to test this. No explicit events to say it is right or wrong. It is a definition.[6] Nor is there any way to test the essential characterization that "man is an individual." Yet, this characterization is my starting point for understanding war and peace.[7]

This untestable nature of much social philosophy is well known and maligned among positivists or behavioralists, many of whom therefore assert the superiority of empirical science in dealing with social problems. However, what some may not appreciate is that quantitative methods also are more or less subjective and arbitrary.

Science provides rigorous methods and precise techniques. True. But it does not provide the *understanding* needed to decide between methods, the *insight* to select the proper techniques, the *intuition* to use the best rules of thumb in using a technique, and the *imagination* to put all these aspects of science together in a creative research design. Understanding, insight, intuition, and imagination must also, therefore, play a role in empirical science.

I will restrain myself with one example. The correlation coefficient seems precise. It gives an exact numerical measurement of the correlation between, say, a state's size and its wars. But consider. There are different ways of measuring size and wars and each could give a quite different correlation; the data, however measured, could be over months, years, or decades; or over states, pairs of states, or systems. Again possibly different results. More important than these obvious operational problems, is that of the correlation itself. Which of a dozen or more ways of calculating a correlation coefficient (product moment, phi, rank, tetrachoric, intraclass, and so on.) does one select? Does one transform data beforehand? Adjust the correlation for random error? And then, how does one evaluate the significance of whatever correlation coefficient is calculated? At what level of significance? What variance?

Behavioralists often mislead themselves and others. Empirical science is a rudderless ship without the command and direction given by insight and understanding. A perspective on war and peace which provides definitions, categories, and insight helps navigate empirical science.

Yet, as mentioned, although philosophy can give the command and direction it is not precise enough to draw the navigation charts. An integrative third way to truth is still needed. This is analytic theory.

A philosophy of man and his war and peace can be given rigor through analytic theory in the sense that a beautiful landscape can be represented on canvas by a selective mixture of colors and lines, a very personal feeling can be partially captured by a word or phrase, or the essence of a complex political situation can be characterized by a cartoonist. That is, analytic (logically or mathematically rigorous)[8] theory captures the structure, the main lines, of a philosophical view, and fits it into a logically articulated whole from which assertions about reality may be made.

Analytic theory adds precision, rigor, and inner consistency to a philosophical perspective, and becomes a rational framework and a precise navigational chart for empirical science. For analytic theory provides the precision to philosophy which can dictate the proper empirical methods, techniques, and operational decisions. And define what will prove or disprove the theory.

Of course, analytic theory by itself is defective, which those who push analytic models like game theory, systems theory, or mathematical communications theory may not always realize. On the philosophical side such models lose much of the richness of understanding provided by great insight and wisdom—

the feel for the nature of war and peace developed by, say, Hans Morgenthau, Quincy Wright, and Raymond Aron. Well-informed insight and intuition help in constructing good analytic theory, but analytic rigor by itself cannot replace such understanding.

Moreover, such theories must be tested and substantiated before they and their implications can at all be accepted. Anyone with some logical or mathematical training can construct an analytic theory (or model) during lunch. But the most intellectually difficult task is to construct an analytic theory which well represents the philosophical essence of war and peace and can be confirmed by empirical science.

In sum, then, the way of determining the *common* aspects of war and peace is through social philosophy, analytic theory, and empirical science. But not as separate ways heaping disparate elements together. Rather as a whole which combines them in some unified picture of man, society, conflict, war, peace. In the final analysis, then, the epistemological problem is to *artfully* paint such a picture. One which will be a communication between our intuition, reason, and experience.

Fortunately, my realization of the limits of science and the need for social philosophy and traditional scholarship in understanding war did not cancel out my previous research. Its theory and results were still valuable, but their interpretation was broadened and given a different context.[9] Much of this early work is integrated here, but anyone comparing something I wrote, say in 1965,[10] with this book will see that the approach and interpretation have altered radically.

At this point, therefore, a review of this research and its relationship to this volume should be useful.

1.2. PREVIOUS RESEARCH

In one way or another, remotely or directly, all my graduate and professional research has been on the problem of understanding war. This has been my single, superordinate passion, regardless of my change in perspective on truth or in political views.[11] Thus, my research over the past 20 years has been accumulative, fitting in various pieces, testing various techniques, establishing certain propositions about war and its context. This volume is the consummation of this work, the integrative (hopefully) volume on the subject of understanding war, the conflict out of which it grows, and peace.

This research followed a number of distinct but related lines. One line involved formal work in international relations which I discovered as an undergraduate was a field of study through which I could focus on war and peace. All my academic study through to a Ph.D. at Northwestern University (in 1963) concentrated on the foundations of international relations, and I have taught various courses on it since.

A second line of research focused on theory, especially the more analytic theories, such as systems theory, game theory, and the analytic theories of Boulding (1962), Coleman (1964), Rashevsky (1947, 1951), L. Richardson (1960, and Wright (1955: chapter 32). Although insightful and helpful in the context within which they were developed, none of these seemed adequate theories of or approaches to war. Learning from such work, however, I then tried to develop my own theoretical approach, which I published in 1965 as "A Field Theory of Social Action." This was meant to be a very general, mathematical theory of social relations, and applicable to international relations in a way to fit war and its causes into a larger social context.

I saw war theoretically as a type of behavior relative to other international behavior within a field of states, and as a consequence of diverse field forces reflected in the relative social, economic, political, culture, and geographic distances between states. The theoretical equation was simple: conflict or war between states equals (is a resolution of) the sum of their weighted vector distances (forces). This equation, much elaborated and clarified, still forms a basic equation of this volume.

I continued this theoretical effort throughout the years, trying in various ways to improve on it and incorporate into it competing theories. These efforts have been published in my *Field Theory Evolving* (1977).

A third line of research involved appropriate methods for operationalizing and testing a theory of war and generating empirical concepts that could be incorporated in such a theory. Multivariate methods seemed most appropriate in this regard, especially factor analysis. The fruits of this methodological research and work on factor analysis (along with empirical findings) was published in my *Applied Factor Analysis* (1970). Through this book I hoped to stimulate others to employ such systematic research to understanding war and to provide for reference a central publication elaborating the basic methodologies I was using.

A fourth line was strictly empirical. Before 1965 I carried out quantitative empirical analyses (1963, 1963a, 1966a, 1972) [12] in order to generate findings and concepts that could subsequently inform my attempt to develop a theory of war. [13] And after such a theory was first sketched in 1965, I then directed this empirical effort to operationalizing concepts in the theory, as published in *National Attributes and Behavior* (1978); and testing the theory, as published in *Field Theory Evolving* (1977).

A fifth line involved understanding man, society, and conflict. Along with my formal work in international relations I had also studied analytic philosophy and the social sciences. But as I focused on the scientific approach, especially on operationalizing and testing field theory, I had little time to spare for indirectly related research or reading.

However, as I began to shift my perspective to one recognizing the value of social philosophy for understanding war I made such study a central part of my research. The result of this was, Volume 1, *The Dynamic Psychological Field* [14] (for philosophical and psychological foundations), Volume 2, *The Conflict Helix* (for sociological and cultural foundations, and an understanding of conflict generally), and Volume 3, *Conflict in Perspective* (for competing theories of conflict).

These five lines of research (international relations; theory; methodologies; empirical analysis; and man, society, and conflict) come together in this book. But there is a sixth line of research not reflected here, no doubt perplexing to my colleagues in peace research, and which will be part of Volume 5. That concerns the implications of all this for eliminating or controlling war generally, and particularly, for avoiding nuclear war.[15]

I am not seeking to understand war out of scientific curiosity. I am devoted to ending war. I was a pacifist in my youth and my life since has been an inner struggle between the hatred of war and the reality of contending interests and powers, aggrandizing leaders and states, and of aggressive antidemocratic and totalitarian ideologies. I simply cannot confront the reality of Hitler's cold-blooded execution of six million Jews and accept the pacifist argument that no war is justified. Nor can I similarly accept the enslavement of tens of millions by communist leaders and their wanton extermination of many more millions than even Hitler killed. Nor can I argue that the risk of war is totally unacceptable and that we should unilaterally disarm, leaving ourselves and the rest of the world vulnerable to similar enslavement. The problem as I now see it is how to minimize the risk of war, especially nuclear war, and still protect what freedoms we have against aggressive totalitarianism.

Accordingly, when in 1975 my empirical research for this *Volume* was completed [16] it seemed that our foreign and defense policies were the opposite of that which would preserve nuclear peace with freedom. I was convinced that the results showed the foreign policy of détente to be based on false premises about international relations and conflict; and that this policy and associated adverse military trends were in fact *increasing* the likelihood of war. And time then seemed critical and still does.

Rather than wait until this volume was finished, therefore, on the basis of the empirical results then available and some additional analysis of the military balance, I wrote the warning, *Peace Endangered: The Reality of Détente* (1976a), for the general public. The results that I have accumulated since are presented here [17] even more confirm my view of our danger.

Those who quantitatively study war and peace are usually quite dovish [18] on questions of U.S.-Soviet relations, if not, as among many European peace researchers, downright hostile to any hint of anticommunism or militarism. This community has received my apostasy with less than open arms and to some even my more scientific writing in this area are right-wing "diatribes."[19]

In any case, this volume presents the premises and evidence for these applied conclusions on détente in as rigorously objective, scholarly, and scientific manner as I could make them. All evidence I could find has been included. Data and cases have been analyzed regardless of region, time, or source. The most objective methods have been used. I have searched the available systematic literature for additional evidence. The results have been given or referenced so that they may be tested or assessed by others, whether from the left or right.

1.3. ON THE ORGANIZATION OF THIS VOLUME

The attempt to merge social philosophy, analytic theory, and empirical analysis in this volume has created a number of organizational problems, especially because I am writing for a diverse audience of interested laymen, concerned professionals, and quantitative analysts. This creates a dynamic tension between understandability and technical arguments, between explanations and supporting data and evidence. And this tension changes from chapter to chapter, part to part. My guiding organizational principle has been to make everything as clear as possible to the layman, and if technical material is presented, to rephrase this in nontechnical terms. Therefore, even the most technical sections will have paragraphs of descriptions or explanations in what, I hope, is plain English.

With this in mind, the conceptual and technical organization is linear: each chapter more or less depends on and assumes the previous chapters, with the technical material interspersed among the chapters. This made dividing the volume into technical and nontechnical halves impractical. Therefore, I followed a compromise course. Wherever possible, I have put the technical or systematic material in a chapter appendix or footnote, with this material restated in nontechnical terms in the body of the chapter.

This is not entirely satisfactory and has led to some repetition. Moreover, some chapters (like chapters 5 and 6) were so integrated that I could not segregate the technical without seriously weakening the presentation.

Table 1.1 may be helpful in guiding the reader. For those with little technical background, it would still be helpful to skim the more technical chapters because, as mentioned, the results and arguments often are restated in nontechnical terms.

There is much packed in this and previous volumes. In order to pull out clearly and concisely what I see as essential I have used five approaches.

One is to reduce the empirical conclusions on international conflict, violence, and war to 54 explicit propositions on their phases, causes and conditions, end, and nature. These are given in the appendices of chapters 15-18.

A second approach is to further abstract from Volumes 1-4 the most general empirical propositions on social conflict (of which international conflict and war are subtypes). These are presented in chapter 19.

A third approach is to distill from these volumes major principles [20] of man, interpersonal relations, society, and international relations which bear on peace and conflict, violence, and war. These constitute the concluding chapter 20. As a nontechnical propositional overview, chapters 19 and 20 might be read first.

TABLE 1.1: Technical Organization of This Volume

PART	CHAPTER/APPENDIX	TECHNICAL SCALE* 1	2	3	4	5
I	Chapter 1					
	Chapter 2	Yes				
	Chapter 3	Yes				
II	Chapter 4		Yes			
	Chapter 5			Yes		
	Chapter 6			Yes		
III	Chapter 7		Yes			
	Chapter 8				Yes	
	Chapter 9	Yes				
	Appendix 9A					Yes
IV	Chapter 10		Yes			
	Chapter 11			Yes		
	Chapter 12	Yes				
	Chapter 13	Yes				
V	Chapter 14	Yes				
	Chapter 15	Yes				
	Appendix 15A			Yes		
	Chapter 16	Yes				
	Appendix 16A	Yes				
	Appendix 16B		Yes			
	Appendix 16C			Yes		
	Chapter 17	Yes				
	Appendix 17A	Yes				
	Chapter 18	Yes				
	Appendix 18A		Yes			
VI	Chapter 19	Yes				
	Appendix 19A		Yes			
	Chapter 20	Yes				
	Appendix I				Yes	
	Appendix II		Yes			
	Appendix III		Yes			

*1 = least technical (laymen's level)
 5 = most technical

A fourth approach is to provide a summary outline of the major points and conclusions of each chapter. This is in the following section, below.

And a fifth approach is to rewrite Volumes 1-4 in entirely nontechnical language for the layman, and introductory undergraduate classes in social conflict and war. This writing is now underway and the result may be published as *In the Minds of Men* (tentative title) in late 1979 or early 1980.

In the original outlines of this Volume I had planned to apply the principles and propositions developed here to analyze several historical and contemporary wars. This would exemplify the value of these results and provide, I felt, another way of concretely understanding their meaning. However, page limitations have forced me to postpone this "historical reconstruction" until the completion of Volume 5.

Because of the omission of such case studies this volume deals almost entirely at the abstract and general level. My primary concern here is to understand war in terms of its common aspects. I am after generalizations. Thus, specific events, conflicts, crises, engagements, and war are data points. Characteristics, personalities, trends, forces, and the like are variables. My question is: *What is it about any particular conflict or war that is common to other conflicts of wars? Specifically, what are the common phases, causes and conditions, ending, and aspects of international conflict?* And I try to answer this through a synthesis of philosophy, theory, and empirical analysis.

Finally, this work and supporting volumes 1-3 are certainly not definitive, but at most simply another scholarly and scientific step towards a socially significant irenology—a science of peace. Perhaps no one can see better than I that this volume raises a host of new questions, new problems, new directions.

I do not pretend to have established any final answers. Truth emerges from the balancing of multiple facts, perspectives, approaches, and interpretations. What is presented here is no more than a few more pieces fitted together in the puzzle of war and peace. My hope is that this volume will challenge other scholars and scientists whose critical evaluation, checking, testing, and reformulation will eventually evolve into a perspective that will give us all the foundation for understanding war and peace in a way to better mankind.

Now, here are my truths. Be at them.

For if they withstand your onslaught, or if you prove them wrong, we shall all gain.

And I will cheer you.

1.4. SUMMARY AND OVERVIEW

Two concluding summaries are given at the end of the volume. One in terms of *propositions* (chapter 19) and the other in terms of *principles* (chapter 20). Here I will outline the major points and ideas that lead up to them, and then concisely abridge both the propositions and principles.

On International Relations

International conflict and war occur within a dynamic field we call international relations. In the opening, substantive chapter 2, I therefore first consider the nature of international relations and conclude the following:

(1) International relations is man's largest *society*.

(2) It is an exchange society dominated by *bargaining power*.

(3) It is governed by a *libertarian political system*.

Thus, international relations is seen as a normatively integrated system with a division of labor, expectations, and status quo. It is neither chaotic nor Hobbes' state of nature.

In chapter 3, I then consider international relations further, and focus especially on its actors. I make these points.

(4) Of all larger societies, international relations is closest to a dynamic *field* of spontaneously interacting members.

(5) One kind of actor is the state-authority, whose behavior contributes to locating the state in the international field.

(6) Other actors are the individual, and leaders of internal and international groups and organizations.

(7) Thus, the international field is a mixture of interstate, intersocietal and interpersonal relations. The field is delimited by the behavior and attributes of individuals, internal or international groups and organizations, and states.

(8) The mixture of relations among the different actors in the field is mainly shaped by and is a consequence of state *power*.

On International Behavior

War is a form of international behavior and understanding it first requires an appreciation of how and why states behave in general. Part II concerns this general behavior, with chapter 4 focusing on its theoretical and empirical components. The conclusions are as follows.

(1) International *behavior* can be meaningfully separated into acts, actions, practices, and reflexes. It has a direction, as to whether it is solidary or antagonistic; an intensity; an extensity; a duration; and, more or less, organization.

(2) These aspects of behavior combine into three *theoretical components* of behavior: *familistic, compulsory,* and *contractual*.

(3) These theoretical components are reflected in a number of independent *empirical components* (or patterns) of international behavior: transactions, relative exports, foreign students, international organizations, alignment, negative behavior, military violence, and antiforeign behavior.

(4) The familistic and contractual empirical components manifest associated *structures of expectations* (as defined and discussed in Volume 2, 1976: passim); the compulsory empirical components manifest the *breakdown and restructuring of expectations*.

(5) Cooperative and conflictful components (or patterns) of behavior are empirically *independent*.

Chapter 4 defines general components of behavior. The problem, however, is to relate these to the individual actor and his *common* behavior. For it is ultimately the common aspects of conflict and especially war that are the focus. This is the job of chapter 5. Its points are these.

(6) The overall, manifest components of behavior delineate the *common behavioral dispositions* of actors in the field.

(7) The *common behavior* of an actor is the product of his *behavioral dispositions* and his *expectations* of the outcome of his behavior.

Expectations are thus central to understanding international behavior, and specifically, conflict and war. But then, this begs the question about what influences or affects expectations and associated dispositions. Chapter 6 continues the analysis of behavior by bringing in the *situation* and argues the following.

(8) Each actor behaves within a *situation* as he uniquely perceives it.

(9) Each actor's *expectations* are related to a specific situation.

(10) An actor's *common behavior within a situation* is a product of his general dispositions and his expectations of the outcome of this behavior within the specific situation.

(11) An actor's *overall common behavior* is an aggregate of his situational behaviors.

Chapter 6 thus unifies within a common framework the crucial concepts of behavior, expectations, perception, and situation.

On the International Field

Part III now explicitly considers the field within which actors behave commonly in terms of perceived situations and situational expectations. The first concern, which is taken up in chapter 7, is the common international, sociocultural components delineating this field for all actors (individual, group, and state). Chapter 7 concludes the following.

(1) The *common space-time components* of the international field are: wealth, power, totalitarianism, authoritarianism, size, social conflict, Catholic culture, density, diversity, and import dependency.

(2) Wealth, power, totalitarianism (versus liberal democracy) and authoritarianism (versus liberal democracy) are the *primary components* of states.

(3) The common components reflect various *structures of expectations* within each state through which actors understand and perceive each other.

(4) The *relative attitudes* and *capabilities* of actors lie along their *distance vectors* on the field's components. These distance vectors (such as the difference in wealth or power) therefore measure *potential forces* in the field.

(5) These potentials (attitudes and capabilities) are transformed into active *interests* and *capabilities* by an actor's *perception* of a *situation*. This perception energizes the disposition of an actor to behave towards another in a certain way. Leaving aside unique influences, behavioral dispositions in a situation are a product of interests and capabilities (distances), and the situational perceptions.

Chapter 8 now makes the equation of interests and capabilities more precise, bringing in explicitly the will of the actor. It argues these points.

(6) The actor is *individualistic*: his particular interests and capabilities, and independent *will* play a role in his behavior. His behavior is partly patterned, partly unique; partly due to common and partly individualistic interests and capabilities; partly to a will influenced by common social forces and partly to an independent will.

(7) As pointed out in chapter 6, behavioral dispositions are a product of interests and capabilities, and the perceived situation. But common behavior is a product of these same dispositions and situational expectations. Therefore, within a *situation* an actor's *common behavior* is partly explained by the product of his common *interests* and *capabilities,* and his situational *expectations* and *perceptions*.

Chapter 9 then integrates chapters 4-8 in order to comprehensively and generally, analytically and empirically, understand the international field. The chapter also has an appendix which shows how the defined relationships and concepts should be measured and empirically specified, and presents comprehensive empirical results. The major empirical conclusions of the chapter are as follows.

(8) Across situations in the field, power is the primary force vector of behavior.

(9) Situations involving perceived coercive power most often also entail expectations associated with possible compulsory behavior. That is, coercive power primarily is a force towards *conflict behavior.*

(10) Of all behavioral dispositions, an actor most often and highly expects desirable outcomes for its *contractual behavior* in terms of his perception of another's interests and capabilities. That is, distance-forces most affect contractual behavior. This is especially true of *political distances.*

(11) In the field, dispositions towards *military violence* are among all behavioral dispositions most subject to unique influences and will.

(12) The most probable situation in the field is one in which *political distance* is a force towards *contractual behavior* (participation in international organizations, diplomatic relations, trade, alliances, and so on.)

(13) As a force, *wealth* (rich-poor gap) is less important than political and power distances. What influences it does have is on contractual behavior.

On the International Conflict Helix

The previous chapters describes the international field in general, centering on common behavior, and its causes and conditions. In part III, I now focus this discussion and the background in Volume 2 on international conflict, violence, and war. The dominant perspective is of conflict as a process through which the parties establish a balance of powers and an associated structure of expectations. This balance and these expectations then define peace and harmony, and enable international cooperation and a division of labor.

The chapters treat successively each phase in the process of conflict. Chapter 10 begins with latent conflict, and makes these assertions.

(1) The components of the international field define the *potentiality* for conflict: the *conflict space*. The potential forces towards conflict are spread throughout this field and are seated in the meanings, values, norms, status, and class of international actors.

(2) As actors become *aware* of each other, potentiality for conflict is transformed into a latent *disposition* to conflict: a *structure of conflict*. This disposition is of opposing *attitudes* (goals and means) and their attendant resources (relative *capabilities*). These latent attitudes and capabilities to conflict lie along the *distance vectors* between actors on the sociocultural components of the field.

(3) Within a perceived *situation,* needs for security, self-assertion, protectiveness, and so on, become stimulated and energize attitudes. That is, stimulated *needs* empower dispositions and transform them into active *interests* seeking gratification. Active opposing interests and relative capabilities which are reflected in the distance vectors between actors define the actor's disposition to conflict within a *situation of conflict.*

(4) How these active dispositions to conflict will be manifested depends on an actor's *situational expectations.*

Interests, capabilities, expectations, and perceived situations define the latent strain towards conflict. In chapter 11 I consider what stimulates and conditions the manifestation of this conflict. I conclude as follows.

(5) The manifestation of a conflict initially requires the *will* to conflict and some *trigger* event. The likelihood of a trigger is a matter of time and the intensity of the active disposition (interests and capabilities) towards action.

(6) The trigger provokes the will, the will decides on action, and preparations are made. This comprises the *situation of uncertainty,* the initial phase of conflict behavior.

(7) This situation of uncertainty is reflected in an *empirical* pattern (component) of conflict behavior.

The situation of uncertainty leads to the balancing of powers, the actual confrontation of opposing interests. In chapter 12 I now detail this balancing and state the following.

(8) International conflict behavior, violence, and war mirror an under-lying *balancing* of opposing *interests, capabilities,* and *wills.* This is a *bargaining process* determining the real goals of the parties, their strength of motivation; their actual relative military and economic power, national morale, and qualities of leadership; and will power.

(9) The balancing of powers entails three *subphases*: status quo testing; and actual test of powers, which may involve coercion, force, or noncoercive balancing; and termination.

(10) The results of status quo testing may lead to a coercive or noncoer-cive confrontation or *termination* of the conflict, depending on what the testing reveals about the others' interests, capabilities, and will.

(11) Once a confrontation occurs, all paths lead primarily to accommoda-tions, except when the conflict escalates to force.

(12) There is a path which is an alternative to coercion in a conflict, which involves the use of bargaining (exchange), intellectual, author-itative, or other *noncoercive powers.* Therefore, some manifest be-havior in the balancing of powers may be *cooperative* (e.g., offers of aid, promises, acceptance of implicit rules governing the conflict.)

(13) The coercive *subphase* in the balancing of power is manifested in three ways: through verbal or written threats (and warnings), through threatening actions, or through applying deprivations or violence.

(14) *Coercion* acts on the will. It is psychological. *Force* acts on the will's means: its body, capability, or resources. Wars often are coercive violence; that is, a psychological manifestation, a test of will.

(15) The *termination* of conflict behavior may be through accommoda-tions, conquest, submission or withdrawal, or conflict behavior may just die away. In any case the outcome is a *balance of powers.*

(16) All conflict dynamics lead eventually to a new *balance of powers,* a new equilibrium of interests, capabilities, and wills, supporting a new structure of expectations—a new peace.

The final chapter in part III compares this dynamics of conflict—the bal-ancing of powers—to those "models" proposed by others, namely Richard Barringer, F.S. Northedge and M. D. Donelan, Quincy Wright, and Herman Kahn. Chapter 13 then concludes the following.

(17) Except for the conflict helix, dynamic models focus wholly on interstate conflict involving the threat or actuality of military vio-lence. They are not meant to be applicable to processes of conflict within states, groups, or between individuals.

(18) All models begin with some conception of *latency,* a situation out of which conflict behavior develops.

(19) The *dynamic elements* differ between models. For some they are wholly physical. For the conflict helix these elements are psycholog-ical, involving shifts in forms of power.

(20) The conflict helix uniquely defines a separate path involving *non-coercive powers,* such as bargaining and persuasion.

(21) The helix uniquely distinguishes *force* from *coercion.*

(22) Only in the helix is a clear outcome in terms of a balance of powers a part of the process; and this balance an explicit part of a larger process of establishing order. In short, conflict, peace, and cooperation are tied together.

On the Empirical Balancing of Powers

Part IV then takes up the empirical propositions on international conflict, violence and war that are either explicit or implicit in previous chapters and volumes. And chapter 14 is simply introductory to this effort. I explain the manner in which the propositions are formulated and the types of evidence, and note this.

(1) The two sources of *evidence* used are (a) the published and unpublished (listed in appendix I) research from my Dimensionality of Nations Project, and (b) the systematic literature on international relations and foreign policy (as listed in appendix III).

(2) The evidence for each proposition is *organized* by case, state, dyad, and system levels, and whether it is static or dynamic.

(3) The evidence is *rated* as to whether it is positive or negative for each proposition and how strongly.

Chapter 15 then presents six propositions on the dynamics of conflict behavior—on its phases. The evidence presented in the appendix to the chapter supports the following.

(4) Conflict Behavior manifests a preconfrontation and uncertainty phase, different coercive versus noncoercive paths in the balancing of powers, different subphases, underlying hostility, reciprocity, and crisis.

(5) Empirically, Conflict Behavior consists of a number of separate and distinct *components*—patterns manifesting the subphases in the process of balancing: antiforeign behavior, preparations, negative communications, negative (nonviolent) actions/sanctions, low-level military violence, bargaining, persuasion, and negotiation.

Chapter 16 next presents empirical propositions on the causes and conditions of conflict, violence, and war, and shows in its appendices (16B and 16C) that the evidence supports the following.

(6) International Conflict Behavior is:

(a) *caused* by opposing interests and capabilities (specific sociocultural differences and similarities between the parties), contact and salience (awareness), significant change in the balance of powers, individual perceptions and expectations, a disrupted structure of expectations, and a will-to-conflict;

(b) *aggravated* by sociocultural dissimilarity, cognitive imbalance, status difference, and coercive state power;

(c) *inhibited* by sociocultural similarity, cognitive balance, status similarity, decentralized or weak coercive state power;

(d) *triggered* by perception of opportunity, threat, or injustice; or by surprise.
(7) In addition to the above general causes of Conflict Behavior, *nonviolent conflict behavior* and *low-level violence* are:
   (a) *aggravated* by cross-pressures;
   (b) *inhibited* by system polarity (centralization of coercive power), and a stable status quo;
(8) In addition to the above general causes of Conflict Behavior, *violence* (including *war*) is:
   (a) *caused* by authoritarian and totalitarian states, status quo disruption, and confidence in success;
   (b) *aggravated* by system polarity (centralization of coercive power), Big Power intervention, weakness of the status quo power, credibility at stake, and honor at stake;
   (c) *inhibited* by cross pressures, internal freedom, strength of the status quo power, and world opinion.
(9) In addition, *war* is:
   (a) uniquely *aggravated* by power parity;
   (b) uniquely *inhibited* by power disparity.
(10) The necessary and sufficient cause of international conflict behavior, violence, and war is a disruption of the structure of expectations between the parties.

Chapter 17 now focuses on the ending of conflict and states seven empirical propositions. The evidence given in its appendix supports the following.

(11) Conflict will end when a *mutual balance* in the *interests, capabilities* and *wills* of the parties has been achieved. This psychological equilibrium in the minds of the participants is the only *necessary and sufficient condition* for ending conflict behavior.
(12) The conditions otherwise facilitating, easing, hastening the end of *war* are domestic opposition, consistent expectations of the outcome between the parties, shift in military power, and ideological devaluation of the conflict.

Chapter 18 finally concludes this empirical Part by extracting from field theory and the previous volumes the propositions concerning the nature of international conflict. The evidence provided in the appendix to the chapter supports the following:

(13) At the highest level of abstraction, *international conflicts* are independent, helixical, uncorrelated with cooperation, and independent of internal conflict behavior.
(14) *Wars* are state specific, cyclic, neither increasing nor decreasing in trend, and their peaks are correlated with the peaks in internal war.

The Conclusion

The final part VI has two purposes. One is to consolidate the propositions presented in the previous part, in Volume 2, and in *Field Theory Evolving* into a set of *primary empirical propositions*. These are presented in chapter 19, which asserts the following.

(1) Overall, for *conflict* (international, internal, interpersonal) the empirical conclusions are that:
   (a) disrupted expectations cause conflict behavior;
   (b) power shapes conflict;
   (c) freedom minimizes violence;
   (d) cooperation and conflict behavior are independent;
   (e) change produces conflict;
   (f) conflict takes place in a situation;
   (g) individual perceptions and expectations condition conflict; and
   (h) sociocultural distances affect conflict.

(2) These empirical conclusions get their meaning and substance from a perspective on conflict, which is:
   (a) conflict is a process of establishing a balance of powers and associated structure of expectations;
   (b) peace, harmony, and cooperation are a structure of expectations congruent with a balance of powers; and
   (c) within a closed system conflict tends to become less intense and frequent and peace more enduring.

Finally, chapter 20 concludes Volumes 1-4 by distilling all into the following few basic principles.[20]

(3) *Psychologically*, man is an individual. His perception is subjective. He behaves to achieve, particularly to enhance his self-esteem, and his expectations of the outcome guide this behavior. And he is responsible for this behavior (he has free will).

(4) *Interpersonally*, through conflict man negotiates a social contract. Now, man communicates as a field of expression, and produces effects. His interpersonal conflict is then a means of communication and a balancing of these effects (powers)—an adjustment of expectations to power. His cooperation then depends on this structure of expectations; and a subsequent gap between these expectations and power causes new conflict. But (other things being constant) in time this conflict will become less intense, peace more lasting.

(5) *Socially*, power shapes conflict. Man's interpersonal principles apply to societies, which are generally trisocial: three types of society congruent with three types of political systems, of conflict, and of peace. A gap between the status quo and power causes social violence. And the more government, the more such violence.

(6) *Internationally*, peace is a social contract. International relations is a social field and an exchange society, in which violence does not occur between internally free states. War requires that at least one of the participants is authoritarian or totalitarian and then is a means for negotiating an alignment of the status quo with the balance of powers.

NOTES

1. For these and the following figures I am drawing on the quantitative compilations and estimates of Beer (1974), Kende (n.d., 1971), Singer and Small (1972), L. Richardson (1960a), and R. Richardson (1966).

2. For a discussion of these cycles and their evidence, see appendix 18A, proposition 18.7.

3. For an intellectual autobiography, see Rummel (1976b).

4. That we see reality through a perspective is a basic philosophical position I have taken in these volumes (of *Understanding Conflict and War*). It is philosophically developed in Volume 1 (1975: chapters 7-8 and *passim*). It is also used as an introductory theme in Volume 2 (1976: section 1.1). The idea of a paradigm captures much of what I have in mind (Kuhn, 1962).

5. See Volume 1 (1975: 8-10) for a relevant discussion of metaphysics.

6. This is the definition of conflict I give in Volume 1 (1975: 238).

7. It is the First Master Principle given in chapter 20.

8. Some readers might think of a mathematical or simulation model in this regard. It should be understood, however, that a model is meant to simply fit empirical reality, whereas an analytic theory is meant to capture the nature of things that underlie the empirical world.

9. For example, in my early factor analyses (Rummel, 1963) the results were seen then as simply empirical dimensions—concepts meant to be integrated eventually into theory. Now, I see these dimensions as underlying latent functions (components), in the sense of Volume 1 (1975: chapters 9-10). Chapters 4 and 7 here also exemplify a more philosophical interpretation of such dimensions.

10. For example, see Rummel (1965), also partially reprinted in Rummel (1977).

11. From non-Marxist socialist to democratic socialist to libertarian. See Rummel (1976b).

12. The basic empirical work published in Rummel (1972) was completed before 1965.

13. At this time there were still very few empirical analyses of war, or international violence and conflict. The only major works were by Sorokin (1937-1941, 1957), Wright (1942), and L. Richardson (1960, 1960a). My 1963 study was the first extensive multivariate analyses across many nations and types of conflict. Thus, there was little accumulated empirical foundation for theorizing. My awareness of this need was my major reason for joining the Dimensionality of Nations (DON) Project in 1962—a strictly empirical effort then—which subsequently became the project framework for most of my research. See, for example, appendix I. The Don project is more extensively described in Hoole and Zinnes (1976: part III).

14. Volume 1 apparently has been confusing to some readers who expected an extensive discussion of conflict and war. The book was not meant to present nor be an analysis of either conflict or war, as was clearly indicated in the introduction. I intended it to stand on its own as a philosophical and psychological analysis of man, and thus be a solid foundation for the later analysis of society and conflict (Volume 2), and international relations as a type of society (this Volume).

Volume 1 was originally written to be published only as *The Dynamic Psychological Field*. But after all but its introduction was completed, Sage suggested (and I accepted) publishing it as part of a series called *Understanding Conflict and War*. At the time I did not know that the series title would be the major title of Volume 1.

15. In other words, Volumes 1-4 have been concerned with the *plane of reality*. Volume 5 will consider the *plane of morality*, especially the region where the two planes overlap. On this distinction, see Volume 2 (section 1.1).

16. I had yet to do the systematic survey of the literature for relevant evidence. See appendix III.

17. All these results are brought together as evidence for Propositions 16.3, 16.18, and 16.21 in appendix 16B; and Propositions 18.2 in appendix 18A. Virtually all the propositions in these appendices are also related in one way or another to assessing détente and U.S.-Soviet relations. In a more abstract fashion, the results given in appendix 9A also are consistent with my criticism of détente.

18. The labels "dove" and "hawk" are of course stereotypes, but do capture a difference in attitudes comprising two perspectives on foreign policy. The dove tends to fear nuclear war above all, and sees a communist threat as much less serious, perhaps even less so than militarism or a resurgent fascism. Moreover, the dove is disposed towards negotiation of differences, cooperative exchanges, and comprehensive arms control agreements and unilateral arms limitation (if not outright disarmament) as the best ways of preserving peace.

The hawk, however, fears both nuclear war and communism about equally, and perhaps communism to an even greater extent for some. The Soviet Union is viewed as driven by an aggressive ideology bent on world domination. And political power and military superiority are seen as the means by which communism can be contained and the nuclear peace preserved. Arms control has a role for many hawks, but it must be negotiated with care that the fundamental balance of power maintaining the peace and Western strength is not upset.

There are, of course, variants and extremes of both positions, from the pacifist and unilateral disarmer at one end to the absolute anticommunist, and "roll them back" advocate, at the other end.

My position, insofar as it can be labelled, is as a moderate hawk. I see nuclear war and communism as twin evils; I view strong Western interests, superior military capability, and resolute will as necessary to preserve the peace with freedom and dignity. But I also perceive this strength as a framework within which arms control can be vigorously pursued in order to lessen the danger of misunderstanding, miscommunication, or accident; and cooperative exchange can be sought, not as a way to peace but for our mutual benefit, and to help open totalitarian communism to the outside.

19. This word was used by a reviewer of my paper on the U.S.-USSR military balance (1977a). One academic peace researcher frankly admitted that even were I correct, even were the risk of nuclear war or Soviet domination made likely by weakening American defenses (among other things), then she still could not support increasing defense expenditures. Clearly, her antimilitary position was an end, not a means. This, it appears to me, is true of so many working in this area.

20. A principle is fundamental, often nonempirical. See the opening quote of Wang Fu-chih in chapter 2.

PART I

INTRODUCTION

Peace makes plentie, plentie makes pride,
Pride breeds quarrel, and quarrel brings warre:
Warre brings spoile, and spoile povertie,
Povertie pacience, and pacience peace:
So peace brings warre and warre brings peace.
                        George Puttenham, *The Art of English Poesie, 1589*

Chapter 2

INTERNATIONAL RELATIONS

At bottom, principle is not a finished product that can be grasped. It is invisible. The details and order of material force is a principle that is visible. Therefore, the first time there is any principle is when it is seen in material force. After principles have thus been found, they of course appear to become tendencies.
Wang Fu-chih, *Ch'uan-shan i-shu* [1619-1692]

International relations, world politics, transnational relations, global society. This sphere of diplomacy and war, treaties and alliances, aid and trade, migration and tourists. This arena of empires, international organizations, states, nations, governments, groups and individuals. This greatest theater of man. What is its essence?

First, *international relations compose man's largest society.*[1] Since the Age of Colonization in the eighteenth century, international relations have encompassed the globe. There is now a worldwide system of communication regulated by international organizations (such as the Universal Postal Union, International Telecommunication Union, and Intergovernmental Copyright Committee), involving mail, telegrams, radio, television, newspapers, periodicals, and books. There is a global transportation system involving international shipping lines, and especially, the airlines regulated by the International Civil Aviation Organization. There is an extensive worldwide trade and division of labor, with states and multinational corporations specializing in extractive industries, forestry, fishing, food crops, or manufacturing. There are international social norms that frame the variety of interaction among states and international groups, some of which have the status of international law. There is a stratification system recognized by all and dividing states into those with wealth, power or prestige, and those without.[2] There is a class system subordinating many states to some others who can command obedience,[3] such as among Soviet satellites. And there is a culture, of which the dominant language is English, with norms emphasizing the sovereignty, independence and equality of states, and valuing truth,[4] education and knowledge, development, science, planning, and the use of governmental institutions and coercion to create equality and social justice.[5]

International society is riven and, in Simmel's (1955) useful expression, "sewn together" by cross-cutting conflicts.[6] In my terms, this society is a moving complex of overlapping and nested structures and situations of conflict, power balancing, balances of powers, and structures of expectations. The keynote is change, alteration, transformation, and the mechanism and manifestation of this is conflict behavior.

As do all societies, international society has two faces. One is of conflict, change, a struggle and dialectic of power. The other is equilibrium, societal norms and structures which at any one point in time appear to describe society. Indeed, without a process or conflict view of international society, the normal state of affairs is stability, of functions maintaining the system and adjusting individuals to it. Indeed, within this snapshot view international conflict appears deviant, an aberration of the system. Consensus and equilibrium rather than conflict would be the defining characteristics of the society.[7]

This perspective, so rightly identified with Talcott Parsons' later work (1958) for societies in general, appears at first to contradict the conflict view of international relations. However, if we consider the equilibrium perspective to be, *essentially,* that international society comprises a system of meanings, values and norms (1) according to which its members regulate their behavior, (2) in which they are socialized, (3) which comprise a relatively persistent equilibrium among their needs and interests, and (4) is at the core a causal-functional (integrated) unity, then at the same time, international society can be seen as changing configurations of power and balancing: a conflict helix.

Now, international actors are continuously entering into new power balances, behaving within existing structures of expectations undergirded by previous balances. These structures exist at different levels of specificity and formalization. Some may be merely intuitive and even unconscious understandings between actors, such as between leaders, diplomats, or international businessmen. As such structures exist through time they can become increasingly crystallized, to develop a rule-inertia, which is the sociological counterpart of habit at the psychological level. Nonetheless, these structures remain informal—personal understandings between individuals.[8]

In international relations, many structures of expectations are formalized, involving written agreements, contracts, or treaties defining the rights and obligations of cosigners. Some structures of expectations (like the UN Charter) formalize *law norms,* which define the membership in the structure, the rights and obligations of members, and authoritative roles (positions). Authoritative roles are those which within the structure of expectations carry the right to give certain commands for their incumbents and the obligation to obey for the other members. They carry the right to punish disobedience. In the development of law norms and authoritative roles evolves the sociological *group.* In international society the state is one such group. International organization is another.

The multitude of groups in society display concretely the major expectations ordering individuals. They show how structures can be nested (a state is in UNESCO which is part of the UN), independent (such as the Catholic church and ASEAN) or overlap (such as NATO and the EEC). But it should be clear that a group is simply a phase in the eternal process of social balancing, albeit of longer duration than less formal structures of expectations. An international group represents but a certain formalization of the balance of interests, capabilities, and expectations of members.

In this sense, a group is a point of equilibrium, a balance of values and norms. Without a knowledge of the prior conflict process or the possible future disruption, a group such as Ethiopia, the Arab League, or the Warsaw Pact may appear stable. Consensus and functional maintenance will appear the case, as indeed it is if one views a group's history only through the existing, formalized structure of expectations. But as within states, where such groups as families end in divorce, churches dissolve in schism and corporations are destroyed, states, international organizations, and the largest of all social groups, the international system, undergo disruption and revolutionary change. But, on the other hand, to focus on the becoming, on the conflict or disruption, is to ignore the periods of order, of regularity, of harmony and consensus identified with a tolerable balance of powers.

International society is then a particular configuration of balances, of structures of informal and formalized expectations, to be sure. But so is a dump a configuration of objects, and a sand pile a configuration of sand grains. There is more to international society than a heap of balances.

The *society* is itself a balance, whether we talk of society as the city, province, state, or international system. International society is that balance which formally confers legitimacy on the diverse sturctures of expectations which comprise it. It is a complex of informal (e.g., one should not lie or aggress) and formal (e.g., treaties) expectations, involving both general social norms and the official law. It has a defined membership (e.g., states), law norms delimiting rights (e.g., sovereignty) and obligations (as defined in systemwide multilateral treaties, like the UN Charter), and authoritative roles (the Secretary-General of the United Nations; the five permanent members of the Security Council).

Second, *international relations form an exchange society.* It is dominated by bargaining power: international trade, treaties, agreements, tourist and student movements, migration, technical aid, capital flows, exchange rates, and so on. All these activities usually manifest some individual, group, or state giving up something they value for something else they want more.

This is not to deny the role of coercion in international society, as in Kissinger's attempt to achieve a lasting Middle East peace in 1974 by threatening to withdraw American aid to Israel if she did not come to terms with Egypt; or the use of state power by the Oil Producing Exporting Countries to establish a cartel and force oil prices many times above the international free market value; or the forced expropriation or nationalization of multinational corporations, as in Chile's 1971 takeover of Kennecott, Anaconda, Cerro, Ford and ITT. Nor is it to deny that whole regions are dominated by coercion, as in Eastern Europe within the Warsaw Pact and Council for Economic Mutual Aid (COMECON or CEMA).[9]

It is to say that of all powers—coercive, authoritative, bargaining, intellectual, altruistic, and manipulative—international and transnational social interactions are governed more by bargaining power establishing an exchange relationship.[10]

In this international exchange society, states are generally free to pursue their own interests; social behavior is normally cooperative and contractual.[11] Rewards and promises are the basis of the society. Treaties, commercial contracts, and written agreements provide its explicit framework.

Third, *international society is governed by a libertarian political system.* States are by international law guaranteed the rights of sovereignty, independence, and equality which take precedence over and limit world government. The United Nations as the executive and legislative core; the International Court of Justice as the judiciary; and the various international organizations, such as the World Health Organization, International Monetary Fund, and World Meteorological Organization; serve as the administrative structure and provide a minimal government. Sanctions are applied, as when the Security Council voted action against the North Koreans' aggression in 1950 and mandatory economic sanctions against the Southern Rhodesian white government after it declared its independence from Britain in 1965;[12] and international military forces are used, as in the peace-keeping operations in Cyprus since 1964, the Congo (1960-1964), and Middle East since 1975. Decision-making is often by consensus, but decisions may even be made by majority vote as in the all-member assembly of the International Civil Aviation Organization; and important decisions by the upper chamber of the world legislature (the Security Council) require the concurrence of the five Big Powers.

This is a confederation, the weakest form of federation, in which each constituent-member state retains sovereignty and a monopoly of force is denied the central government. Its functions are janitorial, meeting international crises when called upon by states; resolving international conflicts when requested; providing judicial judgments upon appeal; and above all, through the network of international governmental *and* nonintergovernmental organizations, providing an administrative structure for international transactions among states, groups, and individuals.

This world political system has four aspects. One is that it is a system open to participation by all states on equal terms. It is politically competitive, and political parties (blocs) are free to form and contest for dominance. The legislative-judiciary functions of the government are ordinarily closed to groups other than states, however, and to individuals, but the administrative network includes not only international organizations for states, but those for groups and individuals as well. [13] There are no elite states, groups or individuals that control this international government, that dictate to the world society, and that are insulated from global political competition and contests for power.

A second aspect of the political system is its nonintervention in the world society. Transactions are carried on among states, groups and individuals without coercive control or regulation by the world government. Attempts to intervene more, especially on behalf of the Third World, are now underway, as in the UN Conference on the Law of the Sea meetings (one aim of which is to internationally govern the mining of resources underlying the world's oceans).

The noninterventive character of world government can be seen easily in comparison to the role governments play within states. On the global level, states, multinational corporations, international churches, professional groups, and individuals pursue their interests without the governmental interference that can be seen within all contemporary states. [14]

A third aspect of world government is that it is normative, rather than positivist, in its law. International law is limited to custom, precedent, and established principles and rights. The way states behave and the norms that have arisen out of their interaction govern the society. To be sure, positivist rules and regulations exist, but as administrative details to fill in the broad laws which are the basis of world government.

The final aspect concerns the past, present, or future orientation of the world government. Generally, the government (in the totality of its functions) acts neither to maintain the traditions of international society; nor to mobilize the society towards, or reconstruct it in the light of, some future image. Rather, world government reflects and represents through its various organs immediate global and national interests. Neither past nor future-oriented, it mirrors current interests as long as they do not conflict with traditional rights and principles (such as the equality of states). [15]

Considering this government, the dominant exchange power, and international behavior, then, *international relations are an exchange society with a libertarian political 'system.* This is the essence of international relations. Other ways of characterizing international relations have been suggested. Raymond Aron concluded in his book *Peace and War* that the "distinctive nature" of international relations "lay in the legitimacy or legality of the use of military force. In superior civilizations, these are the only social relationships in which violence is considered normal." [16] This is a customary view: international relations is seen as a realm of violence, of war, in contrast to state-societies which are perceived peaceful, where the use of violence is abnormal and illegitimate.

But this focus on legitimate violence does not distinguish international relations. Through their police, military, and security forces, state governments employ legitimate violence against internal criminals, insurrections, banditry, terrorism, revolution, and so on. Some urban societies within states are in a perpetual condition of violence, as between rival gangs, residents and police; and the expectation of burglary and muggings is high. [17] Moreover, some state-societies are governed by terror and repression, where arrests, beatings, and torture, and possibly death at the hands of the government is a constant threat. Such societies are ruled by violence, as was Haiti under Duvalier, and the Soviet Union under Stalin, and now Cambodia in 1975-1978 under the Khmer Rouge. Indeed, consider the violence against the Jews within Hitler's Germany.

The crucial term here is "legitimacy." What is legitimate is what people generally think is right or proper, or more formally, what corresponds to the legal norms of society. In international relations aggression is generally considered illegitimate (witness the attempts on the part of all aggressors to label the victim as the aggressor), even though circumstances may justify a preemptory attack or the use of violence to correct injustice (such as is argued by the black African states in supporting guerrilla warfare against white-ruled Southern Rhodesia and the Union of South Africa; or by Egypt in her 1973 attack on Israel to recover lost territory, precipitating the Yom Kippur War). However, the use of violence by states in their defense or to defeat aggression is certainly legitimate. And this does not differ from state-societies, where the police or military legitimately use violence to prevent crime or rebellion.

It is a question whether rule by violence in totalitarian states is legitimate, however. From the perspective of the rulers, violence is legitimate if it maintains control and state security; from the perspective of their constitution, if they have one as in the Soviet Union, such violence may be illegitimate; from the perspective of the ruled also, such violence may be illegitimate, even though there may be some suffering repressive violence who believe it right and proper, but misdirected in their case. [18]

Both within and between states, the legitimacy of violence is a matter of whose ox is gored and the outcome. Had the United States won in Vietnam, the war probably would have been seen eventually by Americans and their allies as legitimate, justified by the foreign policy of Containment, [19] the Truman Doctrine, [20] and the SEATO Treaty. [21] The Vietnam war is now considered an illegitimate use of violence by many Americans. [22] In China, however, the deaths of millions of Chinese from communist violence in imposing and maintaining Mao's regime from 1948 to 1976 is often considered legitimate. [23]

Closely related to the characterization of international relations by the legitimacy of violence is its depiction as a *state of war*. On what this means we could do no better than quote Thomas Hobbes (1958: 106-107):

> Hereby it is manifest that, during the time men live without a common power to keep them all in awe, they are in that condition which is called war, and such a war as is of every man against every man. For WAR consists not in battle only, or the act of fighting, but in a tract of time wherein the will to contend by battle is sufficiently known; and therefore

the notion of *time* is to be considered in the nature of war as it is in the nature of foul weather. For as the nature of foul weather lies not in a shower or two of rain but in an inclination thereto of many days together, so the nature of war consists not in actual fighting but in the known disposition thereto during all the time there is no assurance to the contrary.

Because international relations lacks a central government with a monopoly of power (they do, however, have a central government without such a monopoly, as described above) states are insecure. Their protection depends on themselves and what faith they can put in their allies. This insecurity will breed arms for defense. Moreover, each state must itself right injustice done against it. The reliance on self-help,[24] the *security dilemma*[25] that each state faces, creates a constant disposition to violence, a state of war.[26]

War, however, is by definition, a state of hostile, armed conflict between *states*. To therefore characterize international relations by that already defined as specific to it does not add to our power of discrimination.

Moreover, if we understand that war is a type of social violence and recognize that we are typifying international relations as a *state of violence*, then obviously this would hardly characterize international relations uniquely. Many states with central governments constitute a state of violence. Stalin's Soviet Union, Duvalier's Haiti, and Cambodia's first two years under the Khmer Rouge were states of violence: well-known people would disappear, relatives or friends arrested would never be heard from again, and one's background, associations, or an innocent remark could mean years of prison, torture, or execution. The insecurity and paranoia of totalitarian rulers and their desire to control and regulate, create a constant disposition to violence against their subjects. Indeed, Solzhenitsyn's *Gulag Archipelago* could well be retitled *The State of Violence*.

However, a state of violence is not limited to totalitarian systems. Lebanon since 1975 and Ethiopia since 1976 have been in a state of violence; Burma with its numerous guerrilla bands and factions is in a state of violence, as was Colombia between 1946 and 1957 with its bloody, large-scale disorder (this "La violencia" may have caused 150,000 to 200,000 deaths). Even in the United States, in many urban neighborhoods people must barricade their homes or apartments at night, cannot safely walk the street after dark, and even during the day are afraid to go out alone. In these countries or areas violence was or is an expectation and a disposition.

On the other side of the coin, not all international relations are a state of violence. Among Canada, the United States, United Kingdom, Australia, New Zealand, France, Belgium, Netherlands, Norway, Sweden, and Switzerland there is simply no expectation of nor disposition to violence. Problems arise in their relations, conflicts do occur, but none prepares for or entertains the possibility of violence against the other. Similarly between most countries of the world.

Indeed, the expectation of and disposition to violence between states is limited to very few bilateral relations, the most important of which are the United States and USSR, USSR and China, Israel and her Arab neighbors, NATO and the Warsaw Pact, North and South Korea, India and Pakistan, Thailand and her communist neighbors, Vietnam and both Cambodia and China, Greece and Turkey, Ethiopia and Somalia, and both the Union of South Africa and Southern Rhodesia versus the black African states. In a world of over 8,000 pairs of states, this propensity to violence is remarkably limited.[27] In fact, because of the greater extent of transactions between nations and contractual relations, international relations could better be characterized as a *state of peace*. This, especially in contrast to many states.[28]

F.S. Northedge and M.D. Donelan published a study (1971) of 50 international disputes occurring between 1945 and 1970, such as those within or over Greece (1944-1949), Austria (1945-1955), Berlin (1948-1949), Korea (1947-1953) and Vietnam (1954-1970). These disputes were divided into those within states and those between. One observation they make about such disputes is relevant here.

> In contrast [to those within states], the disputes between states were much less marked by violence. To judge this, let us recapitulate them by loose titles: the German question; Austria 1945-55; Poland 1944-45; the United States and Cuba; the Cuba missile dispute; Mauritania and Morocco; Kuwait and Iraq; Indonesia and Malaysia; the Somalia borders; Trieste; Kashmir; Goa; West Irian; Anglo-Icelandic Fisheries; Sino-Indian Border; Algeria and Morocco; the Anglo-Iranian Oil Company; the Suez Canal; the Panama Canal.

> Two of these disputes, the German question and the Cuba missiles dispute, raised grave dangers to the world in that the great powers were directly involved. Some in which they were indirectly involved raised considerable danger. Many included some form of breach of relations. Some led to fighting. But, on the whole, the remarkable feature of these disputes, for all the drama, bitterness, disruption and waste that they caused, was how little bloodshed was suffered and how little physical damage the antagonists did to each other or even sought to do [Northedge and Donelan, 1971:145].

To characterize international relations as a state of war, however, is often to mean that, in John Locke's words (1955: 14), "Men living together according to reason, without a common superior on earth with authority to judge between them is properly the state of nature."

The state of nature was a favorite concept of Hobbes, and other social contract theorists. It was a tool for understanding international relations used by the early international lawyers, such as Emmerich de Vattel, who argued that: "Since Nations are composed of men who are by nature free and independent, and who before the establishment of civil society lived together in the state of nature, such Nations or sovereign States must be regarded as so many free persons living together in the state of nature." From this state of nature de Vattel concluded that states must be absolutely free and independent.

For the social contract theorists of the seventeenth and eighteenth centuries (Hobbes, Spinoza, Locke, Hume, and Rousseau),[29] the state was formed by agreement among its first subjects and for specific purposes. Man was believed logically prior to and above the state. It was therefore possible to contrast his hypothetical prepolitical life to the advantages and disadvantages of the state.

The time when no state existed was called a state of nature, and at the two extremes, this period was either a propertyless anarchy, a law of the jungle, of Hobbes' "the war of all against all" requiring the absolute state—the leviathan—for each man's security. Or, as for Rousseau, the state of nature was one of innocence in which men's relations were governed by family attachments and not a state of war. But vices existed and man mistakenly formed the state to protect man against them, and thus created a tool of greed and power. In the nineteenth and twentieth centuries our view of prepolitical man moved from hypothesis and speculation to solid knowledge. Anthropology became a recognized discipline, and the fiction of a state of nature lost appeal.[30] That is, except in describing international relations.

International relations are believed to be in a state of nature: the relations between states are seen as though states were so many men living in a condition of anarchy, where each preys on the other and life is brutish and short. Hobbes' perspective dominates. Each state is presumed to be insecure, all in a state of war, violence is the norm, and individual morality is alien.[31] Coercive power is therefore supposed the regulator of international relations and diplomacy and war, its two faces. And a world state, a global leviathan, is thought necessary to provide security and prevent violence. Many do not recognize that this state of nature is a fiction.

Related to the belief in a state of nature is the view of international relations as chaotic. For example, Stanley Hoffmann sees international relations as distinctly the realm of *uncertainty,* and makes much of this in his own work:

> LET US IMAGINE a large gambling place. Around a large roulette table stand players of all sizes and all ages. Behind them are their families. Depending on the stakes, and on the fancies of the roulette ball, the families' fortunes increase or collapse. Sometimes one player dominates, sometimes the struggle focuses on two main rivals, sometimes a great number of players share the bulk of the gains. Occasionally, the accidents of the game do not simply ruin a family but kill it. But the game never stops.

> Such are international relations. They are features, *par excellence,* of the realm of uncertainty [1965: 134].

Now, clearly, statesmen find the future essentially unpredictable,[32] they believe themselves governed by the "chain of circumstance," as Sir Harold Nicolson pointed out (quoted in Sprout and Sprout, 1962: 108-109), and that as

Frederick the Great wrote, "uncertainty, although every time appearing in a different form, holds sway in all the operations of foreign policy, so that in the case of great alliances the result is the very opposite of what was planned." (quoted in Hinsley, 1963: 181-182)

But as with violence, this unpredictability only covers certain relations for particular times. Much of international relations comprises clear expectations, high predictability, strong patterns. Conditions and patterns of trade, tourist regulations and flows, communications and transportation, diplomatic rules and principles, alliances and even the behavior that would cause a war, are known. We could hardly travel to another country or have transactions were it otherwise. And does anyone doubt that at least local war and possibly World War III would follow American tanks knocking down the Berlin Wall or the Soviet Union again secretly trying to implant intermediate and medium range missiles in Cuba.[33]

On the other hand, the predictability of internal (domestic) affairs is less than assumed and not much different than international relations.[34] Was Watergate predictable? The presidential nomination of Jimmy Carter by the Democrats? Clearly, societies are integrated by virtue of mutually reliable expectations—what I call structure of expectations—but there is also much unpredictability, as anyone trying to invest in the stock market soon finds out, where the impact of unpredictable political comments, speeches, decisions and events can cause sudden looses or windfall gain.

No, international relations are not anymore chaotic than affairs within states. They are not anarchic. They are not normless, ruleless, nor lawless. They are not a state of war and violence is not the norm. States are not universally insecure. And coercive power is not the rule.

Rather, international relations comprise a global society and world culture with a limited government. Relations are generally harmonious, contractual. Bargaining power dominates. Reciprocity is the rule. Antagonism, conflicts, and violence exist, but in general are less in intensity than can be expected within many states. The "wonder is, not that nation-states conflict, but that they do not conflict more often and more violently than they do." (Northedge and Donelan, 1971) International relations conform more to Rousseau's than Hobbes' state of nature.[35]

In sum, the essence of international relations is an exchange society based mainly on bargaining power and with a limited, libertarian political system. International relations therefore is a sociocultural *field,* and it is to the clarification of this that I will turn in the next chapter.

NOTES

1. The nature and types of societies are analyzed in Volume 2 (1976: chapter 30), and supporting evidence is given in the same volume (1976: chapter 34).

2. Social stratification and status, especially as relevant to international relations, are analyzed in Volume 2 (1976: chapters 17-18 and section 21.3).

3. By "class" I mean those who either authoritatively command others in an organization, or those who are so commanded. See Volume 2 (1976: chapters 24-25).

4. All cultural systems share an emphasis on truth as a value, although they may differ in basing truth on revelation, intuition, reason, or experience. Even those political systems in which truth is systematically distorted to some end will give lip-service to truth and admit its value, as in charging opponents with being liars. On the different cultural bases of truth, see Sorokin (1957), especially Chapters 13 and 14. For an informed and persuasive philosophical attempt to establish five universal postulates of justice, the first of which is truth, see Brecht (1959: chapter X).

5. Among intellectuals and government leaders today, there is a pervasive faith in socialist methods and principles, even in the United States. Dominant is a belief in government controls, regulations, planning, and economic and social intervention, services, welfare, and subsidies. Among international elites there appears little disagreement over the need for some intervention and control; the disagreement is over the extent of control desirable, with communist systems at one end, India and Sri Lanka-type socialism in the middle, and the American, West German, and Swiss mixed, free-market-socialism, at the other end.

6. For a good coverage and clarification of Simmel's contribution to our understanding of social conflict, see Coser (1956).

7. There is an important intellectual division on this point. Students of international relations emphasize conflict, power, confrontation. A "balance of power" is the major organizing framework for understanding and explaining international behavior. As one whose doctoral work was in this field, my "feel" for international relations is violated by defining it in consensus or equilibrium-of-values terms. It is natural for students of international relations to take conflict as the starting point: a conflict model of the international society dominates.

However, for state-societies, the consensus or equilibrium-of-values perspective in society still prevails, at least in the United States. Marxism, neo-Marxism, and non-Marxist conflict models have made inroads on this, but the influence of Talcott Parson's (1958) system approach is still strong. Conflict is still deviant.

It is the strength of this consensus model which probably explains why so many nonstudents of international relations whose perspective is shaped by a view of society as consensual see then the fundamental explanation of international conflict to be the lack of a strong world government. After all, in this perspective, state-societies are consensual and conflict is unusual, while international relations appears riven by violence. The major difference between these consensual societies and international relations is the existence of a strong government. It follows in this view, then, that a lack of world government explains the difference.

In a conflict view of state-societies, where an equilibrium-in-values is seen undergirded by a balance of power between domestic groups and individuals, however, a strong world government could only institutionalize a particular balance of power and involve more global violence than yet seen in order to consolidate a decisive monopoly of force. And once institutionalized, it could well collapse through international revolution, civil war, or guerrilla warfare.

8. I am not ruling out informal structures of expectations between groups. In my view, such structures always involve individuals, whether acting authoritatively for a group or on their own behalf. Thus, an informal structure of expectations between China and the United States would be between particular leaders.

9. Of course, neither is this to say that bargaining power does not play a role, as in the resistence of East European nations to becoming economically integrated with the Soviet Union and to sacrificing their own economies, as with Rumania, in order to provide raw materials to other COMECON members. Again, I am referring to a dominant and not exclusive power.

10. For my analysis of these forms of social power, see Volume 2 (1976: chapters 19-21).

The ability to bargain is dependent on the resources available to a state. Two empirical dimensions of states measure this ability: their wealth (GNP per capita, energy consumption per capita, telephones per capita, and the like), and their absolute resources (national income, raw resources, energy production, and such). Both of these have been found as primary wealth and power dimensions of states (see section 7.1 and Rummel, 1972). The sheer magnitude of nonconflicful participation of states in the international system is largely a function of these two dimensions (Rummel, 1972, chapter 13). Moreover, their dyadic behavior is also largely a function of both these dimensions (appendix 9A).

However, the elements of the power dimension, which also include defense expenditures, are also a base for coercive power. Thus, the same dimension underlies bargaining behavior (along with wealth) and coercive conflict behavior. This is a fundamental ambiguity in the resources of power, where the same resources, such as energy production, can be used both to bargain and to threaten (as the oil producing Arab states did in the 1973 Arab-Israeli war).

There may be another source of confusion here. In part V, I emphasize the role of coercion in conflict and Primary Proposition 19.2 in chapter 19 (appendix 19A) is that power shapes conflict. Now, the form of power (bargaining, coercive, authoritative) shapes society and the form of conflict it has. And in interstate conflict behavior, coercive power plays the major role. But to assert this in no way contradicts the conclusions that international relations is an exchange society based on bargaining power (no more than the use of coercion in labor-management conflicts or in conflicts between corporations contradicts the statement that the free market is based on bargaining power). Compared to the variety and volume of international behavior, conflict behavior is a small region of international behavior space (see note 11, below).

11. For years I had coded daily the reporting in the New York *Times* of any conflict event (threat, warning, boycott, expulsion of diplomats, border clash, and so on) between any two states. The number of such events was small in comparison to the continuous flow of cooperative behavior between nations, of which trade was only one manifestation.

For example, for 1963, I recorded in total nearly 3,000 international conflict acts for 275 out of 5,671 pairs of sovereign states then existing (Hall and Rummel, 1970). Yet, virtually all these 5,671 pairs had some kind of cooperative interaction during this period, involving at least their delegates to the United Nations and various other international organizations and, for most pairs, trade, communications, tourists, and intergovernmental conferences and discussions.

More specifically, *and focusing only on events* (ignoring cooperative flows and structures, as defined in appendix II) for example, McGowan (1973) found among 14,500 events for 32 black African states (1946-1966) that cooperation comprised 35.2%, participation was 47.1%, and conflict involved 17.7%. For 5,500 events for 1966 for all states, McClelland and Hoggard (1969) found that 33% were cooperative, 35.5% participation, 31.5% conflict. And Hermann (1975) found that for 35 states, 1959-1968, and 11,589 events, 12% were neutral or friendly deeds of one to another, against 3% found hostile.

These data on conflict occurrences contradicts the perception that international relations is an arena of conflicts, a society riven by disagreements, contention, tension, and violence. This perception is no doubt partly due to the daily news emphasizing international conflict and, especially, focusing in depth on international violence wherever it occurs. The constant pulse of cooperative interaction between states is background, recorded in international statistics and documents, only occasionally to be manifested in the news as a new agreement or contract signed, a state visit, an international conference, or a diplomatic party.

On the predominantly cooperative nature of modern foreign policies, see Morse (1970).

12. On the effectiveness of such economic sanctions, see Galtung (1967).

13. The hundreds of nonintergovernmental international organizations are listed and described in the *Yearbook of International Organizations*. For a useful and informative study of the growth in international organizations, see Angell (1969).

14. This may seem contrary to fact. Surely, just to mention a few examples, international airline standards for personnel licensing and rules of the air are determined by the International Civil Aviation Organization, basic postal rates for foreign mail are established by the Universal Postal Union, and international health regulations to control yellow fever, plague, cholera, and smallpox are determined by the World Health Organization. However, it must be realized that these regulations are established among the states themselves by mutual agreement; they are self-regulations. They do not constitute governmental intervention, which would be distinguished by regulations or laws backed by sanctions and with which the subjects may not agree and in which they have had no hand in making. The distinction is between voluntary and coercive regulations.

Another source of confusion is over regulations governing, say, multinational corporations. The states may establish them by mutual agreement over the opposition of the corporations themselves. This would clearly comprise intervention in the interaction among international groups, although not states. An example of such intervention are those state-level agreements governing the international economic system, like the General Agreement on Tariffs and Trade (GATT).

15. The five aspects distinguishing the international libertarian political system are developed in Volume 2 (1976: chapter 31).

16. This is Aron's assessment of his own work. See Aron (1967: 190-191).

17. Just consider the insecurity of the elderly in American cities. "When they go out—if they go out—they listen anxiously for the sound of footsteps hurrying near, and they eye every approaching stranger with suspicion. As they walk, some may clutch a police whistle in their hands. More often, especially after the sun sets, they stay at home, their world reduced to the confines of apartments that they turn into fortresses with locks and bars on every window and door. They are the elderly who live in the slums of the nation's major cities." (Time, November 29, 1976, p. 21, italics omitted)

"In New York, two 16-year-old step-brothers allegedly tried to rape a 75-year-old woman after robbing her (her screams brought help and the youths fled). In Detroit, an 80-year-old woman was jumped in a supermarket parking lot by three youths. When she clung to her purse, they shot her in the face. And the New York couple who committed suicide, Hans Kable, 78, and his wife, Emma, 76, were driven to it by young thugs who repeatedly stabbed Emma Kable in the face with a kitchen fork, demanding money that she did not have.

"Those who survive are increasingly reclusive. 'We find some of them almost starved to death,' said New York City detective Donald Gaffney. 'They're afraid to leave their apartment after a robbery and won't even go to the supermarket.' Some band together for protection, moving in huddled groups and gathering in social clubs—but they are the courageous minority." (Newsweek, November 29, 1976, p. 39)

18. Many communists executed in Stalin's purges of the 1930s felt that the communist party was doing the right thing, although a mistake was being made regarding them personally. Some even aided the purge by giving confessions they knew to be wrong in order not to hurt the communist cause. See Conquest (1968).

Of course, the vast Soviet concentration camp system contained among its many victims communists who even in their suffering thought the system justified. See Solzhenitsyn (1973-1975).

19. This was the American foreign policy of containing communism to the territorial limits it had reached as of 1949. Castro's successful communist revolution in Cuba breached this limit, but after the disastrous U.S.-sponsored Bay of Pigs invasion of Cuba in 1961 Cuba was tolerated as an aberration. Containment was transformed into President Nixon's "Structure of Peace" in 1969 and relabeled détente in the early 1970s.

20. The Truman Doctrine, first enunciated by President Truman before a joint session of Congress on March 12, 1947, expressed the policy of helping free men anywhere threatened by communist aggression. After two decades, in what became known as the Nixon Doctrine, this policy was limited to helping only those who would help themselves. Both the revision of containment and of the Truman Doctrine were influenced by the American inability to win in Vietnam or even achieve the type of status quo, ante bellum resolution that concluded the Korean War.

21. This was the South East Asian Treaty Organization Treaty, signed in 1954 by Australia, France, New Zealand, Pakistan, the Philippines, Thailand, the United Kingdom, and the United States, and ratified in 1955. South Vietnam was included by the parties through a protocol appended to the Treaty.

22. This judgment may change as the cost to the people in Laos, Cambodia and Vietnam of the communist victory eventually is taken into account. In the first year of communist rule in Cambodia alone the death toll from Khmer Rouge terror, forced evacuation from the cities and resettlement, and executions, may have been between 500,000 and 600,000 (Time, April 19, 1976, p. 65) and even may have reached 800,000 (according to Le Monde, as mentioned in a Wall Street Journal editorial on Cambodia, April 16, 1976).

23. The only source I know of which has attempted to tally the toll from communism in China is "The Human Cost of Communism in China," prepared for the Senate Committee on the Judiciary, 92d Congress, 1st Session, 1971 (U.S. Government Printing Office Stock No. 5270-1138), by Richard L. Walker (Director of the Institute of International Studies at the University of South Carolina). Walker calculates the toll to be between 31,750,000 and 58,500,000 dead since 1949 (excluding those Chinese killed in the Korean War).

Although these specific figures are often disputed, most accept that the toll has been around ten million at least. While regrettable, some in the West feel that this number should be weighed against the betterment of Chinese health, nutrition, education, and living conditions since the 1948 takeover.

24. "International politics as a branch of political science has therefore assumed: (a) sovereign, territorial states with conflicting policies exist in contact with one another, (b) the major value of each is its own continuous, independent, existence, (c) the only reliable means available to maintain this value is *self-help* supported by military power and alliances." (Wright, 1955: 137; italics added)

25. Glenn Snyder (1971: 73-74) raises the security dilemma concept to the status of a theory: "This theory has a venerable history, beginning at least as early as Hobbes and elaborated in the modern international context by John Herz . . . , Kenneth Waltz . . . , Herbert Butterfield . . . , Arnold Wolfers . . . , and others. The dilemma is said to arise inevitably out of the fundamental structure of the international system—a 'state of nature,' or a system of decentralized power and multiple sovereignties. Lacking any powerful central authority which can regulate conflict, states are under continual apprehension of attack by other states, and their relations assume the character of a continuous struggle for security in the shadow of war. The dilemma arises because states can never be sure that the security measures of others are intended only for security and not for aggression. Consequently, each state's effort to gain security through power accumulation do tend to increase the insecurity of other states, stimulating them to enhance their power, which then leads to further

apprehension and power accumulation by the first states, and so on. Thus, the very existence of states in a condition of anarchy produces a competition for security which is objectively 'unnecessary' and ultimately futile."

John Herz (1959) makes the security (and power) dilemma "a fundamental condition which underlies all social and political phenomena. . . . Politically active groups and individuals are concerned about their security from being attacked, subjected, dominated, or annihilated by other groups and individuals. Because they strive to attain security from such attack, and yet can never feel entirely secure in a world of competing units, they are driven toward acquiring more and more power for themselves, in order to escape the impact of the superior power of others."

26. For a contemporary treatment of international relations from this perspective see Hoffmann (1965), who in fact titles his work *The State of War.*

27. At the empirical level, overt conflict should reflect the disposition to violence. Yet, we find a small proportion of states manifesting conflict. For example, in 1963, only 4.8% of all pairs of nations showed foreign conflict behavior of any type. See note 11.

28. One statistical analysis (R.P. Richardson, 1966) of 380 conflicts, 1946-1964, found 57 of them were between nations. Of those involving over 100,000 killed, four were guerilla wars, one a limited war; of those involving 10,000-100,000 killed, one was an insurrection, two were guerilla wars, and one was a civil war. Kende (1971) examined 97 wars, 1945-1969, and found only 15 were international (fought across frontiers). Denton (1969: 22) systematically analyzed wars between 1750 and 1960, and concluded "that international violence does not constitute a major portion of organized conflict." Of all pairs of belligerents during this period, 35% were sovereign states opposing each other.

29. On the contract theorists, see Gough (1957) and Barker (1958).

30. A contract theory can be entirely hypothetical, analyzing political arrangements as though government is subservient to man and implied agreements exist. These assumed agreements can then be used to contrast existing government against what ought to be. This is an effective approach in the natural law, human rights tradition. For a current philosophical example, see Rawls (1971).

31. Not only is it asserted that the morality applied within states does not apply between, but it is argued that this ought to be the case. Morgenthau (1962: 854), for example, asserts that: "A foreign policy derived from the national interest is in fact morally superior to a foreign policy inspired by universal moral principles."

The reader is entitled to know my moral "biases" from the beginning. I believe the same morality that applies between individuals must apply to groups, governments, and states. The theory of dual morality—what is immoral for citizens may be moral for governments and states—has been an excuse for the excesses of state power in the service of some higher presumed good, such as development, equality, social justice, national security, or national interest. I object to any but the most limited state power, and then balanced and checked in the maintenance of the maximal liberty. And one check that must apply is the common morality. Governments free to define their own morality in the light of their own definition of national interest are not to be trusted. We should sew on our underwear the understanding that power corrupts, and absolute power corrupts absolutely.

32. Regarding the lack of program planning in the foreign field, the "essential unpredictability of the future is often used as the principal argument for not planning. A Foreign Service career officer, when asked why the State Department did not put more emphasis on planning, replied, 'How can you plan foreign policy when no one can possibly know what Castro is going to do two years, or even two days, from now?' " (Lindsay, 1965: 130)

33. I tested (Rummel, 1977: chapter 5) the predictability of international relations by determining if data for 1955 on 56 kinds of behavior between 182 *selected* and 164 *randomly* chosen pairs of states would predict their behavior for 1963. The overall correlation between 10,192 predictions and actual behavior for all the selected sample data

was .84; for 9, 184 predictions of random sample data the correlation was .80.

For similar prediction studies of Chinese behavior by Sang-Woo Rhee, and the United States and USSR by Chang-Yoon Choi, see Rummel (1977: chapters 12 and 14, respectively). See also chapter 3 (note 11) and appendix 9A in this volume.

34. In comparing the domestic patterns of states for different years, I got high correlations between predicted and actual similar to those for international relations. See Rummel (1972: section 10.1) and (appendix I:3.3). Although the specific concern was determining the reliability of dimensions I found for 1955, the methodology was the same as that used for predicting international behavior and can be interpreted as an assessment of predictability.

35. The dominant contemporary tendency is to contrast international conflict and war to cooperative relations within states. But this is to ignore national crime, murders, riots, revolts, banditry, terrorism, purges, insecurities, and the like. (See notes 11 and 13). Rather, both harmony and conflict among states must be contrasted to both within.

Scholars and laymen alike who have had a fixation on war and contrast its occurrence and expectations with a perceived harmony within states, have an image and goal of an integrated community—a security community—of states. In this, they have committed a common methodological error: neglecting to compare different cases (international relations versus within-state relations) on the same variables in the same units.

To compound this error, there has also been a shift in framework when moving from within the state to the interstate level. Most students of international relations are trained in diplomatic or political history, or political science. It is natural to see international relations in terms of politics, coercive power, antagonistic conflict, and war. However, most have also been educated in a functional and integrated model of national societies. They see a moral community, a basic culture, regulated by norms and laws; the government serves to assure security and apply reason to maintain and improve the common welfare, regulate the economy, and move society towards a better future. The scholar or social scientist therefore shifts models as he moves from within to between states. Oddly enough, he has realized that psychology applies at both levels and our current international relations literature has woven perception, needs, attitudes, expectations, and the like, into the state-of-nature model. But, there is little recognition that the same sociological and anthropological perspectives on state-societies also apply to international relations.

As seen through my previous volumes in this series and this book, I believe the same perspective applies to all societies and groups, whether the family, the church, the corporation, the government, the state-society, or international relations.

Chapter 3

THE INTERNATIONAL ACTORS

One of the most common images is that of an international society in which States each have the attributes of persons within a community. Abnormal psychology, game-theory, value judgments and moral responses then appear to be immediately relevant to international studies. In reality the nation-State is not of this order; if there must be an analogy then it would be at least as appropriate to use mechanics or electronics as sociology. It is only by describing the world system as it operates that there can be any understanding of it: and then it becomes clear why mentally healthy leaders sometimes appear to respond abnormally in the international system, why seemingly moral men take seemingly immoral decisions, why mild and humble members of the leading elite appear aggressive.

Burton, 1968: 36-37

As an exchange society with a libertarian political system, international relations forms a sociocultural *field*.[1] It is a space of states and transnationally related groups and individuals. Its dimensions define world culture, stratification (wealth, power and prestige) and classes. Its medium consists of international meanings, values, and norms. Seated in this medium, its forces are generated by interests.[2] And its dynamics comprise the conflict helix.

Of all modern societies, contemporary international relations is closest to a field. Interactions are primarily spontaneous[3] and free-market processes largely determine fundamental relations. No one plans what the society will be like. There is no overarching organizational structure which coercively commands behavior. And relations among members of the world society comprise multiple and overlapping local, regional, and international expectations dependent on the interests, capability,[4] and credibility (or will) of the parties involved. In other words, the international order is sewn together by diverse and cross-cutting balances of social powers.[5]

Statesmen act towards goals (interests) in a context of these multiple balances; they "speak out of an environment" (Sprout and Sprout, 1962); they are restrained by a complex of rules they implicitly accept; they have finely tuned expectations about the behavior of others; they approach issues gingerly lest some balances somewhere, at some level, be upset, conflict ensues, and a new, unpredictable and possibly less desirable balance results.

But statesmen are not the only actors, nor other statesmen the only concern. Indeed, who, more specifically, are the actors in the international field?

The state is obviously a candidate for actor. The relations between states have been the focus of my attention in discussing the international society. States have status in international law as entities. They are responsible for official actions in their name; they can enter into treaties and make war; they have rights; they have defined territories and people. Of course, all this is legal fiction that has evolved among diverse societies. It is a structure of international relations widely accepted.[6] Men's actions and expectations give hard reality to the legal existence of states.[7]

Nonetheless, although as with domestic corporations states are persons under the law, states do not act.[8] They do not behave. But, they do structure and frame the behavior of men. They give meaningful-causal understanding to diverse behaviors and simplify our apperception of them. Thus, a violent clash between several thousand men on Damansky (or Chenpao) Island on the River Ussuri in March 15, 1969, becomes understandable as a border clash between Soviet and Chinese frontier guards—as a manifestation of the *Sino-Soviet conflict.*

"Power, ultimately is personal." (Berle, 1967: 428)[9] Men do assume authoritative positions in the state and act legally on its behalf; their own behavior is influenced by the development, political system, culture, geographic location, and history of the state; and they must be cognizant of the obligations and commitments made by previous authorities on behalf of the state. Moreover, they do enter into a system of international rules, procedures, and norms governing the behavior between officials representing different states, as in the exchange of diplomats. There are therefore roles—"a clustering of attitudes that share provocations by, or invocation in, the same situation and have a common goal or action" (Volume 1 1975: 203)—associated with authoritative status and these roles tend to override personality differences.[10] Thus, the international behavior of state officials is patterned, is structured, in a fashion understandable by reference to the attributes and relationships of states.[11]

But, men are still acting in the framework of and in reference to legal fictions. The state is still no person; it has no real personality; it does not behave; you cannot kick it. The modern state is a society controlled by a government based on an internal balance of powers, which defines who has authoritative status to act on behalf of the state.

> In the name of the state a policy is formulated and presented to other countries as though it were, to use Rousseau's terminology, the general will of the state. Dissenters within the state are carried along by two considerations: their inability to bring force to bear to change the decision; their conviction, based on perceived interest and customary loyalty, that in the long run it is to their advantage to go along with the national decision and work in the prescribed and accepted ways for its change. The

less good the state, by Rousseau's standards, the more important the first consideration, and in the ultimate case the unity of the state is simply the naked power of the *de facto* sovereign. On the other hand, the better the state, or, we can now add, the more nationalistic, the more the second consideration is sufficient; and in the ultimate case the agreement of the citizens with the government's formulation of foreign policy is complete.

Waltz, 1968: 178

While one may refer to the policy, or commitment, or conflict, of the United States, while meaning the policies, commitments, and conflicts of specific elite,[12] we should keep in mind that at all times individuals are acting in terms of *their* political, bureaucratic, societal balances of powers. This will help avoid the tendency to treat the morality of states as different from that of individuals, and to ascribe responsibility for actions and events to states, rather than individuals. Especially, thinking always in terms of authoritative individuals—or the elite—should help keep in mind the underlying balance of powers within states that supports and structures foreign policies and actions.[13]

In sum, then, one actor in international relations is the authority—the leader—who can, according to his status and international law, speak and write, promise and threaten, and make or break commitments on behalf of his state.

But each state has a complex of authorities who act in its behalf: diplomats and statesmen, trade and custom officials, military men, legislative leaders, cabinet members, prime ministers, presidents, monarchs. Their actions are diverse and divided, sometimes contradictory. Authoritative decisions require implementation by subordinates; decisions must filter down the chain of command; lower level officials may veto by inaction or alter the decision. Therefore, from a complex of authorities ensues a complex of state-actions through complex political and organizational processes.[14]

What gives this complex coherence is a structure of foreign policies, alliances, and treaties determined at the highest authoritative level; the internal balance of powers within which authorities are imbedded; and the roles of all authorities that are framed by the state's geography, economic development, political system, culture, and so on. *To therefore say a state behaves is to say that a complex of authorities acts within a direction delineated by an internal and external structure of expectations.*

It is the internal structure that establishes the hierarchy and policies among the complex of authorities; it is the external structure that provides meaning and understanding to the complex of actions. Thus, we can evaluate and weight a speech by the American President which claims that NATO is strong and can withstand an invasion by the Warsaw Pact versus a speech given elsewhere that same day by the Secretary of the Army who claims that NATO has become dangerously weak.

Further clarification is yet required. All states are, more or less, antifields[15] from the perspective of international relations—they are organizations whose elite have goals, foreign policies to achieve these goals, and an establishment (a complex of state organizations) to articulate these policies. Internally, these states may be less antifields than fields; they may be more spontaneous, free societies than coercively or authoritative ones. But in the state's external relations, around the rim dividing the state-society from the foreign world, elites maintain coercive control. To move anything or anyone *across* this rim—to trade or travel, to emigrate or immigrate, to work or play, is of potential concern to the elite and usually requires their permission. Of this, the passport is a universal symbol.

Externally, states are *fields of expression.*[16] The complex of actions of a complex of authorities, the complex of interests, capabilities and wills, and the complex of state attributes, give the state a behavioral direction and character that define what we mean by Soviet intentions, Chinese behavior, the Japanese attitude, American credibility, and so on. In observing the behavior of state authorities in international relations, we make sense out of the complex in the same way we do a painting. The dynamic field of lines, shapes, shades, and hues are perceptually organized into a mountain or lake or forest. Similarly, the complex field of actions of authorities within a complex of state attributes is given perceptual and cognitive coherence as the Breshnev Doctrine, NATO, American economic aid to India, or an American presidential campaign.

In short, one kind of actor is the state-authority whose actions contribute to a field of expression locating the state in the international field.

Aside from state-authorities, there are three other international actors. First, there is the individual who for personal reasons is involved in international society. Tourists, foreign students, migrants are the most obvious, but also those who correspond with foreigners, watch foreign movies, read foreign books, or purchase foreign goods are part of international relations. And so are pirates, plane hijackers, and dope smugglers who cross international boundaries. More-over, there are the invisible nets of travelling, transacting, communicating scientists, academics, artists, athletes, and businessmen, whose interests and activities transcend state boundaries. All help define and knit together international society.

Second, there is the nonstate group, or group for short, which is involved in international relations or whose organization is cross-national. Here, I have in mind multinational corporations (having foreign subsidiaries), companies with foreign investments, religious organizations like the Catholic church, associations like the International Political Science Association, political groups like the Palestine Liberation Organization, and terrorists like the Che Guevera Internationalist Brigade.

Like states, groups are integrated authoritative structures and legal fictions. They may have a legal identity within domestic law (as does the corporation or church), or within domestic law be extralegal (as the Palestine Liberation Organization), or illegal (as are terrorist organizations). In any case, each group has internal law norms which establish its hierarchy and command structure, and specify who can legally (by group law) represent and commit the group in international relations. The same analysis of the state as actor applies to the group: the actions of group-authorities form a pattern within a direction given by the group hierarchy and policies.

Finally, there are the various intergovernmental and nonintergovernmental organizations, including the United Nations, which have legal identity in international relations. Like states and other groups composing the international society, international organizations are legal fictions represented by authorities who act on their behalf, usually administering rules and regulations governing state, group, and individual international relations.

Thus, the international field is a complex of individuals acting in different international capacities and roles, representing different international groups, and interacting at different international levels.[17] What provides most coherence to this complex is the state, which in international law takes precedence over (can command) all other organizations, at least within its boundaries. Indeed, for totalitarian states, the international relations of all their groups and people are integrated into state policy and rigidly controlled, including the actions of their citizens representing international organizations.

This control by the state and the complex of relations between the diverse international actors can be made more coherent by dividing international relations into *interstate, intersocietal,* and *interpersonal.*

Interstate relations are those authoritative actions, understandings, or commitments of the governmental authorities—the leaders—of one state to or with the governmental authorities of another state or its groups or citizens, either bilaterally or through international organizations. For example, this would not only include the obvious international conferences, military aid, state visits, treaties, and the like, but also nationalizations of foreign business, expelling foreign newsmen, arresting a foreign national, applying duties to foreign goods, censoring foreign magazines. Thus, any authoritative actions of a state's governmental elite against any citizen or group or another state is part of interstate relations.

Intersocietal relations are those authoritative actions, understandings, or commitments of the authorities of groups[18] within one state with those groups or citizens of another state, or those relations within groups whose membership and organizations transcend states. The latter would include, for example, multinational corporations with foreign subsidiaries, the Catholic church, or international professional associations. Also, included in intersocietal relations are companies selling goods to the citizens of other states, contacts between foreign firms, or one company hiring foreign nationals.

And *interpersonal relations* (in international relations) are those relations of or between citizens of different states acting in their personal interests. Tourists, migrants, foreign students, the international jet set, exemplify such interpersonal relations, as do a portion of international mail, telegrams, phone calls, and cross-border air and surface traffic.

International relations are interpersonal, intersocietal, and interstate: the international field comprises interpersonal, intersocietal, and interstate behavior and attributes.[19] States more or less dominate these relations as they are more or less antifields. The more an antifield, the more a state will control the involvement of groups and individuals in international relations.

To picture this, consider first the three major types of state-societies shown at the ends of the triangle in Figure 3.1.[20] For understanding international relations, there are three spheres of power in states. One is that of the (national) government, which in all states is the coercive force monopolizing sphere of states. The second sphere of power is that of social groups (the family, church, corporation, institution, and so on), and the third is that of the individual's personal interests.

As shown in Figure 3.1, in the libertarian state individual interests dominate over social groups and both over the government. The state's agent, the government, is limited by human rights standing above government. These rights, such as of religion, the press, and speech, create the dominating sphere of individual powers (no social group can dominate through governmental control).

No true libertarian state exists today. The United States, West Germany, and Switzerland are perhaps the closest to it, but in each the governmental sphere encroaches on individual liberty and dominates social groups.[21] All Western-style democracies have become welfare-liberal states, with the relative spheres of individual, group, and governmental power a mix between libertarian and totalitarian states. The welfare-liberal state is so shown in Figure 3.1.

In the totalitarian state, the truest manifestation of an antifield at the state level, the political elite controls the society. Most social groups are appendages of the state, and those that are independent have little autonomy. Individuals have no rights above the state; their daily lives are dictated, regulated, or channelled by the elite.

In all communist societies, for example, the state is the major employer, producer, farmer, renter, and landowner. Thus, in Figure 3.1 the governmental[22] sphere is shown to overlay that of individuals and social groups. Moreover, totalitarian state-societies are future-directed and materialist. They are ordered by coercive power. They are *sensate cultures*.[23] Therefore, social groups, such as the family and church, are weak and are shown within a smaller sphere than the individual.

Finally, unlike the others the authoritarian state is dominated by social groups, as illustrated in Figure 3.1. The church, the caste, the tribe, the clan, or the family legitimately controls society through their adherance and representation of widely prevalent customs and norms. Their authoritative power orders social relations within an ideational culture.[24] Government conforms to fundamental principles and traditions, and is often controlled by a family or clan line.

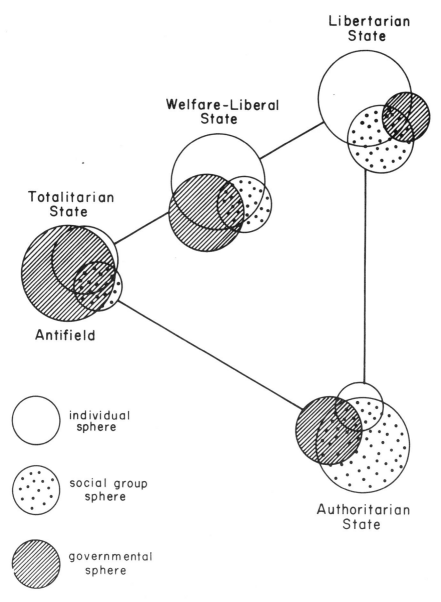

FIGURE 3.1: Types of States and Spheres of Autonomy

INTERNATIONAL RELATIONS

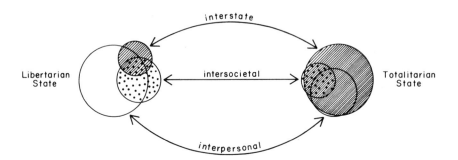

FIGURE 3.2: Scope of Relations between Libertarian and Totalitarian States

Monarchical and hereditary rule are the norm and actual governing is limited to enforcing and maintaining customary law and representing the state in foreign relations.

In an ideational culture—a traditional, group dominated, society—the sphere of individual power is small, as shown in Figure 3.1. Individual interests are circumscribed socially by the traditional norms; politically by the authoritarian government.

Although, therefore, international relations are interstate, intersocietal, and interpersonal, the scope of these relations depends on the type of state. For example, as shown in Figure 3.2, the relations between libertarian and totalitarian states can be interstate, intersocietal, and interpersonal. But, virtually all the foreign relations of a totalitarian state are controlled by the state, including much of the foreign relations of what would be the autonomous international relations of groups and individuals in libertarian societies. Thus, the interstate relations of a totalitarian state compose nearly all its relations, while those of a libertarian state would be of small scope compared to societal and individual relations. This creates a basic asymmetry in the international relations between libertarian and totalitarian states, which can be readily seen from Figure 3.2.

The sphere of state power is the sphere of coercion, threats, force. As the international relations between two states are dominated by interstate relations, so their relations are dominated by coercion, threats, and force. And by violence and war.[25]

It is a major argument of this book that international relations are more violent, more warlike, as interstate relations overspread and permeate all. *International violence is shaped by and a consequence of state power.*[26]

Returning now to my initial questions about who are the actors in the international field, the answer is that there are four kinds: three types of authorities—the elite of states, domestic groups, and international organizations—and individuals acting in their private interests. Each actor is, of course, a person. But when the elite of the state, international organization, or social group are acting in their authoritative roles, they represent the group's policies and reflect its characteristics. It is the complex of the international relations between these actors and their group or personal attributes which define the international field. In other words, *the international field is delineated by the behavior and attributes of the different actors.*

This has profound implications for our image of international relations, so far systematically articulated only by Quincy Wright.[27] For it implies that the state in the international field is not a coherent body, a billiard ball pushed hither and yon by Newtonian-like forces, colliding with other states; nor is it a chess player in an endless tournament for high stakes; nor a family watching its leader bet on the spin of a roulette wheel. It implies that states are not unitary, but segmented in the field into government, groups, and individuals, each with a different location in the field, each manifesting different behavior, each influenced by different forces, each reflecting different interests, will, and capability.

N O T E S

1. In previous volumes I have dealth with the nature and use of a field concept in philosophy and the sciences (Volume 1, 1975: part I), and have applied it to understanding perception psychologically (Volume 1, 1975: part II), and socially (Volume 2, 1976: part II), to expectations and behavior (Volume 1, 1975: part III), social behavior (Volume 2, 1976: part III), and society and culture (Volume 2, 1976: part IV and VIII). Moreover, the concept's mathematical framework has been developed at the psychological level (Volume 1, 1975: part III), at the social level (Volume 2, 1976: chapter 11), and applied to and tested on international relations (1977). At this point, therefore, I will assume that the field concept has been given sufficient exposition and justification.

2. Throughout, an interest will have the precise psychological meaning I gave it in (Volume 1, 1975: chapter 20), and social implications given it in (Volume 2, 1976: sections 19.6 and *passim*). Briefly, an interest is an energized attitude, which has the form "In these circumstances I want to do x with y." It is thus a situation-goal-means complex, a *disposition to behave in a certain way in a specific situation to achieve a particular goal.* An interest is linked to basic human needs through a lattice of interconnected attitudes and (if the attitudes are energized) interests. An attitude becomes transformed into an interest when a connected need is stimulated.

3. I am using spontaneous to mean uncommanded and unmade, with the social meaning given by Hayek (1973), particularly in his chapter 2 discussion of two kinds of order: *made* and *grown* (spontaneous). His distinction is similar to my antifield (Volume 2, 1976: chapter 22) and field.

4. "Capability" involves resources or abilities which can be applied to satisfy interests. At the state level military capability is obviously important, as are economic, technological, and political capabilities. Less obvious is moral (as of the Catholic church) or ideological (as of the Soviet Union and China representing two communist creeds) capability.

5. Social power is a family of powers, including coercive, bargaining, intellectual, authoritative, altruistic, and manipulative. Note that coercive (or at the international level,

what is mainly military) power is only one type. Balances of powers may consist of any one of these types or their combination, although in the international society such balances primarily involve coercive, bargaining, and authoritative powers. See Volume 2 (1976: chapters 19-21).

6. All this stems from the Treaty of Müenster, October 24, 1648, which along with the Treaty of Osnabrüeck made the Peace of Westphalia. The former treaty "provided that differences in the political status no longer exist and that all electors, princes, and states of the Roman Empire are confirmed in and guaranteed their ancient laws, prerogatives, liberties, privileges, free exercise of local law, either spiritual or temporal . . . that they enjoy without contradiction the right of suffrage in all imperial deliberations, especially in the making or the interpretation of laws, the declarations of war." (Mangone, 1954: 31). The Peace of Westphalia originated the modern international system.

7. "To deny personality to the state is just as absurd as to assert it. The personality of the state is not a fact whose truth or falsehood is a matter for argument. It is what international lawyers have called 'the postulated nature' of the state. It is a necessary fiction or hypothesis—an indispensable tool devised by the human mind for dealing with the structure of a developed society." (Carr, 1964, 148-149).

8. My view of states is nominalist, rather than methodological holist (Volume 2, 1976: section 33.4). To me, individuals are the concrete reality and wholes such as groups or collectivities are mental fictions. Nonetheless, wholes do have reality in men's minds. Men do act as though wholes are real. I distinguish, therefore, between the perceiving, interest directed, emotion prone, rational and rationalizing *actor,* who is always an individual, from the cognitive framework and perceptual context of his actions.

9. Adolf Berle's point is better appreciated in context: "As a minor diplomat at the Paris Peace Conference in 1919, spectator and, from time to time, special missioner between wars, assistant secretary of state during World War II, and in government service as the cold war was at its height in 1961, I have observed a substantial sector of twentieth-century American foreign affairs. Included has been opportunity to observe the workings of power. Some instances are recorded here. In substantial measure, they are the basis of one of the propositions set out in this book: power, ultimately, is personal. In each of the recorded cases, the power holder could have made a different decision from the one he made."

10. That roles give structure and constancy to state-level relations is not as obvious as it may seem. Kal Holsti, for example, felt it useful to write an article (1970) on employing the concept of role in foreign policy analysis. For a consistent use of the role concept in analyzing international relations, see Burton (1968). Rosenau (1968) compared the ability of individual versus role variables to explain the behavior of American Senators, and found the role variables more potent.

11. "What baffles [the observer] is the massive continuity of American policy—despite the innumerable verbal clashes, the promises of drastic reform, the temporary oscillations around the main trends, and the headlines announcing crises and bankruptcy. The wrapping changes: the substance remains much the same; images multiply, but the reality they mirror is monotonous. Consequently, there is constant clamor for change." (Hoffmann, 1965: 161)

12. By elite (or leaders) I will always refer to the incumbents of authoritative positions in a group. The elite have a right to command and apply sanctions by virtue of the group's law norms. Thus, the elite are the upper, or superordinate class in the group. In the state those who are the governing elite form its upper class. See Volume 2 (1976: chapters 24-45) for this concept's formulation and grounding in the literature.

My conception of elite combines political and bureaucratic elites and excludes influentials, such as "interest and communication elites." These influentials, insofar as they act on behalf of groups, are group elites. Through their influence and activities, they play a role in international relations, but meaningfully distinct from that of the legitimate, governing elite. Only the latter can legally wield coercive power on behalf of the state.

13. The Vietnam war is a good example of how a domestic balance of powers underlies policy, even that of war. In 1965 when President Johnson formally committed the United States to military action in South Vietnam, he had the support of the American public and Congress, and could justify his actions by the SEATO Treaty, and the policy of Containment. By 1968, militant opposition and public frustration, as well as the defection of significant segments of the Democratic party, administration officials, and former congressional supporters, led to Johnson's withdrawal from the 1968 Presidential race, violent clashes at the Democratic Convention in Chicago, and the defeat of the democratic candidate Hubert Humphrey by Richard Nixon.

By 1974, a new balance of domestic powers had solidified in opposition to U.S. involvement in Southeast Asia, either directly or indirectly through military aid, and to new commitments elsewhere, such as in Africa. Thus, in 1975 Congress defeated attempts by President Ford and Secretary Kissinger to provide 28 million in military aid (in addition to $32 million covertly given by the CIA) to the two non-Marxist independence movements fighting against Agostinho Neto's Popular Movement for the Liberation of Angola (MPLA), which was ultimately supported by 12,000-22,000 Cuban troops and large Soviet aid. This provoked Secretary Kissinger to point out that: "Angola represents the first time since the aftermath of World War II that the Soviets have moved militarily at long distances to impose a regime of their choice. It is the first time that the United States has failed to respond to Soviet military moves outside their immediate orbit. And it is the first time that Congress has halted the executive's action while it was in the process of meeting this kind of threat." (Statement of Secretary Kissinger before the Senate Subcommittee on African Affairs of the Foreign Relations Committee, January 29, 1976)

14. Graham Allison (1969) has distinguished three models of foreign policy through which behavior is seen: as largely purposive value maximizing *choices* of unified national governments (a rational policy model); as routine *outputs* of large governmental organizations with their own goals, programs, and repertoires (an organizational process model); and as *outcomes* of political bargaining and conflicts between bureaucratic groups and individuals within government (bureaucratic politics model).

In my perspective, all national behavior comprises acts, actions, practices, or reflexes of individuals (see section 4.1, below). Of greatest foreign policy relevance are acts and actions, which are always purposive choices (whether personally value maximizing is a wholly subjective matter). Organizational routines and bureaucratic bargaining influence, frame, and may even determine the individual's foreign perception, interests, expectations, and behavioral dispositions. But this does not assume a rational process model, with its assumption of the state represented by a single, rationally choosing, decision maker. While totalitarian states may come closest with the central power of a Hitler, Stalin, or Mao, each of them must still have chosen acts or actions within a policy process and organizational-bureaucratic structure. For example, the actions of each depended on information and intelligence channelled through bureaucratic layers. Moreover, once an action was chosen it could only remain a command until moving down the bureaucratic layers it eventually ensued as a foreign policy act or action.

For a theoretically oriented, former insider's view of the foreign policy process, see Hilsman (1964: 541)

15. Antifield is a central concept, and refers to a coercive organization. It has a command structure—a clear class structure dividing members into those who command and obey—and task-oriented goals according to which the organization is constructed and commands given. It is coercive in that authoritative commands are backed up by negative sanctions. In the pure antifield, membership by the obey-class is also coerced, as exemplified by prisons, concentration camps, draftees in the Army, and communist states (where those attempting to leave without permission may be shot, and if captured, imprisoned). For the development of the concept, see Volume 2 (1976: part VI).

16. For the development of this concept in person-perception, see Volume 2 (1976: part II). All individuals, whether statesmen, or simply citizens, perceive other states holistically: acts, actions, practices, and characteristics give meaning to and take on their meaning from a gestalt. Thus, some see the foreign policy, actions, and capabilities of Soviet rulers as defensive, seeking security, and traditionally Russian; others see them as aggressive, driven by the communist ideology, and seeking world hegemony. Each of these images provides a contextual understanding of Soviet behavior.

17. This all may seem painfully obvious, but in fact it is a perspective different from the most respected contemporary scholarship. Consider Aron's words in his *Peace and War* (1966: 94-95): "An international system, like a party system, involves only a small number of actors. When the number of actors increases (there are more than a hundred states in the United Nations), that of the chief actors does not increase proportionally, and sometimes does not increase at all. We note two super powers in the world system of 1950, at most five or six great powers, actual or potential. Therefore, the principal actors never have the sense of being subject to the laws of the market. The structure of international systems is always *oligopolistic.*"

18. This includes nonnational governments, such as of cities. For example, the city governments of Honolulu and Hiroshima have established official relationships, but these do not represent or involve the American-Japanese national governments, and therefore are not interstate relations. A state-group only can be authoritatively represented by a national government.

19. Mansbach, Ferguson, and Lampert (1976: 275, italics omitted) systematically analyzed the behavior of state and nonstate actors in the Middle East, Western Europe, and Latin America, 1948-1972. In sum, they found that for all dyadic interactions "under half involved nation-states simultaneously as actors and targets, and over 11% involved nonstate actors exclusively!" Their data are cooperative and conflictful events, and therefore do not take into account cooperative flows (trade, student movements, tourists, and so on). Thus, if anything, they overstate formal state-to-state interactions. See also Alger (1977)

20. These types have been developed in Volume 2 (1976: chapters 22-23, and especially figure 31.2).

21. Most influenced by the liberal philosophers (Sir John Harrington, John Locke, Adam Smith, Jeremy Bentham, and John Stuart Mill), England most exemplified a libertarian state in the nineteenth century. The United States was under its Constitution of 1787 founded as a libertarian republic, whose principles at first limited governmental power to the smallest sphere. These principles were three: that each individual has certain inalienable rights standing above government; that all governments carry within themselves the seeds of tyranny which can be checked by a balance of powers and interests (the checks and balances system); and that the purpose of government is mainly to define and administer the customary law.

England has by now become a socialistic society, with government power dominating over social groups and the individual. In the United States governmental power has also grown to dominate. This can be seen by direct and indirect government taxes taking almost 40% of all earned income. On the average, individuals who are employed are now forced to work without pay almost five months of the year for government. And this at the point of a gun, for if you do not turn your income over to the tax collector, your property may be forcefully confiscated and you may be jailed.

22. By government I mean the governing system, and not just the formal or constitutional institutions. As a case in point, in the Soviet Union the Supreme Soviet and its Presidium are constitutionally vested with supreme power; the formal Soviet government at the top comprises The Council of Ministers, which is appointed by the Supreme Soviet and Presidium and accountable to them. By the Soviet Constitution, the Council is the highest executive and administrative organ of the state.

However, the Stalin Constitution also established through Article 126 that the Communist Party (CPSU) "is the leading core of all organizations of the working people, both public and private," and this dominance of the CPSU has been maintained in the just approved Brezhnev Constitution. According to CPSU rules, the "supreme organ" is the Party Congress, which is convened by its Central Committee every four years. The Central Committee, which is ostensibly elected by each Party Congress, elects its own members to its Politburo. By CPSU rules, the Politbureau is responsible to the Central Committee and handles its work between plenary meetings. In practice, however, the Politburo has become the dominant body over all Soviet domestic and foreign policy.

The formal government headed by the Council of Ministers and the Politburo of the CPSU are two parallel structures governing the state, with the formal government by law and practice subordinate to the CPSU. Thus reference to the Soviet government or its governing elite is to this dual structure; reference to the top governing elite is to the members of the Politburo.

23. The concept is Pitirim Sorokin's (1937-1941; 1957) and refers to empirically oriented, sensory, hedonistic, and materialist supercultural systems. The opposing type of system is called *ideational,* and refers to other-worldly, principled, and spiritually ordered cultures. Both the United States and Soviet Union are sensate cultures; early nineteenth century Japan, precommunist China, and contemporary Saudi Arabia were or are ideational. In *Volume 2* (1976: section 30.6) I relate this distinction to the exchange, authoritative and coercive types of society.

24. See note 23.

25. This assertion is subsequently formalized as a proposition. See the Joint Freedom Proposition (16.11) and supporting evidence in appendix 16B.

26. In addition to the proposition noted in note 25, see also in appendix 16B the proposition labeled Joint Power (16.5), Status-Quo Power (16.18), Power Parity (16.21), Freedom (16.27), Totalitarianism (16.30), State-Power (16.31), and Power Vector (16.31). All these propositions are supported by the evidence.

27. See Wright (1955: chapter 32, particularly p. 557). He dealt separately with locations of people, nation, state, and government within his analytic field. His people correspond to my individual actor; his government to my state authorities (except that he also includes the influential elite, such as business of labor leaders). His nation represents the literate population aware of national values and identity; his state the population participating in politics, such as by voting. For me, neither his "nation" or "state" has group identity with distinguishable authoritative actors and roles, and therefore cannot act in international relations.

PART II

INTERNATIONAL BEHAVIOR

On this great stage, the world, no monarch e'er
Was half so haughty as a monarch player.
                    Charles Churchill, The Apology *254*

Chapter 4

INTERNATIONAL BEHAVIOR
SPACE-TIME

if there is a determining spatial dimension to the units being analyzed, that dimension is not territoriality and the units are not disjoint. Instead, the determining spatial dimension our discussion suggests is a behavioral one, where space is thought of as that which acts as a reference point for behavior, which both distinguishes units through differentiation and associates them by contiguity. Propensities, functional interdependencies, and issue-type define behavior-spaces; it is these which distinguish and associate states; and within such spaces, units are interconnected and memberships are overlapping.

Ruggie, 1972: 87

4.1 MEANING OF BEHAVIOR: ACTS, ACTIONS, PRACTICES AND REFLEXES

International society involves a multitude of actors and their diverse behavior. This behavior is social[1] in taking account of other *international* selves: it is behavior intentionally directed at, through, or involving the psychological field of other international actors. Such is a threat of President Carter to General Secretary Brezhnev, the sale of Japanese Toyotas to Brazilians, or a state visit by Cambodia's Premier Pol Pot to China. Even tourism, migration, or foreign student movements are social, in that international actors (such as passport, visa, border and custom officials, transportation terminal clerks, and merchants) must be dealt with.

Ironically, it is when international behavior becomes most organized, most intense, most deadly, that it tends to lose its social character. Such is war. For war often escalates to the application of *force*—of physical power—to overcome, rather than coerce, other wills. This is not to deny that war can be or should be an extension of politics—communist leaders have become contemporary masters of this as evidenced by the Vietnam war[2]—but to point to an aspect of all violence.

Whether war or otherwise, manifest international behavior is infinitely devisible. Simply an international negotiation over a trade agreement can be fragmented into a multitude of different behaviors; the movement of one tourist across an international boundary comprises diverse behaviors (stopping, exchange of greeting with a border official, answering questions, presenting passport, more questions, presenting baggage for inspection, and so on). This diverse behavior is given meaning and unity by its underlying intention, rational meaning, or causation.[3]

Intentional behavior comprises acts or actions. *Acts* are behavior given meaning by an underlying plan, aim, purpose; *actions* are behavior toward achieving the act. Thus, negotiating a treaty is an act, the negotiations the actions; alliance the act, a state visit the action. Of course, what is action in one context may be an act in another, although some behaviors are usually only of one kind or another. For example, violence is generally action—it is to achieve some act (victory, independence, equality, and so on); diplomacy likewise is action toward some goal (containment, détente, peaceful coexistence). However, tourism, migration, and trade are generally acts, although they may sometimes be encouraged or manipulated by the elite to achieve particular goals, such as détente.

Acts and actions are meaningfully unified by their intentions. Reflexes, however, are given causal unity. They are cause-effect, stimulus-response, action-reaction behavior. Prick a person with a pin and he will yell "ouch"; let a mob attack another country's embassy and a diplomatic protest is certain; raise the duties on another nation's goods, and one's own will suffer a similar imposition; go on a military alert against another, and their alert will follow as though governed by some social Newtonian law.

Reflexes are caused by specific changes, events, behaviors. They are not behaviors chosen as part of a larger plan, or to achieve a larger goal. They do not define intentions beyond that of responding to the cause. As an "ouch" is simply a cry of pain, an automatic signal to others that one has been hurt, so a diplomatic protest is often a cry of concern, an automatic warning that a country's interests have been stung.[4]

Finally, there are international practices—behavior that is habitual, customary, rule or norm following, or moral. It is procedural, proper, the right thing to do, the moral way to behave. Rule or norm following behavior is indicated by passports and visas, diplomatic rituals, air transport requirements, world health regulations, exchange rates, customs of the sea, and so on. Moral behavior is partially defined by international law, but also by the moral consensus of the age. In our time, behavior that is internationally good is antiracist, antimilitaristic, antiright (or antifascist), or antinuclear proliferation; and prodevelopment, pro-Third World, proindependence, proenvironment, or proequality. International society is interwoven with practices. They form a structure of expectations within which actors can mutually predict behavior and pursue their individual concerns.

Practices are done *because of* . . . ; they are behavior determined by reasons.[5] Acts and actions are done *in order to* . . . ; they are behavior determined by interests—they are intentional.[6] Reflexes are automatic, causally determined. The *meaning* of international behavior involves understanding it as an act, action, practice, or reflex.[7]

4.2. THEORETICAL COMPONENTS: FAMILISTIC, CONTRACTUAL, AND ANTAGONISTIC

Besides its meaning, manifest behavior also has a *direction,* as to whether it involves common goals and compatible actions and values. *Solidary* behavior is cooperative, helpful, aiding another to achieve his goals. *Antagonistic* behavior, however, is conflictful, hostile, aimed at hindering another. *Mixed* behavior is partly solidary and antagonistic. Technological and financial assistance in economic development is often solidary behavior, as is international cooperation in solving world health or weather problems; war, military actions, boycotts, and the like obviously are antagonistic. Mixed behavior is exemplified by negotiations to end hostilities, or debate and voting in the UN General Assembly.

Moreover, besides its meaning and direction, international behavior may be *intense* (strongly felt, emotional, single minded) as in war or migrating to another country, or superficial (trivial, minor, common) as in buying a postcard in Rome or for President Carter to send a congratulatory message to Fiji upon her tenth year of independence. It may be *extensive,* wide ranging, involving many activities, as in maintaining national security or an alliance; or *narrow* as in exporting copper to Belgium. It may be of long *duration,* as in the Marshall Plan which involved extensive activities over many years, or short in time as in a 15-minute meeting between the French Ambassador and New Zealand's Prime Minister. Finally, it may be organized as in covert intelligence operations, or relatively *unorganized* as in the movement and choices of foreign students.

Thus, the diverse, multitude of interstate, intersocietal, and interpersonal behaviors can be characterized as act, action, practices, or reflexes; as solidary, mixed, or antagonistic; as intensive or superficial; as extensive or narrow; as of long or short duration; or as organized or disorganized. International behavior is a combination of these characteristics, of course. A behavior may be a short, superficial, unorganized, antagonistic act, as a mild warning of the American Ambassador against Japan raising the duty on American television sets. A behavior may be a long, intense, organized, solidary action, as in President Carter's military and economic aid to Israel. Or, a behavior may be a short, intense, organized act, as in the Chinese military shooting down an American reconnaissance plane.

Although international behavior may combine these characteristics in various ways, there are recurring patterns of behavior, particular combinations which can be identified. In general, these combinations can be categorized as *familistic, compulsory,* or *contractual.* Familistic behavior are acts, actions or practices that are solidary, tend to be of long duration, intensive in feeling and extensive in scope. Such familistic behavior has largely characterized the relations between England, the United States, Canada, Australia, and New Zealand, for example. Compulsory behavior, however, is consistently antagonistic acts, actions, or reflexes. It may or may not be intense, extensive, organized or of long duration, and usually involves coercion or force. American and Soviet relations between the Berlin Blockade of 1948 and Cuban Missile Crisis of 1962 were characterized by such antagonistic interaction, or cold war. And then there is contractual behavior, or that which is limited in the range of behaviors involved and in duration, which is mixed solidary and antagonistic in direction, and which involves primarily actions and practices. Examples of this combination of behavior are treaties, contracts, executive agreements, and understandings.

The familistic, contractual, and compulsory types are the most general theoretical components (latent functions)[8] of behavior space-time. They provide the greatest conceptual and meaningful organization to the complex of diverse international behavior. All international acts, actions, practices or reflexes are some combination of familistic, contractual, and compulsory behavior and can be located in a space-time of these dimensions.

This behavior space-time defines the behavioral repertoire of international actors; it delineates their potential behavior. At the most general behavioral level, an international actor is some combination of familistic, contractual, and compulsory components towards other actors. He can cooperate, negotiate, aid, threaten, sanction, attack, protest, exchange, bargain, discuss, visit, and so on. But each act, action, practice, or reflex will have consequences, and how each actor actually will behave depends on his behavioral dispositions and expectations of these consequences, as will be described more fully later.

Two examples, however, will be helpful at this point. An American tourist may be disposed to visit the pyramids in Egypt (a personal act which would necessitate a variety of international contractual actions having to do with the visa, transportation, hotel accommodations, touring the pyramids, and the like), but because she is Jewish and concerned about her reception in Egypt and anti-Jewish terrorists, she chooses instead to tour Buddhist Temples in Japan, which are also of interest to her and which seem to involve no personal risk. Or, Chinese Communist Party Chairman Hua Kuo-feng may be disposed toward a hard line (compulsory action) on China's border disputes with the Soviet Union, but because of growing Soviet strategic power and American weakness, a hard line may provoke Secretary Brezhnev to take military action. Thus, Hua chooses instead to be conciliatory, to signal a more pragmatic policy, and to renew the Sino-Soviet border talks (contractual actions).

4.3. EMPIRICAL COMPONENTS: STRUCTURES OF
EXPECTATIONS AND CONFLICT BEHAVIOR

So far, I have imposed a perspective on international behavior; I have considered different kinds of actors; I have organized behavior by meaning (act, action, practice, reflex), duration, intensity, and so on. I have discriminated three components of international behavior space-time. And I have asserted here (and argued elsewhere) that manifest behavior is a product of expectations and behavioral dispositions. All this is theoretical.

What do we find empirically if we systematically analyze international behavior? I have quantitatively analyzed several dozen international behavioral variables to determine their underlying components. These involved interstate relations (such as aid, threats, treaties, military actions, and alliances), intersocietal relations (such as trade, nonintergovernmental organization memberships, and investments), and interpersonal relations (such as tourism, student movements, and migration). These involved all such dyadic[9] behavior between Brazil, Burma, China, Cuba, Egypt, India, Indonesia, Israel, Jordan, the Netherlands, Poland, the United Kingdom, the Soviet Union, and the United States for the years 1950, 1955, 1960, 1963, and 1965.

In sum, the analysis altogether involved 48,230 behavioral datum defining the manifest diversity of international relations, 1950-1965. They reflect the potential behavior and behavioral dispositions of international actors. Their common variance mirrors the structure of expectations guiding behavior. And their underlying, common components delineate the empirical, behavioral space-time.[10]

The appropriate method to determine the common components is factor analysis and several such analyses were done on the behavioral data, with the results shown in Table 4.1. The technical details and data have been presented elsewhere (Rummel, 1978) and are omitted here.[11] As shown in Table 4.1, eight empirical components were found to span the space-time of international behavior. These measure intercorrelated clusters of behavior and reflect their underlying organization. For example, one such component is transactions, which mirrors a mainly intersocietal pattern of activities involving, among others, exports and NGO comemberships. While its highest correlations are with intersocietal behavior, it also comprises interstate conferences. The component will be more fully discussed below.

What do these eight empirical components show? First, they show that international behavior is highly patterned in definable ways between different actors.[12] It is not random, unpredictable, but orderly and regular, as should be expected of a society. Second, they show that the familistic, contractual and compulsory components of behavior are represented in manifest behavior. Third, they show that interstate, intersocietal and interpersonal relations are reflected in different empirical components—the acts, actions, practices and reflexes of

TABLE 4.1: International Behavior Space-Time Components

THEORETICAL COMPONENT	EMPIRICAL COMPONENT[a]	ILLUSTRATIVE CORRELATED BEHAVIOR $i \rightarrow j$[h]	PRIMARY RELATIONS
familistic	transactions	books, exports, economic aid, investments, mail, NGOs[c], treaties, tourists, migrants, relative embassies	intersocietal
contractual	relative exports	exports/GNP of i, exports/total exports to all nations, tourists/population of i	intersocietal
	foreign students[b]	students, students/foreign students in j, treaties, state visits, IGOs[c]	interpersonal
	international organizations	IGOs/total IGOs of i, NGOs/total NGOs of i, IGOs/total IGO comemberships of i	interstate
compulsory	alignment	UN voting distance common bloc[d] membership	interstate
	negative behavior[i]	accusations negative communications[e] negative behavior[f]	interstate
	military violence	military actions warning and defensive actions days of violence	interstate
	anti-foreign behavior	unofficial anti-foreign actions[g] non-violent and anti-foreign actions	interpersonal

a. The components are from the image analysis, oblique rotation, given in R. J. Rummel, *National Attributes and Behavior*, Beverly Hills: Sage Publications, 1978, Chapter 6.

b. This component was "unnamed" in Rummel, *Ibid*.

c. NGO = comembership in non-intergovernmental international organizations; IGO = comembership in intergovernmental international organizations.

d. Common bloc membership was measured by the existence of a military alliance or treaty with the United States or USSR.

e. This is the total accusations, threats, warnings, protests, and the like, $i \rightarrow j$.

f. This is the total boycotts, expulsions of diplomats, severances of diplomat relations, and other kinds of negative behavior, $i \rightarrow j$.

g. This involves antiforeign boycotts, demonstrations, riots, attacks on foreign nationals and property, and the like.

h. These are a synthesis of the empirical results given in R. J. Rummel, *Ibid*, and R. J. Rummel, *Field Theory Evolving* (1977) and *Dimensions of Nations* (1972), both from Beverly Hills: Sage Publications. All behavior is dyad $i \rightarrow j$, where i stands for the actor and j the object, as in U.S. $\rightarrow$ Brazil.

i. This was named the "negative communications" dimension in Rummel, *National Attributes . . . (op. cit.)*

transnational actors representing the state, social groups, or themselves are not generally correlated. Fourth, the components show the major structures of expectations among international actors. And, finally, they show international conflict behavior and cooperation to be independent.

These last two points deserve expansion. In interacting, actors establish, as in all social systems, an integrated structure of informal understandings, rules, norms, contracts, and treaties regulating their relationship. At its core, this is a *status quo* which defines who owns and gets what, and reciprocal duties and obligations. This structure enables actors to anticipate each other's behavior, to predict the consequences of their actions, and thus to define a social order. It encompasses systems of reliable expectations between actors, and for this reason I call it a *structure of expectations.*[13]

There will be diverse structures of expectations in society involving different interests and a division of labor. Some structures will be nested, some will overlap, all will be within an overarching structure bonding the society together, defining the overall meanings, values, and norms of society, and the status and class of actors. These different structures will be manifest through patterns of covarying familistic and contractual behavior.

Across society as a whole, then, the largest distinct structures of expectations will be defined by the empirical components of behavior, for these will each reflect a different intercorrelated cluster of cooperation.[14] We find from Table 4.1, therefore, that *there are four major international structures of expectations.*

One involves transactions, largely at the intersocietal level. It is a cluster of behavior reflecting a structure of understandings, norms and contracts governing intersocietal relations, and involving such behavior as exports of books, comemberships in NGOs, economic aid,[15] overall exports,[16] mail,[17] and foreign investments.[18] Moreover, this structure also involves to a certain degree interpersonal relations such as tourism and migration, and interstate relations like conferences, NGO comemberships, treaties and relative embassies (as a proportion of the total). These interstate relations are mechanisms for formalizing and regulating the structure of intersocietal expectations.[19]

As a component of behavioral space-time, transactions reflects the broadest structure of expectations. It involves a variety of intersocietal behaviors, as well as that which is related interpersonal and interstate; overall it encompasses more behaviors than any other structure (or conflict component) to be mentioned. This component is what students of international relations often refer to as cooperative or integrative behavior; it is what I am calling familistic. Although a number of contractual behaviors are involved, such as tourists, the general sense of this large pattern of behavior is solidary in direction, and tends to be enduring, extensive (it does involve many behaviors), and intensive in feeling.[20]

Transactions is the only major familistic component. Three independent contractual components also exist, as shown in Table 4.1, each reflecting an underlying structure of expectations. The first is mainly of *relative exports,* or a pattern of exports to specific nations which tends to dominate over all other exports and the exporter's economy. Such is relatively true for the exports of Brazil and Israel to the United States, and Cuba and Poland to the Soviet Union, for example. The second is primarily of *foreign students,* involving also treaties, IGOs, and state visits.

And the third is of *international organizations,* whether IGOs or NGOs. All measures of IGO or NGO comembership are involved in this pattern; and it is independent of all other forms of behavior. And well it should be. This is the structure of expectations comprising international government, overarching and regulating many kinds of behavior, and thus not specifically correlated with any one.

The familistic and contractual components reflect the major structures of expectations: transactions, relative exports, foreign students, and international organizations. There are thus four major kinds of order; four separate patterns of interrelated international behavior.

These expectations develop out of a balancing of powers between actors, an engagement of their interests, capabilities, and wills. This is a conflict of desires, abilities, and determination. And it establishes a working *balance of powers*[21] between the actors, an arrangement with which each can live. This balance of powers undergirds the structure of expectations and its inner status quo.

Conflict behavior and cooperation are therefore complementary. Conflict behavior is a mechanism for establishing a balance, a structure of expectations between actors. And this structure enables these actors to interact cooperatively, to behave contractually and familistically.

While conflict and cooperation are part of the same process (the conflict helix),[22] at the manifest level for the society as a whole, cooperation and conflict behavior will appear uncorrelated.[23] This is because the four major structures of expectations plus numerous smaller ones[24] are in different stages: some provide a solid structure of cooperation; some are in the process of disruption, creating new conflict; some in the process of formation through conflict. Therefore, aggregate conflict behavior will be a sum of conflict behaviors associated with different structures and thus relatively independent of any one.[25] Such is theory; and such is empirically found within state societies,[26] and such is found for the international society.[27]

And this is what the empirical components show. As can be seen from Table 4.1, the compulsory (conflict) components are independent of the familistic and contractual. Indeed, *no* hostile behavior is even moderately correlated with any familistic or contractual component.[28] Cooperation and conflict behavior are not opposites, but complements. They are part of the same process.

To focus now on the separate empirical, compulsory components, each measures a tendency for particular conflict behaviors to go together; each corresponds to *a pattern of behavior in the process of balancing powers,* forming structures of expectations.[29]

The first of these compulsory processes shown in Table 4.1 is *alignment,* a pattern of defense treaties associated with the Cold War, 1950-1965, and voting agreement and disagreement in the UN General Assembly. It mirrors the major bloc conflict to cut across the international system during these years. It reflects the balancing of power—the stabilization of a new international post-World War II order—between the U.S. and Soviet Union and their allies.

The second compulsory component involves both verbal or written interstate negative communications, such as accusations, protests, threats, warnings, and denunciations; and negative behaviors, like boycotts, embargoes, severance of diplomatic relations, expulsion of diplomats, and the like. This component clearly manifests coercive balancing involving warnings or threats and sanctions, and has been named *negative behavior.* [30]

The third compulsory component is of *military violence.* This is either the preparation for such violence through alerts, partial or full mobilization, cancellation of leaves, troop movements, reinforcing frontiers; or the actual involvement in military actions, border clashes, or wars. This component manifests the pattern of violence associated with balancing coercive power and force.

Finally, there is a compulsory, interpersonal component of *antiforeign behavior.* This is a pattern of unofficial violent and nonviolent demonstrations and attacks on the property, citizens or officials, and symbols of another country. It reflects public antagonism and hostility, either covertly organized by the government or political groups, or spontaneously arising from particular events. In any case, antiforeign behavior is a distinct pattern of conflict in the process of forming a balance of powers.

In sum, then, there are a number of common and independent, empirical components that are compulsory, contractual, or familistic; and which span the international behavior space-time. These mirror either the distinct major structures of expectations existing between nations or the process of their formation or disruption.

4.4. HIGHER-ORDER STRUCTURE AND PROCESS

Structures and processes are, however, correlated. The components of Table 4.1 are independent in being separate, distinct, patterns, [31] but not independent statistically. [32] We should expect that structures of expectations and conflict processes would be interrelated into larger, more comprehensive patterns, that finally there should be one overarching *higher-order* structure and another *higher-order* pattern of conflict behavior. What do we find empirically?

Table 4.2 presents the results of an higher-order factor analysis of the components in Table 4.1. [33] Three major higher-order components exist; each is perfectly uncorrelated with the others; each reflects the largest structure of expectations or process of conflict. The first is a familistic-contractual component which shows that, indeed, an overall structure of expectations does encom-

TABLE 4.2: International Behavior Space-Time
Higher Order Components[a]

EMPIRICAL HIGHER ORDER COMPONENT	EMPIRICAL COMPONENT[b]
familistic-contractual	transactions relative exports foreign students international organizations
compulsory I	alignment negative behavior
compulsory II	antiforeign behavior military violence

a. From R. J. Rummel, _National Attributes and Behavior_, Beverly Hills: Sage Publications, 1978, Chapter 6, Table 6.9.
b. These are listed in Table 4.1.

pass all the separate patterns of cooperation: transactions, relative exports, foreign students, and international organizations.[34]

The second and third higher-order components wholly define conflict. The first of these (compulsory I) is a pattern of alignment and negative behavior—a pattern of nonviolent conflict behavior. The second (compulsory II) involves both military violence and antiforeign behavior (which also comprises antiforeign violence). This is primarily a pattern of "saber rattling" and actual violence, with high tension and hostility mixed in. This is a pattern quite apart from the other compulsory component.

These empirical results support the theoretical analysis.[35] The behavior space-time of international actors is spanned by familistic, contractual and compulsory components; and the familistic and contractual components reflect an overall order of rules, norms, understandings, and the like, guiding and regulating cooperative behavior. Moreover, the conflict process involved in forming or reforming these structures manifest behavior components quite independent of these structures. Thus, cooperation and conflict are not opposites, but complements. They are alternative stages in the eternal process of order, disorder; cooperation, conflict; peace, war.

4.5. SUMMARY

International actors behave within a common space-time. There are common conceptual and theoretical components spanning this space, which discriminate among behaviors in terms of their meaning (act, actions, practices, reflexes), direction, duration, intensity, and scope; three common theoretical components span this space: familistic, contractual, and compulsory. These are empirically defined by an analysis of manifest international dyadic behavior, which shows familistic behavior to involve a pattern of transaction; contractual to involve patterns of relative experts, foreign students, and international organizations; and compulsory to involve patterns of alignment, negative behavior, military violence, and antiforeign behavior.

The familistic and contractual patterns (empirical components) reflect the separate structures of expectations between actors, the distinct orders; the compulsory patterns manifest the conflict process associated with the formation and disruption of such structures. Cooperation and conflict are in theory complementary, each a separate stage in the functioning of international society. In theory, conflict behavior should be independent. In fact, this is found true.

4.6. A TERMINOLOGICAL NOTE ON CONFLICT AND COOPERATION

The terms conflict and cooperation are the workhorses of these *volumes* and must be clear, especially in regard to the other behavioral terms developed or used here.

Conflict is a generic term and refers to the opposition of social powers, as defined in Volume 2 (1976: chapters 26-27). Conflict may be latent or manifest, it may be structure, situation, or the balancing—confrontation—of powers. Conflict, therefore, does not necessarily mean overt behavior. When behavior is involved, however, as in "Conflict Behavior," then this means that behavior manifesting the process of balancing powers.

Now, such powers may be coercion or force, but may also be intellectual, exchange, or altruistic, among others. Conflict Behavior, therefore, need not be antagonistic, and may well take place between allied or friendly states.

Cooperative behavior in contrast, refers to one of three types of behavior. There is that behavior comprising *flows* (e.g., tourists, exports, mail) between states, or *structures* (e.g. comembership in international organizations, diplomatic recognition), as discussed in appendix II. Flows and structures are manifest behavior within a structure of expectations.

The third type of cooperative behavior involves *events* (e.g., signing a treaty, offering aid, granting concessions) which are usually part of Conflict Behavior—the balancing of powers—and indeed, in chapter 12 below, such cooperative behavior is defined as an independent conflict path.

Here I have also introduced the terms solidary, mixed, and antagonistic behavior; and familistic, contractual, and compulsory behavior. How do these logically relate to conflict and cooperation? Table 4.3 and 4.4 provide the answering information and relationships.

In Table 4.3, cooperation is shown to combine both the familistic and contractual components. In other words, cooperation is of solidary acts, actions, or practices of long duration, and intensive, as well as mixed solidary and antagonistic actions or practices of limited duration and range. Conflict Behavior

TABLE 4.3: The Relationship Between Behavioral Terms

GENERAL TERMS	COMPONENTS (LATENT FUNCTIONS) OF BEHAVIOR	MANIFEST BEHAVIOR
cooperation	familistic	solidary acts, actions, or practices; of long duration, and intensive
	contractual (cooperative events component)[a]	mixed solidary and antagonistic actions or practices; of limited duration and range
Conflict Behavior		
conflict behavior	compulsory	antagonistic acts, actions, or reflexes

a. A contractual component involving cooperative events is not shown in Table 4.1, since appropriate data were not included in the empirical analysis. Therefore, Table 4.1 shows only contractual components defining cooperative flows and structures.

TABLE 4.4: Taxonomy of Conflict and Cooperation

TERM	MEANING
Conflict	opposing vectors of power; the conflict space, structure of conflict, or balancing of powers; latent or manifest conflict
conflict space	latent space of possible conflicts; realm of potential opposing vectors of power
structure of conflict	latent opposing attitudes
situation of conflict	latent opposing interests
Conflict Behavior	manifest balancing of powers; cooperative (contractual) events and compulsory behavior
conflict behavior	compulsory behavior
conflict process	the development of a conflict through its various phases
cooperation	cooperative structures or flows; familistic or contractual (excluding cooperative events) behavior
cooperative flows	aggregate and repetitive behavior involving the movement of people, goods, services, or aid.
cooperative structures	the cooperative framework of behavior established by agreement (e.g., number of treaties, international organizations, diplomatic recognitions)
cooperative events	specific contractual events (e.g., signing a treaty, offering aid, making a concession)
cooperative behavior	flows, structures, or events

is then of antagonistic acts, practices, or reflexes; or mixed solidary and antagonistic action or practices of limited duration and range. Lower case conflict behavior restricts the term to simply compulsory—antagonistic—behavior.

Table 4.4 shows this meaning of cooperation and conflict behavior in relation to other uses. The terminology delineated therein will be followed throughout this volume and should help avoid confusion.

NOTES

1. I am using social behavior in the sense developed in Volume 2 (1976: part III). The analysis therein and the logic of Volume 2 (1976: chapter 33) underlie this whole chapter.

2. For the doctrinal expression of this in communist military strategy, see Milovidov and Kozlov (1972). Regardless of the dominant political and psychological aspects of communist strategy in Vietnam, the final victory was won by a conventional *force*. Moreover, the Soviet invasions to defeat the Hungarian Revolution in 1956 and the Czechoslovakian "Spring" in 1968 were, after attempted coercion, pure force.

Force is the application of physical power to others in spite of their wills; coercion is the use of threats or sanctions to get another willfully to do or stop doing as demanded. Force works on another's body, resources, or capabilities (such as by killing soldiers, destroying air fields, or bombing factories); coercion on the mind (such as to establish credibility, or to bring another to negotiate, or to concede territory). Of course, no war is pure force or coercion. All are mixtures of social powers. But wars are dominated by one type of power over another. For example, American leaders fought for unconditional surrender by Japan and Germany in World War II, and made that war primarily a test of force.

3. Each of these concepts is developed in Volume 2 (1976: chapter 8).

4. In analyzing 598 diplomatic protests of the United States, McKenna (1962: 195-196) found that the American government "has usually shown an unfortunate inclination toward afterthought rather than forethought . . . action has followed a stimulus-response scheme, based either on a standing policy—requiring, for example, quick protest to defend petroleum interests abroad—or on a deeply ingrained reverance for the law."

5. For example, one gets a passport *because* it is required; a new ambassador follows a particular ritual in presenting his credentials to another government *because* that is the way it is done; airline tickets from Paris to Rome cost a certain amount *because* that is the internationally agreed on price; Nixon cancelled the American ABM program *because* of the SALT I, U.S.-USSR Treaty on the Limitation of Anti-Ballistic Missile Systems; French fishermen do not fish closer than 200 miles off Brazil's shores *because* that is Brazil's fishing zone.

6. Clearly, practices are implicitly intentional in the sense that they are implicitly chosen because of a rule, custom, and so on. In mailing a letter abroad we pay the proper postage, and do so intentionally. We choose to follow the rules. Thus, in returning home after my classes I choose to drive on the right side of the road and this practice enables me to get home safely. Practices, once established, relieve us of making *overt* choices, of deciding what to do in a particular circumstance, of how to decide anew everything at every moment.

Acts and actions, however, directly result from decisions made between alternatives; they are overtly intentional. Thus, to attend a conference in Japan is an intentional act, and to fly there by Pan American is an intentional action. Both involved new decisions; neither involved following a rule, norm, or custom.

7. What about the *outcomes* of bureaucratic processes? A particular behavior may not be what anyone would choose or desire, and it may not accord with any international rules or agreements, but be the outcome of compromises and concessions—a composite of bits and pieces of what different elite with different intentions would do. Therefore, is not this behavior reflexive (the effect of multiple bureaucratic causes)?

Not necessarily. Rarely does anyone behave as he is so disposed. We often must make cost-gain calculations and compromise among competing and sometimes contradictory interests. And often, we settle for the second or third most desirable behavior. Simply as family members, for example, our behavior reflects many compromises with the interests of others. If we thus go with our family to visit relatives rather than to a football game, is the visit any less intentional?

Similarly, in interstate relations some official must always behave on behalf of the nation. And this behavior is no less intentional if it is decided on through bureaucratic compromises. The crucial distinction is not between intentional behaviors and bureaucratic outcomes, but as to whether the behavior is an act, action, practice, or reflex in its meaning.

8. The concept of latent function is basic. I see reality as a "manifold of potentialities, dispositions, determinables, and powers, which comprise *latents* underlying reality's specific and ephemeral *manifestations*. These latents themselves combine in intricate overlapping ways, but nonetheless are reducible by man to patterns enabling him to make sense of his perceptions, to give order to the world, and to predict the consequences of his behavior. These patterns comprise *latent functions,* or *components* of the *spaces* of man." (Volume 1, 1975: 11) This concept is developed in Volume 1, (1975: chapters 8-10).

9. To be clear, dyadic behavior means that of one actor with or towards another, as in United States and France joint membership on the Security Council or U.S. exports to Japan, and symbolized by United States-France, or United States-Japan.

10. This paragraph condenses the logic of Volume 2, (1976: chapter 33). Note that there I am describing a space of sociocultural attributes, while my concern here is dyadic behavior.

11. The results are given a nontechnical description and explanation (especially related to the assumptions of détente) in my *Peace Endangered* (1976a: chapter 5).

12. Technically, empirical components will be delineated for any data matrix, even random numbers. It is not the existence of the components themselves that shows meaningful order in the data, but their size—the percent of variance they define. These eight *common* components account for 42% of the total variation among 53 behavioral variables. For common factor analysis (in this case, the common factor model called image analysis was applied) this is a respectable percent of variance for eight common components, and far greater than what would be found for random data.

13. The structure of expectations is developed as a concept in Volume 2 (1976: section 29.4). What I mean by a structure of expectations is well captured by Luard (1968: 43): "Each of these codes [practices, conventions, morality, law] creates *norms* of conduct, of varying degrees of precision and persuasiveness. The effect of these is to set up expectations in the minds of the members of the group that, in given types of situations, a particular type of response is demanded. They thus come to modify the motives deriving from other sources, innate drives, experience from the past, and others. They establish *rules,* to *regulate* conduct, by setting up *regularities* of behavior. Such rules provide the main instrument of government among all societies. By reducing insecurity and unpredictability, they provide the stability essential to a harmonious and well-balanced existence for each individual member. They contain the essential element of impartiality and objectivity which personal rule in its arbitrary and subjective character may lack. And even apparently coercive authorities depend in practice largely on principles of this type to maintain their power. It is rules, rather than rulers, that everywhere exert ultimate authority."

Luard's work is an excellent treatment of expectations in international relations, especially regarding conflict behavior.

14. I am concerned only with components that are rotated to fit intercorrelated clusters of behavior, as are those in Table 4.1.

15. In *National Attributes and Behavior* (1978) the correlation of economic aid with transactions is ambiguous, but in the *Field Theory Evolving* (1977) studies aid is generally related to it.

16. Russett (1968: 379), for example, found "surprising continuity" over a 25-year period in trading groups. He concludes that trading "relationships are rooted in long-term habits, preferences, and expectations." Such is my view.

17. "The primary focal area [for world mail flows] centers around the North Sea in Northwestern Europe. Within a five hundred mile radius of Brussels are located the capitals or major conurbations of eleven postal countries which, combined, dispatched 40 percent of the world's mail in 1952 and were involved in approximately three-fifths of the world's total mail exchange. This small part of the earth's surface is the principal fountainhead and focus of the flow of international mail. The United States constitutes a secondary world focal area for mail interaction, about an eighth of the world's international mail flow being involved with this one postal country." (Taylor, 1956: 15)

18. Mail and foreign investments were not included in *National Attributes and Behavior* (1978) analysis, but were found correlated with transactions in the analyses reported in my *Field Theory Evolving* (1977).

19. For example, the largest number of treaties is between emigration and immigration states. See Dahl (1968: 348-349, n44).

20. The greatest volume of transactions is among Anglo-Saxon, commonwealth, and common market societies, between whom special bonds of culture, religion, and history exist. The volume of transactions of the United States with Canada and the United Kingdom dominates over that among all other dyads, and it is especially between these states that we talk of a special relationship, of enduring bonds, of—in my terms—familistic behavior.

21. In previous volumes I had used the singular "balance of power." But on working with this concept I found it fundamentally misleading. Power is a family of powers (Volume 2, 1976: chapter 21) and any balance is some combination of these powers, such as the coercive, bargaining and authoritative. Yet, to many a balance of power connotes wholly a balance of force or coercion. For this reason in this volume and subsequently, I will refer to a balance of powers.

22. The conflict helix was the major focus of Volume 2 (1976: section 29.6). See also the Helix Proposition (18.1) in appendix 18A, and the discussion in chapter 18 and Figures 18.1-3.

23. This is subsequently asserted as a proposition. See the Cooperation-Conflict Proposition (18.2) in appendix 18A.

24. Many additional small components exist in the dyadic data which are not shown in Table 4.1. Moreover, were a more extensive collection of behavioral variables included, other components would no doubt emerge, but probably not alter the major components shown in the table. The reason for this confidence lies in the different number of analyses underlying the results, the wide choice of behavioral variables, and the nature of the technique.

25. See Volume 2 (1976: sections 33.3-33.4) and the Cooperation-Conflict Proposition (18.2) in appendix 18A for the logic involved.

26. See Volume 2 (1976: chapter 34)

27. See the Cooperation-Conflict Proposition (18.2) in appendix 18A for the evidence.

28. See Rummel (1978: chapter 6).

29. These compulsory components reflect phases or subphases in the conflict process and balancing of powers. For the development of this perspective, see chapter 13. Appendix 15A presents the empirical evidence.

The compulsory components presented in Table 4.1 are defined in the context of familistic, contractual, and compulsory behavior, and are therefore highly aggregative. Those conflict components presented in Table 15.1, however, are delineated when conflict behavior is analyzed alone, and are therefore more specific. The dependencies between the two sets of components are as follows (with the components of Table 15.1 given in parentheses next to the component of Table 4.1 on which they are dependent): alignment (alignment not shown in Table 15.1), negative behavior (negative communications; negative actions/ sanctions), military violence (preparations; low-level military violence; high-level military violence), antiforeign behavior (antiforeign behavior).

    As explained in section 4.6 and chapter 15, conflict behavior also involves cooperative events along the components shown in Table 15.1. To my knowledge, data to measure such components have yet to be included in the overall analysis of internation behavior, and thus no relevant components are included in Table 4.1.

    30. This was labeled negative communications in Rummel (1978). However, by virtue of the correlations of negative sanctions with the component, it is better to use a more general name here.

    31. Technically, the components are oblique rotated dimensions of an image analysis.

    32. Used is many senses, the concept of independence is a source of constant confusion. Here I mean independence between components in the algebraic sense—as no one component being a linear function of all of the others—as nonperfect correlation. Statistical independence, however, would mean that all the components are mutually and perfectly uncorrelated.

    33. The higher-order components are the orthogonally rotated (eigenvalue-one cutoff) dimensions from a component analysis of the correlations between the components of Table 4.1.

    34. I describe the methodology of higher-order factor analysis in chapter 18 of my *Applied Factor Analysis* (1970). See Figure 18-3 therein for the picture of what is being described here. Each of the different first-order clusters can be considered a separate structure of expectations encompassed by a unifying second-order set of expectations.

    35. The empirical basis of this conclusion rests not only on the analyses presented in Tables 4.1 and 4.2, but also on that for proposition 18.2 in Table 18A.2, such as: Sang-Woo Rhee's (1977) analysis of 7,296 cases of the dyadic behavior of Chinese actors towards as many as 112 other states for the years 1960 and 1965; on Chang-Yoon Choi's (1973) analyses of 4,592 cases of the dyadic behavior of U.S.S.R. actors toward 82 states for 1960 and 1965, and of 4,592 cases of the dyadic behavior of American actors towards the same states for the same years; of Edward Schwerin's (1977) analysis of 1,908 cases of the dyadic behavior of American actors towards 106 nations in 1963; and finally of my analysis (1972a) of 1,539 cases of the dyadic behavior of American actors towards 81 nations in 1955. Although not dyadic, the various results described in Rummel (1972) provide additional evidence. All these studies uniformly found familistic and contractual components independent of compulsory ones.

Chapter 5

EXPECTATIONS AND DISPOSITIONS

Expectations therefore are vital in relations between states. Every social order is based ultimately on expectations.
Luard, 1968: 41

It is in relation to expectations that contemporary theories of politics and international politics have most to offer to the practitioner.
(Burton, 1968: 71)

5.1 BEHAVIORAL DISPOSITIONS

Each of the empirical components of behavioral space-time (Table 4.1) defines a manifest pattern of behavior, an underlying structure or process—so much as been said. Now, each of these patterns comprise a type of behavioral choice available to an actor. He may transact, he may export, he may align, he may threaten, and so on. The eight components therefore span the common behavioral repertoire of actors, the space of common potential acts, actions, practices, and reflexes.

Moreover, each manifest behavioral pattern defined by the components reflects the underlying dispositions of actors to so behave. That is, the different empirical components not only reflect structures and processes, but also likely behavioral dispositions at different points in time.

Thus, the overall disposition of an actor to behave towards another can be visualized as a *time path* in behavioral space-time. The movement of this actor-object dyad through space-time depends on the actor's changing disposition. Figure 5.1 pictures these *actual paths* for the dyadic behavioral dispositions of the United States, USSR, and China dyads, 1950-1965, in the space of transactions and negative behavior—two behavioral components discussed previously.[1]

For Soviet dispositions towards the U.S., the figure shows an interesting movement away from negative behavior towards transactions from 1950 to

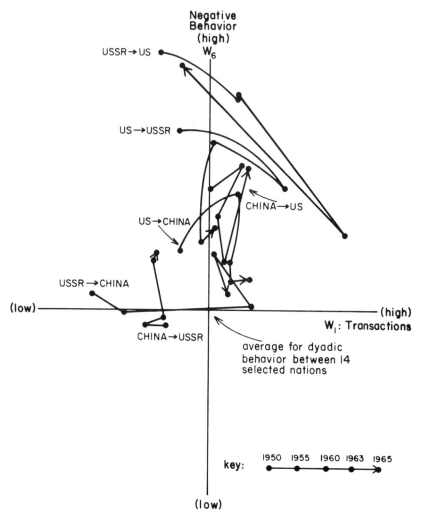

FIGURE 5.1: Space-Time Paths for the Mutual Behavioral Dispositions of China, USSR, and United States, 1950-1965

1963. However, from 1963 to 1965 there was a complete reversal of direction in dispositions—almost a return to the previous status quo. This can well be explained by the escalation of the Vietnam guerrilla war in 1963 to an intense local war between the United States and North Vietnamese by December, 1965, with North Vietnam fully supported by the Soviet Union. This 1963-1965 tendency to retreat from détente with the United States did not parallel American dispositions toward the Soviet Union. The United States also tended towards less negative behavior and more transactions between 1950-1955 (especially after the death of Stalin in 1953), but reversed that disposition after the Soviet suppression of the Hungarian Revolution in 1957, Khrushchev's missile rattling in the Suez War of 1957, the evidence of Soviet ICBM capability with their launching of Sputnik in 1958 and the resulting missile gap scare, the Berlin crisis of 1958, and the U-2 incident of 1960 which broke up the Eisenhower-Khrushchev summit. From 1960 to 1965, however, the U.S. disposition to transact with the Soviets remained about the same, while the tendency towards negative behavior decreased from 1960-1963, and only slightly increased as a result of Vietnam.

The effects of the Sino-Soviet split on their mutual dispositions can also be seen in Figure 5.1, where the Soviet movement towards greater transactions was reversed in 1960, with a greater tendency towards negative behavior (this was partially reversed in the 1963-1965 period, perhaps as a result of a need for a Vietnam war-related cooperation with China). However, China over the same period has simply tended towards more Soviet-directed conflict behavior.

5.2 AND EXPECTATIONS

Given an actor's dispositions, such as those shown in Figure 5.1, how in fact he behaves towards another depends on his assimilated, common expectations of the outcomes.[2] An actor will have such common expectations associated with each of the components and they will weight his associated dispositions. How in fact he behaves will be a result of his overall assessment of outcomes in relation to these dispositions.[3]

Figure 5.2 shows this actual relationship for Soviet dispositions towards the United States in 1963. The location of the disposition vector in 1963 is one point in the USSR →US time path plotted in Figure 5.1.[4] It is a disposition towards both high negative behavior *and* high transactions.

Would the Soviets then move toward a high-level conference with American leaders in 1963? Their common expectations about the outcome of such a conference is shown as the vector β_h in Figure 5.2. The projections of the expectation vector are product-moment correlations.[5] They show that conference expectations have a small, insignificant inverse relationship to those involved in negative behavior; a positive and high relationship (amounting to 36% of the variation in conference expectations)[6] to those expectations involved in transactions. That is, the Soviets see conference outcomes as irrelevant to negative behavior but quite important for enhancing or promoting transactions.

How in fact the Soviets will behave, whether they are likely to seek conferences with American leaders, is a function of both their common dispositions and expectations. Figure 5.2 shows this function at increasing levels of specificity. The actual number of high-level Soviet-American conferences in 1963 resulted from a weighting of Soviet behavioral dispositions by their expectations. This was a vector (dot) product of $w_{USSR \to US}$ and β_h; it was a summation of

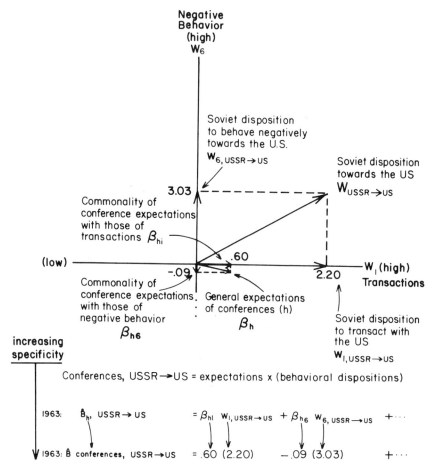

FIGURE 5.2: Soviet Expectations and Behavioral Dispositions Toward the U.S. in 1963

the product of expectations times dispositions on each behavioral space-time component.[7]

In terms of general international expectations and an actor's behavioral dispositions toward another at some specific time, the general equation for an actor's common behavior towards another is

$$\hat{B}_{h,i \to j} = \beta_{h1} w_{1,i \to j} + \beta_{h2} w_{2,i \to j} + \dots + \beta_{hq} w_{q,i \to j}, \qquad [5.1]$$

$$= \sum_{k} \beta_{hk} w_{k,i \to j},$$

where $\hat{B}_{h,i \to j}$ = manifest common behavior h of state, group or individual actor i toward state, group or individual actor j;

$w_{k,i \to j}$ = actor i's disposition to manifest component behavior k toward j;

β_{hk} = relationship of actor's expectation of the outcome of behavior h to those expectations involved in component behavior k;

Σ = summation sign (Σ_k means the values are summed across each component of behavior, k, for all q number of components).

This is a basic equation of international behavior.[8] It connects behavioral dispositions and expectations; it relates common manifest and latent behavior; it spans common cooperation and conflict; it locates actors in a common behavioral space-time. In short, it says that the behavior of one actor to another depends on the actor's dispositions and international expectations.[9]

To understand better the equation and the meaning of common, let me be more precise about the kind of behavioral variation it defines.[10] Figure 5.3 lays out in detail the variation being described. The solid middle bar represents all the dyadic variation in some specific behavior (B_h) of actors towards others. For example, if B_h denotes threats, then "variation" would mean that variation in the threats of the United States towards Albania, Afghanistan, Australia, and so on to Yemen, Yugoslavia, and Zaire; of the USSR towards each of these nations; of China towards each of those nations; and so on.

This variation in behavior is divisible into *common* and *unique,* where common variation refers to that intercorrelated with other behavior (such as negative sanctions, exports, treaties, and so on); unique is then that behavior which is uncorrelated—it is idiosyncratic, individualistic, odd. Variation in a kind of behavior (B_h) is thus a sum of the variation in common ($\hat{B}_h$) and unique behavior. Variation in unique behavior is shown in Figure 5.3, therefore, as $B_h - \hat{B}_h$. The common components of international behavior space-time discussed previously are those of this common variation in all kinds of behavior for all actors.

Now, the variation in common and unique behavior B_h is further divisible into practices and reflexes, and acts and actions as also shown. That is, some of the common variation in behavior partly involves international acts and actions, and partly practices and reflexes. If B_h is threats, then some variation may be due to routine behavior within a conflict process, some may be an automatic reflex, or some may constitute actions towards a goal.

Below the solid bar is indicated the relationship of common expectations and behavioral dispositions to behavior. First, note that these two common factors only relate to common behavior. And second, note that unique behavior is related to factors U other than common expectations and behavioral dispositions. What these might be is specific to the individual, behavior, situation, and object of behavior. For example, President Carter's threats towards the Soviet Union may be less than one would expect given his *common* dispositions and

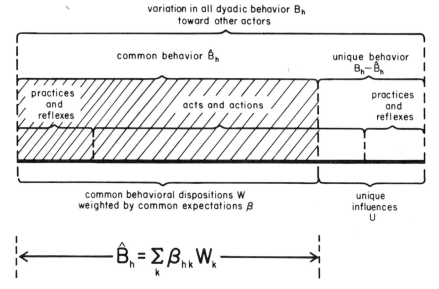

FIGURE 5.3: A Partition of the Variation in Dyadic Behavior into Common Dispositions and Expectations

expectations, due to a personal fear of an arms race and nuclear war with the Soviet Union that is not involved in threats to other nations.

Third and finally, note that all common behavior is assumed a consequence of common expectations and behavioral dispositions. That is, because common behavior is intercorrelated with other behavior there must be underlying expectations and dispositions shared among actors.

With this understood, the *vector* equation in Figure 5.2 should be clear. It is:

$$\hat{B}_h = \sum_k \beta_{hk} W_k,$$ [5.2]

where $\hat{B}_h$ = the common variation in (vector of) an actor's dyadic behavior h towards others;

$\beta_{h \to k}$ = common expectations among actors of behavior h in relation to the expectations involved in component behavior k;

W_k = the common variation in (vector of) dyadic dispositions of actors to manifest behavior h towards others.

Thus, Equation 5.1 given previously defines a specific common behavior h towards a specific state (thus, the subscripts i →j), which is an element in the vector $\hat{B}_h$ of Equation 5.2. The specific behavior, $\hat{B}_{h,i \to j}$, is not shown in Figure 5.3–the figure pictures all the *variation* in specific behavior towards others, rather than just that of i towards j.

To place this discussion of common behavior in the context of the international behavior of all actors, Figure 5.4 divides this space-time as shown. If B refers to the international space-time of all actors, then B is divisible into common ($\hat{B}$) and unique (B-$\hat{B}$) space-time. Then:

$$\hat{B} = W\beta \qquad [5.3]$$

where $\hat{B}$ = the matrix of common international behavior of actors towards others;

β = the matrix of general expectations of actors of the outcome of their behavior;

W = the matrix of common behavior dispositions of actors.

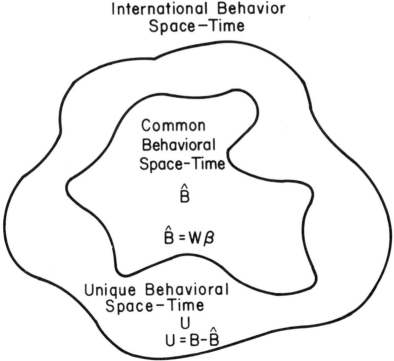

FIGURE 5.4: The Common and Unique Regions of International Behavior Space-Time

Equation 5.3 is the most general equation of expectations and dispositions. It defines the general expectations and dispositions model, which is given detail in vector terms for specific behavior by equation 5.2 and for a specific dyad by equation 5.1. These equations differ only in the level of specificity within the same model. Table 5.1 lists and describes these equations together.

Some words about choice and intentions are necessary here. The equations look deterministic; they seem to imply that given expectations and dispositions cause behavior. In no way is this meant. The equations simply mean that among diverse international actors are commonalities of dispositions and concern over consequences—that each actor will seek to gratify his interests depending on the costs and gains involved. The equations say no more than that given his disposition to behave in a certain way, and his general expectation of the outcome, he commonly will choose a specific behavior. As an historical generalization, a reflection of past data, the equations simply say that an actor has chosen such behavior as a result of certain dispositions and expectations. There is no loss of free will in this equation or in the previous analysis.

TABLE 5.1: **The Equations of Expectations and Dispositions**

LEVEL	EQUATION	TYPE OF EQUATION	DESCRIPTION
International behavioral space-time	$\hat{B} = W\beta$	matrix	The common behavior of actors towards others is a function of an actor's general expectations and common behavioral dispositions
Variation in an actor's common behavior	$\hat{B}_h = \Sigma\beta_{hik}W_k$	vector	The variation in an actor's particular common behavior towards others is a function of common expectations and behavioral dispositions
An actor's specific common behavior towards j	$\hat{B}_{h,i\to j} = \Sigma\beta_{hik}W_{k,i\to j}$	scalar	The specific common behavior of an actor towards another actor is a function of common expectations and common behavioral dispositions

NOTES

1. The plots in Figure 5.1 were generated from a factor analysis (super-P) done on 53 behavioral variables over the years 1950, 1955, 1960, 1963, and 1965 for 182 dyads. The plots are of the factor scores from the orthogonally rotated components of this image analysis. See Rummel (1978) for the specific results and original data.

2. Expectations should not be confused with perception, which I will discuss in the next chapter. On this I agree with Burton (1968: 69) who treats expectations as "analytically distinct from interactions and perceptions because they concern future behavior." I do not understand, however, his following argument that expectations thus give freer reign to "prejudice and preconceived notions because there can be no reality-testing as is frequently possible with perception." Indeed, I would argue that the opposite is the case. Expectations concern specific consequences about behavior and are constantly tested in the process of behaving. It is mutually tested and balanced expectations that forms the structure of expectations. But perceptions form part of our perspective, they constitute a larger framework of behavior, a gestalt that is not well-tested by individual behavior, but which may undergo slow change, or a sudden shift under an accumulation of events discordant with the framework.

3. The use of expectations regarding both cooperation and conflict behavior components may be confusing. The cooperation components reflect a *structure* of common expectations between actor *and* object, which is an implicit or explicit *contract*. These are common expectations mutually "negotiated" through a balancing of powers. Also, however, expectations are commonly associated with conflict behavior as well. An actor warns, threatens, sanctions, or does violence against another in the anticipation of certain consequences. Aspects of such expectations are common to all actors and are developed through common experiences of conflict, and through the culture shared by international actors. A diplomatic protest, for example, is ritualized, its role in diplomacy well understood. The pattern of expectations of which it is a part is familiar: accusations, protests, warnings, threats, ultimatums. Thus, for example, there are expectations locked into a treaty between parties, and there are the common expectations each party has about the actions involved in the negotiating process—the conflictful or balancing phase.

4. The particular behavioral dispositions of an actor to another are denoted here in lower case (e.g., $w_{k,i \to j}$), rather than the upper case W used in previous volumes. The reason is to make the notation simpler and more consistent with other notation to be introduced in subsequent chapters.

5. These values of the expectation vector are the factor loadings of conferences on the (orthogonal) behavioral space-time components. See note 1.

6. This is the squared correlation times 100.

7. Lest this seem overly abstract macro-analysis, the picture is congruent with a micro-analysis—with the psychological space of each actor. See Volume 1 (1975: chapters 13-14, 18). Volume 1 was written to provide the specific psychological foundations for the perspective being presented here.

8. Note that equations 33.1 and 33.3 in Volume 2, chapter 33, are unaccountably in error. They vary the expectations β by actor i and object j, $(\beta_{i \to j})$, when they are supposed to be generalized expectations regarding the outcome of a particular behavior (W_k). The correct specification for expectations is equation 5.1 given in the text.

9. Many operational questions will emerge at this point, the most important of which have been answered in my various publications and this chapter. To consider briefly just a few:

How is this common behavior space-time measured? By a common factor analysis of the widest, most varied dyadic behavior B_h.

How are the p common components W defined? Each W is a primary pattern factor (Rummel, 1970: section 17.1.1) resulting from an oblique rotation of the image analysis factors.

How are the dispositions of each actor to behave toward an object j measured? These are the factor scores of a dyad $i \rightarrow j$ on each factor W.

How are the generalized expectations of actors measured? These are the loadings of each behavior B_h (such as exports, threats, border clashes, state visits, and so on) on the separate factors W. *Thus, the Equation 5.1 is in fact the factor model* (with unique variance omitted and $B_{h,i \rightarrow j}$ assumed to define only common behavior). See Rummel (1970: sections 5.1-5.2). Thus, the expectation vector in Figure 5.1 is the vector of factor loadings for B_h; the disposition vector is the vector of factor scores for dyad $i \rightarrow j$.

How is time brought in? The data matrix is a super-matrix of column behaviors B_h over rows of dyads $i \rightarrow j$ for different time periods. Thus, one row would define US →China behavior 1950, another for 1955, a third for 1960, and so on for the time periods involved and the separate dyads. The logic underlying this space-time analysis is given in Rummel (1977: chapter 8). See Rummel (1978) for a full scale analyses of this space-time matrix.

10. For a fuller treatment of "common" than that given here, especially regarding latents and latent functions (components), see Volume 1 (1975: chapter 10).

Chapter 6

ACTOR AND SITUATION

The prism through which every nation looks at the outside world has been shaped by its own experience. For a policymaker, there is as much truth in Eliot's "Hell is ourselves" as in Sartre's "L'enfer, c'est les autres." How the same challenge (say decolonization) is met by France or Britain tells us much more about the domestic values and political habits of each nation than about the particular external circumstances that distinguish the French from the British problem. Any study of foreign policy that sets goals which cannot be reached so long as the nation does not change its skin and its soul is of limited worth.

Hoffmann, 1965

6.1. AN ORIENTATIONAL NOTE

So far I have shown that common dyadic behavior is a product of common expectations and behavioral dispositions—that the common behavior of, say, China's elite towards Japan is a result of their dispositions toward Japan, weighted by their expectations of the outcome of their behavior.

I could stop here in my analysis, for expectations and dispositions provide insight into behavior, are measurable,[1] equations are specified (such as Equation 5.1), and predictions of behavior can be made.[2] However, the analysis is not sufficiently fundamental or interesting. For while conceptually distinct, on the basis of the previous analysis we can only measure expectations and dispositions from past *behavior*. At the manifest level therefore, we simply have the equation that *behavior begets behavior*.

This clearly will not do, for a full understanding of international relations and conflict requires engaging power, ideology, perception, distance, situation, and the like. Such factors or forces must underlie expectations and dispositions; they must be brought out and their relationship to behavior clearly shown. Much unpacking must be done.

This I did at the conceptual level in Volumes 1 and 2. In Volume 1 I argued that the dynamic psychological field has a tetradic structure: expectations, behavioral dispositions, personality, and situation. An understanding of the relationship between these aspects provide insight into a person's behavior. In Volume 2, I focused this tetradic structure on the social behavior of one person to another, and argued that it takes place in a perceived situation and relative to the sociocultural distances (which include status and class) between actor and object: situation weights distances. And these distances reflect the personality[3] differences between individuals.

Because international relations are social relations among individuals (albeit in different authoritative and individual capacities), the analysis of Volume 2 applies here. Understanding international behavior and conflict means bringing in situation and distances. But in doing so, an approach different from Volume 2 must be taken. For there the concern was conceptual and philosophical, social and psychological understanding. I could ignore precise distinctions, methodological problems, and express only very general equations. Measurement was not of concern, insight was.

Here, however, both understanding and measurement are involved. I have the dual purpose of explaining behavior and rigorously defining this explanation with practical equations. I am after insight and numbers.

These aims create a double burden. I must be more logically discriminating and rigorous than before, but I must tie this logic into an intuitively meaningful explanation. This has been done in the previous chapters, but within the logical framework defined in previous volumes. Now, the framework itself must be extended. To do this, I will begin by focusing on an actor's behavior in a situation as perceived uniquely by him.

6.2. AN ACTOR'S BEHAVIORAL SITUATION

The common behavior of an international actor towards another consists of threats, exports, visits, conferences, and the like. For any period of time, we can define the *number* of an actor's threats, visits or conferences, or the amount of exports, and so on to another. Such is the measurement of $\hat{B}_{h, i \rightarrow j}$ appearing in previous equations. If h denotes threats, then $\hat{B}_{h, i \rightarrow j}$ means the number of common threats of i to j. That is, dyadic behavior is measured as an *aggregate*.

Now, this aggregate is of common expectations and dispositions, of common structures and processes of conflict. The aggregate reflects general international patterns among all actors. And this common level would suffice, if our concern was only with expectations, dispositions, and behavior.

But I am also interested in the underlying field forces—the distances. To focus on these forces toward behavior we must move down to the individual level—to that of an actor in a *situation* as he perceives it. For while the field forces, such as status and class distances, are common across actors, each actor will be influenced by them in his own way.[4] President Carter and Chairman Brezhnev may interact in different situations, such as in reference to arms control, to human rights, or to trade. Each may see these situations differently; to each different forces (power, wealth, ideology, and so on) may be salient.

An aggregate measure of behavior will amalgamate such different situations. The *total* threats of an actor to another over some period, for example, may well be due to one situation or be a combination of many. For this reason we should subdivide common behavior $\hat{B}_{h,i \to j}$ into that specific to each situation.

To wit:

$$\hat{B}_{h,i \to j} = \sum_g \hat{B}_{hg,i \to j}, \qquad [6.1]$$

where g = a situation;

$\sum_g$ = the summation across situations $1,2,3, \ldots, g, \ldots$.

That is, the common behavior of an actor i to another, such as its total threats, is an aggregate of behavior within separate situations $1,2, \ldots, g, \ldots, as$ *i perceives them.* And within each situation distinct common behavior $\hat{B}_{hg,i \to j}$ can be defined. Thus, we can consider, say, the number of threats of Brezhnev to Carter in an arms control situation distinct from those he makes in reaction to Carter's emphasis on human rights.

Now, i's behavior in a situation is subject to the same analysis as made of overall behavior. It is a composite of expectations and behavioral dispositions, except that since the situation is as i perceives it, the expectations will be specific to i as well. Thus,

$$\hat{B}_{hg,i \to j} = \beta_{hig} w_{g,i \to j}, \qquad [6.2]$$

where $w_{g,i \to j}$ = actor i's behavioral disposition toward j in situation g;

β_{hig} = i's expectation of the outcome of behavior h in situation g.

and from Equations 6.1 and 6.2,

$$\hat{B}_{h,i \to j} = \sum_g \beta_{hig} w_{g,i \to j} \qquad [6.3]$$

It should be clear that common expectations β_{hk} and dispositions in Equation 5.1 and β_{hig} and $w_{g,i \to j}$ in the above are not the same. Both are exepctations weighting dispositions; both sum to the same common behavior. One, however, is shared expectations among actors weighting dispositions reflecting common structures of expectations and conflict processes; the other is actor specific situational expectations and dispositions.

The expectations β_{hk} shared by all actors and the situational expectations β_{hig} of an actor are not independent. Each shared expectation is a complex result of the interaction between an actor's situational expectations and dispositions.[5] What is involved here is common to all societies. Each of us perceives social situations differently. Indeed, we may not even agree on what is the social situation. Here we are at the level of situational expectations and dispositions.

However, through interaction with others (the conflict helix) we develop over-arching expectations shared with others, which provide a framework for pursuing our different interests.

The rules of the road provide our everyday example. Each of us may see our automobile differently and we use it within our own perceived situations—to get to work, to shop, to display status, to conduct business, to make love. Each of us will have individual expectations and dispositions regarding our car. But on the road we all have developed shared expectations about the rules of road—about signalling turns, stop lights, passing, and so on. These common expectations enable us to achieve our situational expectations.

Similarly, transactions involve a general structure of expectation among states, or rules, contracts, norms, and the like. However, this structure is an outcome of each actor's specific situational expectations. For the United States, for example, transactions may be the outcome of a philosophy of free trade, a general belief in cooperative interactions and the benefits of an open market. Thus, a multitude of transactions reflect the diverse decisions of private individuals and groups seeking to gratify their own interests. However, for the Soviet Union, transactions may be fully determined by the elite, who see them as a factor in the historical struggle between capitalism and socialism, and particularly, the need for Western trade to overcome Soviet economic deficiencies. Nonetheless, these different situational expectations can lead, and have for the United States and Soviet Union, to shared expectations governing transactions. Thus, one could look at actual U.S.-Soviet transactions as a result of these shared expectations and common dispositions, or as of the situational expectations and dispositions.

To summarize this section, common, overall behavior is an aggregate of behavior in different, actor-perceived situations. And behavior in a situation is a product of situational expectations and behavioral dispositions.

6.3. SITUATIONAL DISPOSITIONS

What is the relationship between the dispositions common to general structures of expectations and conflict processes and the situational disposition? Now, each actor will see the common dispositions as having a particular function or role in a situation. Thus, for Brezhnev his disposition to transact, to export, to behave negatively toward the United States will be weighted in an arms control situation by his expectations specific to the situation. That is, his overall disposition in the situation will be a result of this weighting of such common dispositions by his situational expectations. Similarly, for the United States, Carter's disposition to transact, to export, to behave negatively will be weighted in a situation by his situational expectations.

To better define this,

$$w_{g,i \to j} = \sum_k \beta_{gik} w_{k,i \to j},$$ [6.4]

where $w_{k,i \to j}$ = the common dispositions of Equation 5.1;

β_{gik} = i's expectation of the outcome of behavior $w_{k,i \to j}$ in situation g.

An actor's situational disposition is a composite of his common dispositions weighted by his expectations of the outcome of these common dispositions in a particular situation.

But now *we have two kinds of situational expectations.* Those relating a specific behavior to situational disposition, and those relating situation to common dispositions. These can be put into one equation. From Equations 6.2 and 6.4,

$$\hat{B}_{hg,i \to j} = \beta_{hig}(\sum_k \beta_{gik} w_{k,i \to j})$$ [6.5]

Then, from Equation 6.1,

$$\hat{B}_{h,i \to j} = \sum_g \beta_{hig}(\sum_k \beta_{gik} w_{k,i \to j}).$$ [6.6]

This last equation now shows how aggregate common behavior is divided into the two kinds of situational expectations: those relating to specific behavior h and situational disposition; those relating situation and dispositions.

For example, the equation means that the number of Carter's threats to China is a result of the expectations Carter has of the outcome of threats in each situation he perceives between China and the United States (such as the Sino-Soviet conflict, the danger to South Korea from the North, the stability of Southeast Asia, the Taiwan problem in normalizing U.S.-China relations); and these expectations weight his disposition to behave towards China in a certain way in each situation. Moreover, these situational dispositions themselves result from Carter's expectation of the outcome in each situation weighting his common dispositions toward China—the common structures of expectations and conflict processes between the United States and China.

6.4. THE BEHAVIORAL VARIATION

In Figures 5.3-5.4 of the last chapter, I defined the behavioral variation dependent on common expectations and dispositions. The same clarity is now required here.

Equations 6.1-6.6 focus on the variation in the common behavior of an actor, and defines this variation as dependent upon his perceived situation, as reflected in his situational expectations and dispositions. Figure 6.1 delineates this variation and its elements for an actor.

As for Figure 5.3, the variation of interest is defined in Figure 6.1 by vector notation:

$\hat{B}_{hi}$ = vector of i's common behavior h to object 1, object 2, . . ., object j, . . . ;

W_{gi} = vector of i's behavior dispositions in situations g towards object 1, object 2, . . ., object j, . . . ;

W_{ki} = vector of i's common behavioral dispositions on behavior component k towards object 1, object 2, . . ., object j, ...

The situational expectations β_{hig} and β_{gik} are scalar parameters.

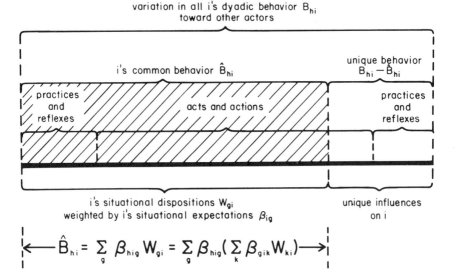

variation in all i's dyadic behavior B_{hi}
toward other actors

i's common behavior $\hat{B}_{hi}$

unique behavior $B_{hi} - \hat{B}_{hi}$

practices and reflexes

acts and actions

practices and reflexes

i's situational dispositions W_{gi} weighted by i's situational expectations β_{ig}

unique influences on i

$$\hat{B}_{hi} = \sum_g \beta_{hig} W_{gi} = \sum_g \beta_{hig} \left(\sum_k \beta_{gik} W_{ki} \right)$$

FIGURE 6.1: **The Partition of the Variation in an Actor's Dyadic Behavior into Situational Dispositions and Expectations**

$$\hat{B}_{hi} = \beta_{hi1} W_{1i} + \beta_{hi2} W_{2i} + \cdots + \beta_{hig} W_{gi} + \cdots = \sum_g \beta_{hig} W_{gi}$$

$$\begin{bmatrix} \hat{B}_{h,j\to1} \\ \hat{B}_{h,j\to2} \\ \vdots \\ \hat{B}_{h,i\to j} \\ \vdots \end{bmatrix} = \beta_{hi1} \begin{bmatrix} w_{1,i\to1} \\ w_{1,i\to2} \\ \vdots \\ w_{1i\to j} \\ \vdots \end{bmatrix} + \beta_{hi2} \begin{bmatrix} w_{2,i\to1} \\ w_{2,i\to2} \\ \vdots \\ w_{2,i\to j} \\ \vdots \end{bmatrix} + \cdots + \beta_{hig} \begin{bmatrix} w_{g,i\to1} \\ w_{g,i\to2} \\ \vdots \\ w_{g,i\to j} \\ \vdots \end{bmatrix} + \cdots = \sum_g \beta_{hig} w_{gi}$$

FIGURE 6.2: **The Vector Equation of an Actor's Common Behavior, Dispositions, and Expectations**

International Behavior
Space—Time B

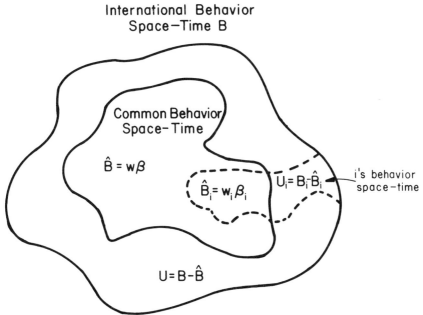

FIGURE 6.3: An Actor's Behavioral Region in International Behavior Space-Time

The equation at the bottom of Figure 6.1 is the vector counterpart of scalar Equation 6.6;[6] the latter defines an element, $\hat{B}_{h,i \to j}$, in the vector $\hat{B}_{hi}$. This should be clear from Figure 6.2, in which the dashed rectangle contains the scalar Equation 6.3, and the vertical brackets define the vectors and their elements. Figure 6.2 is another way of expressing the variation in i's behavior illustrated in Figure 6.1.

Finally, there is the question as to how the behavioral space-time of an actor fits into the overall international space-time of all actors, as pictured in Figure 5.4. Figure 6.3 illustrates that in dealing with an actor alone, I am not defining a new space-time, but only a *region* of the space-time of all actors. Thus, the matrix of i's common behavior, $\hat{B}_i$, is a submatrix of $\hat{B}$,[7] and U_i is a submatrix of U. However, because they are specific to i's perceived situations, the matrices W_i and β_i are not submatrices of W and β. Indeed, the purpose of separating the region $\hat{B}_i$ is to define expectations β_1 and dispositions W_i that are not common to other actors.

6.5. SUMMARY

Table 6.1 summarizes the levels are equations of behavior. Leaving aside the notation and equations, I have simply moved beneath the framework of expecta-

TABLE 6.1: The Behavioral Equation of Situational Expectations and Dispositions

LEVEL	EQUATION	TYPE OF EQUATION	DESCRIPTION
International behavioral space-time	$\hat{B}_i = W_i \beta_i$	Matrix	An actor commonly behaves towards others depending on his situational expectations and dispositions
Variation on an actor's common behavior	$\hat{B}_{hi} = \sum_g \beta_{hig}(\sum_k \beta_{gik} W_{ki})$ $= \sum_g \beta_{hig} W_{gi}$	Vector	An actor commonly varies his specific behavior towards others depending on his situational expectations and dispositions toward them
An actor's specific common behavior towards an object j	$\hat{B}_{h,i \to j} = \sum_g \beta_{hig}(\sum_k \beta_{gik} w_{k,i \to j})$ $= \sum_g \beta_{hig} w_{g,i \to j}$	Scalar	An actor commonly will behave in a specific way toward another depending on his situational expectations and disposition toward the other

tions and dispositions common to actors to those situationally specific to an actor. This enables us to relate situations as perceived by an actor to the particular combination of forces influencing him.

I have argued that in each situation an actor perceives, he is disposed to behave towards another in a certain way. And that this situational, behavioral disposition is a combination of his common dispositions weighted by expectations of the outcomes within the situation. Moreover, I have argued that the actual common behavior of an actor towards another is a combination of the situational dispositions weighted by expectations of the behavioral outcome.[8] All this is prelude to the following chapters.

NOTES

1. See note 9, chapter 5.

2. Such have been done, for example, in my *Field Theory Evolving* (1977: chapter 5).

3. Personality involves temperament and personal abilities, to be sure, but also attitudes, interests, needs, sentiments, values, cognitive structures, and roles. See Volume 1.

4. I am here arguing for Model II of field theory (Rummel, 1977: especially section 4.4 and chapter 16). Model I presumes that common forces operate in the same way for all actors. Although I discarded this for Model II before empirically testing the field theory equations, some "let's see what would happen anyway" empirical assessment of Model I was done using distance vectors. The results showed no better ability to predict behavior overall than guesswork. That is, assuming actors are similarly influenced by underlying field forces (in terms of differences) provides no general ability to predict behavior. Model II is later stated as a proposition (Actor Proposition 16.7) in appendix 16B.

When Model I is used as a framework for linking dyadic behavior to the actors' attributes and absolute or squared distances, however, some moderate relationships do appear. See, for example, appendix I, section 4.

5. From the previous equations and those to follow, the explicit functions can be worked out. They are complex, involving summations, products and quotients of situational expectations and dispositions W_k. I see no need to include these functions here.

6. The vector equation is written in statistical notation for clarity. Introducing vector algebra at this point would only add another layer of symbols (e.g., the vector of parameters β_{gi}) to no manipulative end.

7. Technically, the common behavioral space-time of actors is first determined through common factor analysis. Then that portion of the common space-time defining i's behavior is used in subsequent analyses of situational expectations and dispositions. This is done through employing only i's common behavior dispositions (factor scores on the components of common space-time).

The importance of this approach is that i's common behavior is defined relative to that behavior of other actor's; i's behavior is explained within the common behavioral field. Thus, context is maintained and the results explain not only why i made more threats to object j, than to k, but also why i made more threats than, say, agreements, with object j in comparison to the behavior of other actors to j.

8. All this is consolidated into the Actor Proposition 16.7 in appendix 16B, which the systematic evidence presented there strongly supports.

PART III

THE INTERNATIONAL FIELD

We need "variables which are capable of general treatment." They are to be provided by a general framework defined as a set of interrelated questions, or, as it is sometimes called, a "box," but, if I may say so, a flexible one, and one whose main role is to be put to use. . . .

The most fruitful approach to building such a box is, as Quincy Wright has suggested, to consider the world as a field in which individuals, groups, nations, international organizations, and so on, compete, clash, and cooperate, rather than as a plan designed by God, by history, or by nature, or as an equilibrium, or an organization, or as a community: at any given moment the world might present certain aspects of one of the latter models, but never of all of them, whereas the idea of a field is always a more accurate approximation.

Hoffmann, 1960: 179

Chapter 7

INTERNATIONAL SOCIOCULTURAL
SPACE-TIME

each international organization, national government, association, individual, or other "system of action," or "decision-maker" may be located in a multidimensional field. Such a field may be defined by coordinates, each of which measures a political, economic, psychological, sociological, ethical, or other continuum influencing choices, decisions, and actions important for international relations.

Wright, 1955: 543

7.1 SPACE-TIME COMPONENTS

Structures of expectations and conflict processes are seated in the meanings, values, and norms of each actor and his status and class. Actors differ in religion, philosophy, language, science, fine arts, ethics, and law; in wealth, power and prestige; in being superordinate or subordinate. Each new contact, event, or relationship may therefore involve a clash of different perspectives, of diverse situational expectations and dispositions, and thus a process of working out common expectations—a conflict process.[1]

> Foreign policy objectives are shaped within the whole political idea-system, which in turn is a part of cultural idea-system and of the whole culture. It is hardly possible to understand foreign policy objectives without this cultural perspective and, therefore, they should be analyzed within the context to a society and culture.
>
> Gross, 1954: 63

International behavior therefore takes place within a sociocultural framework, a space-time spanned by components mutually locating actors. These components are the reference points for action; the space bounds and defines the potentiality for conflict.

These components are the main ingredients of theoretical and applied analysis: nations are characterized and compared as to economic development, economic growth, and modernization; as to political development, type of government, and ideology; as to race, religion, and language; as to ethnicity, national character, and culture; as to area, people, and climate. And, of course, as to power, prestige and predominance.

[109]

In summing up his comprehensive overview of international relations, *The Study of International Relations* (1955: 543ff), Quincy Wright tried to define analytically components that would locate states, nations, governments, and people in an international space.[2] He distinguished six *capability* components: rate of economic progress (flexibility versus rigidity), rate of political decentralization (lethargy versus energy), degree of power (strength versus weakness), rate of development of international trade and communication (isolation versus cooperation), rate of technological development (technological advancement versus backwardness), and resources (resource poverty versus abundance); and six additional *value* components: evaluation (objective versus subjective), perception (concrete versus abstract), action (manipulative versus contemplative), relations (restrictive versus liberal), orientation (self-orientation versus situation orientation), and expectations (affirmation versus negation).[3]

In essence, Wright's six capability components define the wealth, power and politics of actors (if we ignore the behavioral component of trade and communications, which is similar to transactions as described in the previous chapter); in essence, his six value components reflect the philosophy and religion, ethics and law, fine arts, science, and language of actors. In short, Wright has distinguished the social and cultural components of status, class, meanings, values and norms.

The purpose of Wright's components was to define the analytical space of international actors within which their position and motion could be envisioned. For Wright saw that the distances between actors in this space[4] and their relative movements implied cooperation or conflict, peace or war.[5]

He determined the components by an intuitive factor analysis of national attributes:

> What continua can most usefully be employed as coordinates for defining this analytical field? The problem is similar to that of determining the factors which account for mental performance, studied by psychologists. C. E. Spearman assumed a single factor, L. L. Thurstone devised methods for determining the minimum number of factors necessary to account for the results of numerous tests of mental ability. He found that factors concerning the use of words, numbers, and visual images were sufficient to account for the results of certain tests. Application of similar methods to a limited body of data suggested that the psychic relations among certain states could be accounted for by four factors—opinions concerning change, ideology, war, and form of government. No such analysis is attempted here. A dozen factors are postulated and relations among them suggested from some familiarity with the field, in the hope that eventually measurement of these factors may permit of correlations to determine the degree of their sufficiency, redundancy, and applicability.
>
> 1955: 545-546

At the time Wright wrote, such first empirical measurements had already been done in the factor analyses of nations by Cattell (1949, 1950) and colleagues

TABLE 7.1: Common Components of International Sociocultural Space-Time

ACTOR	COMPONENT[a]	REPRESENTATIVE CORRELATED ATTRIBUTES[b]
individual	Catholic culture	proportion of Roman Catholics percent divorces proportion of college students in law
	density	number of people to land area proportion of arable land railroad length to land area
individual and group	wealth	energy consumption per capita gross national product per capita literacy rate
group	diversity	number of language groups number of ethnic groups proportion of the population speaking one language
	import dependency	imports to trade imports to gross national product aid received
state	power (coercive)	energy production times population national income military expenditures
	totalitarianism	communist government no political freedom complete censorship
	authoritarianism	one-party rule military participation in government censorship
	size	population area
individual group, and state	social conflict	riots coup d' etats guerrilla warfare

a. The components are from the image analyses of transformed data, orthogonal rotation, given in R. J. Rummel, *National Attributes and Behavior*, Beverly Hills: Sage Publications, 1978, chapter 5.

b. These correlated attributes are a synthesis of the results given in R. J. Rummel, *Ibid.*, and *Dimensions of Nations*, Beverly Hills: Sage Publications, 1972.

(Cattell, Bruel, and Hartman, 1951).[6] The Dimensionality of Nations Project, which began in 1962 and which I directed until it ended in 1975, initially focused on replicating the components Cattell found and better empirically defining Wright's "analytical" space of nations. Data were collected on hundreds of economic, political, demographic, social, cultural, and geographic attributes for all nations; dozens of factor analyses were done; and results were systematically compared with those of Cattell and others doing similar analyses.[7]

The results were described in Volume 2 (1976: chapter 34). The purposes there were to define the sociocultural space of state-societies; measure the structures of expectations within states; and test the hypothesis that theoretical exchange, authoritative, and coercive types were society's major empirical forms.

The common components described in Volume 2, and in detail in my *Dimensions of Nations* (1972) and *National Attributes and Behavior* (1978) are

TABLE 7.2: The Wealth Component

ATTRIBUTE DOMAIN[a]	REPRESENTATIVE CORRELATED ATTRIBUTES[b]
Agriculture	proportion agricultural workers proportion agricultural production
Arts and Culture	motion picture attendance per capita book titles per capita
Communications	newspaper circulation per capita telephones per capita
Demographic	birth rate urbanization
Economic	gross national product per capita energy consumption per capita
Education	literacy proportion of 5-14 age group in primary school
Health	infant death rate heart disease deaths per capita
Science and Technology	proportion science book titles productivity
Social	proportion dwellings with piped water divorce rate
Transportation	roads per square kilometer air passenger kilometers per capita
Values	proportion Protestants proportion female students

a. The domains simply provide conceptual organization to the list of attributes correlated with wealth.
b. See footnote b, Table 7.1.

shown in Table 7.1. They delineate international sociocultural space-time; they locate individuals, groups, and states relative to each other in this space-time; and they enable relative movement and distances to be measured.

I have discussed these components in detail elsewhere.[8] Because of their particular importance in international relations, however, a few details on the wealth, power, totalitarianism and authoritarianism components are warranted.

Wealth has consistently appeared in all empirical analyses as the major component of nations.[9] The range of attributes delineated by this component is shown in Table 7.2. Wealth involves a highly intercorrelated cluster of agriculture, cultural, communication, demographic, economic, education, health, scientific and technological, social, transportation, and value-type attributes. It obviously reflects the sociocultural meanings, values, and norms of individual actors. And it reflects their international status.

Next in empirical scope has consistently appeared the power component, which is given in Table 7.3. This measures the bases of a state's coercive and exchange power, and is identical to "national power" as usually defined in the literature. The elements or factors of national power generally isolated in the literature are correlated with it,[10] including the major indices of power suggested by scholars: size and population (Strausz-Hupé and Possony, 1950);

TABLE 7.3: The Power Component

ELEMENTS OF NATIONAL POWER[a]	REPRESENTATIVE CORRELATED ATTRIBUTES[b]
Military	defense expenditures military personnel
Mass	population area
Economic	gross national product national income
Political	centralization unitary versus federalist government
Resources	energy resources energy resources per capita
Production	steel production total energy production x population
Transportation	railroad length railroad freight per capita

a. Those elements simply provide conceptual organization to the list of attributes correlation with power.
b. See footnote b, Table 7.1.

TABLE 7.4: The Political Components

COMPONENT	REPRESENTATIVE CORRELATED ATTRIBUTES[a]		
totalitarianism	Communist	versus	noncommunist regime
	totalitarian control	versus	constitutionally limited
	mobilizes population	versus	nonmobilizational
	censorship	versus	noncensorship
	no freedom of group opposition	versus	freedom of group opposition
	noncompetitive electoral system	versus	competitive
authoritarianism	no freedom of group opposition	versus	freedom of group opposition
	few political parties	versus	many
	little horizontal power distribution	versus	horizontal power distribution
	totalitarian control	versus	constitutionally limited
	censorship	versus	noncensorship
	elitist	versus	nonelitist
	interventive military	versus	neutral military

a. From R. J. Rummel, *National Attributes and Behavior*: Beverly Hills, Sage Publications, 1978.

national income (Organski, 1958); and energy production X population (Wright, 1955).[11]

And then there are the two political components shown in Table 7.4. One measures the totalitarian versus liberal democratic component of state politics; the other the authoritarian versus liberal democratic. That liberal democracies are a common end to both components empirically reflects the ideological triangle existing in a two-dimensional political space-time.[12] The three points of the triangle are the pure political types: libertarian, totalitarian, and authoritarian (or dynastic). Incidentally, while independent (distinct), the totalitarianism and authoritarianism components are correlated.[13] Thus, some political attributes are correlated with both components, as shown in Table 7.4.

Wealth, power, totalitarianism, and authoritarianism are the primary components of nations. They, plus the other, smaller components shown in Table 7.1 span the sociocultural space. They locate and differentiate international actors. The meanings, values and norms of actors are reflected in the wealth, Catholic culture, diversity, density, totalitarianism, and authoritarianism components; and their statuses[14] and class are mirrored by the wealth, power, size, and import dependency components.

These components do dual service. They delineate the international space-time of actors. *And they reflect the various structures of expectations within each state through which actors understand and perceive other actors.*[15] As should be the case, therefore, there is also an independent social conflict component (the domestic counterpart of the international conflict components discussed in the last chapter) which delineates the conflict process in the formation and disruption of these structures.

7.2 DISTANCES AND SITUATION

Actors are located in a common international space-time by the components. As individuals come from rich or poor, Catholic or non-Catholic, and dense or sparsely populated nations they will have different sociocultural positions; as groups are of rich or poor, homogeneous or diverse states, they will have different sociocultural locations; and as governmental elite are of weak or powerful, of liberal democratic, authoritarian or totalitarian states, they also will be differently placed in the international, sociocultural space-time.

And as actors have different meanings, values, norms, status and class, they will be disposed to behave towards each other in different ways. Their interests, capabilities, and expectations will diverge. Structures of expectations will evolve with more or less difficulty. The tendency will be towards either cooperation or conflict. All this is to say that *sociocultural distances* comprise potential social forces on behavior.[16]

As in Quincy Wright's analyses of war (1942) and international relations (1955), the concept of distance has been basic to my work.[17] I have elaborated it psychologically and sociologically in Volumes 1-3, and mathematically (especially in reference to international relations) in *Field Theory Evolving* (1977). This ground need not be covered again. I should, however, clarify the relationship between distances on different components and the three types of international actors.

Although common components are salient to particular actors, as power is to the elite and wealth to individuals and groups, all actors are part of the same international space-time. Actors therefore will be influenced by and perceive others in relation to all the components. A foreign minister will interact with his counterpart as his interests and capability relate to the power and political perspective of the other, but the other's culture and nation's wealth will also play a role. The cultural matrix (Volume 1, 1975: chapters 7 and 11) through which each sees the other, their attitudes and diverse interests, their ability to communicate, will depend on their overall location in international, sociocultural space-time. But nonetheless, certain components will dominate their relationship, and these will be of wealth, power and politics.[18]

To the observer, distances between actors are the indicators of possible agreement or disagreement, predictable behavior or uncertainty. To the actor distances are perceived.[19] They are potential forces toward behavior. What is also perceived by an actor is the *situation,* the context within which he relates to others. For interests and capabilities are activated and take on different flavor and meaning depending on the perceived context. Sociocultural distances are

therefore weighted by the perceived situation within which actors are interacting. Economic, political, and power distances will reflect different combinations of interests of the U.S. foreign policy elite toward the Soviet Union, for
example, as the perceived situation is a UN General Assembly debate on racism,
a concern for the U.S.-USSR military balance at the global level, or Soviet
violations of a 200-mile U.S. fishing zone.

My concern here is, however, not with specific, nonreccurring situations, but
with the general contextual frameworks within which an actor behaves, such as

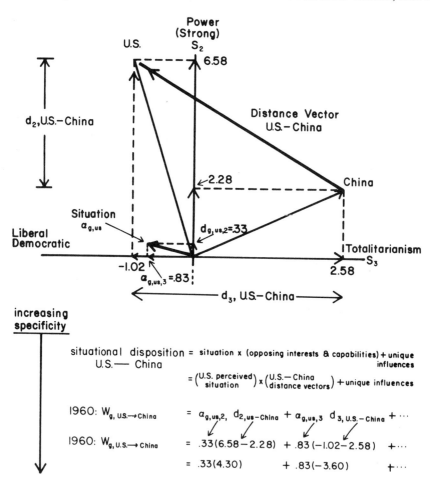

**FIGURE 7.1: U.S. Situational Perceptions of China, and Totalitarian and Power
Distances in 1960**

the cold war or the international market. Regarding such general situations, we can assume that those interests and capabilities (distances) salient for one actor will not be for another in the same situation; that different actors will not perceive situations similarly.[20]

Figure 7.1 shows an actual 1960 relationship between the perceived situations for U.S. actors and distances between the United States and China in a common space of the two international space-time components of power and totalitarianism. Within this space the United States was located as a vector with projections shown by the dotted lines on both components; China also had a location and projections as shown. The distances between the United States and China were then vectors $d_{US\text{-}China,2}$ and $d_{US\text{-}China,3}$ lying along the components. These vectors were then potential social forces affecting the behavior of American actors towards China. In other words, these differences in power and political systems reflected particular American attitudes and potential capabilities towards China, *and therefore a behavioral disposition of American actors.*

These potential forces were activated by the perceived situation g represented by the vector $\alpha_{g,US}$ which was related to power and totalitarianism as shown by the dotted projections. The situation was of a particular pattern (type g)[21] perceived by Americans as salient to relative U.S. power, but seen as largely independent (as shown by the small projection on totalitarianism) of this difference in political systems. In this perceived power dominating situation, particular American interests were activated and disposed American actors to behave towards China in a certain way. That is, the perceived situation activated American interests and capabilities, and the combination of situation, interests, and relative capabilities was then a force towards behavior:

$$1960: \text{disposition}_{g,US\rightarrow China} \longleftarrow \alpha_{g,US,2} d_{US\text{-}China,2} + \alpha_{g,US,3} d_{US\text{-}China,3}.$$

The arrow in the above is simply to indicate a force towards behavior.[22]

Clearly, this behavioral disposition in a situation is a link to the analyses of the previous chapters. There we saw that our actor's behavior was a resultant of situational expectations and dispositions. Now, we have dispositions as a resultant of distances in a situation. But before we draw what appears the obvious conclusion that an actor's behavior is then a function of expectations and distances, some additional behavior is required, especially to bring in the actor's will.

Summary

The common international sociocultural space-time is defined by independent, empirical components reflecting the meanings, values, norms, status and class of international actors. Such major components are wealth, power, totalitarianism, authoritarianism, and size, among others.

The interests and capabilities of actors are reflected in these components, and distances between actors in this space-time mirror their attitudes toward each other and their potential, relative capabilities. These potentials are transformed into actual interests and capabilities by an actor's perception of a situation. And this perception then energizes a disposition to behave towards another in a certain way.

N O T E S

1. All this was developed in Volume 2. See therein chapter 13 on meanings, values and norms, chapters 17 and 18 on status, chapters 19 and 20 on power, chapters 24 and 25 on class, and chapter 29 on the process of conflict.

2. See note 27, chapter 3.

3. In postulating value components Wright was much influenced by Talcott Parson's analysis, especially as described in the working papers on his theory (Parsons and Shills, 1951). The value components defining evaluations, perceptions, relations, and orientations correspond to Parson's four pattern variables: achievement-ascription, particularism-universalism, specificity-generality, and self-orientation-collective orientation. Parsons analysis was built on that of Pitirim Sorokin, and lost clarity and insight in translation. For a close comparison of the two "systems," see Sorokin (1966). In previous volumes I have clearly preferred Sorokin's work. For a comparison of my perspective to Sorokin's, see Volume 3 (1977: especially chapter 6 and section 8.1).

4. Wright termed this space a field. He used field to refer to a totality of interdependent and reciprocal relationships (which is what I call a *relational* field theory). For my analysis of physical, social, and psychological field theories, see Volume 1 (1975: part I). Section 4.6 specifically deals with Wright's theory.

5. Wright had elsewhere analyzed the consequences of changing distances, particularly in his major work, *A Study of War* (1942: 1240ff, 1254, 1433ff, 1471). Wright then used a calculus model to interrelate diverse distances. Over a decade later he incorporated this model into a linear (algebraic) and spatial view of international relations (the differential terms in his equation are components of the space).

By contrast, I moved directly to a linear algebraic perspective in the mid-1960s and allowed the components to reflect (as latent functions) *any* linear term, whether differentials or otherwise. See my *Field Theory Evolving* (1977), particularly chapter 10 which tests Wright's distance hypotheses, among others. See also appendix 9A.

6. As evidenced by his major works on war (1942) and international relations (1955), Wright was a thorough scholar, widely read in many disciplines, and open to diverse approaches and methods. It is not a commentary on the man but on the difficulties of any scholar keeping up with relevant contemporary work in other fields that he should be unaware of Cattell's work (published in psychological and sociological journals) which followed the path of Thurstone and did precisely what Wright saw needed.

7. A description and critical evaluations of the Dimensionality of Nations Project are given in Hoole and Zinnes (1976). For monographs on the project, see Hilton (1973) and Seidelmann (1973). For an autobiographical essay on the project's role in the evolution of the perspective presented here, see my "Roots of Faith" (1976b). The major quantitative results of the project are given in Rummel (1972, 1977, and 1978); the basic methodology in Rummel (1970).

8. My *Dimensions of Nations* (1972) presents the components for 236 variables for 82 nations in 1955, and a systematic comparison with the components found by others. Moreover, the sources of error in the results are systematically assessed. See also my *Applied Factor Analysis* (1970) for the use of such components and related results to exemplify the application of factor analysis. In my *Field Theory Evolving* (1977) the components are

discussed and used to predict dyadic behavior. And in my *National Attributes and Behavior* (1978) the technical details and research design surrounding the delineation of the specific components in Table 7.1 are given, as well as the data. Appendix 9A brings all these results together with regard to international behavior.

9. See the systematic comparisons of the economic development component in Rummel (1972: chapter 10). In light of the subsequent results in Rummel (1978), I changed the name of the component to wealth. The idea of affluence and abundance versus poverty better conceptualize the diverse cluster of attributes delineated by this component.

10. To be clear about a possible source of confusion, the representative correlated attributes were not determined by correlating the component with a mass of variables and selecting out the higher correlations. Nor was the component formed by selecting and scaling the indicated attributes. Rather, hundreds of attributes were factor-analyzed and power was one of the independent components uncovered in this mass of data. In other words, in cross-national data there is a distinct, independent, empirical pattern of attributes which reflect national power, and some of those attributes are shown in Table 7.3.

11. Alcock (1970: 339) found that: "The power of nations as perceived by Canadian subjects is best explained in terms of military expenditures of nations." Military expenditures is also correlated with the power component, as shown in Table 7.3.

12. For the details of this political triangle, see Volume 2 (1976: chapter 31).

13. Because of this correlation, the two components often appear as one political orientation component in orthogonal rotation, or in studies with insufficient political attributes to distinguish the two types.

14. In international relations, the perceived prestige of a state is largely dependent on wealth and power. For an empirical study of this, for example, see Alcock (1970). Therefore, I assume that a state's wealth and power as measured by the components in Tables 7.2 and 7.3 empirically reflect its international wealth, power, *and* prestige.

15. These components measure national character, as reflected by the location of an actor in the common, international space-time. This is not to imply that national character is homogeneous. Rather, national character has different loci within the nation, it is differentiated into individual, group, and state levels. The character of individuals from a wealthy and economically developed state is similar in many respects to those from another wealthy and developed state. Industrialization creates considerable similarity in interests and perspectives. However, the character of the elite between these same states will differ considerably if one is a communist state, the other liberal democratic. The point that national character has different loci is made by Terhune (1970) in his critical review of the national character literature and reformulation of the concept.

16. The role of distance in conflict is later made more specific empirically in appendix 9A, and in appendix 16B through a number of propositions. The relevant evidence is also provided therein. See Propositions 16.6, 16.12, 16.14, 16.21, 16.32 and 16.33.

17. For how I came to realize the importance and use of this concept, see my "Roots of Faith" (1976b).

18. See the Wealth-Power-Politics Proposition (16.33) in appendix 16B for the evidence, which is strongly supportive.

19. In Volume 1, I tried to clarify the psychological nature, aspects, and roles of perception; in Volume 2 I similarly analyzed perception in a social context. Perception is now a well-accepted analytical concept in international relations, as for example in the work of Burgess (1967), Boulding (1959), Burton (1968), and Jervis (1970), and is worked through such ideas as "misperception," "image," "cognitive dissonance," and "cognitive model," all of which play a role in my own analysis.

In brief review, we perceive others along components related to ourselves (as distances from ourselves in psychological space) and in relation to a situation. This perception of *both* ourselves and others and of the situation is shaped by our cultural matrix, by our cognitive models of the world, by our self-images and those of the other, and by psychological forces toward balance and consistency. How these distances between international actors and situations combine to predict international behavior reflects this perception, as will be discussed in the next chapters. But for the moment I will be content to sum up my view in the words of Harold and Margaret Sprout (1965: 224): "values and preferences, moods and attitudes, choices and decisions are relatable to the milieu only via the environed individual's selective perception and his psychological reactions to what is perceived. From the perspective of decisions and decision-making, what matters is how the individual or group imagines the milieu to be, *not* how it actually is."

See the Actor and Perception Propositions 16.7 and 16.29 in appendix 16B.

20. See the Actor Proposition in appendix 16B.

21. In my previous works I have left different situations denotatively implicit. But this has tended to confuse, especially in detailing the precise linkages between behavior, situation and distances. Also, were I able to begin my notation from scratch without the baggage created by my previous publications and conventional notation in factor analysis and canonical analysis, I would denote situation by s rather than α. However, to so drastically alter notation at this point would be to create even more confusion.

22. As with the last chapter, the reader may have many operational questions, some of which may be as follows.

How are the common components of space-time defined? Data are arrayed in an actor (state) by years by attribute matrix, where the columns are defined by attributes. The matrix is factor analyzed (image analysis) and the components rotated to an oblique (biquartimin) solution.

How is the location of each actor i and j defined? Each state i has a location in international, sociocultural space-time defined by its factor scores, $s_{i\varrho}$, on the image components.

How are the sociocultural distances between actor and object measured? This is the difference $s_{i\varrho} - s_{j\varrho}$ in factor scores of i and j on each component.

How is the situation $\alpha_{gi\varrho}$ measured? This is the ϱth canonical coefficient of the gth equation of a canonical regression of dyadic behavior onto the distances. Rummel (1978) empirically exemplifies this design. See also appendix 9A.

Chapter 8

INTERESTS, CAPABILITIES, AND WILL

Policies and distances are clearly interrelated.
Wright, 1942: 1255

8.1 THE EQUATION OF INTERESTS, CAPABILITIES, AND WILL

Now I can be more complete and precise about the relationship between distances (interests and capabilities), situation, will, and behavior. For this I will rely on Figure 8.1, which reproduces Figure 6.1 and adds to it the forces and elements accounting for the variation in an actor's international behavior.[1]

In the previous discussion and Volumes, I have tried to make clear that distance vectors between actors empirically reflect their relative, latent attitudes and capabilities, and that attitudes are transformed into interests through the stimulation of associated needs. Attitudes are therefore inactive interests. And by themselves, distances only define potentiality. All this will be discussed further in section 10.2 regarding the structure of conflict.

However, here and in Figure 8.1, I am concerned with distances in a situation in relation to behavior. A perceived situation stimulates needs; it transforms attitudes into interests, potential capability into actual capability. Therefore, the distances linked to an actor's behavior in a situation will reflect his living interests and relevant capabilities. Of course, not all interests will be weighted in a situation—not all interests will be active. It is the situational weights α that measure the transformation of attitudes into interests and the relative weight these interests will have.

However, between the activation of interests and the utilization of relevant capabilities is the will. The will is an actor's power to actually choose and try to gratify his interests—to bring himself to behave.[2] But not all behavior requires the will. Some behavior is routine, habitual, automatic, reflexive. The will, however, is engaged in interrelating actions and acts, in intentional behavior. Behavior that comprises practices are routine, and habitual, norm and rule following behavior, and therefore due to reasons; behavior that comprises

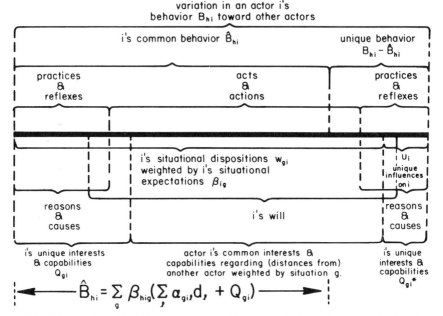

FIGURE 8.1: The Partition of the Variation in an Actor's Dyadic Behavior into that Due to Unique and Common Interests and Capabilities and Situation

reflexes is automatic, due to causes. Thus, Figure 8.1 shows the variation in an actor's behavior as divisible into that brought intentionally about by the will, and that due to reasons and causes. Note also that some unique practices may be also a matter of will; they may be individualistic, against the common grain, and thus require the will to maintain.

With this crucial understanding that an actor's will is engaged in common acts and actions, I can now deal more precisely with the equation of interests, capabilities, and will. In a situation, the variation in behavioral dispositions of an actor towards others will be a function of his common interests and capabilities regarding them and his unique interests and capabilities. In vector terms,

$$W_{gi} = \sum_{\ell} \alpha_{gi\ell} d_{\ell i} + Q_{gi}, \qquad [8.1]$$

where W_{gi} = variation in (vector of) i's behavioral dispositions towards others in situation g;

$\alpha_{gi\ell}$ = the perceived salience in situation g on i's interests and capabilities reflected in the distances along the ℓth common component of international space-time;

$d_{\ell i}$ = i's variation in (vector of) distance vectors[3] from other actors;

Q_{gi} = i's (vector of) unique interests and capabilities in situation g.

Thus, distances and situation tell only part of the behavioral story. Man is also individualistic. He has his particular interests and capabilities and his independent, free will. Note that Q measures the unpredictable part of a behavioral disposition, the part not reducible to a function of situation and distances. Thus Equation 8.1 embodies the belief that behavior is partly patterned, partly unique; partly due to a will influenced by common social forces, partly to an independent will.[4]

Equation 8.1 is the vector equation interrelating the various sources of variation in an actor's common behavior that are shown in Figure 8.1. The *specific* behavioral disposition of an actor towards a specific other is then,

$$w_{g,i \to j} = \sum_{\ell} \alpha_{gi\ell} d_{\ell,i-j} + Q_{g,i \to j}, \tag{8.2}$$

where $w_{g,i \to j}$ = the behavioral disposition of i towards j in situation g;

$d_{\ell,i-j}$ = i's distance vector from j on the ℓth component of international space-time;

$Q_{g,i \to j}$ = i's unique interests and capabilities regarding j in situation g.

8.2 AND BEHAVIORAL EQUATION

Only the behavioral disposition in a situation has so far been specified, not the actual behavior of an international actor towards another. But from the equations of chapter 6, the linkage can now be made.

In words, the specific behavior of an actor towards another is a function of an actor's situational expectations and dispositions, where these dispositions themselves are a function of situational perception and distances. More precisely, for common behavior h, from Equations 6.3 and 8.2,

$$\hat{B}_{h,i \to j} = \sum_{g} \beta_{hig} w_{g,i \to j}, \tag{8.3}$$

$$= \sum_{g} \beta_{hig} (\sum_{\ell} \alpha_{gi\ell} d_{\ell,i-j} + Q_{g,i \to j}).$$

The vector counterpart of this equation is shown at the bottom of Figure 8.1. It is

$$\hat{B}_{hi} = \sum_{g} \beta_{hig} (\sum_{\ell} \beta_{gi\ell} d_{\ell i} + Q_{gi}) \tag{8.4}$$

Equation 8.3 is the basic equation of field theory.[5] To be sure it is understood, Figure 8.2 conceptually defines its elements.

Now to consider again the international sociocultural space-time. Figure 8.3 pictures this space-time, and the inner, common space-time spanned by the

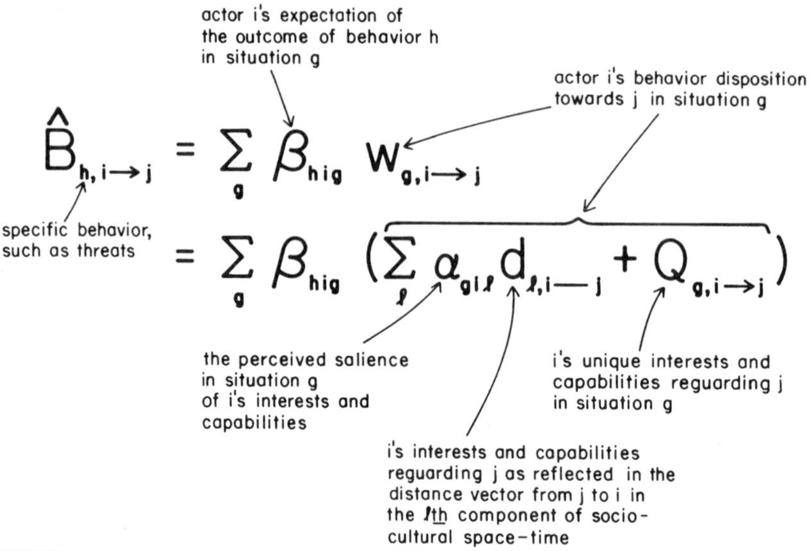

FIGURE 8.2: The Basic Equation of Social Field Theory Conceptually Defined

components of Table 7.1, such as wealth and power. As shown, the common behavior of *an actor* related to *his* distance vectors is a subspace of this common space-time. In other words, *that common behavior of an actor associated with his common interests and relative capabilities is imbedded in sociocultural space-time.* From Figure 6.3 and section 6.4,

$$\hat{B}_i = W_i \beta_i, \qquad\qquad [8.5]$$

where $\hat{B}_i$ = matrix of i's dyadic behavior towards others;

W_i = matrix of i's situational, dyadic dispositions;

β_i = matrix of i's expectations of the outcome of behavior in different situations.

This defines i's region of common behavior space-time, as shown in Figure 6.3. Then for the matrix of i's dispositions,

$$W_i = D_i \alpha_i + Q_i, \qquad\qquad [8.6]$$

where D_i = the matrix of i's distance vectors from other actors on the common components of sociocultural space;

α_i = the matrix of situational perceptions;

Q_i = the matrix of i's unique dyadic interests and capabilities regarding others in various situations.

And from Equations 8.5 and 8.6.

$$\hat{B}_i = W_i \beta_i = (D_i \alpha_i + Q_i) \beta_i$$

$$= D_i \alpha_i \beta_i + Q_i p_i$$

$$\hat{B}_i - Q_i p_i = D_i a_i \beta_i \qquad\qquad [8.7]$$

Thus, as with the expectation and disposition equations of chapters 5-6, there are also matrix, vector and scalar versions of the behavioral equations of interests, capabilities, and situation. These are shown in Table 8.1.

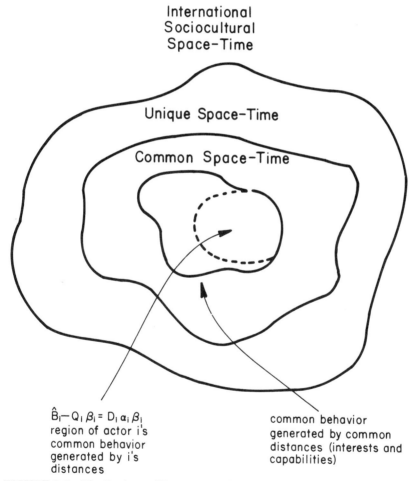

$$\hat{B}_i - Q_i \beta_i = D_i a_i \beta_i$$
region of actor i's
common behavior
generated by i's
distances

common behavior
generated by common
distances (interests and
capabilities)

FIGURE 8.3: The Regions of International Sociocultural Space-Time Generated by Distances

TABLE 8.1: The Behavioral Equations of Situational Expectations, Interests and Capabilities

LEVEL	EQUATION	TYPE OF EQUATION	DESCRIPTION
International Sociocultural space-time	$\hat{B}_i = D_i . \alpha_i . \beta_i + Q_i . \beta_i$	matrix	An actor commonly behaves towards others depending on his situational expectations, perceptions, interests and capabilities
Variation in an actor's common behavior	$\hat{B}_{hi} = \sum_g \beta_{hig} (\sum_\ell \alpha_{gi\ell} d_\ell + Q_{gi})$	vector	An actor commonly varies his specific behavior towards others depending on his situational expectations, perceptions, interests, and capabilities towards others.
An actor's specific common behavior towards object j	$\hat{B}_{h,i \rightarrow j} = \sum_g \beta_{hig} (\sum_\ell \alpha_{gi\ell} d_{\ell, i-j} + Q_{gi+j})$	scalar	An actor commonly will behave in a specific way toward another depending on his situational expectations, perceptions, interests and capabilities with regard to the other.

8.3 SUMMARY

Within a situation, an actor's common interests and capabilities are forces weighted by his situational expectations and perception. These situationally dependent common interests and relative capabilities then explain a portion of an actor's international behavior. Actors, however, also have a will and unique interests and capabilities which also explain common behavior. Any attempt to understand an actor's behavior must bring together both his individuality and commonly shared influences.

Of course, in day-to-day reality, interests, capabilities, and situational expectations and perceptions interact in complex and multifold ways. International behavior in its rich daily variation is neither simple, linear, nor wholly reducible to mathematical functions. Historians have tried to capture this flow of events and activities, this interaction of personalities and situations and often have become convinced thereby that international relations are idiosyncratic, unique, and irreducible to general forces, principles, or laws. At a more abstract level, many who have tried to analyze international relations statistically or mathematically have also become convinced that simple linear equations cannot fit the complex, interdependencies between national behaviors, forces, and conditions.

Here I do not wish to again join this issue.[6] The equations of situational expectations, perception, and distances are meant to represent latent interwoven interests, perceptions, and so on, at the most general, manifest level. Distances and situations are latent functions[7] reflecting patterns in this complex, in the same way the historian or statesman reduces the complex reality of potentials, dispositions, powers, and manifestations to a "balance of power" or "national interest."

The behavioral equations express relationships, interactions, dependencies. But they are not linked into the process of developing international orders, of conflict. The question is central: how do these equations reflect the conflict helix? Answering this is the burden of the following chapters, and will require far more discussion and specificity about the elements of the behavioral equations than yet given.

NOTES

1. This figure is no "taxonomy gone wild." I am trying to reduce distinctions to only those necessary to understand the equations, which have also been kept to a minimum number. And I am also introducing the distinctions in the sections where they serve a role in clarifying the empirical analysis. Thus, the three important variance charts, Figures 5.3, 6.1, and 8.1 have been introduced in this book rather than Volumes 1 or 2, because only here is manifest *dyadic* behavior empirically analyzed.

2. The nature of the will in relation to the self and the question of free will was analyzed in Volume 1 (1975: part VI).

3. The distance is the *difference* between the location of i and the other on a component. This difference can be plus or minus and is a single element vector. The vector

of differences is therefore of vectors. Admittedly, this is clumsy. But the wording is necessary to avoid the ambiguity between distance as magnitude and distance as vector. Throughout I argue that the direction of difference is crucial, as for example whether an actor is the dominant or subordinate power to another. Distance magnitudes ignore direction. Vectors take this direction into account. See the Distance Vector Proposition (16.6) for supporting evidence.

4. As shown in Figure 8.1 unique interests and capabilities explain both some common behavior, Q_{gi}, and unique behavior, Q_{gi}^*. Because the empirical concern is with variation in common behavior, only Q_{gi} is dealt with here.

5. In my development of Model II of field theory published in *Field Theory Evolving* (1977) I had defined the basic equation as (in the notation used here)

$$w_{g,i \to j} = \sum_\ell \alpha_{gi\ell} {}^d\ell_{,i-j},$$

where $w_{g,i \to j}$ = the location of the dyad $i \to j$ in behavior space on a component W_g.

This is the same as Equation 8.2, except for the definition of Q and the subscript g. The addition of Q marks my change in philosophy from determinism to a belief in free will—see my "Roots of Faith" (1976b). The addition of subscript g to α was left undefined in my previous work to avoid introducing another layer of notation, even though it was necessary to define the coefficients of the different canonical equations emerging from canonical analysis.

Here I have now conceptually and substantively defined the terms and subscripts in the basic equations to bring out g as situation, and to relate this basic equation explicitly to specific, common behavior, as in Equation 8.3.

Admittedly, discussion of $w_{i \to j}$ in *Field Theory Evolving* is sometimes inconsistent with its treatment here as *disposition* $w_{g,\ i \to j}$ in *situation* g. Nor am I striving to maintain consistency. The previous theoretical-empirical work antedates by many years that of these Volumes. Then I had only a partial conception of the conflict helix. (see particularly 1977: chapter 9, section 4), and only a hazy view of the dynamic psychological field.

6. I have tried to cover this central issue in various ways, including from the perspective of the major method (1970: section 2.2; 1972, section 2.3.2), from philosophy (Volume 1 1975: chapters 9-10), and from a probabilistic perspective (Volume 2, 1976: chapter 33). See also 1977: chapter 16.

Each age and each discipline has its mindless slogans. One of these particularly dominating quantitative social science work is: "But that is linear." It is not realized that linearity is a concept covering many different types of equations, including those critics ordinarily propose to replace "linear" ones. In my work, a linear equation is of a linear space; it is linear only in the function—the separate terms can be complex. For example, distance d_1 could *reflect* some interconnected complex of forces, such as $d_1 = xy^2(1-z)$, or a differential term dx/dt.

7. Situation is a latent function, operationally, in being defined by the canonical variates. Each canonical variate is, mathematically, an eigevector and interpretable as a component. On latent functions see Volume 1 (1975: chapter 10).

Chapter 9

THE FIELD

Can that essential characteristic—the absence of a tribunal or police force, the right to resort to force, the plurality of autonomous centers of decision, the alternation and continual interplay between peace and war—serve as a basis for a scientific theory, even though it is obvious to the actors themselves and belongs to their own intuitive "sociology" or "political science?" Should not science substitute for everyday notions those concepts that science itself elaborates? It seems easy for me to answer that nothing prevents us from translating the preceding idea into a word or a formula more satisfactory to the "scientists."

Aron, 1967: 192

9.1 THE ANALYTIC FIELD

The international space-time is a *field of relations.* It is bounded by such components as wealth, power, politics, and culture, which reflect the interrelationships (covariation) among actors' attributes. The location of actors within this space-time depends on their *relative* attributes.[1] And their motion in space time depends on their *relative change* in attributes.[2] Moreover, itself imbedded in this space-time, international behavior is delimited by such components as transactions, negative behavior, and military violence, which locate actors by their mutual and relative behavior.

This field of relations is an *analytic map.* It reduces the complex and interwoven manifestations of international relations to a set of coordinates, a space, prominent orienting features, relative locations, and distances. Of course, a map does not capture all the rich variety of the real landscape. Its purpose and function is to reduce this reality to its essential relationships, to enable us to visualize relative and multiple distances.

The field of relations is *dynamic.* It reflects potentialities, dispositions, and powers;[3] it delimits the possible, probable, and actual. Spread throughout the space-time is a common medium of meanings, values, and norms; of status and class. This medium is continuous; it is everywhere in international space-time. *It is the international culture and society.* All international actors are imbedded in it.

Seated in this medium are potential forces on international behavior. Meanings, values, norms, status and class carry forces that when activated influence behavior. Because this medium is continuous throughout international space-time, these forces exist as potentiality everywhere in space-time. And what determines which forces are potentials for an actor are his space-time locations. In other words, wealth, power, totalitarianism, authoritarianism, Catholic culture, and so on, reflect potential forces; the relative wealth, power, and other component-attributes of an actor reflect what potential forces may be actualized.

These forces are complex and multifold and are often dealt with in rich detail by historians and political scientists. Industrial development, armaments, ideology, size, public opinion influence and affect foreign policies and behavior through interests, capabilities, perceptions, and expectations, and these are the kinds of force potentials of which I write. Nonetheless, however complex, these forces exert their strength in a direction. Their principal potentiality lies along the distance vectors between actors. That is, the distance vectors between actors in sociocultural space-time reflect the potential forces affecting their behavior.[4]

This dynamic field is intentional. Seated in sociocultural space-time, directed along the distances between nations, these forces of nations stimulate an actor's *needs* for security, protectiveness, self-assertion, sex, curiosity, gregariousness, hunger, and perhaps pugnacity,[5] and thus transform latent attitudes into living, empowered *interests*.

International actors, as all men, are intentionally directed. They have a superordinate goal that organizes their personality and perception towards the future, towards maintaining and enhancing their self-esteem. Thus, I would argue that Secretary of State Kissinger's behavior fitted into a goal complex. His emphasis on arms control and building a net of agreements with the Soviet Union, to imbedding them in cooperative arrangements which he thought would give them a stake in détente, was part of this superordinate goal: preserve humanity from nuclear war. This goal had the highest moral weight for Kissinger and was thereby most closely connected to his self-sentiment.[6]

International behavior is most affected by these forces through interests they actualize.[7] International acts and actions (section 4.1) are expressions of these interests, as are international practices—routines integrated into a structure of expectations. Thus, there is a congruence of interests and distances. That is, *national interests lie along the distances between nations in wealth, power, totalitarianism, authoritarianism, Catholic culture, density, size, social conflict, import dependency, and diversity. And underlying international forces lie along these same distances.*[8]

The international field is thus relational, dynamic, and intentional. And in all these aspects it begets and shapes contemporary international society. It comprises the spontaneous interactions among actors, their free response to international forces, and their mutual balancing.[9] It generates and shapes a spontaneous process. *It produces the conflict helix.*

But all this is abstract. What, concretely, is the nature of this field, and particularly the conflict helix? The next section and appendix 9A deal with the empirical field: the remainder of the book clarifies the empirical basis and aspects of the international conflict helix.

9.2 EMPIRICAL FIELD FORCES AND SITUATIONS

Within the international field actors behave towards others within situations defined by a structure of expectations or involving the balancing of power—the process of readjustment of what actors want, can do, and will do in the formation of a new structure of expectations.

This behavior, as was described in the last chapter, is a function of situational expectations and perceptions, behavioral dispositions and distance vectors. Now, the uppermost question is how do states manifestly behave? That is, what real content do the field equations have?

Appendix 9A provides the methodology and many systematic *empirical* findings answering this question. Here I can only mention a few of the most interesting results.

(1) Across situations, actors most often and strongly perceive another state's *power*-related interests and capabilities as relevant to the possible outcomes of their behavior. Among the Big Powers this is especially true for the USSR. Among types of states, power is especially important for the poor, weak, totalitarian, or authoritarian. That is, in the field *power is the primary force vector of behavior.*

(2) Situations involving perceived *power* most often and strongly involve also the expectation associated with possible *compulsory* behavior, particularly for the nonpoor, powerful, and nonauthoritarian actors. Where a concrete situation involves perceived power-related interests, and capabilities, the primary disposition is towards conflict. That is, in the field *power primarily is a force towards conflict behavior.*

(3) Of all behavioral dispositions, an actor most often and highly expects desirable outcomes for his *contractual* behavior in terms of his perception of another's *distance*-related interests and capabilities. That is, in the field *distance-forces most affect contractual behavior.* This effect is especially strong for the USSR among Big Powers, and for wealthy, weak, or authoritarian actors in general.

(4) Of the distance-related interests and capabilities most situationally affecting the *contractual* disposition, those perceived along the *political* distance vector are the most potent. That is, in the field *political distance is the force towards contractual behavior.* This is especially true for China, among Big Powers, and middle wealthy, or liberal democratic actors.

(5) Across situations, an actor's expectation of possible *military conflict* behavior is least influenced by his perceptions of *distance*-related interests and capabilities. That is, in the field *military dispositions*

are most subject to unique influences and will. This is due to military conflict behavior being a subphase in the process of conflict (chapters 15-16).

(6) Across situations, *physical* distances (demographic; geographic) have less effect on actors then perceived interests and capabilities associated with *sociocultural* distance vectors. That is, in the field *meanings, values, norms, status, and class most affect behavior.*

(7) Across situations, perceived *wealth* related interests and capabilities are often and highly related to the actor's expectation of possible *contractual* behavior, especially for the USSR among Big Powers, and for poor, or middle powerful states. That is, in the field *wealth is a force towards contractual behavior.*

(8) The most often occurring situational linkage is between perceived *power*-related interests and capabilities and the expectation of possible *contractual* behavior; the highest situational linkages, however, are between perceived *power*-related interests and capabilities, and the expectation of possible *compulsory* behavior. That is, in the field *the most common effect is of power on contractual behavior; the greatest effect is of power on conflict behavior.*

(9) The most likely *situation* for actors is one in which an actor expects that an object's perceived, relative *political*-related interests and capabilities will lead to desirable outcomes for the actor's *contractual* behavior towards it. That is, in the field *the most probable situation is one in which the political vector is a force towards contractual behavior.*

(10) The second most likely *situation* for actors is one in which an actor expects that an object's perceived relative *power*-related interests and capabilities will lead to desirable outcomes for the actor's *familistic* and *contractual* behavior towards it. That is, in the field *the second most probable situation is one in which the power vector is a force towards familistic and contractual behavior.*

(11) Finally, the third most likely *situation* for actor's is one in which an actor expects that an object's perceived geographic closeness implies desirable outcomes for the actor's cooperation or conflict behavior towards it. That is, in the field *the third most probable situation is one in which geographic distance affects behavior.*

In sum, the most potent field force is power, which mainly affects conflict. However, forces generally 'most affect contractual behavior; least affected is military action. Wealth (or a rich-poor gap) is less important than political and power forces, but what influence it does have is on contractual behavior.

And the most probable situation in the international field is one in which political distance is a force towards contractual behavior—international organization, diplomatic relationships, trade, alliances, and the like.

Such is the contemporary international field. Now, I can shift my focus to the major concern of this book. The process, causes, conditions, and termination of conflict, and particularly violence and war, within the field. This is the task of the following chapters.

NOTES

1. Operationally this means that everything in the field is measured relative to all else in the field, including attributes, components, positions, distances, forces, interests, cooperation, conflict behavior. *There is no absolute point of reference.* Even time is relative (Rummel, 1977: chapter 8). Philosophically, this means that the international field is a gestalt, a whole that is more than the sum of its parts and each part takes on greater meaning through its role in the whole. Mathematically, the field is determined through standardizing all data (which measures each datum relative to a mean and standard deviation), forming a matrix of cosines between all attributes (or behaviors) so transformed (which are equal to product-moment correlations), and computing the eigenvectors of this matrix. Scaled by their eigenvalues, these are then the components of the field. Each component is then measured relative to all the others, even though independent.

2. For example, it is not the change in wealth or power itself which will alter the location of an actor relative to others, but the change in relative wealth or power. Thus, if two nations similarly increase their power, their relative positions in international space-time remains the same.

3. Here I mean power as a philosophical category, as the mode of transformation of dispositions to manifestation, such as the power of a thunderclap to be heard, or of nitroglycerin to explode. This category, along with that of potentiality, disposition and manifestation are elaborated in Volume 1 (1975: chapter 8).

4. The distance vector is the actor's score minus the potential object's score on a component (such as wealth), which creates a vector pointed towards the actor. That is, the forces bear upon the actor. This is consistent with my ontology of perception. What we perceive as distances and situation is a balance between the strength of these inward bearing forces toward a specific perception and our perspective straining outward towards manifesting a particular reality. See Volume 1 (1975: part II).

5. All this and the following psychological discussion as been developed in Volume 1, with references to the appropriate psychological studies. Although pugnacity has been uncovered as a need in psychological research, its reality is much less confirmed than the other needs mentioned. See Volume 1 (1975: section 22.11).

6. Kissinger was clear about the nature and goals of his foreign policy. See, for example, his statement before the Senate Committee on Foreign Relations on September 19, 1974. This has been published in *The Department of State Bulletin,* Vol. LXXI (October 14, 1974).

7. Of course, for different actors the same forces (distances, say, in power) will not actualize the same interests. Interests reflect an actor's cultural matrix, learning and experience. For example, power parity between two neighboring states with opposing political beliefs may stimulate the insecurity or protectiveness needs in their elite. What interests are thereby energized, whether arms control, military superiority, or political détente, may differ between them. For each actor, therefore, similar situations will have different salience and weight distances differently. That is, each actor has his unique equation of international behavior. This perspective I have called Model II in my quantitative analyses. See Rummel (1977: particularly sections 4,3, and 4.4).

8. This is not to say that these forces are the only ones relevant to international relations. Purely domestic forces (as those underlying a society's status quo) affect a nation's character, wealth, power, and politics, its location in international space-time. Moreover, domestic forces influence the weight to be given a particular situation. And then there is the force of will which is independent of distances, of domestic pressures, of environmental influences, of social causation. Aside from the will, all is latent disposition, interest and intentions, goals and means. The will is the mode of transformation into acts and actions. The will is the mental power to act in a specific way (Volume 1, 1975: chapter 29).

9. International relations constitutes an exchange, libertarian society in which actors can freely adjust to others in terms of their interests, capabilities, and expectations (chapter 2). The emphasis here is on this type of international society. For were international relations coercively directed, as say in world domination by one elite, then the society would be an antifield. Forces toward behavior congruent with distances would then be blocked by the forces of elite control. That is, international relations would be an *organization*. See Volume 2 (1976: chapter 22) for an analysis of antifields relevant here.

APPENDIX 9A
EMPIRICAL, SITUATIONAL
DISPOSITION-DISTANCE LINKAGES

A number of empirical, canonical analyses have linked the dyadic behavioral dispositions of state-actors to their distance vectors according to the equations of chapters 5-8. The purpose here is to aggregate these results in order to see their major commonalities.

To present these aggregations requires considerable methodological clarification, especially regarding the relationship of factor analysis and canonical analysis to the field equations, and the manner in which the results are aggregated.

9A.1 METHODS AND FIELD EQUATIONS

Factor analysis: The function of factor analysis is to: (1) delineate the components of behavioral space-time for dyads, where the factor scores of dyads then define the dyadic behavioral dispositions $w_{k,i \rightarrow j}$ of Equation 5.1 and the matrix of factor scores is W in Equation 5.3; (2) to delineate the components of international space-time along which the distance vectors (the differences in factor scores on a component) in Equation 8.1 can be determined, and from which the matrix D of distances in Equation 8.6 can be constructed. Factor analysis thus provides the basic input data for the canonical analysis of *an actor.*

Canonical analysis: The function of canonical analysis is more complex to explain, partly because the method is much less known than factor analysis.[1] First, I need to put the field equations in proper matrix form for the canonical model.

Equations 6.4 and 8.2 provide the basic equations for the canonical analysis. Equation 6.4 can be translated into the matrix equality

$$W^*_{nxq} = W^i_{nxq} \beta^i_{qxq} \qquad [9A.1]$$

where W^*_{nxq} = the matrix of i→j dispositions for each of the n dyads (rows) in q different situations (columns);

W^i_{nxq} = the matrix of factor scores on the q components[2] (columns) of behavior space-time for all n i–j dyads with actor i:

β^i_{qxq} = the matrix of i's expectations of the outcome of behavioral dispositions in each of the q situations.

Equation 8.2 also can be translated into the matrix equality

$$W^*_{nxq} = D^i_{nxp} \alpha^i_{pxq} + Q^i_{nxp}, \qquad [9A.2]$$

where D^i_{nxp} = the matrix of distance vectors for the n i→j dyads on p components of the international space-time;

α^i_{nxp} = the matrix of situational perceptions of i in q situations;

Q^i_{nxp} = the matrix of unique influences and will.

From equations 9A.1 and 9A.2 we have, dropping subscripted matrix orders,

$$W^i \beta^i = D^i \alpha^i + Q^i \qquad [9A.3]$$

This is the canonical model, where W^i and D^i are the input data matrices, β^i and α^i are the canonical coeeficients, and Q^i contains the residuals.

The canonical analysis determines a number of equations, each of the scalar form (sticking to my notation):

$$\sum_k \beta_{gik} w_{k,i\to j} = \sum_\ell \alpha_{gi} d_{\ell,i\to j} + Q_{g,i\to j} \qquad [9A.4]$$

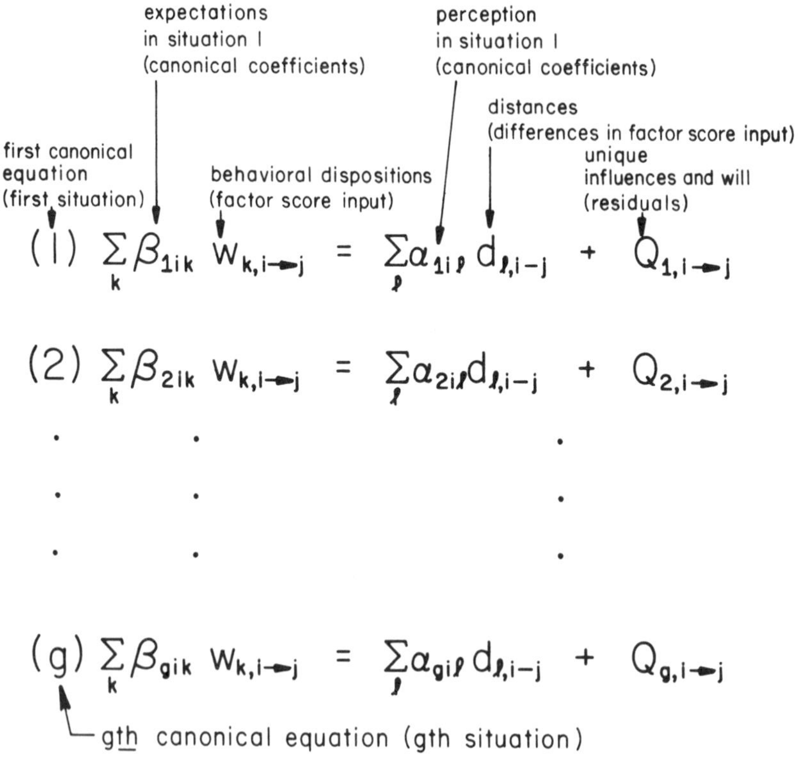

FIGURE 9A.1: Canonical Equations Conceptually Interpreted in Terms of Social Field Theory

where the equality is from Equations 6.4 and 8.2. Each *canonical equation* is defining a different q in (9A.4). That is, *each canonical equation defines a specific situation in which expectations, perceptions, dispositions, and distance vectors are linked.* And each equation is orthogonal.

Thus, canonical analysis solves the operational problem: how does one best define the independent situations in which situational expectations, perceptions, dispositions, and distances (interests and capabilities) are maximally linked. Moreover, canonical analysis also solves the problem of how to measure expectations and perception. These turn out to be the canonical coefficients, and are thus measured in terms of the empirical relationship between behavioral dispositions and distance vectors. [3]

Figure 9A.1 should clarify and summarize all this.

9A.2 AGGREGATING CANONICAL RESULTS [4]

Seventy-one distinct and separately useful canonical analyses have been done on 3,699 dyads in a field theory context. [5] Table 9A.1 provides the essential information on these. Additional information on each is given in appendix III.

These 71 analyses provide 197 canonical equations (situations) linking expectations, behavioral dispositions, perceptions, and distances (interests and capabilities) for 14 different actors (Brazil, Burma, China, Cuba, Egypt, India, Indonesia, Israel, Jordan, Netherlands, Poland, United Kingdom, USSR, and United States). These actors were carefully selected to represent the different types and characteristics of all actors (Rummel, 1978: section 3.1).

Now, each of these 197 equations define a situation in which behavioral dispositions and distance vectors are linked for a specific actor. [6] The aim here is to determine whether general conclusions about situation, dispositions, and distance can be inferred. To do this requires some technique for aggregating these results.

The technique I applied can best be explained through reference to a subset of the equations. Table 9A.2 presents 21 canonical analyses (Rummel, 1977: 95-96, 148-149, 477-478; 1978; Choi, 1973). This organization and format were followed in constructing similar field-equation tables (not given here) [7] for each of the other 13 actors.

First the results are organized on the left by theoretical components, which have been discussed in chapters 4 and 7. Then, these theoretical components are divided into the empirical components which have been delineated in attribute or behavioral data.

Each of the canonical analyses employed empirical components from a factor analysis often done specifically for that canonical analysis. The empirical components thus defined often were similar, but differences also occurred across studies. Therefore, in aggregating the canonical results I had to be sure to keep similar input components together across the 197 canonical analyses. The organization of results by theoretical and empirical components helped in this. To explain this organization: I will consider each theoretical component in turn.

For wealth: a wealth component has been delineated consistently, but in some analyses secondary wealth-related components ("sufficiency"; "welfare"), [8] named "other" here, also have been found.

For (coercive) power: a component merging power and size, the latter a secondary measure of power, has emerged in numerous factor analyses. Separate components of power, size, and smaller "other" secondary components measuring an aspect of power also have been found("disunity'"; "trade dependency"; "domestic conflict"). [9]

For political: a liberal democratic versus totalitarian (or communism) component has commonly emerged, but several factor analyses also have found separate totalitarian or authoritarian components (the "non" prefix is to show the direction of relationship in the

TABLE 9A.1: Description of Canonical Analysis

ANALYSES	SAMPLES	DYADS IN EACH SAMPLE	YEAR(S)	NUMBER OF USEFUL CANONICAL EQUATIONS	CANONICAL CORRELATION RANGE	(AVERAGE) TRACE CORRELATION SQUARED
Rummel (1977, 95-96)	14	13	1955	27	.66-1.00	(.57)
Van Atta & Rummel (1977, 148-149)	14	13	1963	24	.58-.99	(.53)
Rummel (1972)	United States	81	1955	5	.56-.94	(.47)
Schwerin (1977: 308)	United States	106	1963	3	.72-.85	.37
Rhee (1971)	China	81	1955	5	.58-.99	.55
Rhee (1971)	China[a]	81	1955	3	.85-.96	.50
Rhee (1971)	China	55	1955	3	.90-.99	.58
Rhee (1971)	China[a]	55	1955	3	.89-.97	.52
Rhee (1971)	China	81	1963	4	.85-.97	.52
Rhee (1971)	China[a]	81	1963	3	.80-.96	.45
Rhee (1971)	China	55	1963	4	.83-.97	.55
Rhee (1971)	China[a]	55	1963	2	.93-.96	.49
Rhee (1977: 390)	China	456	1950-65	2	.76-.85	.23
Choi (1973)	United States	82	1960	5	.34-.92	.46
Choi (1973)	United States	82	1965	6	.26-.94	.51
Choi (1973)	USSR	82	1960	6	.50-.92	.52
Choi (1973)	USSR	82	1965	4	.63-.97	.46
Rummel (1977: 477-478)[b]	14[a]	65	1950-65	46	.24-.98	(.43)
Rummel (1978)[b]	14[c]	65	1950-65	42	.30-.91	(.37)
TOTALS	71	3699[d]		197		average = .48

a. Transformed data   b. Only partial results given in source   c. Indicators used for canonical analyses rather than factor scores   d. Total dyads across all samples

TABLE 9A.2: USSR Empirical Field Equations

Matrix	Theoretical Components	Empirical Components	12	24	44	45	99	100	101	102	103	104	105	106	107	141	142	143	183	184	185	197	200	(F) entries/possible	(P) points possible
	wealth	wealth	x	x	x	x	x	-6												-6				5/21 5/21	21/189 21/189
		other	-6	-2	-6	x	x								-3					-3	-2			3/4	14/36 0
	power	power + size	x	x	x	-9			-6			-6				-3	-3	-6		-3	-2			7/17 12/21	32/153 6/153 54/189
		power	x	x	x	x																		1/17	2/153
		size	x	x	x	x																		1/17	
		other																					2	4/18	19/162
distance vectors (independent variate)	political	liberal democratic	4						6					6		-3			x	x				2/3	9/27
		nontotalitarian	x	x	x	x	x	x		x	x	x		x		x	x		6	-3		x		1/3 6/21	3/27 28/189
		nonauthoritarian	x	x	x	x	x	x		x	x	x		x			-3			-3		x			
		other	x	x																x	2	x	2		
	cultural	cultural	x	x	x										1			-6				-1		3/19 3/19	9/153 5/171
	physical	demographic	x	x	x						-2							-6			2			3/17 3/21	9/153 9/171
		geographical																				-1		0/10	0/90 0
dyadic behavior dispositions (dependent variate)	familistic	transactions	6	2	6			-3	6	2				6			9		3			x		9/21 9/21	43/189 43/189
	contractual	contractual					x	x			x		x			x				x	2	x		0/4	0/36
		exchange	x	x	x			6	2			6		6		6			6			x		3/17 11/21	10/153 29/153 42/182
		diplomatic	x	x	x						x		6			3	-3		3	-3	2		4	7/17	12/63
		defense			4	6	x	x			x		x		x	3			3	x	6	x	x	4/17	19/36
		conflict behavior	9		x	x	x	9		3	9		x		x	2	3		x	x		x	x	3/4 3/4	19/36
	compulsory	non-military	x	x	x	x	x	9			x		x		x	2	3			3		x		7/17 10/21	35/153 54/189
		military	x	x	x					x	x		x		x				x	x		x		1/7	3/63

Key: numbers are product of: (canonical r² = 1 (.25–.49), 2(.50–.74), 3(.75–1.0)) x (canonical coefficient²
= 1(.25–.49), 2(.50–.74), 3(.75–1.0))
signs are those of the canonical coefficient
x means that the empirical component was omitted from the canonical analysis
Blank = 0
a. Each canonical equation is identified by a code number. These 21 equations are of the 197 defined by the analyses listed in Table 9A.1.
Code numbers exceed 197 due to the omission of several equations.

table), as well as secondary "other" political components ("colonialism"; "USSR aid"; "communist trade"; "U.S. aid"; "equality").

For cultural: this involves the Catholic culture and oriental culture components.

For physical: the previous components reflect sociocultural space-time. However, to determine the relative effect on behavior of merely *physical* differences, demographic components ("density"; "diversity") and geographic ("location"; "distance") components were also included.

For familistic: across the factor analyses a transaction (I) component was usually found. Also included here were secondary or similar components ("private international relations"; "transactions II"; "aid"; "migration"; "informal diplomacy"; "visits").

For contractual: this includes a contractual ("administrative behavior") component, as well as exchange components ("relative exports"; "foreign students"; "economic patronage"; "communication network"; "promise"), diplomatic components ("international organizations"; "diplomatic"; "administrative cooperation"; "proselytizing"), and defense ("alignment"; "military treaties"; "defense patronage").

For compulsory: this includes a "conflict behavior" component, in addition to nonmilitary components ("negative communication"; "negative sanctions"; "antiforeign behavior"; "deterrence"; "UN voting") and a military violence component.

In Table 9A.2, each numbered column defines a canonical equation (a situation) of the type shown in Figure 9A.1, and a rating for each component on it. These ratings measure two aspects of a canonical equation. One is the size of a canonical coefficient for a component; the other is the canonical correlation between the two canonical variates (the correlation between the sum of the left terms and the sums of the right terms, excluding residuals, shown in Equation 9A.4).

The ratings were formed in this way. Each canonical correlation and coefficient squared was transformed to integers as follows:

Integer	canonical correlation or coefficient squared
0	.00 - .24
1	.25 - .49
2	.50 - .74
3	.75 - 1.00

These integers then rate the dependent variance for a component behavioral disposition, or the variance of a component distance involved in a variate.[10] Then, for each component on each variate a rating was calculated, where

rating= (integer for canonical correlation) x (integer for canonical coefficient).

This rating then measures the involvement of a component with the canonical variate, *taking into account the canonical correlation.* Thus, the better an equation fits behavioral dispositions, the more weight is given to the distances and dispositions involved.

These ratings for the 21 USSR equations are shown in Table 9A.2. Zeros are left blank; components omitted from an equation are indicated by an "X"; each rating is given the original sign of the associated canonical coefficient.

For example, the first Equation 12 shows a high relationship between a power (power + size) distance of other states from the Soviet Union and its disposition toward compulsory behavior with them. Keeping in mind the interpretation of Figure 9A.1, then, the first equation shows that for the Soviet Union there is a situation in which (1) Soviet perceptions give high weight to power distance and (2) Soviet expectations give high weight to compulsory dispositions.

The next problem is to *aggregate* these ratings in such a way as to provide an overall view of the results. This can be done in two ways.

First, one can count the frequency of occurrence of nonzero integers to the number that could occur because the appropriate components were included in the analyses. This ratio, labelled F in Table 9A.2, measures the *probability* that a distance or disposition will play some role in some situation. Thus, in Table 9A.2 the F columns show that power distance has the largest probability (12/21) of being situationally relevant for the USSR; contractual dispositions (for all four components = 11.21), the most likely disposition.

A second way of aggregating is to take into account the proportional size of the integers by summing their absolute values and dividing by the maximum possible. The result is the "P" columns in Table 9A.2. This measures the overall proportional salience of distances and dispositions to each other (because the ratings also involve the canonical correlation). Thus, for the USSR, power distance is proportionally (54/189) most salient; compulsory dispositions, proportionally the most salient disposition. Note that F and P thus can give different views of the same result, which is why they are both calculated.

Table 9A.2 is only a preliminary table, however. It now enables me to compute the overall linkages for the USSR, as shown in Table 9A.3. This provides a tabulation of F and P for all possible *cooccurring* distances and dispositions, organized by components. The political and cultural components were combined in the third column, because both together reflect the meanings, values, and norms components of cultural space-time.

The entries in Table 9A.3 define for the USSR the percentage coincidence (F) of disposition and distance, or the cosalience (P) of both. Thus, distance in wealth and familistic behavioral dispositions could cooccur 21 times with a nonzero rating in Table 9A.2, but only cooccurred once. Therefore, $(1/21) \times 100 = 5\%$ (rounded off), which is the figure shown in Table 9A.3. Similarly, to measure the cosalience the sum of the cooccurring distance and disposition rankings for an equation is calculated, summed for all equations, and divided by the maximum possible, which for wealth and familistic is $(6 + 3)/378$, which equals about 2%. For power and familistic disposition, this would be $(2 + 2) + (6 + 6) + (6 + 2) + (3 + 9)$ divided by 378, or 36/378, which rounds off to 10%, as shown.

Thus, from all the entries in the Table, one can see that for the 21 equations power and political distances and contractual defense dispositions are most likely to go together (43% possible for each).

That is: *in situations involving the USSR as an actor, the Soviets expect that the object's perceived power and political system-related interests and capabilities will lead to desirable outcomes for their more or less contractual-defensive behavior towards it.*

Looking at the highest P however, the picture changes. For then power distance and compulsory disposition are shown to have the highest percentage salience (24% of possible). This means that: *of all USSR expectations in situations involving her as actor, those jointly involving compulsory dispositions and her perception of another's power will be most salient.*

On the margins of the table are calculated the overall F and P for the distances and dispositions. Considering just the familistic component as an example, its F is the sum of all the cooccurrences in Table 9A.2 for the indicated distances $(1 + 4 + 4 + 0 + 0 = 9)$ over the sum of the possible occurrences $(21 + 21 + 21 + 17 + 10 = 90)$ in Table 9A.2. The overall F is thus 9/90, or 10% for familistic behavior, as shown on the margin in Table 9A.3. Similarly, the sum of the cosalience in Table 9A.2 for the familistic disposition $(9 + 36 + 43 + 0 + 0 = 88)$ is divided by the sum of the maximum possible points $(378 + 378 + 378 + 306 + 180)$ in Table 9A.2, which is 88/1620, or a rounded 5% as also shown on the margin.

From these marginals note that the USSR expectation of defense-related, contractual dispositions had the highest situational linkages to perceived distances; contractual-exchange

TABLE 9A.3: **USSR Empirical Distance and Behavior Linkages**

Behavior Dispositions	Score[b]	wealth[c] (1)	power[d] (2)	political + cultural[e] (3)	political[e] (4)	demography (5)	geography (6)	(1)+(2)+(3) +(5)+(6)[f]
				DISTANCE VECTORS[a]				
(1) familistic	F	5	19	19	19	0	0	10
	P	2	10	11	11	0	0	5
(2) contractual	F	19	29	29	19	6	0	19
	P	10	10	12	9	1	0	8
(3) contractual	F	0	0	12	12	6	0	4
exchange	P	0	0	7	7	1	0	2
(4) contractual	F	24	29	24	12	0	0	18
diplomatic	P	13	11	8	5	0	0	7
(5) contractual	F	29	43	43	43	0	0	23
defense	P	12	14	17	17	0	0	9
(6) compulsory	F	14	38	14	10	12	0	18
	P	8	24	5	4	5	0	9
(7) compulsory-non-	F	18	29	18	12	12	0	17
military	P	10	19	6	5	5	0	9
(8) compulsory-	F	14	14	14	14	0	0	9
military	P	7	5	5	5	0	0	3
(1)+(2)+(6)[g]	F	13	29	21	16	6	0	
	P	7	15	9	8	2	0	

a. Numbers are percent of cooccurring F or P in Table 9A.2. See text for full explanation.
b. F = entries/possible
P = points/possible
c. "Wealth" and "other" empirical components
d. "Power+size," "power," "size," and "other" empirical components
e. "Liberal democracy," "nontotalitarian," "nonauthoritarian" and "other" empirical components.
f. This is the percent number of cooccurrences or points for the five distances over the total possible
g. This is the percent number of cooccurrences or points for the three components over the number possible

the least. Moreover, looking at the bottom margin, perception of distance in power was the most predictive, or potent, distance vector in accounting for expected outcomes (dispositions); geographic distance the least.

The importance of Tables 9A.2-3 here is in illustrating the process of synthesizing and aggregating the 197 canonical equations.[11] I can now turn to the overall results.

9A.3 COOCCURRENCES AND COSALIENCE OF SITUATIONAL DISTANCES AND DISPOSITIONS

Table 19A.4 presents the overall situational linkages for distances and dispositions. These are the marginal totals for behavior and distance and show which disposition is most situationally involved with distance vectors; which is least. Similarly, the totals indicate which perceived distance vectors are most and least potent for expectations. The values for the USSR are those given in Table 19A.3, and thus provide an initial point of comparison for understanding the calculation of all these numbers.

TABLE 9A.4: Overall Distance and Behavior Linkages

Actors	N	Score	BEHAVIOR DISPOSITIONS								DISTANCE VECTORS					
			familistic	contractual	exchange	diplomacy	defense	compulsory	non-military	military	wealth	power	political + cult.	political	demography	geography
all actors	14	F	13	22	9	14	13	13	9	5	12	24	22	18	10	8
		P	6	10	4	7	5	6	4	2	6	11	10	9	3	3
China		F	18	17	6	12	11	13	12	2	5	22	23	23	4	0
		P	4	8	2	5	5	7	6	0	2	11	11	11	1	0
USSR[a]		F	10	19	4	18	23	18	17	9	13	29	21	16	6	0
		P	5	8	2	7	9	9	9	3	7	15	9	8	2	0
United States		F	17	12	10	7	9	13	4	10	8	19	22	16	15	3
		P	5	5	4	4	4	5	1	3	3	7	18	7	5	1
wealthy	4	F	14	22	6	12	16	14	8	7	11	21	23	19	13	2
		P	6	8	4	6	5	7	3	2	6	9	10	10	5	1
middle	5	F	12	22	10	15	10	13	11	3	10	25	22	20	6	10
		P	6	11	6	8	5	6	5	1	5	13	11	10	3	5
poor	5	F	13	30	10	16	16	11	6	5	16	26	19	12	15	12
		P	5	12	4	7	6	4	4	1	9	11	6	5	3	5
powerful	4	F	12	16	7	19	12	14	10	7	8	23	22	19	9	1
		P	5	7	3	5	5	7	5	2	4	9	10	9	3	0
middle	6	F	15	26	11	23	19	12	6	3	16	23	23	17	10	11
		P	8	13	6	12	7	5	2	1	10	11	11	9	4	4
weak	4	F	14	30	12	16	13	12	9	4	16	28	18	14	17	13
		P	5	12	4	7	5	5	2	1	8	12	7	5	3	6
liberal democracy	5	F	16	19	9	13	12	12	4	5	12	21	24	18	13	4
		P	7	9	5	7	5	5	2	2	7	9	10	9	3	1
middle	5	F	14	28	11	15	16	12	7	5	16	25	19	14	15	13
		P	6	11	5	6	5	5	2	1	8	10	7	6	3	6
nonliberal democracy	4	F	10	19	7	15	14	15	13	5	8	25	22	19	6	6
		P	5	9	3	7	6	6	7	1	5	11	10	10	4	3

a. From Table 9A.3

Again, these numbers are derived from the coefficients of 197 canonical equations, where the behavioral coefficients refer to expectations linking behavioral dispositions to situations in which an actor's perception gives weight to specific distances. Figure 9A.1 must be kept in mind. Thus, to observe that Table 9A.4 shows the contractual disposition is, for all actors, the most dependent on distance vectors *means that in the diverse situations in which international actors behave, an actor's expectations give most weight to its contractual dispositions in terms of its situational perception of the distances (interest and capabilities) of the object state from it.*

In describing the results here and in subsequent tables, I will usually leave implicit the reference to situational expectations and perceptions and describe the results in terms of dispositions-distance linkages. With this in mind, from Table 19A.4 a variety of conclusions can be drawn, a few of which are as follows.

(1) The *contractual* disposition is most often (F) and tightly (P) linked to distance vectors; military disposition the least.[12]
(2) *Power* is the most potent distance vector; *geographic distance* the least.
(3) For China and the United States, the *familistic* disposition is most often linked; for the USSR it is defense related, *contractual* dispositions.

TABLE 9A.5: Behavioral Linkages By Distance Vector: Wealth, Power, and Politics

Distance Vectors and Behavioral Dispositions[b]

Actors	Score	WEALTH								POWER								POLITICAL							
		familistic	contractual	exchange	diplomacy	defense	compulsory	non-military	military	familistic	contractual	exchange	diplomacy	defense	compulsory	non-military	military	familistic	contractual	exchange	diplomacy	defense	compulsory	non-military	military
All 14	F	8	19	8	16	13	9	5	3	21	25	12	11	16	25	21	12	14	28	13	28	18	10	7	3
actors	P	4	10	5	8	5	5	2	1	10	10	5	4	5	13	10	4	7	14	7	14	8	5	3	1
China	F	0	10	0	8	10	5	5	0	20	13	10	5	20	33	30	10	13	40	10	32	20	15	14	0
	P	0	3	0	3	3	2	2	0	9	5	2	2	8	20	19	1	6	19	4	15	12	8	6	0
USSR[a]	F	5	19	0	24	29	14	18	14	19	29	0	29	43	38	29	14	19	19	12	12	43	10	12	14
	P	2	10	0	13	12	8	10	7	10	10	0	11	14	24	19	5	11	9	7	5	17	4	5	5
United	F	13	10	0	0	10	0	0	0	13	10	25	0	0	33	16	24	13	20	8	24	20	13	4	8
States	P	4	5	0	0	4	0	0	0	4	3	8	0	0	14	5	10	6	10	6	13	9	7	1	2
Wealthy	F	10	16	5	13	10	7	5	2	14	19	7	11	15	31	20	15	19	26	14	21	25	13	5	7
	P	4	7	3	7	4	4	3	1	6	6	2	4	4	16	9	7	9	13	9	12	11	7	2	2
Middle	F	5	18	7	16	7	7	5	0	24	21	14	5	13	29	30	16	14	34	14	35	20	12	11	0
	P	4	10	4	8	3	3	2	0	13	10	8	2	5	15	15	3	7	18	8	18	12	6	5	0
Poor	F	10	25	12	21	21	14	6	6	25	41	18	21	21	12	9	3	8	24	12	24	9	4	3	0
	P	6	12	7	10	8	8	2	2	11	17	6	8	6	6	3	1	3	10	5	11	2	1	0	0
Powerful	F	6	13	2	10	11	6	6	2	18	17	9	9	16	33	24	16	16	29	11	26	23	13	9	6
	P	2	6	1	5	5	3	3	1	8	6	3	3	5	19	14	6	8	14	6	13	11	6	4	2
Middle	F	13	28	15	29	15	7	3	0	20	31	12	15	15	16	18	10	15	26	15	29	23	13	9	6
	P	9	17	10	17	6	4	1	0	13	13	6	5	4	7	5	2	8	15	9	18	11	6	4	2
Weak	F	7	24	8	15	12	17	8	9	29	39	27	12	19	15	15	4	10	29	15	31	8	2	4	0
	P	3	11	3	7	4	10	3	3	12	18	9	5	6	7	5	1	3	13	6	14	1	0	0	0
Liberal	F	13	19	11	15	9	4	0	0	16	22	11	10	12	24	15	13	16	25	14	28	19	12	2	4
democracy	P	7	12	9	9	4	3	0	0	9	9	2	4	3	11	5	5	7	13	9	15	8	6	0	1
Middle	F	10	24	12	18	15	14	9	5	25	39	18	12	21	12	9	5	10	25	15	26	12	6	6	0
	P	5	11	6	9	5	7	3	2	11	14	6	5	6	5	2	1	4	12	6	14	4	2	1	0
Nonliberal	F	3	14	0	16	15	9	8	4	22	19	11	11	19	35	33	17	3	11	8	6	4	3	3	0
democracy	P	1	8	0	8	7	4	4	2	10	8	5	4	7	14	18	4	2	4	5	2	2	1	1	0

b. Numbers are percent cooccuring F and P. See text for full explanation
a. Based on Table 9A.2

(4) For the USSR, *power* is the most potent distance; for China it is the *political*; for the United States it is the *political and cultural*.

(5) For wealthy states, the *contractual* disposition is most often and tightly linked.

(6) For the poor, the *wealth power*, and *geographic distances* are more potent, while *political* distance is more potent for the wealthy.

(7) For weak states the *contractual* disposition is more often and tightly linked to distance, and *military* disposition is linked less than for the powerful.

(8) For the weak, the *wealth power, demographic,* and *geographic distances* are more potent, while *political* distance is more important to the powerful states.

(9) For liberal democratic as opposed to authoritarian (middle) and totalitarian states, the *familistic* disposition is most often linked, and the *compulsory, nonmilitary disposition* is the least linked; and *power* distance is least potent.

(10) For authoritarian states, the *contractual* disposition is most often linked, while *wealth, demographic,* and *geographic* distances are the most potent.

(11) For totalitarian states, the *compulsory* disposition is most often tightly linked, *familistic* the least; while *wealth* and *demographic* distances are the least potent.

Besides the overall results shown in Table 9A.4, of even greater interest is the cooccurrence and cosalience of specific distances and dispositions. These are shown in Tables 9A.5

TABLE 9A.6: Behavioral Linkage by Distance Vector: Cultural, Demographic and Geographic

Distance Vectors and Behavioral Dispositions[b]

Actors	Score	Political & Cultural								Demographic								Geographic							
		familistic	contractual	exchange	diplomacy	defense	compulsory	non-military	military	familistic	contractual	exchange	diplomacy	defense	compulsory	non-military	military	familistic	contractual	exchange	diplomacy	defense	compulsory	non-military	military
All 14 actors	F	17	34	15	30	22	14	10	6	11	15	8	7	10	5	3	4	5	10	1	3	4	9	1	1
	P	7	16	8	15	10	6	3	1	4	5	3	3	4	1	1	1	2	4	1	2	2	3	0	0
China	F	13	40	10	32	20	15	14		0	3	8	10	5	0	0	0	0	0	0	0	0	0	0	0
	P	6	19	4	15	2	8	6		0	1	3	4	2	0	0	0	0	0	0	0	0	0	0	0
USSR[a]	F	19	29	12	24	43	14	18	14	0	6	6	0	0	12	12	0	0	0	0	0	0	0	0	0
	P	11	12	7	8	17	5	6	5	0	1	1	0	0	5	5	0	0	0	0	0	0	0	0	0
United States	F	27	20	8	24	20	20	4	16	24	16	17	12	15	4	0	4	4	0	0	0	0	4	0	4
	P	10	10	6	13	9	8	1	3	7	7	7	7	6	1	0	1	1	0	0	0	0	1	0	1
Wealthy	F	24	29	14	26	25	17	7	11	19	13	11	6	10	7	5	2	2	2	0	0	3	2	0	2
	P	10	14	9	14	11	7	2	3	6	5	5	4	4	3	2	1	0	0	0	0	1	0	0	1
Middle	F	16	37	20	35	20	13	12	0	3	14	7	9	10	0	0	0	6	14	4	8	0	11	4	0
	P	8	19	10	18	12	6	5	0	2	6	4	4	4	0	0	0	4	7	2	5	0	5	1	0
Poor	F	10	35	12	29	21	12	9	3	15	21	6	6	9	13	6	10	8	15	0	3	10	12	0	0
	P	3	14	5	13	7	3	2	0	2	5	1	2	3	1	1	5	3	6	0	2	4	5	0	0
Powerful	F	20	31	11	28	23	16	10	10	10	10	10	5	9	5	3	2	2	0	0	0	0	2	0	2
	P	8	15	6	13	11	7	4	2	3	4	4	2	3	2	1	1	0	0	0	0	0	0	0	1
Middle	F	19	35	18	32	26	17	6	3	11	17	6	12	12	3	0	3	7	14	3	3	6	12	3	0
	P	8	17	10	19	12	7	2	0	4	8	4	6	4	0	0	0	4	5	2	2	1	4	1	0
Weak	F	10	37	19	35	15	7	12		0	15	27	8	8	8	8	9	6	19	0	9	9	12	0	0
	P	3	16	7	16	5	1	2	0	3	4	2	3	3	1	1	1	3	10	0	5	3	6	0	0
Liberal democracy	F	22	31	14	30	21	18	4	8	21	12	9	7	12	4	2	2	4	4	0	0	4	4	0	2
	P	8	14	9	16	9	8	1	2	7	6	4	5	4	1	1	0	1	1	0	0	1	1	0	1
Middle	F	14	33	18	29	21	10	9	3	14	22	6	9	12	8	6	10	7	17	3	6	10	14	3	0
	P	5	16	8	16	8	2	2	0	3	6	1	3	4	1	1	2	4	8	2	4	4	6	1	0
Nonliberal democracy	F	15	35	14	31	26	14	14	4	3	11	8	6	4	3	3	0	3	10	0	4	6	0	0	0
	P	8	17	7	15	14	6	6	1	2	4	5	2	2	1	1	0	2	5	0	2	1	3	0	0

b. Numbers are percent coocurring F or P. See text for full explanation.

a. Based on Table 9A.2

and 9A.6. To help make rapid sense of all the figures, Table 9A.7 consolidates the more important results from these two tables, as well as from Table 9A.4.

A few of the many more important conclusions that might be drawn from these specific results are as follows.

(12) The *power* distance vector is most often and tightly linked to the *compulsory* disposition, especially for the nonpoor, powerful, or nonauthoritarian states.
(13) The political distance vector is most often and tightly linked to the *contractual* disposition, especially for China, middle wealthy, or liberal democratic states.

TABLE 9A.7: **Consolidated Linkages**[a]

Actors	Score	Overall[b] (familistic)	(contractual)	(compulsory)	Overall (wealth)	(power)	(politics)	By Distance Vector[c] — Wealth (familistic)	(contractual)	(compulsory)	Power (familistic)	(contractual)	(compulsory)	Politics (familistic)	(contractual)	(compulsory)
all 14 actors	F		(22)			(24)		(19)					(25)		(28)	
	P		(10)			(11)		(10)					(13)		(14)	
China	F	18				23		10					33		(40)	
	P	8			11	11		3					20		(19)	
USSR	F		(19)			(29)		(19)					(38)	19	19	
	P		(9)			(15)		(10)					(24)		11	
United States of America	F	17				19		13					33		20	
	P	5	5		7	7		5					14		10	
wealthy	F		22		21			16					31		26	
	P	8					10	7					16		13	
middle	F		22			25		18					29		(34)	
	P		11			(13)		10					15		(18)	
poor	F		(30)		(26)			(25)					(41)		24	
	P		(12)			11		(12)					(17)		10	
powerful	F	16				23		13					33		(29)	
	P	7	7		9	9		6					19		14	
middle	F		26			23		(28)				31			26	
	P		(13)			11		(17)				13	13		(15)	
weak	F		(30)			(28)		24					(39)		(29)	
	P		12			12		11					(18)		13	
liberal democracy	F	19			21			19					24		(25)	
	P	9			9	9		(12)					11		(13)	
middle	F		(28)		(25)			(24)					(39)		(25)	
	P		(11)		10			11					(14)		12	
nonliberal democracy	F	19			(25)			14					35		11	
	P	9			(11)			8					(14)		4	

a. Only the highest F and P in *each row* of a *set* (rectangle), or those tied for highest, are shown. The highest F and P in a whole set are shown in parentheses.

b. From Table 19A.4

c. From Table 19A.5

(14) The wealth distance vector is most often and tightly linked to the contractual disposition, especially for the USSR, poor, or middle powerful states.

(15) Of all linkages for the major powers and for the types of states, the power-contractual linkage most often situationally occurs for the poor; and the power-compulsory linkage is the tightest for the USSR.

However, the purpose here is not to distill propositions or conclusions from these tables. Rather, I only wish to present them along with the underlying logic so that others might, in terms of their own interests and at least for these actors and for this time period, use them to assess the relationship between an actor's situation expectations, behavioral dispositions, perceptions, and distance vectors (interests and capabilities); and to show that field theory and the *field equations of behavior have an operational and empirical structure.*

9A.4. THE MOST GENERAL EMPIRICAL EQUATIONS OF SITUATIONAL DISTANCES AND DISPOSITIONS

The previous approach provides a specific and precise measurement of the linkages between distance vectors and behavioral dispositions. There is another way, however, of aggregating these equations, and that is in terms of the most general equations latent in all these results. Given all the 197 equations, which best represent the overall, situational linkages?[13]

First, consider how a complete matrix of canonical equations would look for all significant equations and actors, as shown in Figure 9A.2. Each cell of the matrix would contain the canonical coefficient of the column attribute distance or disposition on the row-equation for a particular actor. For the analysis here this matrix was filled in with all canonical coefficients for 39 of the most significant equations across all 14 actors.

When we ask for the most general equations in the results, in effect, we mean to ask about what distances and behaviors most often cluster together in the matrix of Figure 9A.2. This is a question about the pattern of covariation in the table, and can be answered using factor analysis: a way of determining systematically the most general equations for the canonical results is to factor analyze the matrix of canonical coefficients (the canonical structure matrix).[14]

The results of doing this are shown in Table 9A.8.[15] Each of the four columns gives a general equation (situation) linking distances and dispositions latent in the 39 significant equations (p ≤ 05, two-tailed) found for the 14 actors. Thus, for the first column we find

$$.86 \text{ (IO)} \doteq -.40(\text{wealth}) + .93 \text{ (totali.)} + .96 \text{ (authori.)}$$
$$+ .48 \text{ (diversity)} -.84(\text{density}) -.44(\text{Catholic culture}),$$

and this equation accounts for 22.5% of the variance in all the coefficients (measuring situational expectations and perception) among the 39 equations.

According to this equation, then: in general the wealthier, denser, more Catholic, less totalitarian, less authoritarian, and diverse the object state relative to the actor, the more an actor is disposed to join IO's with it.[16] To turn this around, comemberships in international organizations tend to be a function of wealthy, densely populated, homogeneous Catholic, and democratic societies.

Or, in terms of the theoretical components and the higher coefficients: contractual dispositions are mainly a function of political and demographic distance vectors.

Finally, now bringing in the theoretical meaning of the coefficients and equation, this first equation says: *there is a situation between states in which an actor expects that an object's perceived, relative political and density-related interests and capabilities will lead to desirable outcomes for the actor's contractual behavior towards it.* This is the most general equation to be found in all the canonical linkage equations. And these are the three

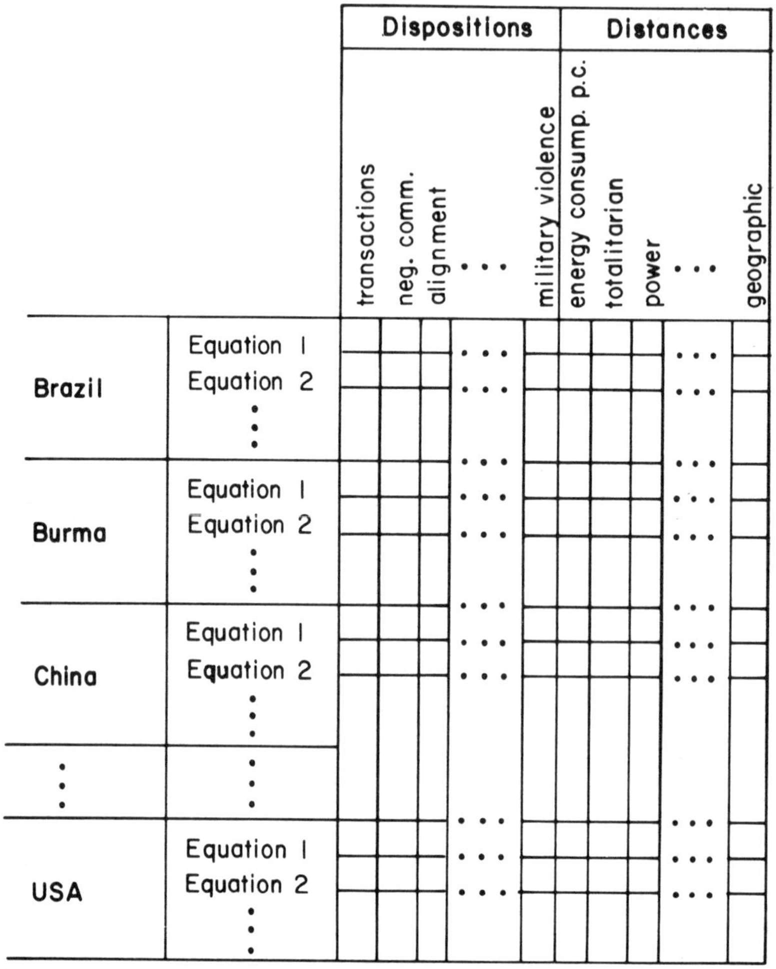

FIGURE 9A.2: The Data Matrix ofCanonical Coefficients Linking Dispositions and Distances

increasingly abstract ways (in terms of empirical components, theoretical components, or the expectations-disposition-perception-distance equation) in which it may be interpreted.

Turning now to the second most general equation in column four of Table 9A.8, which accounts for 15% of the variance, there is no need to lay out the equation here. We can simply interpret it as showing that: the weaker, smaller, stable, and more dependent on imports the object state relative to the actor, then the less an actor tends to transact with and export relatively to it.[17] In terms of theoretical components: the less the power of the object states, the less an actor is disposed toward familistic and contractual behavior with it. And in terms of the theoretical meaning of the equation: *there is a situation between states in which an actor expects that an object's perceived relative power-related interests and capabilities will lead to desirable outcomes for the actor's familistic and contractual behavior towards it.*

The third most general equation accounting for 11.5% of the variance is shown in column 2 of Table 9A.8. This is purely a geographic distance linkage: the closer the actor is to the object states, the more disposed an actor to transact, align, and export relatively toward it. Or: the greater the familistic, contractual, and compulsory (nonviolent preparatory) [18] disposition toward it. That is: *an actor's perception of the geographic closeness of an object defines a situation in which it expects desirable outcomes of familistic, contractual, and compulsory behavior towards it.*

The next general equation (column 3 of Table 9A.8) ties wealth and power to conflict. The poorer and weaker the object states relative to the actor, the less disposed the actor to

TABLE 9A.8: **Most General Equations Linking Distance and Behavior**[a]

MATRIX (SPACE)	THEORETICAL COMPONENTS	EMPIRICAL COMPONENTS	EQUATIONS					h^2
			1	2	3	4	5	
distance vectors	wealth	wealth	−.40		.50		.54	.78
	power	power			.44	.77		.91
		size				.80		.85
		domestic conflict				.64	−.42	.62
		import dependency				−.54		.47
	political	totalitarianism	.93					.88
		authoritarianism	.96					.95
	cultural	Catholic culture	−.44				.64	.73
	demographic	diversity	.48					.53
		density	−.84					.74
	physical	geographic		−.50				.43
dyadic behavior dispositions	familistic	transactions		.76		−.58		.94
		aid					.57	.35
	contractual	inter'l org.	.86					.90
		relative exports		.76		−.56		.93
	compulsory	alignment[b]		.72				.65
		negative communications			−.83			.72
		anti-foreign behavior			−.49			.36
		military violence			−.61			.41
		%total variance	22.5	11.5	11.1	15.0	9.0	

a. These are the orthogonally rotated dimensions of an image factor analysis of the matrix partially given in Rummel (1978, Table 8.3). The matrix factored comprised all the complete significant equations, where the matrix cells were the correlations between variables and equations.

Where an equation lacked a score (for example, since many developing states do not give aid, aid had to be omitted from the analysis for those states), a correlation of .00 was inserted.

Only loadings greater or equal to an absolute .40 and only those dimensions involving both distances and dispositions are shown.

b. Scale reversed. Higher magnitudes mean closer UN voting distance.

direct negative communications, antiforeign behavior, and military violence towards it. And in terms of the theoretical meaning: *there is a situation between states in which an actor expects that an object's perceived, relative wealth and power will lead to desirable outcomes for its compulsory behavior towards it.*

The last general equation concerns aid: the poorer, more unstable, and non-Catholic the object state relative to the actor, the more aid the actor directs towards it. Or: some familistic behavior is a function of wealth, power (stability), and culture. And, finally: *there is a situation between states in which an actor expects that an object's perceived, relative wealth, power, and cultural-related interests and capabilities will lead to desirable outcomes for the actor's familistic behavior towards it.*

In summary and considering only the larger coefficients of the distances in Table 9A.8 and the empirical components, we find general situations (equations) separately linking dyadic conflict (excluding alignment) and cooperation. For conflict, we find a *conflict-wealth-power situation* where dyadic conflict is purely related to the wealth-power-distances.

For cooperation, we find four different general situations. The most general is an *I.O.-politics-density situation,* where the tendency toward comemberships in international organizations is largely a function of the democratic political characteristics of the object and its relative density. Second, we have a *transactions-alignment-exports-geographic distance situation* whereby closer states are disposed toward more cooperative interaction. Third, there is a general *transaction-export-power-size situation,* relating dispositions toward dyadic transactions and relative exports mainly to power and size. Finally, the weakest linkage is an *aid-wealth-stability-Catholic situation.*

These five general situations underlie the 39 significant equations (situations) for the 14 actors, 1950-1965. These show that the data contain patterned relationships between distance vectors and important international, empirical, behavioral dispositions. Wealth, power and politics indeed relate to transactions, conflict, trade and alignment—to familistic, contractual, and compulsory dispositions.[19] Clues to some of these relationships are suggested in Tables 9A.4-8.

Finally, there is one more aspect of Table 9A.8 to note: the communalities (h^2). The larger the communalities, the more involved a distance vector in the general situations (equations) or the more a behavioral disposition is weighted by situational expectations. Thus, we find that the distance most involved in these general situations is authoritarianism (.95), next is power (.91), and totalitarianism (.88) is third. By far, expectations most highly weight dispositions to transact (.94), export (.93), and to cojoin international organizations (.90). The worst distance (in finding general, across actor situations) is geographic; the worst disposition is aid.

Considering dyadic international behavioral dispositions as a whole, then, *the most productive distances to focus on are political and power.* Indeed, these are the elements students of international relations have traditionally used to explain international behavior. And those behavioral dispositions most tied to these distances are transactions, exports and international organization comemberships.

9A.5. THE MOST COMMONLY SHARED EMPIRICAL EQUATIONS AMONG GROUPS OF ACTORS

The previous section has shown what general situations exist among the 39 significant dyadic situations for the 14 actors. This section will focus on the similarity between actors in the situations they manifest. Are some situations similar to China and the USSR; what about the USSR and the United States? Is there a similarity in situation between developed and underdeveloped, nontotalitarian and totalitarian, or powerful and weak actors? The way to determine this is to Q-factor analyze the same complete matrix of canonical coefficients exemplified in Figure 9A.2 and used to generate Table 9A.8. We factor by rows (the actors and equations) rather than by columns (the distance vectors and behavioral dispositions), and the resulting dimensions (when rotated) define the clusters of actors with similar equations (situations).

These results are shown in the upper half of Table 9A.9, where the coefficients are the correlations between the actors and each of the common groups (columns). The bottom half of the table presents the general equations (factor scores) manifesting the situational similarity of actors within each group.

There are seven groups of actors, the first being by far the largest. It includes all of the 14 actors except the Netherlands, USSR and United States; and Brazil and Indonesia are central members. Regarding the equation for this group, the signs of the factor scores can be interpreted the same as the coefficients of Table 9A.8.[20] We, therefore, can read the general equation for those actors in this group and the empirical components as: the less the object's power, and the greater its diversity and Catholic culture relative to these actors, the more these actors tend to join international organizations with, and the less they are disposed to transact with and relatively export to, the object. This is a group of actors which tend to focus their cooperation on international organizations to the exclusion of exports and transactions *if* the object state is weak, diverse and Catholic relative to them. Power here is the main distance vector.

The theoretical meaning of this equation is this: *there is a situation between states in which Brazil and Indonesia, especially, but also Israel, India, United Kingdom, Jordan, Egypt, Cuba, Burma, China, and Poland expect that an object's perceived, relative power, Catholic culture, and diversity-related interests and capabilities will lead to desirable outcomes for their comembership in international organization, and undesirable outcomes for their transactions with and relative exports to the object.*

The second group (column 2 in Table 9A.2) also includes most states, but now China, Egypt, Jordan and the USSR are omitted. United Kingdom, Netherlands, Brazil, Israel and the United States are central members, making this appear a dominantly Western group. This group cooperates with other states mainly in line with their wealth. Specifically, the wealthier the object state relative to them and the less authoritarian and the denser it is, the greater their transactions and relative exports to it and the more they cojoin international organizations with it. Theoretically: *there is a situation between states in which the United Kingdom, Netherlands, Brazil, Israel, and the United States particularly, but also Indonesia, India, Cuba, Burma, and Poland expect that an object's perceived, relative wealth, non-authoritarianism, and density-related interests and capabilities will lead to desirable outcomes for their transactions and international organizations comemberships with, and relative exports to, it.* This collection of actors can be called a *cooperation-wealth situational* group.

The third group (column 3 in Table 9A.9) involves Egypt, Israel, Jordan and the Netherlands, and appears mainly a Middle East group. To these actors the relative totalitarianism of the object states is crucial in their alignments. That is, the less totalitarian and import dependent the object state and the further away, then the more they are inclined to align with it. Leaving out the theoretical interpretation, this may simply be labeled an *alignment-politics situational* group.

The remaining groups involve two actors. There is one for China and the USSR, showing that they both transact and align with, export more to, and send lesser negative communications to relatively poor, weak, totalitarian and authoritarian states. They form a *cooperation-wealth-politics-power situational* group. Another group comprises Egypt and Jordan, who align and have conflict more with object states, the more relatively import dependent, non-Catholic and closer geographically they are. Egypt and Jordan constitute a *cooperation-conflict-geographic distance situational* group. Finally, the two groups involving only the

TABLE 9A.9: Groups of Actors Showing Common Situations Involving Distances and Dispositions

ACTOR	GROUPS[a]						
	1	2	3	4	5	6	7
Brazil	.93	.93					
Indonesia	.92	.83					
Israel	.88	.93	.92				
India	.79	.84					
U.K.	.75	.97				.90	.70
Jordan	.75		.60	.84			
Egypt	.73		.74	.91			
Cuba	.71	.75					
Burma	.69	.76					
China	.69				.92		
Poland	.63						
Netherlands		.77	.74				
United States		.97				.82	.87
USSR		.89			.84		

Associated Equations[b]

Matrix	Components								
	theoretical	empirical							
	wealth	wealth	2.02	−1.79			1.41		
	power	power					1.70		
		size			1.51	−1.64		−1.21	−1.51
		domestic conflict							−1.41
		import dependency							

TABLE 9A.9: Groups of Actors Showing Common Situations Involving Distances and Dispositions (Cont.)

			(1)	(2)	(3)	(4)	(5)	(6)	(7)	(8)
distance vectors	political	totalitarianism	-1.52		1.60			-1.13		1.17
		authoritariansim		1.05				-1.35		1.01
	cultural	catholic culture					1.06			1.08
	demographic	diversity	-1.36						-2.37	1.94
		density	-1.32						-1.08	
	physical	geographic			1.26	-1.93				
	familistic	transactions	-1.44	1.73				1.34		
		aid								
	contractual	inter'l org	1.75	1.80						
		relative exports	-1.40	1.77			1.23			
dyadic behavior dispositions		alignment[c]			2.82	1.82	1.62			
		neg. communications			1.78		-1.72			
		anti-for behavior						-2.00		
	compulsory	military violence			1.66	2.35		-1.01		

a. These groups result from a Q-factor analysis of the complete matrix employed to determine the common linkages shown in Table 9A.8 Component analysis was used, and the groups shown in the table are the orthogonally rotated components. Only loadings greater than or equal to an absolute .60 are shown.

Note that each actor may appear with high loadings in more than one group, since each had more than one canonical equation (more than one row of matrix). If an actor has more than one high loading on the same factor, only the highest is shown.

b. This part of the table gives the factor scores of each empirical component on the actor group shown above. Only factor scores greater than or equal to an absolute 1.00 are shown.

In the original computer output some actors had negative loadings on the group factor. This only indicated that their equations had all the signs reversed from those for the positive loading actors. These negative loadings were therefore all made positive, which in no way affects our interpretation of the results.

c. Scale reversed. Higher factor scores mean closer distance in UN voting.

United Kingdom and the United States show that they have two different linkage equations, or situations, in common. One shows that they have more military violence with the larger, relatively more diverse and denser object states; the other shows that they direct less negative communications to and join fewer international organizations with object states, the less totalitarian, authoritarian, diverse and Catholic they are and the more unstable and import dependent. The United Kingdom and United States form *conflict-stability-diversity situational* groups.

In summary, we find that certain actors share specific situations in which they are similarly affected by distances. The same distances are linked to the same dyadic behaviors in the same ways. There are seven such groups of actors, some showing common situations involving organization memberships and relative power; involving cooperation and relative wealth; involving alignment and relative politics; involving cooperation and relative wealth, politics and power; involving cooperation and conflict and geographic distance; and involving conflict, stability and diversity.

NOTES

1. For the mathematical development of the canonical model in relation to field theory, see Rummel (1977: section 4.4).

2. Technically, I am assuming that the number of canonical variates (situations) will equal the number of input components in the dependent (behavioral dispositions) matrix. This is a necessary assumption of the theory, where a certain measure of free will and specific influences are involved in each situation. Thus, theoretically, the trace correlation should never be 1.00: all the common variance in behavioral dispositions should never be completely dependent on distance vectors, and the number of variates will equal the number of behavioral components. A second auxiliary assumption is that the number of input behavioral components is less than or equal to the number of distance vectors. This is a theoretical assumption: common behavioral space-time is a subspace of the common international (attribute) space-time and therefore its dimensionality cannot exceed that of attributes, i.e., the number of distance vectors.

3. Both my ontology and epistemology are inseparably linked through this approach, which was philosophically developed in Volume 1. That is, expectations and perceptions are aspects of the dynamic psychological field. They can be only indirectly known by observers from their manifestations—their traces on the plane of phenomena. Here, the manifestations are the linkages between behavioral disposition and distance vector, i.e., the canonical coefficients. As to why this particular linkage should display expectations and perceptions was the burden of Volumes 1-2 to establish. For example, see Volume 1, 1975: part III.

4. Reported here for the first time are part of the results of Project 7.3, described in appendix I.

5. Many more canonical analyses than these have been done, but not all are distinct enough to include here. For example, some simply involved reanalyzing the same data with minor changes in methodology.

6. A number of criteria entered into selecting each equation from those generated in the analyses: its canonical correlation, significance test, meaningfulness, and the size of its canonical coefficients.

7. Available on request.

8. The names in parenthesis here and below are those given by the scientist to the relevant component in his analysis.

9. In previous works and in chapter 4 I kept the primary power component separate from other components, such as domestic conflict and trade dependence, which have a

secondary relationship to a state's coercive power. Here, however, empirical components are classified under the most relevant theoretical label for the purpose of linking them to behavioral dispositions, and the secondary nature of the empirical component is then crucial.

10. Generally, structural canonical coefficients were used. These are correlations between component and variate, and thus their square measures their variance in common.

11. There is a difference between some of the F and P values shown for the USSR in Table 9A.3 (and also for the U.S. in subsequent Tables 9A.4-7) and those values in Tables 5 and 7 of my "Soviet Strategy and Northeast Asia," *Korea and World Affairs: a Quarterly Review,* Research Center for Peace and Unification, Seoul, Korea (Vol. 2, Spring, 1978). Where differences occur, those in the article are in error (i.e., for USSR demographic weights and U.S. wealth and geographic distance weights in Table 5; and for all except U.S. cooperative weights in Table 7). The corrected figures (weights) do not in any way alter the points made in the article, and if anything slightly strengthen the conclusions.

12. The reason for this low linkage of military action to distance vectors is that it is a phase in conflict behavior. Distances affect the initiation, and to a certain extent, the intensity of conflict; but whether a conflict will escalate to violence is related to a number of contextual, nondistance-vector, factors. See appendix 15A and 16B, particularly Propositions 15.3, 16.9-11, 16.16-22.

In general, cooperation (familistic *and* contractual behavior) has a better linkage to distances (Table 9A.4) or attributes (Rummel, 1972; chapter 13) than conflict (compulsory behavior). See also Vasquez (1975: Table 12). The reason for this is that cooperation is a particular fit to attributes (interests and capabilities), whereas, conflict is the universal means by which this matching takes place.

13. The following is a revision of Rummel (1978: chapter 9).

14. In the analysis, the correlations between variables and canonical variates were used (the canonical *structure* matrix) rather than coefficients.

15. I am indebted to Peter Sybinsky for originating all the analyses reported in this section and the next.

16. The distance vectors can be interpreted easily by reference to the object nation if the sign of the distance coefficient is reversed (see Rummel, 1978: chapter 8). Thus, contractual disposition $_{i\to j}$ = +.63 (wealth distance $_{i-j}$), can be interpreted as: the *less* wealth of j, the more the disposition of i to contract with j. If the sign of .63 were originally negative, then the equations would read: the *more* wealth of j, the more the disposition of i to contract with j.

17. The relationship between import dependency and dyadic, relative exports is not tautological. A State may have relatively low imports to its total trade (thus being trade-independent), while another is sending to it high exports relative to that state's GNP. Indeed, were there any tautological relationship, it should be the opposite of that shown.

18. Alignment is a preparatory phase of conflict behavior. See chapter 15.

19. This is a revision of Rummel (1978: chapter 10).

20. See note 16.

PART IV

THE INTERNATIONAL

CONFLICT HELIX

Thus the size of the body politic being purely relative, it is forced to compare itself in order to know itself; it depends on its whole environment and has to take an interest in all that happens. In vain it wishes to stay within its own bounds, neither gaining nor losing; it becomes big or small, strong or weak according to the extent that its neighbour expands or contracts, grows stronger or weaker.

Rousseau, Extract 3: The State of War

One fact emerges clearly from the analysis: it is the persistent reassertion of the balance or equilibrium of power as the irreducible if changing central dynamics of international relations.

Liska, 1960: 143

Chapter 10

LATENT CONFLICT

Things are seldom what they seem
Skim milk masquerades as cream
　　　　　　W.S. Gilbert, H.M.S. Pinafore *II*

Interaction between international actors is a process of balancing and balance, of disorder and order, of conflict and cooperation. Expectations are disrupted, overt conflict breaks out, new expectations are reformed, peace and cooperation ensue.

This process is continuous. Although structures of expectations may be stable for generations, interests shift, capabilities wither or increase, will becomes emboldened or timid, and expectations once aligned with interests, capabilities, and will, have only habit and inertia to withstand opposing forces. Only a trigger is needed to break up the old, initiate a new balancing, bring about a new structure of expectations. Such is an aspect, a turn on the conflict helix. Change is the constant of life.

The full process of conflict—the conflict helix—is pictured in Figure 10.1 and has been elaborated and detailed in Volume 2. My interest in this chapter is to make the latent conflict phase of this process more explicit in terms of the space-time components and behavioral equations outlined previously in Table 8.1. The elements, empirical concepts, and notation of the conflict helix to be discussed here are presented in Table 10.1.

10.1. CONFLICT SPACE

The sociocultural space-time defines the level of *potentiality* for conflict; the potential forces towards conflict spread throughout this space-time and seated in the meanings, values and norms, status and class,[1] of international actors. The components of this space-time (shown in Table 10.1) are a set of (linear) independent probability functions—latent functions—based on manifest attributes, and reflecting the underlying lines of sociocultural potentiality. An actor i is located in this space-time by his values ($s_{i\varrho}$) on each component (S_ϱ) and this location defines behavioral force potentials—latent forces toward or away from conflict.

For example, the people of the Pacific Island nation of Tonga and the land-locked Central African Republic will be similarly or differently located in international space-time as they are similar or different in their state's wealth and power, politics and social conflict, culture and diversity, and so on. These relative locations reflect shared and distinct meanings, values, and norms; convergent and divergent status and class; and thus congruent, opposing, and different interests, capabilities, and expectations. Neither peoples may be in contact; neither may be aware of each other. But, these relative similarities and differences divide potential conflict and cooperation. Place a Tongan and a Central African next to each other, have them share a dormitory room while both are attending a foreign university, and this potential for conflict and cooperation will become actual.

Through acculturation, socialization and individual experience, international actors develop a lattice of attitudes.[2] These are clustered around an actor's superordinate goal, delineate his sentiments, and define his role dispositions.

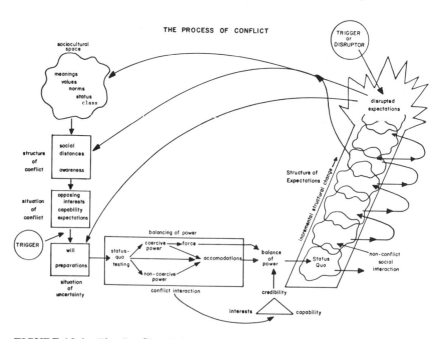

FIGURE 10.1: The Conflict Helix

TABLE 10.1: The Latent Conflict Phase of the Conflict Helix

SUBPHASE	THEORETICAL ELEMENTS[b]	EMPIRICAL CONCEPTS	NOTATIONAL AND EQUATION
sociocultural space-time (conflict-space)	meanings	common *sociocultural space-time*	s_ℓ
	values	common space-time *components*:[a]	s_1
	norms	wealth	s_2
	status: wealth	power (coercive)	s_3
	power	totalitarianism	s_4
	prestige	authoritarianism	s_5
	class	size	s_6
		Catholic culture	s_7
		density	s_8
		diversity	s_9
		import dependency	s_{10}
		social conflict	
		international *actors*	i,j
		actor's space time *location*	$s_{i\ell}; s_{j\ell}$
structure of conflict	awareness	contact, communication	
	opposing attitudes	sociocultural distance vectors	$d_{\ell,i-j} = s_{i\ell} - s_{j\ell}$
	relative capabilities		g
situation of conflict	stimulation of needs	situation	$\alpha_{gi\ell}$
	opposing interests	situational perception of actor i	
	relative capabilities	sociocultural distance vectors	$\alpha_{gi\ell}d_{\ell,i-j}$
	expectation	situational expectation	β_{hig}

a. From Table 7.1

b. Become of the division of the Table into theoretical elements and empirical concepts (elements), there is same difference from the elements shown in Figure 29.1, Volume 2.

Attitudes are goal and means potentials transformed into dispositions. Their development structures the *conflict space*. Attitudes make possible the *structure of conflict.*

10.2. THE STRUCTURE OF CONFLICT

Through a variety of means—education, movies, television, radio, ethnic jokes, travel, contact, transactions—international actors become aware of each other. Awareness transforms potential opposition into opposing dispositions. It creates the *structure of conflict.* Awareness is the first theoretical element[3] in this structure, the second level of latent conflict.

The structure of conflict is the disposition or tendency to conflict. Along with awareness, it comprises opposing attitudes (inactive—dispositional—interests) between actors and their attendant means (relative capabilities). On the empirical plane, it consists of mutual sociocultural distance vectors.

Now attitudes lie along the sociocultural distances between actors: their differences and similarities in meanings, values, norms, status and class define their opposing attitudes.[4]

And these distances reflect vector forces in the psychological space of an actor. They define latent motivations toward behavior.

The distance vectors between all actors on all the sociocultural components then embody the variety of motivational (attitudinal) forces latent within the conflict structure.

To retrace the logic, international actors have differing latent attitudes expressing their ends, wants, and goals, and the means to achieve them. Within the structure of conflict these attitudes are inactive; they are dispositional forces waiting for stimulation. Moreover, attitudes cluster into particular patterns which lie along the components of sociocultural space. There are attitudes involved with wealth, politics, power, and so on. Therefore, the differences and similarities between actors in their attitudes are along these components. And it follows, then, that the distances between them on these components then embody these differences in attitudes.

But do differences mean opposing attitudes? To answer this, consider again the sociocultural components delineating the space-time of international actors. The poles of the components are wealth versus poverty, powerful versus weak, totalitarian versus liberal democratic, authoritarian versus liberal democratic, Catholic versus non-Catholic, and so on. Clearly, these poles denote potentially opposing attitudes, and distances on these dimensions then reflect this.[5]

However, this is not to imply that only differences on these components measure opposition. Similarity in high power status may as well (Volume 2, 1976: chapters 17-18) reflect opposing attitudes, that of the strong who may see their strength as means of manifesting their differing attitudes along other components.

As a final point of clarification, note that attitudes comprise goals, that which an actor wants. But again, these are latent, inactive goal dispositions. At this level distance vectors reflect the opposition towards which actors are disposed by their latent goals.

A third theoretical element in the structure of conflict is *capabilities*,[6] the base or resources for power in all its forms, whether coercive, bargaining, authoritative, or (as in much violence and war) physical. Here the wealth, type of political system, size, culture, and the like, of an actor's state, as well as his individual abilities and resources, are all relevant, depending on the situation, form of power, and object. These capabilities relative to another actor lie along the distance vectors.

Distances in power (coercive), in wealth, totalitarianism, authoritarianism, size, and so on, not only describe opposing attitudes but capabilities as well. For example, the distance along the power component between two actors measures the difference in national income, energy resources, energy production X population, political centralization, defense expenditures, and armed forces—all capabilities for coercion or force.[7]

Such is the *structure of conflict,* as shown in Table 10.1: awareness, and distances reflecting attitudes and relative capabilities.[8] It defines the tendency to oppose, to conflict, to struggle. But this tendency is inactive, without strength.

10.3. THE SITUATION OF CONFLICT

The stimulation of the needs for security, self-assertion, protectiveness, and so on, energize attitudes. Stimulated needs empower dispositions and transform them into interests, vectors of power toward gratification.

But needs are not stimulated in a vacuum. They are linked to a *perceived situation* g, such as the threat of aggression, loss of human rights in another country, possibility of a profitable investment, and the like. Perceived situations stimulate needs and transform structures into actual conflict,[9] attitudes into empowered interests. Such stimulation is the first theoretical element in the situation of conflict; for an actor at the empirical level it is defined by a situational parameter $\alpha_{gi\varrho}$ of Equations 8.1-8.3, as shown in Table 10.1.

Interests—energized attitudes—are the second, essential theoretical element in the conflict situation and major forces towards behavior. These define the excited purposes, activated roles, felt sentiments, and most important, an actor's driving superordinate goal. Also essential is the third theoretical element, the means ingredient of interests, the *relative capabilities* of international actors—their differing coercive, authoritative, bargaining, and physical powers.[10] Both opposing interests and relative capabilities are reflected in the sociocultural distances between actors. Which interests are stimulated and which relative capabilities are salient depend on the perceived situation.

Because both opposing attitudes and potential capabilities were reflected in sociocultural distances, opposing interests and relative capabilities are likewise manifest. Distances measures both dispositional and dynamics levels, both the structure and situation of latent conflict. What distinguishes the two levels, what separates possible attitudes and potential capabilities from active empowered interests and salient capabilities is the perceived situation. The product of perceived situation α and distance vector d discriminates between structure and situation.[11] This is shown in Table 10.1.

Therefore, a particular product αd means: *the actor's situational perception of an object's relative (to the actor) interests and capabilities.*[12]

The perceived situation is latent, however. While interests are engaged within a situation, behavior yet remains unaffected. Conflict is there, but beneath the surface. Therefore, the variation in $\alpha_{gi\varrho d\varrho,i-j}$ for different others j has yet *no necessary correlation* with the common, manifest behavior of i to j.

In a specific *perceived situation of conflict* g, the common interests and capabilities are theoretical, a cognitive framework for understanding the process of conflict at the level of dispositions and powers. Dynamic interests and relative capabilities transform behavioral potentials into an active tendency, a psychological force towards threatening, protesting, snubbing, attacking, accusing, sanctioning, and so on. But this behavioral disposition, while empowered, is yet latent.

How a behavioral disposition will be manifested in what specific behavior depends on the actor's *expectation* within the situation, the final element in the situation of conflict. Situational expectations of outcomes alter, suppress, or strengthen dispositions; they determine the final manifest behavior to follow from interests and relative capabilities. This situational expectation, β_{hig}, has been discussed in Chapters 6 and 8 and articulated in Equations 6.2-6.6 and 8.3-8.4; it is also listed in Table 10.1.[13]

However, note again that the situation of conflict is latent. Theoretically, the sociocultural distances d define the forces toward conflict behavior—the strain to conflict. But there may be no manifest interaction between actors or they may be interacting in some manner incidental to or independent from the conflict situation g. For the forces reflected in d have yet to be manifest: they are powers toward manifestation and it is the next stage in the process that makes these forces—opposing interests and relative capabilities—determinate.

NOTES

1. Class is an element of the sociocultural space-time, but was accidently omitted from Figure 29.1, Volume 2, 1976: 266.

2. The attitudinal lattice is detailed in Volume 1, 1975: chapter 21 (see especially Figures 21.1-2).

3. In Volume 2, 1976: Figure 29.1, awareness was listed second in the structure of conflict. Here I have listed awareness first in order to highlight its role in transforming potentiality into disposition.

4. Beware of automatically interpreting large distances as large attitudinal opposition. Actually, similar distances may reflect predisposition to want the same thing, and thus conflict; large distances may mean that individuals have different interests and thus no opposition. For such an analysis of differences and similarities, see *Volume 3*, 1977: chapter 6. All I have done at this point is say that opposing interests lie along sociocultural distances, but I have not specified their direction of correlation.

5. Note that wealth versus poverty, and totalitarianism versus liberal democratic, comprise the North-South and East-West poles currently applied to explain major global conflicts.

6. Capability is a dispositional concept: it means the capacity or faculty for carrying out or doing something specific.

7. See Table 7.3.

8. In Figure 29.1 of Volume 2, reproduced here as Figure 10.1, I was only concerned with displaying the major conceptional elements in the conflict helix. Because my task is now to divide out those aspects of the helix which are empirical and operational and reflect underlying *theoretical* elements, a greater precision is required. Thus, the structure of conflict in Figure 29.1 was composed of sociocultural distances and awareness; now, awareness is considered theoretical, and contact and communications are defined as its empirical indicators, and distances are defined as empirically reflecting opposing attitudes and relative capabilities. Changes in subsequent aspects of Figure 29.1 are similarly explained, unless otherwise noted.

9. Actual conflict may not be manifest. Here I am concerned with conflict which is felt, recognized, but yet does not display itself through behavior. I am concerned with dispositions. The operational nature of this situation regarding general and actor-specific behavioral dispositions, including conflict, and their empirical content are developed and shown in appendix 9A.

10. Relative capabilities also appears as a theoretical element in the structure of conflict. But there it is a weak, dispositional element, at the same level of latency as the unstimulated attitudes. In the situation of conflict relative capabilities are now "on alert," strongly disposed towards gratifying stimulated interests.

11. Henceforth, I will leave the subscripts off these terms as long as they are clear in context.

12. See appendix 9A, sections 9A.3-5, for the operational working of this product and empirical results for behavioral dispositions.

13. See appendix 9A for the operationalization of expectations and their joint working with perceptions, behavior dispositions, and distances. Sections 9A.3-5 provide empirical results for general and other specific situations.

Chapter 11

TRIGGER, WILL AND PREPARATIONS

the policymaker must be concerned with the best that can be achieved, not just the best that can be imagined. He has to act in a fog of incomplete knowledge without the information that will be available later to the analyst. He knows—or should know—that he is responsible for the consequences of disaster as well as for the benefits of success.
Kissinger, 1973: 527

Conflict may remain latent between international actors. Leaders may change, domestic interests may shift, new ideologies may become ascendent, weapons purchases or developments may alter relative capabilities. But patterns of interaction may persist. Emerging interests may become absorbed into or submerged by overriding goals.

For example, the need for Western technology and aid has persuaded Soviet leaders to ignore some short-run interests that may create new conflicts with the West. The uncertainty of American commitments and support following the fall of South Vietnam in 1975 caused President Marcos of the Philippines to ignore latent conflicts with the Soviet Union and China, and seek new patterns of cooperative relations with them. Directors of multinational corporations like IBM have often submerged their many interests in conflict with communist leaders in order to make large, profitable deals with them. And so on.

Still, situations of conflict do involve active, empowered forces towards conflict. In spite of overriding interests or because the situation is independent of such interests, pressures in the situation may burst forth in manifest conflict behavior. Two conditions bring this about: some event (occasion) and the will's consequent decision to manifest the opposing interests.

11.1. THE TRIGGER

Phase I in the conflict helix involved levels of potentiality, inactive dispositions, and active powers toward manifestation; of space, structure, and situation.

The second phase is that of *uncertainty*. It is the initiation of conflict phase, with all the objective uncertainty about an object's real goals, capabilities, responses, and stakes in the conflict. Although an actor may be subjectively certain of success, may calculate or intuit that the costs of the conflict will be acceptable, such expectation is always conditional. The precise moves of the other are unsure; the subsequent course of actual events speculative.

My intent here is to make more precise the theoretical elements and their relationships in this *situation of uncertainty*.

Now, this phase is initiated via a decision of the will triggered by some event. This trigger transforms the situation of conflict into a situation of uncertainty involving the will and preparations to assert one's interests. How can this trigger be made more precise?

First, consider that a trigger is a random event. It may be some final straw, some objectively minor or major happening that finally tilts an actor towards action, provokes such action, or makes it unavoidable (like the capturing of one's ship, as in the Pueblo or Mayaquez incidents involving the United States). It may be unintended communication from the other by word or deed that shows a lack of will or ability to defend some opposing interest. Any event is potentially a trigger, depending on the situation of conflict, on the subjective fields of those involved. And these events may be unique, only important to or perceived by the actor. Therefore, we must deal with a space of potential events; we must define a trigger probabilistically and within the actor's perceived situation.

Let T_g denote the occurrence of a trigger stimulating the will to action in a situation of conflict g. Let T_{gf} be a specific trigger f which *would* provoke i's will within this situation. Then,

$$T_g = 0, \text{ if } T_{gf} = 0, \text{ for all f};$$ [11.1]

$$T_g = 1, \text{ if } T_{gf} = 1, \text{ for at least one f},$$

where 0 = nonoccurrence;
1 = occurrence;
g = situation of conflict
f = a specific, potential trigger.

The question now concerns the probability of $T_g = 1$. To assess this consider that situations of conflict can be more or less empowered. They can be tense, hostile situations existing barely beneath the surface, overlaid by a patina of routine, cooperative interaction, an explosion seeking a spark. Little in the way of a trigger—an excuse, really—is needed to surface this conflict. Then there are situations that involve weak, secondary and tertiary interests: a situation one is willing to live with unless these interests are provoked by some rare, and really disruptive occurrence.

Therefore, the likelihood of a trigger occurring is a function of the situation's intensity. The stronger the forces towards action, the more explosive the associated situation, the more powerful the situationally perceived interests and capabilities $(\Sigma \alpha d)$,[1] then the greater the probability at that moment that some trigger will excite the will to action. Consequently, we can define

$$p_{gt}(T = 1) = \delta_g + \gamma_g (\underset{t}{\Sigma} e_{gt}) (\underset{\ell}{\Sigma} \alpha_{gi\ell} d_{\ell,i-j}),$$ [11.2]

where $p_{gt}(T_g = 1)$ = the probability at time t that T = 1, in situation g;

   δ_g, γ_g = situational parameters;

   e_{gt} = the tth time interval e (e.g., days, months, years) since the situation g of conflict came into being.

The notation e_{gt} defines the passage of time. According to the equation, *the probability of T being unity is a linear function of the product of the passage of time since the inception of the situation and the intensity of the disposition $(\Sigma \alpha d)$ towards action.* No matter how much time passes, if there is no situation of conflict, there can be no trigger; if the situation of conflict is intense, only a small passage of time will suffice for a trigger to occur.

The probability p_{gt} (T = 1) is therefore a transition probability—the likelihood of a latent situation of conflict being transformed into conflict.

Equation (8.3) can now be elaborated to include the trigger:

$$\hat{B}_{h,i \to j} = \underset{g}{\Sigma} \beta_{hig}(T_g \underset{\ell}{\Sigma} \alpha_{gi\ell} d_{\ell,i-j} + Q_{g,i \to j}).$$ [11.3]

Thus, if no trigger occurs for situation g, then $T_g = 0$ and,

$$\hat{B}_{hg,i \to j} = \beta_{hig} Q_{g,i \to j},$$

and from Equation 8.2

$$w_{g,i \to j} = Q_{g,i \to j}$$

That is, without a trigger the disposition to behave in a situation g is a result of interests and capabilities independent of the situation of conflict, and common behavior in this situation is then due to this independent disposition weighted by situational expectations.[2] With the occurrence of a trigger, T = 1, Equation 11.3 is transformed into Equation 8.3.[3]

11.2. THE SITUATION OF UNCERTAINTY

The trigger provokes the will, the will decides on action, and preparations are made. At the personal level such preparations may be psychological, a mutual girding for action. At the state level, however, such preparations will involve some sort of behavior. For the elite it may be intense, high-level interaction, staff work, and late meetings. Decisions may ensue to cancel military leaves, reinforce strategic points, disperse vulnerable targets (such as bombers), mobilize the reserves, inform the press, and alert the public.[4] Or if it is a matter of, say, preparing to cancel aid or expelling a diplomat, explanations and press releases may be prepared and appropriate ambassadors informed of the forthcoming action.

The decision to confront or to initiate conflict may involve an immediate threat or opportunity, or long-range one. For the long range, armaments may be increased and new programs undertaken; alliances, and defensive pacts may be negotiated.[5] In any case, the situation of uncertainty will involve preparations, the first behavioral manifestation of conflict.

The situation of uncertainty is detailed in Table 11.1. It is the transition stage between latent and manifest conflict, between accepting existing relationships and the balancing of power, between Phase I and III of the conflict helix shown in Figure 10.1. Before turning to the latter phase, however, the manifest reality of preparations in the situation of uncertainty should be assessed. If, indeed, such is a distinct element, then *it should be evident as a separate component among conflict behavior.*

11.3. CONFLICT BEHAVIOR COMPONENTS

As discussed in chapter 4, compulsory components define an independent region of common conflict behavior between international actors (see Table 4.1).[6] The question is then whether in focusing on this region of conflict alone we find a specific conflict component reflecting the *situation of uncertainty for conflict events.*[7]

In doing this two concepts must be kept clear. *Compulsory components* refer to those defining conflict behavior in the overall behavior space-time, that is, in the context of diverse nonconflict behavior. "Compulsory" is a theoretical term. A *conflict component,* as I will use it here, is an empirical component of conflict behavior. Only the conflict behavior region of space-time is analyzed to delineate these components. Conflict components describe the covariation between conflict behaviors; compulsory components underlie the covariation between international behaviors.

Now, relevant analyses have been done for all the reported conflict behavior of state actors and dyads for 1955 and 1963.[8] Data were coded as threats, warnings, antiforeign demonstrations, clashes, discrete military actions, troop

TABLE 11.1: The Initiation Phase of the Conflict Helix: Phase II

SUBPHASE	THEORETICAL ELEMENTS	EMPIRICAL CONCEPTS	NOTATION AND EQUATIONS
transformation from situation of conflict	trigger	trigger: occurrence nonoccurrence probability	T $T_g = 1$ $T_g = 0$ $p_{gt}(T_g = 1) = \delta_g + \gamma_g(\sum_t e_{gt})(\sum_\ell \alpha_{gi\ell} d_{\ell,i-j})$
situation of uncertainty	will preparations	common preparations: warning and defensive acts armaments alliances	$\hat{B}_{hg,i\to j} = \beta_{hg}(T_g \sum_\ell \alpha_{gi\ell} d_{\ell,i-j} + Q_{g,i\to j})$

movements, alerts, boycotts, and so on. These codings were then merged into 23 to 26 variables, depending on the amount of data, and the variables were factor analyzed to delineate the conflict components. This analysis was done for the total threats, warnings, sanctions, and so on, of state actors;[9] for interstate dyadic behavior, such as that of U.S. leaders to China;[10] for conflict data aggregated by year; and for data disaggregated by year; and for data disaggregated by month.[11] The analyses were done using various approaches[12] and systematic comparisons of the results were made between studies and to similar studies by others.[13]

Table 11.2 summarizes the results of these and other similar analyses.[14] Consistently across the various analyses, six components of conflict behavior

TABLE 11.2: Components of Conflict Behavior[a]

EMPIRICAL COMPONENTS	ILLUSTRATIVE CORRELATED CONFLICT BEHAVIOR[b]
Preparations (warnings and defensive actions)	alerts, mobilizations, troop movements, maneuvers, cancellation of leaves
Low-level military violence	clashes, discrete military actions, continuous low-level military engagements
High-level military violence	war, number killed
Negative communications	threats, warnings, accusations, denunciations, diplomatic protests
Negative (nonviolent) actions/sanctions	severance of diplomatic relations, expulsion of diplomats, boycott, embargo, cancellation of state visit, diplomatic rebuff
Antiforeign (unofficial) behavior	attacks on foreign citizens or property; antiforeign riots or demonstrations; attacks on embassies; unofficial boycotts

a. These are the kinds of behavior coded and aggregated into conflict variables.
b. These are the components of antagonistic conflict behavior and are a subset of these defining the balancing of powers given in Table 15.1.

were found. *And one of these is a warning and defensive actions component that well manifests interstate preparations for conflict.* The situation of uncertainty involving an immediate threat or opportunity, the first phase of the conflict helix that may manifest underlying conflict, is therefore reflected at the empirical level.[15]

A situation of conflict develops; a trigger provokes the will into action; preparations for conflict are made. This is summarized in Table 11.1.

NOTES

1. I am omitting the subscripts on the terms if context allows. It should be understood, therefore, that $\Sigma\alpha d$ means the summed product of an actor's perceived situation weighting his distance vectors from others, as in Equation 8.2.

2. I have tested Equation 11.3 in several unpublished projects (appendix I: Projects 4.2-4.8). The results overall were mixed, and especially ambiguous because the underlying model was usually inappropriate (Model I rather than Model II). Nonetheless, when the concept of trigger is properly formulated in propositional form and related to the variety of analyses available, the ideas developed here have considerable empirical support. See Propositions 16.1, 16.10, 16.28-16.29 in appendix 16B.

3. Of course, this logic applied to the scalar equations also applies to vector equations, such as 8.4, as well.

4. Analyses of conflict behavior for dyads generally find such warning and defensive acts intercorrelated highly and consistently defined as an independent component of conflict. See chapter 15, and particularly the Uncertainty Proposition in appendix 15A. Among 45 relevant empirical analyses, 84% favor the proposition. Table 11.2 incorporates these findings.

5. Alliances and arms increases have also been found as empirically distinct patterns from conflict behavior, as should be the case if these assertions are correct. That alliances are a separate pattern can be seen from Table 4.1. The sources of evidence for this are given in Table 15A.2 for Proposition 15.1.

6. The compulsory components shown in Table 4.1 were delineated for dyadic conflict *events* and cooperative dyadic flows and structures. On these data, see appendix II. The concern here, however, is in conflict events alone, and in the conflict components which may have been lost in the macroview of overall behavior space-time. To be clear on my use of the concepts "conflict behavior" and "compulsory," see section 4.6.

7. A focus on events excludes alliance structures and arms increases, except in terms of their initiation. Therefore, alliances and armaments are not included in Table 11.2.

8. For 1955, data sources were The New York *Times* Index, New International Yearbook, Keesing's Contemporary Archives, Facts on File, and Britannica Book of the Year. The data collection indicated that these sources generally were redundant against the New York *Times,* and only this source was used for the 1963 data.

9. Oliva and I (1969) analyzed 24 conflict variables for 107 nations on 1963 data; I analyzed (1967a) 26 conflict variables for 82 nations on 1955 data.

10. Hall and I (1970) analyzed 24 conflict variables for 275 dyads for 1963 data.

11. Phillips (1969) analyzed (super-p analysis) 23 conflict variables across the 12 months of 1963 for 267 dyads.

12. Orthogonal and oblique rotations were done; component and image analyses also were applied.

13. See Hall and Rummel (1969, 1970), Phillips (1969), Oliva and Rummel (1969), Keim and Rummel (1969).

14. See those listed in Table 15A.3.

15. For an explanation of these different components (why do they occur? what do they mean regarding conflict?), see chapter 15.

Chapter 12

THE BALANCING OF POWER

Here is the place to set forth the principles of British policy towards Europe which I had followed for many years and follow still. . . . For four hundred years the foreign policy of England has been to oppose the strongest, most aggressive, most dominating Power on the Continent, and particularly to prevent the Low Countries falling into the hands of such a Power.

Churchill, 1948: 207

the struggle for power is universal in time and space and is an undeniable fact of experience.

Morgenthau, 1962: 68-69

International Conflict Behavior[1] is the surface turbulence, the visible bubbles and waves caused by the underlying balancing of opposing interests, capabilities, and will. This balancing is a bargaining process which determines the real goals of participants and their strength of motivation. It measures relative military and economic power, national morale, and qualities of leadership. And above all, it gauges will.

This balancing entails three subphases. One is the *status-quo testing* phase, through which participants assess each other's stakes in the conflict, willingness to give ground before threats or warnings, and desire to negotiate opposing interests. For example, when national leadership changes, the new prime minister or president will be tested by adversaries to determine whether and in which way his interests and will may differ from his predecessor. Thus, President Kennedy was tested by Chairman Khrushchev; President Carter by Chairman Brezhnev.

The second subphase is of the actual test of power, which may involve *coercion, force,* or *noncoercive* balancing. And finally there is the third subphase, termination, perhaps through *accommodations*—a negotiated end to manifest conflict—and the resulting new balance of powers.

[175]

12.1. STATUS QUO TESTING

The status quo is a central concept in understanding social interaction, including international relations. It defines the *mutually perceptible* distribution of rights and privileges.[2] It answers the question as to who owns and can do what.

At the interstate level, the status quo is mainly defined spatially, in terms of territory and rights thereto. The geographic boundaries of a state, its sphere of control (as the Soviet Union over Eastern Europe and the United States over the Trust Territories of the Pacific) or interests (including Cuba for the Soviets and South Korea for the United States), or its rights (as the Four Power rights in Berlin). The status quo is a mutual recognition of what is "theirs." and what is "ours."

We know that East Germany is Soviet dominated, it is theirs. And they know we know this. Thus, any American attempt to aid a liberalization movement in East Germany will be seen by Soviet leaders as a premeditated attack on the U.S.-Soviet status quo. On their side, the Soviets recognize that South Korea is ours, in the sense that it is within our sphere of security interests, and we know they know this (indeed, we have through treaty commitments, the stationing of American troops in South Korea, military aid, frequent official pronouncements, tried to prevent any ambiguity on this). Thus, any attack on South Korea would be an attack on this status quo.

The territorial status quo between states defines what each is willing and able to defend; between hostile states it defines the threat of violence and war. Statesmen know what will risk war: to unilaterally try to change the territorial status quo.

The status quo is not limited to territorial-based rights, however. It includes any mutually agreed or perceived rights or limits. Thus, in the SALT I, 1972, Limitation of Antiballistic Missile Systems Treaty, the United States and Soviet Union agreed to limit antiballistic missile (ABM) deployment to two widely separated regions, one for the national capital and the other for the defense of ICBMs. In total, each agreed to deploy no more than 200 ABMs. This treaty defined a mutually perceived status quo regarding ABMs. To openly violate this status quo would cause much tension and nonviolent conflict behavior (accusations, warnings, protests, increased expenditures on arms, and so on). This potential conflict could be seen in the deep concern shown in Congress and the American defense community over alleged Soviet violations of the companion strategic arms Interim Agreement.

The status quo also includes patterns of behavior that have become mutually recognized, perhaps not explicitly, but by virtue of past accommodations, implicit acceptance, or lack of counteraction. Such may be overflights of surveillance aircraft, covert aid to rebellious groups, and political bribery by multinationals. These patterns will be predictable and mutually understood as accepted. Therefore, to change them, either one's own pattern or that of the other, can provoke a response—and conflict behavior.

We thus have three types of status quo: territorial, contractual, and behavioral. *It is only attempts to change the territorial status quo by hostile states that risks violence and war.* Unilateral violations of treaties, agreements (not involving territory), or changes in patterns of behavior, may provoke conflict, and raise tension, but not endanger violence unless such violations reflect on the will of the parties to protect the territorial status quo. If one party allows the other to make significant violations of a treaty or agreement, then this may suggest that the territorial status quo may be violated with impunity as well. Thus, the North Vietnamese systematically violated the 1973 Paris Agreement with the United States and knew that such were perceived as violations by American leaders. The lack of a meaningful response in conjunction with the Congressional cut in military aid to South Vietnam must have suggested that American leaders no longer had the will or desire to oppose further North Vietnamese attempts to militarily alter the status quo in South Vietnam. And so it was.

As described so far, the status quo is unambiguous: there is no doubt as to who is permitted what, who has what rights. But a status quo not only depends on a mutual recognition of the distribution of rights, but on the interest, capability, and will to defend them. If one side seems to show by some action that they will no longer defend the status quo or react strongly to unilateral alterations, this may trigger the will to action by the other side—the situation of uncertainty as outlined in the previous chapter. But moves to unilaterally alter the status quo based on a reading of another's *change* in goals, strength, and determination, is risky. Mistaken perceptions, distorted expectations, could initiate the chain of events leading to war.

Thus, status-quo testing. Minor incursions, small challenges to the status quo easy to deny or withdraw from, enable the risk to be gauged. A *prompt* and *proportional* counter response by the other side will communicate the interest and determination to maintain the status quo—to struggle against its alteration. A weak, much delayed, response or none at all will invite stronger tests or an attempt to finally alter that in question. Or, weak responses to attempts to alter the status quo may encourage an attack on the status quo not previously contemplated. Thus, weak responses by Kennedy to communist attempts to alter the status quo in Laos and Berlin may have given the final encouragement to Khruschev to radically alter the strategic status quo by setting up missiles and medium range bombers in Cuba in 1962.

However, a status quo may not be in place to test. That is, the *actual* status quo may be in question. At the level of major states, this often occurs when a power vacuum is created in some region. States formerly accepted as having rights over a territory may withdraw, as did the colonial powers from much of

Africa and Asia. Moreover, a status quo may be completely altered through war, bringing to regional or global dominance new states who will have to work out a new status quo.

World War II thus created a power vacuum in many regions of the world. The 1946-1950 years of intense conflict between the United States and Soviet Union—the Iranian Crisis, Czechoslovakia coup, Greek civil war, Berlin Blockade, and many other crises and tests including the North Korean invasion of the South in 1950—was a shaking out period, a determination of a new territorial status quo between the United States and Soviet Union. Leaders of each were unsure of what the other defined as their rights and limits in Europe and Asia; they were unsure of the other's will. There was, in other words, no immediately obvious, mutually perceptible, status quo globally in place after World War II.

Thus, probing and testing was necessary to assess the status quo—to judge stakes, will, and capability—to fill in the vacuum. Thus, the crisis upon crisis, challenge upon challenge of those early cold war years.

In sum, the status-quo testing subphase of the balancing of power lessens uncertainty about opponents reactions to asserting one's interests. It helps define risk and costs. The result will suggest one of four courses of action: coercion, force, noncoercive (nonantagonistic) conflict, and accommodations.

12.2. COERCION

Coercion is the use of threats to get another to do what he otherwise would not do. The threats may be explicit, such as Harold Brown, Secretary of Defense, pointing out after the failure of the March, 1976, SALT II talks that "the United States would have to increase spending on strategic weapons by 'several billion dollars' a year if it finds the Soviet Union unwilling to settle for the kind of nuclear parity sought in the Carter administration's arms limitation proposals."[3]

The threat may be implicit, as in President Idi Amin's warning that: "As long as false statements continue to be broadcast by the BBC (British Broadcasting Corporation), then the Ugandan government will bring pressure to bear on British and American citizens who are the sources of the false information."[4]

The threat may be verbal, written, or implied in actions underway, as in President Anwar Sadat's summer, 1976, buildup of nearly 20,000 troops, 250 tanks and 80 war planes on the Libyan border following his accusation that Libya's President Col. Mu'ammar al-Qadhafi was training terrorists to overthrow him.[5]

The threat may be of actions to follow, such as severance of diplomatic relations, cancellation of an agreement, boycott, military action. Or, the threat may be of a continuation of negative sanctions or deprivations until what is wanted is done, as in the Arab oil boycott of 1973. This boycott was maintained against oil dependent European nations and Japan until their foreign policies were changed to support the Arab position against Israel.

While a threat may be a specific we will do x (or stop doing x) if you do y, in the language of diplomats a threat is often indirect, given as a warning: "we will view such actions seriously . . . ," "Soviet involvement would be inconsistent with détente . . . ," or "if Israel does not return captured Arab territory, we will take all necessary steps. . . ."

The most serious threat among states is that of war. It appears in two ways. First, the threat may be implied purposely by actions underway, as President Sadat's above mentioned movement of military forces to the Libyan border or President Kennedy's mobilization of American forces and substantial military movements to Florida during the Cuban missile crisis of 1962; or it may be explicit as in the American treaty commitments to defend Western Europe if attacked by the Soviet Union. By word or deed, one side can intentionally communicate a threat to the other.

Second, however, the threat may be implied from previous actions, or may be implicit in current behavior. Thus, the fact that the Chinese entered the Korean War in November, 1950, at great cost to themselves when North Korea was threatened with total defeat, gave credibility to the implied threat of her intervention in the Vietnam war were South Vietnam and the United States to counterinvade the North. Thus, an intention to develop a nuclear first-strike capability against the United States explains the Soviet strategic military buildup in the 1970s.[6] Such are not threats made intentionally by one to another in a specific conflict. They comprise one's expectations or perceptions of the other.

For example, the October 2, 1950, communication of Chou En-lai to Washington, through the Indian Ambassador K.M. Pannikar, that China would enter the war if American troops crossed the 38th Parallel, was a threat.[7] The possibility of China also entering the Vietnam war if the North were invaded was, however, an expectation. The two must be kept distinct, for the first constitutes conflict *behavior* (the threat to . . .); the second defines a threat's *credibility*. Threat as behavior and threat as credibility serve different functions: one communicates intention, the other determines the faith we can have in such communication.

In sum, the coercive subphase in the balancing of power is manifested in three ways: through verbal or written threats (and warnings), through threatening actions, or through applying deprivations or violence (with the threat to continue them unless x is done).

12.3. FORCE

Coercion acts on the *will*. Force acts on the will's *means*: its body, capabilities, or resources. Coercion is psychological; force is physical. When the will cannot be coerced, force is the ultimate recourse.

From this, however, we cannot conclude that violence and war only result from the failure of coercion. The reason is that coercion itself may embody violence and war. Presidents Kennedy, Johnson, and Nixon fought the Vietnam war as a test of will against North Vietnamese leaders. Military violence was employed to prevent the success of Hanoi's forces in the South while, for Johnson and Nixon, also threatening to destroy these forces and Hanoi's military-economic capacity in the North. The American aim was to coerce North Vietnam's leaders into accepting a sovereign and independent South Vietnam, or at a minimum ending their aggression against the South.

In Korea in 1950, however, General McArthur crossed the 38th Parallel with his divisions in pursuit of the retreating North Korean armies, not to coerce their will, but to totally and militarily defeat them—that is, to remove any choice except unconditional surrender. However, once the Chinese armies entered the war and forced a retreat of our divisions from much of North Korea, the character of the war changed. It became a coercive test of wills on both sides.

The Japanese militarily attacked Pearl Harbor on December 7, 1941, to destroy the American Pacific fleet and coerce the American government into accepting a new Japanese order in Asia and the Pacific. They realized they could not destroy the United States militarily and the American capacity to rebuild her Pacific fleet, but believed they could work on a perceived weakness of will. A negotiated settlement granting a much expanded Japanese sphere of influence in Asia was their aim. The bad timing of their declaration of war, which unintentionally was delivered shortly after the Pearl Harbor attack, and the widely perceived immorality of "this stab in the back", galvanized American war sentiment and made limited war aims impossible. The Japanese fought a *war of coercion*; the United States fought from the beginning a *war of force*: to so destroy Japanese military and economic power that unconditional surrender was the only option.

Therefore, in spite of war's great physical destruction and loss of lives; its profound physical commitment of a nation's spirit, people and resources; and its awesome geographic, mechanical, and technological dimensions; *wars often are a psychological manifestation, a test of will.*

But wars have also been fought as a test of might: not to coerce opponents into accepting certain conditions, but to physically deny their wills any other choice but complete surrender. Thus, Hitler invaded Poland in 1939 to crush her militarily and rule her politically. This was not a test of will, but of might. Thus, the Allies invaded Germany in 1944 to totally defeat Hitler. Thus, the armies of Mao Tse-tung fought the last stages of the Chinese civil war against Chiang Kai-shek's Nationalist troops for total victory; thus, Kim Il-sung's North Korean Army invaded the South in 1950; thus, the North Vietnamese launched their largest and finally successful offensive against South Vietnam in 1975.

That war is a continuation of politics by other means is the classic observation of Karl von Clausewitz (1943). By this he means that political policy dominates the pursuit of war and its strategy, that war is part of the political bargaining between states. War is not strictly military (the art and science of force), but involves political issues and requires political decisions be made along with those purely military. It melds the art of coercion and science of force. The choice of an invasion route, the use of a weapon (as the atomic bombs on Hiroshima and Nagasaki), or the supplying of an ally, will involve military factors to be sure, but also can have political consequences for the subsequent peace. In my terms, war is part of the balancing of interests, wills, and capabilities from which a structure of expectations—a new order—emerges.

But this is not to say that war of coercion is political and a war of force is purely military. Political policies can dominate both types of war. The military means selected in a war of force can be determined on both political and military grounds. To defeat another's will, to destroy him or leave him no option but surrender, can be done without turning the conduct of the war entirely over to the generals and admirals. The allied war aims in World War II against Hitler did not necessitate an invasion of France at Normandy, instead of an invasion up through the "soft underbelly of Europe"—through Greece and into Eastern Europe, thus possibly saving a number of Eastern European countries from postwar, Soviet domination.

My classification of wars into those of coercion and of force is not along a political versus military dimension, but rather *along a dimension of power*. At one end is the war of coercion, such as President Johnson fought against North Vietnam; at the other end is the war of force, such as that fought by Presidents Roosevelt and Truman against Germany and Japan.

The threat of war may lead to a war of coercion or of force, if the threat is called. Or a war of coercion may turn into one of force, as did the Vietnam war. Until American forces were withdrawn, the war for the North Vietnamese was a test of U.S. will; afterwards, it became a conventional war of force against the South.

In any case, a war of force may escalate from the use of coercion. *If the will cannot be deterred or violently persuaded, physical force is the last resort and ultimate challenge.*

Although in contrasting coercion to force I have emphasized the role of violence and war in coercion, violence is the extremity of coercion usually applied only after a range of nonviolent threats and deprivations have been employed. Coercion is present if some means are being used intentionally to pressure another into action they would not otherwise take. Coercion may be thus manifested by boycotts, embargoes, freezing another's assets, expelling ambassadors, and so on. The key to coercion is the *intentionally* stated or implied threat of more or worse to follow.

12.4. NONCOERCIVE BALANCING

Power comes in many forms, (Volume 2, 1976: chapter 21). The same behavior may, *depending on an actor's intention,* manifest different powers. A higher tariff on goods from another state may be to coerce the other into lowering their tariff or it may be the expression of legal reciprocity and thus of authoritative power. A diplomatic protest over a hostile public demonstration and attack on one's embassy may carry a warning of possible retaliation unless a form of apology is forthcoming and the leaders of the attack are punished. This is coercion. Or a protest may be an expression of legal right, as in a dispute over commercial rights, and thus be an instrument of authoritative power; or it may be a carefully researched and reasoned review of the background and factors in a dispute and the strength of one's position, and thus relying on intellectual power.

National elites have a great variety of means—of actions—to manifest their interests in opposition to another state, some of which I have already discussed. They can, of course, make war. But they can also boycott, embargo, or blockade another; support terrorism against the other, provoke border clashes or engage in limited military action. They can, verbally or in writing, formally or informally, threaten, warn, protest, represent, accuse, denounce, or issue an ultimatum. They can mobilize, move their forces, cancel leaves, alert their troops, maneuver, or strengthen forces, all as preparation for contingencies or to threaten or warn another. Leaders can show the flag, display the fleet, overfly fighters or bombers, or cause a few sonic booms over another's capital. They can sever or suspend diplomatic or economic relations, expel diplomats or the other's nationals, and restrict the internal movement and actions of diplomats. They can rebuff or snub the other diplomatically, discontinue giving or reject aid, abrogate treaties or commitments, freeze assets, seize another's property, or impose high tariffs. They can walk out of a conference, cancel a state visit, try to take the other state to court (the International Court of Justice), invoke international action against it through international organizations, or have it expelled from certain organizations. They can form defensive or hostile alliances, aid the other's enemies, give aid and training to subversive or rebellious groups, propagandize its people, disseminate false information, spy and subvert, and sabotage. Or they can unofficially organize public outcry and demonstrations against the other; attacks on its property, citizens and embassy; cross-border "tribal" attacks or "banditry," or private boycotts. Clearly. The means are many and this short list could be lengthened many times.[8]

Conflict behavior, however, is not necessarily hostile or antagonistic. It may be what is ordinarily considered helpful, cooperative, or solidary. Elites not only threaten, deprive, sanction, retort, or retaliate, but also bargain, trade, cooperate, or aid another or exchange with them as part of the balancing. Presidents

Johnson and Nixon used the stick and carrot approach to Vietnam, offering postwar rehabilitation aid if Vietnam would negotiate a satisfactory end to the war. The Nixon-Kissinger policy of détente stressed jointly the use of American power to deter Soviet aggression and the use of trade, aid, and cooperative agreements to give them a stake in a relaxation of tensions.

How are all these overtly antagonistic or cooperative means to be classified? What scheme can we impose on them to bring out their inherent logic and meaning? I have searched the literature on international relations without finding any extensive definitions, classifications, and analysis of the variety of conflict related, international actions. Introductory texts are too general, books on international politics focus on violence and the threat of war, and works on international law concern conflictful actions only as they exemplify the legal basis of such behavior.[9] The "list" of actions mentioned previously were developed empirically as I recorded daily all conflict actions reported in The New York *Times* from 1963 to 1968.

One approach to such actions is to organize them in terms of their latent functions—their inherent patterns of occurrence. This was the approach in my empirical work on foreign conflict, the results of which are given in Table 11.2. While this approach provides a significant classification and understanding of the covariation in conflict behavior to be discussed in more detail in chapter 15, it does not provide meaning and insight. For that, we must again go beneath the surface, not probabilistically to define components this time, but to uncover the logic of such behavior.

And the logic is that of power. I have dealt with the literature of power in Volume 2 (1976: chapters 19-21), and the essence and forms of power. My conclusion was that power is a vector towards manifestation that takes different forms depending on whether it is intentionally directed, directed to another self, its basis (such as legitimacy or credibility), and its means (such as threats or promises). Thus, I discriminated identive, assertive, and physical power; the social forms of power, which are coercive, bargaining, intellectual, authoritative, altruistic, and manipulative powers; and the physical form of power—force— oriented to overcome and not change another's will.

The balancing of powers phase manifests the confrontation of these diverse forms of power. Except for force, all actions are oriented towards another's psychological field. They derive their meaning, not from their physical quality— the empirical nature of the action—but from their intention. For this reason the same *physical action*, such as a formal diplomatic protest, can be meant as a threat (coercive power), as a legally justified request (authoritative power), as a persuasive argument (intellectual power), to trap the other into accepting one's definition of the situation (manipulative power), or as an appeal to universal morality (altruistic power). It is the psychological intent of an action, the form of power it reflects, that defines the underlying logic of the balancing of powers phase.

On the balancing of power mankind has focused great attention. War, the threat of war, revolutions, rebellions, and other forms of social violence have been the focus of innumerable scholarly and literary works. My argument here is straightforward. These phenomena, showing the full range of man's barbarism, cruelty, courage, cowardice, love, and hate reflect a process of conflict, most of which is an unseen balancing of interests, capabilities, and wills.[10]

12.5. ACCOMMODATIONS AND TERMINATION

Conflict and cooperative interaction in the balancing process are an implicit negotiation and adjustment between the parties. Mutual interests (goals, desires, stakes) are judged. Diverse capabilities (skills, qualities, resources, leadership, armament) are proved. And wills (resolution, determination, courage, grit) are tested. This implicit negotiation may become explicit. Diplomatic negotiations may take place, third parties may intervene to mediate, international organizations may become involved and intervene, the conflict may be adjudicated before the International Court of Justice.[11]

In any case through implicit and explicit negotiations, *compromises* between the desires of both sides may be struck or *awards* may be determined for one side or the other to settle the conflict. In other words, accommodations between the parties have been determined; a new treaty, contract, agreement, or understanding may be signed to define a new *balance* of powers.

Negotiations may achieve no formal accommodations, however. The outcome of the balancing of power may be *conquest,* the complete victory over and mastery of the other. At the state level this may involve the disappearance of the other state and absorption of its people and territory by the winner, as happened in the Soviet Union's conquest of Lithuania in 1939 or North Vietnam's conquest of the South in 1975. The outcome may be the *submission* of one side to the other, as in Japan's and Germany surrender in 1945, or it may involve the *withdrawal* of one party to the conflict, as for the Angola-based Kantagan rebels who retreated from their invasion of Zaire in 1977.

Or their may be no clear termination. The conflict may drag on with alternating hot and cold periods, or just die away without any clear win or loss or accommodations—an uneasy acceptance of the status quo antebellum.[12] For example, Burma remains riven by decades old guerrilla and civil warfare; the violent conflict between mainland China and Taiwan remains frozen, as of 1978; the overarching conflict between Arabs and Jews initiated with the creation of Israel in 1948 remains *generally* unsettled, although it has burst fourth in the four Middle Eastern wars of 1948, 1956, 1968, and 1973; and the Korean conflict is frozen as well with an uneasy negotiated armistice of the 1950-1953 hot war in place.

Both the Middle Eastern and Korean conflicts exemplify the narrowness of focusing on a specific war as constituting a conflict. The particular issues involved (which for the Middle East concern the existence, borders, and rights of the state of Israel in an Arab region; and for Korea concerns the unification of a communist North Korea and authoritarian, anticommunist, South) may not be settled by a war. The war may end in a stand-off or a victory for one side which may increase its advantage or leverage, but not decisively settle the basic dispute. Its outcome may be a temporary balance of power—a tactical pause—within the overall and continuing balancing of powers.

The continuing Middle East conflict—the four wars, the interwar feints and probes, military actions and clashes, accusations and threats, and regional arms races—exemplify this underlying balancing which may occasionally reach great heights of violence, but do not resolve the underlying major issues, the situation of conflict.

Such *durable* conflicts simply point out *the nested and overlapping nature of balances of powers.* Conflict and war may take place *within* a stable balance of powers; the balancing may concern lower order interests. As a case in point, one aspect of the Vietnam war was a regional balancing of powers between American and Soviet leaders. American military forces fought the regular North Vietnamese Army and guerrilla Vietcong, both mainly supplied with weapons by the Soviets; some of the SAM batteries that shot down American planes over North Vietnam may have been manned by Soviet "technicians," some of whom may have been killed when such batteries were bombed. Yet, this local confrontation took place under an umbrella, global balance of powers, manifested in a variety of cooperative activities and agreements. On the other hand, conflict behavior and war may take place as phases or aspects of a larger, continuing balancing of powers, as already discussed with regard to the Middle East. The violence may be terminated. But the underlying situation of conflict continues.

To summarize, the termination of conflict *behavior* may be through accommodations, conquest, submission or withdrawal, or such behavior may die away. In any case, the outcome of the process is a balance of powers. This is a locking together in a formal or informal, explicit or implicit, equilibrium of the interests, capabilities, and wills of the parties. This balance may be short-lived or durable. It may be of wide scope covering diverse interests, or it may be narrow, involving one interest (e.g., a nationalization of foreign property). It may be intense, involving the fundamental values and norms of participants (as that concluding a world war), or it may concern peripheral values and norms (as the settlement of a minor issue raised in a protest note).

Regardless. The balance creates and undergirds a new structure of expectations, a momentary *order* in some of the relations between the parties.

12.6. SUMMARY

Figure 12.1 summarizes the dynamics of conflict *behavior.* Note the following.

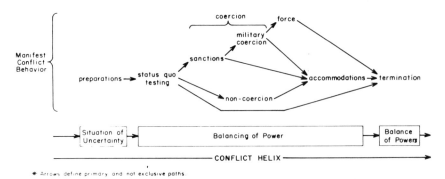

FIGURE 12.1: Dynamics of Conflict Behavior

(1) Conflict behavior reflects a process toward establishing a balance of power and itself has internal dynamics.

(2) The results of status-quo testing may lead to a coercive or noncoercive confrontation or termination of the conflict, depending on what the testing reveals about the others interests, capabilities, and will.

(3) Once a confrontation occurs, all paths lead *primarily* [13] to accommodations, except when the conflict escalates to force.

(4) There is an alternative path to coercion in a conflict, which may involve the use of bargaining (exchange), intellectual, authoritative, [14] and other noncoercive powers. Therefore, some manifest behavior in the balancing of powers may be, what is generally termed, cooperative (e.g., offers of aid, promises, implicit acceptance of rules governing the scope and limits of conflict behavior).

(5) Coercion has a nonmilitary and military aspect.

(6) Force is a noncoercive (an attempt to bypass or destroy the other's will after failure to coerce it) escalation of military coercion.

(7) All paths lead to a new balance of powers, a new equilibrium of interests, capabilities, and wills, supporting a new structure of expectations.

NOTES

1. Conflict Behavior, capitalized, refers to the whole balancing of powers phase; conflict behavior, lower-cased, connotes the antagonistic balancing with this phase. See section 4.6.

2. My definition of the status quo is the same as Payne's (1970), whose treatment of the threat of war, the role of the status quo, the nature of bargaining through conflict, the importance of risk and uncertainty, and the statesman's calculus (gains minus costs minus risks) is close to my own. Indeed, his book with its many historical examples, shows the implicit operation of a conflict helix between hostile states, and could well be supplementary reading for this volume.

3. Baltimore Sun, April 2, 1977, p. 2. The Carter administration later retreated from its own proposals, thus negating its threat and slicing away a piece of its credibility.

4. Honolulu *Star Bulletin,* March 14, 1977, p. A-7 *(AP)*

5. *Newsweek,* September 13, 1976, p. 69. This buildup eventuated in the Egyptian-Libyan border war almost a year later.

6. I am not saying that the intent is to launch a first strike, but to develop the capability as a threat to back up political demands or initiatives and, in case it is needed, to preempt a "last gasp attack by dying capitalism." See my "Will the Soviet Union Soon Have a First-Strike Capability?" (1976c).

7. Halle (1967: 222).

8. Most of the actions mentioned were part of my foreign conflict coding sheet (Rummel, 1966). For many years I personally collected daily foreign conflict data on all states, which I then aggregated and factor analyzed to delineate such components of foreign conflict as shown in Table 11.2. See, for example, (Rummel 1967a, 1968). Appendix II provides an overview of such "event data" coding and analysis.

9. Thus, international law defines such conflict behavior as international *delicts* (violations of international law), *sanctions* (obligations to right the wrong done by a delict), *reprisal* (a particular sanction legally permitted against a delict) and *retortion* (a legal act to repair injury done by a legal act of another—i.e., a nondelict).

10. By will here, I mean the will to make and follow through on threats or promises. This is from the actor's perspective. From the perspective of the object or an observer, this will define the actor's credibility.

11. For a discussion and analysis of the outcomes of conflict I will consider here, see K.J.Holsti (1966) and Hannah (1968, 1972). On the termination of conflict generally, see Coser (1961). Specifically on the termination of war, see Carroll (1969, 1970); Ikle (1971); Kahn, *et al,* (1968); Klingberg (1966); Phillipson (1916); Randle (1972); and Weiss (1961). K.J.Holsti (1977) has a useful overview of concepts and findings on conflict resolution. Systematic studies on war and conflict termination are relatively rare compared to those on the causes and nature of war, as could be seen by comparing the evidence available for the causes and conditions of conflict (Table 16C.3) and for its ending (Table 17A.3).

12. See Etzioni (1964).

13. "Primary" is used in the sense of what usually occurs. For example, force may be unsuccessful and therefore either deescalated to military coercion or negotiations may ensue. However, in many applications of force the outcome is termination without negotiations and accommodations.

14. The use of authoritative power, for example, would be an attempt of one party to have a conflict placed on the Agenda of the Security Council in the hope that the UN would intervene in its behalf.

Chapter 13

COMPARATIVE DYNAMICS

The balancing of power is the power process among the participants in an arena. . . .
[It] is a component of every social process.

Lasswell and Kaplan, 1950: 250-251

Whether in fact conflict displays the theoretical, behavioral dynamics shown in Figure 12.1 is a question yet to be answered. There are two sides to such an answer. One is whether this dynamic model is consistent with these proposed by others. And the second side is whether systematic, empirical analyses of Conflict Behavior confirms the dynamics. This chapter will consider the former question, leaving the empirical one to the next part and chapter.

Studies of the outbreak of war abound; analyses of war causation are even more numerous. But few inquiries have been published on the stages, process or dynamics of conflicts involving or threatening war,[1] apart from military strategy. Of those which have been published, the ones by Barringer, Northedge and Donelan, Wright, and Kahn are especially relevant here.[2]

13.1 RICHARD E. BARRINGER

The study by Richard E. Barringer (1972)[3] is particularly concerned with empirically investigating the systematic factors accounting for a transition of conflict from one stage to another, especially to violence. I will make reference to his empirical findings at appropriate points; here I am concerned only with his model of the conflict process (1972: chapter 1) which is presented in Figure 13.1.[4]

Barringer sees war ("hostilities") as one of many policy options introduced into an ongoing dispute and viable only after some "military mobilization and preparedness" has been undertaken (1972: 16-17). Once the possibility of war is being considered the dispute may still be settled nonviolently, but the character of the dispute has been fundamentally changed.

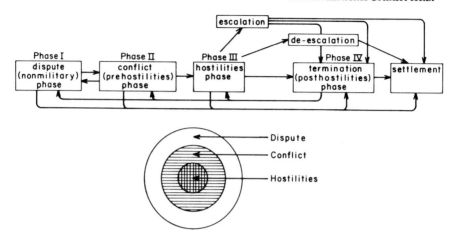

FIGURE 13.1: Barringer's Model

In Barringer's words, conflict is 'the subset of all disputes between parties capable of waging war in which the military option has been introduced, and at least one party perceives the issues at stake in partially, if not wholly, military terms." (1972: 17) A dispute is a "felt grievance by a party capable of waging war that, in its eyes, demands some more tolerable accommodation with another party than presently exists."

A dispute, then, turns into a conflict when a military option has been introduced, and the conflict turns into hostilities when war has, *de facto,* been initiated.

Before moving on to his other phases, note first that a dispute is a latent and initiating phase (a "felt grievance") in which no manifest conflict behavior may occur. It thus corresponds to the *conflict situation* of the helix. Second, he defines a prehostilities phase in which the war option has been introduced and which involves preparations thereto. This is similar to the *situation of uncertainty* of the helix, in which the will has made the decision to confront the other and undertaken preparations of various sorts, and in which manifest conflict behavior short of violence therefore may occur.

Third, Barringer is focusing on the process entailing at least the option of war. His dynamic model is not meant to delineate the generic phases of all social conflict (in my terms), but only those phases of interstate disputes in which a resort to war is being considered. Thus, his model does not apply explicitly to a dispute between husband and wife, General Motors Corporation and the Department of Justice, or Eritrean separatists and the Ethiopean government—as does the conflict helix.

And finally, at the interstate level, Barringer collapses coercive and negative, nonviolent, behavior by parties *not considering a war option* into his dispute phase. Because this behavior may involve boycotts, embargoes, severance of diplomatic relations,[5] accusations, and so on, his dispute phase is overloaded. It involves a felt grievance, which may be latent without manifest behavior, and actual and perhaps quite antagonistic conflict behavior.

Moving on to Barringer's third phase, it involves "the organized and systematic violence . . . undertaken by the armed forces of any party to the dispute as a purposeful instrument of policy." (1972: 20) Within this phase may occur two subphases (see Figure 13.1): escalation and deescalation, depending on "a gross change in the existing rules of the game governing the conduct and limitation of hostilities." (1972:20)

The final, fourth phase is the termination of organized hostilities between the parties, although the dispute "is as yet unresolved and is perceived in military terms by at least one party and could generate renewed hostilities either immediately or after a prolonged period of cease-fire and renewed preparations for combat." (1972: 20) The model thus allows for conflict to iterate or cycle around hostilities or even return to the dispute stage.

Of course, hostilities or escalation could lead directly to the settlement of the dispute by "some form of accommodation between the parties, annihilation of one or more of them, loss of saliency, or other means." (1972: 20)

The model also allows for disputes that could lead directly to settlement without conflict (in Barringer's terms), and a settlement of a conflict might be achieved without hostilities.

In addition to the previous comparisons with the conflict helix the following are significant. Barringer does not distinguish between stages of coercion and force, but only between levels of physical violence correlated with the "rules of the game." But "rules" about such limits as sanctuaries and weapons within a conflict may change as the war escalates, without a change in the form of power involved. That is, the intent still may be to coerce, not overcome, another's will.

Moreover, status-quo testing, coercive means short of violence, and noncoercive means are not part of his process.

In sum, Barringer's model is concerned with the objective transformation of a dispute—its changes from a psychological to *physical* character and back again. Thus, the dispute (psychological) is transformed into a conflict (psychological and physical) to hostilities (physical) to escalation (physical) to deescalation (physical) to termination (physical) to settlement (psychological).

By contrast, the balancing of power phases in the conflict helix are all psychological; they are defined by psychological factors and distinguished by forms of power. Thus, conflict situation (psychological) is transformed into the will to conflict involving preparations (psychological) to status-quo testing (psychological), to coercion or noncoercion (psychological) to force (psychological)[6] to accommodations (psychological) to a balance of powers (psychological). Of course, the psychological phases may involve physical elements, as in preparations or blockade, but *they are epiphenomena of shifts in the psychological field.*

13.2 F. S. NORTHEDGE AND M. D. DONELAN

Northedge and Donelan (1971) studied 50* international disputes occurring between 1945 and 1970 in order to determine why some disputes escalate to military action and war.[7] They see this question as requiring answers to four others: what is an international dispute, what brings them about, how do they escalate, and how are they resolved? Their analyses of these questions provide helpful insight into the nature and process of disputes.

In their analysis of disputes they separately consider "origins" and "development." They do not articulate a flow model of disputes, as does Barringer, but their discussion clearly defines stages in disputes and enables their underlying model to be constructed.

At the outset, Northedge and Donelan distinguish between dispute and situation, where a situation is "a state of potential conflict, where all the ingredients of a dispute exist but where the dispute has neither been formulated nor crystallized" (1971: 2). A dispute is then "a formulated difference of opinion as to matters of law, fact or justice arising in the mutual relations of states." (1971: 2-3)

As a "diffuse condition of tension or potential tension," their situation defines the *structure of conflict* within the conflict helix. It is a latent stage in which parties are aware of each other, there is an opposition of attitudes, friction exists, but the conflict is uncrystallized. Interest have yet to become focused, the lines of cleavage sharp. The dispute is then the crystallization of differences. In my terms, it is the generation of opposing interests, which is the *situation of conflict* in the helix.

Now, these differences among states in a dispute are of particular kind. They "are essentially a clash of convictions about 'ours' and 'theirs'." (1971: 40) They are, therefore, about the status quo, in both Northedge and Donelan's words and my own.[8] And in the helix it is conflict over the status quo which carries the potential for violence.

A *manifest* dispute[9] begins with a demand or response (1971: 136)[10] to which a state's leaders must reply. They cannot ignore an issue of rights because to ignore it is first to concede the other's claim or argument, and second, to weaken credibility for protecting one's own (1971: 137). Therefore, the challenge elicits a response and the dispute is manifestly joined.

This leads to the first stage (phase) of a dispute: diplomatic argument. Both sides make their case, either "implicitly or explicitly, they indicate to each other the possible costs of an unyielding stand and of a protracted conflict." (1971: 137)

The dispute may then be settled immediately, it may drift, or it may escalate to "heights of bitterness." Which way it goes depends on the importance of interests engaged, whether honor is involved, the impact on credibility ("reputation for power"), and whether the parties are competitors or enemies.

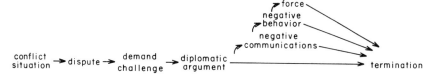

FIGURE 13.2: Northedge and Dunelan's Development of a Dispute

If the dispute deepens, the next stage is denunciation and propaganda (1971: 148)—negative communications, in my terms. After this, comes the stage of negative behavior, the behavioral expression of condemnation, which may involve a breach of diplomatic relations, refusal to recognize a government, a breach of commercial relations, boycotts, sanctions, and the attempt to enlist third parties to intervene (1971: 149-152). The dispute may then escalate to the next stage of force (in their terms), after which the dispute may terminate, be settled, or drag on for many years until it lapses.[11]

Figure 13.2 summarizes their stages.[12] A dispute may move from a diffuse conflict situation, to formulated opposition (dispute), to manifest confrontation (demand, challenge), to debate (diplomatic argument), to hostile (negative) communications, to hostile (negative) behavior and nonviolent coercion, and to military action (force). Termination can occur, of course, at any stage.

Once a dispute has surfaced, the emphasis is on the type and intensity of behavior between the parties, as with Barringer. Thus, military action is a final stage, whether coercive or pure force, or whether really a probing, status-quo testing behavior. Northedge and Donelan sequence their development of a dispute in terms of physical manifestations, rather than in terms of psychological phases and forms of power, as in the conflict helix.

13.3. QUINCY WRIGHT

Quincy Wright's comprehensive *A Study of War* (1942; 1964), and *A Study of International Relations* (1955) have informed this volume in many ways, and where my intellectual indebtedness can be made specific appropriate citations to these studies have and will be made. Here I am concerned with Wright's subsequent study of conflict escalation, which unfortunately was severely compressed into one article appearing in *The Journal of Conflict Resolution* (1965).[13]

He begins by pointing out that in a "*broad sense*" conflict between states "may be divided into four stages: (1) awareness of inconsistencies, (2) rising tensions, (3) pressures short of military force, and (4) military intervention or war to dictate a solution." (1965: 434) Conflict is latent during the first two stages and corresponds to the structures and situations of conflict within the helix.

In the *"narrow sense"* (1965: 435) conflict involves the last two stages, when conflict is manifest in opposing actions. In focusing on manifest conflict, Wright expands these two stages into four, which he articulates in a pair of reaction equations developed from Richardson's arms race model.[14] Wright's equations are

$$dx/dt = (Nx + Fy) - (Cx + Wx) + (Px - Py) - (Vx - Vy),$$ [13.1]

$$dy/dt = (Ny + Fx) - (Cy + Wy) + (Py - Px) - (Vy - Vx),$$

where x, y   = states x and y;

dx/dt, dy/dt   = growth rate of hostility for x, and for y;

Nx, Ny   = perception of its national interests by x, and by y;

Fx, Fy   = perception by x of forces immediately available to x, and by y;

Cx, Cy   = perception by x of costs of hostilities and preparations, and by y;

Wx, Wy   = perception by x of world pressures for peace, and by y;

Px, Py   = perception by x of its and y's long run power position, and by y;

Vx, Vy   = perception by x of its vulnerability to destruction, and by y.

The stages formulated in the equation has been succinctly expressed by Wright:

> The magnitude of the positive or negative value of the growth rates of hostility (dx/dt or dy/dt) at a given moment indicates the degree of willingness of *x* and *y* respectively to escalate or to stop hostile activities. These equations imply that the course of a conflict, in the narrow sense, is influenced by the emergence of new considerations by the participants as it proceeds through four stages indicated by the parentheses. The formula does not attempt to predict the probable duration of these stages.

> Once *x* takes action to solve the conflict, it will develop forces in readiness for further action at a rate (dx/dt) in proportion to the intensity of its national interest in the issues (Nx) and its apprehension of the obstacles presented to realization of its policy by y's preparation of forces to resist (*Fy*). In the second stage, *x* will consider the increasing costs of its preparations and, if hostilities are in progress, its losses in life and property (*Cx*); it will also consider the pressures of world opinion, including the intensity of opinion both at home and abroad demanding maintenance of peace or termination of hostilities, the effectiveness of the organization of that opinion, and the adequacy of the procedures which that opinion proposes in the particular situation (*Wx*). These considerations may induce willingness in one or both participants to accept a cease-fire and to negotiate or adjudicate. If, however, hostilities continue, *x* is likely to consider the long-run power position in military forces, economic capability, political morale, and potential allies of itself (*Px*) and its enemy (*Py*), and to escalate or negotiate as that position seems favorable or unfavorable. If hostilities continue to the final stage, *x* will consider its

vulnerability to destruction by the military resources available to the enemy (Vx), comparing this with what it perceives as its enemy's vulnerability to destruction by its own attack (Vy). It is assumed that the satisfaction of visiting huge destruction upon its enemy will seem sufficient compensation for its own heavy losses and that, therefore, the party most vulnerable will surrender—i.e., a state will surrender before its total destruction unless it has a good prospect of totally destroying its enemy. Unilateral suicide will be avoided, but mutual suicide may seem preferable to surrender.

Party y will progress through the same stages as those just described for x. Each stage may be terminated by escalation, cease-fire, negotiation, surrender, or protracted stalemate in which each awaits a favorable opportunity to renew hostilities.

Foresight about the later stages may influence behavior in the earlier stages. Thus, x may have a lesser interest in the issues of the conflict than y, and may be behind in forces in readiness, but x may believe that y's economy will not permit of much escalation, that world opinion is going to turn against y, and that in the long run it can gain allies and marshall much greater power y, and that y will be vulnerable to total destruction by nuclear weapons which only its side (x) will possess. On the other hand, x may take a more pessimistic view of the future and seek a cease-fire while it still has an advantage; but governments are often unrealistically optimistic about the prospects of hostilities. If both sides see it this way—i.e., if the signs of both dx/dt and dy/dt are positive—the conflict will probably escalate. [1965: 435-436]

Figure 13.3 graphs Wright's equation for one party x. Wright is clear: the stages in a conflict are characterized not by activity, but "by the degree of attention likely to be directed to the future and to the ultimate outcome." (1965: 436) As in the conflict helix, the process is psychological, not physical. Wright emphasizes this: "the important variable in determining willingness to escalate or to negotiate is the *perception* of the situation by the decision-making authority, not the objective reality." (1965: 437)

But unlike the helix in which overt conflict subphases are distinguished by transitions in intentions (form of power), Wright's stages are shifts in the salience of particular variables to the perceived outcome. These shifts are shown at the bottom of Figure 13.3. The process moves from national interests and perception of resistance, of costs and world opinion, of long-run relative power, to the perception of relative vulnerability to destruction, and finally to the perception of the outcome and future.

Wright tested his equations against the stages of 45 international conflicts, beginning with World War I. Although his measurements were subjective (but often statistical data were taken as a starting point) and admittedly "educated guesses," (1965: 441) the equations do have "considerable predictive value when applied to situations which have come to an end." (1965: 441)[15]

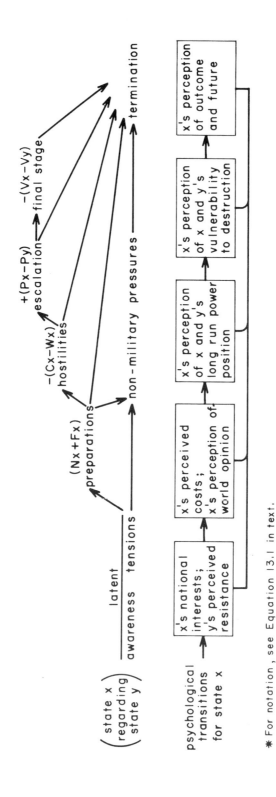

* For notation, see Equation 13.1 in text.

FIGURE 13.3: Wright's Equation of Conflict Escalation

13.4. HERMAN KAHN

In 1965 Herman Kahn published his *On Escalation: Metaphors and Scenarios.* Although the work is mainly concerned with the escalation to and through nuclear war, it provides a carefully worked out escalation ladder whose lower rungs can be usefully applied to interstate conflicts.[16]

Kahn's escalation ladder contains 44 rungs, as shown in Figure 13.4. It is "a linear arrangement of roughly increasing levels of intensity of crisis. Such a ladder exhibits a progression of steps in what amounts to, roughly speaking, an ascending order of intensity through which a given crisis may progress." (1965: 38) In actual conflict, rungs of the ladder may be bypassed or the parties may go down as well as up. (1965: 40)

The ladder stands on a base of disagreements and cold war. Kahn does not pay much attention to this base, but from the context of his brief discussion this appears a latent situation of conflict, an underlying disagreement of interests and perspectives. In Kahn's terms, "the environment is such that any disagreement could easily result in either a slow or rapid climb up the ladder." (1965: 53)

In this situation a disagreement can turn into an ostensible crisis, an actual exchange of warnings and threats, and an attempt on both sides to make them credible. This is the first rung of the ladder. The second rung involves various negative actions designed to put pressure on the other, such as recalling an ambassador, launching a vigorous propaganda campaign or denouncing a treaty.

The third rung follows with solemn and formal declarations that thereby embody a credible commitment and resolution. It is a clear communication that one party is willing to escalate further, if the other so chooses. This is a watershed rung. After it, the crisis becomes deeper, war becomes a distinct possibility, and each side competes in the manipulation of the risk of war. (1965: 62-65)

The fourth rung is then an hardening of position, a confrontation of wills. Negotiations "take on a much more coercive than contractual character." (1965: 67) Both parties have "locked in," which may be manifested by more extremes of negative communications and actions.

The next rung is the actual show of force, a direct or indirect communication of one's willingness and capability to use military force through, say, well-publicized military movements, maneuvers, or overflights of a disputed area.

The sixth rung comprises a significant mobilization, usually beginning with a cancellation of leaves and discharges, and the calling up of important reserve units. Other measures may also be involved whose purpose is to harden one's actual fighting capability and show resolve.

This may be followed by a seventh rung, legal harassment—retortions. These are actions one can take against the citizen or property of the other party to show (or as a manifestation of) extreme hostility. Blockades, embargoes, boycotts exemplify such actions.

A Generalized (or Abstract) Scenario

_____ Aftermaths _____

	44.	Spasm or Insensate War
Civilian	43.	Some Other Kinds of Controlled General War
Central	42.	Civilian Devastation Attack
Wars	41.	Augmented Disarming Attack
	40.	Countervalue Salvo
	39.	Slow-Motion Countercity War

(City Targeting Threshold)

	38.	Unmodified Counterforce Attack
	37.	Counterforce-with-Avoidance Attack
Military	36.	Constrained Disarming Attack
Central	35.	Constrained Force-Reduction Salvo
Wars	34.	Slow-Motion Counterforce War
	33.	Slow-Motion Counter-"Property" War
	32.	Formal Declaration of "General" War

(Central War Threshold)

	31.	Reciprocal Reprisals
Exemplary	30.	Complete Evacuation (Approximately 95%)
Central	29.	Exemplary Attacks on Population
Attacks	28.	Exemplary Attacks Against Property
	27.	Exemplary Attack on Military
	26.	Demonstration Attack on Zone of Interior

(Central Sanctuary Threshold)

	25.	Evacuation (Approximately 70 per cent)
Bizarre	24.	Unusual, Provocative, and Significant Countermeasures
Crises	23.	Local Nuclear War--Military
	22.	Declaration of Limited Nuclear War
	21.	Local Nuclear War--Exemplary

(No Nuclear Use Threshold)

	20.	"Peaceful" World-Wide Embargo or Blockade
	19.	"Justifiable" Counterforce Attack
	18.	Specacular Show or Demonstration of Force
Intense	17.	Limited Evacuation (Approximately 20 per cent)
Crises	16.	Nuclear "Ultimatums"
	15.	Barely Nuclear War
	14.	Declaration of Limited Conventional War
	13.	Large Compound Escalation
	12.	Large Conventional War (or Actions)
	11.	Super-Ready Status
	10.	Provocative Breaking Off of Diplomatic Relations

(Nuclear War is Unthinkable Threshold)

	9.	Dramatic Military Confrontations
	8.	Harassing Acts of Violence

FIGURE 13.4: Kahn's Escalation Ladder

```
Traditional     7.  "Legal" Harassment--Retortions
Crises          6.  Significant Mobilization
                5.  Show of Force
                4.  Hardening of Positions--Confrontation of Wills

                    (Don't Rock The Boat Threshold)

Subcrisis       3.  Solemn and Formal Declarations
Maneuver-       2.  Political, Economic, and Diplomatic Gestures
ing             1.  Ostensible Crisis

_____Disagreement--Cold War_____
```

*From Kahn (1965, p. 39)

FIGURE 13.4: Kahn's Escalation Ladder (Cont.)

The eighth rung moves from nonviolent, legal harassing acts to illegal or violent ones. "Unofficial" bombing against the other's property may take place, mob attacks on his embassy, violations of the other's territorial sovereignty by war planes, support for terrorism, a border intrusion, and the like. Although Kahn does not particularly emphasize this rung (1965: 73-74), I should note that a fundamental threshold has been crossed. Illegal acts (within international law) and especially military violence form a mutually recognizable boundary to conflict, a mutually understandable barrier to further escalation. As long as manifest conflict is kept within this barrier, there is a clear stopping place for escalation, as a river is a natural division between opposing armies. But once illegal actions and violence has been initiated, quantitative escalation may easily take place until a new qualitative barrier is reached, such as in terms of types of weapons (e.g., tactical nuclear weapons), natural geographic boundaries, military personnel (introduction of uniformed soldiers), and so on. Parties to a conflict will not escalate to this rung unthinkingly and easily.

The following ninth rung involves dramatic military confrontations. A full military alert in a contested area or across a border may occur, with both sides instantly prepared to fight on command. Or this rung may involve a strategic alert by the major powers in a deepening crises. Regardless of whether the confrontations are local or global, they "are direct tests of nerve, committal, resolve, and recklessness. They are also dramatic enough to make all the participants and observers take note of what has happened." (1965: 74) These confrontations indicate to both sides that war is thinkable and possible.

The following 10 rungs (see Figure 13.4) define an intense crisis. They move from a provocative breaking of diplomatic relations through super-ready status, large conventional war (or actions), large compound escalation, declaration of limited conventional war, barely nuclear war, nuclear "ultimatums," and so on. There is no need here (although clearly important in another context) to deal with all these rungs. For the purpose of comparison, we can collapse the escalation rungs after super-ready status into war and subsequent escalation.

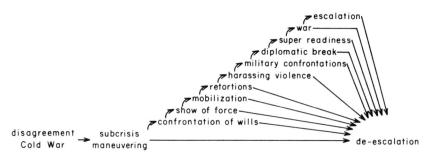

FIGURE 13.5: Kahn's Crisis Dynamics

What about deescalation or termination? Kahn is careful to point out (1965: 230-231) that deescalation may not be a simple descending of the escalation ladder, because actions and signals may be involved which have no escalatory counterpart. And he spends a chapter discussing aspects of deescalation, including the means the parties can use to escape the costs of further conflict while insuring themselves against further escalation or loss of important values. Clearly, deescalation is part of his model.

Kahn conceives of his escalation ladder as most applicable to a, U.S.-Soviet crisis. Deescalation appears therefore a return to the normal situation of conflict—an end to the crisis, but not conflict. Escalation and deescalation have, therefore, no termination, no accommodations, no settlement (nor do such words appear in his index).

Figure 13.5 summarizes Kahn's relevant crisis dynamics. His stages are differentiated by the intensity and scope of actions and their role in communicating the intensity of mutual threat and resolve. Kahn's metaphor of a physical ladder is apt: each rung is a higher physical level of intensity and communication.

Kahn's ladder differs significantly from the helix in two respects. First, the balancing of power phase is a general process and its subphases are meant to apply to all crises, engagements, confrontations, and so on. The subphases are therefore more abstract and less refined than Kahn's ladder, which is specialized to a U.S.-Soviet crisis. Second, Kahn's dynamic framework nonetheless emphasizes physical shifts in intensity rather than psychological transition points. Status-quo testing is of course involved in Kahn's lower rungs, but does not clearly differentiate them; coercion, bargaining, and force (in my usage) are involved in later rungs, but not as clear stages or separate, dynamic lines of development.[17]

13.5. COMPARISONS

For explicit comparison to the conflict helix, Table 13.1 orders the four dynamic conflict "models"[18] considered, such that similar "stages" are in the same, approximate, temporal phase. Figure 13.6 then shows the dynamic process, stages, and lines of development in each model, again compared to the conflict helix.

A careful study of Table 13.1 and Figure 13.6 should bring out the important, detailed differences and similarities. At the most general levels, I should note the following.

(1) Except for the conflict helix, the models are of interstate conflict involving the threat or actuality of military violence. They are not meant to be applicable to processes of conflict within states, groups, or between individuals as in the conflict helix.[19] Some of the differences between the conflict helix and the other models are explicable simply on this basis.[20]

(2) All models begin with some conception of latency, a situation out of which conflict behavior develops.

(3) The dynamic elements differ between models. For the conflict helix, they are psychological, involving shifts in forms of power. They are also psychological for Wright's model, comprising the perception and salience of different variables (interests, costs, power, and so on). For Northedge and Donelan, the process is in forms and intensity of behavior, as it is for Barringer and Kahn. Overall, the basic distinction is between psychological and physicalistic models.[21]

(4) The conflict helix uniquely involves a separate line of development involving noncoercive powers, such as bargaining and persuasion. Of course, cooperation within a conflict process is discussed by the others and Kahn is particularly concerned with the tacit rules of the game the parties establish and their implicit and explicit bargaining, but these behaviors are not treated separately from the stages and are not considered an alternative conflict route.

(5) The helix uniquely distinguishes force from coercion. The relevant dividing stages for the other models is between nonhostilities, hostilities, and escalation ("force" in the Northedge-Donelan model means military action); they move from low-intensity action to high-intensity action, from (to measure this) no killed to some killed to many killed. But in the helix, the later state (force) might actually involve as much or less intense hostilities. It may be more costly in immediate physical terms to persuade the other party to concede or compromise than to destroy their ability to resist.

(6) Only in the helix is a clear outcome in terms of a balance of power considered a part of the process. Within the helix conflicts terminate or are resolved such that a new cooperative relationship, a new structure of expectations, is established.

(7) Finally, only in the helix is the conflict dynamics explicitly part of a larger process of establishing order, rebalancing expectations. That is, the dynamics of conflict behavior is linked to stability, peace, harmony, order. In short, conflict and cooperation are tied together.

TABLE 13.1: Comparative Dynamics of Conflict Behavior

CONFLICT HELIX			BARRINGER	NORTHEDGE-DONELAN	WRIGHT	KAHN	
latent situation			dispute	latent situation	latent awareness & tensions	disagreement cold war	↑
preparations				demand or challenge	preparations and pressures short of military force	ostensible crisis	
status quo testing				diplomatic argument		political, economic, and diplomatic gestures	
non-coercion	coercion	sanctions	prehostilities	negative communications		solemn and formal declarations	
				negative behavior		confrontation of wills	
						show of force	
						retortions	Time
		military coercion	hostilities	"force"	hostilities	harassing acts of violence	
						intense crises	
						provocative diplomatic break	
						super-ready status	
						war	
	force		escalation		escalation	compound escalation etc.	
					final stage		
accommodations			deescalation	termination	termination	deescalation	
			termination				
balance of powers			settlement				↓

[202]

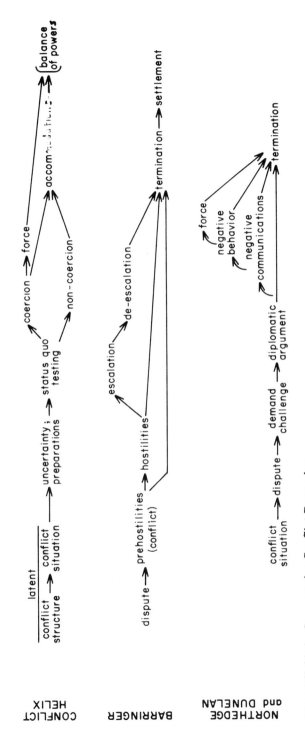

FIGURE 13.6: Comparative Conflict Dynamics

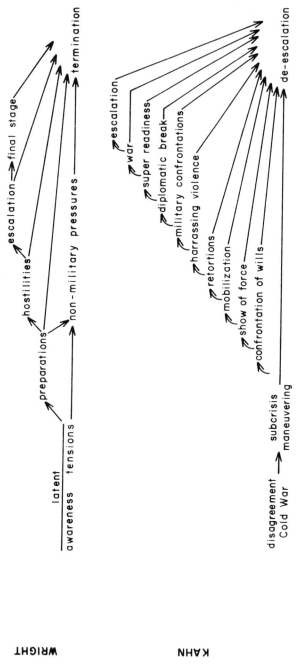

FIGURE 13.6: Comparative Conflict Dynamics (Cont.)

NOTES

1. This is, of course, consistent with the lack of scholarly or scientific literature on the termination of conflicts. Most students appear concerned with preventing conflict, especially war, and not with how conflicts are waged. Or ended.

2. Other systematic studies of escalation or conflict phases include Azar (1972); Field (1972); Fitzsimmons (1969); Leng and Goodsell (1974); McClelland (1968, 1972); D. McCormick (1975), Phillips and Lorimore (n.d.); Tanter (1974).

3. Dr. Barringer was associated with a series of research studies conducted by the Arms Control Project of the MIT Center for International Studies, partially sponsored by the U.S. Arms Control and Disarmament Agency. The model of conflict dynamics used by Barringer in his study also was employed in the MIT research. See particularly the Bloomfield and Leiss study (1967) prepared for ACDA and their subsequent book (1969).

4. Based on Barringer's Figure 2.1 (1972: 21) and drawing (1972: 17).

5. War is not necessarily an option underlying a severance of diplomatic relations. When several of the Arab leaders severed diplomatic relations with European states during the fourth, 1973, Middle East War, I doubt they were thinking also of the possibility of making war on, say, Japan or West Germany.

Barringer is inconsistent, however. After the paragraph defining conflict as that "in which the military option has been introduced" (1972: 17), he also defines conflict as that in which a party "begins to conceive of the conflict at hand as an actual or potential military issue and takes steps to prepare for that contingency." And also several pages later he describes the conflict phase as that "in which a dispute is perceived by at least one party thereto in active or abnormal military policy terms (for example, through arms buildup, troop mobilization, or force deployment)." (1972: 20)

Now, introducing a military option into policy considerations and perceiving the possibility of military action are not the same. In severing diplomatic relations with the United States in 1973 Arab leaders no doubt considered the possibility of this and the subsequent Arab oil boycott as risking a U.S. or joint U.S.-European military takeover of the oil fields. But that did not make such a war an option for the Arabs. Nor is it likely that the Arab severance of diplomatic relations with the United States provoked a war option to be considered by President Nixon, although I suspect that the oil boycott did.

6. Force is the use of physical means to bypass the other's will (section 12.3). The intention of the actor distinguishes force from coercion. Therefore, the transformation from coercion is at the psychological level.

7. For case histories of these disputes, see Donelan and Grieve (1973).

8. The "starting point from which states, like individuals, think on the issue of justice is existing possession, the *status quo*. Whoever has a thing, it is his unless another can show cause why not. Whatever the existing position, that is right until someone can show better. If a state which demands or makes change cannot show this, it is suspect as a force for chaos. Alarm for security in the widest sense is instantly aroused. The *status quo* has a prima facie justification against the revisionist in all eyes, usually even his own. The onus is on the revisionist." (Northedge and Donelan, 1971: 77).

9. The authors are not that clear about what is latent or manifest in a dispute. My use of manifest is an interpretation of their analysis.

10. The demand or challenge appears most often to follow "an uncertain probing of the ground by one side, hardly noticed by the other." (1971: 87) This appears like the initial status-quo testing subphase within the balancing of powers, especially since Northedge and Donelan almost immediately point out that "states still make their initial decisions in deep uncertainty as to relative power." (1971: 87) However, they do not discuss this probing at all in their focused analysis of the development of a dispute in chapter 7. They begin with the challenge, and it is not clear whether the challenge is issued after probing or is part of it.

11. The logical flow of Northedge and Donelan's analysis is not always explicit. From

the context, however, force seems to follow negative behavior as the most intense manifest stage of the dispute, after which termination in some form will occur. See (1971: 152-156).

12. As indicated in note 10, the stages are not as clearly articulated as the Figure suggests. It is my interpretation of their development. However, I am sure that Northedge and Donelan do not see a dispute as necessarily following a linear-time course. A dispute may deescalate from one stage to a previous one. Figure 13.2 is only meant to represent a dispute's main, developmental stages.

13. For a critique of Wright's article, see Carroll (1969). I have reanalyzed Wright's variables and data, including a variety of additional measures. See appendix I (Project 7.1).

14. See Lewis F. Richardson (1960), particularly chapter 2. Wright had been one of the earliest students of international relations to recognize the value of Richardson's work. See Wright (1942, Vol. 2, appendix XLII). An excellent critique of Richardson's model has been published by Rajan (1974).

15. For a systematic analysis of Wright's stages and variables, as well as the background conditions, see (appendix II: 7.1). I found escalation most dependent on perceived national interests, and secondarily on power parity (the closer in power, the more likely escalation), relative vulnerability, and differences in wealth. Political-cultural differences appear to play no role in escalation.

16. Kahn's "phases" are conceptually postulated and untested. They are meant to be "metaphorical," and are neither developed from an explicit survey of a given sample of conflicts, as for Northedge and Donelan, nor tested against such conflicts, as were those of Barringer and Wright. This is not to depreciate Kahn's contribution. An innovative conceptual distinction can be potent to the understanding and provide new insight into empirical work.

   Moreover, I should make clear that the ladder is formulated primarily for U.S.-Soviet confrontations and "is in some senses an American rather than a Soviet ladder." (1965: 53)

17. For example, regarding the transition from rung 3 Kahn says: "As soon as negotiations take on much more of a coercive than contractual character, I would argue that we have reached Rung 4." Now, to describe either objectives or tactics, Kahn uses the terms *contractual, coercive, agonistic, stylistic,* and *familial* (1965: 15-22). Translating to my terms, his contractual refers to bargaining behavior; his coercive to coercion, force, and practices (e.g., retortions to reciprocate or sanction the actions of another according to international law); his agonistic to practices (rule following behavior); and his familial to, indeed, what I call familistic behavior. Coercion for Kahn involves the use of threats and punishments, but such are employed not only at rung four, but in subcrisis maneuvering as well. Even at rung one, Kahn emphasizes implicit or explicit threats and concern for their credibility (1965: 54) as the rung's keynote. Given that he does not emphasize the role of coercion, contractual behavior, and such, in distinguishing escalation rungs beyond the above quote, and this one quote seems inconsistent with his *prior* characterization of lower rungs, I do not consider it a serious part of his dynamics.

18. Only Barringer uses the term *model* for his conflict dynamics.

19. Northedge and Donelan do consider the development of disputes within states (1971: chapter 6), but their *model* is less explicit and differs from their interstate one.

20. This is important to keep in mind, for the comparisons being made are not meant to be invidious but descriptive.

21. The reader might object to this characterization of Kahn's ladder, because he seems so basically concerned with perception, expectations, credibility, and such. But Kahn himself points out that "intensity" is the underlying criteria (1965: 38). The only question is whether he means intensity in behavior or psychological variables. From his discussion of the rungs of the ladder and even their labels, it is clear that for him it is physical action that differentiates the rungs.

PART V

THE BALANCING OF POWERS:
DYNAMICS, CAUSES, CONDITIONS,
AND HELIX

Man is not a circle with a single center; he is an ellipse with two foci. Facts are one, ideas are the other.

Victur Hugo, Les Miserables *VII.i.*

Chapter 14

INTRODUCTION TO PROPOSITIONS
AND EVIDENCE

The great tragedy of Science—the slaying of a beautiful hypothesis by an ugly fact.
T.H. Huxley, Biogenesis and Abiogenesis

In previous volumes, I have delineated the generic process of conflict within social fields and provided relevant evidence. In Volume 1, I focused on the psychological and philosophical foundations, and gathered together the systematic, psychological evidence on the dynamic field of motives, attitudes, and goals (1975: part IV). There, I was especially concerned with a solid, empirical foundation for needs and sentiments, especially the integrated self, against which prevailing theories about the drive for power, aggression, authoritarian personality, and so on, could be evaluated.

In Volume 2, I described the social field and its process that is the conflict helix, and focused my discussion at the level of state-societies. A number of general propositions about social conflict were drawn from the analysis and all the systemic, empirical evidence I could find for and against the propositions was presented (1976: chapters 34-35).

In Volume 3, I was concerned with contending theories and views on conflict and presented no systematic evidence. However, the ability of social field theory and its conflict helix to confront or absorb other perspectives as was shown is itself a form of evidence.

Finally, in this Volume 4, I have focused on one exchange society, one social field: international relations. The nature and components of the international field and behavior within the field have been presented and discussed (1979: chapters 4 and 7), and the process of international conflict has been delineated (1979: chapters 8-13). Many empirical results already have been presented, especially bearing on the components of the field and behavior (1979: chapters 4 and 7, appendix 9A, and chapter 11). However, these results were used descriptively, except for some asides, and not as evidence for field theory.

Descriptive empirical results are assumed to *map* some aspect of reality. There is, of course, the question of validity and reliability; and the user of descriptive results should know and present the evidence for and against a particular description, such as that wealth is a major component of states. However the descriptive results by themselves are not meant as evidence for a theory, but as the empirical foundation or framework for such evidence.

For example, to assert that components in a social field are forces towards behavior first requires an empirical description of the components. This description neither confirms or denies the theory, but provides the base for assessing the theory. Once the empirical mapping determines the components of the field, then the relationship among these field and behavioral components can be used as empirical evidence for and against the proposition that behavior is dependent on the field components.

The *test* of whether results are used descriptively or evidentially depends on whether in principle the results could falsify the theory, hypothesis or propositions. Any possible, properly determined set of empirical components would comprise components of the international field, but not all possible empirical results would satisfy the proposition that behavior is dependent on field components.

In the following chapters, I will present a number of propositions about conflict drawn from the field theory and its conflict helix. And I will provide the evidence for each proposition. The purpose of this chapter is to present the variety of considerations that will inform and guide this effort.

14.1 WHY PROPOSITIONS?

Why not continue the progress of the previous chapters, dealing next with the balance of power and structure of expectations, international order and law, and then conclude with a number of conflict-related generalizations abstracted from the discussion? And this all can be made so impressively empirical by reference to systematic findings and descriptive results.

However, the result would be a partial picture, an incomplete argument. The "truths" presented might be intuitively convincing and theoretically sound, and the reader might therefore be persuaded. But truth stands on three legs: intuition, reason (theory), and experience (the empirical world). Therefore, a complete and persuasive picture of the field requires a systematically ordered confrontation with reality. Not a descriptive mapping, but hard and comprehensive *tests* against data with the greatest potential for falsifying a "truth." And this confrontation cannot be selective. All relevant evidence must be found and the criteria for what is relevant should be biased, if at all, towards a negative finding. But this is saying no more than we must be good scientists in dealing with evidence.

Granted the need for such evidence, then, to what is the evidence to be related? Theory, theorems, hypotheses, or propositions? The field theory presented here and in the previous volumes is a comprehensive *perspective* involving hard theory (equations and explicit logic) integrated within a philosophical, metasocial and intuitive framework. The theory in its totality cannot be tested empirically. Aspects of the theory, such as the analytic core, can be tested, however, and in their accumulated results add empirical confirmation to the intuitive and rational persuasiveness of the overall structure.[1]

Because of this intuitive-rational-empirical nature of the theory, theorems cannot be derived from the whole and therefore tested; although they can be from aspects of the theory, such as that involving status.[2] The problem is that theorems require a formal theory, which is an explicit analytic system of axioms, rules of deduction, and theorems. However, aspects of my perspective are matters of feeling, perception, and an orientation towards international reality. Such are not reducible to an axiomatic system, but are rather the context or framework for such a system and its theorems. But here I wish to go beyond what is merely axiomatic, for analytic systems overly constain what can be asserted and tested about international relations. While in some research contexts, these constraints are desirable, here I am concerned not only with the scientifically *deducible and predictable,* but also with generally understanding conflict and war. While the two overlap, they are not the same.

Then why not test hypotheses? Hypotheses can be made precise and related to both hard and soft theory. However, an hypothesis is a statement that is tentative; it is an assumption, a speculation, a starting point for research. And this is not what I will be asserting.

The statements about conflict that can be made on the basis of field theory are more than provisional suppositions. They are *propositions,* definite affirmations about conflict grounded in a perspective on man's psychology, society, and conflict.

Moving from the empirical descriptions of the previous chapters to empirical propositions will serve a number of purposes. First, the most important, empirical aspects of the international field and its conflict helix can be made specific and indexed as propositions. Second, propositions provide organization to a mass of empirical results and findings of which various dimensions, levels of meaning, and significance might otherwise be lost. And third, propositions serve as foci for arraying all the positive *and negative* empirical results bearing on a statement, and thus help in avoiding selective bias.

14.2 THE APPROACH

In order to facilitate the presentation of propositions and their evidence, they are organized into a number of chapters. Chapter 15 presents the propositions and evidence on the manifest dynamics of conflict, such as that manifest conflict involves a number of subphases. Chapter 16 focuses on propositions about the causes and conditions of conflict, violence, and war. Chapter 17 offers several propositions about ending conflict. Chapter 18 defines propositions about the conflict helix itself—about the whole process of conflict within the international field. Finally, a concluding chapter 19 will overview the propositions and evidence and abstract the primary propositions of international conflict and war.

There is a greater tension here than in previous volumes between the scientific requirement to explicitly present methods and evidence and my desire to make these results useful and understandable to the nonspecialist. It is the usual conflict between the need to communicate to both the technical and general reader; the strain between the requirements of evaluation and communication.

In what follows I have tried to resolve this tension by (1) giving in each chapter a nontechnical summary and discussion of the propositions and their evidence, (2) consigning the specific proposition-by-proposition technical considerations of the evidence to a chapter's appendix.

In order to evaluate the evidence for a proposition in the appendices, I will define the proposition, discuss its theoretical basis, present the relevant evidence, and state a conclusion about the proposition's empirical status. The whole purpose is to provide the maximum information in the shortest space. The style may therefore be too systematic and formal—lacking in life—for some, but the reader might consider it penance for the soaring, metasocial prose he may have noticed elsewhere.

14.3. SOURCES OF EVIDENCE

There are two major sources of evidence. One is the accumulated research of my Dimensionality of Nations Project (DON)[3], through which I tried to map the international field and determine the conditions and causes of manifest conflict. The published results will be referenced as are other published sources. However, many of DON's results are unpublished, but nonetheless bear significantly on the propositions of concern. Therefore, in appendix I, I have organized these unpublished results as separate projects (along with unpublished studies I have done independently of DON) and detailed the essential information for each. As relevant, these empirical results will be referenced as appendix I and by project, e.g., (appendix I: 2.3).

A second source of evidence is the systematic literature—books, monographs, articles, conference papers, and so on—on international relations and foreign policy. The literature and the parameters of this relevant research are given in appendix III. The appendix also describes the manner in which these sources were selected and the considerations governing their description. It also includes the published reports of the DON project.

14.4. NATURE OF THE EVIDENCE

Through appendix III the evidence is already organized by source, cases, data periods, and method. However, additional dimensions are also important for evaluating the evidence, as shown in Table 14.1. The horizontal dimension in the table defines whether the evidence is static or dynamic. *Static* evidence is for one period in time (e.g., all states in 1968) or for entities regardless of time (e.g., primitive tribes or societies; all wars); *dynamic* evidence involves the change in an entity or its behavior through time (e.g., trend in violence; correlation between American economic growth and its wars).[4]

As shown by the vertical dimension in Table 14.1, the evidence can be also organized by case, states, dyad, or system. *Case* refers to evidence based on the analysis of specific conflicts, incidents of violence, crises, or wars. For example, Butterworth (1976) analyzed 310 management attempts in 274 conflicts during 1945-1974. This was a *static* analysis of *cases* of conflict.

States refers to the analyses of sovereign or independent societies, whether nation-states, city-states, or primitive tribes. The unit of analysis underlying evidence at this level is the state, its behavior or attributes.

The *dyadic* level concerns the behavior, similarities and differences, geographic distance, and so on, *between* states. These usually will be dyadic (involve

TABLE 14.1: **Important Dimensions of the Evidence**

	Static	Dynamic
Case		
State		
Dyadic		
System		
Surveys		

a pair of states) or triadic relations reducible to dyads. The unit of analysis will generally be a pair of states, such as the relations between China and Japan, Bolivia and Argentina, or North and South Korea.

Finally, there is the *system* level, which refers to the character of a system of states (e.g., the European system; the international system) and the aggregate, overall behavior within the system. An example of system level (and static) evidence would be the results of Singer and Small's (1966) analysis of the relationship between the number and character of alliances in the international system and the number of wars, 1815-1945.

At the bottom of Table 14.1 a place is given to *surveys* which have collected, summarized, or given an overview of relevant systematic results.

There are nine cells in Table 4.1, or nine different kinds of evidence for a proposition.[5] Not all cells may be relevant to a proposition (e.g., static evidence would be irrelevant to a dynamic proposition), but ideally, a solid proposition would have positive evidence for it in all relevant cells. So that the reader also may assess the support for each proposition, positive and negative evidence will be presented on a cell by cell basis.

14.5. THE QUALITY OF THE EVIDENCE

It is relatively easy to count sources with positive or negative results. It is an *art* to weigh and evaluate different results and conclude whether they are *on balance* strongly positive, positive, ambiguous, negative, or strongly negative on a proposition. Consider some of the elements of such an evaluation.

- Whether the results are manifestly positive or negative.
- The competance of the analysis.
- The methods used and their appropriateness.
- Nature, validity, and reliability of the data used.
- The "degrees of freedom," that is, the degree to which negative results could have appeared.
- The scope of the analysis, or the number and quality of the cases, states, dyads, or systems concerned.[6]
- The importance and significance of the results.

The element concerning the data is of particular importance. Much of the evidence to be presented is based on *event data*, a count or scaling of occurrences of different kinds of conflict and cooperative behavior. This type of data provokes many questions about data sources, validity, reliability, methods of analysis, and so on. Because of the importance of event data here, in appendix II I discuss and overview such data for both the general and technical reader.

Regarding the whole list of elements, each source of evidence could be rated on each and even an overall summary rating could be developed. But this would be misleading. The rating and method of forming the overall scale would be fundamentally subjective and involve an implicit weighting. I prefer to admit that these elements all will be gauged and weighted subjectively and the final judgment about a proposition will be an intuitive synthesis—guided by method, to be sure, but no less intuitive.

Thus, the best I can do here is to make my sources of evidence and their parameters clear and to present my logic as explicitly as possible. Whatever biases or selectivity involved may therefore become evident.

NOTES

1. See my *Field Theory Evolving* (1977), especially chapter 16, for empirical tests of the analytic structure of field theory in international relations.

2. In the years when I considered myself a logical positivist (Rummel, 1976b), I had driven toward an axiomatic field theory from which theorems could be derived and tested. For the first such effort, see Rummel (1965), republished in (1977: chapter 2). The last gasp of this effort was my status-field theory (1977: chapter 9).

3. Reviews of the project are given in Hilton (1973), and Seidelmann (1973), and Hoole and Zinnes (1976). For the autobiographical background, see Rummel (1976b). After 13 years, the project was terminated in June, 1975.

4. More precisely, the evidence is based on analyses in which time is an explicit or implicit variable. It is explicit if an actual time variable is used, say, in regression analysis. It is implicit if the data is organized and analyzed by time units, such as in a matrix of U.S.-U.S.S.R. negative communications for each year, 1946-1977.

5. There are some studies which do not fit easily into the table. Sample survey analyses, public opinion studies, or content analyses are classified as at the state level if assessing the attitudes, perceptions opinions, and the like of one or a number of states. If, however, these studies have analyzed such variables for a state *toward* a specific other, they are considered dyadic. The classification is made easier if it is kept in mind that the focus is not on attitudes, perceptions, or opinions, per se, but on what they manifest about cases, states, dyads, or systems.

6. This is more than a statistical degree-of-freedom question, which is only concerned with the number of cases versus the restraints of the statistical techniques used and the number of variables. Keeping techniques and variables constant, a study involving 22 wars spread through three centuries may be far more important than one of 22 incidents of military violence in 1971.

Chapter 15

EMPIRICAL CONFLICT DYNAMICS

the Balance of Power is a system of political dynamics that comes into play whenever a society articulates itself into a number of mutually independent local states.
Toynbee, A Study of History, *III*

International Conflict Behavior is not a spasmodic, aimless, reactive flailing of hostile leaders, bent on simply hurting or destroying each other. Violence is not necessarily stupid or irrational. War is not necessarily insane.

Conflict Behavior is usually calculated to coerce, persuade, or bargain with the other's will. Or to overcome it through force.

Conflict Behavior is aimed toward the gratification or protection of some interests in opposition to those of others. Such behavior manifests a balancing of powers with distinct subphases and a determinate outcome—the balance of powers.

In Conflict Behavior we should find, therefore, patterns—regularities—which mirror the underlying process. And we do, indeed.

The evidence presented in appendix 15A confirms that Conflict Behavior manifests:

- a preconfrontation and uncertainty phase
- different coercive versus noncoercive paths in the balancing of power
- different subphases
- underlying hostility
- reciprocity
- crisis.

Empirically, Conflict Behavior consists of a number of separate and distinct components—patterns underlying the phases and process of balancing. Table 15.1 summarized the patterns found by a large number of studies and indicates the typical behaviors involved in each.[1]

The relationship of these manifest patterns to the underlying process of conflict is shown in Figure 15.1. The solid bars in the Figure outline the

TABLE 15.1: Patterns (Components) of Conflict[a]

COMPONENT	TYPICAL ACTIONS
C_1: antiforeign (unofficial) behavior	mob attacks on embassy, on foreigners, on foreign property; private boycotts; antiforeign demonstration
C_2: preparations (warning and defensive actions)	alerts; mobilizations; cancellation of leaves; troop movements
C_3: negative communication	threats; warnings; protests; denunciations; accusations
C_4: negative (nonviolent) actions/sanctions	boycotts; embargoes; severance of diplomatic relations; expulsion of diplomats; cancellation of aid; abrogation of treaty
C_5: low-level military violence	clashes; discrete military action; continuous low-level military engagements
C_6: high-level military violence	war; many killed in violence
C_7: bargaining	offer; limit; reward; exchange
C_8: persuasion	justification; presentation; argue; urge
C_9: negotiation	agree; meet; present; propose

a. Components C_1 to C_6 are listed in Table 11.2 for antagonistic conflict behavior

theoretical process of conflict. Moving from left to right, the latent situation of conflict is triggered into a situation of uncertainty involving preparations. This phase is transformed into the manifest balancing of powers, beginning with status-quo testing. Two paths lead from this subphase, as shown by the horizontal division in the Figure. One path involves coercion, the other noncoercion. Coercion is divided into nonmilitary and military coercion, as shown. Force is a subsequent subphase, with accommodations as the final subphase in the balancing of powers. As discussed in chapters 12-13, a conflict may not traverse each subphase, and may actually return to a previous subphase (see Figures 12.1, 13.6). However, for simplicity, the subphases are simply shown as sequential in Figure 15.1.

The bars in the Figure are open at each end because only part of the conflict process (that involving the situation, initiation, and balancing of powers) is shown.

Between double lines, on each side of the theoretical process, are shown the *empirical* components—patterns[2]—of international conflict listed in Table 15.1. The left-right extension of the double lines is vertically correlated to the theoretical underlying phases and subphases shown between solid bars.

The first component pattern is *antiforeign behavior,* the unofficial actions of individuals or groups against another state, its nationals or its property. Such

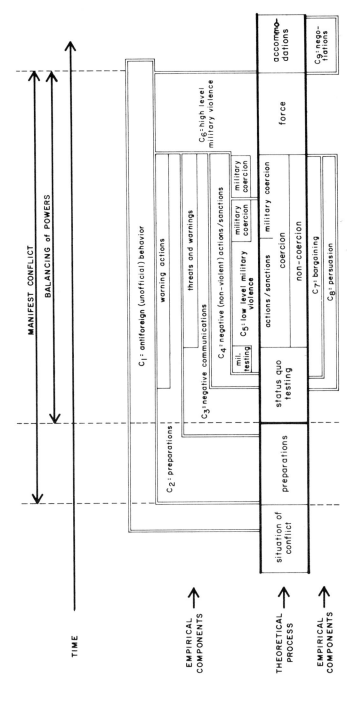

FIGURE 15.1: The Relationship of Manifest Conflict Components to the Underlying Process of Conflict

reflects the hostility engendered *by* a conflict,[3] and such manifest hostility may occur at any point in the process (as shown in Figure 15.1), even during part of the accommodations stage when some individuals or groups may be upset at leaders entering into negotiations. Moreover, hostility may bubble to the surface within a situation of conflict, when there is no overt interstate conflict.

The second component is *preparations,* involving mobilizing the public for possible confrontations, strenthening forces, alerts, troop movements, and the like. Such are usually concentrated during the preparations phase, but may also occur during subsequent subphases as a party prepares to escalate the conflict.

An aspect of this pattern is warning actions,[4] which may occur during the testing and coercive subphases. This possibility is indicated by the subregion (rectangle) delineated within the double lines in Figure 15.1. This also reflects the dual implication of preparations. They indicate a decision has been made to prepare for hostile and possible violent contingencies, but they also often are *meant* as a warning to the other side that a decision has been made to escalate, if necessary.

The next component is *negative communications,* an aspect of which involves the verbal or written threats and warnings which usually occur during the coercive subphase of a conflict. A fourth component pattern is *negative actions/ sanctions,* which comprises retaliatory acts, physical expressions of displeasure, retortions, and so on.

Military violence consists of two components, one being *low-level military violence.* This may involve either the use of military means to probe the other's interests and will (e.g., an apparently spontaneous, but secretly planned border clash), or the use of military coercion. Both possibilities are shown by inner boxes in the Figure. Military action, however, may neither be a test nor coercive, but simply an expression of the conflict. Thus, an aircraft of one party straying over the territory of the other may be shot down, or a surveillance ship may be boarded or sunk.

The second military component is that of *intense, high-level, military violence.* A war. As shown in the Figure, such high-level violence may constitute either military coercion (as in the Vietnam war) or force (as in World War II).

Moving now to the cooperation components there are three.[5] The first of these (C_7 in the Figure) reflects *bargaining* power. Aid may be offered, as it was by the United States to Hanoi in the Vietnam war, and promises may be made. Moreover, both sides may implicitly agree to limits on their conflict. Sanctuaries may be allowed, weapons limited, tactics restrained, and so on. That is, a conflict may manifest a balancing through antagonistic behavior and a bargaining and "contract" over the limits of this behavior.

A second cooperative component involves *persuasion:* intellectual power, with authoritative and altruistic powers mixed in. Each party may clarify its position and demands, justify its case, argue that justice and the good of humanity is on its side, apply logic, cite precedent, appeal to international law, and so on.

And finally, the last component is *negotiation,* the actual formal or informal attempt to resolve the conflict through mutual accommodations.

Nine empirical component-patterns reflect underlying international conflict. As components, they delineate a *Conflict Behavior space-time* within which states can be located in terms of their relative conflict and conflict dynamics. This is a subspace of international behavior.

In summary, the process of conflict may move through phases, paths, and subphases. These usually involve the confrontation of different forms of power in the process of establishing a balance of powers, a structure of expectations.

This process is latent; it is what gives meaning and understanding to Conflict Behavior. Reflecting this process, Conflict Behavior separates into nine space-time components. These are patterns of intecorrelated behavior defining the hostility generated by a conflict, preparations for confrontation or escalation, negative communication, negative actions and sanctions, low-level military violence, intense violence, bargaining, persuasion, and negotiations.

NOTES

1. Not all studies would agree on these components, but they represent the central tendency of those listed in Table 15A.2 of appendix 15A. Most studies have focused on the antagonistic conflict components (C_1-C_5). Where conflict and cooperative data have been analyzed together they have consistently divided into separate components. Those studies including appropriate variables often find the three cooperative patterns merged into one (e.g., McClelland and Hoggard, 1969). In some a pure negotiations pattern has emerged (e.g., Kegley, *et al.,* 1974).

2. These are components in the sense of latent-functions, as I have developed the concept in previous volumes. Pattern also is used here because each component (as a simple structure, rotated dimension of component or common factor analysis) defines a separate and clear cluster of interrelated space-time behavior, as confirmed in appendix 15A.

3. Contrary to popular belief, conflict usually does not develop out of public hostility. Rather it is the other way around. For example, see Buchanan and Cantril (1953).

4. Thus, empirical studies have usually labeled the pattern "warning and defensive acts." See, for example, Hall and Rummel (1970).

5. Again, a warning. The empirical reliability of these three patterns are much less established than for the antagonistic ones, because relatively few studies have employed the proper variables.

APPENDIX 15A

PHASING PROPOSITIONS ON INTERNATIONAL

CONFLICT AND EVIDENCE

Six phasing propositions are presented in Table 15A.1. Each will be treated separately below in terms of supporting theory, predictions, evidence, and conclusion. This approach,

TABLE 15A.1: **Phasing Propositions on International Conflict**

		PROPOSITIONS	
No.	Name	Abstract Description	Empirical Description
15.1	Uncertainty	Conflict Behavior begins in uncertainty	Preparations for conflict form a separate and distinct pattern for Conflict Behavior.
15.2	Conflict Paths	Coercion and noncoercion are independent conflict paths	Conflict Behavior manifests different coercive versus noncoercive paths in the balancing of powers.
15.3	Conflict Subphasing	Conflict Behavior manifests different subphases	Conflict patterns manifest separate status quo testing, nonviolent coercion, violent coercion, force, and accommodation subphases in the process of balancing power.
15.4	Hostility	Hostility reflects latent and manifest conflict	Manifest hostility reflects the situation of conflict, uncertainty, and the balancing of powers.
15.5	Reciprocity	Conflict behavior is reciprocal	Negative communications, negative actions and sanctions, and violence, are reciprocated.
15.6	Crisis	Crises are distinct behavior patterns signalling escalation	The threat of imminent escalation in a subphase is manifested through an intensification and diversification of conflict behavior.

as well as the manner in which the evidence is handled, is described in chapter 14 and in appendix 16C.

Major evidence for each proposition will be discussed in order to communicate the quality and nature of the analyses drawn upon and the basis for the ratings. Space does not allow that this be done for all propositions in this book, however, and in subsequent appendices in which propositions are presented, the evidence usually can only be collectively presented.

15A.1 PHASING PROPOSITIONS

Proposition 15.1 (Uncertainty):
Conflict Behavior begins in uncertainty.

Preparations for conflict form a separate
and distinct pattern of Conflict Behavior.[1]

Theory: As discussed in section 11.2 and chapter 13, preparations manifest the uncertainty–initiation–phase of the balancing of powers, the girding of the will. No further Conflict Behavior may be manifest, for the underlying conflict may be resolved through accommodations or abnegation, or preparation may be followed by an actual confrontation of some kind. What Conflict Behavior will follow preparations is unclear at the initiation stage (thus, the uncertainty). It may only be status-quo testing; or possibly negative actions, such as boycotts, embargoes, severance of diplomatic relations; or even coercive violence.

Therefore, (1) preparations should comprise specific behaviors, such as strengthening forces, alerts, cancelling leaves, troop movements, partial or full mobilizations; (2) preparations may or may not eventuate in confrontation; and (3) what kind of confrontation (balancing) will occur, if any, is unknown. It follows that preparations should form empirical patterns (latent functions) of behavior separate and distinct from other forms of Conflict Behavior.

Prediction: A factor or component analysis of diverse, static or dynamic Conflict Behavior data should delineate empirical patterns of preparations. Moreover, preparations and other kinds of Conflict Behavior should be relatively uncorrelated (bivariate or multivariate).

Moreover, if such data are included, alliances and increase in armaments (such as in military expenditures) should form a separate pattern from short-run preparations (such as alerts or mobilizations).

Evidence: See Table 15A.2.

In crises periods, a "warning and defensive acts" component is statistically independent of other types of behavior, and involves a variety of preparatory-type actions (Phillips and Hainline, 1972; Phillips and Lorimore, n.d.). In precrises phases the same component also exists (Phillips and Lorimore, n.d.), as it must if there is such a preparatory phase.

Considering preparations to involve a variety of military growth or decline factors (e.g., growth in defense expenditures), then U.S. and USSR preparations by year, 1948-1968, have no high correlation with the cold war. Indeed, most correlations are negative (Väyrynen, 1973: 132).

For states, a statistically independent component almost uniquely delineating prepatory actions and called "warning and defensive acts" existed in 1955 (Rummel, 1967; Keim and Rummel, 1967); and in 1963 (Phillips, 1973; Oliva and Rummel, 1969). Moreover, such a pattern exists in both the conflict behavior a state directs towards others (previous citations) and that *received* from other states (Phillips, 1973).

In other factor analyses studies on conflict behavior, an insufficient number of preparatory variables were included for such a pattern to emerge, but in both Rummel (1963) for 1955-1957 data and Tanter (1966) for 1958-1960 data, troop movements and mobilizations

(text continues on page 226)

TABLE 15A.2: Evidence on the Phasing Propositions on International Conflict

Level[a]	Source[b]	Importance[c]	1	2	3	4	5	6
Case – Static	Phillips & Hainline (1972)	H	SP		A	SN		PI
	Fitzsimmons (1969)	M		P	P			
	Burrowes & Garriga-Pico (1974)	M		SP				
	"United..." (1968)	H	SP					SP
	Haas, M. (1974)	H			P			SP
	Holsti, O. (1972)	M			P			P
	Lentner (1972)	L						PI
	Naroll (1974)	H	P					
	Triska & Finley (1968)	M					P	
	Brecher (1974)	M					P	P
	Tanter (1974)	M						SP
	Midlarsky (1975)	H	PI					
Case – Dynamic	Phillips & Lorimore (n.d.)	H	SP		SP	A		SP
	Vayrynen (1973)	H	SP	SP				
	Fitzsimmons (1969)	M		P				
	Burrowes & Garriga-Pico (1974)	M		SP				
	McClelland, et al. (1965)	M					P	SP
	Field (1972)	L					P	
	McClelland and Hoggard (1969)	M						SP
	McClelland (1972)	M						SP
	Azar (1972)	M					P	PI
	Denton (1969)	H	N					
	Goldman (1973)	H				PI	SP	
	McCormick, J. (1975)	M					N	
	Smoker (1969)	M			SPI			
	Leng & Boodsell (1974)	H		P	P		P	
	McClelland (1968)	M						SP
State – Static	Keim & Rummel (1969)	M	SP		A	A		
	Phillips (1973)	M	SP		P	A	SP	
	Oliva & Rummel (1969)	M	SP		SP	SP		
	Rummel (1963)	M	P		N			
	Tanter (1966)	M	P		N			
	Burrowes & Spector (1973)	M		SP	SN			
	McClelland & Hoggard (1969)	M		SP	SP			
	Salmore & Munton (1974)	M		SP	SP			
	Salmore, et al. (1974)	H		SP	P			
	Moore, J. (1970)	H		A	P			
	Kegley, et al. (1974)	M		A	A			
	McGowan (1973)	M		A				
	Rummel (1967a)	M			SN	SP		
	McClelland & Ancoli (1970)	M			A			
	Hazelwood (1973)	M			N			
	Phillips (1970)	M					SP	
	Alcock (1970)	M	P					
	Naroll (n.d., 1966)	H	PI		SPI			
	Weil (1975)	M	P					
State – Static (Cont.)	Haas, M. (1974)	H	P		P			
	Brady (1974)	H		P				
	Hermann, C., et al. (1973)	M					P	
State – Dynamic	Keim & Rummel (1969)	M	SP					
	(appendix I: 1.6)	H	SP		P	SP		
	Wilkenfeld, et al. (1972)	M	SP					

TABLE 15A.2: Evidence on the Phasing Propositions on International Conflict (Cont.)

Level[a]	Source[b]	Importance[c]	Propositions[d]					
			1	2	3	4	5	6
	Wilkenfeld, et al. (1977)	H		A				
	Phillips (1970)	M			P	SP		
	Haas, M. (1974)	H	N					
	Choucri & North (1974)	H	PI				SP	
	Cattell (1953)	H	P					
	Mahoney (1976)	H					SP	
	Gibb (1956)	L	P				SP	
Dyadic – Static	Rummel (1967a, 1968)	M	SP			SP		
	(appendix I: 1.2)	H	P		P	P		
	(appendix I: 1.4)	M	SP		A	N		
	Rummel (1965)	M	SP		P	SN		
	Hall & Rummel (1970)	M	SP		SP	SP		
	(appendix I: 1.1)	M	SP		P	SP		
	Phillips (1969)	M	SP					
	(appendix I: 2.3)	M	SP	SP		SP		
	(appendix I: 1.5)	M	SN		P	SP		
	(appendix I: 1.3)	H	A		P	SP		
	(appendix I: 2.3)	M		SP	A	SP		
	McGowan (1973)	M			P			
	Sullivan, I. (1972)	M	P					
	Teune & Synnestvedt (1965)	M	P					
	Leavitt (1968)	L	P		P			
	Moore, I. (1970)	M					SPI	
	Russett (1967)	H	P					
	Schubert (1975)	M			A			
	Van Atta & Rummel (1972)	M	SP					
Dyadic – Dynamic	Hall & Rummel (1970)	M	SP					
	Phillips (1969)	M	SP		P	SP		
	Phillips & Hainline (n.d.)	H	SP		SP	SP	SP	
	(appendix I: 1.3)	H	P		SP	SP		
	Omen (1975)	M	P			SP		
	Park & Ross (1971)	M			SP	SP		
	Wilkenfeld, et al. (1972)	M			A		SP	
	Azar (1975)	M					SP	
	Azar, et al. (1974)	M					SP	
	Phillips & Crain (1974)	H					SP	
	Milstein (1972)	M					SP	
	Holsti, et al. (1969)	L					SP	
	Duncan & Siverson (1975)	L					N	
	Mahoney (1977)	H					N	
Dyadic – Dynamic (Cont.)	Pool (1951)	L					SPI	
	Moore & Young (1969)	M					P	
	Vayrynen (1973)	H					P	
	Mogdis (1970)	M	P				N	
	Peterson (1972)	M					P	
	McCormick, J. (1975)	M					P	
System – Static	Wallace (1973)	H	SN					
	Zinnes (1971)	M	N					

TABLE 15A.2: Evidence on the Phasing Propositions on International Conflict (Cont.)

Level[a]	Source[b]	Importance[c]	Propositions[d]					
			1	2	3	4	5	6
Summary	Vasquez (1975, 1976)	L	P					
Studies	Weede (1977a, 1977b)	M	P					

a. These levels are discussed in section 14.4.
b. All sources are referenced at the end of the book and characterized in appendix III, with the exception of references to unpublished projects in appendix I clearly so identified, e.g. (appendix I: 1.3)
c. This is a measure of the importance and centrality of the source *for the propositions given here*, where:
   H = high importance
   M = moderate importance
   L = low importance
   It is not an evaluation of the work itself nor its competence.
d. Numbers refer to the propositions listed in Table 15A.1. The evidence is coded: SP = strongly positive, P = positive, A = ambiguous, N = negative, SN = strongly negative. An I after the assessment means that results are positive for a proposition by inference—they are what would be expected were the proposition true.

have low correlations with other conflict behavior, no high loading on conflict components, and low communalities (h^2).

Dynamically, Keim and Rummel (1967) found that a preparatory pattern of conflict showed the most stability between 1955 and 1963. A super-P component analysis of state conflict behavior for 13 months, 1976-1977, delineated a statistically independent, preparations pattern (appendix I: 1.6). A dynamic (super-P) analysis of six Middle Eastern states, separately and together, for 217 months (1949-1967) delineated a preparations pattern (Wilkenfeld, *et al.* 1972).

For dyads, a preparatory pattern also existed in the conflict behavior of states towards specific others in 1950 (appendix I: 1.2), 1955 (appendix I: 1.4; Rummel, 1965; Hall and Rummel, 1970), in three-month periods of 1963 (Phillips, 1969), and in 1967 (appendix I: 2.3).

However, in the analysis of 24 types of conflict behavior of 305 dyads for 1965 no preparatory pattern emerges: it combines with a pattern of violence (appendix I: 1.2). Moreover, when common factor analysis is done on 16 variables for 1955 (for apparently 341 dyads), only two distinct patterns emerge: military violence and negative communications. Finally, a warning and defensive actions variable was included in the analysis of conflict for 1950, 1955, 1960, 1963, and 1965. Its communality tended to be relatively low, although in 1955 and 1965 it correlated highly with a violence pattern.

Dynamically, at the dyadic level a preparations pattern (Hall and Rummel, 1970) is stable between 1955 and 1963 (product moment is .89). When dyadic conflict behavior is analyzed by month for 1963 (using super-P analysis), a distinct preparations pattern is found (Phillips, 1969). Such a statistically independent pattern also exists in the dyadic behavior between the United States, USSR, and China for 72 months, 1962-1968 (Phillips and Hainline, n.d.). Finally, super-P analysis of the years 1950-1965 (appendix I: 1.3) showed a warning and defensive action variable to have relatively low correlation with other conflict variables (h^2 = .59; highest loading = .68); in a *common* super-P, factor analysis of the same data, its variance in common with the other conflict behavior was shown (Omen, 1975) to be quite low (h^2 = .27).

In sum, and including those studies not mentioned above, there are 50 analyses bearing on the Uncertainty Proposition. These are classified by category in Table 15A.5. (for discussion of this method of classification, see appendix 16C), located near the end of the appendix. Twenty-one of these studies are direct and strongly positive; six of them are from important studies; 12 are my own analyses. An additional 22 analyses support the proposition, 19 of which are direct, 10 important, and three my own. Only five analyses are at all negative—two strongly so.

Conclusion: In those studies including a number of preparations-type conflict behavior variables an empirical, statistically independent pattern of short-run preparations was found to exist in all but one study, regardless of level and whether static or dynamic. Moreover, 86% of the evidence supports the proposition (almost half of this strongly so). Therefore, it appears safe to conclude that: *the evidence strongly supports the proposition.*

Proposition 15.2 (Conflict-Paths): Coercion and noncoercion are independent conflict paths.

Conflict Behavior manifests different coercive versus noncoercive paths in the balancing of powers.

Theory: The balancing of powers includes coercion (which is the path to force), bargaining power, and intellectual power, as manifested in their means: threats or deprivations, promises, and persuasion. Fundamentally, therefore, we can divide the process of conflict along two tracks: coercion (and force) and noncoercion.

This does not mean that Conflict Behavior moves exclusively along one path or the other. Rather, these are two time-components of such behavior. For example, a person can both work at a career (such as journalism or the military) while getting a degree in law. These would be two separate paths underlying and explaining the complex of the person's day-by-day behavior. But they are divergent paths, not leading necessarily to the same goal. As an example of convergent paths, I both teach and do research. Each is a separable path of behavior, but each for me is a convergent process towards a better understanding of my subject. Similarly, in a violent conflict between states, as in the Vietnam or Korean Wars, along with the threats negative actions, and violence, also may occur offers of aid, attempts at persuasion, and tacit bargaining: convergent paths in the balancing of powers. See section 12.4 for a discussion of the noncoercive path.

Prediction: Two separate, empirical patterns of static and dynamic Conflict Behavior should exist, regardless of level. One should be predominantly of coercive (and forceful) conflict behavior; the other of noncoercive, cooperative behavior.[2]

This cooperative, noncoercive, behavior is part of the *balancing* of powers, and therefore manifested through particular cooperative *events,* such as a promise, offer, compliment, explanation, assurance; or aid, support, help, assistance. Such behavior is different from that constituting accommodations and negotiations, such as signing agreements, which are the end—the accommodations—subphase of the noncoercive path. Moreover, such cooperative events are different from familistic and contractual *flows* and *structures,* such as the flow of mail, trade, tourists, or comembership in intergovernmental international organizations.

Therefore, the noncoercive path in the balancing of power should be manifested by a pattern of primarily exchange and intellectual type of behavior, distinct from accommodative-negotiative behavior and familistic-contractual flows and structures (see appendix II, section II.1).

Moreover, we should find little correlation between coercive behavior and force on the one hand, and cooperative balancing on the other.

Evidence: There is a terminological problem here that may create confusion in surveying the evidence, and which I anticipated in section 4.6. Most of the literature (including my own studies) label coercion and force as conflict *behavior,* and noncoercion within a conflict as *cooperation.* We thus have the set of conflict behaviors constituting the balancing of power, with the subsets of conflict behavior and cooperation. Surely, this is confusing.

Therefore, in presenting the evidence I will continue to use the following translation rules. The term "Conflict Behavior" will refer to the balancing of powers, encompassing both what the sources call conflict and cooperation (events); "conflict behavior" will refer to coercion and force, as it usually does in the literature. Now, for the relevant sources of evidence for Proposition 15.2, see Table 15A.2.

For 16 international conflicts involving violence or its threat, Fitzsimmons (1969) found one-third of the events to be cooperative, a number of which are conciliatory in the abatement stages of a conflict. In the beginning, duration (of violence), and abatement stages of conflict, two of three correlations between violence variables and conciliatory acts are nonsignificant.

Burrowes and Garriga-Pico (1974) did a variety of factor analyses of 4,500 events for 63 two-week periods in the Middle East, 1965-1967. They found an Arab conflict behavior pattern, three separate Israel-Arab conflict behavior patterns, and three distinct, Arab cooperative patterns. They also (using O-factor analysis) determined distinct periods of Middle East conflict, and then did an analysis within each, finding again separate cooperation patterns.

Still at the case level, Väyrynen's (1973) super-P component analysis of East-West conflict, 1948-1968, found a cold war pattern, a global violence pattern, and a separate US-USSR cooperative behavior pattern (involving also flows and structures).

Moving now to the state-level, Burrowes and Spector (1973) analyzed a variety of Syrian behavior over 74 four-week periods (1961-1967) and found that Syria's foreign conflict behaviors have higher intercorrelations than with cooperative behavior. Moreover, a component analysis of Syria's foreign behavior showed conflict and cooperative (event) behavior to be statistically independent.

The WEIS coding approach to event data involves both cooperative and conflict behavior and has been much used (see appendix II, section II.2). McClelland and Hoggard (1969) found one-third of foreign events (WEIS) data to be cooperative for 83 states in 1966. Component analysis revealed a separate, statistically independent cooperation pattern among 47 types of Conflict Behavior. Similar log transformed (WEIS) data for 73 nations, 1966-1969, showed a distinct cooperative pattern to exist, regardless of how the data was aggregated (Salmore and Munton, 1974). Moreover, when differently collected or aggregated data sets are analyzed, cooperation still emerges (Salmore, et al, 1974). Moore (1970) also found for 40 months, 1966-1969, for 86 nations, a distinct cooperation pattern. However, it also had some conflict behavior (deny, warn, and reduce relationship) correlated with it. Finally Kegley, et al (1974) factor analyzed WEIS coded CREON data (see appendix II, section II.2) and found a statistically independent negotiations pattern, with cooperation behavior also highly correlated with it.

For 14,500 acts of 32 black African states, 1964-1966, cooperative events comprise 35% of their behavior (McGowan, 1973). Moreover, cooperation forms two distinct patterns (accept; increase relationship) and is independent of nonmilitary and diplomatic conflict patterns. However, there is a mixture of reward behavior with force and subversion, and participatory with conflict behavior. In no case do conflict and cooperative behavior appear negatively correlated.

I am aware of only one state-level, dynamic study (Wilkenfeld, 1977). A super-P component analysis over the years 1966-1970 shows a clear cooperation pattern (with a few correlated conflict behaviors) in the behavior of 56 states. However, the Conflict Behavior received by states involves a large, mixed conflict-cooperation pattern (accounting for 58% of the variance) and a separate yield and reward pattern. These results for received Conflict Behavior are ambiguous, and may be due to an insufficient number of factors being extracted from the data.

At the dyadic level, separate positive communications and bargaining, cooperative patterns exist for 182 state-dyads in 1967 (appendix I: 2.3). Moreover, for these dyads conflict behavior has little ability to predict cooperative behavior (canonical analysis, trace correlation squared is .10; highest-squared canonical correlation is .18).

As tabulated in Table 15A.5, there are in total nine strongly positive, four positive, and four ambiguous analyses, all of which are direct. There are no unambiguous negative results. Of the important studies, two are strongly positively, two positive and two ambiguous.

Conclusion: No unqualified negative results appear. In McGowan (1973) a combined cooperative-conflict pattern appears, but so do purely cooperative patterns; in Moore (1970) some conflict behavior and cooperation are intercorrelated, but this is within a dominant cooperation pattern, and in Kegley, *et al.* (1974) negotiation and cooperation go together, but independently of conflict behavior.[3] And in Wilkenfeld (1977) a combined conflict-cooperative pattern was found in received behavior, but this balanced by cooperation being a distinct pattern in sent behavior. In any case, when cooperation and conflict behavior are correlated, it is usually in a *positive* direction, as should be expected if they are part of a conflict process.

These ambiguous results should be compared to the nine different sources of unambiguous, positive evidence for the existence of a clear and distinct cooperative pattern. The conclusion follows: *the evidence strongly supports the proposition.*

Proposition 15.3 (Conflict Subphasing): Conflict behavior manifests different subphases.

Conflict patterns manifest separate status-quo testing, nonviolent coercion, violent coercion, force, and accommodations subphases in the process of balancing powers.

Theory: The balancing of powers involves two paths and a number of phases initiated by status-quo testing, as described in chapters 12 and 13. The noncoercive path leads to accommodation, while the coercive one has a number of phases:[4] nonviolent coercion (negative actions and sanctions, negative communications), coercive violence (the use of violence to coerce the other party into concessions and settlement), and force (the effort to overcome the other party).

No one necessarily follows another and, indeed, the process may return to previous phases (e.g. force may deescalate to coercion). Moreover, accommodations may follow from any nonforce phase. Accordingly, the separate phases should be manifest in separate patterns of conflict behavior.

Predictions: Separate, empirical patterns of conflict behavior exist, discernable as status-quo testing, nonviolent coercion, violent coercion, force, and accommodations.

Evidence: Assessing the evidence presents problems. No study has used data coded specifically to test the proposition. We can, however, locate relevant studies with results bearing on the proposition, but their results require interpretation. Moreover, the studies differ in whether they include data which would allow a specific pattern to emerge. It is no negative result to find a pattern missing when the appropriate variables are omitted.

Another problem is that at the level conflict events are usually coded, the same event may be a manifestation of different phases, as for example, a threat may reflect status-quo testing and nonviolent or violent coercion; military action may mirror status-quo testing, coercion, or force. Escalation to more intense conflict behavior does not mean a termination of actions at a lower level. Nonviolent negative actions may continue even after escalation to coercive violence.

What makes the proposition empirically tractable, however, is that each phase is reflected in a deescalation of some kind of coded-conflict events and escalation of some other kinds, as shown in Table 15A.3. Probing and testing behavior should be most intense during the status-quo testing period, and although there will be testing in other phases, it will be dominated by other forms of behavior.

Negative communications may reflect some status-quo testing (as in probing with a verbal threat to test a new leader), but should be intense in the nonviolent coercion and

TABLE 15A.3: **Conflict Subphases and Conflict Events**

CODED EVENTS	STATUS-QUO TESTING	NONVIOLENT COERCION	VIOLENT COERCION	FORCE
probing; testing	escalation	decrease	decrease	none
threats; warnings; protests; accusations	some	escalation	escalation	decrease
nonviolent negative actions and sanctions	some	escalation	continuation	decrease
clashes; discrete military action; low intensity violence; few killed	some	none	escalation	escalation
intense military violence, many killed	none	none	some	escalation

even more in the violent coercion phase, when such communications are essential to conveying the threat and desired response. But when force is used, the aim is to overcome and there is less concern with reaching the mind of the other. Thus, negative communication should decrease.

For negative actions and sanctions, such as severance of diplomatic relations, boycotts and embargoes, they may be used in testing, but should be the primary behavior during the nonviolent coercive stage, and continue as the emphasis shifts to violence.

Low-level military action, such as clashes and discrete military action (e.g., shooting down another's aircraft) will usually reflect military coercion, although it may also sometimes simply be a testing operation. Coercion may also be manifested in extreme violence (as in the Vietnam war), but force will always be reflected by intense violence.

Considering then that these different kinds of behavior will serve different functions and correlate differently in different phases of conflict, we then should expect—if indeed these are actually phases—that five empirical patterns of conflict behavior should be found: testing, negative communications, negative actions and sanctions, low-level violence, and intense violence.

Moreover, there should also occur a separate accommodations pattern involving negotiations, concessions, yielding, agreements, and the like.[5]

To best organize the evidence, Table 15A.4 presents most sources of static or dynamic results by level. A number of elements are involved in the assessments shown: number and types of variables, factor-patterns, communalities,[6] and factor techniques. The right most column gives the rating shown for the analyses in Table 15A.2.

Different social scientists probably would evaluate the evidence differently in a number of cases. Overall, I have attempted to be conservative, and therefore trust that others would *on balance* arrive at the same conclusions, although perhaps even with more conviction.

Overall, looking at the totals in Table 15A.5, there are forty relevant analyses, of which ten are strongly positive (eight are direct and four from important studies). There are five negative analyses, two strongly so.

Conclusion: The most rigorous test of the proposition is whether all possible patterns emerged in the different studies, which it did in 38% of those listed in Table 15A.4. The majority of negative results were due to violence forming a single pattern in most of the

TABLE 15A.4: Breakdown of Evidence for Conflict Phases and Subphases

Level[a]	Source[b]	Sub-Study[c]	1	2	3	4	5	6	Evaluation[e]
Case-static	Fitzsimmons (1969)		Yes	Yes	X	X	Yes	X	P[f]
	Phillips & Hainline (1972)		No	No	X	Yes	X	X	A
Case-dynamic	Phillips & Lorimore (n.d.)	precrisis	Yes	Yes	X	Yes	X	X	P
	Phillips & Lorimore (n.d.)	Crisis	Yes	Yes	X	Yes	X	X	SP } SP
	Phillips & Lorimore (n.d.)	postcrisis	Yes	Yes	X	Yes	X	X	SP
	Leng & Goodsell (1974)		Yes	Yes	X	X	X	X	P
State-static	Oliva & Rummel (1969)		Yes	Yes	A	Yes	X	X	SP
	Keim & Rummel (1969)	1955	Yes	Yes	Yes	Yes	X	X	SP } A
	Keim & Rummel (1969)	1963	No	No	Yes	No	X	X	N
	Rummel (1963)		No	No	No	Yes	X	X	N
	Tanter (1966)		No	Yes	No	No	X	X	SN
	Rummel (1967a)		Yes	Yes	No	No	Yes	X	SP
	McClelland & Hoggard (1969)		No	No	X	Yes	Yes	X	A } A
	McClelland & Ancoli (1970)	ME	No	Yes	X	No	Yes	X	P
	McClelland & Ancoli (1970)	World	Yes	Yes	A	Yes	No	X	SP } P
	Phillips (1973)	sent	No	Yes	No	Yes	X	X	A
	Phillips (1973)	received	No	No	No	Yes	X	X	N
	Hazelwood (1973)		No	No	X	Yes	Yes	X	A
	Kegley, et al (1974)		No	No	X	No	X	X	SN
	Burrowes & Spector (1973)		No	No	X	Yes	Yes	X	A } P
	Salmore, et al (1974)	WEIS	Yes	Yes	X	X	Yes	X	SP
	Salmore, et al (1974)	SAS	Yes	Yes	X	Yes	Yes	X	SP
	Salmore & Munton (1974)	g	No	Yes	X	No	Yes	X	P
State-dynamic	Phillips (1970)	sent	No	Yes	No	Yes	X	X	P } P
	Phillips (1970)	received	No	Yes	No	Yes	X	X	P
	(appendix I: 1.6)		No	Yes	Yes	No	X	X	P

EVIDENCE[d]

TABLE 15A.4: **Breakdown of Evidence for Conflict Phases and Subphases (Cont)**

Level[a]	Source[b]	Sub-Study[c]	EVIDENCE[d] 1	2	3	4	5	6	Evaluation[e]
Dyad-Static	Rummel (1965)		No	Yes	No	Yes	X	X	P
	Hall & Rummel (1970)	1963	Yes	Yes	Yes	Yes	X	X	SP ⎫
	Hall & Rummel (1970)	1955	Yes	Yes	Yes	Yes	X	X	SP ⎬ SP
	McGowan (1973)		A	X	X	Yes	Yes	X	P
	(appendix I: 1.1)	1950	No	Yes	No	Yes	X	X	P
	(appendix I: 1.3)	1955	No	Yes	No	No	X	X	P
	(appendix I: 1.3)	1960	No	Yes	Yes	No	X	X	N
	(appendix I: 1.3)	1963	No	Yes	No	Yes	X	X	P ⎫
	(appendix I: 1.3)	1965	No	Yes	No	No	X	X	P ⎬ P
	(appendix I: 1.4)		No	No	X	Yes	X	X	A
	(appendix I: 1.5)	g	No	Yes	Yes	No	X	X	P
	(appendix I: 2.3)	23DON	No	No	No	No	X	X	SN ⎫
	(appendix I: 2.3)	12 WEIS	Yes	Yes	X	Yes	X	X	SP ⎬ A
	(appendix I: 1.2)	1950	No	Yes	Yes	No	X	X	SP
	(appendix I: 1.2)	1955	No	Yes	No	Yes	X	X	P
	(appendix I: 1.2)	1960	Yes	Yes	No	Yes	X	X	P ⎫
	(appendix I: 1.2)	1963	No	Yes	No	Yes	X	X	SP ⎬ P
	(appendix I: 1.2)	1965	No	Yes	No	Yes	X	X	P
Dyad-Dynamic	Phillips (1969)	g	No	Yes	No	Yes	X	X	P
	Park & Ross (1971)	A to A	No	Yes	No	Yes	X	X	P
	Park & Ross (1971)	N to A	Yes	Yes	Yes	Yes	X	X	SP ⎫
	Park & Ross (1971)	A to N	Yes	Yes	Yes	Yes	X	X	SP ⎬ SP
	Wilkenfeld, et al (1972)		No	Yes	X	No	X	X	A
	Phillips & Hainline (n.d.)		Yes	Yes	X	Yes	X	X	SP
	(appendix I: 1.3)		Yes	Yes	Yes	Yes	X	X	SP

TABLE 15A.4: Breakdown of Evidence for Conflict Phases and Subphases (Cont)

Level[a]	Source[b] $\dfrac{\text{Yes}}{\text{No. of Studies}}$ (in percent)	Sub-Study[c]	EVIDENCE[d]						Evaluation[e]
			1	2	3	4	5	6	
System	None								
			38	81	41	72	100	X	72
					$\dfrac{\text{SP} + \text{S}}{\text{No. of Studies}}$ (in percent)				

a, b, See notes, Table 15A.2.

c. A source may have more than one analysis. Each substudy is identified by a study-specific characteristic, such as the data-year, number of variables, or number of cases.

d. The numbered columns define six kinds of results, as follows:

No.   Result

1. Possible and appropriate patterns are delineated.
2. Violence and nonviolence are separate patterns.
3. Violence separates into high (intense) and low-level patterns.
4. Nonviolence separates into negative communications and negative action/sanction patterns.
5. Accommodations is a separate pattern.
6. Testing is a pattern.

With regard to these possible results, the analyses are coded

Yes, No, A = ambiguous, X = irrelevant.

e. Evaluation involves an overall assessment of whether the source is positive, ambiguous, or negative on the proposition. SP = strong-positive; P = positive; A = ambiguous; N = negative; SN = strong-negative.

f. Table 17 with the factor analysis results was missing from my copy, and was therefore reconstructed from the discussion. Were it not for this problem in interpretation, I would consider the results strongly positive.

g. The evaluation is a synthesis of diverse analyses.

[233]

studies in which it could have divided into the stipulated high and low patterns. Otherwise, the results would usually support the proposition.

Considering, then, the above and the overall analyses tabulated in Table 15A.2, 67% were at least positive and 13% negative, the conclusion is that *the evidence supports the propositon.*

One final note to provide statistical perspective. The evidence results from diverse factor analyses of usually a dozen or so types of conflict behaviors. There is nothing in the method to force out of the data artificial patterns even dimly approximating those postulated. In one study of two dozen types of conflict variables the probability of getting by chance even *one* of the expected patterns for 50 cases, states, or dyads is surely over a trillion to one (the one-tailed probability of just one *correlation* over .44 between two variables for 50 cases in over 2,000 to one.) Then to find two expected patterns in most of the studies and all in about one-third, surely can only be explained by some underlying, substantive factors—such as the theoretical subphases in the balancing of power.

Proposition 15.4 (Hostility): Hostility reflects latent and manifest conflict.

Manifest hostility reflects the situation of conflict, uncertainty, and the balancing of powers.

Theory: International conflict usually engenders animosity, enmity, antagonism. While leaders themselves can be cool and calculating, racial and religious hatreds, cultural animosities, invidious propaganda, and ideological-nationalistic fervor, may create a naked, mass hostility against the "enemy."

Such hostility is not necessarily correlated with any phase of conflict, and may even occur in the situation of conflict, before leaders act overtly.

This hostility is a psychological variable, a strong emotional mix of hatred, anger, and self-righteousness. It may be manifested against another state in many ways: mass demonstrations, private boycotts (e.g., refusal to load the other's ships or buy their products), harassing their nationals, destruction of their property, attacks on their embassy, assassinations, bombings, and the like.

Prediction: Because hostility may be manifest at any phase or subphase in the conflict process, hostile acts—"antiforeign behavior"—will form an empirical pattern uncorrelated with other empirical conflict patterns.

Evidence: Table 15A.2 presents the sources of evidence.

At the case level, Phillips and Hainline's (1972 component analysis of 21 crises showed antiforeign behavior involved in separate patterns with protests and with severance of diplomatic relations. This is a clear negative result.

When the stages of 47 crises are component analyzed, Phillips and Lorimore (n.d.) found antiforeign behavior mixed with expelling and recalling ambassadors in the precrisis period, mixed with severance of diplomatic relations during the crisis period, and a purely separate pattern in the postcrisis. These are ambiguous results.

At the state level, I found (1967) a clear antiforeign behavior pattern for 26 conflict variables for 82 states in 1955. But for the same year and 13 variables, Keim and Rummel (1967) delineated antiforeign behaviors mixed with the incidence of violence, although for 1963 a separate and clear antiforeign pattern was found. For 1963 also, 24 conflicting variables, and all states, Oliva and Rummel (1969) found that same uncorrelated pattern; Phillips (1973) also uncovered the same pattern in behavior *sent* by states, but for *received* behavior antiforeign behavior was mixed with negative communications.

Some dynamic, state-level evidence is also available. Phillips' (1970) super-P component analysis of 12 months in 1963 for 65 states showed a clear antiforeign pattern in both sent and received conflict behavior. A similar analysis of 13 months, 1976-1977, also identified the same separate patterns (appendix I: 1.6).

Moving now to the dyadic level, a separate antiforeign behavior pattern appears for all dyads manifesting conflict for four of the five different years analyzed (appendix I: 1.2) and for all years in a more refined data analysis (appendix I: 1.3). This pattern also was delineated by different studies for 340 dyads in 1955 (Rummel, 1967), 289 dyads in 1960 (appendix I: 1.1), 275 dyads in 1963 (Hall and Rummel, 1970), and 183 dyads for 1967 (appendix I: 2.3). For common factor analyses (appendix I: 1.5) of 16 conflict variables, 1955 data, antiforeign behavior was unique—uncorrelated with common patterns of conflict behavior.

Finally, some dynamic evidence is available. A super-P component analysis of the years 1950-1965 delineated separate antiforeign patterns (appendix I: 1.3), which became unique in a similar *common* factor analysis (Omen, 1975). Phillips' (1969) super-P analysis of 12 months in 1963 for 267 dyads delineated an uncorrelated antiforeign pattern. Such a pattern was also found by Park and Ross (1971) for Asian dyadic monthly conflict behavior, 1962-1968; and for separate analysis of foreign behavior was shown to be uncorrelated with other patterns. And a similar analysis (Phillips and Hainline, n.d.) of 72 months of the dyadic behavior between China, USSR and the United States also brought out a separate antiforeign pattern.

Overall, as shown in Table 15A.5, of the 24 analyses bearing on the proposition, most (16) are strongly positive and direct (four are from important studies). There are three negative analyses, two strongly so.

Conclusion: The evidence strongly supports the proposition. Even the negative findings lend support: there is no pattern across studies to the correlation between antiforeign behavior and the other conflict patterns. The few correlations that did occur involved warning and defensive actions (appendix I; 1.4; Rummel, 1965), negative communications (Phillips, 1973), violence (Keim and Rummel, 1967), and negative actions (Phillips and Hainline, 1972; Phillips and Lorimore, n.d.).

Proposition 15.5 (Reciprocity): Conflict Behavior is reciprocal.

Negative communications, negative actions and sanctions, and violence, are reciprocated.

Theory: Structures of expectations enable mutually reliable predictions between two actors. When this structure is disrupted it involves both actors; both are then parties to the balancing which establishes new expectations. Much of their confrontation will then involve an action-reaction process: coercion will be met with coercion, violence with violence. Moreover, by definition accommodative (negotiating) behavior will involve the opposing parties.

However, preparations may not be met with opposing preparations (the other side may try appeasement or simply be unaware of such activities), status-quo testing may not be met by opposing behavior—actually, no response may result. Moreover, while violence may be met by violence, one side may be applying force, the other coercive violence.

Nonetheless, certain types of conflict behavior which reflect different phases of conflict (as shown in Table 15A.3) should be reciprocal. These are negative communications, negative actions/sanctions, low-level violence, and high-level violence.

The behavior of the parties to a conflict may be momentarily out of alignment as one side moves to escalate or deescalate the confrontation, but this should soon be met by an adjustment by the other side, and an action-reaction, lock-in at a new or prior phase will occur.[7]

Prediction: Empirical patterns of negative communications, negative actions/sanctions, low-level violence, and high-level violence will be reciprocal. That is, each party tends to manifest behaviors similarly during the same period.

Evidence: Table 15A.2 presents the sources of evidence. The nature of the evidence can be illustrated by selecting a few of the analyses. At the case level, McClelland (1965) did a super-P factor analysis of the Taiwan Strait crises during 1950-1964. He found a high reciprocity in behavior, although the study does not make clear how this breaks out along the patterns. In the 12 days of the Sino-Indian Conflict in 1962, Field (1972) found a high correlation between the actions on each side.

For states, Phillips (1970) compared the canonical correlations between their sent and received conflict behavior to the (1) canonical correlations of present and past received, and (2) present and past sent. Not only was the canonical correlation of sent and received behavior high ($r = .80$), it was much higher than for the prediction of present from past behavior.

In a similar study, Phillips (1973) did a canonical analysis of sent and received behavioral patterns and found that military violence sent best linked to military violence received ($r = .98$); negative communications and actions/sanctions to negative communications ($r = .94$); negative communications minus negative actions/sanctions to negative sanctions ($r = .74$) and warning and defensive actions to warning and defensive ($r = .35$).

For dyads, Wilkenfeld, et al. (1972) found that over 217 months, the best predictor of the conflict behavior of a Middle East state was the conflict received. Also dealing with the Middle East, and the United States and USSR in addition, Azar (1975) found a state's past behavior and that received from the other jointly predict its behavior (89% fit between observed and predicted). In a more comprehensive and detailed study of 12 dyads, Azar, et al. (1974), showed that past behavior accounts for only about 25% of the variance and that behavior received is the best predictor (but the most effective model includes both an actor's past behavior and that received from the other).

Finally, in Phillips and Hainline's (n.d.) canonical time-series analyses of conflict behavior between the major powers, they found that an object's behavior explained more of the actor's behavior to it than did the actor's past behavior; and that the mutual behavior of actor and object in the same month tended to be similar.

In sum, considering the twenty-nine analyses rated in Table 15A.2 in regard to the proposition and totaled in Table 15A.5, most are strongly positive and direct (12). Five of seven important studies are strongly positive. There are four negative analyses.

Conclusion: Considering that 48% of the evidence is strongly positive and 86% at least positive, then I argue: *the evidence strongly supports the proposition.*

Proposition 15.6 (Crisis): Crises are distinct behavior patterns signalling escalation.

The threat of imminent escalation in a subphase is manifested through an intensification and diversification of Conflict Behavior.

Theory: A coercive phase in the balancing of powers is a behavioral lock-in by the parties. As the parties perceive that escalation is likely, they will intensify current behavior in the hopes of avoiding escalation and to signal its imminent possibility. Moreover, behavior will become more diverse. Warning and preparatory actions (troop movements, alerts, and the like) may be involved, as well as attempts at bargaining in order to avoid escalation. The imminence of the escalation also means that time is short, decisions must be made soon, and this will also tend to increase the tempo of activities.

Crises may occur in any phase; it involves a threatened escalation to a next and higher phase. Thus, a crisis may occur in a situation of conflict, threatening an outbreak of overt conflict; in the situation of uncertainty, threatening violence; or in the coercive violence subphase, threatening force. *In other words, crisis is a behavior pattern separate and distinct from the phases and subphases conflict.*

Predictions: A crisis period during a conflict phase will manifest intensified (volume) and more diverse behavior. In studies employing crises variables, crises should be delimited as a distinct behavioral pattern.

Evidence: Table 15A.2 presents the evidence. Generally, studies of crises have not subdivided conflict into the theoretical phases posed here and isolated the crises within each. Such studies have been of imminent threats of violence. Nonetheless, they usually provide direct evidence on the proposition.

Again, some of the analyses will be selected to illustrate the evidence.

To begin with the case level, in the Bendix analysis ("United . . . ; 1968) of conflict, 1945-1966, no crises pattern was found for 52 conflict variables and 351 conflicts. But many of these conflicts were riots, bloodless coups, international incidents, and the like. When only conflicts involving more than 99 killed were analyzed, a separate crises pattern of behavior emerged. Phillips and Hainline's (1972) component analysis of 21 crises found seven components, more than usually found for conflicts and thus indicating greater diversity. Moreover, for all except the first, the variance accounted for is fairly level across the components, again suggesting diverse behavior.

At the dynamic-case level, McClelland (1965) showed an increase in positive acts during the Taiwan Straits crises. McClelland and Hoggard (1969) also found an increase in conflict behavior in the Berlin and Taiwan crises; and McClelland's (1972) study shows that the change from noncrisis to crisis is in a greater variety of behavior. Azar's (1972) analysis of the 1956 Suez conflict showed that the crisis involved an increase in reciprocity and an increase in behavior ("events") above a normal range. Finally, Phillips and Lorimore's (n.d.)

TABLE 15A.5: Evidence: Subtotals and Totals

Category	Rating	PROPOSITIONS[a]						Total	%[b]	ONE-LEVEL DECREMENT[c]	
		1	2	3	4	5	6			Total	%[b]
Overall	SP	21	9	10	16	14	8	78	45 80	0	0 45
	P	22	4	17	2	11	5	61	35	78	45
	A	2	4	8	3			17	10	61	35
	N	3		3	1	4		11	6 9	17	10 19
	SN	2		2	2			6	3	17	9
Direct	SP	21	9	8	16	12	8	74	46 79	0	0 46
	P	19	4	17	1	11	2	54	33	74	46
	A	2	4	8	3			17	10	54	33
	N	3		3	1	4		11	7 11	17	10 21
	SN	2		2	2			6	4	17	11
Important	SP	6	2	4	4	5	3	24	40 82	0	0 40
	P	10	2	8	2	2	1	25	42	24	40
	A	2	2	1	1			6	10	25	42
	N	2				1		3	5 8	6	10 18
	SN	1			1			2	3	5	8
Rummel Studies	SP	12	2	3	11			28	56 77	0	0 56
	P	3		6	1			10	21	28	56
	A	1		3	1			5	10	10	21
	N			1	1			2	4 10	5	11 21
	SN	1		1	1			3	6	5	10

a. Blanks = 0
b. All percentages are rounded off and therefore may not sum to 100%
c. All ratings reduced one level to compensate for hypothetical bias

TABLE 15A.6: Summary of Conclusions on the Phasing Propositions

| PROPOSITIONS | | CONCLUSIONS ABOUT THE EVIDENCE[a] | | |
Name	No.	Strongly Supportive	Supportive	Ambiguous Negative Strongly Negative
Uncertainty	15.1	Yes		
Conflict Paths	15.2	Yes		
Conflict Subphasing	15.3		Yes	
Hostility	15.4	Yes		
Reciprocity	15.5	Yes		
Crises	15.6	Yes		
Totals		5	1	0

a. Yes = evidence unanimous

study of precrisis, crisis, and postcrisis periods found that crises involve more conflict patterns and more diverse behavior (they could use 22 conflict behavior/variables to analyze a crises, but only 15 for precrises and 16 for postcrises).

In total, there are 13 relevant crises analyses, as totaled in Table 15A.5, of which six are direct and strongly supportive, and three of these are from important studies. There are no ambiguous or negative analyses.

Conclusion: The evidence strongly and unanimously supports the proposition.

15A.2. OVERALL CONCLUSION

The evidence is totaled for all propositions in Table 15A.5. Appendix 16C explains the categories in the Table and the use of the one-level decrement to assess the effect of possible coding bias.

As can be seen, regardless of category, the totals come out clearly the same across the six phasing propositions. This indicates that the conclusions are independent of the directness of an analysis, importance of a study, or whether I did the analyses or not. Moreover, even when the one-level decrement is applied, the results are still favorable by more than 2 to 1.

Of course, the totals in Table 15A.5 are only a rough guide. Qualitative considerations also bear on the assessment, and these were taken into account in assessing each proposition. Table 15A.6 presents the quantitative-qualitative judgment on each proposition. As can be seen, when judged individually, the propositions are with one exception strongly supported.

One aspect of the results should be noted. The balancing of powers is a dynamic process involving several subphases. It is therefore interesting and important to note in Table 15A.2 that out of 47 relevant *dynamic* conflict analyses, only six were negative.

On balance, then, the evidence supports all the propositions. *And by virtue of the propositions being theoretically imbedded in the field perspective the evidence supports this view of international conflict as well.*

NOTES

1. "Conflict Behavior" refers to that behavior involved in the balancing of power; "conflict behavior" refers to that Conflict Behavior which is antagonistic. See section 4.6,

2. Herein lies a source of terminological confusion. Cooperation and conflict are commonly seen as either opposed, or at least separate. It therefore seems nonsensical to talk of cooperative conflictful behavior (i.e., the noncoercive path). In the section on evidence I will try to straighten out this terminology. See also section 4.6.

3. Unlike the coercive-force path, cooperation leads to accommodation. Force, however, may simply lead to a termination of the conflict without accommodations, such as the total victory of the Allies in World War II.

4. These are subphases in the balancing of power phase of the conflict helix. However, because the focus is on the dynamics of the balancing, I will simply refer to them as phases, leaving the "sub" understood.

5. A review of chapter 12, especially of Figure 12.1 should be helpful at this point.

6. This refers to h_j. Even if a statistically independent pattern of, say, negative actions does not emerge, low communalities for the variable(s) indicate that negative actions/sanctions is separate from the other patterns.

7. Note especially that preparations, such as increasing armaments, is excluded from this action-reaction process.

Chapter 16

CAUSES AND CONDITIONS OF INTERNATIONAL CONFLICT AND WAR

> *War arises because of the changing relations of numerous variables—technological, psychic, social, and intellectual. There is no single cause of war. Peace is an equilibrium among many forces. Change in any particular force, trend, movement, or policy may at one time make for war, but under other conditions a similar change may make for peace. A state may at one time promote peace by armament, at another time by disarmament; at one time by insistence on its rights, at another time by a spirit conciliation. To estimate the probability of war at any time involves, therefore, an appraisal of the effect of current changes upon the complex of intergroup relationships throughout the world.*
> *Wright, 1965: 1284*

16.1 THE CAUSES AND CONDITIONS

What causes war? Why international violence? International Conflict? The answers are specific.

International Conflict Behavior is *caused* by:

- opposing interests and capabilities (specific sociocultural differences and similarities between the parties),
- contact and salience (awareness),
- significant change in the balance of powers,
- individual perceptions and expectations,
- a disrupted structure of expectations,
- a will-to-conflict.

It is *aggravated* by:

- sociocultural dissimilarity,
- cognitive imbalance,
- status difference,
- coercive state power,

It is *inhibited* by:

- sociocultural similarity,
- decentralized or weak, coercive state power.

It is *triggered* by:

- perception of opportunity, threat, or injustice,
- surprise.

Such are the *general* causes and conditions of international Conflict Behavior whether nonviolent conflict behavior, violence, or war. But, as pointed out in the previous Chapter, Conflict Behavior manifests a series of subphases in the balancing of powers. Each subphase involves different kinds of behavior. What, then, uniquely characterizes each subphase *within* the above framework of general causes and conditions.

In addition to the general causes of Conflict Behavior, *nonviolent Conflict Behavior and low-level violence,* are *aggravated* by:

- cross-pressures.

They are *inhibited* by:

- system polarity (centralization of coercive power),
- a stable status quo.

In addition to the general causes of Conflict Behavior, violence (including war) is caused by:

- authoritarian and totalitarian states,
- status-quo disruption,
- confidence in success.

It is *aggravated* by:

- system polarity (centralization of coercive power),
- Big Power intervention,
- weakness of the status-quo Power,
- credibility at stake,
- honor at stake.

It is *inhibited* by:

- cross-pressures,
- internal freedom,
- strength of the status-quo Power,
- world opinion.

War is a particular type of intense violence and what generally causes, aggravates, and inhibits violence so affects war. In addition, war is uniquely *aggravated* by:

- power parity,
- class conflict.

It is *inhibited* by:

- power disparity.

This list immediately raises a number of questions: How are cause and condition defined? What is the theoretical foundation for the list? What do the particular causes and conditions mean, such as power parity or class conflict? What is the evidence?

These are central questions, and must be answered. To best organize the relevant technical material and answers, three appendices have been prepared. Appendix 16.A defines cause and conditions and considers their particular use here. Appendix 16B presents 33 propositions stating the specific framework for understanding each cause or condition, the theoretical basis, prediction, and evidence. Appendix 16C provides methodological detail and the sources for evaluating the evidence used in appendix 16B.

16.2 THE PHASE MAP

A necessity for understanding the causes and conditions of international Conflict Behavior, violence and war is an appreciation that they operate as part of a field. They are field forces, conditions, and states. This means that these causes and conditions are interrelated, part of a whole, a process, and an equilibrium. In other words, they operate *contextually* within the conflict helix, as pictured in Figure 10.1. The whole character of Volumes 1-3, my *Field Theory Evolving* (1977), and the previous chapters of this volume therefore underlie as foundation, analysis, and evidence,[1] the list of causes and conditions.

Against this background and within the social field context, the causes and conditions of antagonistic[2] international conflict behavior are shown in a *phase map* in Figure 16.1. The base of this map pictures the theoretical and empirical supported *phases* of conflict and the *subphases* of conflict behavior discussed in the previous chapter. Therefore, the figure is mapping the flow and process of conflict through time, from past to future, from left to right.

The level between double lines just above the phases, map as horizontal lines *behavior* manifesting a particular phase or subphase of conflict. The *length* of each line is congruent with the phase or subphases the associated behavior reflects. Thus, the line plot for intense military violence shows it to be congruent with a portion of the coercive violence subphase and the whole of the force subphase.

Above these phase plots for behavior, the causes and conditions are then mapped in ascending levels. Each cause or condition is shown as a line congruent to both the phase or subphases *in which it operates* and the conflict behavior *it could produce or influence*. A vertical line drawn anywhere in the phase-map, therefore, will locate:

- the phase or subphase of conflict,
- the types of conflict behavior a phase or subphase manifests,
- the manifest causes and conditions of these behaviors,
- the causes and conditions operating together in any phase or subphase of conflict.

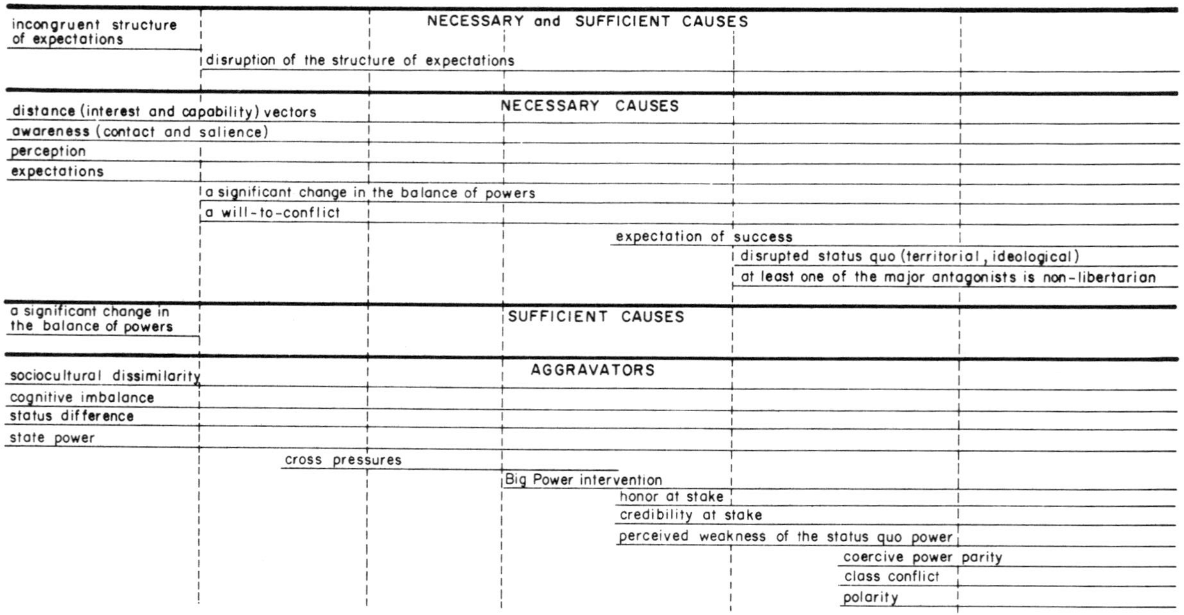

FIGURE 16.1: A Phase Map of Conflict

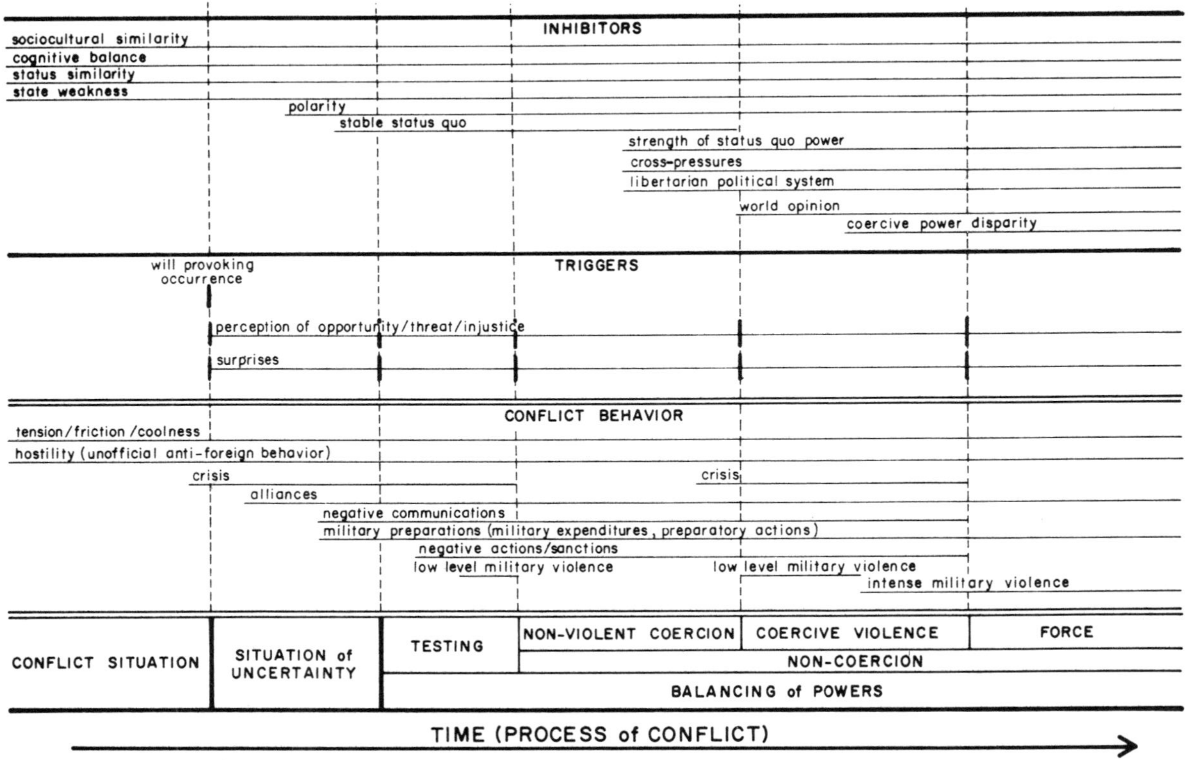

FIGURE 16.1: A Phase Map of Conflict (Cont.)

INHIBITORS

sociocultural similarity
cognitive balance
status similarity
state weakness
polarity
stable status quo
strength of status quo power
cross-pressures
libertarian political system
world opinion
coercive power disparity

TRIGGERS

will provoking occurrence
perception of opportunity/threat/injustice
surprises

CONFLICT BEHAVIOR

tension/friction/coolness
hostility (unofficial anti-foreign behavior)
crisis
alliances
negative communications
military preparations (military expenditures, preparatory actions)
negative actions/sanctions
low level military violence
crisis
low level military violence
intense military violence

CONFLICT SITUATION	SITUATION of UNCERTAINTY	TESTING	NON-VIOLENT COERCION	COERCIVE VIOLENCE	FORCE
				NON-COERCION	
			BALANCING of POWERS		

TIME (PROCESS of CONFLICT)

This phase map is the basic organization (model) for interrelating the causes and conditions of international conflict. [3] And I will now focus on it in brief.[4]

16.3 NECESSARY AND SUFFICIENT CAUSE:
INCONGRUENT AND DISRUPTED EXPECTATIONS

As shown at the top level of the *phase map,* there are two *necessary and sufficient* causes. The first is an *incongruent structure of expectations* which is correlative to the conflict *situation.* [5,6]

A structure of expectations is based on a particular balance of powers between states. The balance may shift in time, however, and aggravated by sociocultural dissimilarity and cognitive imbalance, will produce incongruent expectations. *Without such incongruency* between two states there would be no conflict situation. There would be no mutual antiforeign riots or demonstrations, and tension, friction, and coolness in relations.

When incongruency occurs, such a conflict situation is produced; tension and hostility are generated.[7]

Incongruency is a latent situation of conflict ripe for disruption, for an eruption into manifest confrontation. This disruption divides in time, and thus in the *phase map,* the conflict situation from the situation of uncertainty and the balancing of powers. The *disruption of expectations* is the necessary and sufficient cause of intentional, state Conflict Behavior, whether negative communications, sanctions, or war. *International Conflict Behavior assumes such a disruption has occurred; its occurrence produces Conflict Behavior.*

There are no other jointly necessary and sufficient causes. Incongruency and disruption are thus basic, and have been given considerable theoretical analysis in previous chapters and volumes, especially in terms of the conflict helix: structure of expectations become incongruent with the balance of powers, making disruption likely; disruption generates the balancing of powers, which determines a more realistic, mutually perceived balance of powers; this new balance forms a new, congruent structure of expectations; this structure becomes in time incongruent; and so on.

16.4 NECESSARY CAUSES

A necessary cause of Conflict Behavior is *that without which the conflict behavior would not occur.* There are a number of necessary causes which operate throughout or in various phases and subphases of the conflict process, as shown in the *phase map.*

Considering the necessary cause of Conflict Behavior in general first (these are the lines beginning with the conflict situation or situation of uncertainty and running completely across the *phase map*), one is the *distance vectors* between states in sociocultural space. These mirror the basic opposition between national interests and capabilities—they measure the relative position of states in their meanings, values, norms, status, and class. Opposing interests are necessary to the latent conflict situation and for manifest balancing.[8]

Another necessary cause is mutual awareness, a *contact* between states and mutual *salience*.

In addition, perceptions and expectations specific to each actor (as described in chapter 5) are necessary to its conflict. What the situational content of these might be depends on the actor.[9]

Two necessary causes specifically underlie the disruption of the structure of expectations and the consequent situation of uncertainty and balance of powers. One is a *significant change in the balance of powers*. This is a change in interests, capabilities, or will (credibility) that causes one or both parties to feel that their understandings and agreements, the distribution of rights and benefits, duties and responsibilities—in short the structure of expectations—are wrong, and should and can be altered to their advantage.

The second necessary cause of disruption is a *will-to-conflict*. No Conflict Behavior can occur unless the parties are willing to confront each other.

So far then, for Conflict Behavior to occur between two states there must be a particular combination of sociocultural distances between them (an opposition of their interests and capabilities), mutual awareness (contact and salience), a significant change in their balance of power, disrupted expectations, and a will-to-conflict.

Besides these necessary causes of Conflict Behavior of all kinds, violence uniquely assumes the existence of three additional necessary causes, as shown in the *phase map* (Figure 16.1). One is the *expectation of success*. In their own subjective calculus of gains and losses, each party believes that the outcome of violence will be advantageous.

A second necessary cause of violence is a disrupted *status quo*. The status quo defines for states the ideological and territorial distribution of who has what. It is the core of the structure of expectations. Without a disruption in the status quo the issues are neither important or clear enough to warrant violence.

The third necessary cause is that a party to the conflict be *nonlibertarian* (authoritarian or totalitarian). Violence will not occur between two libertarian states: domestic constraints, cross-pressures and libertarian bonds makes violent alternatives unthinkable. Such is not the case for nonlibertarian states.

16.5 SUFFICIENT CAUSES: A SIGNIFICANT CHANGE IN THE BALANCE OF POWERS

A sufficient cause of conflict is one whose occurrence produces conflict. There is only one such cause, and it is of a conflict situation, not formal or official conflict behavior. This is *a significant change in the balance of powers*.

Such change therefore has a dual effect. It produces a conflict situation, perhaps manifested in tension, hostility, friction, coolness, and antiforeign demonstrations. Interstate relations remain "correct," but beneath the pot is boiling. And this change is a necessary cause for the subsequent Conflict Behavior (as shown in the *phase map*), once expectations have been disrupted.

Note that there is a logical relationship between incongruent expectations as a necessary and sufficient cause of hostility and tension, and a significant change in the balance of powers as a sufficient cause. "Significant" is defined in terms of those changes in the interests, capabilities, and wills comprising a balance of powers that creates a gap with regard to expectations. That is, what states want, can get, or are resolved to get are no longer consistent with their understandings or agreements. In other words, such significant change produces incongruent expectations.

16.6 AGGRAVATING CONDITIONS

Aggravating conditions worsen a conflict, make outbreak, escalation and intense conflict more likely.

Four such conditions affect international Conflict Behavior generally, regardless of phase or subphase. One is *sociocultural dissimilarity,* which makes opposing interest more likely and aggravates communications between parties. The second is *cognitive imbalance,* or the imbalance in relationships or status between parties. Such can create a pressure towards misperception and miscommunication, and necessitate a conflict aggravating readjustment.

A third aggravator is the overall *status difference* (distance vector), or rank between parties. Relative status is a basic force between states, as between individuals, and differences in wealth (e.g., a rich-poor gap), in power, and in prestige can interject status considerations into a conflict. And make it far more difficult to resolve.

And fourth is the coercive *power of state.* The more relative power a state has the more global its contacts and interests and the more concern over its reputation for power. Great power is not necessary or sufficient for conflict behavior. Weak states do conflict; do go to war. But power does stimulate and aggravate issues, giving them a more global significance. And centralized state power means also that resources can be controlled and directed towards a conflict and domestic restraints manipulated. The more power the parties have in a conflict, the more conflict behavior there is likely to be.

The other aggravating conditions only affect certain phases and kinds of conflict. The first of these is *cross-pressures,* which deepens the situation of uncertainty, provoking status-quo testing and stimulating nonviolent conflict behavior and low-level violence.

While affecting some nonviolence also, most of the remaining aggravators primarily act on violence. First of these is *Big Power intervention* in the conflict, which may transform a local dispute into one involving the status quo among the Powers, and thus raise the stakes at issue. Such intervention also injects into the conflict greater resources for confrontation.

Two additional aggravating conditions of violence are the injection of *honor* and *credibility* (reputation for power) into conflict. If a leadership perceives its or the nation's self-esteem at issue, or if it feels that the outcome of a conflict will determine how others perceive their will and capability, then the conflict is more likely to escalate, be more intense, and be more difficult to resolve.

Another aggravating condition is the perceived *weakness of the Status-Quo Power.* A status quo will always involve some perceived unequal distribution of rights and benefits. As long as the major benefactor—the Status-Quo Power—has the strength to defend the status quo, however, this distribution is likely to remain stable. But if the Status-Quo Power becomes weak (a significant change in the balance of powers) and its ability to defend the status quo is questionable, then attempts the realign the status quo are encouraged. And violence is ascerbated.

Finally, *polarity* also aggravates Conflict Behavior and violence. International systems in which power is highly centralized assure that once conflict breaks out, it can easily involve the fundamental status quo and become a test of the organizing power, thus encouraging escalation and extreme violence.

Two conditions particularly aggravate intense violence and war. One is (coercive) *power parity.* The more equal in power two states are, the more objectively ambiguous the outcome and the more both sides can believe in success.

The second is *class conflict.* Class is a relationship of power regarding the status quo, where the superordinate class most benefits from the status quo. The subordinate class comprises the "outs." The more this class division puts states in the same one-up or one-down position on international rights, privileges, and benefits, the more likely conflict will become intensely violent.

16.7 INHIBITING CONDITIONS

Inhibiting conditions restrain conflict, making outbreak, escalation and intense conflict less likely.

Many of the aggravating conditions of Conflict Behavior are inhibitors if their values are reversed. Whereas, dissimilarity aggravates, *similarity* inhibits. Likewise, cognitive *balance,* status *similarity,* and *weak state power* are the general inhibitors of Conflict Behavior.

Focusing now on particular subphases of conflict, there are only two inhibitors of nonviolent conflict behavior and low-level violence. One is *polarity,* or the centralization of power within the internal system. In centralized systems, except for extreme violence Conflict Behavior tends to be dampened and repressed. Such conflict is largely controlled, for it might escalate and involve the major power(s), or affect the general status quo. Polarity is a dual condition, therefore. It dampens nonviolent conflict behavior and low-level violence while aggravating violence.

The second inhibitor of low-level conflict is a *stable status quo.* Even though there may be an intense nonviolent dispute, as long as the status quo between the parties is unquestioned, the conflict is restrained and escalation to violence is unlikely. Except for isolated low-level violence, coercive violence and force are over a disrupted status quo. Therefore, the line representing a stable status quo in the *phase map* must end where a disrupted status quo (the necessary cause of violence) begins.

Turning now to inhibitors of violence (which may also inhibit some nonviolent Conflict Behavior), the first is the *strength of the Status-Quo Power.* Its weakness aggravates conflict, making violence and escalation more likely. And its strength inhibits the escalation of conflict into violence and war.

The second inhibitor is *cross-pressures,* which like polarity has a dual causal role, but in opposite directions. As a result of diverse, contending interests, cross-pressures encourage Conflict Behavior, but bleed off, segment and confuse this conflict so that violence and war are inhibited.

A generator of cross-pressures, *libertarian political systems,* inhibit the involvement of libertarian states in extreme conflict and violence, especially in initiating violence. It is usually in defense of the status quo against authoritarian or totalitarian initiatives or aggression that libertarian states will be involved in violence, if at all.

Finally, there is *world opinion,* which if vocal and focused can inhibit the occurrence and escalation of violence. Allies can threaten to withdraw support; friendly countries can turn hostile, thus affecting other issues besides those in the dispute. In other words, world opinion can raise the cost of a conflict to the parties.

Aside from the inhibitors of violence, war as a type of violence has only one special inhibitor: coercive *power disparity.* Power disparity makes escalation to and in war more likely. The ambiguity of power enables both parties to expect success. A power disparity that makes clear the power dominance of one party over the other tends to discourage war.

16.8 TRIGGER CAUSES

Conflict Behavior is directly caused by some trigger that provokes the will of one or both parties to action, finally disrupting an incongruent structure of expectations. The trigger can be any event fitting into one of two overlapping classes.

One class is of those events *perceived* by one or both parties as showing *opportunity, threat,* or *injustice.*

Opportunity could be indicated by some event displaying the weakness of the other party, such as its withdrawal from a local conflict with an apparently inferior party, mutiny of a garrison, or a coup d'etat. Threat may be perceived in an assassination plot financed by the other party, or discovery of the development of a secret weapon, or declared alliance between the other party and another adversary. And injustice may be seen in the other sinking one's passenger liner, harboring or supporting terrorists, or refusing to concede territory one feels the other illegally occupies.

The second class of triggers are those which *occur suddenly, provoking surprise,* and crystallizing will and opposition. These are the crises creators. The events which were not foreseen, but which cannot be ignored and change or threaten to change the relationship between the parties. The sudden discovery by the United States that the Soviet Union was putting missiles and bombers in Cuba in 1962, threatening to alter the balance of powers was such a trigger. So was the sudden blockade of West Berlin by the Soviet Union in 1948, the erection of the Berlin Wall in 1961; and the nationalization of the Suez Canal by Egyptian President Nasser in 1956.

Note on the *phase map* that triggers conveying perceptions of opportunity threat, or injustice, and surprise may operate also to escalate the subphases of conflict.

16.9 THE CAUSES OF WAR

What causes war? This question has been answered above, but the range and nature of all the causes and conditions may not be clear, because the discussion moved across phases and subphases of conflict and types of causes.

War is generated by a field of sociocultural forces seated in the meaning, values, and norms of states. Specifically, war is an outcome of an imbalance among these forces in international space-time. And is the process through which a new field equilibrium is established.

The causes and conditions of war, therefore, operate within this field. They are interrelated; their operation is relative to the space-time. War is therefore not the product of one cause, or x number of causes operating independently. War is a social field phenomenon, and its causes and conditions must be understood as aspects of this field—as contextual, situational.

With this understanding, an answer to "What causes war?" requires first stating the conditions that must be met for war to be possible. These are the necessary causes of war.

For war to occur between two states they must have some *contact* and *salience,* some awareness of each other. They must also have some opposing interests, something to fight about, and capabilities to fight. Such is obvious. What is not so clear is the more abstract but operational statement of this: they must have *specific sociocultural distances (vectors).*

What opposing interests are necessary for war depend on the actor and situation. But there is one characteristic, however, which can be defined. At least one of the potential combatants must be *nonlibertarian.* Shared domestic restraints, cross-pressures and bonds, ideology, preclude war between libertarian states.

For war to occur, however, there are still additional requirements. There must be a significant change in the *balance of powers* supporting the *status quo*. Interests, capabilities, and will singly or in combination must have changed sufficiently that the status quo is now felt to be unjust, threatened, or ripe for readjustment. This change has created a tension, a cold or hostile climate between the parties. It is obvious to informed observers that if something is not done to prevent it violence and possibly war will break out.

Second, there must be a *will-to-war*. That is, each potential combatant must have a will to fight either in defense of or to change the status quo. Abnegation, surrender, concessions can avoid war, at least for the short run. Such, of course, may be at a cost in honor, benefits, potential gain, or freedom greater than a leadership is willing or able to bear; and thus stimulating a subsequent will-to-war.

And third, each potential combatant must *expect success* as he defines it. That is, each must believe that if war does occur as a result of the increasingly unstable status quo, then he will be able to achieve his war aims (desirable slice of territory; defeat the other's border attack; force acceptance of a new sphere of interests; establish control over trade routes, and so on).

These, then, are the rock bottom, generally necessary causes for war: contact and salience, opposing interests and capabilities, nonlibertarian enemies, significant change in the balance of powers underlying the status quo, a will-to-war, and a belief in success if war occurs.

Wherever present between states on the globe, these causes demarcate the *war potential zones,* the possible global fronts of extreme violence.

Yet, war may not occur. For a final necessary cause also must be present. This is the *disruption of the status quo*. Some, perhaps *surprising,* event will communicate injustice, threat, or opportunity in a way to crystallize the conflict situation and provoke the will-to-action for one or both parties. The change in the balance of powers has created tension, a recognition of the possibility of war over a status quo. The *trigger* event brings this to a head, provoking a crises in which war is the outcome, or directly stimulating the decision to attack.

Disruption of the status quo is both necessary *and sufficient*. Such disruption will not occur unless the requirements for war are present (opposing interests, significant change in balance of powers, and so on). The decision to go to war takes preparation and months may go by in which tension grows or, through the subterfuge of one party or another, seems to abate before the attack.

Such are the necessary and sufficient causes of war, what in the abstract must be present or happen for war to occur.

However, it should be clear that all these requirements for war may be present, and still no war may break out. Moreover, the war that does occur can be a short, intense confrontation on a border, or a full-scale war between the parties involving bombing raids on each other's capital city and invasion, or a general war in which many states are involved.

There are three groups of aggravating conditions which increase the likelihood of war, given the presence of the necessary conditions, or increase its intensity once it has occurred. One group is of those conditions which worsen Conflict Behavior generally, whether negative communications, sanctions, violence, or war. These include the *sociocultural dissimilarity* between the parties, their *cognitive imbalance* and *status difference* and the *coercive power* of the parties. All these acerbate opposing interests and with regard to war, tend to destabilize the status quo, and increase the likelihood of its disruption.

A second group of aggravating conditions uniquely influence violence and war. One of these is the *polarity* of the system, which defines the generality of the status quo and increases the probability that a state's violence, wherever it occurs, will involve Big Power interests. A second is *Big Power intervention* itself, which may inject into local conflicts larger status-quo interests and resources and provoke violence or its escalation.

Another aggravating condition is the *weakness of the Status-Quo Power.* Given the presence of the necessary causes, if the Status-Quo Power seems to display an unwillingness or inability to defend an already unstable status quo, then this makes more likely its disruption and the escalation of violence and war, once they occur.

Finally, there is *honor* and *credibility.* If these are at stake in a conflict situation, it becomes more explosive, making violence and war more likely, more intense once they occur, and more difficult to resolve.

The third group of aggravators is unique to war. These make disruption and war more likely, given the necessary causes, and make the escalation of war more probable. One is *power parity,* or a sufficient equality of coercive power and force such that each side believes that it can successfully oppose the power of the other.

The second aggravator is *class conflict.* Class in international relations defines the authoritative, status-quo rights of the parties. As there is increasingly one division separating those who have from those who want; those with wealth, power and prestige from those who are poor, weak, and unrenowned; and those states who command and those who obey; then this division worsens conflict, makes war more likely, and tends to turn a war, once it occurs, into a general war.

In total, the three groups of aggravating conditions push toward war. But, singly or collectively, they will not *in general* cause war by themselves. The necessary causes must be present; the status quo must be disrupted. However, these aggravating causes can turn potential into disposition and disposition into a war seeking an excuse to happen.

In any conflict, however, there are always two sets of conditions present. Those promoting confrontation; those discouraging it. For war, also, there are a variety of inhibiting conditions which oppose its occurrence and escalation. These also comprise three groups, depending on whether they operate in all Conflict Behavior subphases, only violence and war, or only on war.

The first group comprises those aggravators that when reversed act also as inhibitors. Thus, sociocultural *similarity, cognitive balance, status similarity,* and *state weakness* restrains the tendency toward Conflict Behavior, violence and war.

The second group contains a number of inhibitors which act on violence, only one of which is the reverse of an aggravator. This is the *strength of the Status-Quo Power.* If in spite of a change in the balance of powers, the supporter of the status quo appears willing and able to defend it, this tends to work against its disruption. Even then disruption and consequent violence or war may occur. The *AntiStatus-Quo Power* may believe it can successfully change the status quo over the other's resistance. But, the threshold for this is raised.

Another inhibitor in this group is *cross-pressures.* These involve diverse interests that may segment the particular opposing interests of the parties. Violence or war may be desirable for these interests, but other interests may therefore be compromised or lost. Some interests push toward war; some pull away from it.

Related to this is *internal freedom*—a libertarian political system—as an inhibitor of violence and war. Libertarian states do commit violence and go to war; but reluctantly, usually against totalitarian or authoritarian threats or aggression, and often with considerable domestic opposition.

A final inhibitor in this group is *world opinion,* the pressure that allies and neutrals can bring to bear to prevent or check violence and war.

The final group is of those conditions uniquely inhibiting war. It has one member: *power disparity.* Power parity worsens a war-potential situation; power disparity restrains it. War still may occur, in spite of a gross inequality in military forces and resources. Other factors, such as honor, credibility, survival, or determination may make the difference, as they have in the Israeli-Arab Wars. Success may be pegged to the potential for Big Power intervention; or success may be measured not in terms of winning, but in actually having fought the other to a standstill or in unifying a nation. Or a state may calculate that the other side will use only a small part of its power, as small North Vietnam correctly did in fighting a war against a Superpower, the United States.

These, then, are the causes and conditions of war. Table 16A.1 in appendix 16A pulls them all together, by level and group. Figure 16.1 shows these causes operating by phase and subphase. And the basic picture of the conflict helix in Figure 10.1 portrays the process of conflict, and thus of war as well.

In order to be as clear as possible, however, I have also constructed Figure 16.2. This brings together in one Figure all the necessary and sufficient causes and the aggravating and inhibiting conditions of war, in their relationship to each other and to the underlying process of conflict. Causes and conditions are shown in lower case; descriptive terms for this process are capitalized.

The core of the structure of expectations—the *status quo*—is shown as a bar with regard to which a gap (*incongruence*) is created by a *change in the balance*

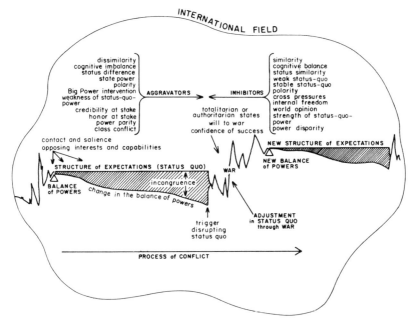

FIGURE 16.2: Causes and Conditions of War

of powers (necessary cause). This assumes mutual *contact* and *salience*, and *opposing interests and capabilities* (necessary causes). A *trigger* (cause) disrupts the status quo (necessary and sufficient cause) and war results, assuming a *will-to-war, confidence in success,* and that *totalitarian or authoritarian* states are involved (necessary causes). The war then determines a new balance of mutually recognized powers and a congruent status quo as shown in Figure 16.2. Also as shown, a number of aggravating and inhibiting conditions operate on the process.

Such, then, is a well-confirmed perspective on war.

NOTES

1. There are two levels of evidence. One level is the statement of the cause, such as "x causes y." Such are the propositions given in appendix 16B. The other is the premises of the statement. For example, one might assert that because of premises a,b,c, and d, then "x causes y." Now, if a,b,c, and d are supported by the evidence, then the derivation of "x causes y" gives the statement a truth value over and above the empirical evidence bearing on the statement alone. Only true deductions can be logically derived from true premises. Appendix 16B presents the evidence for the statements (propositions) involving the causes and conditions. The previous chapters and volumes provide the evidence (such as the psychological evidence from multivariate psychology in Volume 1 and the cross-national evidence for the general conflict propositions in Volume 2) for the premises of the statements.

2. Although the general causes and conditions refer to Conflict Behavior, which involves both the coercive and noncoercive paths, where the latter may comprise cooperative behavior (see Figure 12.1), I have restricted the phase map to the former for simplicity.

3. Attempts to visually model causes of war usually employ an arrow diagram to show the causal relationship between independent and dependent variables. The *phase map* in Figure 16.1 is an alternative model which allows dynamic interrelationship among variables to be simultaneously shown at different phases in process.

4. A complete, detailed discussion of each cause, theoretically and empirically, would obviously entail a volume by itself. However, because each basic concept (e.g., structure of expectations, power, libertarian political system) has been defined and analyzed in previous volumes and chapters, and because appendix 16B focuses this previous analysis on each propositional statement of a cause or condition, I can be brief here.

5. Because this is a necessary and sufficient cause of an international *situation* of conflict and not *behavior,* it does not appear in the list of causes and conditions in Table 16A.1, nor in the propositions listed in Table 16B.1.

6. As I discuss these causes and conditions, such as incongruent expectations, I will be moving up and down the vertical region in the *phase map* whose width is defined by the horizontal line which plots a specific cause or condition. Thus, for incongruent expectations, note that the vertical region encompasses at the base the conflict situation; such behaviors as UN voting, and antiforeign behavior; and such aggravating conditions as sociocultural dissimilarity and cognitive imbalance. The vertical region also includes, as sufficient cause, a significant change in the balance of powers, which I have just pointed to in the text as producing incongruent expectations. This approach underlines the interrelatedness of the causes and conditions, behavior, and latent process.

7. Hostility, manifested in unofficial antiforeign behavior, and tension or friction *reflect* a latent situation of conflict. They are not intentional state acts or actions necessarily connected to the specific situation. Indeed, hostility and tension are a matter of atmosphere and feeling, not a specific behavior. In the situation of uncertainty and balancing of powers, however, conflict acts and actions are willful, intentional confrontations regarding the conflict.

8. This is not a trite nor tautological assertion, for the cause is defined in terms of distance vectors in sociocultural space. Interests are therefore given a specific empirical manifestation and operational meaning distinct from empirical conflict behavior.

9. Appendix 9A provides some related useful results on situational expectations and perceptions.

APPENDIX 16A

ON CAUSES OF INTERNATIONAL CONFLICT

There are a variety of schemes for assessing the causes of conflict: remote versus immediate, necessary versus sufficient, significant versus trivial, structural versus situational. Moreover, there is the question as to what one means by cause: an event (an occurrence) that can be dated, a condition, a mathematical relationship. There is finally the question of whether causes actually exist in social behavior, are statistical regularities, or are projections of our minds on that behavior.

My concern here is not to philosophically analyze the meaning of cause, but to cut through the various perspectives and interpretations and simply ask: "given my field interpretation of conflict and the conditions and forces presumably operating, what do I mean by, for example, x causes or is a condition of war?"[1]

A number of aspects of the international field bear on an answer to this.

(1) Possible causes and conditions are interrelated and relative within a gestalt comprising the process of conflict (the conflict helix).
(2) We are dealing with states as parties to conflict, where "state behavior" comprises an outcome of a complex process of domestic and foreign decision-making, organizations, and processes (this process has been the focus of this book up to this chapter).
(3) Decision makers are basically teleological: mainly deciding in order to satisfy interests rather than because of specific causes (thus the emphasis on *process* and *balancing*).
(4) The field may be in a state of local equilibrium or disruption, thus influencing the salience of possible causes or conditions.

Moreover, in defining causes and conditions I am concerned with their systematic, empirical evidence.

With this in mind, I will demand of a "cause" or "condition" that it:

• have a logical (or statistical) relationship to conflict,[2]
• have a theoretical explanation as to why it should affect conflict,
• be empirically and scientifically testable.

Now, define a cause as x, and the conflict behavior it affects as y. Then, logically, a cause *in my terms* can have one of three meanings. First, the cause can be *sufficient* for y: if x then y. Whenever x occurs, y follows. But y can also be an effect of other causes, so that if x is sufficient for y, we cannot say that not-x, then not-y. If heavy drinking is a sufficient cause of automobile accidents, this does not mean that sober driving implies no accidents. For accidents also are caused by excessive speed, falling asleep, mechanical breakdowns.

Second, the cause x can be *necessary* for y: if y then x. If y occurred, then x must have also occurred. Or, y would not occur without x being present. Thus, gravity is a necessary cause for one to fall on an icy sidewalk. But gravity is not sufficient. Even though gravity is present you may not slip and fall.

Third, a cause may be *necessary and sufficient:* y if and only if x. That is, y will occur only when x occurs. For example, the launching of American ICBMs involves a complex set of simultaneous procedures to be carried out by more than one person. These procedures have been designed so that together they are necessary and sufficient for a launching: a launching would not occur without following these procedures, either by accident or will.

There is a special type of sufficient cause that I will call a *trigger*. This is a class of causes x that operates within a system of conditions highly favorable for producing y, such that any member of the class x could have produced y and would not have been a cause without these conditions. The trigger is often called the proximate or immediate cause. Any kind of spark (class x) may trigger an explosion once sufficient explosive gas has accumulated; any additional car (class x) on a bridge may trigger its collapse, given it is already overloaded. Any overt attack (class x) on a regime, such as an assassination, may trigger a revolution or war, if the political conditions are ripe.

Specific triggers are therefore random causes. They are not of intrinsic interest except as a *class* of events. What is of interest are the causes and conditions that must cooccur for triggers to be successful and the specific, sufficient causes that make certain that some random trigger will spring y.

Then there are conditions z of y. Conditions, in my sense, retard or enhance the operations of a cause. Setting a match to kindling is a sufficient cause of fire. But, if the (condition of the) wood is wet, the sufficient cause will be hampered, possibly defeated. If the (condition of the) wood is desert dry, the wood could burst into vigorous flame at the touch of a match. World opinion similarly could inhibit or aggravate violence depending on

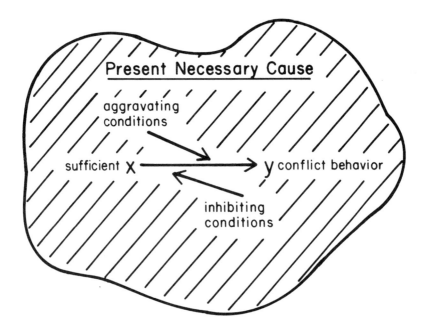

FIGURE 16A.1: The Theoretical Causal Model of Conflict Behavior

TABLE 16A.1: Causes and Conditions of International Conflict Behavior*

		CAUSES AND CONDITIONS				
Necessary Causes	Sufficient Causes	Necessary & Sufficient Causes	Aggravating Conditions	Inhibiting Conditions	Classes of Trigger Events	Effect
change in the balance of powers (3)		disrupted expectations (1)	dissimilarity (12)	similarity (12)	perception of opportunity, threat or injustice (29)	Conflict Behavior (including violence and war)
contact (4) & salience (5)			cognitive imbalance (13)	cognitive balance (13)	surprise (28)	
sociocultural distance vectors (6)			status difference (14, 33)	status similarity (14, 33)		
perception and expectations (7)			state power (31, 32)	state weakness (31)		
will-to-conflict (8)			cross-pressures (15)	polarity (23) stable status quo (26)		nonviolent Conflict Behavior and low level violence

TABLE 16A.1: Causes and Conditions of International Conflict Behavior* (Cont)

| | CAUSES AND CONDITIONS | | | | | |
Necessary Causes	Sufficient Causes	Necessary & Sufficient Causes	Aggravating Conditions	Inhibiting Conditions	Classes of Trigger Events	Effect
nonlibertarian states (11)			polarity (20)	cross-pressures (24)		
status quo disruption (10)			Big Power intervention (19)	internal freedom (27)		
confidence in success (9)			weakness of Status Quo Power (18)	strength of Status Quo (18)		violence (including war)
			credibility at stake (17)	world opinion (25)		
			honor at stake (16)			
			power parity (21)	power disparity (21)		war
			class conflict (22)			

*Numbers in parentheses are the numbered propositions (appendix 16B) containing the cause or condition. See especially Table 16B.1.

whether it was strongly opposed (as in Vietnam) or favorable (as regarding white-controlled Rhodesia)

In theoretically explaining conflict behavior, then, the causal model I will use treats *causes and conditions as operating within a field and through a medium of meanings, values, and norms.* The model is illustrated by Figure 16A.1.

With this understanding of causes and conditions of Conflict Behavior in mind, then, Table 16A.1 organizes the *theoretical* causes and conditions of Conflict Behavior. The proposition relating them to conflict and discussion of their meanings are given in appendix 16B; the evidence is given in appendix 16C.

In reading the table it should be kept in mind that Conflict Behavior includes violence or war. Therefore, what is a necessary cause for Conflict Behavior would also be so for war. What causes or conditions are specified in addition for violence or war are therefore those that theoretically discriminate them from other Conflict Behavior. Thus, given that the necessary causes have occurred, then nonviolent conflict escalates to military action and war if neither party is libertarian, the status quo has been disrupted, and each is confident of success. This escalation will be made, more or less, intense depending on the presence of the tabulated aggravating and inhibiting conditions. Especially, escalation to war will be probable if the parties have power parity and it is a widescale class conflict.

NOTES

1. The work that comes closest to my view on causation is Bunge (1963). He argues that causal determination is just one of many forms of determination; that cause-effect cannot be considered purely a logical or statistical relationship; that cause-effect does imply a nonlogical bond or link of some kind between the cause and effect.

2. I do not intend to *define* cause logically, for the laws of logic imply causal relationship that few would be willing to accept (for example, see Bunge, 1963: 242-243). I am using logic only to clarify the types of theoretical causal connections of concern. The logic is therefore an organizing principle and not a rigid formalization.

APPENDIX 16B

THEORETICAL PROPOSITIONS ON THE CAUSES AND CONDITIONS OF INTERNATIONAL CONFLICT BEHAVIOR AND THEIR EVIDENCE

16B.1 INTRODUCTION

The theoretical propositions on the causes and conditions of conflict behavior are given in Table 16B.1.

The first column defines the types of cause or condition, as described in Appendix 16A: necessary and sufficient cause, sufficient cause, necessary cause, trigger cause, aggravating condition, inhibiting condition, and relative aggravators.

TABLE 16B.1: **Propositions on the Causes and Conditions of Conflict Behavior**

Type of Cause & Conditions	No.	Name	PROPOSITION	
			Abstract Description	**Empirical Description**
necessary and sufficient	16.1	Disrupted Expectations	Conflict Behavior if and only if disrupted expectations	Conflict Behavior occurs if and only if a mutual structure of expectations is disrupted
sufficient	16.2	Change/ Tension	Change produces tension and hostility	Tension and hostility occur if there is a significant shift in the balance of powers (interests, capabilities, will)
necessary	16.3	Change/ Conflict	Conflict behavior assumes change	Conflict Behavior occurs only if there is a significant shift in the balance of powers (interests, capabilities, will)

TABLE 16B.1: **Propositions on the Causes and Conditions of Conflict Behavior (Cont)**

Type of Cause & Conditions	No.	Name	PROPOSITION	
			Abstract Description	Empirical Description
(and aggravating)	16.4	Geographic	Conflict Behavior assumes contact	Geographic distance is negatively correlated with Conflict Behavior
(and aggravating)	16.5	Joint Power	Conflict Behavior assumes salience	Joint Power is positively correlated with Conflict Behavior
	16.6	Distance Vector	Distances are the force vectors of conflict	Conflict behavior is most correlated with sociocultural differences and similarities (distance vectors)
	16.7	Actor	Individual perceptions and expectations condition conflict force-vectors	The potency of interests (sociocultural distance vectors) depends on an actor's individual perceptions and expectations
	16.8	Will-to-Conflict	Conflict behavior demands will	Conflict behavior will occur only if there is a will to conflict
	16.9	Confidence	Violence assumes confidence	Intense violence will occur only if there is an expectation of success
	16.10	Status-Quo Disruption	Violence assumes a disrupted status quo	Violence is over a status quo
	16.11	Joint Freedom	Libertarian systems mutually preclude violence	Violence will occur between states only if at least one is nonlibertarian
Aggravators	16.12	Dissimilarity	Dissimilarity aggravates conflict	Sociocultural dissimilarity is positively correlated with Conflict Behavior
	16.13	Cognitive Dissonance	Cognitive dissonance aggravates conflict	Cognitive dissonance is positively correlated with Conflict Behavior

TABLE 16B.1: **Propositions on the Causes and Conditions of Conflict Behavior (Cont)**

Type of Cause & Conditions	No.	Name	PROPOSITION	
			Abstract Description	Empirical Description
	16.14	Status	Status distances are force vectors of conflict	Differences in status (wealth, power, prestige) are positively correlated with Conflict Behavior
	16.15	Cross-Pressures/ Conflict	Cross-pressures generate nonviolent conflict	Cross-pressures are positively correlated with nonviolent Conflict Behavior
	16.16	Honor	Honor at stake risks escalation in violence	Involvement of a state's honor is positively correlated with violence
	16.17	Credibility	Credibility at stake risks escalation in violence	Involvement of a state's reputation for power (will) is positively correlated with violence
	16.18	Status-Quo Power	Weakness of the Status-Quo Power risks escalating violence	An actual or growing weakness of the status-quo-party compared to the anti-status quo party is positively correlated with violence
	16.19	Intervention	Big Power intervention risks escalating violence	Big Power intervention in a conflict is positively correlated with violence
	16.20	Polarity/ Violence	Polarity stimulates intense violence	Polarity is positively correlated with intense violence
	16.21	Power Parity	Power parity makes escalation to war more likely	Power-parity is correlated with war
	16.22	Class	Class conflict is the cauldron of general war	Class conflict is correlated with general war
inhibitors	16.23	Polarity/ Conflict	Polarity inhibits non-violent conflict behavior and low level violence	Polarity is negatively correlated with non-violent conflict behavior and low level violence

Type of Cause & Conditions	No.	Name	PROPOSITION	
			Abstract Description	Empirical Description
	16.24	Cross-Pressures/ Violence	Cross-pressures inhibit intense violence	Cross-pressures are negatively correlated with intense political violence
	16.25	World Opinion	World Opinion inhibits violence	Opposition of world opinion is negatively correlated with violence
	16.26	Status Quo	Status-quo stability inhibits nonviolent conflict behavior	A stable status quo is negatively correlated with the intensity of non-violent conflict behavior
	16.27	Freedom	Freedom inhibits violence	The more libertarian a state, the less it tends to be involved in violence
trigger	16.28	Surprise	Abrupt opportunity, threat, or injustice risks catalyzing and escalating conflict behavior	Abrupt perception of opportunity, threat, or injustice is positively correlated with crises and with the occurrence and escalation of conflict behavior
	16.29	Perception	Opportunity, threat, or injustice stimulates Conflict Behavior	Perception of opportunity, threat, or injustice is positively correlated with Conflict Behavior
relative-aggravators	16.30	Totalitarianism	Political distance (vector) most affects totalitarian states	The more totalitarian a state, the more correlated its Conflict Behavior with political differences (distances)
	16.31	State-Power	Power breeds conflict	National coercive power is positively and among attributes, most correlated with conflict behavior

TABLE 16B.1: **Propositions on the Causes and Conditions of Conflict Behavior** (Cont)

Type of Cause & Conditions	No.	Name	PROPOSITION	
			Abstract Description	Empirical Description
	16.32	Power Vector	Power distance is the most potent force vector towards conflict	Difference in coercive power is most highly correlated with conflict behavior
	16.33	Wealth-Power-Politics	Wealth, power, and political distances are the most potent force-vectors of conflict	Differences (distance vectors) in wealth, power, and politics are of all differences the most correlated with conflict behavior

The relative aggravators refers to propositions describing the operation of an aggravating condition relative to other such conditions. Thus, of all attributes of nations, (coercive) power attributes are theoretically most highly correlated with conflict behavior (Proposition 16.31); of all differences between nations, differences in power, wealth, and politics are most highly correlated with conflict behavior (Proposition 16.33); among these three, power is most correlated (Proposition 16.32); and the more totalitarian a state, the more correlated its conflict with political differences (Proposition 16.30).

Each proposition in the Table is given a number and name for easy identification and each is given both an abstract and empirical description. The "empirical" (or operational) description is specific about how the causes or conditions relate to conflict, observationally. It is the description that a social scientist would probably prefer.

The "abstract" description is the general and compelling way to describe the proposition. It is more intuitive, in a sense poetic. It would probably appeal more to the historian, social philosopher, or polemicist.

The abstract and empirical descriptions of the same proposition are not just alternative statements. They are meant to describe the causes and conditions through different perspectives, each of which is believed true, and both of which together give a fuller appreciation of the cause or condition.

In some cases there is virtually no difference between the empirical and abstract description, except the latter is shorter, as in Proposition 16.1. In other cases, the difference is such as to apparently involve dissimilar propositions, as with Proposition 16.31.

As in appendix 15A, each proposition will be discussed from the perspective of *theory, prediction, evidence,* and *conclusion.* The evidence for all the propositions is presented in Tables 16C.3-4. Appendix C also discusses this evidence in general terms, and considers several sources of possible bias. Appendix C would be useful reading, before moving into the individual propositions here.

16B.2. PROPOSITIONS, EVIDENCE, AND EVALUATION

Proposition 16.1 (Disrupted-Expectations:
Conflict behavior if and only if disrupted expectations.

Conflict Behavior occurs if and only if a mutual structure of expectations is disrupted.
    Theory: The character of *Understanding Conflict and War* as a whole underlies this

proposition, and particularly part VII of Volume 2 dealing with the conflict helix. In short, peace and order exist within a structure of expectations based on a balance of powers. As this underlying balance becomes incongruent with the structure of expectations, the probability increases that some trigger will disrupt expectations. Manifest conflict then will occur as a new balance of powers and associated structure of expectations are determined.

This disruption of a structure of expectations is a *necessary and sufficient* cause of international Conflict Behavior. Necessary, in that I assume by theory that Conflict Behavior could not take place without a relevant structure of expectations having been disrupted.

I am assuming that all international relations now take place within mutual or multiple structures of expectations; that new structures are transformations of previous ones. Even new states adopt existing structures as a first approximation and develop, in the process of negotiating independence, new structures to fit their situations.

In social relations within states it is possible for people to first meet, develop initial expectations from their perceptions of each other's field of expression (Volume 2, 1976: part II), yet have not worked out relevant structure of expectations. This will come out of subsequent conflict which may or may not involve Conflict Behavior. Thus, the conflict helix in Figure 10.1 is shown with a structure of conflict leading to a situation of conflict, to balancing, and to a structure of expectations. In this case Conflict Behavior could occur without the disruption of a structure of expectations, because none was yet in place.

In international relations we no longer have the "strange new boy on the block." The globe has become integrated through modern communications and trade; international elite are acquainted with each other's cultures and societies through travel, foreign residence, education, and involvement in the United Nations. Diverse nonintergovernmental organizations involve in some way all countries, whether independent or not. And some multilateral international legal and economic arrangements are initial structures within which new states must operate. Past is the historical meeting and confrontation of societies and cultures completely new to each other. The age of discovery and exploration is over: international conflict now functions to reorder structures of expectations, rather than establish them *de nova*.

The disruption of structures of expectations also is a *sufficient* cause of Conflict Behavior: disruption implies some kind of international Conflict Behavior.

While in personal relations tacit adjustments may take place in a balance of power without Conflict Behavior—one accepts the other's advantage or submits to the changed situation, fearing the consequences—states are not people. They are collections of balances of powers among diverse interests. Therefore, no breakdown in a structure of expectations will be accepted without some kind of manifest conflict and adjustment—accusations, protests, offers, promises, alliances, troop movements, negotiations, agreements. Nor does it mean that the behavior is necessarily antagonistic or violent. It does mean, however, that some disruption-related, conflict-reflecting behavior will occur.

Prediction: Because disruption is both necessary and sufficient, the occurrence of any International Conflict behavior implies that some structure of expectations has been disrupted; the disruption of any structure of expectations implies Conflict Behavior will follow.

This is the ideal causal relationship for correlational analysis, because the product-moment correlation or its variants best reflect necessary and sufficient causation, if it exists. While a high correlation between x and y does not imply causation, of course, if x is a necessary and sufficient cause for y, however, then they should have a high (or perfect, if one assumes no measurement, collection, and manipulative errors) correlation.

Therefore, the prediction is of a high (or moderate, if much operational slippage exists) positive correlation between disruption and Conflict Behavior in samples involving some members without Conflict Behavior.

If in the mixed sample the conflict variable is measured in any other way but as a dichotomy, then the correlations are predicted to be near zero or moderate positive. The reason for this in the case of disrupted expectations is discussed in appendix 16C with regard to Figure 16C.1.

In samples in which all members have Conflict Behavior (e.g., a sample of war dyads), then disrupted expectations should be present in *all* cases. Technically, disrupted expectations would be a constant and the product-moment correlation coefficient would then be indeterminate. But conceptually the correlation should be zero: the two variables (vectors) are orthogonal.[1] Of course, cross-tabulation should immediately display this lack of relationship.

Similarly in samples involving no Conflict Behavior. There should be no disrupted expectations, and therefore in this sample the correlation should be zero, conceptually, between disrupted expectations and lack of conflict behavior.

Evidence: As shown in Table 16C.3, there are seven analyses bearing on the proposition. The most powerful support is given by Sorokin's work on historical movements in war and peace (1957), and Blainey on the causes of war (1973). Melko's (1973) analysis of 52 peace societies also lends considerable indirect support. Indeed, the sum total of both Melko's and Sorokin's findings cannot be well understood without assuming the correctness of the Disrupted Expectations Proposition.

All except one of the sources of evidence are important studies (see Table 16C.4), and over half bear directly on the proposition. Moreover, most analyses did not violate the Model II and distance vector assumptions of the social field. And five of the seven relevant analyses provide strong positive support for the proposition; and all five were done by others than myself.

Finally, special attention should be given to Sorokin's historical-cultural analysis of war (see especially Sorokin, 1937-1941), and his overall analysis of cultural change. His theory is that revolution and war manifest the breakdown in the values and norms of sociocultural systems; the shift to a new system. Peace then is a condition of crystallized values and norms. On this theory he brings to bear a diverse collection of positive historical evidence. Clearly, as I discussed in Volume 3 (1977: section 8.1) Sorokin's theory is easily rewritten in terms of conflict helix: the nature of his whole work provides strong support for the Disrupted Expectations Proposition.

Conclusion: While only a comparatively small number of analyses relate to the proposition, the importance of these analyses and their strong support for the proposition give it solid credibility. Therefore: *the evidence strongly supports the proposition.*

Proposition 16.2 (Change/Tension): Change produces tension and hostility.

Tension and hostility occur if there is a significant shift in the balance of powers (interests, capabilities, will).

Theory: No disruption may occur in the structure of expectations, but the balance of powers and expectations can have become so incongruent that the climate of relations—the atmosphere—can be altered. In short, tension is in the air, hostility is felt. There may be no specific conflict behavior to point to, but relations *feel* strained.

Change should satisfy two conditions before it produces such tension and hostility. First, it must be in the balance of interests, capabilities, and will. One party may have lost interest in maintaining a status quo, its will may have weakened, or the other party may have grown considerably in military power. The old balance of powers has been altered; but the old structure of expectations remains in place. Thus, tension.

This leads to the second condition: the rate of change in the structure of expectations and balance of powers must differ significantly. Structures of expectations evolve as the parties interact. If this evolutionary change is in line with changes in the underlying balance of powers, then no tension or hostility should result. But if the change in expectations does not keep pace with that in the balance of powers, then eventually this growing incongruency will cause tension and hostility (Volume 3, 1977: section 8.5). Such change is thus a *sufficient* condition.

What about Conflict Behavior generally? Such change is not a sufficient condition for Conflict Behavior generally, nor for antagonistic Conflict Behavior, because a disruption in the expectations has not yet, or may not at all, occur. The incongruency may be there, tension may be in the air, but no suitable trigger may have yet occurred to disrupt the expectations, or *adjustments* in expectations or the underlying balance may lessen the incongruency. Interests may be revitalized; will reaffirmed; armaments cut back.

Conflict may not always be thus avoided, nor may it always be desirable to do so. But this does point out that there is no inevitability to incongruency producing conflict behavior.

Prediction: A significant change in the balance of power should be positively correlated with the occurrence of tension and hostility. But what about Conflict Behavior generally?

Now, tension and hostility can be present without specific, manifest Conflict Behavior; moreover, manifest conflict behavior can occur without tension and hostility (e.g., a mild protest of the United States to Canada). However, in general, high or intense antagonistic conflict behavior will be associated with tension and hostility. Therefore, in a mixed sample a positive correlation should be expected, as shown in Table 16C.1. Similarly for a conflict scale.

For nonviolent conflict behavior, however, tension and hostility may be present or absent for cases above or below the mean, thus meaning the predicted correlation is random: it hinges on the peculiarities of the sample.

For all other samples and conflict variables, the results are irrelevant. This is because high violence and war transcends tension and hostility, and these terms are no longer applicable.

Evidence: Four analyses are relevant (Mahoney, 1976; Abravanel and Hughes, 1973; Buchanan and Cantril, 1953; M. Sullivan, 1970). Three have strongly favorable results, one is ambiguous. All the positive evidence is indirect; and the studies are not important ones relevant to the propositions. Nonetheless, there are no negative results.

Conclusion: the evidence supports the proposition.

Proposition 16.3 (Change/Conflict): Conflict Behavior assumes change.

Conflict Behavior occurs only if there is a significant shift in the balance of powers (interests, capabilities, will).

Theory: International Conflict Behavior implies that a relevant structure of expectations has been disrupted. This could occur only if there were some incongruence between the balance of powers and the structure of expectations. And this incongruence is produced by significant change in associated, relative interests, capabilities, and will. Therefore, conflict behavior implies change. Or, to turn this around: a significant change in the balance of powers is a necessary cause of conflict behavior.

Why not sufficient? A structure of expectations may be incongruent, but no trigger may have yet occurred to disrupt it or steps may have been taken to readjust the balance, thus reducing the incongruence (by a gradual increase in arms, reemphasis on relevant national interests, revitalized will).

In social science parlance, disruption is an intermediary variable whose presence is necessary before change causes conflict behavior.

Prediction: Assessing this necessary condition is empirically complex. It must be present in all conflict behavior, so that if measured as a dichotomy it should easily show up in cross-tabulations of presence-absence against the conflict variables. But even here there is a problem. What constitutes significant change?

First, the change must be in interests, capabilities, or will.

Second, the change must be significant to the parties involved: it should be such that (1) one or both parties are dissatisfied with the formal or implicit contract governing their rights and obligations—the structure of expectations—and (2) believe that the shift in the balance of power favors their revising the contract to their advantage.

Third, the change must be relative to that in some structure of expectations. Absolute change may be irrelevant, because a structure of expectations itself may have slowly evolved congruent with this change in the balance of powers.

Clearly, empirical studies must be designed with this proposition in mind to adequately test it. For this reason I cannot specify the correlations that should occur for relevant variables in a mixed sample, except when Conflict Behavior is measured as a dichotomy as shown in Table 16C.1.

By theory, all Conflict Behavior manifests significant change in the balance of powers. Therefore, for all cases with Conflict Behavior significant change should have occurred. Thus, as shown in Table 16C.1, such change will be present for all conflict variables in the conflict, violence, and war samples.

But in the mixed sample for the *non*conflict cases, some may have significant change but Conflict Behavior has yet to occur, or some may have no significant change in their balance of powers. The tendency of the correlation, then, should be moderate positive for the dichotomous conflict variable.

For all other conflict variables of the mixed sample, conflict behavior could occur beneath the mean (see Figure 16C.1), thus complicating the prediction of what correlations to expect. If change has occurred, but the associated conflict behavior is beneath the mean, then this would contribute to a negative correlation—even though both significant change and conflict are present. For this reason, I simply assumed a random correlation for all other conflict variables in the mixed sample.

Because for the conflict, violence, and war samples, change should be present in all cases, the correlations then should be near zero between significant change and all conflict variables *in the samples*.

Evidence: The evidence is all positive (four analyses) or strongly positive (four analyses). Almost all are direct and more than half come from important studies; most are in design consistent with field theory; all are done by others than myself.

As with the Disrupted-Expectations Proposition, there are also some studies here whose character and importance give them special weight, namely the analyses of peace societies by Melko (1973) and Sorokin's (1957) comprehensive historical analysis.

Conclusion: Considering that the evidence without exception is consistent with the proposition and weighing the nature of the studies involved, then the conclusion: *the evidence unanimously supports the proposition.*

Proposition 16.4 (Geographic): Conflict Behavior assumes contact.

Geographic distance is negatively correlated with Conflict Behavior.

Theory: Contact is a necessary cause of conflict; it is an empirical concept in latent conflict (see Table 10.1). It generates the awareness necessary to transform a conflict space into a structure. Awareness is present in all conflict.

One dimension of contact is the physical or functional geographic distance between states: their contiguity; their air distance; the type of terrain between them; the transaction distance (the time it takes or the relative expense of shipping goods between them); the number or size of states between them. Geographic distance is thus a complex concept referring to the ease and likelihood of two states directly communicating with each other.

It is also necessary to keep in mind that contact is a necessary cause with a gradient. This is like gravity, which is necessary for a fall, but which also varies in degree (by height above sea level, or by planet). Contact should not only be present in all Conflict Behavior, but the more diverse and intense the Conflict Behavior between parties, the more likely (operationally) the parties are close; and (theoretically) the more their mutual awareness.

That is, the scope and intensity of awareness, while not sufficient for conflict, enhances the operation of other causes, and makes conflict behavior more likely in occurrence, scope, and intensity once the appropriate conditions are present. The stronger the pull of gravity (within a certain gravitational range), the more likely one will slip on ice, if not careful. The more international contact, then the more: important and diverse the opposing interests, likely diverse structures of expectations, likely associated conflict in their formation and disruption, diverse and intense the manifest conflict.

Degree of contact therefore also acts as an aggravating cause (as indicated in Table 16A.1), while contact per se is a necessary cause. Contact is always present, and even more so in the upper ranges of Conflict Behavior.

Geographic distance is one operational dimension of contact. A second is joint power, which is formulated in the next proposition.

Prediction: Because contact is a necessary cause that can vary in degree, contact should not only be present in all Conflict Behavior, but the more diverse and intense the Conflict Behavior between parties, the more likely (operationally) the parties are close; and (theoretically) the more their mutual awareness.

In the mixed sample for the dichotomous conflict variable, cases with conflict should be, on the average, closer geographically (where closer means less difficult passage between them) than states without Conflict Behavior.

This should not be a high correlation, however, because some states without Conflict Behavior between them may also be close. They may have stable structures of expectations, some of the other necessary causes for conflict may be absent, or they may have an incongruent structure of expectations yet to be triggered.

Therefore, at best, the correlation between geographic distance and conflict behavior should be moderately negative, as shown in Table 16C.1. The same logic applies to the conflict scale.

There also should be a moderate, negative correlation of geographic distance with the conflict scale in the conflict and violence samples. Above the mean conflict behavior on the scale will be more diverse in scope and type and more intense and this should be correlated with the scope and degree of contact. This may not be true in the war sample, however, where parties with war and intense conflict of other kinds can be below the mean on the conflict scale. There is a threshold beyond which degree of awareness may no longer discriminate in Conflict Behavior, and I assume that is in discriminating between intensity of wars and violence.

For this reason, and because the below-the-mean Conflict Behavior on the other conflict variables can be itself intense or diverse in scope (see Figure 16C.1), the resulting correlations are assumed random with regard to the proposition: they will depend on the particular sample's peculiarities.

Evidence: The evidence is usually positive (17 out of 25 analyses) and direct (all but three). Important studies split for and against, while those studies which do not violate the field assumptions (Model II and distance vectors) are usually favorable (9 to 2); and most of my own studies have also been favorable (8 to 4). Some of my results are given in appendix 9A.

This is the first proposition for which negative evidence has appeared, and in their light the expected correlations should be reconsidered. How serious is a negative result here?

Important, but not critical. The reason is that geographic distance has usually been measured as air distance between capital cities, state boundaries, political boundaries (including colonies), contiguity or not, or as the number of political boundaries. In some of my studies I have also measured it as transaction distance (cost of shipping).

In all those measurements, geographic distance roughly reflects contact and awareness. One should expect a negative correlation; but it need not be high (as argued in the prediction section, above), and it may be low.

Moreover, contact and awareness are not purely a matter of geographic distance, no matter how measured. For distance also depends on the resources of states to transcend distance: their joint power, as formulated in the next proposition. Therefore, the specific characteristics of cases included in a sample can also affect the relationship between geographic distance and Conflict Behavior.

Theoretically, correlations should still be positive in general, otherwise there would be no Geographic Proposition. However, the occurrence of some negative correlations is understandable.

Conclusion: The weight of the evidence in Table 16C.3 is positive and the qualitative nature of this evidence lends further support. Therefore, the conclusion: *the evidence supports the proposition.*

Proposition 16.5 (Joint Power): Conflict Behavior assumes salience.

Joint power is positively correlated with Conflict Behavior.

Theory: Conflict Behavior assumes contact. True. But, it also assumes salience, a mutual importance of the states.

Salience is an aspect of awareness. Not only are states in contact, their leaders mutually aware of each other, but they each have a mutual salience: a mutual importance of interests, capabilities, and will. This salience qualifies the impact of geographic distance, for states at a considerable distance may be more salient than those closer to home.

Salience is reflected along many dimensions of behavior: the degree of transactions, the existence and degree of diplomatic relations, prominance in the media, state visits and conferences, and the like. There is a more fundamental measure of salience, however, that relates to all these and should be positively correlated with conflict behavior. This is the *joint power* of two states.

Power in terms of combined national income, resources, area, population, and defense expenditures reflects the interest of national leaders in other states and the interest of other states in it (as a possible aggressor, if for no other reason), *plus* the ability of leaders to transcend geographic distance.

Power bases (or coercive power potential) is thus by itself a gradient of a nation's global saliance, and should be related to Conflict Behavior. This is one source of the State Power Proposition (16.31), to be considered below. The mutual salience of two states is thus measured by their joint power: the power of one plus that of the other.

Conflict behavior assumes salience. It assumes that states have sufficient power to transcend their distances or are given such power by other parties (such as in the American-aided South Korean military action against North Vietnam in the Vietnam war); or Soviet-aided Cuban military action against Somalia in the Ethiopian-Somalia War.

As with geographic distance, salience is also a gradient. And the more salient two states, the more it can worsen a conflict between them and increase the intensity of Conflict Behavior. Therefore, salience can also be considered an aggravating cause, as shown in Table 16B.1.

Prediction: In my research I have measured power as either the factor scores on the power (bases) component, or by national income or population indicators. Joint power was measured then as the power of the actor plus that of the object state. *Or,* as this sum divided by geographic distance (sometimes squared). This latter operationalization also measures what is called "the social gravity" of two states.

Studies measuring joint power as any reasonable variant of the above types of measures (such as the power of one times that of the other) are considered relevant to the proposition.

The expected correlations shown in Table 16C.1 and their supporting arguments are the same as for the Geographic Proposition; except for joint power the correlations should be opposite to geographic distance.

Evidence: The evidence is mostly supportive (10 out of 12 analyses), and is mainly direct (6 out of 7). Only two important studies bear on it, however, but both are positive. Excluding studies inconsistent with Model II and the distance vector assumptions of field theory, five are for, none against. My own analyses have been positive, except for one ambiguous result.

In addition, I have found that joint power has been an empirically strong correlate of dyadic conflict behavior, sometimes appearing as the best predictor or strongest correlate in regression and factor analyses.

Conclusion: the evidence supports the proposition.

Proposition 16.6 (Distance Vector): Distances are the force vectors of conflict.

Conflict Behavior is most correlated with sociocultural differences and similarities (distance vectors).

Theory: The medium of the international field is the meanings, values, and norms of international actors. Seated in this medium are the potential field forces of international behavior: the sociocultural distance vectors between actors. This is the analytic level.

Substantively, actors have different and often opposing interests and capabilities. Interests provide the field's energy; they are the actor's need-connected goals and means. Stimulation of needs generates the motivational energy, and interests direct this energy.

All this has been developed in Volume 1 (1975 part IV), Volume 2 (1976 chapter 6), and in chapter 8. As pointed out, the axes of opposing interests and capabilities between actors lie along their distance vectors. *Component distance vectors are therefore forces because they reflect interests and capabilities;* the vector forces are seated in meanings, values, and norms because the component distances are on the sociocultural components of the international sociocultural space-time, such as wealth, power, totalitarianism, Catholic culture, and the others discussed in chapter 7 (Table 7.1).

By theory conflict is a balancing of opposing interests and capabilities, and by theory this opposition should be reflected in the international space-time distances between actors. In other words, of all types of independent variables (distance magnitudes; internal variables; system variables; actor characteristics alone), distance vectors should best account for the variance in Conflict Behavior.

This does not mean that distance vectors are necessary and sufficient for Conflict Behavior. Distance vectors are necessary causes. They may reflect the structure of conflict and, in relation to perceived situation (see Table 10.1), the situation of conflict; but they still may be held in check by a congruent structure of expectations or by a lack of a trigger if the structure is incongruent with the associated balance of powers.

Distance vectors in their effect are analogous to a tight web of rubber bands, tied together and stretched between many sticks. The web is a balance of pulling forces along the taut rubber bands. The forces are there, but are latent until one band is cut. Then, there will be a sudden readjustment of the web in line with the pulling forces. Likewise, when an international structure of expectations is disrupted, conflict occurs in line with the distance vectors.

Prediction: The prediction is that distance vectors will best account for the variance in Conflict Behavior. In analyses using many different types of independent variables, distance vectors should be the most effective; in studies using only distance vectors, they should account for a significant (practical or statistical, depending on the analysis) amount of variance.

A high correlation may occur but cannot be generally expected: *distance vectors are only necessary, not sufficient, for Conflict Behavior.* Appropriate vectors may reflect a structure or situation of conflict, but for lack of other necessary causes, no conflict may occur.

When there is conflict behavior, however, it should occur in line with the distance vectors (opposing interests and capabilities).

Direction of correlations is irrelevant: This proposition only states the potency of distance vectors. Other propositions (e.g., Propositions 16.12, 16.14, 16.30, and 16.32) give direction in correlation and substantive interpretation to certain distance vectors.

The variance in distance vectors should be most correlated with the variance in each conflict variable listed in Table 16C.1, regardless of sample.

One source of confusion. In the analyses of a dyadic sample involving the same actor, variation in distance vectors is equivalent to variation in the object state's attributes. Therefore, analyses of object attributes provide evidence for the Distance Vector Proposition.

Evidence: On balance the evidence favors the proposition: overall there are 18 analyses for (with five strongly positive), six against. Most of the positive evidence is inferential, however, and when excluded, there remain six for and five against.

The important studies are generally positive (6 to 1); and excluding model I studies leaves a favorable balance of evidence (8 for to 3 against). Most of the favorable analyses are my own (12 out of 15), and so are half the negative analyses (3 out of 6).

Thus, 75% of the evidence supports the proposition and 21% is strongly positive; 25% is negative, 8% strongly so. Two out of eight important analyses are negative.

Moreover, there is a feel I have developed for distance vectors from my own research and that of others. Often, distance vectors added to an analysis make the difference between accounting for much or little variance in conflict behavior; between having highly significant regression coefficients or barely significant ones.

Conclusion: The proposition is consistent with most of the evidence, but there is still sufficient negative evidence to qualify the conclusion. Therefore: *the evidence tends to support the proposition.*

Proposition 16.7 (Actor): Individual perceptions and expectations condition conflict-force vectors.

The potency of interests (sociocultural distance vectors) depends on an actor's individual perceptions and expectations.

Theory: This is the basic assumption of Model II of field theory: states are influenced by distances (opposing interests and capabilities) in the light of their own experiences, domestic systems, leadership, and so on. In short, perceptions and expectations will vary by state and differently weight distance and behavioral disposition vectors (see chapter 10). The important role of actor dependent perceptions and expectations has been a theme of the previous volumes.   Conflict promoting perceptions and expectations are necessary, but not sufficient, for conflict behavior, however. They can create a situation of conflict, but a structure of expectations based on a stable balance of powers may still maintain a stable peace. When conflict does occur, however, perceptions and expectations should be the parameters of its direction and intensity. This is detailed in Propositions 16.9, 16.28, and 16.29.

Now, I should be clear that I am asserting something more than that perceptions and expectations are an important necessary cause of Conflict Behavior. This is:

(1) expectations and perceptions in their causal relationship to conflict behavior differ by actor (Model II),

(2) expectations and perceptions are parameters weighting behavioral dispositions (among which are dispositions to conflict) and distance vectors (see appendix 9A),

(3) the proper model of conflict behavior is one involving directed dyads and the same actor (Model II).

Prediction: The prediction closest to theory is that the trace correlations (canonical analysis) of a Model II fit of international behavior (including conflict behavior) will be significant (as shown in appendix 9A), and more so than alternative models of international behavior. And this should hold regardless of sample or conflict variable.

Those analyses involving expectations or perceptions as *variables* across actors are also relevant, and should find a moderate correlation (because perception and expectation are necessary causes) between them and the conflict variables.

Evidence: With the exception of one ambiguity, the evidence is uniformly positive; the majority (11 out of 21) strongly positive. Indeed, strongly positive results predominate also for the direct and important studies as well. Moreover, most of this evidence is from analyses other than my own.

This evidence is congruent with my experience in testing Model II on a variety of data (see 1977: chapter 16): it has generally accounted for about 50% of the variation (canonical trace correlation) in international behavior (including conflict), and first canonical correlations were often greater than .90.

Conclusion: the evidence strongly supports the proposition.

Proposition 16.8 (Will-To-Conflict): Conflict behavior demands will.

Conflict behavior will occur only if there is a will to conflict.

Theory: There can be no antagonistic conflict behavior withour the will-to-conflict. There can be appeasement, acceptance, submission, abnegation, surrender.

Will is an explicit part of the process of conflict. It initiates the uncertainty phase, the point at which the decision is made to confront, or oppose another's interest, or pursue one's own in spite of opposition. And will (or credibility) is one of the three elements, along with interests and capabilities, involved in the balancing of powers; and in the balance underlying the structure of expectations.

While the will to conflict may be there, however, interests may be confused and capabilities insufficient. Will is not sufficient, therefore, but it is necessary.

Prediction: Strength of will should be positively correlated with the conflict behavior variable or conflict scale for the mixed sample shown in Table 16C.1. But, otherwise, because strength of will may vary across types of conflict behavior and along conflict behavior components (e.g., negative sanctions), and because much of this behavior can lie below the mean for the other conflict variables and samples, the resulting correlations are random.

A serious problem lies in measuring will. It cannot be measured by the occurrence of conflict behavior, for then the analysis would be tautological with regard to the proposition. But will could be measured by a complex of previous behavior showing a tendency, say, to withdraw or appease when confrontation occurs; by party platforms, public statements, official appointments, or expert ratings. In any case, its measurement must have been kept separate from the dependent variable to be relevant to the proposition.

Evidence: No evidence is available other than in Blainey's (1973) nonquantitative, historically "soft" systematic analysis of war and peace since 1700.

There may be three reasons for this. One is that will is considered too difficult to measure. I doubt this, however, because I do not recall the problem even being discussed and there has been a variety of attempts to measure other equally soft concepts, like perception.

A second reason may be that will is considered obviously a part of conflict, too self-evident to mention or require analysis. Perhaps. But I suspect that it is less a matter of obviousness than of perceived irrelevance. To many social behaviorists, will is a metaphysical concept; not quite respectable for "scientific" interest. Moreover, conflicts are often assumed to be occurrence, happenings, like highway accidents, or sickness, while will implies a conscious choice to conflict. A third and related reason may be that will is nondeterministic, implying freedom of choice. Most behaviorists are conscious or unconscious determinists who leave no room in their philosophy for a will as first cause.

In any case, whether because it is obvious, irrelevant, or rejected, I am aware of no systematic evidence on the role of will in conflict.

Conclusions: there is insufficient evidence.

Proposition 16.9 (Confidence): Violence assumes confidence.

Intense violence will occur only if there is an expectation of success.

Theory: The expectation of success is a necessary cause of intense violence, whether large scale military action or war. Escalation of violence, launching a war, or defense against such, is a subjective cost-gains calculation. It is rational in the sense that in the actor's calculus, violence will succeed in preserving, enhancing, or achieving some subjective stake.

This stake may be territory, independence, self-determination, a homeland, religion, national identity, an ideology, honor, credibility, domestic power. It may appear irrational to outsiders. But regardless of content, the actor believes or feels that the stake is worth the violence, and that violence will succeed.

Violence is a threshold in conflict behavior. It indicates an intense opposition of interests; a struggle over the status quo. Negative sanctions, accusations, protest, threats, and the like, can occur between states for whom mutual military violence is presently inconceivable, such as the United States, Canada, Great Britain, Australia, and New Zealand. This threshold is crossed when border clashes, discrete military actions (shooting of a border guard, downing a surveillance plane, capturing an intelligence ship) occur. But the violence and costs are minor: few if any deaths occur, and the violence can often be shrugged off officially as caused by mistaken identity, local commanders, or hotheads.

Such actions may be probes to assess the success of more direct or intense action, they may be limited actions of low risk and possible high gain, or they may be spontaneous local engagements. Nonviolent conflict behavior can also be probes, sanctions, retortions, communications, and the like. The status quo may not even be involved.

However, when intense violence is selected, when large military formations are engaged for more than a day and the killed range upward from the hundreds, a second threshold has been crossed. Now, the costs can be severe, major national values can be lost, a leader's head may be on the line, and only major stakes and a belief in success can justify the danger.

Overt conflict begins in a situation of uncertainty. But by the time war is chosen, at least the uncertainty of success is dispelled. For both major parties.

Prediction: Expectations of success may or may not be present in nonviolent conflict or low-level violence, while always present in high-level violence. Therefore, it should be correlated positively with the intensity of violence and conflict scale for the mixed, conflict, and violence samples.

For the frequency of war variable, for both the mixed conflict samples, however, war and intense violence will appear below the mean (see Figure 16C.1) and can thus cause the correlation to range from a near zero to a moderate plus.

For the war sample, expectation of success should be present in all cases.

Evidence: The evidence amounts to three analyses, two positive and one strongly positive. One is Blainey's (1973) analysis, a second is Wright's analysis of escalation (1965), and third was my own (appendix I: 7.1) systematic analysis of Wright's data, augmented by attribute and distance data. All are important studies; two of the three are direct.

Conclusion: Although the number of relevant analyses is small, they are consistent. Thus the conclusion: *the evidence unanimously supports the proposition.*

Proposition 16.10 (Status-Quo Disruption): Violence assumes a disrupted status quo.

Violence is over a status quo.

Theory: The status quo is the division in rights and duties, what is ours and theirs. It is the hard core of any structure of expectations, usually well-defined, and the major values in any interaction.

In international relations the status quo is defined by who has sovereignty over, control over, or the actual or implied allegiance of the people living on a *territory.* A conflict may be over a border area (e.g., Vietnam versus Cambodia in 1977-1978), the independence of a colony (e.g., the Algerian War, 1954-1962), the independence of a state (e.g., the Korean War, 1950-1953), and the control of a state (e.g., the Soviet invasion of Czechoslovakia in 1968). Moreover, a terriotrially defined status quo is often the source of conflict, as over the rights of Greek versus Turkish Cypriots.

Ours and theirs may refer to the allegiance or ideology of territorially defined peoples. We "lost" Cuba to the Soviet Union; they are "gaining" Angola. The "free world" now consists of . . . ; NATO will be "weakened" if Italy has a communist government. And so on.

The disruption of the status quo may not cause violence. A new status quo may be determined nonviolently, as in the Panama Canal Treaty negotiated by the United States and Panama (although there were anti-American riots and demonstrations and potential violence was an argument used by the Carter Administration in seeking Senate ratification, the settlement was achieved nonviolently), and the granting of independence to many former colonies.

However, the status quo defines the high stakes, and only the status quo is worth violence.

What comprises nonstatus quo expectations? This is the whole complex of implicit and formal understandings, agreements, and treaties governing the relationship and interaction between parties, which do not define who has what rights and duties over what territory. Trade agreements, counselor understandings, disarmament treaties, diplomatic norms, and the like, are the nonstatus quo part of our international structure of expectations.

Prediction: A disrupted status quo is a necessary condition of violence. That is, all violence should be over some territorial sovereignty, control, allegiance, or territorial-based rights (as over ethnic group or national group rights in a territory).

For the nonconflict behavior sample, nonconflict behavior implies that a disrupted status quo is absent, as shown in Table 16C.1.

For the mixed sample and conflict variable, no disrupted status quo should appear below the mean, while above the mean cases can also have nondisrupted status quos. The correlation can therefore range from near zero to moderate positive.

For nonviolent conflict, however, status-quo disruption can appear above and below the mean in frequencies depending upon the sample's specific characteristics. This is because nonviolent conflict may or may not reflect a disrupted status quo, while below the mean occur violent cases with disrupted status quo and nonconflict cases without such disruption.

For other conflict variables, there should be a moderate correlation.

The logic is the same for the conflict variables in the conflict sample, while for the violence and war samples disrupted expectations should be present in each case.

Evidence: All ten sources of evidence support the proposition, four strongly and directly so. Moreover, most of the evidence are from important studies, are consistent with field theory, and all are from studies other than my own.

Conclusion: the evidence unanimously supports the proposition.

Proposition 16.11 (Joint-Freedom): Libertarian systems mutally preclude violence.

Violence will occur between states only if at least one is nonlibertarian.

Theory: Totalitarian and authoritarian states are the sources of military violence. Power is centralized, and in the hands of a small group or leader. Control over the communication media can be used to direct and intensify public opinion against another state: domestic interest groups can be controlled; and dissidents in the elite can be jailed.

In open systems, however, initiating a war or military action is usually precluded by the restraint of public opinion and opposition of interest groups, unless there is a clear and present danger to the state or its security by military aggression or a unilateral change in the status quo (e.g., Egypt's takeover of the Suez Canal in 1956). Then public opinion and the elite unify behind defense, or at least the party in power will support its leadership in the near term.

However, between libertarian states there is a fundamental sympathy of their peoples toward each other's system, a compatibility of basic values, an existence of cross-pressures and overlapping groups and organizations, and a suffusion of power and interests.

Between exchange societies and their libertarian political systems exist the same conditions minimizing violence (Proposition 16.24) that operate within societies.

Therefore, a necessary condition of violence between two states is that at least one be totalitarian or authoritarian.

Prediction: The prediction is narrowly specific: only jointly libertarian states will be without violence. This makes assessing correlation especially difficult. For simplicity, I will call two jointly libertarian states a *libertarian dyad*. *Nonlibertarian dyads* are any pair of states, at least one of which is nonlibertarian in the sense developed in Volume 2 (1976: chapter 31).

For the nonconflict sample, both libertarian and nonlibertarian dyads can be without conflict.

For the mixed sample and conflict variable, both libertarian and nonlibertarian dyads can appear randomly above and below its mean, because both types of dyads may or may not have conflict behavior. Therefore, a random correlation is expected. Similarly for the nonviolent conflict variable.

However, for the frequency of violence or war variables, libertarian dyads should be at the bottom of the scale and the correlation should therefore be negative. At this point, what independent variables are correlated with the conflict variable should be carefully considered.

There are three types of potentially relevant independent variables. The closest to the proposition would be a *dichotomous variable separating libertarian dyads from nonlibertarian.* Correlation between this independent variable and the frequency of violence or war for the mixed sample should, by theory, be moderately negative. The reason that a perfect negative correlation cannot be assumed is that the frequency of violence or war variables would have violence also occurring below their means (see Figure 16C.1), and nonlibertarian dyads also may be without violence.

If the independent variable is the *absolute political distance* between actor and object state, the correlation could be random regarding the Joint Freedom Proposition, because this measurement does not distinguish between libertarian and nonlibertarian dyads, and the proposition does *not* imply that similar political systems (e.g., two totalitarian states) should be involved in violence more or less than dissimilar ones (e.g., totalitarian and authoritarian or authoritarian and libertarian states).

If the independent variable is *vector distance,* the same point applies, except when all dyads have the same actor (Model II). Then, in effect the distance vector is measuring the variation in the object's political system. And when the actor is libertarian, then this variable should be correlated moderately and negatively with the violence in the dyad.

Keeping in mind, then, that the independent variable is a dochotomy or vector distance in Model II for libertarian actors, we should also find that the violence intensity and conflict scale variables are moderately and negatively correlated.

The same logic applies to the conflict sample. For the violence and war samples, however, there should be no cases of libertarian dyads having violence or war, and therefore, these dyads should be absent from the samples.

A final consideration. Violence here refers to low or high-level violence. In a crises or war situation involving other nations a discrete military action or clash may occur between libertarian states, such as the Israel attack on a U.S. surveillance ship during the 1973 Yom Kippur War. Usually the attack will not be given official sanction and apologies will be made. Such events should be rare and ought not to be given significant weight in assessing the proposition.

Evidence: Nine analyses (three strongly) support the proposition; three are negative. Highly significant is that no important analysis is negative, and two of the three negative results were indirect—inferences I made from rather complex statistical manipulations involving samples and variables which, themselves, only indirectly measure what is of concern here. This is, of course, true for the indirect positive evidence as well. However, the importance of this point is that in contrast to these weak negative results some of the direct positive results are clear and absolute, especially regarding wars where with one ambiguous and explicable exception (the War of 1812 between the United States and Great Britain), wars simply have not occurred between libertarian or partially libertarian systems (see appendix I: 7.5; Babst, n.d., 1972).

Conclusion: the evidence supports the proposition.

Proposition 16.12 (Dissimilarity): Dissimilarity aggravates conflict.

Sociocultural dissimilarity is positively correlated with Conflict Behavior.

Theory: The more distant states are in the international space-time, the more likely their interests will conflict and the more difficult communication and negotiation will be (see Volume 3, 1977: chapter 6).

Such absolute distances are not sufficient or necessary for conflict, however. Nations close in space-time may have territorial, ideological, or theological disputes (as between Catholic states in Europe during the Middle Ages or communist states today); moreover, states quite distant may have little contact and salience. But given the occurrence of the conditions embodied in propositions 16.1-11, then sociocultural distance aggravates the conflict, making resolution more difficult.

Prediction: Dissimilarity (as absolute sociocultural distance) should be positively and moderately correlated with the conflict behavior variable in the mixed sample.

However, for nonviolence, the frequency of violence, or frequency of war, and considering the other conditions operating, dissimilarity alone would appear not to have any uniform correlation. For the violence variables this is in effect saying that while conflict is acerbated, there is no necessary relationship between the degree of dissimilarity and the intensity of *overall* conflict as embodied in a conflict scale.

If this is confusing, consider again Figure 16C.1. While more intense conflict in general will appear above the mean for the conflict variables, for the violence and war frequency variables, cases with intense nonviolent conflict, or intense war (for the violence variable), or intense low-level conflict, can appear far below the mean (possibly at zero).

The predicted correlations for the other samples follow the same logic.

Evidence: All the relevant analyses bear directly on the proposition and ten are supportive versus four against. Of the important studies the balance is almost even, four to three (but two of the three are strongly negative).

Conclusion: the evidence supports the proposition.

Proposition 16.13. (Cognitive Dissonance): Cognitive dissonance aggravates conflict.

Cognitive dissonance is positively correlated with conflict behavior.

Theory: I have considered cognitive dissonance, or imbalance, theoretically in Volume 1 (1975: chapter 12) and particularly with regard to status and behavior in Volume 2 (1976:

section 18.2). In short, there are two aspects of cognitive dissonance relevant to national leaders.

First, leaders will tend to adjust their policies to maintain a psychological balance in their perceived relations with other states. If, for example, leaders perceive an ally is also allied to an hostile state, then they will tend to readjust their policies accordingly. But such readjustment may provoke conflict, for it will involve different behavior and a new structure of expectations.

Second, leaders will tend to see their state in terms of its highest status and other states in terms of their lowest. Because leaders of different states are then emphasizing different components of their relationship, this makes communication more difficult, conflict more likely, and settlement more difficult. Therefore, cognitive dissonance aggravates conflict.

Prediction: Cognitive dissonance can be operationalized as either status incongruence (Volume 2, 1976: 142) between states or a triadic imbalance in relations (dissonance: Volume 1, 1975: 124-128). So measured, cognitive dissonance will be positively correlated with the conflict behavior variable and with the conflict scale for the mixed, conflict, and violence samples, as shown in Table 16C.1. For the other variables,. I see no theoretical reason for cognitive dissonance being correlated with one type of conflict intensity versus another, and therefore expect correlations to vary from one study to another.

Evidence: The evidence is almost uniformly supportive (ten analyses for to one against), but usually indirect. Six out of seven of the analyses were from important studies.

The one negative study was also direct. It involved a time-series analysis (Mogdis, 1969, 1970) of Sino-Soviet interaction and perception and analyzed the effect on their behavior of a cognitive imbalance in the triangular Soviet-China-United States relationship.

Conclusion: Although the evidence is almost unanimous, it is mainly inferential and there is one important negative study. Nonetheless, I can say simply that: *the evidence supports the proposition.*

Proposition 16.14 (Status): Status distances are force vectors of conflict.

Differences in status (wealth, power, prestige) are positively correlated with Conflict Behavior.

Theory: Status vectors are forces toward conflict. The theoretical justification for this was the burden of Volume 2 (1976: chapters 17-18).

But these forces are neither sufficient nor necessary. They act within the context of the other forces (causes) and conditions given in Table 16A.1. They are forces which worsen conflict, making conflict behavior more likely and more intense.

Status is defined by wealth, power, and prestige. These are esteemed, desired components. Power, however, has also particular importance in its own right.

Absolute difference in (coercive) power, or the degree of power parity, indicates the likelihood of escalation in war (Proposition 16.21). The centralization of (coercive) power stimulates extreme violence (Proposition 16.20) and inhibits low-level conflict (Proposition 16.23). Together, these propositions imply that of all attributes, power is the most correlated with conflict (Proposition 16.31), and that power is the most potent force toward conflict (Proposition 16.32).

Here, however, the interest is in status distance. Parity or polarity will be considered irrelevant (but not power distance vectors) for this proposition.

Prediction: Status distance (vector) in some sense should be positively correlated with all the conflict variables in the mixed and conflict samples, except for the frequency of low-level conflict.

For this variable other kinds of intense conflict will occur below the mean and this should not generally be compensated for by a high relationship of status distance to the intensity of low-level violence. Status is too gross a force to make a great difference in whether states have, say, few or many border clashes. Therefore, the expected correlation is random.

For the violence and war samples, much of the variance in the effect of status on nonviolent conflict behavior has been eliminated. Therefore, I expect that the correlation will also be random for this variable in those samples.

Evidence: Status has been a focus of many studies, and thus relatively much evidence exists. And virtually all analyses (16 to 1) support the proposition. Most evidence is strongly positive, all of which is direct. Even for important studies, the evidence is mainly positive, most strongly so.

Conclusion: the evidence strongly supports the proposition.

Proposition 16.15 (Cross-Pressures/Conflict): Cross-pressures generate nonviolent conflict.

Cross-pressures are positively correlated with nonviolent Conflict Behavior.

Theory: The theoretical function of cross-pressures (and crosscutting) is presented in Volume 2 (1976: *passim* – see index). There are two aspects to consider: the impact on nonviolent conflict, and on violence. Cross-pressures act to increase one and reduce the other. The former impact is considered here; the latter is embodied in the Cross-Pressures/Violence Proposition (16.24).

Simply put, diverse, overlapping meanings, values and attitudes in society create a variety of opposing interests and the necessity to achieve many different, associated structures of expectations. There will thus be many small scale conflicts – a hubbub of Conflict Behavior.

For example, consider a societywide market in which prices are determined by free competition. There will be a variety of cross-pressures operating in the market and many associated conflicts between buyers and sellers, management and labor, and producer and consumer groups, not to mention the competition between businesses. A free market is a field of such conflicts.

In an authoritarian or coercive system, however, issues are generally decided by tradition and authority or by coercion (as in socialism). The function of diverse, competing and opposing interests and capabilities – of *cross-pressures* – is therefore subdued. People are harmonized by class, ethnic group, region, religion, or coercion.

At the international level, the more cross-pressures can operate in the international system, the more nonviolent conflict will be present. Highly polar systems (coercive systems) or those divided into a few alliances or religious groupings (authoritative systems) should have relatively less nonviolent Conflict Behavior overall.

Between states (dyadically) cross-pressures should operate similarly. The more cross-pressures, the more confused interstate relations and the more likely nonviolent conflict as multiple balancing is required. But the very existence of these cross-pressures also inhibits the formation of a single, dominant dispute along which interests could polarize and cause intense conflict and extreme violence.

See also the theoretical discussion for Propositions 16.20, 16.23, and 16.24.

Prediction: The expected correlations for each sample must take into account the complementary Cross-Pressure/Violence Proposition (16.24) and is discussed in general terms for that proposition. The expected correlations will be the same for both propositions.

Evidence: The only evidence I could find was in the Vasquez (1975, 1976) sifting of quantitative results, which was negative.

Much of the explanation for this lack of evidence is that research on or involving cross-pressures is almost always on violence, and that it is not widely appreciated that cross-pressures have a dual role in inhibiting violence and aggravating nonviolent conflict.

Conclusion: The one negative result, especially because it is from a summary, suggests the conclusion: *insufficient evidence.*

Proposition 16.16 (Honor): Honor at stake risks escalation in violence.

Involvement of a state's honor is positively correlated with violence.

Theory: At the core of interests lies the self-sentiment, man's self-image. Man acts to enhance and develop self-esteem. One of the sources of power for state leadership is that citizens generally link their self-esteem to their nation. Its gains are their gains; its losses they suffer, psychologically. In this sense, nations are like hometown teams. We identify with them, cheer them on to victory and are ecstatic when they win; depressed, sometimes violent, when they lose. That about a state which is linked to the self-esteem of its people defines its *honor.*

Because self-esteem is the superordinate goal of all men (Volume 1, 1975: section 21.5) honor is a central variable in a state's relations with others and in the genesis of violence. It is an aggravating cause.

A festering *humiliation* over past defeat may aggravate a dispute or stimulate another war, as in the Egyptian-Syrian launched attack on Israel in 1973. *Outrage* over a surprise attack may crystallize war sentiment and make negotiated peace impossible, as in Japan's attack on Pearl Harbor in 1941. A people may feel insulted by another state, their sense of *dignity* at stake.

States may surely have material interests in a conflict, power and credibility may be at stake. But the strength and nature of a conflict will not be well understood unless the engagement of honor (self-esteem) is also considered.

Two possible sources of misunderstanding should be clarified. First, honor is an *interest,* as discussed in *Volume 1* (1975: section 21.5) in terms of self-esteem. The reason I emphasize the term honor here is because of its general use and understanding in international relations. Therefore, honor is not simply an emotion (although pride or a feeling of injustice will be involved) to be opposed to national interests. Honor is a national interest of high order.

Second, honor is sometimes confused with credibility. Clearly, there is an overlap in meaning. A nation's reputation for justice, fulfillment of promises, and discharge of military commitments is an aspect of its honor. But honor as self-esteem and credibility as will to meet promises or threats are distinct. More on credibility below, regarding the next proposition.

Prediction: Honor operates at the higher levels of conflict, specifically to aggravate violence. It is generally irrelevant to nonviolent conflict in all samples. Also, it should have no general correlation one way or another with the frequency of low-level violence, simply because honor may be highly correlated with the violence that appears below the mean for the variable (see Figure 16C.1).

The other conflict variables, however, should be positively correlated with honor being at stake.

Evidence: The only evidence (which is direct, important, and strongly positive) is the nonquantitative semisystematic analysis of disputes since 1945 by Northedge and Donelan (1971). Honor has simply been ignored by quantitative researchers.

Conclusion: Insufficient evidence.

Proposition 16.17 (Credibility): Credibility at stake risks escalation in violence.

Involvement of a state's reputation for power (will) is positively correlated with violence.

Theory: The more involved in a conflict is a state's credibility for defending its interests or meeting its commitments to defend others, then the more intense and prolonged the conflict may become.

Now, the status quo is certainly involved in violence (Proposition 16.10). That is what it is being fought over. However, a state's *reputation for power,* the image a state projects of a will to protect its interests and follow through on threats is also at stake. For leaders realize that what a state does in a current conflict is recorded on an international ledger to be consulted by others interested in pushing their own status quo interests. To show weakness of will, like the boy in the schoolyard who submits, crying, to the taunts and slaps of a bully, is to invite a broad assault by many on one's interests.

State's fight not only to win a current conflict, but to avoid or reduce the costs of the next. For example, the credibility stake became a major variable explaining U.S. military involvement in Vietnam under President Johnson.

Prediction: The predictions for the involvement of credibility are the same as for honor. Both operate similarly and at the same conflict levels.

Evidence: There are two sources of evidence. One is direct and important, and is the Northedge and Donalan (1971) nonquantitative analysis. It strongly supports the propositions.

The other source is also direct and important, and is Barringer's (1972) rigorously systematic work. His results support the proposition and show that the perception of some public commitment at stake is one of the variables discriminating between hostilities and lower-level conflict.

Conclusion: Because there are *two* important analyses, both supporting the proposition, the conclusion: *the evidence supports the proposition.*

Proposition 16.18 (Status-Quo Power): Weakness of the status-quo power risks escalating violence.

An actual or growing weakness of the status-quo party compared to the antistatus-quo party is positively correlated with violence.

Theory: A structure of expectations has at its core the status quo which defines rights: what is ours versus theirs.

Over the status quo may grow a latent conflict between that state which benefits most from the status quo and believes it is just or right, and one who opposes it as unjust or undesirable. However, the antistatus quo party will continue to acquiesce in the status quo as long as it feels attempts to change it will be unsuccessful or too costly. In other words, as long as the original balance of powers undergirding the status quo does not shift to favor the antistatus-quo party, the structure of expectations is stable.

However, if the status-quo party significantly weakens in will, interests, or capability for coercive power, then the balance in powers will shift. And a disruption of the status quo will likely occur as the antistatus-quo party is triggered to pursue a more favorable status quo.

This does not make the weakness of the status-quo party a sufficient condition for violence, however. For nonviolent accommodations may take place; both parties may be libertarian (which would preclude violence, as stated in Proposition 16.11); in spite of a disrupted status quo and extreme nonviolent conflict, the antistatus-quo party may be deterred from violence by an uncertainty over success or the costs (as in the deterrent effect of nuclear weapons on both the United States and USSR behavior during the 1962 Cuban Missile Crisis).

Nonetheless, the weakness of the status quo party is a potent aggravator of conflict, making violence more likely and more intense. This because the issues deal with territory, core rights, and perceived justice.

Prediction: Operationally, there are three primary variables involved in a balance of power: interests, will or credibility, and capabilities. And the overall strength of the status-quo party is a multiple of these variables. Thus, a status-quo party can become weakened by a shift in one, two, or all three variables. Thus, to lose will through the election of a pacifist leader would create weakness; to reduce the salience of a specific status-quo interest (such as American loss of interest in defending freedom elsewhere) would create weakness; and, as everyone knows, to reduce military power would create weakness.

What should also be clear is that weakness is comparative: the status-quo party could actually remain as strong or be increasing in strength. But if the antistatus-quo power increases power (interests, will, capabilities) faster, then a weakness of the status-quo party would still be produced; a dangerous gap between the status quo and the supporting balance of power would occur.

Weakness is an aggravating cause of violence, as are the involvement of honor and credibility.

Thus, the expected correlations shown in Table 16C.1 follow the same logic.

Evidence: Six different analyses bear on the proposition as tabulated in Table 16C.3, four of them are important and five direct. All six support the propositions; three do so strongly. And all these analyses are by others than myself.

Conclusion: the evidence unanimously supports the proposition.

Proposition 16.19 (Intervention): Big Power intervention risks escalating violence.

Big Power intervention in a conflict is positively correlated with violence.

Theory: Local conflicts are a balancing of power among non-Big Power states contiguously or regionally involved. A Big Power then intervening to aid one side will likely inject into the local conflict the question of the status quo between the Big Power and its status-quo adversary.

Certainly, what a Big Power gains is not necessarily the loss of another. But when Big Powers intervene they raise the stakes involved in the local conflict. The outcome will determine what is within the Big Power's territorial or ideological sphere of influence and support. Therefore, such intervention usually does not go unanswered: The Big Power's adversary will counterintervene covertly or directly. A local conflict then becomes a balancing of the status quo between Big Powers.

Even were another Big Power not to counterintervene, intervention is usually on behalf of the losing side and will forestall its defeat and encourage an escalation of the local conflict.

Simply, intervention aggravates local conflict, risking an escalation in violence.

Prediction: Big Power intervention is an aggravating cause of violence. As a variable, its expected correlations are the same as for honor and credibility (Propositions 16.16-17) and the justification is similar.

Evidence: Two direct analyses strongly support the proposition. One is important and is Barringer's (1972) systematic analysis of variables discriminating the phases of conflict. The other is Kende's (n.d., 1971) statistical survey of 97 local wars, 1945-1969.

Conclusion: the evidence supports the propositon.

Proposition 16.20 (Polarity/Violence): Polarity stimulates intense violence.

Polarity is positively correlated with intense violence.

Theory: Polarity refers to the centralization of coercive power in a system. It is a state (as in "state of the system") variable, without application at the dyadic or nation-state level.[2]

Polarity as a variable does not distinguish the type of international societies involved. Unipolar systems may be authoritarian or coercive, but are in any case nonlibertarian. Bipolar (two major competing centers of power) or multipolar (more than two competing centers of power) or multipolar (more than two competing centers of power) systems may be a mixture of societies. Each pole maybe one type (as the American alliance since 1950 has been largely libertarian, while the Warsaw Pact has been coercive) and the overall system can be libertarian, as it is now (chapter 2).

Polarity is a distinct concept from cross-pressures. The latter may operate at the dyadic or nation-state level, and describe the state of the system as well. It means simply that for an individual state the existence of diverse, contending interests will usually work against any one being the basis of all out conflict. Overlapping and pluralistic groups and relationships define this essentially psychological variable.

Theoretically, however, there is a complementary relationship between polarity and cross-pressures. As a system is centralized (from multipolar to bipolar to unipolar), there is a decrease in the diversity of independent groups and relationships. Interests become aligned towards the poles; issues and disputes increasingly become part of the status quo—a class division—between the poles. If the system is unipolar conflicts still occur along the front between classes (the status-quo "ins" and the antistatus-quo "outs").

However, while increasing polarity decreases cross-pressures, decreasing polarity may not be followed by increasing cross-pressures (it may be a traditional, authoritative social system with a culture aligning interests along, say, religious lines as in Islamic society). Moreover, an increase in cross-pressures does not mean that polarity is decreasing. The increase may be due to increased economic and technological development.

Polarity and cross-pressures, in other words, are theoretically and conceptually distinct and need not be highly correlated empirically.

Nonetheless, they have opposite effects. Cross-pressures aggravate nonviolent Conflict Behavior (Proposition 16.15) while inhibiting violence (Proposition 16.24); polarity inhibits nonviolent Conflict Behavior (Proposition 16.23), while aggravating intense violence (Proposition 16.20).

Now to focus on the proposition of concern here. Polarity reduces cross-pressures and links otherwise ordinary conflicts into the more general status quo. Conflicts become a question of class power. Increasing polarity generalizes class conflict (in my terms, as developed in Volume 2, 1976 chapters 24-25) to the system and increases the salience and scope of this division to each state's interests (see also Proposition 16.22).

Therefore, more becomes at stake in a conflict, the issues are more burning, and the potential intensity and scope of violence is increased. That is, polarity aggravates violence. It makes intense war more likely. It makes a general war more probable. See also the theoretical discussion for Proposition 16.23.

Prediction: The expected correlations for each sample must take into account the complementary Polarity/Conflict Proposition (16.23) and is discussed in general terms for that proposition. The expected correlations will be the same for both propositions.

Evidence: There are three direct, strongly positive, and important analyses; one direct, positive, and important, as shown in Table 16C.4. But there are also two direct, important negative analyses, and three ambiguous ones. And all studies are consistent with the field theory Model II.

Why the negative evidence and unusual ambiguity? A major problem lies in the measurement of polarity. As a theoretical system variable, polarity varies with the centralization of the system, as shown in Figure 16B.1. At the point a system becomes unipolar, there may still be considerable dispersion of power. Consider that under the Articles of Confederation the American states formed a unipolar system during the Revolutionary War and under the Constitution of the United States which followed in 1787, the federation was much more centralized. Then compare this initial unipolar system with the centralized dominance of the American federal government today. Then compare this current unipolar system, which still

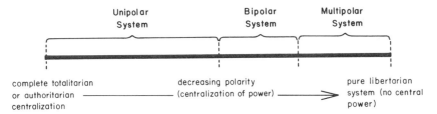

FIGURE 16B.1: Variation of Power with System Polarity

has considerable libertarian disperson of power, with the extreme centralization (polarity) of theocratic, authoritative Saudi Arabia or the totalitarian Soviet Union. Yet, all these systems (including the U.S. Confederation) would be unipolar.

Similarly counting the Roman Empire, the ancient Chinese Empire, the Persian Empire, the Holy Roman Empire, the German Confederation, the Napoleonic Empire, the Soviet Empire, and the like as unipolar is to collapse important variance related to conflict and violence.

Unfortunately, most quantitative studies measure polarity by a count of poles of power, and this may well account for the ambiguous and negative results. For when polarity is considered within states and is measured on a scale capturing the relevant variance, the relationship between polarity and violence (antiregime *and* that of a regime against the people) is positive: authoritarian and totalitarian states manifest more violence (Volume 2, 1976: chapter 35).

Conclusion: On balance the evidence supports the proposition, but the three ambiguous and two negative analyses, which are direct and important, suggest caution. Therefore, the conclusion: *the evidence tends to support the proposition.*

Proposition 16.21 (Power Parity): Power parity makes escalation to war more likely.

Power parity is correlated with war.

Theory: That power is related to war is one of the central beliefs of international relations. But on the precise nature of this relationship there is much dispute. Some argue that relative power parity stabilizes relations and is a force for peace. Others argue that power parity is a cause of war. The proposition argues the latter position: power parity is an aggravating cause of war.

A conflict that has reached the stage of violence (but not yet war) is over deeply held, status-quo interests (Proposition 16.10). Already costs have been incurred, the stakes are high, and further success or losses depend on the balance of coercive power or force. If one side is clearly superior in will and existing military capability and potential, then the other side is likely to avoid escalation, if necessary by negotiating a resolution to the conflict. Of course, if the stakes warrant it, the stronger side is likely to push its war threat chip forward to pressure the other, and in the expectation of success if called.

Power parity is an ambiguous situation of coercive power in which both sides simultaneously can believe that war will be victorious. War clears up this ambiguity.

Note that power here is not simply existing military capability. It is also military potential, which reflects economic power and probable third-country support. And it is strength of interests and will. Outweighed on paper by the combined Arab military forces, Israel nonetheless balanced the equation to her favor by a sharply focused and powerful desire for national and religious survival; and a national will rooted in Jewish history.

Note also that parity tends to convert low-level violence to war, but in theory is systematically unrelated to nonviolent Conflict Behavior or low-level violence. War involves the core national interests, possibly survival. Relative power becomes critical. Other forms of conflict are not so central and indeed may be peripheral to major national interests. Weak states can often pursue conflict with a much stronger one without worrying about the other's full power being brought to bear. The issue may not be that important for the stronger or it may be restrained by concern over provoking the involvement of a Big Power.

Finally, parity is an *absolute* distance variable.

Prediction: Parity should be positively correlated with the intensity of war: the more ambiguous the relative power, the more both parties can believe in success (Proposition 16.9); and the more ambiguous the relative power, the more intense tends to be the war. At that point when relative power becomes clear to both, when one of the sides who thought they would win now realize that defeat is a near certainty, it is the beginning of the end. Third-party conciliation and negotiation may now be fruitful.

As a cause of war, power parity then is irrelevant for all the nonviolent and low-level violence variables and the expected correlation is random in all samples, as shown in Table 16C.1. This is true also for the war frequency variable, which may be surprising. But consider. For the mixed, conflict, and violence samples, the zero point on the war frequency scale (as shown in Figure 16C.1) may involve cases with high or low parity (because parity is theoretically unrelated to conflict, except for war), and some cases of war below the mean may be intense conflicts which by theory should be highly related to parity. Each war is counted as one in the war frequency variable, thus equating such conflicts as the 1977-1978 Cambodian-Vietnam war, Vietnam war, 1973 Yom Kippur War, and World War II. The combination of nonwar cases and possible intense wars beneath the mean implies that in general the correlation will be random.

However, only war is involved in the war sample and although intense wars still may appear below the mean, the higher frequencies above the mean with the likelihood of their involving more of the intense wars, make probable a positive correlation with parity.

For the violence intensity and conflict scale in all samples, a positive correlation is predicted because of the increasing weight of intensity above the mean.

Evidence: As totaled in Table 16C.4, a large variety of analyses—37 to be exact—have been done involving parity and war. Of these one-fourth are negative (only one is strongly so), all but two of which are unimportant studies that I have done.

My studies have usually involved factor scores for military violence, with parity measured as absolute differences in national income or population. Moreover, the analyses were usually done for one year, especially for 1955, during which no intense war occurred in the sample. Obviously, the sample and measures are gross regarding the proposition and not too much should be made of the negative findings.

On the other side, 65% of the evidence is positive; 30% is strongly positive. Virtually all this evidence is direct, and most from important studies. Indeed, for important studies, which are usually those which have analyzed wars over a long historical period, 78% of the evidence is positive, most of which is strongly positive.

Conclusion: the evidence supports the proposition.

Proposition 16.22 (Class): Class conflict is the cauldron of general war.

Class conflict is correlated with general war.

Theory: A class is a latent or manifest group that stands in either a consistent superordinate or subordinate position regarding the status quo—in a command or obey position regarding the law norms of a society, as defined and developed in Volume 2 (1976: chapters 24-25).

Historically, international relations has been a sequence of orders (general structures of expectations) based on a balance of powers. Each order is a particular distribution of rights, of a status quo, distributing command and obey status. The command is usually an explicit: "These are my territory, my people, my sphere of influence, my privileges. Keep off and beware!" In each order a particular state or group of states most benefit and in effect form the superordinate, upper class. These are the status-quo powers.

As the same distribution of rights and privileges covers more international relations states, as the same states in more and more relationships are similarly up or down with respect to each other, an international class division is increased and enhanced.

The division of an order into classes is an aggravating cause of *general* war. Small wars escalate; more states are drawn in. This class division is a political fault line between the major international forces, and once the fault begins to slip at one place, pressures will be exerted to cause it to shift all along the line.

A general war is one involving the Big Powers, and a number of lesser states as well. The war is nearly unlimited in territory and weapons. Examples of general wars are the Thirty Years War, the Napoleonic Wars, World War I, and World War II.

Theoretically, class formation is closely related to polarity and cross-pressures (Propositions 16.20 and 16.24). Increasing polarity—the centralization of coercive power—increasingly divides society between those who command and those who obey. And increasing polarity decreases cross-pressures in the system, making the class division a societal wide front between opposing interests.

Prediction: The postulated relationship is of class formation with general war, a subcategory of intense wars (a very intense war may not be general, but limited to small states, such as the 1973 Yom Kippur War), where intense wars form a subcategory of Conflict Behavior. Much caution is indicated in predicting empirical correlations.

Table 16C.1 includes no general war variable, for the simple reason that analyses usually focus on war frequency or intensity. Singer and Small (1974) do consider the number of nations involved in a war, which does loosely measure generality, but this and other work by Singer and Small are an exception.

Therefore, simply given the variables included in Table 16C.1, what are the predictions? Assuming that absolute intensity of conflict behavior will itself have a correlation with general war (as an unnormed variable, e.g., number of killed is not divided by the populations involved), then class will operate correlationally like power parity. The expected correlations will be the same in both cases, except that they should be weaker for class, because we are dealing with a subcategory of intense wars.

Evidence: Only three different analyses (Denton, 1969; Kende, n.d., 1971; Barringer, 1972) are relevant. Two are important, one is direct, all are positive.

Conclusion: the evidence supports the proposition.

*Proposition 16.23 (Polarity/Conflict): Polarity inhibits
nonviolent conflict behavior and low level violence.*

Polarity is negatively correlated with nonviolent conflict behavior and low-level violence.

Theory: Polarity has already been discussed with regard to the Polarity/Violence Proposition (16.20), which states that polarity aggravates intense violence by creating a system-wide schism between opposing interests. The Polarity/Conflict Proposition, however, points out that polarity inhibits nonviolent and low-level behavior.

The centralization of power into a few poles, or into a unipolar system, suppresses the diversity of interests that lead to frequent nonviolent conflicts and occasional low-level violence. The Big Powers which form the poles, as have the United States and Soviet Union since World War II, try to avoid conflict behavior among allies and satellites, and especially conflict behavior between members of the opposing blocs which could escalate into a confrontation between the bloc leaders. Polarity creates continents of relative surface harmony.

Prediction: In predicting the correlations for polarity and conflict behavior there are three theoretical considerations. These are brought together in Figure 16B.2. The curves are theoretically standardized, which means that each is hypothetically plotted as a variation from its own mean.

First, polarity increases the likelihood of extreme violence (Proposition 16.20). This is violence measured, say, as the total killed in the system from war, other military violence; and in increasing importance as polarity increases, a regime's violence against individuals and groups under its control. Thus, the theoretical, standardized curve for violence in Figure 16B.2 is at its highest for unipolar systems and decreases to approach some minimum as multipolarity increases.

Second, a component of violence is war, especially intense wars like World Wars I and II. Intense wars are increasingly likely as there are fewer poles to the point of a bipolar system of rough power parity. A unipolar system is less likely to have an intense war due to domination by one center of power. This war intensity curve is similar to the empirical curve found for domestic political systems, where *group* violence is greatest at the middle range of political coerciveness.[3]

And third, another component of violence is the number of wars. Now, war constitutes violence which to the participants may be quite intense. But in system terms, the war may be minor. For example, a war between two tribes of 500 members each may leave 25 dead on a field and live in the memory of generations, but in the international system such a war does not merit notice. The short border war between Libya and Egypt in 1977 killed less than a thousand, perhaps. The declared war of Rhodesia's neighbors against her white-ruled government has by 1978 cost less than a thousand killed. And then in 1978 there are the current wars between Cambodia and Vietnam, and Ethiopia and Somalia, where the death toll runs at least into several thousand. Yet in the international system these wars are still relatively minor. None of these has cost as many lives as the mass killing of its people by the Cambodian Khmer Rouge regime in the period 1975-1977, for example.

And then at the other end of the scale are the very intense, general wars costing millions of lives.

Now, theoretically, the *number* of wars should be least in a polarized system, but if any wars do occur the polarity almost guarantees that they will be extremely intense guerilla, revolutionary, or civil wars. As polarity decreases, power is decentralized, more independent states are formed and more wars are likely. But because there will be an increasing plurality of interests, the likelihood of these wars being intense *in the system,* or generalized to many states, decreases. Thus, the theoretical frequency curve shown in Figure 16B.2.

Polarity aggravates intense violence; but it inhibits lower level violence and, of course, nonviolent conflict behavior. With this background, the expected correlations are shown in Table 16C.1. What has to be kept in mind is that polarity has opposing effects on different

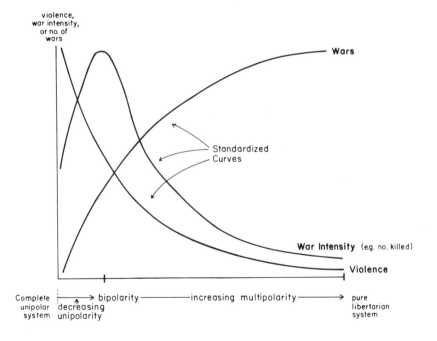

FIGURE 16B.2: Curves of Violence and War with Decreasing Polarity

conflict variables. For this reason, I predict the correlations with the conflict behavior and conflict scale variables to be random in all samples.

The frequency of low-level violence and war is inhibited by polarity and therefore should be higher in multipolar systems, indicating a negative correlation for all samples. The intensity of violence should be higher as polarity increases, and the expected correlation should therefore be positive.

One final consideration. Studies have used diverse measurements of polarity, which creates a problem in assessing evidence. Fortunately, these different measurements can be classified into two types. There are those measuring polarity by some power variables, such as the number of poles of power or number of Big Powers. And there are measurements of interstate relations from which is inferred polarity. For example, the distribution of trade, intergovernmental organization memberships, or diplomatic ties, may be taken to measure polarity.

The fault with measuring polarity by such relations, however, is that they are reflecting cross-pressures and not necessarily polarity. While increased polarity should decrease the diversity of such relations, it does not follow that decreasing polarity will increase this diversity (see the theoretical discussion for Proposition 16.20). Moreover, different systems at the same level of polarity may have more or less dispersed relationships between members, depending in part on whether the political systems are authoritarian, libertarian, or coercive.

Therefore, I have treated all measurements of polarity in terms of behavioral relationships as really measurements of cross-pressures and have related the results to the cross-pressures propositions.

Evidence: The only evidence is in the studies by Haas (1974) and Weede (1975), the former being important and direct. Both are positive.

Conclusion: The evidence supports the proposition.

Proposition 16.24 (Cross-Pressures/Violence):
Cross-pressures inhibit intense violence.

Cross-pressures are negatively correlated with intense political violence.

Theory: This is the counterpart to the Cross-Pressures/Conflict Proposition (16.15). Multiple overlapping interests generate varigated conflicts. But, the cross-pressures and segmented interests restrain conflict from coalescing, inhibit the formation of a societywide conflict front, and therefore constrain the intensity of violence.

At the international level, cross-pressures cause (aggravate) conflict and inhibit intense violence.

Prediction: Cross-pressures and polarity have a theoretically complementary relationship, although they are distinct concepts (see the discussion for Proposition 16.20). The positive or negative correlations expected for cross-pressures are the opposite of those expected for polarity.

Evidence: There are six direct, positive analyses (one strongly so), five of which are important, versus one direct and important negative analysis. And there are three analyses with ambiguous results.

Conclusion: In spite of there being only one negative analyses, this plus the ambiguous analyses make up 40% of the total. Therefore, the more restrained conclusion: *The evidence tends to support the proposition.*

Proposition 16.25 (World Opinion): World Opinion inhibits violence.

Opposition of world opinion is negatively correlated with violence.

Theory: World opinion consists of the public and elite opinion in other states opposing a conflict *and* the interests their leaders express in seeing the conflict ended. This opinion tends to dampen conflicts for two reasons.

First, world opinion provides spiritual support and political ammunition to those interest groups and that public working against their state's involvement in a conflict, as happened in the United States during the Vietnam war. In the short run, however, the government may ignore domestic clamor if the leadership perceives the dispute to be critical, as did British Prime Minister Eden in his approval of an invasion of Egypt in 1956 after President Nasser took over the Suez Canal.

Second, world opinion indicates possible difficulties a state will have in its future relations with other countries if it continues in or escalates a conflict. Statesmen are sensitive to the interdependence of all international relations, to its *field* nature. Pushing a dispute here may negatively affect the negotiation of a treaty there. Or request for economic aid. Or an arms sale agreement. Or trade.

Thus, affronting world opinion, especially of those states that matter in some way, introduces a different set of costs into a conflict which a leadership must weigh against the potential gains (including a reputation for not knuckling in under world opinion, which may sometimes be generated by the propaganda agencies of the opposing states). The stronger and more vociferous this opinion, the more salient it becomes and the more attention will be paid by the parties to the implied costs.

Prediction: World opinion operates best once violence has occurred and at the higher levels of violence. Border clashes or minor military engagements often occur over one or several days and usually are not that important at a global level. They will escalate to a war before usually attracting world attention and before opinion can be worked up. Therefore, there should be no systematic relationship between world opinion and the *occurrence* of low-level violence, meaning that the predicted correlations will be random in all samples, as shown in Table 16C.1.

However, once war is underway, it always attracts world attention; and because it is usually ongoing for months, war gives world opinion a chance to crystallize, and to thus inhibit escalation. Therefore, both the intensity of violence and the conflict scale should be negatively correlated with world opinion in all samples.

Because world opinion focuses on war, world opinion should have no systematic relationship to conflict behavior in general or to nonviolent conflict behavior: the expected correlations are random for these variables.

Evidence: The evidence is all positive, direct, and important, but only consists of three analyses. One is Wright's (1965) analyses of escalation. A second is my reanalysis of Wright's data with my own added (appendix I:7.1). And the third is the Northedge and Donelan (1971) nonquantitative, but systematic analysis.

Conclusion: the evidence supports the proposition.

Proposition 16.26 (Status-Quo): *Status-quo stability inhibits nonviolent conflict behavior.*

A stable status quo is negatively correlated with the intensity of nonviolent conflict behavior.

Theory: A structure of expectations is composed of both core status-quo agreements, treaties, understandings and surrounding norms, practices, and implicit conventions. Conflict may occur over these nonstatus quo expectations, while the status quo itself remains stable. The dispute may be over airline landing procedures, the terms of a trade agreement, payment for damage done by a tanker spilling oil, lack of consultation or warning about a change in foreign policy, hostile propaganda, and so on. Territorial issues are not involved; in a widely evident sense, what is ours versus what is theirs is not at stake.

As long as the status quo remains stable, conflicts over other issues will be inhibited from escalation. The reason is that a stable status quo—one which is congruent with the balance of powers—is mutually satisfactory and thus both sides will tend to inhibit the intensity and range of their dispute so as not to endanger the status quo.

This proposition is complementary to the Status-Quo Disruption Proposition (16.10), which states that status quo disruption is a necessary condition for violence. So long as the status quo is stable, nonviolent conflict is inhibited and violence should not occur. But if the status quo itself becomes part of the dispute and is disrupted, then the door to extreme conflict and violence is opened.

Prediction: As a variable in this proposition, status quo ranges from stable to very unstable, with disruption at the extreme end. The prediction is, therefore, that status quo stability will be negatively correlated with nonviolent conflict behavior and the conflict scale for the mixed and conflict samples. For the violent samples, by theory (Proposition 16.10) the status quo has been disrupted and therefore a stable status quo should be absent for all variables.

For the frequency of violence and war and the intensity of violence variables, disruption should have occurred for all nonzero values (see Figure 16C.1), while the zero values can involve a stable status quo. Therefore, the correlation should be a moderate negative for each variable in the mixed and conflict samples.

Evidence: The Barringer (1972) analysis, which is direct and important, is the only one relevant to the proposition. His results are strongly positive.

Conclusion: Because there is only one relevant analyses, the conclusion: *insufficient evidence.*

Proposition 16.27 (Freedom): Freedom inhibits violence.

The more libertarian a state, the less it tends to be involved in violence.

Theory: Libertarian states *are* involved in warfare, military intervention, and other kinds of international violence. This is usually reactive violence, a response to perceived aggression from nonlibertarian states or movements, where aggression also means unilateral attempts to change the status quo, as in Egypt's 1957 seizure of the Suez Canal; or attempt to stabilize a political situation from which opposing ideologies could benefit, as in the U.S. intervention in the Dominican Republic in 1965, or Lebanon in 1958.

Nonetheless, *in comparison to other states,* libertarian states have natural inhibitors on involvement in violence: the responsiveness of elected leaders to domestic interest groups and public opinion, which ordinarily will oppose violence, tax increases, and conscription, unless there is a clear and present danger. Libertarian states will defend their basic interests, and with violence if need be, if the aggressors are nonlibertarian (as defined in Joint Freedom Proposition 16.11). But domestic interests set limits and libertarian leaders often lack the power or will to take violent initiatives or make moves escalating violence, unlike their authoritarian and totalitarian counterparts.

Prediction: A prior question has to do with the kind of violence limited by libertarian systems. Libertarian systems are the natural enemies of authoritarian and totalitarian states. By their example and the products of freedom they are naturally subversive of authoritarian or totalitarian systems; and these freedoms seem to make libertarian states defenseless against unilateral changes in the status quo. Thus, libertarian states are often involved in reactive and defensive violence against the initiatives of nonlibertarian states. Therefore, in general, I do not expect that there will be a correlation between libertarianism and the frequency of involvement in war or violence. Nor should there be for the conflict behavior variables. The predicted correlations for these variables are therefore random, and for all samples as shown in Table 16C.1.

However, once a libertarian state is involved, domestic forces will usually begin to coalesce against increased violence and for a settlement of some sort. The growth in anti-Vietnam war sentiment and its impact on the American leadership's war policies and decisions are a paradigm case of the Freedom Proposition. It follows that the intensity of violence variable (which measures the scope, occurrence, and degree of violence) and the conflict scale (which has intense violence at the extreme) should be negatively correlated with libertarianism for both the mixed and conflict samples.

For the violence and war samples, however, it is not clear whether there should be a general negative correlation or a random correlation. The prediction is therefore indeterminate.

Evidence: There are 25 relevant analyses, all but two of which are direct. Thirteen analyses support the proposition with 10 opposed; four are strongly for, six strongly opposed. The proportions change much more in favor of the proposition when only important studies are considered, or when limited to those which are not inconsistent with the Model II distance-vector assumptions of field theory.

Conclusion: The negative evidence is substantial and does not allow for unqualified support for the proposition. Therefore, the conclusion: *the evidence tends to support the proposition.*

Proposition 16.28 (Surprise). Abrupt opportunity, threat, or injustice risks catalyzing and escalating conflict behavior.

Abrupt perception of opportunity, threat, or injustice is positively correlated with crises and with the occurrence and escalation of conflict behavior.

Theory: "Surprise" is a characteristic of a class of trigger events (not all trigger events) whose occurrence suddenly focuses perception of opportunity, threat, or injustice. These are the crises creators, the disruptors of the structure of expectations, the stiffeners of will. They are the immediate, the proximate causes of conflict or escalation.

What such a spark might be is unpredictable. It could be an assassination, a terrorist hijacking, a ship blown up, a sighting of dangerous weapons secretly mobilized in neighboring territory, a unilateral change in the status quo, a coup d'etat, and so on.

Prediction: Surprise should be positively correlated with crises, with the initiation of conflict behavior or its escalation. There may be considerable conflict as part of the process of balancing without there being surprising trigger events correlated with it. Surprise is initiating or escalatory. Thus, the positive correlations should be with nonviolent conflict behavior, violence frequency, violence intensity, and the conflict scale, in all samples.

Evidence: Two analyses (Phillips and Hainline, 1972; Brady, 1974), directly support the proposition, one strongly so.

Conclusion: the evidence supports the proposition.

Proposition 16.29 (Perception): Opportunity, threat, or injustice stimulates Conflict Behavior

Perception of opportunity, threat, or injustice is positively correlated with Conflict Behavior.

Theory: This is a broad class of trigger events whose occurence disrupts an incongruent structure of expectations (Proposition 16.1).

The distribution of obligations, benefits, and rights locked into a structure of expectations become incongruent with the reality of power. Dissatisfaction develops. And then some event which involves a perception of opportunity (such as a mutiny and breakdown in law and order in an opposing state which indicates weakness) a threat (such as the other side unveiling a new weapon in a military parade), or injustice (such as discovery that the other side has been systematically violating a treaty) brings an increasingly unhappy situation of conflict to a head. And Conflict Behavior may ensue.

The trigger is thus a proximate or immediate cause of Conflict Behavior.

Not all such triggers occur abruptly, as in the Surprise Proposition 16.28. Some may be the looked for event in an increasingly tense situation in which the parties had gradually grown to expect some kind of outbreak. The trigger is like an excuse. Some triggers may be a final straw in a growing list of grievances, or the last bit of evidence to conclusively prove duplicity or subversion.

Triggers which appear abruptly (Proposition 16.28), surprising the parties and catalyzing conflict, are not only a subclass of disruptors, but also can escalate conflict once underway. Disruptors, however, act only on the structure of expectations.

Prediction: A trigger disrupts expectations because it causes a perception of opportunity, threat, or injustice. The trigger event occurs and disappears proximate to the outbreak of Conflict Behavior, but the perception stimulated by the event will remain through the early stages of conflict, if not throughout.

Thus, this perception should be present for all conflict variables and all samples. And the more intense the conflict, the more intense should be this perception of opportunity, threat, or injustice. Thus, the correlation with all conflict variables should be positive.

Evidence: The evidence overwhelmingly and directly supports the proposition, with 20 analyses for (and eight strongly); two against (one strongly); none ambiguous.

Conclusion: the evidence strongly supports the proposition.

Proposition 16.30 (Totalitarianism): Political distance (vector)
most affects totalitarian states.

The more totalitarian a state, the more correlated its Conflict Behavior with political difference.

Theory: Totalitarian states are coercively unified by an enforced definition of the true and just—by an ideology. By a *political formula.* Competition with this formula is not permitted, critical assessments are not allowed. The people are taught one truth, one justice.

Therefore, totalitarian leaders are most sensitive to the ideologies of other states, whether these be revisionist or heretical deviations from the one truth, or competing ideologies. And whether those be actively competing ideologies or those competing by example. In any case, the mere existence of alternative political formulas is a threat to the one truth.

Thus, totalitarian states will be particularly affected by political distance, for this is the axis along which opposing ideologies lie. For these states more than others political distance is an aggravating cause of conflict.

Prediction: The more totalitarian a state, the more its conflict will be correlated with political distance vectors. This positive correlation should appear for all samples and conflict variables.

To be clear, this is not to say that this correlation will be higher than for other distance vectors. It is to say that ignoring other distance vectors, that correlation for political distance will be higher for totalitarian states than it will be for authoritarian or libertarian states.

Evidence: Six analyses are relevant, five of which support the proposition; four strongly so. All direct studies strongly support the proposition; all important studies are supportive. The only negative evidence is my own (appendix I:7.3), some of which is shown in appendix 9A.

Conclusion: the evidence strongly supports the proposition.

Proposition 16.31 (State Power): Power breeds conflict.

National coercive power is positively and, among attributes, most correlated with conflict behavior.

Theory: Power breeds conflict. Power shapes conflict. Such were conclusions of Volume 2. For interstate relations, no less than for their internal affairs, power is the most significant variable in the genesis and form of conflict behavior.

The balancing of power underlies conflict dynamics; the balance of power undergirds a structure of expectations; the change in power creates incongruence with expectations and the likelihood of disruption and a new outbreak of conflict (Proposition 16.2); the power to transcend distance makes conflict possible (Proposition 16.5); the decentralization and pluralism of power in a state inhibits violence (Proposition 16.27), while such between two states precludes violence between them (Proposition 16.11); the role of power in status is a force toward conflict (Proposition 16.14); the reputation for weakness in power risks escalation in violence (Propositions 16.17-18); the polarization of power stimulates intense violence (Proposition 16.20) while inhibiting lower-level conflict behavior (Proposition 16.23); the relative distribution of power defines a class division, which is the cauldron of general war (Proposition 16.22); the perception of power can trigger conflict (Proposition 16.29) and escalation (Proposition 16.28); and the power parity between states can make the escalation to war more likely (16.21).

Of course, power takes many forms and should be understood as the product of interests, capabilities, and will. But between the governments of states, which are the agents of coercion, coercive power capability is the primary ingredient. Therefore, among states (coercive) power breeds conflict.

Prediction: National coercive power should be both positively correlated with conflict behavior, and among a state's attributes, the most highly correlated. This correlation should hold for all samples and all conflict variables, as shown in Table 16C.1.

Evidence: There are 46 analyses bearing on the proposition, 40 of them positive (18 strongly so). Most of these provide direct evidence, but are mainly from unimportant studies. Of the important evidence, 13 favor (8 strongly) the proposition; 4 are strongly negative.

There is only one negative study which does not violate the Model II, distance-vector assumption of field theory.

Conclusion: The evidence strongly supports the proposition.

Proposition 16.32 (Power Vector): Power distance is the most potent force vector towards conflict.

Difference in coercive power is most highly correlated with conflict behavior.

Theory: This is a counterpart proposition to Proposition 16.31. Power breeds conflict and it is *relative state power* that is the force involved. Absolute power is largely irrelevant in international relations. The total income, resources, armaments, and the like, of states have meaning only in *time* and *space* relative to other states. The power of Egypt in 1978 would have made it the supreme power of 1878 and would make it now the dominant regional power in Latin America, were it located there. The power of China relative to Vietnam is one thing; relative to the Soviet Union is another.

This relativity itself is not absolute. The magnitude of the difference in power (i.e., power parity) is only relevant to behavior in making the escalation to war more likely (Proposition 16.21). It is the direction of difference and its magnitude that is generally a force toward antagonistic conflict behavior. That is, a state's conflict behavior towards another state is affected by whether the other is stronger or weaker in coercive power and by how much—by the distance vector.

Prediction: Among all distance vectors, the power distance vector between states should be *most* highly positively or negatively correlated with their conflict behavior. This should hold true for all samples and all conflict variables.

Power refers to coercive power. It may be measured by power-in-being, such as existing armaments and deployment. Or it may comprise, in addition, the power potential of a state—the totality of its resources, national income, population, area, leadership, morale, political unification and control.

Evidence: Twenty-one different analyses are relevant, 19 directly. Fifteen are strongly positive and three positive; only one is negative. Ten important studies are strongly positive; two ambiguous; none negative. Overall, this is the strongest relative support that any proposition has received. Some of my own important and strongly positive evidence is given in appendix 9A.

Conclusion: the evidence strongly supports the proposition.

Proposition 16.33 (Wealth-Power-Politics): Wealth,
power, and political distances are the most potent force vectors of conflict.

Differences (distance vectors) in wealth, power, and politics are of all differences the most correlated with conflict behavior.

Theory: Power influences conflict in a variety of ways, as mentioned in the State Power and Power Vector Propositions (16.31-32). Wealth affects conflict through its role in status (Proposition 16.14), especially in relative status (e.g., rich-poor gap); in sociocultural distances (Proposition 16.6); and in dissimilarity (Proposition 16.12). Moreover, relative wealth defines the exchange system between states, the potential dependency of one state's trade on another.

Political distance is potent for totalitarian states (Proposition 16.30), but as with wealth, also affects conflict through its contributions to sociocultural distances. Moreover, political distance for libertarian states defines the limits of conflict (Proposition 16.11).

Together, power, wealth and political distance reflect the primary lines of opposition among interests and the relative capabilities of states. Together, they define the major axes of the interstate balancing of powers.

Prediction: The wealth, power, and political distance vectors between states together should be more highly correlated with conflict behavior than any other sociocultural distance vectors, singularly or in the aggregate. This should be true for all conflict variables and all samples.

Evidence: Of 15 analyses, all but one direct, 13 support the propositions–strongly so. The one negative I inferred from a less than important (in this context) study by Salmore and Hermann (1970). Some of the positive evidence from my own work is shown in Appendix 9A.

Conclusion: the evidence strongly supports the proposition.

16B.3. OVERALL CONCLUSIONS

Table 16C.4 of appendix 16C totals the evidence by category of evaluation from the 186 analyses and 390 ratings tabulated in Table 16C.3. Moreover, as explained in appendix 16C, a one-level decrement is shown in the totals to conservatively compensate for my possible bias in evaluating each analysis. Does the Table show any significant variation in totals by category which indicates possible bias which could alter the conclusion?

First, note that the percent distribution of evaluations do not vary much by category. What variation there is argues against serious bias. The direct evidence hardly varies in percent positive or negative from that overall, and the strongly positive evidence even increases proportionately. Rather than evidence being skewed positively by unimportant studies, it is the other way around: important studies are more strongly positive.

Moreover, as should be the case if field theory provides the best framework for understanding conflict, studies which do not violate the Model II and distance vector assumptions of the field, are of all most proportionately positive. Out of 202 such ratings, only 8% are negative; 85% are positive.

Finally, if I have been biased toward the proposition in my own analyses then my results should be most favorable. But in fact, my results are least favorable. Of 99 ratings of my results, 23% are negative (compared to 16% overall); 72% are positive (compared to 79% overall).

TABLE 16B.2: Summary of Conclusions on the Causal Propositions

PROPOSITIONS		CONCLUSION ABOUT THE EVIDENCE[a]					
Name	No.	Strongly Supportive	Supportive	Ambiguous	Opposed	Strongly Opposed	Insufficient Evidence
Disrupted Expectations	16.1	yes					
Change/Tension	16.2		yes				
Change/Conflict	16.3		YES				
Geographic	16.4		yes				
Joint Power	16.5		yes				
Distance Vector	16.6		yes*				
Actor	16.7	yes					yes
Will-to-Conflict	16.8		YES				
Confidence	16.9		YES				
Status-Quo Disruption	16.10		yes				
Joint Freedom	16.11		yes				
Dissimilarity	16.12		yes				
Cognitive-Dissonance	16.13		yes				
Status	16.14	yes					
Cross-Pressures/Conflict	16.15						yes
Honor	16.16						yes
Credibility	16.17		yes				
Status-Quo Power	16.18		YES				
Intervention	16.19		yes				

TABLE 16B.2: Summary of Conclusions on the Causal Propositions

PROPOSITIONS		CONCLUSION ABOUT THE EVIDENCE[a]					
Name	No.	Strongly Supportive	Supportive	Ambiguous	Opposed	Strongly Opposed	Insufficient Evidence
Polarity/Violence	16.20		yes*				
Power-Parity	16.21		yes				
Class	16.22		yes				
Polarity/Conflict	16.23		yes				
Cross-Pressures/Violence	16.24		yes*				
World Opinion	16.25		yes				
Status Quo	16.26						yes
Freedom	16.27		yes*				
Surprise	16.28		yes				
Perception	16.29	yes					
Totalitarianism	16.30	yes					
State-Power	16.31	yes					
Power Vector	16.32	yes					
Wealth-Power-Politics	16.33	yes					
Totals		8	21	0	0	0	4

a. YES = evidence unanimous
*"tends to support"

Also, note that in Table 16C.3 even when the one-level decrement is applied, all percents still favor the proposition; about three to one for field theory consistent studies; over two to one for important studies.

The conclusion about bias seems clear. If bias is influencing the results, it must be nonsystematic or operate in ways not measured by the division in Table 16C.3. However, *both* as a result of what is shown in Table 16C.3 and my evaluation procedures, I feel confident that the conclusions are not unconsciously distorted. Indeed, *I feel that I was probably too cautious* in the evaluation and understated the positive evidence.

Now, for the overall conclusions. As tabulated in Table 16C.3, 79% of 390 ratings support the propositions; 35% of the total do so strongly. Quantitatively, recognizing all the dangers and assumptions in treating each analysis as the same, the total evidence overwhelmingly supports the propositions.

To avoid dependence on overall counts alone, qualitative distinctions can be introduced, as was done in classifying the evidence by the categories in Table 16C.3. But, as can be seen, each category by itself leads to the same positive conclusion.

Another qualitative-quantitative way of assessing the overall evidence is by separately assessing each proposition. The resulting conclusions are listed in Table 16B.2. Each of these conclusions took into account the quantitative evidence and my subjective evaluation of the analyses involved, their research designs, adequacy of data, and the like. As can be seen, overall the evidence is supportive, with no negative conclusions.

Therefore, *the overall conclusion: the empirical evidence overwhelmingly supports the propositions. And thereby, field theory and the conflict helix.*

NOTES

1. Technically, upon standardization the vector (variable) with constant values disappears into the origin of the space defined by the cases. Because any null vector is orthogonal to any other vector, the orthogonality condition for zero correlation is met.

2. To be clear, I am referring to the "cut of the data," and discriminating among system, dyadic, and state levels (research designs). This should not be confused with the applicability of polarity to the societies within states. See Volume 2 (1976: chapter 32) for such an application.

3. This is violence in terms of riots, revolutions, guerrilla war, and the like (see Volume 2, 1976: section 35.3). The systematic violence of a regime against its people has not been included in empirical studies. Were such violence included, then the violence curve of Figure 16B.2 is what should be found.

APPENDIX 16C

THE EVIDENCE FOR THE CAUSES

AND CONDITIONS OF CONFLICT BEHAVIOR

There are two kinds of discussion required before I can present the evidence for the propositions. One concerns what evidence is relevant and what quantitative form it should take. The second involves how the evidence was sifted for the propositions.

16C.1 PREDICTING THE QUANTITATIVE FORM OF THE EVIDENCE

Table 16C.1 presents the quantitative form the evidence should take for each proposition. Through the table I have tried to grapple with four quantitative problems in assessing the evidence.

First, the propositions involve different ranges of conflict behavior. Some refer to conflict behavior in general, such as negative accusations, sanctions, border clashes, and war. This can be seen in Figure 16.1 of this chapter, where different causes and conditions are shown overlapping or involving the different types of conflict behavior. Only for those propositions about conflict behavior in general, then, would evidence bearing on any kind of conflict behavior bear on the proposition. Moreover, some propositions concern only specific conflict behavior, such as war. Evidence thus concerning nonviolent conflict behavior or low-level violence, like border clashes, would be irrelevant.

A *second* problem is that the evidence will be based on different conflict samples, of which four kinds must be discriminated, as shown in Table 16C.1.

NonConflict Sample: a sample in which no members have conflict.

Mixed Sample: A sample in which some members have and others do not have the conflict behavior in question (e.g., a sample of dyads, some of which have no conflict behavior).

Conflict Sample: a sample in which all members have conflict behavior, but not all have violence or war (e.g., a sample of dyads all of which have some kind of conflict behavior).

Violence Sample: a sample in which all members manifest violence, but not all have war (e.g., a sample of conflicts in which more than 100 were killed).

War Sample: a sample in which all members manifest wars (e.g., a sample of dyads involved in wars).

Not each sample will be relevant to each proposition; and if relevant the nature of the sample may limit the kind of evidence that can be used. For example, for reasons discussed regarding the Disrupted Expectations Proposition 16.1 in appendix 16B, I expect that the correlation would be positive between disrupted expectations and conflict behavior for the mixed sample, while near zero between this cause and any type of conflict behavior for all the other samples. These expectations are shown in Table 16C.1.

TABLE 16C.1: Quantitative Requirements for the Evidence on the Propositions

Sample/c	Conflict Variable/b	Propositions/a																																
		1	2	3	4	5	6	7	8	9	10	11	12	13	14	15	16	17	18	19	20	21	22	23	24	25	26	27	28	29	30	31	32	33
non-conflict sample	no conflict behavior	A									A																							
mixed sample	conflict behavior	C+	C+	C+	C-	C+	C	C	C+	C+	C*	R	R	R	C+	C+					R	R	R	C-	C+	C- R	C- R	R	C+	C+	C+	C+	C+	C
	nonviolent conflict behavior	C*		R	R	R	C	R	R	C+	R	C-	R	R	C-	C-					C- R	R	R	C-	C+	C- R	C- R	R	C+	C+	C+	C+	C+	C
	violence frequency	C*		R	R	R	C	R	C*	C+	R	C-	R	R	C+	C+	R	R	R	R	C-	R	R	C+	C+	C- R	C- R	R	R	C+	C+	C+	C+	C
	violence intensity	C+		R	R	R	C	C	R	C+	C+	C-	R	R	C+	C+	C+	C+	C+	C+	C+	C+	C+	C+	C-	C-	C-	C-	R	C+	C+	C+	C+	C
	conflict scale	C*	R	C	C-	C+	C	C	R	C+	C+	C-	C+	C+	C+	C+	C+	C+	C+	C+	R	C+	R	R	C+ R	C- R	C-	C-	C+	C+	C+	C+	C+	C
conflict sample	conflict behavior	P		P	R	R	C		R	C*	R	R	R	C+	C+						C- R	C-	C-	C-	C+ R	C- R	C- R		C+	C+	C+	C+	C+	C
	violence frequency	P		P	R	R	C		R	C+	C+ C-	C-	R	C-	C-		R	R	R	R	C-	R	R	C-	C+	C- R	C- R	R	C+	C+	C+	C+	C+	C
	War frequency	P		P	R	R	C		R	C+	C+ C-	C-	R	C+	C+	R	R	R	R	R	R	R	C+	C+	C+	C-	C-	R	R	C+	C+	C+	C+	C
	violence intensity	P		P	R	R	C		R	C+	C+ C-	C-	R	C+	C+	C+	C+	C+	C+	C+	C+	C+	C+	C+	C-	C-	C-	C-	C+	C+	C+	C+	C+	C
	conflict scale	P		P	C-	C+	C		R	C+	C+ C-	C+	C+	C+	C+	C+	C+	C+	C+	C+	R	C+	R	C+ R	R	C- R	C-	C-	A	C+	C+	C+	C+	C	C
violence sample	conflict behavior	P		P	R	R	C		R	P	A	R	R	R							R	R	R	C-	C+ R	R	A	R	A R	C+	C+	C+	C+	C+	C
	violence frequency	P		P	R	R	C		R	P	A	R	R	C-							C- R	R	C-	C+	C- R	A	A	R	A R	C+	C+	C+	C+	C+	C
	war frequency	P		P	R	R	C		R	P	A	R	R	C+	C+	C+	C+	C+	C+	C+	C-	R	C-	C+	C- R	R	P	A	P	R	C+	C+	R	C	C
	violence intensity	P		P	R	R	C		R	C+	P	A	R	R	C+	C+	C+	C+	C+	C+	C+	C+	C+	C+	C-	C-	C-	A	C+	C+	C+	C+	C+	C
	conflict scale	P		P	C-	C+	C		R	C+	P	A	C+	C+	C+	C+	C+	C+	C+	C+	R	C+	R	C+ R	R	C- A	C- A	A	C- A	C+	C+	C+	C+	C	C
war sample	conflict behavior	P		P	R	R	C		R	P	P	A	R	R							R	R	R	R	C- R	R	A	R	A R	C+	C+	C+	C+	C	C
	violence frequency	P		P	R	R	C		R	P	P	A	R	C-	C-						C- R	R	C-	C-	C+	R	A	R	A R	C+	C+	C+	C+	C	C
	war frequency	P		P	R	R	C		R	P	P.	A	R	R	C-	C+	C+	C+	C+	C+	C+	C+	C+	C+	C-	R	A	R	A R	R	C+	C+	C+	C	C
	violence intensity	P		P	R	R	C		R	P	P.	A	R	R	C+	C+	C+	C+	C+	C+	C+	C+	C+	C-	C-	C-	A	C-	A	C+	C+	C+	C+	C	C
	conflict scale	P		P	C-	C+	C		R	P	P	A	R	C+	C+	C+	C+	C+	C+	C+	R	C+	R	R	C+ R	C- A	C- A		C- A	C+	C+	C+	C+	C	C

[301]

a. For a full statement of the propositions see Table 16B.1. The proposition number here corresponds to its decimal number, e.g., proposition 1 is 16.1 in Table 16B.1.

The codes used here are as follows:

blank = irrelevant or indeterminate
0 = low to zero correlation
A = absent (correlation = 0)
C = correlation (C+ = moderate or high positive; C- = moderate or high negative;
C* = near zero or positive)
P = present (correlation = 0)
R = correlation random (can be zero, positive or negative)

b. Conflict variables are operationalized as follows:

conflict behavior = a dichotomy (no conflict behavior vs. conflict behavior)

nonviolent conflict behavior = frequency (e.g. number of threats)

violence frequency = frequency of low level violence (e.g., number of border clashes)

war frequency = number of wars

violence intensity = scale of violence (none to high)

conflict scale = scale of conflict intensity (none to high)

See Table 16C.2 for fuller definitions.

c. For the definitions of samples, see text.

The *third* quantitative problem concerns the conflict variable. Various analyses measure conflict behavior in different ways. In general, we may classify these measurements as shown in Table 16C.2. Some measurements of some conflict variables may be relevant to a proposition, but not all may be. These three dimensions along which to weigh the evidence—proposition, sample, conflict variable—are cross-classified in Table 16C.1.

The *fourth* problem in evaluating the evidence is the diverse techniques of analysis employed across the studies surveyed. Correlation techniques (regression, factor analysis, correlation coefficients) are the most common and some techniques can be easily interpreted correlationally (chi-square, t-test). Therefore, in each cell in the table is indicated whether the actual or underlying correlation should be plus (C+), near zero (P or A), or minus (C-). If the correlation can be anything (that is, the sample and conflict variables are irrelevant for the proposition) an R is inserted. In order to facilitate this assessment, each proposition in the Table of Propositions (16B.1) is stated empirically, usually in correlational terms. Each proposition is discussed theoretically and empirically in appendix 16B and the relevant evidence is more fully considered there.

Figure 16C.1 may help to understand why certain correlations are predicted for each proposition. To predict the correlations between two variables, one must consider the measurements of each and the nature of the cases that will lie above and below each variable's mean. Correlations, after all, are simply reflecting whether the cases for two variables are similarly above and below the mean (yield a C+); or whether when one is above, the other is usually below (C-).

Figure 16C.1 shows the cases which will be above and below the mean for each conflict variable, and the numerical scale also involved. The mean is placed arbitrarily on each scale, and is only meant to show that for many of the conflict variables some of the cases that manifest a high conflict will nonetheless be below the mean on the specific conflict variable.

As an example of the problem here, consider correlating disrupted expectations (Proposition 16.1) with the frequency of violence. Let disrupted expectations be measured as a dichotomy (0=absent; 1=present). Now, the proposition implies that disrupted expectations should always be present, whatever the conflict *behavior*. All cases above the mean on violence therefore should have disrupted expectations. But, all those cases below the mean with nonviolent conflict behavior *and* with lower than average violence also will have disrupted expectations. But, all those cases below the mean with nonviolent conflict behavior *and* with lower than average violence also will have disrupted expectations. Only those cases with no conflict behavior will have no disrupted expectations. This means that *if the proposition is correct* the correlation between disrupted expectations and violence intensity will vary from near zero to *moderate* positive (C*), depending on relatively how many cases with no conflict behavior are included in the analysis.

The result of similarly predicting the correlation for each proposition for each sample for each conflict variable with regard to Figure 16C.1 is shown in the cells of Table 16C.1.

TABLE 16C.2: Measurements of Conflict Behavior

CONFLICT VARIABLES	MEASUREMENTS
Conflict Behavior	dichotomy (e.g., 0 = nonconflict behavior; 1 = any conflict behavior)
Nonviolent Conflict Behavior	dichotomy (e.g., 0 = nonconflict behavior; 1 = any nonviolent behavior)
	frequency of some nonconflict behavior (e.g., negative sanctions)
	factor scores (or scale) of a nonviolent conflict dimension (e.g., negative accusations)
Violence Frequency	frequency of nonwar-like violence, or low-level violence (e.g., border clashes, discrete military actions, terrorist acts)
	factor scores (or scale) on a low-level violence dimension
War Frequency	number of wars
	number of war battles
	number of war days
Violence Intensity	number killed in violence
	factor scores (or scale) of an intensity dimension
Conflict Scale	number of conflict acts
	a scale of conflict intensity (from little low-level conflict behavior to intense warfare)
	factor scores on the first unrotated dimension of conflict behavior or on the scores summed across all dimensions of conflict

16C.2 SELECTION CRITERIA AND EVIDENCE BY PROPOSITION

In sum, Table 16C.1 thus presents my way of handling the four problems I mention: different conflict variables, samples, measurements, and techniques of analysis. But there is a *fifth* problem, which cannot be easily reduced to a table and is the most subjective of all.

Some analyses in part may be *incorrectly or incompetently done.* These I ignore (e.g., Haas, 1974),[1] or reanalyze with the information supplied in the analysis.

Some analyses may have *conclusions contrary to their tabulated results and data.* I ignore the conclusions and accept the analyses. In some cases, I have redone their analysis (e.g., Naroll, Bullough, and Naroll, 1974).

Some analyses may give *more weight to results* than I do. For example, from a correlation of .32 an analyst may conclude that there is a positive relationship between borders and conflict. Within the context of the analysis, however, I may conclude that this

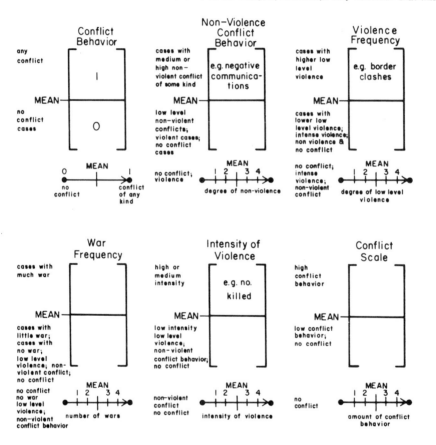

FIGURE 16C.1: Distribution of Cases Around the Mean on the Conflict Variables

correlation, for practical purposes, is near zero and therefore not a C+ as I define it. I would like to set a rigid threshold for what correlation I will accept as a positive or negative result, but this is contextual. It depends on the sample, variables, degrees of freedom, techniques, and that "feeling" a researcher develops for important relationships. For me this is often a correlation near plus or minus .50.

Some analysis do not supply sufficient information to assess their correlations (e.g., Phillips and Hainline, n.d.). Sometimes I will accept these correlations, if the work seems otherwise competently done and the correlations are not crucial. However, especially important correlations are ignored if I cannot confidently reconstruct the analysis.

Some analysis *operationalize concepts in a way quite different* from their meaning here, such as operationalizing system polarity in terms of trade. Then, I will translate the results in terms of their meaning here (polarity means for me centralization of command into opposing camps). In the case of polarity measured by trade, then, I would relate the results to the Cooperation-Conflict Proposition 18.2 in chapter 18 rather than to the two Polarity Propositions 16.20 and 16.23 of this chapter.

With all the above in mind, Table 16C.3 presents the evidence on Propositions 16.1 to 16.33. It is organized by level, and by study. The parameters of most of the published studies are given in appendix III.

In evaluating this evidence, it is important to understand how it was collected.

First, since 1958 I have been putting on index cards the results of published systematic analyses relevant to my interests in conflict.

Second, after writing chapters 2-13, but before writing these empirical chapters and stating the propositions, I surveyed all the empirical analyses I could find (see the discussion in appendix III), including many of those I had previously indexed, and recorded major relevant correlations and results on index cards. "Relevant" means bearing on international conflict behavior in some way. Of course, I could not record all results (such as a large correlation matrix), and no doubt some relevant to the subsequently formulated propositions fell through the screen.

Third, after the survey, which took about a year, I stated the propositions given in chapters 15-18. Now, the propositions are meant to make concrete my theoretical analyses of conflict here and in Volumes 1-3. *They are not meant to summarize, to reflect, or to consolidate the studies surveyed. Nor were any propositions taken from any other studies.*

However, because the propositions were formulated *after* the survey, it is possible and likely in some cases that in their statement I may have been unconsciously responsive to the accumulated findings of others, not to mention my own past empirical analysis. Therefore, Table 16C.3 should be considered more *evidence for,* than independent *tests of* the propositions.

Fourth, after the propositions were stated, I then organized all the indexed evidence by proposition and level as shown in Table 16C.3. Because a study may have undertaken more than one level of analysis, it may appear more than once in the Table.

Fifth, if my *indexed* evidence were ambiguous or I suspected that the study had much more evidence on the propositions than I had recorded, I went back to the study and worked directly from it if possible. If not, I discarded the evidence.

Nonetheless, I must have missed considerable evidence (minor in the context of an analysis and not part of its conclusions) that bear on the propositions. A careful survey of each study's correlation matrices, factor tables, regression coefficients, and the like would likely increase significantly the evidence in Table 16C.3. But the direction of the evidence I did tabulate is so strong, as I will discuss below, that it seems highly unlikely that a finer screening would alter the overall conclusions.

I suspect that the authors of the studies tabulated in Table 16C.3 and their students will be especially interested in how their results relate to the propositions. Moreover, I hope

TABLE 16C.3: Evidence on the Causes and Conditions of Conflict Behavior

Level[a]	Source[b]	Importance[c]	I	II	A	V	1	2	3	4	5	6	7	8	9	10
static-case	Bremer, et al. (1973)	L	Y													
	Babst (n.d.; 1972)	H														
	Denton (1969)	H		Y												P
	Haas, M. (1974)	M		Y												
	Jarvad (1968)	L														
	Kende (n.d., 1971)	M														
	Naroll, et al. (1974)	H	Y													
	Melko (1973)	H					SPI		SP							
	Phillips & Hainline (1972)	H														PI
	Richardson, L. (1960a)	H		Y												PI
	Singer & Small (1966)	H														
	Singer & Small (1972)	H														
	Starr (1972)	H														
	Triska & Finley (1968)	M														
	Wallensteen (1973)	H														
	Wallensteen (1968)	M														
	Wesley (1969)	H								SP						
	(appendix I:7.5)	H														
	Blainey (1973)	H					SP							P	P	
	Ahn (1977)	M														
	Moore, et al. (1975)	M														PI
	Michalka (1976)	H										P				
dynamic case	Brecher (1974)	L										SPI				
	Bremer, et al. (1973)	M			Y							N				
	Field (1972)	M	Y									P				
	McCormick, J. (1975)	M	Y													
	Russett (1971; 1974)	H	Y													
	Sullivan, M. (1972)	L	Y										A			
	Tanter (1974)	L														
	(appendix I:7.1)	H		Y						N				SP		
	Barringer (1972)	H		Y	Y	Y										SP
	Wright (1965)	H		Y	Y									PI		SP
	Northedge & Donelan (1971)	H														SP
	Harf (1974)	M	Y		Y					P						
static-nation	Alcock (1970)	L	Y													
	Brady (1974)	M	Y													
	Brady (1975)	M	Y													
	Broch & Galtung (1966)	H								SP						
	Cattell (1949)	H	Y													
	Cattell & Gorsuch (1965)	H	Y													
	Cattell, et al. (1951)	H	Y													
	Choucri (1974)	L	Y													
	Dahl & Tufte (1973)	L	Y													
	East (1973)	M	Y													
	East & Hermann (1974)	M	Y													
	East & Gregg (1967)	M	Y													
	Eckhardt (1975)	H														
	Eckhardt (1969)	L														
	Gitelson (1974)	L						SP								
	Hazelwood (1973)	M	Y													
	Midlarsky (1975)	H	Y													
	Moore, D. (1974)	M	Y													
	Moore, D. (1974a)	M	Y													
	Naroll (1966)	M	Y							SNI						
	North & Choucri (1971)	L	Y													
	Otterbein (1968)	L														

11	12	13	14	15	16	17	18	19	20	21	22	23	24	25	26	27	28	29	30	31	32	33
																				PI		
SP											PI									SP		
	P									A								P		PI		
							SP				P											
						Pg				Pg						SP						
									P				P				SP					
	P																			SP		
																				SP		
																				SP		
		SP								PI								P		P		
																		P				
SP										SP								SP				
								SP														
							SPI			SP			SP									
																				PI		
																	SP					
																	P			PI		
			P														SN					
	N									P				SP								SP
PI						P	SP	SP		SP	PI			P	SP			P				
					SP	SP				SP				P				SP		PI		
	P																					
																	P					
																P	P					
																				PI		
															SP					SP		
	P																			SN		
															N					SN		
																				SN		
																				PI		
																				P		
																				P		
															P					P		
															P							
															SP							
															P							
															P					SP		
															A							
		SPI																	SPI			
																			SP			SP
																					PI	
															SNI							

[307]

TABLE 16C.3: Evidence on the Causes and Conditions of Conflict Behavior (Cont)

Column groupings: Importance[c]; Model[d] = I, II; Distance[e] = A, V; followed by columns 1–10.

Level[a]	Source[b]	Importance[c]	I	II	A	V	1	2	3	4	5	6	7	8	9	10
	Otterbein (1970)	M	Y													
	Phillips (1973)	L	Y													
	Rubin & Schainblatt (1969)	M	Y													
	Rummel (1963a)	L	Y													
	Rummel (1972)	M	Y													
	Russett & Monsen (1975)	M	Y													
	Salmore & Hermann, (1970)	M	Y													
	Sorokin (1957, 1937-41)	H		Y												
	Vincent (1971a)	M	Y													
	Vincent (1971c)	M	Y													
	Vincent (1971b)	M	Y													
	Vincent (1968)	M	Y													
	Vincent, et al. (1973)	M	Y													
	Vincent (1977d)	M	Y													
	Wallace (1970)	M	Y													
	Weede (1970)	M	Y							PI						
	Weil (1975)	M	Y													
	Wright (1942)	H	Y													
	(appendix I:3.1)	M	Y													
	Haas, M. (1974)	H	Y													
	Hermann, C. et al. (1973)	M														
dynamic-nation	Cattell (1953)	M		Y												
	Choucri (1974)	L						PI								
	Choucri & North (1974)	H		Y									SP			
	Mahoney (1976)	M		Y			PI	P								
	Singer & Small (1974)	H														
	Sorokin (1957, 1937-41)	H		Y		SP		SP								
	Midlarsky (1975)	H														
static-dyadic	Adelman (1972)	M														
	Abravanel & Hughes (1973)	L					PI									
	Buchanen & Cantril (1953)	L					PI									
	Choi (1973)	H	Y		Y					SN	SPI	SP	P			
	Denton (1969)	H														SP
	Dowty (1970)	H											SPI			
	Dowty (1971)	H														
	East (1970)	M								SP						
	Galtung (1966)	M														
	Gleditsch (1969, 1970)	M	Y		Y	Y				SP		SN				
	Holsti, et al. (1973)	H	Y		Y		A			SN						
	Park, T. (1969)	M	Y								P					
	Powel, et al. (1974)	L	Y		Y					N						
	Rhee (1977)	H	Y		Y						PI	SP				
	Rosenau & Hoggard (1974)	M														
	Rummel (1969)	M	Y	Y		Y				SN		SP	SP			
	Rummel (1965)	L	Y		Y					P	A					
	Rummel (1972)	M	Y	Y	Y					P	PI	N				
	Russett (1967)	H		Y						P						
	Schwerin (1977)	M	Y		Y						PI					
	Siverson (1970)	L														
	Sullivan, M. (1970)	M					A									
	Van Atta & Rummel (1977)	M	Y			Y						SP	SP			
	Vincent, et al. (1973)	H	Y		Y								SP			
	Vincent (1967a, 1977b)	H	Y	Y	Y								SP			
	Vincent (1977c, d, f)	H	Y	Y	Y							SN				
	Wallensteen (1968)	L														
	Weede (1975)	M							P							SP
	Weil (1975)	M							P	P						

[308]

11	12	13	14	15	16	17	18	19	20	21	22	23	24	25	26	27	28	29	30	31	32	33
																P						
																				P		
																				SP		
																				SN		
																SN			PI	SN		SP
																SN				P		
																				SPI		SNI
																SP						P
																						P
																						SP
																						P
																				SP		
																				SP		
		PI														N				SP		
																				SP		
																P				P		
																SN				P		
																SN		P				
																		P				
																SN						
																				PI		
																					P	
																				SN		
		SPI	SP																			
			A																			
																		N	SP		SP	SP
	P																					
										SP												
										SP												
		SPI	SP																			
	P	PI																SP		SPI		
	A																					
	N																			P		
																					SP	SP
			SP													Pg						
										N										SP		
			SP							P											SP	A
	SN									SN												
			SP							SP									SP	SP	SP	
										P												
			SP																SP		
			N																A		
	SN									SP									SP		
P			SP							A								SP	SP	A	P
			SP																P		
										P										P		

TABLE 16C.3: Evidence on the Causes and Conditions of Conflict Behavior (Cont)

Level[a]	Source[b]	Importance[c]	I	II	A	V	1	2	3	4	5	6	7	8	9	10
	(appendix I:4.1)	M	Y			Y							SPI			
	(appendix I:4.2)	M	Y	Y						P		PI	SP			
	(appendix I:4.3)	M	Y		Y		PI				P	PI				
	(appendix I:4.4-4.7)	M	Y		Y							SI	SP			
	(appendix I:4.8)	M	Y		Y							PI	PI			
	(appendix I:4.9, 4.10)	L	Y		Y						P	PI	PI			
	(appendix I:5.1)	M	Y		Y					P		PI	PI			
	(appendix I:5.2, 5.3)	M	Y		Y					NI						
	(appendix I:6.1)	M	Y		Y					P		PI				
	(appendix I:6.2-6.4)	M	Y		Y					P	SP	PI				
	Park, Y. (1975)	H	Y	Y		Y							P			
	(appendix I:6.7)	H	Y		Y							N				
	Chadwick (1972)	L	Y		Y							PI				
dynamic-dyadic	Ferris (1979)	H	Y						P							
	Holsti, O. (1965)	L										PI				
	Holsti, O. (1962)	M														
	Mahoney (1977)	H	Y										P			
	Mogdis (1969, 1970)	H	Y		Y		P						P			
	North & Choucri (1971)	H	Y													
	Omen (1975)	M	Y		Y											
	Phillips (1969)	M	Y	Y	Y						SN					
	Rhee (1977)	H	Y		Y							PI				
	Richardson, L. (1960)	H														
	Rummel (1977: chap 15)	H	Y		Y					N		PI	SP			
	Singer & Small (1974)	H	Y					SP								
	(appendix I:6.7)	M	Y	Y	Y	Y						N				
static system	Denton (1969)	H														
	Haas, M. (1974)	H														
	Haas, M. (1970)	H														
	Hart, J. (1974)	M														
	Midlarsky (1974, 1975)	H														
	Sullivan, M. (1970)	M	Y													
	Wallace (1972)	H														
	Wallace (1973)	H														
	Weede (1975)	M														
	(appendix I:6.5)	M								P						
	East (1970)	M														
	East (1972)	M														
	Healy & Stein (1973)	M														
	de Mesquita (1975)	H														
	Singer & Small (1966)	H														
	Singer & Small (1968)	H														
	Singer & Small (1974)	H														
	Sorokin (1957)						SP									
	Tung (1975)	M													PI	
	Levine (1973)	H					SPI									
Surveys	Haas (1965)	L														
	McGowan & Shapiro (1973)	H								P		P				
	Rummel (1977: chap. 16)	H	Y		Y							SP				
	Sullivan, M. (1976)	H														
	Vasquez (1975, 1976)	H										PI				
	Zinnes (1972)	M														
	(appendix I:7.3)	H								P						
	Weede (1977a)	M														

11	12	13	14	15	16	17	18	19	20	21	22	23	24	25	26	27	28	29	30	31	32	33
P										N											N	P
	P									P												
										N												
SPI										SP												
NI										P												
										P												
PI										NI												
PI										NI										PI		
PI			P																			
A	SP		SP							A										SP		
		SP								SPI												
										N												
										ph												
																		P		PI		
		SN								AI								SP			SP	
																			SP	SP	SPi	
																					P	
NI																					SP	
										P												
																				SP	P	
							SP															
N										N										SPI		
									SP													
									SP			P										
									A													
							P															
									SP	P												
										N												
		PI											P									
									A				A									
												PI	P									
	P																					
			PI																			
			PI																			
		PI																				
													.									
										N			P									
													A									
										A			P									
										N												
	P	PI	PI							P						P				P		
			P													A		P			SP	
		P								SP						P						
			A	N			PI						N			N		SP		SP		
																		P				
																			SN			
									PI			P				N					SP	SP

a. These levels are discussed in section 4.4.
b. All sources are referenced at the end of the book and characterized in appendix III, with the exception of references to unpublished projects in appendix I clearly so identified, e.g., (appendix I:1.3).
c. This is a measure of the importance and centrality of the source *for the propositions given here.*
    H = high importance
    M = moderate importance
    L = low importance
It is not an evaluation of the work itself or its competence.
d. *Model I* implicitly or explicitly treats parameters across actors as constant (forces affect all actors similarly).
    Model II implicitly or explicitly treats parameters as varying by actor (forces may affect actors differently)
    Y = yes; blank = no, ambiguous, or irrelevant
e. A: uses absolute distances or their equivalent
    V: uses vector distances or their equivalent
    Y = yes; blank = no, ambiguous, or irrelevant
f. For a full statement of the propositions see Table 16B.1. The proposition number here corresponds to its decimal number, e.g., proposition 1 is 16.1 in Table 16B.1. The relevance of the evidence is coded as follows: SP = strongly positive, P = positive, A = ambiguous, N = negative, SN = strongly negative, blank = irrelevant. An I after the assessment means that the results are positive for a proposition by inference – they are what would be expected were the proposition true.
g. Based on a reanalysis I did of their data.
h. This is from his conclusion, p. 123. Crucial aspects of his methodology are unclear, as for lack of correlation between disparity and escalation to war (p. 73).
i. Regarding the object's population, which in Model II is equivalent to the distance vector in power.

others will track through such studies to check my tabulation and develop their own. In any case, where the tabulated evidence in Table 16C.3 differs from what the reader believes a study presents, the following should be checked:

- the sample (see Table 16C.1),
- the conflict variable (see Table 16C.1 and Figure 16C.1),
- the correlational evidence relevant to a proposition (see the cells of Table 16C.1),
- whether an author's conclusions really follow from the analysis (I usually did my own interpretation of an analysis, regardless of an author's assessment),
- the possibility of different weights on the results (e.g., I may have interpreted a .35 correlation as near zero rather a C+),
- whether insufficient technical information may cause an analysis to be omitted,
- whether operationalizations differ from those given or implied here.

16C.3 OVERALL EVIDENCE AND SOURCES OF BIAS

Table 16C.4 presents the overall results by proposition and in total.

Although these numbers give an air of precision, they should be interpreted loosely. The numbers equate different kinds of studies at different levels involving different variables, techniques, and competencies.

Moreover, because there are so many results for some propositions, a small number, say one or two, for some other propositions may appear insufficient for a conclusion. Yet, these few results may be from a large-scale team effort involving years of data collection, precise research designs, and careful analysis, far overshadowing anything done elsewhere. Such possibilities are taken into account in the proposition-by-proposition assessment of appendix 16 B.

Nonetheless, aside from the necessary subjectivity of my ratings, there are sources of bias in the overall totals in Table 16C.4 that can be checked quantitatively.

One is that the studies are not equally important. Clearly, an analysis of 100 variables for all wars since 1812 is more significant than one of threats and trade in 1955. Also, even for studies of the same general importance, they may differ in relevance to the propositions. To provide an assessment of this, I classified in Table 16C.3 each study according to its importance. The totals for the studies rated important are given in Table 16C.4, and indicate that the only significant effect of segregating important evidence is to raise the overall percentage of strongly positive evidence, from 35% to 40%.

An additional source of bias is that the evidence may be more or less direct. That is, results may bear directly on a proposition or may indirectly or by inference relate to a proposition. To enable the reader to control for this, whenever evidence was indirect or I inferred relevance to a proposition, I inserted an "I" in Table 16C.3 after the rating.

To determine the effect of this indirect evidence, all the totals were recounted for only the direct evidence. Table 16C.4 shows that overall the indirect evidence had little effect on the totals.

Another source of bias is that studies are not all independent. Many are on similar data sets, some on the same data, and some are research variations of basically the same analyses. To control for this, *I eliminated from Table 16C.3 any analysis that did not provide reasonably independent evidence.* Nonetheless, many studies remain that are from the same project or data sets, and therefore weight the overall totals.

There is also a small additional bias introduced by including the eight surveys, which are assessing overlapping literature. I included them, nonetheless, because they provide different perspectives on much the same results. And in the case of these surveys, I used *without change their distillations of the basic findings in the literature.*

Of course, there is also a possible source of bias in including my own analyses, which since 1965 have been explicitly designed with regard to the social field theory of international relations generating these propositions. There are 167 separaté studies listed in the Table; 35 are mine (Rummel, colleague and Rummel, Dimensionality of Nations, or appendix I). This is 21% of the total, which is hardly sufficient to cause the distribution of overall results shown in Table 16C.4.

In any case, Table 16C.4 shows the total ratings for my analyses. Interestingly, my results are the least positive and most negative of all the categories, indicating that if there were bias for or against the propositions operating in my work, it probably was on the side of overly narrow or constraining research designs.

A source of bias also exists in the type of research designs underlying all the evidence. The propositions are stated within the context of a Model II perspective on state behavior: behavior is dyadic, directed by actor i to object j, and each actor is affected by his own perceptions and expectations. That is, different actors have different parameters weighting the forces toward behavior. Moreover, each actor's interest lie along the distance vectors between i and j. Many studies, however, employ a Model I perspective: the same numerical parameters affect different actor's behavior or use absolute distances instead of distance vectors.

Table 16C.4 shows the totals when all studies using a Model I approach or absolute distances are excluded: the evidence is then slightly more favorable and much less negative.

A final consideration. I evaluated the evidence as strongly positive, positive, and the like, depending on a number of considerations; such as the magnitude of results, degrees of freedom, and nature of the conflict variables. I surely may have tended to give positive evidence a higher ranking than negative evidence. There is an obvious conflict of interests in my doing this rating, which ideally should be done by one who strongly disagrees with the

TABLE 16C.4: Evidence: Subtotals and Totals*

Propositions[a]

Category	Rating	1	2	3	4	5	6	7	8	9	10	11	12	13	14	15	16	17	18	19	20
Overall	SP	5		4	3	3	5	11		1	4	3	1	4	10		1	1	3	3	3
	P	1	3	4	14	7	13	10	1	2	6	6	9	6	6			1	3	1	1
	A	1	1			1		1				1	1	1	1						3
	N				4		4					3	2		1	1					2
	SN				4	1	2						2	1							
Direct Evidence[a]	SP	3		4	3	2	5	9		1	4	1	1	1	10		1	1	2	3	3
	P			3	13	4	1	6	1	1	2	2	9	1	3			1	2		1
	A	1	1			1		1				1	1	1	1						3
	N				3		4					1	2		1	1					2
	SN				3	1	1						2	1							
Important Studies[b]	SP	5		3	2	1	3	5		1	3	2		3	3		1	1	3	1	3
	P			2	3	1	3	4	1	2	4	2	4	3	2			1	2		1
	A		1										1		1						3
	N				2		1						1		1	1					2
	SN				2		1						2	1							
Excluding Model I or Absolute Distance[c]	SP	5		3	3	2	4	6			3	2		3	5		1	1	1	3	3
	P		3	3	6	3	4	6	1	1	4		3	4	5				2	1	1
	A	1						1					1	1							3
	N				1		2								1	1					2
	SN				1		1							1							
Rummel	SP					1	3	6		1		2	1		4						
	P		1		8	3	9	3				4	2		2						
	A					1						1									
	N				3		3					2	1								
	SN					1															

propositions to begin with: then if the distributions were to come out as in Table 16C.4, it would be even more impressive.

To at least see what would happen were I systematically biased, by *hypothesis* assume that I interpreted strongly negative results as negative, negative results as ambiguous, ambiguous results as positive, and positive as strongly positive. Assume also *no* strongly positive results. To see the consequences of ·such possible bias, Table 16C.4 reduces each rating one level. Even then the overall evidence still favors the propositions.

NOTE

1. This is only in reference to some of Haas's many analyses. For specifics, see Rummel, "A Warning on Michael Haas's *International Conflict*" (1978a), which was written as a result of screening his analyses for this part.

TABLE 16C.4: Evidence: Subtotals and Totals* (Cont.)

21	22	23	24	25	26	27	28	29	30	31	32	33	Total	(%) [f]	One-Level Decrement [d] Total	(%) [f]
11			1	1	1	4	1	8	4	18	15	7	136	35	0	0
														79		35
13	3	2	5	2		9	1	12	1	22	3	6	173	44	136	35
4			3			2					2	1	23	6	173	44
8			1			4		1			1		32	9	23	6
														16		22
1						6		1	1	6		1	26	7	58	16
10			1	1	1	4	1	8	3	16	14	7	121	40	0	0
														77		40
12	1	1	5	2		9	1	12		12	2	6	113	37	121	40
3			3			2					2	1	22	7	113	37
6			1			3		1			1		26	9	22	7
														16		23
1						5		1		6			21	7	47	16
3			1	1	1	4	1	5	2	8	10	3	84	45	0	0
														79		45
6	2	1	4	2		2		4	1	5		2	64	34	84	45
2			3			2					2		15	8	64	34
1			1			2		1					13	7	15	8
														13		21
1						1				4			12	6	25	13
6			1			4	1	7	2	7	9	4	86	43	0	0
														85		43
6	1	2	5	1		4		6		9	2	1	84	42	86	43
*1			3			1					2		14	7	84	42
			1			2		1					11	5	14	7
														8		15
						2		1		1			7	3	18	8
1				1						1	7	2	30	30	0	0
														72		30
5									1	2		2	42	42	30	30
1												1	4	4	42	42
7											1		17	17	4	4
														23		27
						2			1	2			6	6	23	23

*From Table 16C.2. Counted are the number of indicated ratings regarding a proposition.

a. Excluding all ratings with an "I".

b. All studies rated "H" in importance.

c. Excluding any studies with "Y" for Model I, or Distances A, or both.

d. All ratings reduced one level to compensate for hypothetical coding basis.

e. Blanks = 0

f. All percentages are rounded off and therefore may not sum to 100%.

Chapter 17

ENDING CONFLICT AND WAR:
THE BALANCE OF POWERS

It is easy to begin a war, but very difficult to stop one, since its beginning and end are not under the control of the same man. Anyone, even a coward, can commence a war, but it can be brought to an end only with the consent of the victors.
Sallust, Jugurtha *LXXXVIII*

Once conflict is initiated, what ends it? In general, *Conflict Behavior ends when a new balance of powers has been determined.* The balancing of powers which we see as Conflict Behavior will not end until a balance is achieved; then, conflict ends. A new balance is therefore a necessary and sufficient condition for termination.[1]

More specifically, what constitutes this new balance of powers? First, it is a mutual balance between the *interests* of the conflicting parties—between wants, desires; between goals and intentions. It may be over something as abstract as what God a people will believe in; or as concrete as whose flag will be raised over a specific, small island.

The exchange mutually communicates the relevant interests of each party and their strength of purpose. A new balance then means that both parties better perceive their mutual interests engaged in the conflict and are willing to live with whatever satisfaction of interests that results from the confrontation.

Except in the case of the total victory of one side, conflicts end in some sort of implicit or explicit compromise, where the costs of additional conflict no longer can be justified by the interests involved.

This does not imply that the parties to a conflict are computing machines, weighing explicit costs against articulated interests. Nothing so precise. Conflicts between states are between systems of decision makers and bureaucratic organizations, psychological fields, and societies and cultures. Emotion, jingoism, nationalism, ideology, hate, and all may be involved to some degree. Nonetheless, there is some definition of the interests engaged, simply from the need of bureaucratic organizations and groups to define some specific goals and the demands of internal groups that costs be justified. And costs are weighed, not necessarily as an investor calculating the return in interests, but more as a sense for proportionate costs given the aims.

But interests are only one element in a new balance. A second is the capabilities of each side to continue to pursue the conflict and achieve their interests. Of great importance is the function of the conflict in measuring these relative capabilities: what previously was ambiguous, uncertain, is now clearer as a result of this *reality-testing*. The new balance of powers is also a new, mutual realism about each party's capabilities to achieve the interests involved.

And third, the new balance is also a fresh, mutual appreciation of each other's *wills,* the most elusive and ambiguous of psychological variables. The resolution and determination of each party to pursue its interests and its capability to do so have now been made clear by the conflict.

Therefore, *a new balance of powers is a psychological equilibrium in the minds of the participants,* not a relative inventory of military hardware and personnel, with some ratio comprising the balance. Rather, a new balance of powers is a mutual willingness to accept the outcome as a result of the mutually perceived interests, capabilities and wills, and because of the expectation of the costs of further conflict.

There are no other necessary or sufficient causes of an end to conflict behavior. We can, however, discriminate several accelerating conditions for which evidence is available (see appendix 17A). The following conditions facilitate, ease, and hasten the end of war:

- domestic opposition,
- consistent expectations of the outcome,
- shift in military power, and
- ideological devaluation.

Domestic opposition to the pursuit of a war by a leadership has a number of aspects to it. Public opinion may shift away from support. Interest groups may withdraw support and directly agitate against the war. The opposition party may make ending the war a party platform. And the leadership may be replaced by those with a more dovish outlook. The effect of such processes on the ending of war was seen in the U.S. involvement in the Korean and Vietnam wars, in France during the Algerian War of Independence, and in Great Britain during the Suez War (1957).

A second accelerator is the development of *mutually consistent expectations of the outcome* of the war. When the reality of battle has brought both sides to expect the same winner and loser, or a draw neither can alter, then an end should be near. Wars begin in objective uncertainty over the balance of powers and in subjective certainty of success (Proposition 16.9). Battle proves one or both parties wrong about success and establishes the outline of a new balance of powers.

Related to this mutual perception is a third accelerator: the *shift in military power*. One party obviously begins to physically dominate and the other side has no prospect of overcoming the inequality either through its own means or by third party intervention.

Finally, the end of war is accelerated by its *ideological devaluation*. Wars sometimes are tests of strength between political formulas and religions—of "communism versus the free world," "democracy versus fascism," "Christianity versus Islam," "racism versus antiracism," "colonialism versus anticolonialism." Ideology gives a war significance beyond the immediate, objective status quo issue. It becomes a matter of universal truth and justice. To devalue this content of war is to make its resolution easier in terms of concrete status quo issues.

Such are those conditions helping to terminate war. Individually, or collectively, they will not always bring war to an end. They do not cause termination. But they do generally make it easier for such to occur.

Wars will end if and only if a new balance of powers is determined. This determination is helped by opposing domestic interests, mutual expectations of outcomes, shift in military power, and ideological devaluation.

War is a process of physical and psychological negotiation in a situation of extreme uncertainty. Although the initiation and escalation of wars are caused and conditioned by a number of attributes and sociocultural distances, the ending of war is dependent on the process itself. War will end when the process clarifies, unambiguously, a new balance of powers.

Thus, the accumulated number of causalities is not a good indicator of wars end. The duration of war is independent of its casualities (proposition 17.6 in appendix 17A).

Thus, the attributes of the parties—their wealth, power, politics culture—and their differences and similarities are unrelated to the duration of a war, the settlement procedures used, or the specific outcome.[2]

The end of war is situational, the outcome of balancing powers between adversaries. But as a process, it does have the common accelerators mentioned.

And its end does have a cause: the determination of a new balance of powers.

NOTES

1. For the definition of this type of cause, see appendix 16A.

2. This lack of relationship is best displayed in Hannah's work (1972) and is supported by a variety of other studies. See Proposition 17.7 in Table 17A.3 of the appendix.

APPENDIX 17A

PROPOSITIONS AND EVIDENCE ON THE CAUSES AND CONDITIONS OF ENDING CONFLICT BEHAVIOR

17A.1 THE CAUSES AND CONDITIONS

The ending, or termination subphase, of Conflict Behavior is empirically distinct and therefore should have causes and conditions specific to it.

The definition and discussion of necessary and sufficient *causes* given in appendix 16A are relevant here, but regarding *conditions* a terminological change is required to avoid confusion. I will define any conditions conducive to the end of Conflict Behavior, violence or war as *accelerating conditions*.

TABLE 17A.1: **Causes and Conditions of Ending Conflict Behavior**[a]

NECESSARY CAUSES	SUFFICIENT CAUSES	NECESSARY & SUFFICIENT CAUSES	ACCELERATING CAUSES	EFFECT
		a new balance of powers (1)		Conflict Behavior (including violence and war)
			domestic opposition (2)	
			consistent expectations (3)	
				war
			shift in military power (4)	
			ideological devaluation (5)	

a. Numbers in parenthesis refer to propositions in Table 17A.2

The causes and conditions of ending conflict behavior are listed in Table 17A.1.

There is one necessary and sufficient cause, and no other causes which are necessary or sufficient. In other words, *there is only one general cause of the termination of Conflict Behavior.*

A number of accelerating conditions are listed, all of which refer to war. Because of the paucity of empirical research on ending other kinds of conflict behavior only the theoretical war accelerators are given.

Table 17A.2 lists the propositions associated with the cause and accelerators in Table 17A.1. Each of these propositions will be discussed in turn, as in appendix 16B for conflict behavior. But, before doing this, one clarification is necessary.

The ending of Conflict Behavior, violence, or war means that only the overt behavior ends. To participants or observers, only the fighting may have stopped (as in the four Arab-Israel wars since 1948), but no resolution of the dispute has occurred. No peace treaty may be signed; no negotiations may take place. The fighting may have terminated by mutual agreement, or may have tapered off without public contact or agreement between the participants. The issue or dispute is frozen, unresolved, or so it appears.

On the other hand, a resulution of the conflict, a negotiated settlement may be congruent with the termination of conflict behavior.

Therefore, what is meant here by "ending" covers a variety of routes through which conflicts are resolved or terminated.

17A.2 THE PROPOSITIONS

17A.1. Proposition 17.1 (Balance of Powers):
Conflict will be ended by a new balance of powers.

Conflict Behavior will end when both parties have established a new structure of expectations consistent with their relative powers (interests, capabilities, and wills) as defined by the confrontation.

Theory: Conflict Behavior is caused by a disruption of a structure of expectations (Proposition 16.1) which has become incongruent with a changing balance of powers (Proposition 16.3). The Conflict Behavior is then a process through which is determined a new, mutually perceived balance of interests, capabilities, and wills—a new structure of expectations.

The key to theoretically understanding Conflict Behavior, therefore, is as a balancing of powers. It can end only when a new balance both parties are willing and able to live with is defined; the mutual determination of such a balance ends the Conflict Behavior.

Prediction: If the Balance-of-powers proposition is true, a number of consequences should be empirically evident. There should be a clear shift in the structure of expectations before and after a conflict. That is, the Conflict Behavior should be a transition period between two different sets of understandings, rules, agreements, treaties, and the like.

Moreover, during the process of conflict a clear balance of powers should become evident to observers. Either one side will begin to show, unambiguously, the stronger power, where power = (interests) X (capabilities) X (will); or neither side will be shown to have a clear, decisive edge. Then the ending of the conflict should be a matter of time and face saving arrangements for one or both sides.

Evidence: Table 17A.3 lists the evidence for this and the other propositions. The evidence is organized as in appendix 16C.

The only evidence bearing on the proposition is Randle's (1972) detailed and analytical analysis of the outcome of 46 wars (selected from 60 studied). This study is directly relevant and important and it provides positive support.

TABLE 17A.2: Propositions on the Causes and Conditions of Ending Conflict Behavior

Type of Cause & Conditions	No.	Name	PROPOSITION	
			Abstract Description	Empirical Description
necessary and sufficient	17.1	Balance of Powers	Conflict will be ended by a new balance of powers	Conflict will end when both parties have established a new structure of expectations consistent with their relative powers (interests, capabilities, and wills) as defined by the confrontation
accelerator[a]	17.2	Domestic Interests	The ending of a war is strongly influenced by domestic interests and opinion	Contending domestic interests and opinion will be correlated with the termination and settlement of war.
	17.3	Outcome	War will likely be terminated when both sides have come to expect the same outcome	The end of war is correlated with a mutually consistent expectation of the outcome.
	17.4	Military Power	A decisive shift in military power to one side in a war will enhance termination	The end of war is correlated with a decisive shift in military power to one side
	17.5	Ideological Devaluation	Ideological devaluation hastens war termination and settlement	The end of war is correlated with its ideological devaluation
descriptive propositions	17.6	Duration	War is not terminated because of its casualties	War's duration is uncorrelated with its intensity
	17.7	Situational	The termination of war is primarily situational	The manner in which war is terminated and settled is uncorrelated with the attributes of the parties or their relative differences (distance vectors)

a. Two types of propositions from Table 16B.1 also are relevant here. One type specifies aggravators whose reverse values (e.g., similarity in place of dissimilarity) inhibit conflict (Propositions 16.12-14; 18; 21; 31-33). The second specifies inhibitors of conflict and thus accelerators of conflict termination (Propositions 16.23-27).

TABLE 17A.3: **Evidence on the Cause and Conditions of Ending Conflict Behavior**

Level[a]	Source[b]	Importance[c]	1	2	3	4	5	6	7
			PROPOSITIONS[d]						
Static-case	Fitzsimmons (1969)	L						SP	
	Richardson, R. (1966)	H							P
	Singer & Small (1972)	H						SP	PI
	Starr (1972)	H							PI
	Weiss (1963)	M						PI	
	Hannah (1972)	H							SP
	Haas, E., *et al* (1972)	M							P
	Klingberg (1966)	M						N	
	Rosen (1972)	M						PI	PI
	Ahn (1977)	M						SP	
Dynamic Case	Barringer (1972)	H		SP	SP	SP			SP
	Cannizzo (1975)	H							SP
	Randle (1972)	H	P	P			P		P
	Weiss (1963)	M						N	
	Horvath (1968)	M							P
	Harf (1974)	M							SPI
Static System	Haas, M. (1970)	H							P

a, b, c See footnotes, Table 16C.3
d. For a full statement of the propositions, see Table 17A.2. The proposition number here corresponds to its decimal number, e.g., Proposition 1 is Proposition 17.1 in Table 17A.2. The relevance of the evidence is coded as in Tables 15A.2 and 16C.3.

Conclusion: As in the previous chapters, I will not consider one analysis as sufficient to say a proposition is supported or not. Therefore: *there is insufficient evidence for the proposition.*

Proposition 17.2 (Domestic Interests): The ending of a war is strongly influenced by domestic interests and opinion.

Contending domestic interests and opinion will be correlated with the termination and settlement of war.

Theory: War is a balancing of interests, capabilities and wills through coercion and force. Integral to this balancing is the support of domestic public opinion and interests. If there develops a shift in opinion and interest groups away from support of the war, then the ability of a leadership to pursue the war should be weakened, and the original war aims themselves should be revised downward. An example of this is President Johnson's loss of his domestic support for continuing the Vietnam war after the North Vietnamese-Vietcong Tet offensive of 1968.

Prediction: There should be a positive correlation between (1) shifts in domestic public opinion and interests groups against a state's involvement in war and (2) the effort of its leadership to end the war on terms previously unacceptable. Moreover, such a positive correlation should also be found with (3) the changing war aims of the leadership, which should be scaled downward; or with (4) a change in leadership toward those with a more dovish view.

Evidence: Two direct and important dynamic analyses support the proposition. Randle's (1972) analysis documents the significance of domestic interests. Barringer's (1972) analysis shows the end of hostilities is discriminated by the establishment of a new leadership for the losing side.

Conclusion: The evidence supports the proposition.

Proposition 17.3 (Outcome): War will likely be terminated when both sides have come to expect the same outcome.

The end of war is correlated with a mutually consistent expectation of the outcome.

Theory: Wars begin only when both sides expect they will be successful. This is the Confidence Proposition (16.9). Clearly, these mutual expectations are inconsistent.

War is then a process through which this inconsistency is removed. The expectations of both sides about the war's outcome are brought together. Both sides come to agree as to who has the dominant power and is likely to win. Or both have come to realize that neither has the power to decisively defeat the other.

In either case, the mutual agreement on the outcome removes the ambiguity of power initially involved and helps establish the balance of powers that is necessary and sufficient for conflict to end.

This recognition is an accelerator, not a necessary or sufficient cause. Some leaders may refuse to surrender in spite of obvious defeat and hoping for a miracle fight to the bitter end, as did Hitler in World War II. Some peoples may believe in fighting to the end for their nation, religion or ideals.

Prediction: Through content analysis of official statements and the historical analysis of foreign affairs documents, the trend lines in official thinking during war time could be established. This should usually show for the defeated state a definite recognition of impending defeat, an acceptance of the victory claims of the enemy, before war is terminated.

Evidence: As shown in Table 17A.3, Barringer's (1972) analysis provides important, direct, and strong support for the proposition. He finds that the single variable most discriminating the settlement of hostilities is that the outcome of the dispute is now apparent to both sides. Neither side, moreover, expects that escalation will change the situation or encourage further third party help.

Conclusion: Still, one study is not enough for me to say the proposition is supported. Therefore: *insufficient evidence.*

Proposition 17.4 (Military Power): A decisive shift in military power to one side in a war will enhance termination.

The end of war is correlated with a decisive shift in military power to one side.

Theory: Again, war begins in a situation where power = (interests) X (capabilities) X (will) is ambiguous enough for both sides to expect success. War ends in a new, mutually recognized balance of powers.

A decisive shift in military capability to one side helps eliminate ambiguity about power and communicates the likelihood of defeat to the other. Moreover, it weakens the other's ability to alter this outcome by escalation or perseverance.

Of course, this shift in military capability may be compensated for by an opposite shift in will or interests. This happened in Vietnam after the Tet Offensive of 1968 by the North Vietnamese and their Vietcong front. The offensive ended in a clear military defeat which indicated a significant shift in military power to the United States and South Vietnam. However, the psychological and political impact of Tet, magnified by the American news media, caused an opposing shift in American interests and a weakening of American will to continue the war. This is to say that a military shift increases the likelihood of termination, but other factors may intervene.

Prediction: When physical capability shifts decisively (the relative power is not obvious) to one side in the course of war, termination is likely. This shift, therefore, should be positively correlated with the war's end.

Evidence: Barringer (1972) presents important and direct evidence. He finds that the termination phase of hostilities is distinguished by one party no longer having adequate logistic support for ongoing military operations; imbalance in troop strength, attack aircraft and medical facilities; control by one of all population and area involved in the conflict; and elimination of the base support of the other.

Conclusion: Again there is only one study. Therefore: *insufficient evidence.*

Proposition 17.5 (Ideological Devaluation): Ideological devaluation hastens war termination and settlement.

The end of war is correlated with its ideological devaluation.

Theory: Political ideology is a complex of beliefs about how man should be governed and the ideal social system. Its core is a political formula, an "ism," such as fascism, socialism, Marxist-Leninism, and Libertarianism, which claims a solution to fundamental injustice, inequality, tyranny, and the like.

Wars, such as World War I for the United States, World War II, Korean (1950-1953) or Vietnam, are often seen as ideological confrontations over which political formula will govern a country or region. Such confrontations are most intense, for they engage fundamental beliefs in the true and just. These are struggles not easily resolved by compromise or subdividing a territory. Only exhaustion or clear and decisive military victory will terminate the war.

Such is also true of religious wars. Religion is an ideology of reality and morality. And where religion ends and political ideology begins is not always easy to discern, as for Marxism-Leninism.

In any case, ideological devaluation, or reducing the ideological importance of a dispute to the parties, accelerates the termination of the war.

Prediction: Ideological devaluation can be measured by the analysis of official public statements or the trends in ideological themes or symbols. Internal propaganda and external justification for a war should reflect ideological escalation or devaluation.

Evidence: The only evidence bearing on this proposition is Randle's (1973) direct and important analysis.

Conclusion: Insufficient evidence.

Proposition 17.6 (Duration): War is not terminated because of its casualties.

War duration is uncorrelated with its intensity.

Theory: Wars are fought over a status quo; they are an engagement of interests, capabilities and will. A measure of the intensity of this confrontation is the number killed and wounded.

Except when a leadership has exhausted available combatants and must therefore end hostilities, the accumulated casualties of both sides do not indicate whether: there has occurred a decisive shift in power, domestic interests and opinion maintain their support, a change in expectations of the outcome has occurred, ideology has been devalued, or a balance of powers is about to be achieved. In other words, casualties are too gross a measure to indicate any of those changes during a war that accelerate or presage its end.

Prediction: The casualties (killed, or killed and wounded) of a war (absolutely, or proportionate to the populations involved) should be uncorrelated with its duration.

Evidence: Seven analyses are relevant here, three of them directly. Only one is of an important study (Singer and Small, 1972). Two analyses are strongly positive, two positive, and two negative.

Conclusion: Because there is only one important source of evidence, and the direct evidence divides into two strongly supporting and two negative, caution is required. Therefore, I will only say that *the evidence tends to support the proposition.*

Proposition 17.7 (Situational): The termination of war is primarily situational.

The manner in which war is terminated and settled is uncorrelated with the attributes of the parties or their relative differences (distance vectors).

Theory: While a variety of attributes and differences commonly affect the onset and escalation of war, its ending is primarily a matter of the direction and outcome of the shifting struggle between the parties. There are commonalities to this struggle which enable one to gauge whether and in what manner an end is in sight: breakdown of domestic support, mutual perception of outcomes, shift in military power to one side, and ideological devaluation. But these commonalities should be generally independent of the characteristic of each party, such as its wealth, power, political system, culture, or the initial differences and similarities between the parties. That is, the termination of war and its settlement depend on the situational dynamics.

Prediction: The ending of a war can be measured by its duration. War can be terminated or resolved through international organizations, judicial decision, bilateral negotiation, or mediation. It can end by judicial award, conquest, being frozen, or compromise and resolution. In any case, the end or manner of such termination should be uncorrelated with the attributes or socioculture distances (vectors) between the parties.

Evidence: Twelve analyses support the proposition. None are negative. Of the twelve, four are strongly supportive, eight are direct and eight are also important. This is the best-supported proposition of all in Table 17A.4.

TABLE 17A.4: Evidence: Subtotals and Totals

Category	Rating	PROPOSITIONS[a] 1	2	3	4	5	6	7	Total	%[b]		ONE-LEVEL DECREMENT[c] Total	%[b]	
Overall	SP		1	1	1		3	4	10	40	92	0	0	40
	P	1	1			1	2	8	13	52		10	40	
	A								0	0		13	52	
	N						2		2	8	8	0	0	8
	SN								0	0		2	8	
Direct	SP		1	1	1		3	3	9	47	89	0	0	47
	P	1	1			1		5	8	42		9	47	
	A								0	0		8	42	
	N						2		2	11	11	0	0	11
	SN								0	0		2	11	
Important	SP		1	1	1		1	3	7	47	100	0	0	47
	P	1	1			1		5	8	53		7	47	
	A								0	0		8	53	
	N								0	0	0	0	0	0
	SN								0	0		0	0	

a. Blanks = 0
b. All percentages are rounded off and therefore may not sum to 100%
c. All ratings reduced one level to compensate for hypothetical bias

Conclusion: Because of the number of relevant analyses and the lack of any ambiguous or negative results: *the proposition is strongly supported by the evidence.*

17A.3. GENERAL CONCLUSION

Tables 17A.4-5 summarize the results.

As Table 17A.4 shows, the overall evidence overwhelmingly favors the propositions, even when only the direct or important sources of evidence are isolated. Moreover, when a one-level decrement is applied, the last columns of Table 17A.4 indicate that in general the evidence still favors the propositions.

Table 17A.5 simply summarizes the conclusions on the propositions.

TABLE 17A.5: Summary of Conclusions on the Ending Propositions

PROPOSITION		CONCLUSIONS ABOUT THE EVIDENCE					
Name	No.	Strongly Supportive	Supportive	Ambiguous	Opposed	Strongly Opposed	Insufficient Evidence
Balance of Powers	17.1						Yes
Domestic Interests	17.2		Yes				
Outcome	17.3						Yes
Military Power	17.4						Yes
Ideological Devaluation	17.5						Yes
Duration	17.6		Yes*				
Situational	17.7	Yes					
TOTALS		1	2	0	0	0	4

*"tends to support"

Chapter 18

THE INTERNATIONAL CONFLICT HELIX

Peace comes to an end because systems in their very nature change, and change requires adjustments that will upset the delicate balances on which peace had rested.
Melko, 1973: p. 141

At the highest level of abstraction, international conflicts are:

- independent,
- helixical,
- uncorrelated with cooperation,
- independent of internal conflict behavior.

And wars are:
- state specific,
- cyclic,
- neither increasing nor decreasing,
- correlated peak to peak with internal war.

These assertions are formalized as propositions and given along with their evidence in the appendix (18A) to this chapter.

That conflict is a process has been a theme of these Volumes. Within a sociocultural field, conflict is a process of mutually communicating, negotiating, and adjusting a new balance of powers supporting a cooperative structure of expectations. The resulting order, however, in time may become incongruent with the underlying power balance, and be disrupted by some trigger event. A new series of conflict and cooperation is thus initiated.

At first look this rhythm appears circular; a constant alternation of conflict and cooperation, war and peace. And so it might seem from any fast reading of world history. However, leaders and people learn from past conflict and expectations, and cultures and institutions incorporate this learning.

Assuming that the framework of conditions within which two states interact remains largely and relatively unchanged, then the process of adjustment—

balancing–becomes successively easier, and itself develops tacit or formal rules as to the limits and process of conflict. Diplomatic protests, for example, follow certain form and are conveyed according to certain procedures. Violence may be ritualized, or tacitly limited to certain weapons and geographical area. States may develop certain rules about conducting war, as to its declaration, legal responsibilities of belligerents and neutrals, treatment of prisoners, protection of combatants, and the like.

Moreover, the disruption of a structure of expectations does not wash out the memory or disposition of the parties. Each structure will have previous expectations and balances as a base of mutual recognition and understanding to build upon. Systems of relationships thus *evolve* towards greater coordination of

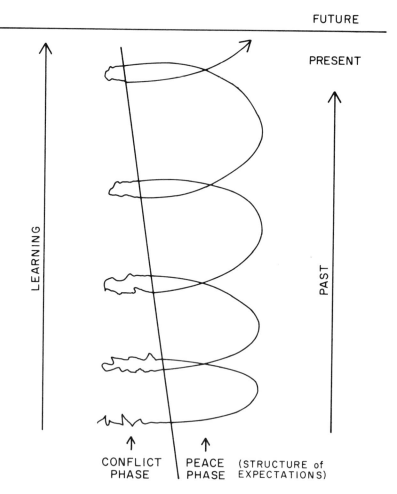

FIGURE 18.1: The Conflict Helix as a Coil Moving Upward on a Path of Learning

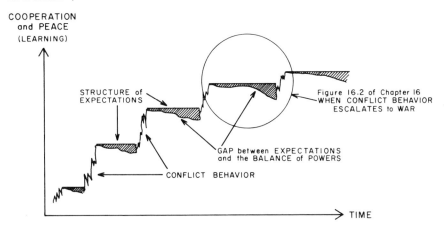

FIGURE 18.2: The Conflict Helix Uncoiled through Time

disparate interests and capabilities, and successive periods of international peace and cooperation will tend to last longer.

Thus, societies develop; cultures evolve. No one plans them. They are not made.[1] They are rather the outcome of iterative adjustments: the process of conflict and cooperation. *Through time conflict becomes less intense, peace more lasting.* This is the helix.

This helixical process is shown in Figure 18.1, where the circular process is really a coil moving upward on a path of learning. Each turn through peace and cooperation takes longer; each twist through conflict is less intense.

This helix is uncoiled in Figure 18.2 to show this process.[2]

The helix assumes that the system does not undergo major changes or shocks. If one of the parties has a revolutionary change in government, as Castro's takeover in Cuba in 1959, then the helix begins anew as shown in Figure 18.3. A whole new series of intense conflicts are therefore initiated. Such changes may also be caused by external events, a general or regional war impacting on the pair of nations, an international economic breakdown, an internal collapse of a state, political shifts or internal war in neighboring states, sudden hostile alliances, and so on.

Change, of course, will always take place. But as long as such change does not affect the foundations of a relationship, as long as it is gradual, even though in the balance among interests, capabilities, and will which supports a structure of expectations, then conflict is helixical.

There is thus two types of change affecting international conflict: that gradual change in the balance of powers to which conflict is a periodic, helixical adjustment; that radical change which sets the helix back and initiates a new sequence of adjustments.

Among radical changes there are several intrinsic to states and which themselves are periodic. The first is the periodic change in national leadership. This

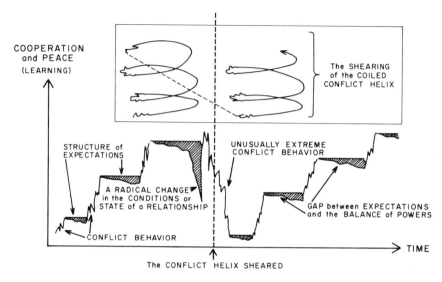

COOPERATION
and PEACE
(LEARNING)

The SHEARING
of the COILED
CONFLICT HELIX

STRUCTURE of
EXPECTATIONS

UNUSUALLY EXTREME
CONFLICT BEHAVIOR

A RADICAL CHANGE
in the CONDITIONS or
STATE of a RELATIONSHIP

GAP between EXPECTATIONS
and the BALANCE of POWERS

CONFLICT BEHAVIOR

TIME

The CONFLICT HELIX SHEARED

FIGURE 18.3: The Shearing of the Conflict Helix

change brings into office new personalities, perspectives, expectations; it elimi-
nates some of the learning the previous incumbent had accumulated. While
institutions, public opinion, interest groups, and the very important bureaucracy
will insure a certain consistency and incorporate and carry over previous experience, the new leadership must undergo new tests, new conflicts with other
states. A change in leadership, depending on how much of a departure it is from
the previous one, causes a regression, more or less, of the helix about every
decade.

However, generally a more radical departure involves the change over in
generations which occurs around every 25 years. The old pass away and the
young with their different beliefs, perceptions, and experiences come into
power; not only in the leadership, but also in the bureaucracy, interest groups,
communication elite, and public. Those who vividly remember the last big war,
who remember well its lessons, pass out of power and influence. Each new
generation, it seems, must learn for itself the lessons of history.

Finally, as generations pass, new institutions develop, new organizational
rules, new norms, new expectations, new ideas. What had become incorporated
in the culture and the society as a result of the last big war itself becomes
transformed. Although year-by-year changes are incremented, perhaps un-
noticed, over a long period of time the system becomes radically changed. Such
probably occurs every two generations or around 50 years.

Therefore, the progress of a conflict helix between states is jolted about every
10 years by leadership change, then by generational turnover about every 25
years, and finally by system change about every 50 years.

The effect of these changes is to produce cyclic patterns of war within international relations. General war is a watershed within and between states. It marks leadership change in most states among defeated and victors alike. The horrors of war are manifest, searing a generation with unforgettable lessons. And all states undergo internal institutional and political changes as a consequence. This creates a *tendency* for leadership, generational and system changes that affect the helix to be correlated across states.

All this is to say that *wars in the international system form three cycles:* about every 10, 25, and 50 years[3] there are upsurges of warfare—*a rephasing of the conflict helix.*

Although cyclic, nonetheless, the helix seems to imply that the war tends to fade away. This is not the case. Although in the short run war may appear to diminish, the overall effect of leadership, generation, and system changes is to shear the helix. Every two generations the process of adjustment begins anew.

The long-term trend in warfare within the international field is thus level: neither increasing nor decreasing throughout the centuries.[4]

Now, this assertion must be hedged. The necessary causes of war channel the occurrence of these cycles and trends. There are certain requirements (causes), as presented in chapter 16, that must be met before leadership, generation, and system turnover create war. For example, as long as two states remain libertarian, then war between them is extremely unlikely regardless of the other internal changes in either country.[5]

Moreover, the probability of war breaking out for any state differs. Although all states will undergo leadership, generational, and system changes, *states have different propensities for war*[6] as a result of their sociopolitical organization (such as whether libertarian or not), their coercive power potential, and relative location in sociocultural space-time.

In sum, then, there are periodic, radical changes intrinsic to states which break down the iterative process of adjustment among them—the conflict helix— and produce cycles in warfare.

This process of adjustment, of balancing of powers, takes place at different levels and along different dimensions. It may concern trade, multinational corporations, tourists, international airline pricing; or diplomatic rights, spying, border territory, spheres of influence, or global or regional power. When it involves general war, however, as in the Thirty Years War, the Napoleonic Wars, the World Wars I and II, then the general structure of expectations, the international status quo, is at issue. And all other structures of expectations between the warring parties and many between the allies are involved.

A breakdown in the international order manifests peaks in warfare within the system. Separate wars coalesce, casualities are the highest, and few states within the field are left untouched. Such a breakdown is also a disruption of structures of expectations internal to those involved. General war and the resulting balance sharply alter the conditions of internal stability in defeated and victorious states alike. Millions have new experiences and change interests and personality. Interest groups are reshuffled; class and status distinctions broken down and reordered; governmental power is increased; weapons become widely available; and dissidents, independence, and revolutionary movements are encouraged to strike. A crescendo of internal war breaks out and may reach its peak after the general war has been terminated.

Peaks in international war, therefore, are correlated with peaks in internal warfare.[7]

This does not mean that there is a general correlation between external and internal, foreign and domestic, *conflict behavior.* In general, the external and internal conflict helixes operate along separate paths—the balancing of powers within states goes on independently of international processes. For some states at some times, these two levels may be linked, as with the United States in the Vietnam war, France in the Algerian War, and South Korea's frozen war with the North. Moreover, internal revolutionary changes in regimes can disrupt a state's relations with others and initiate several rounds of conflict. And, as stated previously, at their extremes, external and internal war do come together.

But across states and times, external and internal conflict are independent processes; they are uncorrelated.[8] That is, internal conflict—a disruption of an internal structure of expectations—is neither a necessary of sufficient cause or condition of external conflict. And vice versa. Nor are they mutually aggravating or inhibiting conditions. Thus, internal conflict is not among the causes and conditions presented in chapter 16.

There are two more general assertions about international conflict that follow from field theory and its conflict helix. One is that international *conflicts are independent processes.*[9] That is, each conflict is specific to a particular, disrupted structure of expectations. Unless these structures between different states are themselves related, as security, aid, and trade may form interdependent nests of expectations in a group of nations, then there is no *general* reason for the balancing of power between, say, Rhodesia and Mozambique to be related to that between Morocco and Algeria, Cambodia and Vietnam, India and Pakistan, or North and South Korea.

Conflict is neither contagious nor emulated. To assert such is to believe leaders blindly or pathologically strike out at other states. Rather, they behave toward another states in a specific situation and regarding *their* interests, perceptions, and expectations.

Conflict elsewhere may of course change the conditions of this relationship and alter interests, as Cuba's military involvement in African wars in 1978 has affected its relationship with the United States. However, such is not a general necessity.

Finally, the *aggregate international conflict of and between states is uncorrelated with their cooperation.*[10] This is a most significant assertion, for it denies a basic assumption of American foreign policy, which is that increasing the cooperation between states will reduce the tension and conflict between them.[11]

The logic is this. Cooperation (flows and structures) and conflict are complementary, two sides of a continuous process of adjustment and interaction: the conflict helix. However, the link between particular conflict and cooperation is specific to a structure of expectations. American-Japanese conflict over Japanese exports of television sets to the American market and resulting imposition of higher American duties is independent of the American-Japanese conflict over Carter's declared intention to withdraw American troops from South Korea, and his resulting assurances to Japan and reiteration of the American security commitment to Korea.

For a pair of states, therefore, their aggregate Conflict Behavior will be accumulated across diverse situations and processes of mutual adjustment, each of which may involve one type or another of more or less intense Conflict Behavior. Moreover, aggregate cooperation will similarly be accumulated across diverse structures of expectations, involving one type or another of more or less cooperation. Consequently, there is no necessary relationship between the aggregate conflict of a state and its aggregate cooperation.

That is, from a state's overall cooperation with another—its exports, treaties, cultural exchanges, comemberships in international organizations, state visits, conferences, tourists, aid, students, migrants, mail, telephone calls, and the like, to and with the other—you cannot in general deduce its level and type of conflict with the other.

In summary then, international conflict is an iterative process of establishing a structure of expectations through which cooperation can take place, a helix. This conflict in the aggregate is uncorrelated with cooperation and internal conflict, although at the extreme, peaks of international warfare correspond to peaks in internal war. Moreover, international conflict across states are themselves independent.

And as for war, in the long term it is neither increasing or decreasing, although around this trend are three cycles corresponding to leadership, generational, and system change. Finally, the probability of any state engaging in war at a particular time is specific to that state. That is, it is a function of its leader's perception, expectations, interest and capabilities, and behavioral dispositions. And, of course, will.

NOTES

1. A most thorough, contemporary argument for this evolutionary view of societies is Hayek (1973-1976).

2. A simpler version of this figure is given in Volume 1 (1975: 150, Figure 15.1) for generalized interpersonal conflict.

3. On balance the evidence supports the existence of cycles that range in periodicity around 10, 25 and 50 years. There is no consistent agreement across studies, however, on the precise periodicity involved (e.g., whether 9.6 or 11.2 years), nor should we expect such until our measurement and historical, quantitative data on war are improved. For this reason

the assertion in the text is one example of where less precision is better than more. See Proposition 18.7 in the appendix.

4. See Proposition 18.8 in the appendix. All empirical analyses of war support this assertion, of which one of the best examples might be given: "Looking first at secular trends, contrary to what might have been expected, no trend, either upward or downward, is evident. That is, whether we concentrate upon frequencies, magnitudes, severities, or intensities, we do not find appreciable more or less war in any of the subepochs covered. Of course, there were more battle deaths in the twentieth century than in the nineteenth (thanks to the impact of the two World Wars and the Korean conflict), but when the figures are normalized for the number of nations in the system, this trend disappears. International war, therefore, appears to be neither waxing nor waning" (Small and Singer, 1970: 147). Their full results and data are given in Singer and Small (1972).

This lack of upward or downward trend may be perplexing, because war frequencies seem unaffected by the growth of democracies, civilization, techniques of warfare, weapons, and so on. When it is realized, however, that war is one manifestation of a universal process of balancing of powers—a balancing intrinsic to man's interaction and that the conflict helix is limited by periodicities inherent in society, than the lack of upward or downward trend is explicable.

5. To say the least, there is much need for careful analysis here, for the lack of any historically downward trend in war raises the question as to whether wars can ever be reduced in number or intensity, or eliminated altogether. This is not the appropriate point at which to make this analysis, which will be done in Volume 5.

6. See Proposition 18.5 in the appendix. This assertion, systematically supported by two relevant empirical studies, is consistent with our appreciation of the war potential of different states. Surely, the probability of Israel, South Africa, or South Korea being involved in war in 1979 (next year) is greater than that of New Zealand, Switzerland, or Sri Lanka.

Also, this assertion is an aspect of the field perspective: that states behave within their own frames of reference. See the Actor Proposition 16.7, appendix 16A.

7. All relevant systematic, empirical research of which I am aware supports this. See Proposition 18.6 in the appendix.

8. This independence has been the result and focus of at least 46 systematic analyses, and strongly substantiated. See Proposition 18.3 in the appendix.

9. See Proposition 18.4 in the appendix. This assertion is similar to the randomness proposition for conflict in society (Volume 2, 1976: section 35.1). The evidence is, without exception, strongly supportive.

10. See Proposition 18.2 in the appendix. At least 51 systematic analyses bear on this assertion, over two-thirds of which support it. This independence can be seen in the separate components of behavior space-time shown in Tables 4.1-4.2.

11. This is the policy of détente, begun in the early years of the first Nixon Administration and continued with little variation through the Ford and into this second year of the Carter Administration. This whole chapter in general and this assertion in particular underlie my *Peace Endangered* (1976), an attempt to warn about the fallacies of détente and the increased danger of nuclear war inherent in such a policy conjoined with a then continuing unilateral disarmament.

APPENDIX 18A
DESCRIPTIVE PROPOSITIONS
ON INTERNATIONAL CONFLICT

18A.1 PROPOSITIONS

I offer eight descriptive propositions about international conflict, which are given in Table 18A.1. The format for considering the evidence for each proposition will be the same as in previous chapters.

Proposition 18.1 (Helix): Conflict is helixical.

Within a closed system Conflict Behavior will decrease in intensity through time and structures of expectations will last longer.

Theory: A structure of expectations becomes incongruent with the associated balance of powers (Change/Conflict Proposition 16.3) producing tension and hostility (Change/Tension Proposition 16.2). The greater this incongruence, the more likely the structure of expectations will be disrupted by some trigger (Surprise and Perception Proposition 16.28 and 16.29). Disruption creates conflict (Disrupted Expectations Proposition 16.1); and conflict negotiates a new structure of expectations more in accord with the changed balance of powers—a structure which provides a framework for cooperation. And this new structure may in time become incongruent, be disrupted, again creating conflict.

Thus, cooperation-conflict-cooperation-conflict . . . the process seems circular, periodic. Conflict appears cyclic.

However, no conflict begins nor is a structure of expectations created de novo, without history. Leaders and peoples learn. Each conflict is informed by previous ones. The next structure of expectations is built on the experience of those that went before. Conflict becomes ritualized or institutionalized, as various tacit understandings, rules, and limits govern conflict behavior. Successive structures of expectations tend to last longer as they become based on deeper and wider experience and communication between the parties.

As shown in Figure 18.1 of the text, the conflict-cooperation cycle is therefore theoretically a helix. Each successive turn from cooperation to conflict is at a higher level of experience and insight between the parties; each turn incorporates what was learned before.

But this assumes a closed system. That is, the relationship between parties neither suffers from internal shocks (a revolution or ideological coup d'etat, for example) nor external shocks, intervention or challenges. The successive conflict and cooperation between the parties thus can gradually adjust and increasingly find a long-run equilibrium, like a tribe isolated in a wilderness or a couple in a small farming community.

An ideological change in a state's regime, the intervention of a Big Power in a state's affairs, a breakdown in the international economic system, a producer's boycott (as with oil in 1973) affecting all states can create new conditions and require a whole new order of balancing and expectations between the parties.

TABLE 18A.1: Descriptive Propositions on International Conflict

		PROPOSITIONS	
Number	Name	Abstract Description	Empirical Description
18.1	Helix	Conflict is helixical	Within a closed system Conflict Behavior will decrease in intensity through time and structures of expectations will last longer.
18.2	Cooperation-Conflict	Conflict occurs across diverse structures of expectations	Cooperative flows and structures are uncorrelated with aggregate Conflict Behavior
18.3	Internal-External	Internal and external conflict are independent processes	The internal and external conflict behavior of states is uncorrelated.
18.4	Conflict-Independence	Conflicts (and wars) are independent	Within any time period, the occurrence and intensity of conflicts (and wars) are independent (random).
18.5	War Probability	War is state specific	States differ in the probability of their going to war
18.6	War Peaks	A disruption of the general international structure of expectations is also a disruption of the internal structure of expectations	Peaks in international war will be correlated with peaks in internal war.
18.7	War Cycles	War is cyclic	War's frequency and intensity are correlated with leadership, generational, and system turnover.
18.8	War Trend	Wars are neither increasing nor decreasing	There is no long-term trend towards an increase or decrease in the number of wars

All this is the conflict helix which has been developed previously in Volume 2 and presented here.

Prediction: As long as the conditions surrounding a relationship change gradually then the periods of cooperation between two states should last longer and the conflicts that do occur should decrease in intensity.

"Cooperation" here means cooperative *flows,* such as trade, tourists, students, migrants, mail, messages, aid, cultural and scientific exchange; as well as cooperative *structures,* such as the comembership in governmental and nongovernmental organizations, and the framework of treaties and agreements between the parties.

There is a potential confusion here between these and a second kind of cooperation—that which is part of the balancing of powers, the process of conflict. Promises, negotiation, offers, signing a treaty, accepting tacit rules of conflict, and so on, play a role in the process of conflict (as discussed in section 12.4 and for Proposition 15.2 in appendix 15A) and do not necessarily reflect the structures of expectations determined by the conflict.

The proposition says nothing about this cooperation which is part of Conflict Behavior. It does say that the cooperation which is part of the structure of expectations established by conflict should, internal and external conditions remaining relatively constant, become more durable.

Evidence: Table 18A.2 presents the evidence on all the propositions; Table 18A.3 tabulates the accumulated evidence by proposition and category, as discussed in appendix 16C.

As can be seen, the Helix Proposition or hypotheses similar to it have not been tested in the literature, nor do systematic results generally relate to it. Two studies, however, have results close enough to the proposition for me to *infer* support.

One is by Most and Starr (n.d., 1976). For three different data sets on war, 1946-1965, they apply a Poisson or Modified Poisson approach to analyze the diffusion of war. In their words (1976: 34),

> The analyses here indicate that nations which were at peace generally tended to remain at peace. Nations which were at war in one period may have had higher rates of proneness to subsequent new war participations, but they appear to have followed some natural "regression" toward [if not actually to] peace so that they became involved in fewer war participations in subsequent intervals.

The second study is by Azar et al. (1974). They analyzed reactive process models for 11,664 events transformed into a cooperative-conflict scale for the years 1950-1971 and 12 dyads. Were the Helix Proposition correct, then dyads which are acting *primarily with each other in view* (i.e. major-major, or minor-minor powers acting within a defined structure of conflict) should move towards a closer linkage of their cooperation and conflict through their mutual learning—the helix. That is, their reactivity coefficients should increase in time. Azar, *et al.,* found that eight out of nine appropriate dyads have positive regression coefficients when their reactivity coefficients are regressed on time.

Conclusion: Of the two sources of evidence, both are indirectly relevant and are important. But the level of indirect support is not strong in either case. Caution therefore dictates the conclusion: *the evidence tends to support the proposition.*

Proposition 18.2 (Cooperation-Conflict): Conflict occurs across diverse structures of expectations.

Cooperative flows and structures are uncorrelated with aggregate Conflict Behavior.

Theory: Conflict Behavior begets a balance of powers and associated structures of expectations. And this structure is the framework for cooperation. But structures of expectations may become incongruent with the supporting balance, some trigger then may disrupt the structure, producing Conflict Behavior through which a new balance and structure of expectations is negotiated. Thus, cooperation and conflict are complementary aspects of a process of mutual communications, adjustment, and cooperation.

But there are many overlapping and layered structures of expectations. For example, a trade treaty between two states may exist within an overarching mutual-security treaty and also be within the framework of a multinational agreement on trade. There may be related, subordinate, or superordinate understandings, agreements or treaties on aid, military basing, off-shore fishing, foreign investment, and so on.

Conflict can occur in the formation of, or because of, the breakdown in any of these structures of expectations. Which is to say that conflict in the aggregate (e.g., the number of accusations, warnings, sanctions of one state to another) reflects diverse balancings of powers; cooperation in the aggregate occurs within diverse structures of expectations. There

TABLE 18A.2: Evidence on the Descriptive Propositions

Level[a]	Source[b]	Important				PROPOSITIONS[d]				
			1	2	3	4	5	6	7	8
Static Case	Horvath & Foster (1963)	L				SP				
	de Leon, et al. (1969)	M			P					
	Naroll, et al. (1974)	M		P						
	McGowan & Rood (1975)	L				SP				
	Nye (1971)	M		N						
	Richardson, L. (1960a)	H				SP				
	"United . . ." (1968)	M			SP					
Dynamic Case	Burrowes & Garriga-Pico (1974)	M		SP						
	Goldman (1973)	L		A						
	Denton (1966)	H						SP	P	
	Denton & Phillips (1968)	H						SP	P	
	Denton (1969)	H								
	Dewey (1962, 1964, 1966, 1969, 1970, 1971)	H							SP	
	Most & Starr (n.d., 1976)	H	PI			SP				
	Richardson, L. (1960a)	H					SP		N	
	Rosecrance (1963)	H			NI					
	Singer & Small (1972)	H				SP	SP	P	PI	SP
	Sorokin (1957)	H			SP	SP	SP	P	A	SP
	Wright (1942)	H							N	SP
Static Nation	Cattell (1949)	M			SP					
	Cattell, et al. (1951)	L		A	SP					
	Cattell & Gorsuch (1965)	M			SP					
	Collins (1973)	M			N					
	Copson (1973)	M			P					
	Cutler (1970)	H							P	

TABLE 18A.2: Evidence on the Descriptive Propositions

Level[a]	Source[b]	Importance	PROPOSITIONS[d] 1	2	3	4	5	6	7	8
	East & Gregg (1967)	M			P					
	Gregg & Banks (1965)	M			P					
	Haas, M. (1974)	H		SP	SP					
	Hazelwood (1973)	M			N					
	Hill (1977)	L			P					
	Hopple, et al. (1976)	M		P	P					
	Naroll (n.d., 1966)	M		SP						
	Phillips (1973)	L						P		
	Rummel (1963, 1963a)	M			SP					
	Rummel (1972)	H		SP	SP					
	Tanter (1966)	M			SP					
	Terrell (1971)	M			SP					
	Wilkenfeld (1972)	M			A					
	Wilkenfeld (1973)	M			P					
	Wilkenfeld et al. (1977)	M			A					
	(appendix I: 3.1)	H			SP					
	Kegley (1974)	L		P						
	Weil (1975)	M		P	P					
Dynamic-nation	Burrowes & Spector (1973)	H			SP					
	Cattell (1953)	H		SP						
	Cattell & Adelson (1951)	M		P						
	Gibb (1956)	M		A						
	Holsti et al. (1969)	L		A						
	Onate (1974)	M			P					
	Richardson, R. (1966)	M								P
	Sorokin (1957)	H							A	
	Stohl (1975)	H			N					

TABLE 18A.2: Evidence on the Descriptive Propositions

| Level[a] | Source[b] | Importance | \|\| PROPOSITIONS[d] | | | | | | | |
			1	2	3	4	5	6	7	8
	Wilkinfeld (1972)	H			P					
	Wilkinfeld & Zinnes (1973)	M			A					
	(appendix I: 3.1)	H			SP					
	Moore, J. (1970)	L		P						
	Vincent (1971a; 1971b)	L			P					
Static-dyad	Gleditsch (1969, 1970)	M			P					
	Holsti, O., et al. (1973)	M		N	P					
	Kegley & Howell (n.d.)	L		P						
	Leavitt (1968)	L		P						
	Park, T. (1969)	M		N						
	Richardson, L. (1960a)	M		P						
	Rosenau & Hoggard (1974)	H		SN						
	Rummel (1969)	H		SP						
	Russett (1967)	H		N						
	Schubert (1975)	M		SN						
	Schwerin (1977)	M		SP						
	Sullivan, J. (1970, 1972)	L		P						
	Sullivan, M. (1970)	M		SP						
	Teune & Synnestvedt (1965)	L		P	P					
	Vincent (1976a, 1977b)	H			P					
	Weil (1975)	M		SP						
	(appendix I: 5.3)	M			P					
	(appendix I: 6.1)	M			P					
	(appendix I: 6.8)	M			P					
	(appendix I: 6.7)	M			P					
	Choi (1973)	M		SP						
	Rummel (1972)	M		SP						

TABLE 18A.2: Evidence on the Descriptive Propositions

Level[a]	Source[b]	Importance	1	2	3	4	5	6	7	8
								PROPOSITIONS[d]		
Dynamic-Dyadic	Azar, et al. (1974)	M	PI							
	Bobrow (1969)	M		P						
	Caspary (1968)	L		PI						
	Mahoney (1977)	M		P						
	Mogdis (1969, 1970)	M		P						
	Park, Y. (1975)	M		P						
	Väyrynen (1973)	M		SP						
	Singer & Small (1974)	M		SN						
	Rhee (1977)	M		SP						
Static system	Hart, J. (1974)	M		P						
	Sullivan, M. (1976)	M		P						
	(appendix I: 2.6)	M		SP						
Dynamic system	Harf, et al. (1974)	H		A						
	Singer & Wallace (1970)	M		A						
	Singer & Small (1974)	M		SP						
Summaries	Zinnes (1976)	H			P					
	Sullivan, M. (1976)	H		P	P					
	Haas (1965)	L			P					
	McGowan & Shapiro (1973)	H		N	P					
	Vasquez (1975, 1976)	H		P	P					
	Weede (1977b)	M		SP	A					

a, b, c. See footnotes, Table 16C.3
d. For a full statement of the proposition, see Table 18A.1. The proposition number here corresponds to its decimal number, e.g., proposition 1 is proposition 18.1 in Table 18A.1. The relevance of the evidence is coded as in Tables 15A.2, 16C.3 and 17A.3.

TABLE 18A.3: Evidence: Subtotals and Totals

Category	Rank	| PROPOSITIONS 1	2	3	4	5	6	7	8	| Total %			| One-Level Decrement Total %		
Overall	SP		16	12	5	2	2	1	3	42	33	78	0	0	33
	P	2	21	25				3	5	1	57	45		42	33	
	A		6	4				2			12	10		57	45	
	N		5	5				2			12	10	12	12	10	22
	SN		3								3	2		15	12	
Direct Evidence	SP		16	12	5	2	2	1	3	41	34	78	0	0	34
	P		20	25				3	4	1	53	44		41	34	
	A		6	4				2			12	10		53	44	
	N		5	4				2			11	9	12	12	10	22
	SN		3								3	3		14	12	
Important Studies	SP		6	6	3	2	2	1	3	23	48	81	0	0	48
	P	1	2	6				2	5		16	33		23	48	
	A		1					2			3	6		16	33	
	N		2					2			5	10	12	3	6	
	SN		1								1	2		6	12	18
Rummel or Appendix I	SP		4	4							8	67	100	0	0	67
	P			4							4	33		8	67	
	A										0	0		4	33	
	N										0	0		0	0	
	SN										0	0	0	0	0	0

is therefore no necessary relationship between the type and level of *aggregate* conflict and the type and amount of *aggregate* cooperation.

Moreover, there is no reason within field theory to expect in general a certain type and volume of cooperation to follow from a balance of power established through a specific kind or intensity of conflict. In theory, the expectation is to the contrary. Because conflict is situational and functions to communicate and adjust different interests, capabilities, and wills, the kind and level of conflict should be uncorrelated across dyads or nations with the kind or level of cooperation which it begets.

Putting these last two paragraphs together, then, in the aggregate conflict and cooperative flows and structures should be uncorrelated.

Prediction: Across levels (cases, states, dyads, and systems) and across time, one should find that various dimensions, components, or factors of cooperative flows or structures are uncorrelated with types or subphases of Conflict Behavior.

Evidence: Tables 18A.2 lists fifty-one different analyses bearing on the Cooperation-Conflict Proposition. Table 18A.3 divides them by category. As can be seen, sixteen analyses are strongly positive and direct, with six being from important studies; twenty-one are positive, and all but one directly bear on the proposition. Only two of the positive analyses, however, are from important studies. There are eight negative analyses, three of these strongly so.

Conclusion: Since 73% of the analyses support the proposition and only 16% are against, it follows that: *the evidence strongly supports the proposition.*

*Proposition 18.3 (Internal-External): Internal
and external conflict behavior are independent processes.*

The internal (domestic) and external (foreign) conflict behavior of states is uncorrelated.

Theory: Conflict within states usually reflects the formation and breakdown of diverse, wholly internal structures of expectations (Volume 2, 1976: part IX). Similarly, a state's foreign conflict usually concerns wholly international structures of expectations. That is, in general.

Of course, there are situations in which internal and foreign structures overlap or mutually influence each other, as will be discussed for the War Peak Propositions. Additionally, abrupt changes in the ideological character of a government, a shift in domestic interest group power, can affect the global or regional Big Power status quo and balances of powers. The victory of Castro in Cuba in 1959 is a case in point. Moreover, foreign conflict can certainly affect domestic structures, as did the Vietnam war on U.S. politics, especially the balance of powers between Congress and the President.

However, specific linkages a correlation do not make. The fact that numerous examples of a relationship between internal and foreign conflict behavior can be shown does not invalidate the theoretical argument: in general the states' border divides two different and *usually* independent processes.

There are other considerations. Aggregate internal and external conflict behavior are associated with the formation of diverse expectations. Even if in the formation of a particular structure of expectations there is a relationship between internal and external conflict behavior, other, ongoing balancing independent of these structures will also contribute to the aggregate behavior. Moreover, as with the Cooperation-Conflict proposition, there is no theoretical reason to expect that a particular type and intensity of internal conflict behavior should be associated with a specific type and intensity of external conflict behavior, even when across states the same kind of internal-external structure is involved.

Prediction: There should be no aggregate correlation between internal and external conflict behavior and dimensions or types. There is one exception to this prediction. At the dynamic system level there should be a positive correlation between war peaks and the intensity of internal conflict behavior, as explained in the War Peaks proposition (18.6).

Evidence: There are 46 analyses bearing on the proposition as listed in Table 18A.2 and totaled in Table 18A.3. Twelve are direct and strongly positive, six of which are from important studies; twenty-five analyses are direct and positive, and six of these are also important studies. There are five negative analyses, four of which are direct, one is important.

From the earliest (1963) publication, the facet of my work which has attracted the most attention has been the finding of a statistical independence between internal and external conflict behavior. As can be seen in Table 18A.3, this independence has been a consistent finding in my subsequent analyses, as well.

Conclusion: Of the evidence 80% is positive; 28% is strongly so. Only 11% is negative; none strongly. Therefore: *the evidence strongly supports the proposition.*

Proposition 18.4 (Conflict-Independence): Conflicts (and wars) are independent.

Within any time period, the occurrence and intensity of conflict (and wars) are independent (random).

Theory: Conflict Behavior is unlike an infectious disease sweeping through the community of states. Nor when conflict breaks out between two states is it emulated by others. Rather, Conflict Behavior is a process of balancing intrinsic to the life stream of two states. Whether Conflict Behavior breaks out between them depends on the congruence between their diverse expectations and associated balances of powers.

Now, it clearly may be that these expectations and balances overlap or are entwined with other states, as the U.S. and South Korean structures are interrelated with the security structure between Japan and the United States; or as the expectations between the United States and Egypt, Egypt and Israel, and Israel and the United States have become entwined under President Carter.

There are scattered throughout the globe nests of expectations and power balances involving several, and sometimes, numerous states, such as in the Middle East, Western, or Eastern Europe. Conflict Behavior anywhere in this nest can spread throughout by its effect on the balances of powers or as a trigger. However, there is no reason for Conflict Behavior to spread from one nest to another, unless, and this is the only reason, it escalates to involve the general regional or global structures or expectations. General war affects all balances and causes multiple outbreaks which, while intrinsic to particular dyads, become absorbed in the larger confrontation.

With the exception of general war, then, the distribution of Conflict Behavior and intensities around the globe at any one period is independent. The reason for this and the exception are given by the conflict helix.

Prediction: One should find that the frequency and intensities of conflict behavior within some time period do not significantly differ from a Poisson distribution.

Alternatively, the *average* temporal correlations between the conflict behaviors of dyads (e.g., the by-month correlation between the conflict between Libya and Egypt with that of Ethiopia and Somalia, 1970-1975) should be low in general, although for some specific clusters of dyads the correlations will be high, reflecting their interlocking expectations.

Evidence: Overall, there are five directly relevant analyses, all strongly supporting the proposition. Three are from important studies (Richardson, 1960b; Most and Starr, n.d., 1976; Singer and Small, 1972).

Conclusion: the evidence strongly supports the proposition.

Proposition 18.5 (War Probability): War is state specific.

States differ in the probability of their going to war.

Theory: The logic here should be clear. States form different structures of expectations and supporting balances within situations of conflict. Situations will differ by state, as will the kind of balances of power and structures of expectation they form (Actor Proposition 16.7). Moreover, the incongruence of these structures should also differ, as would their probability of disruption.

All this is to say that states differ in their probability of going to war—that war is state-specific.

Prediction: States will differ significantly in the frequency with which they engage in war.

Evidence: Two direct and important analyses strongly support the proposition (Most and Starr, n.d., 1976; Singer and Small, 1972). There is no negative evidence.

Conclusion: The evidence supports the proposition.

Proposition 18.6 (War Peaks): A disruption of the general international structure of expectations is also a disruption of the internal structure of expectations.

Peaks in international war will be correlated with peaks in internal war.

Theory: Usually, internal and external structures of expectations are independently formed—they are separate streams of activity. However, sometimes there is a flood and the international stream crosses over to engulf the other. This occurs when the general international status quo is disrupted—when a general war occurs. Or when a number of regional wars reflect the breakdown in the international order.

Any state-society is a balance of powers between different groups. A breakdown in the international system and the requirements and destabilizing effects of intense war upset this balance and cause power to be reordered. Internal unrest, and revolutionary activity—internal war—is often the result. This may not occur during the external war, when diverse internal groups may be united in defense, in pursuing the war, or be holding back waiting for the uncertainty of war to be clarified. Among victors, neutrals, and losers alike, internal conditions and power balances will be sharply altered by the war. And new balances more consistent with the new international status quo must be determined.

Prediction: Within the international system or within isolated regional systems of states, peaks in international war tend to cooccur with peaks in internal war.

Evidence: Two important (Denton and Phillips, 1968; and Denton, 1969) longitudinal analyses of wars strongly, and directly, support the proposition. Three other analyses, two of which are important, also directly support the proposition. There is no negative evidence.

Conclusion: The proposition is strongly supported by the evidence.

Proposition 18.7 (War Cycles): War is cyclic.

War's frequency and intensity are correlated with leadership, generational, and system turnover.

Theory: Holding other conditions relatively constant (that is, the system is closed or isolated), wars for a state, dyad, or international system, should decline in number and intensity in time and the periods of peace should increase in duration. This is the Helix Proposition 18.1.

The reason for this is that people learn from previous wars and structures of expectations. No war or structure of expectations begins anew. All are the present thrust of a past stream of conflict and cooperation.

Organizations, through their law norms, rules and procedures; and societies, through custom, practices, and norms; all incorporate past experience and frame it for the present. States are always thus guided. Nonetheless, states do not make decisions. Leaders and peoples do. And there is a constant turnover of leadership and generations of people. Thus, the mistakes of the past tend to be repeated. The lessons of history tend to be ignored.

Therefore, the frequency and intensity of war has certain cyclic patterns. One cycle should be associated with the pattern of turnover in leadership within states. This of course will differ from state to state, but it appears that the leadership of a state changes on the average every four to six years. In 1955 the average age of the previous two governments for 82 states was 4.88 years, with a standard deviation of 4.12 (Rummel, 1972: 182, variable no. 74).

Change in leadership is change in psychological fields, in perspectives, in interests. Most important, it is a change in the sense for a state's role and position—the nuances of its balance with others. But the affect of this change on the state's structures of expectations should not be immediate, except in the case of a revolutionary turnover. New leadership takes time to get in the saddle, and their change in interests, will, and capabilities take time to produce conflict. Probably the most intense conflict associated with a breakdown in the expectations inherited by a new leadership and relearning lessons that passed out of office with the old will occur towards the end of their average term. The new leadership that then comes in will probably have the task of completing the building of new structures of expectations. Thus, the effect of change in leadership should be seen most in conflict behavior about every eight to twelve years.

At first thought, leadership changes would appear across states to be uncorrelated. However, such changes should have a rough correlation associated with two changes in a system of states. One is the occurrence of general or regional wars, which is usually the cause of a massive turnover in leadership among victors and defeated alike (War Peak Proposition 18.6). Second, a breakdown in the international economic system, as in 1932, will cause widespread leadership turnover.

Of course, such associated cross-national turnovers still leaves a bureaucracy in place. But intense regional and general wars deeply and permanently affect all; all within a society learn from them. War creates pacifists as no abstract lesson ever can.

Moreover, the lessons of the war—how it occurred, and the consequent expectations—are also deeply and widely learned. The so-called Munich model, as to how Britain's appeasement of Hitler's demands in 1938 led to World War II, had an iron grip on American thought and policies regarding Soviet behavior for decades after the war.

Thus, a generation becomes imbued with a perspective and an ethos. But generations change and with them goes their sense for the past. As any parent knows, the new generation simply must learn by themselves many hard lessons. This is no less true for the generational shift in leadership throughout the state.

But what constitutes a generation in time? This is an empirical, rather than theoretical question. The UN *1971 Demographic Yearbook* tabulates live births by age of mother for most countries in the world (Table 24). The highest proportions of births occurs within 20-24 and 25-29 age groups. The proportions in these two age groups are often close, usually higher in the first age group, with notable exceptions (Switzerland, Ireland, Italy, Netherlands, Albania, Jordan, and Japan, among others). The definition of a generation thereby closest to actual international birth statistics appears to be 25 years.

Leaders change, generations turnover, and eventually, the social and political systems also undergo significant change. Weakened and altered are the lessons of the past which were consciously and unconsciously incorporated into the society's institutions and culture, prevailing world view and sense for foreign policy and defense. This world view sets a framework for policy and opinion.

Two generations, about 10 leadership turnovers, or 50 years appears sufficient for incremental internal and international changes to add up to a major, indeed, revolutionary departure from the past. That is, the general and specific frameworks of expectations formed out of an upsurge of wars and violence about 50 years later no longer reflect the multiple internal and international balances of power.

Prediction: The frequency of wars, the casualties, the number of battles in the international system, should show significant cycles, irrespective of trend. These should be within a few years of 10, 25 and 50-year cycles; that is, cycles in leadership, generations, and system.

Because three superimposed cycles are predicted, what precisely would constitute positive or negative evidence for the proposition? As a procedure, any analysis is negative which does not uncover (when it is possible to do so) at least one of these three cycles, while within the design it is not possible to pick up the other cycles. Any analysis is ambiguous which fails to uncover one or two of the cycles when it was possible to do so, while finding the other cycles. Any analysis is positive which shows at least one of these cycles to be present, while within the design it was not possible to uncover the other cycles.

Evidence: There are six important, positive analyses bearing on the proposition, all but one of which are direct. Two important, direct negative analyses also exist (Richardson, 1960b; Sorokin, 1957).

I have categorized the six cycle studies of Dewey published over nine years (1962-1971) as one analysis. This is because they all deal with the same historical data on the frequency of battles (600 B.C.-1957A.D.), even though Dewey refines his cyclic analyses as he goes along. He finds (1970) a 11.24 year cycle (p=.0018) over the whole period; a 21.98 year cycle from 524 B.C. through 1938 (p=.0008); a 53.5 year cycle from 1700 to 1913 (p=.032). His analysis provides the only strongly positive evidence.

Conclusion: The evidence supports the proposition.

Proposition 18.8 (War Trend): Wars are neither increasing nor decreasing.

There is no long term trend towards an increase or decrease in the number of wars.

Theory: In a closed system where international conditions remain relatively constant, wars should decrease in number and severity. This is the Helix Proposition 18.1.

However, conditions are seldom unchanging, except among isolated tribes with strong, authoritative cultures sufficient to overcome the effect of leadership and generational changes. Otherwise, leadership, generational, and system changes are sufficient to wash out the mutual learning and balances established between states. The iterative process of gradual adjustment through periodic conflict—the conflict helix—must begin anew. Thus, there are cycles in war. *Thus, the long-term trend in warfare will not significantly change.*

Prediction: Regardless of the cycles existing in data on the frequency of war, the long-term secular movement in warfare in international relations should show neither a decreasing nor increasing *trend.*

Any analysis which shows the long-term secular trend to be significantly increasing or decreasing is a negative result. Long term means over a century; that is, over two full 50-year cycles, which are the longest theoretical cycles (the War Cycles Proposition).

Evidence: Three important and direct analyses strongly support the proposition (Richardson, 1960b; Singer and Small, 1972; Sorokin, 1957). R. Richardson (1966) found no trend in the frequency of 380 conflicts, 1946-1964. Although this finding was limited in time to 18 years and covered a variety of violence, it showed the proposition to have a short-term validity also. However, as evidence this was considered only positive and others may wish to exclude it altogether. In any case, exclusion would not affect any of the conclusions drawn here.

Conclusion: The evidence strongly supporters the proposition.

18A.2 OVERALL CONCLUSION

In summary, see the total and percent columns of Table 18A.3. They show by category that 33% of the evidence strongly supports the eight descriptive propositions; and about four-fifths is supportive. Only about 12% is negative. When a one-level decrement is applied, most of the evidence is still supportive for each category.

There is little change in the percentages between categories, except for my own analyses, all of which were supportive. The reader may wish to exclude these as possibly showing bias (because they depart from the proportions in the other categories). However, these comprise only 12 out of the 126 analyses and their exclusion would not change the overall conclusions.

Table 18A.4 summarizes the conclusions on the separate propositions. *Overall, the descriptive propositions are strongly supported by the evidence.*

TABLE 18A.4: Summary of Conclusions on the Descriptive Propositions

PROPOSITIONS

Name	No.	Strongly Supportive	Supportive	Ambiguous	Opposed	Strongly Opposed	Insufficient Evidence
Helix	18.1		Yes*				
Cooperation-Conflict	18.2	Yes					
Internal-External	18.3	Yes					
Conflict-Independence	18.4	Yes					
War Probability	18.5		Yes				
War Peaks	18.6	Yes					
War Cycles	18.7		Yes				
War Trend	18.8	Yes					
TOTALS		5	3	0	0	0	0

* tends to support

PART VI

CONCLUSION

If you will be persuaded by me, pay little attention to Socrates, but much more to the truth; and if I appear to you to say anything true, assent to it; but if not, oppose me with all your might, taking good care that in my zeal I do not deceive both myself and you.

Socrates in Plato's Phaedo

Chapter 19

CONCLUSIONS ON CONFLICT AND WAR

War, n. *A by-product of the arts of peace.*
                    Ambrose Bierce, The Devil's Dictionary

From this and previous volumes and related works, we can draw several basic empirical conclusions about man's conflict with each other. These conclusions have been stated as primary propositions in appendix 19B and therein related to the propositions established in this book (for which the evidence is summarized in appendix 19A), in Volume 2, and in *Field Theory Evolving.*

In all, the empirical conclusions are that:

- disrupted expectations cause conflict behavior
- power shapes conflict
- freedom minimizes violence
- cooperation and conflict behavior are independent
- change produces conflict
- conflict takes place in a situation
- individual perceptions and expectations condition conflict
- sociocultural distances affect conflict.

These empirical conclusions get their meaning and substance from a perspective on conflict. This is:

- conflict is a process of establishing a balance of powers in a social field
- peace, harmony, and cooperation are a structure of expectations congruent with a balance of powers
- conflict tends to become less intense and frequent and peace more enduring.

The empirical conclusions and this perspective apply to interpersonal conflict, social (collective) conflict within societies, and international conflict. They constitute together a view of conflict scientifically confirmed by the historical and contemporary record of man's social and international conflicts.

Yet, one must ask, of what moment are these conclusions? Of what value? From them what can we assert about eliminating or managing conflict, violence, and war? And especially, how do they help us avert World War III? This is the concern of the next volume. But before moving on to this, a final chapter is necessary to pull these volumes and propositions together in a set of principles which make explicit and organize simply and clearly the assumptions, theory, and findings explicit in this work.

APPENDIX 19A
OVERALL EVIDENCE ON 54
SOCIAL FIELD PROPOSITIONS ON
INTERNATIONAL CONFLICT

In the chapters 15-18 appendices 54 propositions from the social field theory were presented. These were divided into four types and evaluated with regard to 714 ratings based on the several hundred empirical studies listed in appendices I and III.

Table 19A.1 summarizes the total ratings for the four kinds of propositions and provides a grand total. Several aspects of this summary are noteworthy.

(1) The grand totals vary little by category, suggesting that the conclusions are unaffected by whether the evidence is direct, important, or from my analyses.

(2) Overall, 37% of the evidence is *strongly* positive and another 43% is positive. This contrasts with the 13% overall negative.

(3) For the three subcategories (direct, important, and Rummel), the number of strongly positive results exceeds those just positive.

(4) Except for Rummel (where it ties the ambiguous), the strongly negative ratings are the fewest in number.

Finally, Table 19A.2 summarizes the evaluations of each of the 54 propositions. As can be seen, no proposition is evaluated as ambiguous or unsupported by the evidence. That is, no proposition is rejected. On half the propositions I concluded that the evidence supported them; on an additional 19 (35%), I concluded that the evidence was strongly supportive.

In sum, the propositions appear empirically and scientifically sound. Moreover, because they were either derived from field theory or developed within this field orientation toward international conflict, their support also gives credibility to social field theory.

Of course, all this evidence on field theory is circumstantial. But

Some circumstantial evidence is very strong, as when you find a trout in the milk.
(Thoreau, *Journal,* November 11, 1854)

TABLE 19A.1: Summary of Evidence on Fifty-Four Field Propositions

		PROPOSITIONS														
Category[a]	Rank[b]	Phasing[c] Total	%		Causal[d] Total	%		Ending[e] Total	%		Descriptive[f] Total	%		Grand[g] Total	%	
Overall	SP	78	45	80	136	35	79	10	40	92	42	33	78	266	37	80
	P	61	35		173	44		13	52		57	45		304	43	
	A	17	10		23	6		0	0		12	10		52	7	
	N	11	6	9	32	9	16	2	8	8	12	10	12	57	8	13
	SN	6	3		26	7		0	0		3	2		35	5	
Direct Evidence	SP	74	46	79	121	40	77	9	47	89	41	34	78	245	41	79
	P	54	33		113	37		8	42		53	44		228	38	
	A	17	10		22	7		0	0		12	10		51	8	
	N	11	7	11	26	9	16	2	11	11	11	9	12	50	8	13
	SN	6	4		21	7		0	0		3	3		30	5	
Important Studies	SP	24	40	82	84	45	79	7	47	100	23	48	81	138	44	80
	P	25	42		64	34		8	53		16	33		113	36	
	A	6	10		15	8		0	0		3	6		24	8	
	N	3	5	8	13	7	13	0	0		5	10	12	21	7	12
	SN	2	3		12	6		0	0		1	2		15	5	
Rummel and Appendix	SP	28	56	77	30	30	72	0	0		8	67	100	66	42	77
	P	10	21		42	42		0	0		4	33		56	35	
	A	5	10		4	4		0	0		0	0		9	6	
	N	2	4	10	17	17	23	0	0		0	0		19	12	18
	SN	3	6		6	6		0	0		0	0		9	6	

a. These are the categories used in the tables of summary evidence for each type of proposition (Tables 15A.5, 16C.4, 17A.4, and 18A.3).
b. SP = strongly positive; P = positive; A = ambiguous; N = negative; SN = strongly negative.
c. Regarding six phasing propositions from Table 15A.5.
d. Regarding thirty-three causal propositions from Table 16C.4
e. Regarding seven ending propositions from Table 17A.4
f. Regarding eight descriptive propositions from Table 18A.3
g. Percentages are rounded off and may not sum to 100.

TABLE 19A.2: Summary Evaluations of Fifty-Four Field Propositions

Type of Propositions	CONCLUSIONS ABOUT THE EVIDENCE					
	Strongly Supported	Supported	Ambiguous	Opposed	Strongly Opposed	Insufficient Evidence
Phasing[a]	5	1	0	0	0	0
Causal[b]	8	21	0	0	0	4
Ending[c]	1	2	0	0	0	4
Descriptive[d]	5	3	0	0	0	0
Totals	19	27	0	0	0	8
%	35	50	0	0	0	15

a. From Table 15A.6
b. From Table 16B.2
c. From Table 17A.5
d. From Table 18A.4

APPENDIX 19B
PRIMARY PROPOSITIONS
ON SOCIAL CONFLICT

In a related work on field theory I concluded with five general propositions (FTE: *Field Theory Evolving*, 1977: 497) on international relations. These are given in Table 19B.1 and labeled for easy identification later. A few words on each might be helpful.

TABLE 19B.1: Previously Stated Propositions on International Relations[*]

NO.	NAME	PROPOSITIONS
FTE-1	International Relations	International relations is highly structured into clear and meaningful patterns of nation attributes and dyadic behavior.
FTE-2	Components	The three dominant patterns of attributes comprise wealth, power, and ideology; the dominant patterns of dyadic behavior are transactions, alignment, international organizations, and negative communications.
FTE-3	Behavioral-Equation	About half of the variation in a nation's patterned dyadic behavior is accounted for by its similarities and differences (distances) from the object nation. The particular function relating an actor's dyadic behavior to such distances is $w = \Sigma \, \alpha d$, where w is the patterned behavior, d is a particular distance (vector) on one of the attribute patterns, and α is a parameter specific to the actor.
FTE-4	Model II	Although all actors are similarly affected by distances in total, which distances relate to which behavior depends on the actor. That is, parameters generally vary by actor.
FTE-5	Distance Vector	Although overall, distances account for about 50% of the actor's patterned dyadic behavior, some particular distance relationships explain about 80% to 90% of their variation in such behavior.

[*]From R. J. Rummel, *Field Theory Evolving*, 1977: 497 (FTE).

The International Relations Proposition has found additional support from the results given in appendix 9A and from the positive, systematic evidence for the 54 propositions (appendix 19A).

The Components Proposition is exemplified by the empirical components presented in chapter 4 for behavior (particularly Table 4.1) and chapter 7 for attributes (especially Table 7.1), and further supported by the additional analyses mentioned therein.

The Behavioral-Equation Proposition is empirically exemplified in appendix 9A and forms a framework for the theoretical discussion in chapter 8.[1]

The Model II Proposition is also a basic perspective of this whole work, and is of particular focus in chapter 6. The findings in appendix 9A and the positive evidence for the related Actor Proposition 16.7 provide additional support for it.

Finally, the Distance Vector Proposition is a more general (but in variance terms, more specific) statement of the Distance Vector Proposition 16.6 presented here for international conflict. Of course, the strong support for Proposition 16.6 also additionally helps confirm the FTE one.

Besides these general proposition on international relations, I have also stated in Volume 2 (TCH: *The Conflict Helix*, 1976: chapters 32 and 35) general propositions on collective or social violence, *of which international conflict is a species.* These are given in Table 19B.2.

In Volume 2, as in this one, I related all my available evidence to these seven propositions. All were well supported (Volume 2, 1976: chapter 35).

The question here is then how these three sets of propositions (the five from *FTE*, the seven from *TCH*, and the 54 from this volume) are interrelated and what primary propositions will incorporate all three sets.

Eight *primary propositions* of conflict are listed in Table 19B.3. *These are meant to be the most general scientific propositions about conflict, violence and war supported by my work and that of others.* Their selection and statement articulate most generally my ontological perspective on conflict developed in these volumes.

For each primary proposition is listed those propositions from the three sets which underlie its statement. The diverse empirical support explicitly shown for these underlying propositions in this and the other works then collectively provide confirmation of the primary propositions.

Each of the primary propositions will be discussed briefly in turn. The underlying propositions will be woven into this discussion and identified when appropriate with regard to Table 19B.3.

TABLE 19B.2: **Previously Stated Propositions on Social Conflict**[*]

NO.	NAME	PROPOSITIONS
TCH-1	Random	Manifest conflict is random
TCH-2	Change	Change produces conflict
TCH-3	Power	Power shapes conflict
TCH-4	Dimensionality	There are three dimensions of conflict
TCH-5	Exchange Society	Exchange societies manifest pluralist conflict
TCH-6	Authoritative Society	Authoritative societies manifest communal/ traditional conflict
TCH-7	Coercive Society	Coercive societies manifest elite repression/purges

[*]From R. J. Rummel., *Volume 2 (The Conflict Helix)*, 1976: chapters 32 and 35 (TCH).

TABLE 19B.3: Primary Propositions on Conflict

NO.	NAME	PRIMARY PROPOSITIONS	UNDERLYING PROPOSITIONS	
19.1	Disrupted-Expectations	Disrupted expectations cause Conflict Behavior	16.1	Disrupted Expectations
			16.10	Status-Quo Disruption
			17.1	Balance of Powers
			18.1	Helix
			18.6	War Peaks
19.2	Power	Power shapes conflict	TCH-3	Power
			16.5	Joint Power
			16.21	Power Parity
			16.22	Class
			16.31	State Power
			16.32	Power Vector
			17.1	Balance of Powers
			17.4	Military Power
19.3	Freedom	Freedom minimizes violence	TCH-4	Dimensionality
			TCH-5	Exchange Society
			16.11	Joint Freedom
			16.20	Polarity/Violence
			16.24	Cross-Pressures/Violence
			16.27	Freedom
19.4	Cooperation-Conflict	Cooperation and conflict behavior are independent	TCH-1	Random
			15.2	Conflict Paths
			18.2	Cooperation-Conflict
19.5	Change	Change produces conflict	TCH-2	Change
			16.2	Change/Tension
			16.3	Change/Conflict
19.6	Situation	Conflict takes place in a situation	16.1	Disrupted Expectations
			16.7	Actor
			16.10	Status Quo Disruption
			16.26	Stable Status Quo
			17.7	Situational
19.7	Perception Expectations	Individual perceptions and expectations condition conflict	FTE-4	Model II
			16.7	Actor
			16.9	Confidence
			16.28	Surprise
			16.29	Perception
			17.3	Outcome
			18.5	War Probability
19.8	Distances	Sociocultural distances affect conflict	FTE-3	Behavioral Equation
			FTE-5	Distance Vector
			16.6	Distance Vector
			16.12	Dissimilarity
			16.14	Status
			16.22	Class
			16.32	Power Vector
			16.33	Wealth-Power-Politics

a. FTE propositions are given in Table 19B.1; TCH in Table 19B.2; Propositions numbered 15.x are given in Table 15A.1; 16.x in Table 16B.1; 17.x in Table 17A.1; and 18.x in Table 18A.1.

Primary Proposition 19.1 (Disrupted Expectations):
Disrupted expectations cause Conflict Behavior.

The underlying Proposition 16.1 stated that "Conflict Behavior if and only if disrupted expectations." By dropping the "only if" (because we are dealing with conflict at all levels and cannot assume that all parties had developed a structure of expectations–some may be meeting for the first time) I have raised this to a primary proposition.

The role of the structure of expectations in conflict has been a central theme of this and the previous volumes. Its formation defines peace, harmony, cooperation; its disruption precipitates manifest conflict–violence, if the status quo is involved (Proposition 16.10); and intense internal and external violence if it be the general status quo (Proposition 18.6). Through Conflict Behavior and possibly violence a new balance of powers (Proposition 17.1) is determined and associated expectations structured.

This conflict-balance-conflict-balance is a rhythm of social interaction. But individuals learn and previous adjustments are not forgotten. Therefore, within a closed system this process changes through time (Proposition 18.1): conflict becomes less intense, cooperation more enduring.

Primary Proposition 19.2 (Power): Power shapes conflict.

Power is fundamental to conflict in diverse ways. The type of power which dominates a society determines the type of manifest conflict it has (TCH-3). The amount of power of an actor predicts its degree of conflict involvement (Proposition 16.31); and its difference in power from other actors determines the direction and amount of manifest conflict (Proposition 16.32).

Moreover, the joint power of two actors measures their salience and thus potential conflict (Proposition 16.5), while their power parity indicates the likelihood that their conflict will escalate to violence (Proposition 16.21). And then the significant shift in military power to one of them will signal a termination of hostilities (Proposition 17.4).

Finally, the distribution of power in a society defines its class structure. And the more the society is divided along class lines, the more likely general violence or war (Proposition 16.22).

All this contributes to the balancing through which actors adjust their interests, capabilities, and wills and establish a balance of powers (Proposition 17.1).

Primary Proposition 19.3 (Freedom): Freedom minimizes violence.

The freedom of a people from government coercion is directly related to conflict. First, free–exchange–societies manifest a particular dimension of conflict (TCH-4): pluralist, spontaneous conflict (TCH-5). Second, the freedom of a people limits the foreign violence in which they are involved (Proposition 16.27); and third, mutually free people simply do not engage in violence or make war on each other (Proposition 16.11).

A major reason for this relationship of freedom to violence is due to the effects of power polarity and cross-pressures. An increasing polarity in coercive power will polarize interests and create a class front along which issues escalate to violence (Proposition 16.20). Cross-pressures, on the other hand, are an aspect of exchange societies. Diverse, overlapping interests segment issues and drain off or contain conflict which might escalate to wide-scale violence (Proposition 16.24).

Primary Proposition 19.4 (Cooperation-Conflict):
Cooperation and Conflict behavior are independent.

This raises Proposition 18.2 to the status of a primary. Here conflict is meant in two senses. *Aggregate* conflict behavior is statistically independent of that *aggregate* cooperation (flows and structures) reflecting structures of expectations (TCH-1; Proposition 18.2); and *coercive* conflict behavior is independent of that *cooperative* (noncoercive) behavior involved in the balancing of powers (Proposition 15.2).

Primary Proposition 19.5 (Change): Change produces conflict:

This raises the Change Proposition (TCH-2) in Volume 2 to the status of a primary. Change in the interests, capabilities, or wills of those involved in a structure of expectations may create a gap between these expectations and the supporting balance of powers. This gap produces tension and hostility (Proposition 16.2) and risks a conflict producing breakdown in the structure of expectations (Proposition 16.3).

Primary Proposition 19.6 (Situation): Conflict takes place in a situation:

The situational nature of behavior has been an important theme in this book, as particularly discussed in sections 6.3 and 7.2 and operationalized in appendix 9A.

Specifically, the inception and process of conflict depends on the particular situation an actor perceives and the expectations he has of the outcomes of his behavior in the situation (Proposition 16.7). Moreover, the ending of conflict as well, especially war (Proposition 17.7), is situational. While situations generally will vary by actor, one situation is common to most conflict behavior: for those parties who have sufficiently interacted in the past to form mutual expectations, conflict occurs within the context of a disrupted structure of expectations (Proposition 16.1); their violence within the context of disrupted core expectations—the status quo (Proposition 16.10). A stable status quo inhibits violence (Proposition 16.26).

Primary Proposition 19.7 (Perception-Expectations):
Individual perceptions and expectations condition conflict.

Individual perceptions and expectations are central to understanding man (Volume 1) and his social relations (Volume 2-3). The individuality of perception and expectations has been formalized in the Model II interpretation of field theory (FTE-4) and assumed throughout this book, as presented particularly in chapters 6 and 8 and operationalized in appendix 9A.

Perceptions and expectations enter into conflict in a number of ways. First and basically, an actor behaves according to his perception of the situation and expectations of the outcome of his behavior (Proposition 16.7). For this reason the probability of war varies by actor (Proposition 18.5). Perception of opportunity, threat, or injustice stimulates him to conflict (Proposition 16.29); and if this perception is abrupt conflict may be catalyzed or escalated (Proposition 16.28).

Moreover, expectations play a role in violence, which assumes an expectation of success (Proposition 16.9); and war, as a type of violence, will be terminated when both sides have come to expect the same outcome (Proposition 17.3).

Primary Proposition 19.8 (Distances): Sociocultural distances affect conflict.

That sociocultural differences between actors are forces on their behavior has been a conclusion of my theoretical and empirical research on international relations (FTE-3), and a motif of these volumes, as particularly discussed in section 7.2 and operationalized in appendix 9A (see also Volume 1, 1975: chapter 16; Volume 2, 1976: part V; Volume 3, 1977: chapter 6).

Different kinds of sociocultural distances affect conflict in different ways. For one thing, the *overall* distances between actors play a role in their conflict. As vectors these distances reflect the opposing interests and capabilities between actors (Proposition 16.6): perceptions weight distance vectors within a situation. As absolute distances they aggravate conflict (Proposition 16.12).

In addition, status distance between the parties especially aggravates conflict (Proposition 16.22); and among types of status, power (Proposition 16.32) and class (Proposition 16.22) distance play particularly important roles in explaining conflict.

Among all the different kinds of distances, those that most influence conflict involve distances in wealth, power, and politics (Proposition 16.33).

NOTE

1. What might be confusing is the single term (w) on the left of the equality in the proposition, while in appendix 9A there are a number of such terms on the left, each weighted with a parameter (expectations). This confusion can be avoided by keeping in mind that in the proposition w is a sum of these terms on the left. Technically, it is a canonical variate.

Chapter 20

PRINCIPLES OF PEACE AND CONFLICT

But each for the joy of working, and
each in his separate star
Shall draw the Thing as he sees It for
the God of Things as They are.

Kipling, When Earth's Last Picture is Painted

In previous volumes, I discussed a variety of levels and aspects of man as foundation to understanding his peace and conflict. This covered ontology and epistemology, as well as analytic and synthetic systems. And a normative framework ("Intentional Humanism") was sketched preliminary to the next volume (Volume 1, 1975: part VII; Volume 3, 1977: chapter 10).

I have systematically drawn on this previous work in comprehending international conflict, violence, and war in this volume. The empirical (phenomenological) aspects of the resulting understanding have been stated in 54 propositions on international conflict (appendix 19A) and eight primary propositions on general social conflict (appendix 19B).

However, these propositions are limited in encompassing the full understanding of man, conflict, and peace developed here. By the very virtue of being empirically operationalizable, testable, and falsifiable, these propositions do not fully capture the *essence* of conflict and peace. They cannot be fundamental enough.

What is needed now is a set of *principles* that define the ontological framework of these volumes and the ingredients of this perspective on man, society, international relations, conflict, and peace. These principles should stand at that intersection between intuition, reason, and experience; between philosophy, analytic theory, and empirical science.

Twenty-three such principles are presented in Table 20.1. Table 20.2 indexes where in these volumes the theory, ideas, and facts have been presented which clarify and support each principle; and which of the 54 propositions empirically manifest each principle. Several things about these principles should be noted.

(1) These are *ontological principles* in the sense of fundamental assumptions and metaphysical truths[1] which are the building blocks of these

TABLE 20.1: Principles of Peace and Conflict*

LEVEL	NO.	NAME	MASTER PRINCIPLE	PRINCIPLE
Psychological	20.1	Subjectivity		Perception is subjective
	20.2	Intentionality		Man behaves to achieve
	20.3	Self-Esteem		Man strives for self-esteem
	20.4	Expectations		Expectations guide behavior
	20.5	Responsibility		Man is responsible for his behavior
	20.6	Individuality	Man is an individual	
Interpersonal	20.7	Communication		Man communicates as a field of expression
	20.8	Causal		Man produces effects
	20.9	Conflict		Conflict is a balancing of powers
	20.10	Cooperation		Cooperation depends on expectations aligned with power
	20.11	Gap		A gap between expectations and power causes conflict
	20.12	Helix		Conflict becomes less intense, peace more lasting
	20.13	Interpersonal	Through conflict man negotiates an interpersonal contract	
Social	20.14	Universality		Man's interpersonal principles apply to all societies
	20.15	Trisocial		Societies are generally trisocial
	20.16	Violence		A gap between the status quo and power causes social violence
	20.17	Polarity		The more government, the more violence
	20.18	Power	Power shapes peace	
International	20.19	Field		Free actors comprise a social field
	20.20	Exchange		Free relations form an exchange society
	20.21	Freedom		Violence does not occur between free societies
	20.22	War		A gap between the international status quo and power causes war
	20.23	Peace	Through conflict states negotiate a social contract	

*These principles are nontechnically elaborated and popularized in R. J. Rummel, *In the Minds of Men*, (tentative title), forthcoming 1980-1981.

TABLE 20.2: Bases and Related Propositions for the Principles of Conflict and Peace

No.	Name	Basis of Principle[b]	No.	Name
	PRINCIPLE[a]			RELATED PROPOSITIONS[c]
20.1	Subjectivity	Vol. 1: Part I; Chap. 11, 16	16.7	Actor
		Vol. 2: Chap 5	17.7	Situational
		Vol. 3: Part I	19.6	Situation
20.2	Intentionality	Vol. 1: Chap. 20-21, 26; Part VII		
		Vol. 2: Chap. 6		
		Vol. 3: Part I		
		Vol. 4: Chap. 4		
20.3	Self-Esteem	Vol. 1: Chap. 21		
20.4	Expectations	Vol. 1: Part III	16.7	Actor
		Vol. 3: Sec. 4.3	16.9	Confidence
		Vol. 4: Chap. 5	17.3	Outcome
20.5	Responsibility	Vol. 1: Chap. 30-31		
20.6	Individuality	Vol. 1: entire; Chap. 33	FTE	Model II
			16.7	Actor
			17.7	Situational
			18.5	War Probability
			19.7	Perception-Expectations
20.7	Communication	Vol. 1: Chap. 16		
		Vol. 2: Part II		
20.8	Causal	Vol. 1: Chap. 7-8		
		Vol. 2: Chap. 19-21		
20.9	Conflict	Vol. 1: Chap. 15	16.2	Change/Tension
		Vol. 2: Chap. 28-29	16.3	Change/Conflict
		Vol. 3: entire	17.1	Balance of Powers
		Vol. 4: Chap. 12	17.4	Military Power
20.10	Cooperation	Vol. 1: Chap. 15		
		Vol. 2: Sec. 29.4		
20.11	Gap	Vol. 1: Chap. 15	TCH-2	Change
		Vol. 2: Sec. 29.5	16.1	Disrupted-Expectations
		Vol. 3: Chap. 8	16.2	Change/Tension
			16.3	Change/Conflict
			19.1	Disrupted-Expectations
			19.5	Change
20.12	Helix	Vol. 2: Part VII	18.1	Helix
		Vol. 3: entire		
20.13	Interpersonal	Vol. 1: Sec. 15.3		
		Vol. 2: Sec. 29.4		
		Vol. 3: entire		

TABLE 20.2: **Bases and Related Propositions for the Principles of Conflict and Peace (Cont)**

PRINCIPLE[a]			RELATED PROPOSITIONS[c]	
No.	Name	Basis of Principle[b]	No.	Name
20.14	Universality	Vol. 1: Parts V, VII Vol. 2: Part VII		
20.15	Trisocial	Vol. 2: Parts VIII-IX		
20.16	Violence	Vol. 2: Sec. 27.2; Chap. 29 Vol. 3: Chap. 8	16.10 16.18 16.26	Status-Quo Disruption Status-Quo Power Status-Quo
20.17	Polarity	Vol. 2: Part VI; Chap. 32, 34 Vol. 3: Chap. 5, 10	16.11 16.20 16.24 16.27 19.3	Joint Freedom Polarity/Violence Cross-Pressures/Violence Freedom Freedom
20.18	Power	Vol. 2: Sec. 28.5; Chap. 29 Vol. 3: Chap. 5 Vol. 4: Chap. 9, 12	TCH-3 16.2 16.3 16.5 16.14 16.20 16.21 16.22 16.23 16.27 16.30 16.31 16.32 16.33 17.1 17.4 19.2	Power Change/Tension Change/Conflict Joint Power Status Polarity/Violence Power-Parity Class Polarity/Conflict Freedom Totalitarianism State Power Power Vector Wealth-Power-Politics Balance of Powers Military Power Power
20.19	Field	FTE: entire Vol. 1: Parts I, V Vol. 2: Part IV Vol. 4: Chap. 9		
20.20	Exchange	Vol. 2: Chap. 30-31 Vol. 4: Chap. 2		
20.21	Freedom	Vol. 2: Part VI, Chap. 32, 34 Vol. 3: Sec. 7.1, Chap. 10	16.11 16.27 19.3	Joint Freedom Freedom Freedom
20.22	War	Vol. 2: Chap. 24-25, 27-29 Vol. 4: Chap. 12	16.10 16.22 17.1 18.7 18.8	Status-Quo Disruption Class Balance of Powers War Cycles War Trend

20.23   Peace   Vol. 1: Sec. 15.3
                         Vol. 2: Sec. 29.4
                         Vol. 4: Chap. 12

a. From Table 20.1

b. Referenced are books (*FTE* = *Field Theory Evolving*; *Understanding Conflict War*, Volumes 1-4), parts, chapters (chap.) and Sections (Sec.) in which the theory ideas, concepts, and evidence underlying a principle have been most discussed.

c. | Proposition No. | Appendix in which discussed | Table in which stated |
|---|---|---|
| FTE-X | 19B | 19B.1 |
| TCH-X | 19B | 19B.2 |
| 16.X | 16B | 16B.1 |
| 17.X | 17A | 17A.2 |
| 18.X | 18A | 18A.1 |
| 19.X | 19B | 19B.3 |

volumes. And they are the philosophical origin of the propositions given in chapter 15-19.

(2) The principles span the psychological, interpersonal, social, and international levels and therefore are meant to be comprehensive *within a direction:* understanding conflict, violence, and war; and peace.

(3) One *master principle* defines the essence of each level and assumes and incorporates the other principles at the previous levels. Thus, "Man is an individual" is for me the most basic and significant psychological principle for understanding his conflict, and entails the other, previously stated principles—his Subjectivity, Intentionality, Self-Esteem, and Expectations.

(4) The principles form a chain. Each assumes the previous principles and levels; each master principle assumes the previous master principles.

(5) There are no ethical principles (principles of Intentional Humanism as briefly mentioned in the forthcoming Volume 5, part VII); that is, principles which state what *ought* to be done about conflict, violence, and war given these ontological principles and empirical propositions. Those will be the focus of Volume 5.

(6) I have stated these principles in the simplest and most general language possible (for me), omitting any technical or philosophical jargon. I mean them to communicate widely and be generally useful.

(7) I am preparing a companion, entirely nontechnical, popular book (tentatively titled *In the Minds of Men*) which will present and elaborate these principles. This simple summary presentation of Volumes 1-5 should be published in 1980 or 1981.

Only a brief presentation of each principle can be given here. Extended discussion on the theory and ideas composing each principle can be found in the

volumes by reference to Table 20.2; or in more simple terms in the afore-
mentioned *In the Minds of Men.*

20.1. PSYCHOLOGICAL PRINCIPLES

Principle 20.1 (Subjectivity):
Perception is subjective.

Man perceives the world through a dialectical balance between his perspective—an outward vector of his dynamic psychological field—and the powers of
reality which, as an inward vector, try to impose a perception on him. Perception is thus each person's unique balance with reality.

Principle 20.2 (Intentionality):
Man behaves to achieve.

Man generally behaves to achieve future goals. His behavior is intentional, the
free outcome of a self consisting most fundamentally of id, ego, and superego.
Man's interests are the active interface between this basic organization of the self
and his teleological behavior.

Principle 20.3 (Self-Esteem):
Man strives for self-esteem.

The most basic goals of man's behavior are integrated with his personal
self-esteem. He centrally behaves to maintain, enhance, and increase his view and
opinion of himself. And this superordinate goal organizes, screens, and weights
his needs and associated interests.

Principle 20.4 (Expectations):
Expectations guide behavior.

Man is disposed to behave in a certain way by virtue of a situation he
perceives within his psychological field of motivations (needs and interests),
temperaments, moods and states. How in fact he does behave depends on his
expectations of the potential outcome of this disposition.

Principle 20.5 (Responsibility):
Man is responsible for his behavior.

On the basis of his morality, and for practical ends we must assume that man
has free will. That he has moral choice. Whether in fact he does we can never
know, but we can treat free will as a necessary hypothesis of reason. And such a
conditional acceptance of free will also assumes that man is responsible for his
behavior.

Master Principle 20.6 (Individuality):
Man is an individual.

Each man is one of a kind. His subjectivity is unique; his intentions are specific to his psychological field; his self-esteem fundamentally orients his actions; his expectations guide his behavior; he has free will. In short, he is an individual who alone can best assess his interests, and who cannot be unjust to himself.

20.2. INTERPERSONAL PRINCIPLES

Principle 20.7 (Communication):
Man communicates as a field of expression.

Man conveys his feelings, emotions, desires, and intentions to others through a variety of languages, such as his speech, tone, gesture, dress, stance, actions. All these languages contribute to a field of expression—a totality—which others learn to read through trial and error. Thus, verbal or written language is only one aspect of this field; behavior is only another aspect. In communication the totality of languages must be considered as each understands them within his own psychological field.

Principle 20.8 (Causal):
Man produces effects.

As an individual man is not passive, but an active agent in nature. He is a cause. He exercises power which comes in many forms. Of these identive, assertive, physical and force are the nonsocial powers. The social powers are coercive, bargaining, authoritative, intellectual, altruistic, and manipulative. Exercising these powers—producing effects—is an equation: power = interests x capabilities x will.

Principle 20.9 (Conflict):
Conflict is a balancing of powers.

Through conflict man learns to read and mutually adjust to each other's subjective fields of expression, and to mutually balance their individual powers. And through this balance man produces social effects. A balance of powers is basically a balance of mutual interests, capabilities, and wills; and achieving this is a process of mutual adjustment, implicit negotiation, and trial and error. A process of conflict.

Principle 20.10 (Cooperation): Cooperation
depends on expectations aligned with power.

Through conflict man balances with others his individuality and develops mutually reliable expectations, a structure of expectations, of correct predictions—based on a balance of powers. At the core of these expectations is a status quo which defines mutual rights, obligations, and duties; who gets what, when, and how. Overall, these mutual expectations define the social division of labor, enable and facilitate cooperation, and delineate islands of harmony and social peace. Cooperation and conflict are therefore complementary.

Principle 20.11 (Gap): A gap between
expectations and power causes conflict.

Change is the constant of life. And when the interests, capabilities, and wills defining a balance of powers significantly change, a gap between their mutual balance and the associated structure of expectations can form. This gap will create a strain toward realigning expectations (benefits, agreements, rights, obligations, and the like) with the new balance of powers. The situation is then ripe for some event to trigger a disruption of expectations and conflict—balancing—through which expectations are adjusted to the changed reality of power.

Principle 20.12 (Helix): Conflict becomes
less intense, peace more lasting.

Each new readjustment of expectations through conflict does not begin with an empty mind. Previous conflicts and expectations form a base of experience upon which a new structure of expectations is determined. As this background of mutual adjustments and expectations is built up and filled in conflicts become less intense. Adjustments are easier; expectations last longer because they fit better to the interests, capabilities, and wills of the parties. This assumes that there are no radical changes in the conditions of a relationship which would trigger a whole new sequence of adjustments.

Master Principle 20.13 (Interpersonal):
Through conflict man negotiates an
interpersonal contract.

A structure of expectations is an implicit or explicit contract worked out through a balancing of powers. Conflict behavior in a broad sense is the manifestation of this balancing and a means for negotiating the contract between individuals. This contract establishes peace and cooperation between the different individuals.

20.3. SOCIAL PRINCIPLES

Principle 20.14 (Universality): Man's
interpersonal principles apply to all societies.

Society is a division of labor formed out of the diverse structures of expectations of its members. These expectations merge into general structures and core status quos which are the backbone of a society, such as the basic institutions, customs, and common and public law of a state-society. As individual relations, these general structures are based on balances of powers. If expectations in society get far out of line with the underlying balance between individuals, groups, and classes, a trigger event may disrupt expectations, thus creating a societywide conflict and, perhaps, a violent readjustment of rights, benefits, and duties to the new reality of social powers.

Principle 20.15 (Trisocial):
Societies are generally trisocial.

Societies are usually glued together by some combination of three powers: bargaining, authoritative, coercive. Each power can be identified with its own type of society: exchange, authoritative, coercive. Each of these societies has its own type of political system: libertarian, authoritarian, totalitarian. Each society manifests a particular dimension of conflict: pluralistic (spontaneous), communal/traditional, elite repressions/purges. And each society has its own structure of peace: an exchange structure, an authoritative structure, a coercive structure. Thus, generally, three powers, three societies, three political systems, three dimensions of conflict, three structures of peace.

Principle 20.16 (Violence): A gap between
the status quo and power causes violence.

A social status quo concerns the most fundamental values and goals. It defines rights (such as property), benefits, duties. A gap between the status quo and the supporting balance of powers can lead to conflict over vital, rock bottom interests which may be resolved only by the ultimate test of violence. The most significant social violence of this kind is between classes, where a class is an authoritative division of power in a group between those who command and those who obey.

Principle 20.17 (Polarity): The more
government, the more violence.

When government is small, decentralized, and one of many centers of authority and coercion in society (as for the United Nations in the international society), diverse relationships, groups, classes, and structures of expectations segment and cross-pressure interests and wills. Conflict and violence are thus restrained, localized, and drained off. However, the more government is the center of authority and coercion, the more individuals and classes are polarized along an axis of political power, then the more disputes will involve the fundamental class division of society. Local conflicts can and do then escalate to intense violence along this societalwide, class front.

Master Principle 20.18 (Power):
Power shapes peace.

Power structures society. It molds politics. It forges conflict. Thereby, power shapes the social contract which is peace.

20.4. INTERNATIONAL PRINCIPLES

Principle 20.19 (Field):
Free actors comprise a social field.

The free and spontaneous interactions among actors, whether individuals, groups, or societies, form a social field. Balances and associated structures of expectations among actors are generally determined without outside coercion or force. These balances depend largely on the interests, capabilities, and will of the actors involved. By virtue of their sovereignty and independence, modern states are such free actors and international relations thus comprise a social field. These relations take place in a medium of meanings, values, and norms, which are defined by the sociocultural components of international actors, including their wealth, power, and politics. And this medium is the seat of forces potentially affecting international behavior. The field locally or as a whole is in a state of equilibrium (balance of powers, structure of expectations, peace, cooperation) or disequilibrium (Conflict Behavior). Conflict is a field process by which equilibrium is reestablished, once expectations (equilibrium) get out of line with the supporting balance of powers. As a field, international relations evolves out of the spontaneous interaction of its members and their diverse expectations.

Principle 20.20. (Exchange):
Free relations form an exchange society.

The free and voluntary relations between actors which are largely unregulated by government and in which bargaining power dominates form an exchange society, a particular type of social field akin to the free market. Such is international relations. It is a society in which bargaining and promises play the dominant role in establishing expectations. It has a libertarian government (the United Nations system) and pluralistic conflict. Its structure of peace is neither coercively imposed on the whole system nor authoritatively accepted by all members. It is generally an exchange structure of peace.

Principle 20.21 (Freedom): Violence does
not occur between free societies.

Quite simply, violence should almost never occur between exchange societies due to cross-pressures, the diversity of internal groups and interests, and the limited and responsive nature of libertarian government (Polarity Principle). In others words, open, pluralistic democracies with limited government form islands of nonviolent relations.

Principle 20.22 (War): A gap between the
international status quo and power causes war.

As is true generally in society where a breakdown in a social status quo can
lead to extreme violence (Violence Principle), a breakdown of the status quo in
international relations can lead to war. War is then the means for negotiating a
new status quo more aligned with the changed balance of powers.

Master Principle 20.23 (Peace): Through conflict
states negotiate a social contract.

Through conflict, violence, and war, international actors mutually adjust their
expectations to their changing interests, capabilities, and wills. The result is a
balance of powers and a correlated structure of expectations—that is, a social
contract. This contract then establishes a region of mutually reliable expectations, a region of peace and cooperation.

NOTE

1. For my view on metaphysical truths, see Volume 1, 1975: section 1.2.

APPENDIX I
UNPUBLISHED PROJECTS

Over the years 1965 to 1977, my assistants and I completed a number of relevant research projects of which results are unpublished in any form, including research reports. These projects have been consolidated in the following list under general headings for easy reference. A few introductory definitions should be helpful.

Project No: this identifies the relevant computer output and files, which have been clearly labeled with the Project No. Note that this number does not imply project sequence, e.g., Project No. 30 was not necessarily done after Project 10.

Models I and II: these are two alternative models for assessing the dependence of dyadic international behavior on attributes. Model I assumes that the attributes influence different actors similarly; Model II assumes that the influence of attributes varies by actor (Rummel, 1977: sections 4.3, 4.4).

Dyads: a pair of states.

Directed dyad: the behavior of one state toward a specific other, e.g., exports of an actor toward object state.

Symmetrical dyad: the mutual behavior of two states toward each other, e.g., the total trade of two states with each other, or the total threats they make toward each other.

Assistant: the person working under my general or specific supervision in completing a project.

Data Sources: unless otherwise specified, sources are diverse as listed in Rummel (1972: chapter 5; 1978: appendices).

References to these projects are made in terms of this appendix, general listing, and specific list number. Thus, for example, (appendix I: 2.3) refers to this appendix, general listing 2 titled "Dimensions of International Behavior," and the third listed project titled "Dyadic Foreign Conflict and Cooperation Dimensions." The specific list number and the project number (Project No. 5 in this case) will generally differ because projects have been reordered here to place similar analyses under the same general heading.

I.1. DIMENSIONS OF FOREIGN CONFLICT BEHAVIOR

1.1. "Dyadic Foreign Conflict Dimensions." *Samples:* all directed dyads with reported conflict behavior = 289. *Data Year:* 1960. *Data Sources:* New York *Times Index* using Rummel (1966) code sheet. *Variables:* 21 kinds of foreign conflict behavior. *Analysis:* (A) a component analysis of the 21 variables and orthogonal rotation of all factors with eigenvalues greater than 1.00; (B) a reanalysis of a reduced set of 15 variables. *Results:* dimensions delineated in both the 21 and 15 variable analyses are (1) negative communications and negative sanctions, (2) military violence, (3) warning and defensive acts, and (4) boycotts and embargoes and aid to object's enemy. *Assistant:* George Omen. *Project No. 2.*

1.2. "Dyadic Foreign Conflict Dimensions" *Samples and Data Years:* all directed dyads with reported foreign conflict behavior for 1950 (286 dyads, 19 variables), 1955 (341 dyads, 16 variables), 1960 (290 dyads, 21 variables), 1963 (276 dyads, 24 variables), 1965 (305 dyads, 24 variables). *Data Sources:* daily The New York *Times,* New York *Times Index,* using Rummel (1966) code sheet. *Variables:* as indicated (the variation in the number of variables was due to some being omitted because of an insufficient number of events). *Analysis:* (A) a separate component analysis and orthogonal rotation of factors with eigenvalues over 1.00 for each year; (B) a super-P component analysis of all years together— same rotation. *Results:* dimensions delineated for all years were (1) negative communications, (2) military violence; in addition, consistenly appearing for a number of years were (3) incidence of violence, (4) negative sanctions, (5) warning and defensive acts, (6) antiforeign demonstrations, and (7) aid to rebels. *Assistant:* Sang-Woo Rhee. *Project No. 4.*

1.3. "Dyadic Foreign Conflict Dimensions." *Samples and Data Years:* the samples for the years indicated in 1.2 (Project No. 4) were augmented by additional collection and corrected where errors were found and, in addition, an hypothetical peace dyad without any conflict was added to the sample for each year to give in total: 1950 (285 dyads, 16 variables), 1955 (336 dyads, 15 variables), 1960 (286 dyads, 15 variables), 1963 (275 dyads, 15 variables), 1965 (366 dyads, 16 variables). *Data Sources:* same as in 1.2 (Project No. 4), above, augmented by *Keesings Contemporary Archives, Facts on File,* and other sources as necessary. *Variables:* as indicated above. *Analysis:* (A) a separate component analysis and orthogonal rotation of seven factors (the seventh had an eigenvalue around 1.00) for each year; (B) a super-P image analysis, with rotation same as above (results published in Omen, 1975). *Results:* dimensions delineated in all analyses are: (1) negative communications, (2) military violence; in addition, consistently appearing in a number of analyses were (3) antiforeign demonstrations, (4) aid to rebels, (5) expelling or recalling diplomats, (6) boycotts and embargoes, and (7) war. *Assistant:* George Omen. *Project No. 3.*

1.4. "Dimensions of Dyadic Foreign Conflict" *Sample:* 47 symmetrical dyads with conflict. *Data Years:* 1955-1957. *Data Sources:* diverse (see Rummel, 1963). *Variables:* 12 foreign conflict variables measured as presence or absence. *Analysis:* component analysis and orthogonal rotation of eigenvalues over 1.00. *Results:* dimensions of mobilization and military violence, negative communications, troop movements and antiforeign demonstrations, and negative sanctions accounted for about 73% of the variance. *Assistant:* Mary Hirschoff. *Project No. 27.*

1.5. "Dyadic Foreign Conflict Dimensions." *Sample:* all directed dyads with foreign conflict behavior. *Data Year:* 1955. *Data Sources:* Same as 1.2 (Project No. 4), above. *Variables:* 16 (same as 1.2, above, for 1955). *Analysis:* (A) common factor analysis, image factor analysis, canonical factor analysis, and alpha factor analysis—all with the same rotations and eigenvalue-one criteria for the number of factors; (B) a comparison of the above results to each other and to component analysis. *Results:* (A) common and image analyses delineate military violence and negative communications as independent factors; (B) alpha, canonical, and component analysis essentially agree on military violence, negative communications, negative sanctions, antiforeign demonstrations, and diplomatic protests as independent dimensions. *Assistant:* unrecorded.

1.6. "Assessing Political Risk." *Sample:* All states with significant political conflict (= 82). *Data Periods:* June 1, 1976-August 31, 1977. *Data Sources:* diverse public media. *Variables:* 21 foreign conflict scales. *Analysis:* super-P (time series) component analysis with orthogonal rotation of factors with eigenvalues over 1.0. *Results:* (1) dimensions of negative communications and action, foreign intervention, warning and defensive acts, antiforeign demonstrations, clashes and discrete military action, and killed; (2) the first unrotated dimension accounts for 21 percent of the variance and is general to all the variables. *Assistant:* Gary Murfin. *Project No. 15.*

I.2. DIMENSIONS OF INTERNATIONAL BEHAVIOR

2.1. "Dimensions of International Behavior." *Sample:* 348 directed dyads, 182 of which were nonrandomly selected. *Data Year:* 1955. *Variables:* 40 diverse types of international behavior. *Analysis:* (A) component analysis of the raw data and orthogonal and oblique rotation of factors with eigenvalues over 1.00; (B) higher order image analysis. *Results:* (A) 10 dimensions delineated, which are general transactions, alliances (UN voting and bloc membership), relative exports, embassy and legations, mail and emigration, students, relative mail, relative international organizations, negative sanctions, and military violence and negative communications: (B) conflict and cooperative behaviors are independent; (C) all higher order dimensions are weak, indicating a near complete independence among all behavioral dimensions. *Assistant:* M. Hart. *Project No. 22.*

2.2. "Dimensions of International Behavior." *Sample:* 182 selected, directed dyads. *Data Years:* 1950, 1955, 1960, 1963, 1965. *Variables:* 50 diverse types of international behavior. *Analysis:* separate image and component analyses of the raw data for each year and orthogonal rotation of eigenvalues around 1.00. *Results:* (A) consistent dimensions for each year involve exports/GNP, students, emigrants, UN voting, relative international organizations, embassy or legation, aid, tourists, military violence, negative actions and negative communications; (B) cooperative and conflict behaviors are consistently independent. *Assistant:* Yong-Ok Park. *Project No. 23.*

2.3. "Dyadic Foreign Conflict and Cooperation Dimensions." *Sample:* 182 selected, directed dyads. *Data Year:* 1967. *Data Source:* daily The New York *Times,* New York *Times Index. Variables:* (A) 23 foreign conflict variables aggregated from Rummel (1966) code sheets; (B) 22 WEIS (appendix II, Table II.2) event variables, which involved 10 cooperation and 12 conflict ones. *Analysis:* (A) separate component analyses and orthogonal rotation of different numbers of factors of 23 foreign conflict variables, 22 WEIS event data variables, 12 WEIS conflict variables, and 10 cooperation variables; (B) canonical analysis of the similarity in factors from the 23 foreign conflict variables on the one hand and the WEIS factors on the other; (C) canonical analysis of the similarity of events collected for the 23 variables on the one hand and for the WEIS variables on the other (Phillips, 1972). *Results:* (A) there is about a 60% overlap between conflict events collected for 23 Rummel variables and 12 WEIS conflict variables and similar dimensions can be delineated in each; (B) there are two dimensions of cooperation (positive communication, bargaining); (C) there is little relationship between the cooperation and conflict events; (D) the dimensions of the 23 Rummel foreign conflict variables are negative communications and sanctions, military action plus warning and defensive actions, aid to rebels, antiforeign demonstrations, and expel or recall diplomats plus sever diplomatic relations; (E) the dimensions of the 12 WEIS foreign conflict variables are negative communications and sanctions, military action, threat communication. *Assistants:* Warren Phillips and Mike Zavatsky. *Project No. 5.*

2.4. "International Behavioral Groups." *Sample:* 182 selected, directed dyads. *Data Year:* 1955. *Data Sources:* the component analysis of international behavior results published in Rummel (1969a). *Variables:* standardized distances between dyads on (A) unweighted 10 dimensions of international behavior for raw data, and (B) unweighted 11 dimensions of data transformed towards normality. *Analysis:* separate direct component analyses of distance matrices on raw data and on transformed data dimensions, and orthogonal rotation in each case. *Results:* (A) for each analysis, seven distinct clusters of dyads were defined; (B) in each analysis, one cluster's profile involved high negative communications, great UN voting distance, low tourists, low relative emigrants, low relative students, low exports/GNP, but medium to high relative international organization comemberships, and low to medium relative (to total for actor) embassies and legations. *Assistant:* Betty Bockelman. *Project No. 24.*

2.5. "Peace Systems of International Behavior." *Samples:* (A) 139 selected, directed dyads with no conflict behavior; (B) 151 randomly determined, directed dyads with no conflict behavior. *Data Year:* 1955. *Variables:* 36 diverse types of nonconflict, international behaviors. *Analysis:* two separate component analyses of each sample (and orthogonal and oblique rotations) of (A) raw data, (B) data transformed towards normality. *Results:* most consistently delineated across the four analyses were the dimensions of treaties, bloc alliances, UN voting, relative exports, students, diplomatic (embassies and legations), emigrants, and international organizations. *Assistant:* M. Hart. *Project No. 17.*

2.6. "Conflict Systems of International Behavior." *Sample:* 43 selected, directed dyads with conflict behavior. *Data Year:* 1955. *Analysis:* two separate component analyses (and orthogonal and oblique rotation) of (A) raw data, (B) data transformed toward normality. *Results:* (A) conflict behavior is an independent dimension; (B) international organizations, embassies and legations, alliances (UN voting and bloc membership), are independent dimensions; (C) tourists, mail, and relative exports are independent dimensions. *Assistant:* M. Hart. *Project No. 18.*

2.7. "Peace versus Conflict Systems of International Behavior." *Sample:* 182 selected, directed dyads. *Data Year:* 1955. *Data Source:* results of 2.5 and 2.6 (Projects 17 and 18) listed above. *Variables:* component dimensions for (A) 36 raw data variables, (B) 36 transformed data variables. *Analysis:* (A) raw data, peace system dimensions were transformed into the space of the conflict system (using the factor comparison method of Ahmnaavara (Rummel, 1970: section 20.2.3) in order to compare and contrast the two systems; (B) same analysis for transformed data dimensions. *Results:* (A) international organizations, embassies and legations, treaties, alliances, and UN voting distances form patterns that change little between the two systems; (B) in the conflict system, exports more directly link into treaties, mail, and tourists, relative mail and emigration form a dimension not existing in the peace system, and tourists and translations also form a dimension not found in the peace system; (C) the behaviors most changing their patterns from peace to conflict system are (in decreasing order of change) foreign mail/domestic mail, relative translations, emigration, relative tourists, and exports. *Assistant:* M. Hart. *Project No. 19.*

I.3. DIMENSIONS OF STATES

3.1. "Consistent Dimensions of States." *Samples and Data Years:* 72 states (1950), 82 states (1955), 87 states (1960), 107 states (1963), 113 states (1965). *Analysis:* for each year, component analysis and separate orthogonal rotation of dimensions with (A) eigenvalues over 1.00, and accounting for about 90% of total variance. *Results:* (A) consistent dimensions across all five years are wealth, (liberal democracy versus) totalitarianism, power bases, diversity, authoritarism, and density, (B) the largest dimensions are wealth, power, and politics (totalitarianism) accounting for about 29 percent of total variance. *Assistant:* Sang-Woo Rhee. *Project No. 37.*

3.2. "Principal Space-Time Components of States." *Sample and Data Year:* same as 3.1 (project no. 37), above. *Variables:* 90 diverse attributes of states listed in Rummel (NAB) plus a time variable. *Analysis:* systematic comparison of the unrotated results of (A) component analyses of raw and transformed data (rotated results reported in Rummel, 1978), (B) image analysis of transformed data (rotated results reported in Rummel, 1978). *Results:* wealth, power, and politics are consistently the largest space-time (unrotated) principal axes (components). *Assistant:* none. *Project No. 42.*

3.3. "Stability of Dimensions of States: Cross-time." *Sample:* 82 states. *Data Years:* 1955, 1963. *Variables:* 79 variables common to both the 1955 dimensions published in Rummel (1972) and the 1963 component analysis of 3.1 (Project No. 37), above. *Analysis:* (A) component analysis or raw data for each year and orthogonal rotation; (B) factor comparison using Ahmnaavaara's method (Rummel, 1970: section 20.2.3); (C) canonical analysis to determine predictability of 1963 dimensions from 1955. *Results:* the same largest dimensions of wealth, power bases, and totalitarianism exist for both years, but over all the dimensions there was a considerable shift in correlation and some dimensions were unique to each year. The 1955 dimensions (loadings) predict about 47% of the variation in the 1963 dimensions. *Assistants:* Paul McCarthy and Dennis Hall. *Project No. 38.*

3.4. "Stability of Dimensions of States: Cross-models." *Sample:* 113 nations. *Data Year:* 1965. *Variables:* 90 diverse attributes used in 3.1 (Project No. 37), above. *Analysis:* (A) image analysis and orthogonal rotation; (B) comparison to results of component analysis, described in 3.1 (Project No. 37) above. *Results:* major and important minor dimensions are similar for each model. *Assistant:* Sang-Woo Rhee. Project No. 39.

3.5. "Stability of Dimensions of States: Cross-missing Data Estimation Techniques." *Sample, Data Year and Variables:* same as in 3.1 (Project No. 37), above. *Analysis:* parallel component analysis for each year and super-P component analysis on data with missing data (A) estimated through least squares; B) estimated through a randomized procedure ("pseudoestimates")–see Wall and Rummel (1969). *Results:* essentially similar across missing data estimation techniques. *Assistants:* Sang-Woo Rhee and George Omen. *Project No. 40.*

3.6. "Higher Order Space-time Dimensions." *Sample, Data Year, and Variables:* same as 3.1 (Project No. 37), above. *Analysis:* a higher order component analysis (and orthogonal rotation) of the super-P, image analysis of transformed data published in Rummel (1978: chapter 5). *Results:* Data too complex for a good higher order (oblique results do not achieve simple structure), implying that the unrotated results should be emphasized. *Assistant:* George Omen. *Project No. 41.*

3.7. "Taxonomy of States." *Sample and Data Year:* same as 3.1 (Project No. 37), above. *Variables:* 87 standardized, diverse attributes (listed in Rummel, 1978). *Analysis:* (A) separate Q-component analysis and orthogonal rotation of (1) full data matrix and (2) transformed data matrix; (B) Q-component analysis and orthogonal rotation of 10 trans-formed indicators of the dimensions of states listed in Rummel (1978). *Results:* 3 major empirical types of state-societies exist: coercive, authoritative, and exchange (see Rummel, *Volume 2,* 1976: chapter 34). *Assistant:* Yong-Ok Park. *Project No. 46.*

I.4. TESTING DIFFERENT PREDICTION MODELS OF INTERNATIONAL CONFLICT

4.1. "Model I: Distance Vectors versus Squared Magnitudes." *Sample:* 182 selected, directed dyads. *Data Year:* 1955. *Variables:* (A) factor scores on four conflict dimensions of dyadic international behavior from Rummel (APSR); (B) basic indicators of 13 dimensions of 236 state-attributes from Rummel (1972). *Analysis:* (A) regression analysis of the dependence of conflict dimensions on distances (j-i differences) and, separately squared distances; (B) canonical analysis of the dependence of conflict dimensions on distances (j-i differences) and, separately, squared distances. *Results:* (A) differences account for almost no variation in dyadic conflict behavior (canonical traced squared = .03); (B) squared differences explain about 28% of the variation in conflict behavior; (C) disparity in power, similarity in development, and relative freedom most significantly explain dyadic conflict. *Assistant:* Dave McCormick. *Project No. 7.*

4.2. "Model II and the Conflict Helix: Distance Magnitudes and Time." *Samples:* 14 selected samples of directed dyads, each with the same actor and 13 different object states. *Data Year:* 1955. *Variables:* (A) factor scores on the five dimensions of 16 foreign conflict variables for 340 dyads reported in Rummel (1967a, 1968); (B) eight theoretical, absolute distances variables, including time since last formation of the structure of expectations for a dyad. *Analysis:* regression analysis. *Results:* (A) average of 35% of the variation in dyadic conflict explained by the eight variables; (B) parity rather than disparity in power best explains conflict and is the most significant of all independent variables—next in importance is political dissimilarity. *Assistant:* Tong-Whan Park. *Project No. 8.*

4.3. "Model I and the Conflict Helix: Distance Magnitudes, Power, Time, and Time Interaction." *Sample:* 182 selected, directed dyads. *Data Year:* 1955. *Variables:* (A) factor scores on the dimensions of 16 foreign conflict variables for 340 dyads reported in Rummel (1967a, 1968); (B) 19 theoretical variables, including power parity and time since the formation of the last structure of expectations for a dyad, absolute distances, distances x time, and joint power. *Analysis:* (A) common factor analysis of the 22 conflict and theoretical variables and orthogonal rotation of factors with eigenvalues over 1.00; (B) regression analysis with each conflict dimension as a dependent variable and the theoretical variables as independent. *Results:* (A) conflict forms a dimension clearly independent of the theoretical variables; (B) about one-fourth of the conflict is explained by the independent variables. *Assistant:* Tong-Whan Park. *Project No. 9.*

4.4. "Models I and II and the Conflict Helix: Distance Magnitudes and Time." *Sample:* 182 selected, directed dyads. *Data Year:* 1955. *Variables:* same as 4.2 (Project No. 8), above. *Analysis:* canonical analysis of (A) all dyads; (B) all dyads with Israel as actor; (C) all dyads not involving Israel as actor. *Results:* (A) dyadic conflict has a very low fit to distance magnitudes and parity (trace correlation squared across actors = .02); (B) best fitting canonical variates for all actors have a correlation of .48, with military violence and negative communication most dependent on language and political dissimilarities; (C) Israel's conflict makes no difference in results overall, but analysis of the Israel dyads alone show Israel's conflict well predicted (trace correlation = .67), especially by language dissimilarity and time since the last structure of expectations was formed with her Arab antagonists. *Assistant:* Tong-Whan Park. *Project No. 10.*

4.5. "Model I and II and the Conflict Helix: Distance Magnitudes and Time." *Sample, Data Year, and Variables:* same as 4.4 (Project No. 10), above. *Analysis:* (A) regression analysis with each conflict factor as dependent variable and distance magnitudes and time as independent; (B) a profile analysis of largest and smallest regression residuals; (C) a rerun of the regression for all dyads having Israel as actor; (D) a rerun of the regression for all dyads not having Israel as actor. *Results:* (A) about 12% of the variance in conflict is accounted for by distance magnitudes and time; (B) power parity and political distance are the most consistent predictors of conflict; (C) power parity, Time, and economic distance account for the best predictions (smallest residuals) of military violence: (E) power disparity, little time since the formation of the structure of expectations, and political distance best account for the poor predictions (largest residuals) of military violence. *Assistant:* Tong-Whan Park. *Project No. 11.*

4.6. "Model I and the Conflict Helix: Curvilinear Test of Distance magnitudes and Time. *Sample, Data Year:* same as 4.4 (Project No. 10), above. *Variables:* (A) same as 4.4 (Project No. 10) above; (B) all independent variables transformed to natural logrithms. *Analysis:* (A) regression analysis, with each conflict factor as dependent and log distance magnitudes and log time as independent; (B) canonical analysis of conflict factors against log distances magnitudes and log time. *Results:* (A) there is little curvilinear relationship of conflict to distance magnitudes across actors; (B) the best relationship is that involving political distance and racial-language similarity which account for about 23% of the variation in military violence and negative communications; (C) power parity significantly predicts separately to military violence and negative communication. *Assistant:* Tong-Whan Park. *Project No. 12.*

4.7. "Models I and II and the Conflict Helix: Interaction of Distance Magnitudes and Time." *Sample, Data Year:* same as 4.4 (Project No. 10), above. *Variables:* (A) dependent same as 4.2 (Project No. 8), above; (B) eight theoretical absolute distance variables multiplied by the time since the last structure of expectations was formed, in addition to time by itself. *Results:* (A) overall about 8% of conflict behavior is explained; (B) parity x time is a significant predictor of conflict behavior, especially military action. *Assistant:* Tong-Whan Park. *Project No. 13.*

4.8. "Model I and the Conflict Helix: Distance Magnitudes and Time." *Sample:* 166 randomly selected, directed dyads. *Data Year:* 1955. *Variables:* same as 4.2 (Project No. 8), above. *Analysis:* regression of the different conflict factors onto distance magnitudes and the time since the last formation of the structure of expectations for a dyad. *Results:* (A) little variance in conflict predicted (average $R^2 = .05$); (B) power parity is the most significant predictor (3 of the 4 significant regression coefficients). *Assistant:* Tong-Whan Park. *Project No. 14.*

4.9. "Model I: Theoretical Variables." *Sample:* 91 selected, symmetrical dyads. *Data Years:* 1955-57. *Variables:* (A) dependent are the factor scores on four rotated and first unrotated dimensions of dyadic foreign conflict delineated in 1.4 (Project No. 1.4), above; (B) independent are UN voting similarity, economic similarity, power parity, overall similarity, and joint power. *Analysis:* regression analysis. *Results:* (A) similarity in UN voting and joint power are the best predictors (especially for negative communication); (B) power parity is a poor predictor; (C) overall, about one-third of the variation in negative communications, and warning and defensive acts is dependent on the five predictors. *Assistant:* Betty Bockelman. *Project No. 28.*

4.10. "Models of the Conflict Helix." *Sample, Data Year:* same as 4.9 (Project No. 28), above. *Variables:* (A) dependent same as 4.9 (Project No. 28), above; (B) independent are models of the (logged and unlogged) latent conditions underlying the conflict situation and the conditions theoretically correlated with conflict behavior. *Analysis:* bivariate regression analysis. *Results:* log of conflict behavior most related to logged prediction model of conflict behavior (accounts for 31% of the variance), and the model of the conflict situation moderately predicts (27% of the variance) the log of conflict behavior. *Assistant:* Betty Bockelman. *Project No. 29.*

I.5. TESTING DIFFERENT PREDICTION MODELS OF INTERNATIONAL BEHAVIOR

5.1. "Model I: Squared Distance Magnitudes." *Sample:* 182 selected, directed dyads. *Data Year:* 1955. *Variables:* (A) factor scores on 12 orthogonally rotated factors of a component analysis of dyadic behavior of 182 dyads on 44 variables (see Rummel, 1969a); (B) distance magnitudes on 14 indicators of the factors of a component analysis of 236 variables for 82 nations (see Rummel, 1972) plus two geographic distance variables. *Analysis:* (A) curvilinear regression analysis of each dimension of dyadic behavior onto the squared 14 distance variables, plus geographic distance; (B) curvilinear regression analysis of each dimension of dyadic behavior onto the log of wealth and power distances, squared distances for the remaining dimensions, plus geographic distance. *Results:* (A) about 24% of the variation in international behavior (20% in conflict behavior) is explained by distance magnitudes; (B) power parity, political similarity, and geographic distance significantly predict to negative sanctions; (C) power disparity and political dissimilarity significantly predict to military violence plus negative communications; (D) political disparity, rich-poor gap, and geographic distance significantly predict to UN voting distance; (E) wealth, power, and political distances are most significant for predicting international behavior. *Assistant:* none. *Project No. 16.*

5.2. "Model I: Attributes, Distance Magnitudes, and Joint Power." *Sample:* (A) 182 selected, directed dyads; (B) 166 randomly determined, directed dyads; *Data Year:* 1955. *Variables:* (A) 21 to 30 types of international behavior as dependent variables; (B) 23 independent variables, including actor's attributes, absolute distances, and joint power.

Analysis: canonical analysis. *Results:* (A) attributes and distances account for about 26% of the variation in behavior; (B) an actor's wealth and power, plus the joint power and overall dissimilarity between actor and object, predict to about 90% of the variation in a pattern of mail, transactions, tourists, migrants, and negative communications. *Assistant:* Paul McCarthy. *Project No. 30.*

5.3. "Model I: Distance Vectors and Squared Magnitudes." *Sample:* 182 selected, directed dyads. *Data Year:* 1955. *Variables:* (A) dependent variables are factor scores on 12 dimensions of international behavior delineated through component analysis; (B) independent variables are indicators of 15 dimensions of cross-national attributes delineated through component analysis (see Rummel, 1977, chapter 4 for a discussion of these independent and dependent variables); (C) geographic distance and power parity. *Analysis:* (A) separate regression analyses onto distance vectors and squared distance magnitudes; (B) separate canonical analyses involving distance vectors and squared distances, plus geographic distance and power parity. *Results:* (A) differences (distance vectors) in general account for little (13%) of international behavior across dyadic actors, the best being difference in wealth and power (see Rummel, 1977: 90-91, and Gleditsch, 1970, for some of these results); (B) squared distances account for about 30% of the variation in behavior, the best being squared distances in power and political freedom. *Assistant:* Dave McCormick. *Project No. 25.*

5.4. "Model I: Theoretical Predictors." *Sample:* 42-105 randomly selected, directed dyads with no missing data. *Data Year:* 1955. *Variables:* (A) dependent are factors scores or indicator variables of dimensions of foreign conflict and international behavior from Rummel (1969a), merged into scales of total cooperation, total behavior (cooperation plus conflict), and net cooperation (cooperation minus conflict); (B) independent are distance magnitudes plus geographic distance and joint power. *Analysis:* regression analysis. Results: (A) cooperation (or cooperation plus or minus conflict) highly dependent (86% of the variance); (B) best predictors are joint power (71%), power parity (4%), political similarity (3%), and racial similarity (3%). *Assistant:* Betty Bockelman. *Project No. 26.*

5.5. "Model I: Testing Theoretical Linkages Between International Behavior and Attributes." *Samples:* (A) 182 selected, directed dyads; (B) 166 randomly determined, directed dyads. *Data Year:* 1955. *Variables:* separate raw and transformed 80 variable data sets of (A) 44 types of diverse international behaviors; (B) 36 characteristics of a dyad, involving (1) attributes of the actor, (2) absolute distances on the indicators of the dimensions of 236 national attributes (see Rummel, 1972), (3) rank distance, (4) distance on Russett's socioeconomic dimensions (1967), (5) joint power of actor and object, (6) measures of geographic distance, (7) racial, language, and religious similarities. *Analysis:* target rotation: factors linking 44 behavior and 36 attributes rotated to a best fit to theoretical linkages involving wealth, joint power, geographic distances, and cultural similarity. *Results:* Negative—actors are not similarly influenced by the indicated variables in the theoretical direction. *Assistants:* L. Levine and M. Hart. *Project No. 31.*

I.6. THE LINKAGE OF INTERNATIONAL BEHAVIOR
TO NATIONAL ATTRIBUTES AND DISTANCES

6.1. "Model I: Attributes and Absolute Distances." *Samples:* (A) selected sample of 182, directed dyads; (B) randomly determined sample of 166, directed dyads. *Data Year:* 1955. *Variables:* (A) for international behavior: factor scores of 12 dimensions of behavior for the selected sample (Rummel, 1969a), and 11 dimensions of behavior for the random sample; (B) for attributes and absolute distances: 26 variables measuring an actors attributes, absolute distances between actor and object, cultural similarity, and geographic distance. *Analysis:* (A) a component analysis of 26 measures of attributes and absolute distances separately for each sample; (B) a canonical analysis of the dependence of behavioral factor scores on the factor scores for the attribute and absolute distance dimensions, done separately for each sample. *Results:* (A) in general, national attributes and absolute differences across dyads explain about 18% of the variation in dyadic international behavior; (B) rank distance (absolute differences in power and wealth) and political distance are the best predictors of behavior across actors, accounting for about 50% of some components of behavior. *Assistant:* Paul McCarthy. *Project No. 1.*

6.2. "Model I: Components of National Attributes and Behavior." *Sample:* 348 directed dyads, 182 of which were nonrandomly selected. *Data Year, and Variables:* same as 5.5 (Project No. 31), above. *Analysis:* component analysis and orthogonal rotation of all dimensions with eigenvalues over 1.00. *Results:* no strong linkages appear: an actor's wealth and power have a small link to his volume of transactions; power distance to diplomatic importance; political similarity to UN voting agreement and alliances; contiguity to military violence. *Assistant:* M. Hart. *Project No. 21.*

6.3. "Model I: Common Factors of National Attributes and Behavior." *Sample, Data Year, Data Source, and Variables:* same as 5.5 (Project No. 31), above. *Analysis:* (A) two separate common factor analyses (orthogonal and oblique rotations) for each sample of (1) raw data, (2) data transformed towards normality; (B) a factor comparison of all four sets of common factors, using the method of Ahmnaavara (Rummel, 1970: section 20.2.3). *Results:* (partially described in Rummel, 1972: 407-410): (A) the only strong linkage appearing is of UN voting similarity and alliances to socioeconomic similarity: (B) consistent weak relationships across the four analyses involve (1) transactions linked to wealth, power, political similarity, and geographic closeness, (2) conflict linked to the actor's power, rank distance, total distance across all attributes, and joint power of actor and object, and (3) UN voting distance linked to Catholic culture distance, and political distance. *Assistants:* L. Levine and M. Hart. *Project No. 20.*

6.4. "Model I: Common Components of National Attributes and Behavior." *Samples, Data Year, and Variables:* same as 5.5 (Project No. 31), above. *Analysis:* component analysis of the raw data of each sample and orthogonal rotation of eigenvalues over 1.00. *Results:* (A) similar to those for 6.3 (Project No. 20), above; (B) unrotated components show (1) general transactions have significant dependence on power, wealth, and geographic distance; (2) independently, general conflict has a significant dependence on power, wealth, and political distance, (3) two secondary transaction components are dependent on geographic distances. These five components account for about 50% of the variation in the 70 dyadic behavioral and attribute variables. *Assistant:* L. Levine. *Project No. 32.*

6.5. "Model I: Most General (Higher Order) Factors of National Attributes and Behavior." *Sample, and Data Year:* same as 5.5 (Project No. 31), above. *Variables:* biquartimin factors and components from the common and component factor analyses of 6.2 and 6.3 (Projects No. 21 and 20), above. *Analysis:* second and third-order image factor analyses. *Results:* similar to those for unrotated components listed in 6.4 (Project No. 32), above. *Assistant:* L. Levine. *Project No. 33.*

6.6. "Peace Versus Conflict Behavioral System Linkages to Attributes and Distances." *Sample:* (A) 139 selected, directed dyads with no conflict behavior; (B) 43 selected directed dyads with conflict behavior. *Data Year:* 1955. *Variables:* same as 5.5 (Project No. 31), above. *Analysis:* (A) separate common factor analysis and orthogonal and oblique rotation of raw and transformed data for each sample; (B) peace system linkages compared to conflict linkages by (1) transforming peace results into conflict space (Ahmnaavara's factor comparison technique), and (2) separately transforming into the general space of the results listed in 6.3 (Project No. 20), above. *Results:* (A) the attributes most changing in their linkages to dyadic behavior between conflict and peace systems are racial, religious, and language similarity; (B) shift in patterns between peace and conflict systems along which conflict occurs involve transactions, political distance, and geographic distances. Power, wealth, overall dissimilarity, or joint power linkages do not distinguish peace and conflict systems. *Assistant:* L. Levine. *Project No. 34.*

6.7. "Models I and II: Dependence of Space-Time, International Behavior on Distance Magnitudes." *Sample:* 186 selected, directed dyads. *Data Years:* 1950, 1955, 1960, 1963, 1965. *Variables:* (A) absolute distances on the factor scores for 11 dimensions of national attribute space-time and dyadic factor scores on eight dimensions of behavioral space-time (from Rummel, 1978); (B) indicators for above dimensions used in place of factor scores for attributes and behavior. *Analysis:* (A) separate cannonical analyses of A and B sets of variables for all dyads for each year (Model I); (B) separate canonical analyses of A and B sets of variables across all years for each subsample of 13 dyads with the same actor (Model II). *Results:* (A) for all dyads (Model I), behavior is most dependent on absolute political distances, especially bloc alignment and UN voting agreement; (B) absolute economic and power distances (power parity) have little relationship to behavior; (C) for actor specific analyses, absolute political distance still most important determinant of behavior, especially of trade, aid, UN voting, bloc alignment, and international organization comemberships; (D) distance magnitudes predict behavior almost as well as differences (distance vectors) for individual actors (Model II), and are much better predictors over all dyads (Model I). *Assistant:* Yong-Ok Park. *Project No. 43.*

6.8. "Model II: U.S. Foreign Relations and Absolute Distances." *Sample:* 81 object nations of U.S. behavior. *Data Year:* 1955. *Variables:* (A) absolute distances between United States and object nations on 14 indicators of dimensions of national attributes from Rummel (1972); (B) factor scores from Rummel (1972a) of 81 dyads with United States as actor on six dimensions of U.S. dyadic behavior. *Analysis:* (A) canonical analysis of dependency of U.S. dyadic behavior on U.S.-object, absolute distances; (B) rerun of cannonical analysis with distances on indicators of wealth and power log transformed; (C) rerun of canonical analysis with all distances log transformed. *Results:* (A) overall, absolute distances accounted for 40% of U.S. behavior; (B) power parity and, secondarily, similarity in wealth are tightly linked to Western European cooperation or, secondarily, negative communications and military violence; (B) similarity in political system, dissimilarity in religion, and geographic closeness are linked to diplomatic cooperation. *Assistant:* Richard Van Atta. *Project No. 36.*

I.7. MISCELLANEOUS

7.1. "Correlates of Escalation." *Sample:* major opponents in 39 historical conflicts. *Data Years:* World War I to 1965. *Data Source:* Wright (1965). *Variables:* (A) one variable measuring four levels of escalation; (B) twenty variables involving four from Wright's escalation model, five descriptive of the conflicts, and 11 measuring absolute distances between antagonists. *Analysis:* (A) component and image analysis and orthogonal and oblique rotation of factors with eigenvalues greater than 1.00, (B) higher order factor analyses and orthogonal rotation–same factor cutoff. *Results:* (A) escalation is independent of absolute political and cultural distances across actors and the absolute differences in size; (B) escalation depends on the perception of the parties of their national interest that is involved and (to a lesser extent), their comparison of their relative vulnerability, power parity, and absolute difference in wealth; (C) escalation is more likely in recent years. *Assistant:* L. Levine. *Project No. 6.*

7.2 "Testing the Empirical Assumptions of Détente." *Sample:* (A) 24 distinct canonical analyses of the dependence of dyadic behavior on attribute differences (distance vectors), some published in Rummel (1977, 1978), involving as actors China, USSR, United States; (B) 86 distinct canonical equations involving 14 national actors. *Data Years:* 1950-1965. *Data Sources:* diverse (see Rummel, 1978). *Variables:* about 350 diverse, underlying behavioral and attribute variables. *Analysis:* a systematic comparison of the canonical linkages found empirically against those linkages assumed by détente (as formulated by Henry Kissinger) for both samples A and B. *Results:* (A) the assumption that power is related to conflict is correct, but not as power parity; rather, the greater the power of the object nation, the more conflict directed towards it; (B) the assumption that transactions are inversely related to conflict is falsified (these results underlie the assertions of Rummel, 1976a). *Assistant:* none. *Project No. 44.*

7.3. "Synthesizing Empirical, International Behavior, Space-Time linkages." *Sample:* 197 canonical equations for 14 selected nation-actors linking dyadic behavior and attribute differences (distance vectors). *Data Years:* 1950-1965. *Variables:* about 350 underlying behavioral and national attribute variables. *Analysis:* a systematic tabulation and cross-tabulation of all the linkages regarding (A) coincidence of linkages (scope), (B) strength of co-incidence (intensity). *Results:* (A) for differences in power, politics and wealth, the first has the greatest influence on dyadic behavior, the third the least; (B) for dyadic contractual, familistic, and conflict behavior, the first is most dependent on attribute differences; the first and third are less and equally dependent; (C) the strongest linkages are between power and political differences and contractual behavior; the weakest is between wealth and political differences and conflict behavior; (D) considering the linkages by type of actor, the strongest linkages are between power difference and contractual behavior for poor, weak, or authoritarian actors; (E) the weakest linkages are for political differences and conflict behavior for the poor, weak, or totalitarian actors; and wealth difference and familistic behavior for totalitarian actors. See appendix 9A for partial results. *Assistant:* Lei Rummel. *Project No. 45.*

7.4. "Test of the Conflict Helix for International Behavior." *Samples:* results of 2.1, 2.5, 2.6, 6.2, 6.3, 6.4, and 6.6 (Projects No. 22, 17, 18, 21, 20, 32, and 34, respectively), above. *Data Years:* 1955. *Variables:* see projects listed under samples, above. *Analysis:* a systematic comparison of unrotated dimensions for peace versus conflict systems to test (1) hypothesis that peace systems are more generally integrated by a dominant structure, while being much more pluralistic in behavior, (2) hypothesis that peace has a more general linkage to attributes while having overall more independent of attributes (the conflict system will have more diverse linkages and less unique behavior). *Results:* hypotheses confirmed. *Assistant:* none. *Project No. 47.*

7.5 "Libertarian Systems and War." *Samples:* 50 interstate wars. *Data Years:* 1816-1965. *Data Sources:* Singer and Small (1972). *Variables:* political system (libertarian, authoritarian, totalitarian), number of wars, number killed. *Analysis:* cross-tabulation. *Results:* There were no wars between libertarian (and ambiguously libertarian) systems, 14 wars between libertarian and authoritarian systems, and 36 between nonlibertarian systems. *Assistant:* none. Project No. 48.

APPENDIX II
EVENT DATA: BASES OF
MANIFEST CONFLICT ANALYSIS

II.1. EVENT DATA

Any assessment of the political significance and consequences of, say, the July, 1977, Egyptian-Libyan mini-border war requires information on

- what happened during the war;
- what events preceded the war;
- how preceding events and the war compare in nature, scope, and magnitude with those between other countries.

Any good journalist or analyst can uncover information on the first two. It is the comparison that becomes difficult. How does the war compare to others fought? To other border wars? To other conflicts in Africa or the Middle East? Have similar wars occurred recently? If so, have they been preceded by the same events? Was the sequence of events leading up to the July war atypical, a product of President Col. Muammar el-Qaddafi and President Sadat? Or, was progression of events similar to that preceding other wars, suggesting certain events foreshadow war, as particular economic events warn of recession? And so on.

It is the complexity of comparison that often defeats journalists and experts alike. For comparison requires mentally scanning similar events, similar periods, similar cases; and here the mind is overcome with detail, memory misleads, and hopes and wishes, biases and suppositions, have free play.

To ease comparison, the mind will always find patterns in events, somehow. These patterns will involve an explanation of why the events occur, and provide examples of similar events. They are part of one's political and social culture. Thus, some may see the July war as Sadat's complicity in a Western plot to overthrow Quaddafi, and compare it to Chile; some may see it as Sadat's reaction to Moscow's massive arming of Libya, support for Quaddafi, and encouragement of the Libyan ruler's subversive plots in Egypt and Sudan; some may see it as simply one more indication of Quaddafi's instability and imprudence, another President Idi Amin of Uganda.

Whatever explanation applied, usually the underlying comparisons select events to buttress the explanation and ignore contrary events. Such is natural the way the mind, unaided, patterns and explains reality. But there are aids to the mind which can increase the validity and realiability of such comparisons. The aid is science.

Science, in a nutshell, is a method for making comparisons that provide a reliable view of reality; it is a means of aiding the mind in assessing patterns, in comparing events, whether in nature or man made. The essence of science is comparison, and it now appears almost inevitable that scientific methods would eventually have been applied to political events to improve their understanding, to add the comparative third link to knowledge of an event and of those that precede it.

The stuff of comparison is data, and the heart of science is data that have been collected according to consistent rules and operations. This insures that all relevant data have been included (whether for or *against* an hypothesis or belief), and that others can check or criticize the data underlying results or conclusions. The purpose is to arm the critic of one's results with the best ammunition. For results that then withstand a critical onslaught have credibility worthy of notice.

The application of scientific methods to political events, then, has been aided by the development of event *data*. That is, data for which the rules of inclusion and exclusion of political events are clear and consistently applied to all events. For example, Table II.1 presents event data covering July 1, 1962, to June 30, 1963, for several internal conflict events on a sample of states (this is from a collection for all states given in Rummel, 1965). To give a flavor for the rules governing the collection or riot data, a riot was defined as:

> Any violent demonstration of at least one hundred people. A mob or crowd of people clashing with police or troops or attacking private property is counted as a riot, as long as such violence appears to be spontaneous. Riotous clashes between rival political groups, racial clashes, and the like, are categorized under "clashes." Riots of a distinct antiforeign nature are not counted here. The term "violence" refers to the use of physical force, and the existence of a riot is generally evidenced by the destruction of property, people being wounded or killed, or by the use of police or riot control equipment such as clubs, guns, or water cannons. Arrests per se do not indicate a riot. [1965: 205]

Of course, not all may agree on this definition, but at least all riot data will have been collected in adherance to it, and others can determine with what they disagree, exactly.

The value of the event data in Table II.1 is immediately evident. It can be noted easily that Peru was the most unstable among the six states, having many demonstrations, riots, plots, and attempted or successful coups; that instability in Argentina was at the top, involving plots and coups, and not mass violence; and that India by comparison had its instability in the street, with numerous riots and demonstrations.

Event data, then, are collected according to some consistent and explicit definition of behavioral political events within or between states. Through such data collected across a number of possible events, an internal or external conflict profile of a state (or directed dyad, for external conflict) can be developed, as that for Argentina in Table II.1. Moreover, if such data are collected for a number of states, then comparisons among them in the number of riots, coups, and so on, can be made.

TABLE II.1:   Selected Events Data, July 1, 1962, to June 30, 1963

	DEMONSTRATIONS	RIOTS	PLOTS	COUPS*	ASSASSINATIONS*
Argentina	0	0	1	2	0
Brazil	2	1	0	0	0
France	0	2	1	0	1
Ghana	0	0	0	0	2
India	5	4	0	0	0
Peru	6	2	1	2	0

*Attempted and Successful.
SOURCE: Rummel (1965, appendix II)

Of course, several problems immediately arise. How useful is a numerical count of such events, of which significance, intensity, and even meaning will vary across states and years? Moreover, how can five riots of about 100 people each in Cleveland, Ohio, be considered five times more significant than one riot of 10,000 people in Washington, D.C.?

How reliable can such counts be; how valid the source of data? How can one reduce such diverse events and multidimensional data to clear patterns? The investigation of such questions has occupied many since the early 1960s and a background on this will be given shortly.

First, however, *event data,* should be discriminated from three other kinds of data on nations. One is of *behavioral flows,* that is, statistical aggregates measuring many kinds of uniformly occurring transactions, such as trade, economic aid, tourists, migrants, and the like. The signing of a treaty or agreement establishing such flows is event data, the resulting daily, monthly, or annual exchanges usually are not considered events.

Second, there are *behavioral structures.* These are existing, formal behavioral relationships, such as a treaty, alliance, or common membership in an international organization. The signing of a treaty or alliance, or the act of joining an international organization is an event. But the outcome is a formal structural relationship which then remains constant for a period of time. Thus, if one counts the number of treaties a state is a party to, then behavioral structures are being measured. The results, as should be clear, would not be necessarily correlated with the number of treaties signed during the same period. State A, for example, may be a party to few treaties, but then sign many new ones in a year (perhaps consequent on a new government), while state B which is a party to many treaties may sign fewer treaties than State A in the same period.

And third, there are *attribute data,* which measure or define the magnitude of a nation on some characteristic. Such data are widely used, as of gross national product, population, area, military expenditures, and so on. Table 4.1 presents the results of factor analyzing mainly flow and structural data; Table 7.1 presents similar results for attributes. For both analyses, event data were employed for the conflict variables.

In sum, we can generally distinguish between

- events: discrete political happenings (e.g., a coup threat, military clash);
- flows: state behavior with continuity in time (e.g., trade);
- structures: formal behavioral relationships (e.g., membership in international organizations)
- attributes: a characteristic of a state (e.g., area).

II.2. THE SCIENCE OF EVENTS

As part of the attempt to study more systematically conflict and war, two scientific projects in the early 1960s began to collect and analyze event data. One was directed by Charles McClelland at the University of Southern California, who was interested in quantitatively mapping behavioral events between states, especially in crises. He developed a coding system for tracking the tempo and magnitude of cooperative and conflictful events in a political crisis (McClelland, *et al.,* 1965) that involved 63 types of events organized into the 22 broad categories shown in Table II.2. He found that crises were clearly indicated by a rise in their intensity of events and the range of types of events. Indeed he developed a threshold coefficient for events above which crises clearly were underway (McClelland, 1968).

McClelland's coding scheme, called WEIS (for World Event/Interaction Survey), has been seminal and the bases for much scientific and applied research. Besides his continuing research on international crises (McClelland, 1972; McClelland and Hoggard, 1969), either his data, data collected by others using his scheme, or a variant thereof, have been applied to

TABLE II.2: McClelland's World Event/Interaction Survey Categories

1.	Yield	13.	Protest
2.	Comment	14.	Deny
3.	Consult	15.	Demand
4.	Approve	16.	Warn
5.	Promise	17.	Threaten
6.	Grant	18.	Demonstrate
7.	Reward	19.	Reduce Relationship
8.	Agree		(as negative sanction)
9.	Request	20.	Expel
10.	Propose	21.	Seize
11.	Reject	22.	Force
12.	Accuse		

assess the Berlin crises of 1948-1949 and 1961 (Tanter, 1974); the patterns of foreign cooperation and conflictful events (Kegley, *et al.,* 1974); the dependency of cooperative and conflictful events on national development, size, political system, and stability (Wilkenfeld, et al., 1977; Rosenau and Hoggard, 1974; and Powel, *et al.,* 1974).

Moreover, the WEIS data have been useful simply to map the nature and frequency of cooperative and conflictful events among nations. For example, McClelland and Hoggard (1969) claim that for 1966 there were 5,550 foreign cooperative and conflictful events for all states recorded in the New York *Times Index* (I will get to the reliability and validity of such sources subsequently). Twenty states accounted for 70% of the events; five (the United States, USSR, China, United Kingdom, and France) accounted for 40%. Conflict events comprised 31.5% of the total.

The WEIS approach has been used by corporations doing government contract research on internal and external conflict, such as by General Electric (Rubin, 1969), Consolidated Analysis Centers Inc. (Rubin, 1973), and Decisions Designs, Inc. (Andriole, 1976). An overview of events data research ("The Utilization . . .", 1971), especially that supported by The Department of Defense (Advance Research Projects Agency), was written under the guidance of Robert Young when he was at Consolidated Analysis Centers Inc. Both Young and Andriole have been active in interesting defense and military analysts and decision makers to use the WEIS system to assess and forecast foreign conflict and crises. McClelland and colleagues (1971) and Andriole (1976) have proposed systems for forecasting crises using events data.

Parallel to McClelland's early work, the Dimensionality of Nations Project (DON) which I directed from 1962 until it ended in 1975 (for an overview of DON, see Rummel, 1976; for critical assessments, see Hazelwood, 1976; Hilton, 1973, 1976; Seidelmann, 1973; Van Atta and Robertson, 1976), developed an approach for collecting and analyzing event data on the internal and foreign conflict of nations. This amounted to a frequency count of particular events for nations, such as riots, threats, or military clashes, and their component analysis (Rummel, 1970, section 5.3), to reduce the data to the basic event-patterns. From this early effort a foreign conflict event code sheet was developed (Rummel, 1966), and the resulting data have been much used by others.

The DON data or approach to coding has helped determine the dimensions of international crises (Phillips and Hainline, 1972), crises dynamics (Phillips and Lorimore, n.d.), the reciprocity in conflict behavior between nations (Phillips, 1973), as well as conflict patterns (Rummel, 1963; Hall and Rummel, 1970; Hazelwood, 1973), and dynamics

(Wilkenfeld, et al, 1972), and simply for mapping conflict (Taylor and Hudson, 1972). Numerous studies have been done to replicate my finding (Rummel, 1963) that foreign and internal conflict have little general relationship (Tanter, 1966; Wilkenfeld, 1973; Burrowes and Spector, 1973; Collins, 1973; Wilkenfeld and Zinnes, 1973). The most important use of the DON event data, however, has been in determining its interelationship with the behavioral flows and structures between states as shown in Table 4.1, and dependency upon differences between states in wealth, power, and political system (Rummel, 1972, 1977, 1978), which results are consolidated in appendix 9A.

The WEIS and DON event data approaches encouraged and influenced a number of large scale event data projects that began in the late 1960s and early 1970s, and a number of comparisons and discussion of such projects have now been published (Azar, 1970; Sigler, *et al.*, 1972; Kegley, *et al.*, 1975; "The Utilization . . .", 1972). For concise summary and comparison of eleven such projects see Kegley's 1975 study. The largest of these projects are currently the Conflict and Peace Data Bank (COPDAB) under Edward Azar (1970, 1972, 1975) at the University of North Carolina, and the Comparative Research on the Events of Nations (CREON) (Hermann, et al, 1973; Hermann, 1975) project under Charles Hermann at Ohio State University. Both these projects have focused on foreign events.

Focusing on internal events have been the influential projects of Ivo Feierabend (Feierabend and Feierabend, 1966; Feierabend, *et al.*, 1972) at San Diego State College, and Arthur Banks (1971), Director of The Center of Comparative Research, State University of New York at Binghamton. Moreover, the work of Ted Gurr (1969) at Northwestern University on internal conflict is especially within the event data movement (for the utilization of a broad range of internal event data studies for evidence on internal conflict propositions, see Volume 2, 1976: chapter 35).

The generation and analyses of events data has become an academic and scientific subdiscipline. (See Azar, 1970; Hermann, 1972; and Brady 1971 for a description of the events data movement and extensive bibliographies. A bibliography devoted exclusively to event data studies has also been published by Wynn, 1973). Its research can be found in diverse professional journals and has focused many panels of the annual American Political Science Convention. A Foreign Policy and Events Data Section has been created within the International Studies Association. Books, monographs, and numerous articles have been written on or employing event data, a portion on which are referenced here and in appendix III. Schools within the subdiscipline have developed, utilizing different events data approaches (WEIS, DON, COPDAB, CREON, and so on) and associated with different universities.

The scientific interest in events data was not wholly for basic scientific research, even at the beginning. A major purpose was to eventually provide a global monitoring system which, much like weather reports, would map, track, and forecast internal and, particularly for many, international conflict, crises, and violence. It was and is with this potential in mind that the Department of Defense has given so much support to event data research, and the Department of State has undertaken its own event data based The Foreign Relations Indicator Project (Burgess and Lawton, 1975: 116).

Towards an eventual monitoring system, events data and methods have been developed to analyze and track Middle Eastern conflict (Azar, 1972; Milstein, 1972; J. McCormick, 1975; Burrowes and Garriga-Pico, 1974); to predict the future behavior of the Soviet Union to South Korea (Choi, 1976); to analyze the assumptions of détente and the implications of U.S.-Soviet arms trends (Rummel, 1976a); to weigh the effect of Israeli reprisals on Arab violence (Blechman, 1972); to determine the causes and conditions of instability in Africa (Copson, 1973; Collins, 1973), Asia (Schubert, 1975), Latin America (Bwy, 1972), and globally (Gurr, 1969); to delineate the patterns of U.S. naval responses to instability and conflict abroad ("United States Naval . . .", 1968); to predict foreign conflict (Azar, 1975; Azar, et al, 1974); to provide an operational crises forecasting system (Andriole, 1976); and to assess political risks for investors (Haendel, et al., 1975).

II.3. SOURCES: THE VALIDITY OF EVENT DATA

All the event data projects have collected their data from public sources. WEIS has been mainly from the New York *Times Index,* DON data from the daily New York *Times,* COPDAB from several sources, including the *Times Index,* and CREON form *Deadline Data.* Projects have also used *Keesings Contemporary Archives, Facts on File,* as well as regional and other national sources, such as the *Times* of London.

Of course, two questions immediately follow. How good are these sources? Does one get a different picture from different sources? These questions have been the subject of much research (Azar, 1970; Gamson and Modigliani, 1971; Burrowes, 1974; Hazlewood and West, 1974; Hoggard, 1974; Smith, 1969). In sum, research and analyses have shown that the daily New York *Times,* or its *Index,* suffice to capture most events, particularly the more intense and significant ones. It tends to omit events in the middle or lower range, which can be found in regional sources, such as the *Middle East Journal* or *Asian Recorder.*

Moreover, assessments relying on frequency counts (such as a comparison of the number of threats by India and South Africa) or employing percentages of events (such as in observing that 30% of international threats are made by the United States) are most prone to error when the data are taken from only a few sources.

The most valid approach to event data—the one least susceptable to source bias—is to assess patterns of events (Hazelwood and West, 1974), especially from multiple sources, including the New York *Times* (Hoggard, 1974). This is the approach used in some of DON's early studies (Rummel, 1963) and especially in subsequent work I have collected data from a wide variety of media, including regional sources (appendix I: 1.6). Reliance on many sources and event data patterns is the best possible guarantee against source bias.

One final question. Even if event patterns (components) are focused upon and many sources used, will not censorship, a nation's lack of development, low international interest in a country, and such other possible influences affect the news? I investigated this question systematically for all nations for event data from the New York *Times Index, Keesings Contemporary Archives, Facts on Files, New International Yearbook,* and *Britannica Book of the Year* (Rummel, 1963, 1972: section 9.3.3), and concluded that patterns in internal and foreign conflict events were independent of such possible effects. Undeniably, censorship, development, and so on, influence and distort the news. But their impact on the patterns of events observed in the news appears random. Conclusions based on these patterns should be valid.

The straight forward result of all these validity studies is that the internal and foreign conflict patterns presented in these volumes (such as those in Table 11.2 and 11.5), or underlying the analysis of manifest conflict, are most likely valid—surely more so than alternative ways (as by frequency counts or percentages) of systematically or subjectively assessing conflict events.

II.4. CODER RELIABILITY

Aside from whether event data collected from the media really reflect current events is the question of data reliability. Can different coders produce the same data? The real world is messy and ambiguous and news reports about them often capture their ambiguity and color them with the particular interpretations of a newspaper, journal, or newsman. After seven years of experience coding events daily, I humbly admit that cold and hard definitions and classifications, no matter how often revised, often do not fit reported events and some thought and analyses by a coder are required before what is reported can be defined as, say a riot, political clash, or nonpolitical clash; as a threat, warning, or protest; as terrorism, guerrilla warfare, or rebellion.

Much research has also been done to assess reliability (Burgess and Lawton, 1975; Taylor and Hudson, 1972; Hermann, 1971; Azar, 1970; Sigler, 1972; Rummel, 1966). The results have shown event data coding, in general, to be highly reliable; different coders can be trained to produce the same data from the same sources, with about 80%-90% accuracy. The stress is on training. Reliability increases sharply as coders develop a feel for their sources and an understanding of the rules and definitions applied.

The most stringent test of reliability and validity combined have been systematic comparisons of event data sets collected by different projects employing different coders and using somewhat different definitions and overlapping sources. Phillips (1972) systematically compared the WEIS and DON event data for 1967 on the conflict between 182 pairs of states and found similar conflict patterns in each (see also appendix I: 2.3). That is, for either set the conclusions about conflict event patterns would have been much the same.

However, when one works at the more detailed level of correlations between events, different event data sets might yield different conclusions. Chan (n.d.), for example, found that the CREON and WEIS sets had lack of empirical correspondance for U.S., China, Vietnam, and USSR interactions, both in terms of event magnitude and composition.

Again, these assesments of reliability point to the importance of relying on an analysis of event patterns.

II.5. CODING EVENT DATA

There are two major ways of coding political events. One can code events by type, such as done in Table II.1. The event data then consists of the *frequency* of events of each type, such as the number of coups for Argentina. Such was the WEIS and DON approach, and it is the approach of the CREON project. These codings may differ only in their definitions, their scope (WEIS and CREON cover both cooperative and conflictful external events; DON covers conflictful internal and external events), level of classification, and sources.

The second approach is to classify events and scale (weight and accumulate) them in some manner to reflect their importance or intensity. The event data is then *scaled*. Such is the approach in Azar's COPDAB set, the data developed by Gamson and Modigliani (1971) to analyze the cold war, and in my own later work (appendix I: 1.6).

There are advantages and problems in both frequency and scaled event data. Frequencies stay close to events, minimize assumptions, and allow the data themselves to show their patterns. But, frequencies give all events of a certain type equal weight and their quantitative analysis is a confession of substantive ignorance. Scaled events enable qualitative insight to play a role and weight events of the same type by their political significance. However, this enables subjective bias and a priori beliefs to influence the results.

Event data analysis has matured scientifically. As a scientific subdiscipline, it is vigorous and its products are remaking our knowledge of internal and external politics, conflict, and violence. As an approach it has proven its worth and established its credibility.

APPENDIX III

CHARACTERISTICS OF PUBLISHED QUANTITATIVE
INTERNATIONAL RELATIONS STUDIES

Following is Table III, which lists 317 published, quantitative, international studies and their essential characteristics. Table III provides these characteristics in one place and thus avoids the necessity of repeating them in the text when a study's results are used or referred to several times.

A number of qualifications and considerations should be taken into account in using Table III.

(1) It is not a comprehensive list of quantitative studies in international relations, nor does it necessarily include all such relevant studies. Before writing the empirical parts of this book, I took a year to review all the quantitative international relations studies available in the University of Hawaii Library and my personal collection (both reduced in number by student-colleague attrition), and noted those studies with relevant and competent results. [1] Thus, the table includes only studies personally available in Hawaii and whose quantitative results were used in this book.

(2) Cross-national, comparative, quantitative studies are ordinarily excluded, unless their results also involve relevant international relations and foreign policy variables.

(3) Some mainly qualitative studies or surveys are included if they provide a systematic review of the literature or results, or tabulate relevant data.

(4) One or more studies by the same author may be listed together, (e.g., Dowty, 1970, 1971) if they share most of the same characteristics and most of their results overlap. Multiple listing does not mean the studies are identical, however.

(5) The characteristics tabulated for each study are the essential parameters for gauging the usefulness of its results: sample, data periods, variables, and methods. Clearly, a study of war and alliances for 10 states for 1951 will be less important for most purposes here than one for war and 40 independent variables for all known empires since 2,000 B.C.

(6) The characteristics tabulated are only for the results used here, and not necessarily for the central analysis of a work. My purpose is to relate these characteristics to the evidence I use, and not to characterize a publication for general usage.

(7) A study is listed in Table III if it is listed in one of the six tables of evidence: 9A.1, 15A.2, 15A.4, 16C.3, 17A.3, 18A.2. The only exception to this is the additional 48 unpublished studies (projects) referred to in appendix I and described therein.

TABLE III: Characteristics of Published Quantitative International Relations Studies

AUTHOR (YEAR)[a]	SAMPLE[e]	DATA PERIODS[f]	VARIABLES[b]	METHODS[c]	COMMENTS[d]
Abravanel & Hughes (1973)	17 dyads	1955-1965	d: conf-coop events; i: public opinion	ed, ss/s	applies Balance Theory
Adelman (1972)	US-USSR: 2 crises	1961-1962	content of public documents	co/s	ULO
Addo (1974)	all states	1960-1970	diverse coop	ag/s	tests Galtung's Model
Ahn (1977)	26 A. conflicts	1945-1970	d: conf resolution	ag/s	
Alcock (1970)	42 states	1960	d: mil exp	ag/r	
Andriole (1976)			ed; crises	ed/o	designs crisis forecasting system
Atkinson (1967)	research results	1960-1966	attitudes		ULO; PI
Azar (1970)	ME dyads	1955-1958	coop-conf ed	ed/s	COPDAB data; applies Signal Accounting Model
Azar (1972)	Egypt dyads	Suez, 1956	ed	ed/s	COPDAB data; conf dynamics
Azar (1975)	Israel-Egypt US-USSR	36 mo: 1975-1977 36 mo: 1965-1977	d: conf-coop scale	ed/r	COPDAB data; applies Signal Accounting Model
Azar, *et al.* (1972a)	Israel, Egypt	1955-1958	ed	ed/s	COPDAB data; ed source comparison
Azar, *et al.* (1974)	12 dyads 11,664 events	276 m, 1950-1971	d: conf-coop scale	ed/s, r	COPDAB data; applies Richardson Model
Babst (n.d.; 1972)	116 wars	1789-1941	i: political systems	ag/s	
Barringer (1972)	18 conflicts	20th Century	300 var	ag/d	conf dynamics
Beer (1974)	all wars	3600BC-1974AD		ag/s	war statistics

TABLE III: Characteristics of Published Quantitative International Relations Studies (Cont)

AUTHOR (YEAR)[a]	SAMPLE[e]	DATA PERIODS[f]	VARIABLES[b]	METHODS[c]	COMMENTS[d]
Blainey (1973)	all wars	1700-	—	hi	
Blechman (1972)	Israel dyads	1949-1969	d: conf & coop i: reprisals	ed/s	reprisal dynamics
Bloom (1974)	464 subjects	1970s	IR questions	ss/d	cross-national subjects
Bloomfield & Leiss (1967, 1969)	over 50 small wars	since 1945	d: conf control	ed/s, o	
Bobrow (1969)	120 China dyads	1960-1964	IR beh	ag/s, d	
Bobrow & Wilcox (1966)	NORC surveys	1963-1964	IR questions	ss/d	U.S. subjects
Brady (1974)	35 states 11,583 events	1959-1968	30 ed variables	ed/d, v	CREON data
Brady (1975)	35 states	1966-1969	d: coop & conf i: bureaucratic	ed, ag/s	WEIS data
Brecher (1974)	7 Israel cases	20 years	decision related	cs/s	
Bremer, et al. (1973)	73 wars	1816-1965	i: population density	ag/s, v	Singer-Small data
Broch & Galtung (1966)	652 societies	unrestricted	d: war character	fd/s	
Buchanan & Cantril (1953)	11,000 people 9 states	1948	21 questions	ss/s	
Burrowes & Spector (1973)	Syria 4,710 events	74m, 1961-1967	int & ext conf & coop	ed/d, r	
Burrowes & Garriga-Pico (1974)	ME dyads 4,500 events	Six-Day War 1967	26 conf & coop	ed/d	
Butterworth (1976)	274 conflicts	1945-1974		ag/s	310 management attempts

TABLE III: Characteristics of Published Quantitative International Relations Studies (Cont)

AUTHOR (YEAR)[a]	SAMPLE[e]	DATA PERIODS[f]	VARIABLES[b]	METHODS[c]	COMMENTS[d]
Cannizzo (1975)	30 wars	1816-1965	d: war attr / i: power .	ag/s, r	Singer-Small data
Carroll (1969)			war termination		ULO
Caspary (1968)	USSR; US	1946-1963	coop & conf ed attitudes	ed, ss/s	Gamson-Modigliani data
Caspary (1970)	7 US surveys	early 1950s	conf attitudes	ss/d	
Cattell (1949)	69 states	1837-1937	72 attr	ed, ag/d	
Cattell (1953)	Great Britain	1837-1937	48 attr	ed, ag/d	dynamic dimensions
Cattell & Adelson (1951)	US	1845-1945	44 attr	ed, ag/d	dynamic dimensions
Cattell, et al. (1951)	40 states	1837-1937	72 attr	ed, ag/d	
Cattell & Gorsuch (1965)	52 states	1953-1958	48 attr	ed, ag/d	
Chadwick (1972)	182 dyads	1963	d: IR beh / i: attributes	ed, ag/r	DON data; applies Rummel models
Chan (n.d.)			ed	ed/s	cf. CREON, WEIS & COPDAB data
Choi (1973)	82 US dyads / 82 USSR dyads	1960; 1965	d: IR beh / i: attr distances	ed, ag/d, c	DON data; tests Rummel Model II
Choucri (1974)	45 conflicts	1945-	d: conflict var / i: population var	ag/s	ULO; PI;
Choucri & North (1974)	6 states	1870-1914	d: arms race, alliance, violence	ag/s, r	
Clemens (1966)	USSR	1950-1963	arms control var	ag/s	
Cobb & Elder (1970)	1386 dyads	1952-1964	d: coop	ag/s, c	

TABLE III: Characteristics of Published Quantitative International Relations Studies (Cont)

AUTHOR (YEAR)[a]	SAMPLE[e]	DATA PERIODS[f]	VARIABLES[b]	METHODS[c]	COMMENTS[d]
Cobb (1973)	U.S. Senators	1967	d: votes / i: def. exp. in district	ag/s	
Collins (1973)	33 African States	1963-1965	17 ext. conf. / 22 int. conf.	ed/r, d	
Coplin & Kegley (1971)					ULO
Coplin & Rochester (1972)	118 disputes	1920-1968	d: resolution	ed, ag/s	
Copson (1973)	African States	1964-1969	ext. & int conf	ed/s	
Cutler (1970)	US Surveys	1946-1966	d: IR attitudes	ss/s	
Dahl & Tufte (1973)	113 states	1964c	i: size	ag/s, r	
Denton (1966)	101 wars	1820-1949	36 characteristics	ag/d	Richardson war data
Denton (1969)	296 conflicts / 660 dyads	1950-1960	diverse	ag/s	war trends
Denton & Phillips (1968)	375 wars	1480-1900	time	ag/s	Wright war data; war cycles
Deutsch, K. & Senghaas (1973)				s	ULO
Deutsch, M. & Biener (1969)	subjects from 8 states		nation ratings	ss/d	
Dewey (1962, 1964, 1969, 1970)	all battles	600 BC-1957AD	time	ag/s	war cycles
Dewey (1966)					ULO re war cycles
Dowty (1970, 1971)	470 states / 237 conflicts	280 BC-1914AD	diverse dyadic	ag/s	

TABLE III: Characteristics of Published Quantitative International Relations Studies (Cont)

AUTHOR (YEAR)[a]	SAMPLE[e]	DATA PERIODS[f]	VARIABLES[b]	METHODS[c]	COMMENTS[d]
Dowty (1972)	115 guarantees 219 states	1815-	d: effectiveness	ag/s	source: diplomatic notes
Duncan & Siverson (1975)	India-China	1961-1964	coop & conf; time	co/o	
East (1970)	115 states	1950-1964	status var, conf.	ag/s	
East (1972)	120c states 381 conflicts	1948-1964	d: violence i: status discrepancy	ag/s	
East (1973)	32 states 4,448 events	1959-1968	d: conf & coop i: size	ed, ag/s	CREON data
East & Gregg (1967)	82 states	1955	d: conf & coop i: situation & condition	ed, ag/s	DON data
East & Hermann (1974)	33 states 4,475 events	1959-1968	d:conf & coop i: size, wealth, politics	ed, ag/s	CREON data
Eckhardt (1969)	261 people	mid-1960s	IR attitudes	ss/d	ULO
Eckhardt (1975)	400 societies	unrestricted	500 att&beh	fd/s	ULO
Erb (1968)	N.&S. America	1950-1965	61 att	ed, ag/d	
Ferris (1973)	42 wars	1850-1966	d: war; i: power	ag/s, d, r	Singer-Small war data
Field (1972)	India-China	Oct 21-31, 1962	ed; perception	ed, co/s, r	
Fitzsimmons (1969)	16 conflicts 2,747 events	1945-	ed coop & conf	ed/s, d	WEIS data, conf dynamics
Galtung (1965)	Norway		attitudes	ss/s	
Galtung (1966)	NATO vs Warsaw Pact		d: conf & coop i: status attr	ag/s	

TABLE III: Characteristics of Published Quantitative International Relations Studies (Cont)

AUTHOR (YEAR)[a]	SAMPLE[e]	DATA PERIODS[f]	VARIABLES[b]	METHODS[c]	COMMENTS[d]
Gameson & Modigliani (1965, 1968, 1971)	US-USSR dyad	1946-1963	coop & conf	ed/s	tests Soviet foreign policy models
Gibb (1956)	Australia	1906-1946	40 attr	ag/d	dynamic dimensions
Gitelson (1974)	African states	1957-	d: sev. dip. rel.	ag/s	
Gleditsch (1969, 1970)	82 states 182 dyads	1955	d: conf & coop i: rank vs field theory	ed, ag/c	DON data; tests Rummel models
Goldman (1973)	Europe	1946-1970	d: tension	co, ag/s	
Greaves (1962)	30 conflicts 21 wars	1944-1962		ag/s	war statistics
Gregg & Banks (1965)	all states	1950s	68 attr	ed, ag/d	
Haas, E. et al. (1972)	146 complaints to IO	1945-1970	d: IO success	ag/s	
Haas, M. (1965)					ULO
Haas, M. (1970)	21 IR systems	1648-1963	diverse systems & war attr	ag/d	Richardson & Wright war data
Haas, M. (1974)	diverse states, dyads, systems	diverse	500 + diverse	ed, ag, cs/s, d	diverse analyses
Hall & Rummel (1969)	615 dyads	1955-1963	16 conf. var.	ed/r, d	DON data; conf dynamics
Hall & Rummel (1970)	275 dyads	1963	24 conf var	ed/r, d	DON data
Halle, N. (1966)	3 state surveys		d: IR attitudes i: social position	ss/s	
Hannah (1968)	77 conflicts	1919-1965	29 settlement var	ag/d	DON data; applies Rummel models

TABLE III: Characteristics of Published Quantitative International Relations Studies (Cont)

AUTHOR (YEAR)[a]	SAMPLE[e]	DATA PERIODS[f]	VARIABLES[b]	METHODS[c]	COMMENTS[d]
Hannah (1972)	98 conflicts	1914-1965	44 settlement & system var	ag/d, r, c	DON data; applies Rummel models
Harf (1974)	68 conflicts	1946-1963	d: conf resolution	ag/s, d, o	Wright (1965) data
Hart, et al. (1974)	wars	1816-1965	d: war, i: system vs ext attr	ag/s	Singer-Small war data
Hart, H. (1946)	12 time series	19th & 20th C	diverse	ag/s	fits logistic trends
Hart, H. (1948)	political empires	recorded history	time	ag/s	fits logistic trends
Hart, J. (1974)	dyads, systems	1870s	d: conf-coop scale	ed/o	Graph Theory
Hazelwood (1973)	74 states	1950s	d: conf	ed, ag/c, d, r, o	cf sources
Hazelwood & West (1974)	20 SA States	1955-1960	5 conf var	ed/s, d	
Healy & Stein (1973)	982 events	1870-1881	coop & conf scale alliances	ed/s	Balance Theory
Hefner, et al. (1967)	Detroit Survey 558 interviews	1964c	perceived similarity of 17 states	ss/d	
Hermann, C. (1975)	35 states	1959-1968	conf & coop; size, wealth & politics	ed/s, o	CREON data
Hermann, C. et al. (1973)	35 states	1959-1968	conf & coop	ed/s	ULO; CREON data statistics
Hermann, M. (1974)	10 heads of state		d: conf; i: personality & politics	ed, ag, ss/s	CREON data
Hill (1977)	109 states	1965	d: mil. exp.	ed, ag/s; r	
Hollist (1977)	US-USSR dyad	1948-1970	d: mil. exp.	ag/r	applies Richardson Model
Holsti, K. (1977)	conflicts	1919-1975	conf attr; settlements	ag/s	conf statistics

TABLE III: Characteristics of Published Quantitative International Relations Studies (Cont)

AUTHOR (YEAR)[a]	SAMPLE[e]	DATA PERIODS[f]	VARIABLES[b]	METHODS[c]	COMMENTS[d]
Holsti, O. (1962)	434 US documents	1953-1959	hostility & perception	co/s	
Holsti, O. (1965)	USSR, China 78 documents	1959-1963	conf & cohesion	co/s	applies Balance Theory
Holsti, O. (1972)	2 crises	1914, 1962	crises var	co/ag/s	
Holsti, O. et al. (1969)	US-USSR dyad 25 documents	1962 Cuban missile crises	d: violence potential; i: perception	co/s	
Holsti, O. & Sullivan (1969)	All China & French IR actions	1950-1964	IR beh	ag, ed/s	
Holsti, O. et al. (1973)	alliances	1815-1939 1950-1969	coop & conf, alliances, attitudes	co, ss, ag/s	
Hopple, et al. (1976)	56 states	1966-1970	coop & conf; attr	ed, ag/s, d	WEIS data
Horvath (1968)	315 wars 3317 U.S. strikes	1820-1949 1961	conf termination	ag/s	Richardson's data; fits Weibull distribution
Horvath & Foster (1963)	war coalitions	19th & 20th C.	time	ag/s	
Jarvad (1968)	ICJ cases	1946-1966	diverse	ag/s	
Jensen (1966)	171 subjects		d: elite IR attitudes	ss/s	
Jones & Singer (1972)					ULO
Kean & McGowan (1973)	114 states	1966-1969c	d: IR beh; i: attr	ed, ag/s, o	WEIS data
Kegley (1974)	20 Asian states	1965c	17 IR & attitude var.	ed, ag/d	
Kegley, et al. (1974)	25 states	1959-1968	28 conf & coop var.	ed/d	ULO
Kegley & Howell (n.d.)	52 SEA dyads	1968-1971	9 beh & attr var.	ss, ag/d	
Keim (1971)	all states	1963	conf, distance, power	ed, ag/s, d	DON data

TABLE III: Characteristics of Published Quantitative International Relations Studies (Cont)

AUTHOR (YEAR)[a]	SAMPLE[e]	DATA PERIODS[f]	VARIABLES[b]	METHODS[c]	COMMENTS[d]
Keim & Rummel (1969)	all states	1955-1963	13 conf var	ed/d, r	DON data; conf dynamics
Kende (n.d., 1971)	97 wars	1945-1969	war attr	ag/s	war statistics
Klingberg (1966)	major wars	1618-1914	d: termination i: casualties	ag/s	
Köhler (1973)	64 dyads	13 years	conf & war	ed/s	prediction study
Laulicht (1965, 1965a)	1484 Canadians	1962-1963	d: IR attitudes	ss/d, s	
Leavitt (1968)	110 dyads	1955	11 coop & conf var	ed, ag/d	
Leng & Goodsell (1974)	5 conflicts	1816-1965	coop & conf	ed/s	conf dynamics
Lentner (1972)	US State Dept		crises perceptions	ss/s	
de Leon, et al. (1969)	49 conflicts	1931-1965	situational attr	ag, cs/s, r, d	
Levine (1973)	all states	1880-1965	29 attr.	ed, ag/s, d	system dynamics
Mahoney (1976)	215 US actions	1946-1975	d: pol-mil operations	ed, ag/s	ULO; uses COPDAB data
Mahoney (1977)	Europe, US, USSR	1946-1973	attitudes & conf	ss, ed, ag/s, r	ULO; uses COPDAB data
McClelland (1968)	Berlin crises	1948-1963	conf & coop	ed/s	WEIS data
McClelland (1972)	crises		conf & coop & crises	ed/s	WEIS data
McClelland, et al. (1965)	Taiwan Straits Crises	1950-1964	conf & coop	ed/d, s	WEIS data; crisis dynamics
McClelland & Hoggard (1969)	5,550 events	1966	63 conf & coop var	ed/s, d	WEIS data
McClelland & Ancoli (1970)	8 ME states	1966-1969	conf & coop var.	ed/s, d	WEIS data
McCormick, D (1975)	Arab-Israel documents	pre & during 1967 & 1973 wars	conf & perception	co, ag/s	
McCormick, J. (1975)	ME dyads	Suez & Six Day wars	conf var	ed/s	crisis dynamics

TABLE III: Characteristics of Published Quantitative International Relations Studies (Cont)

AUTHOR (YEAR)[a]	SAMPLE[e]	DATA PERIODS[f]	VARIABLES[b]	METHODS[c]	COMMENTS[d]
McGowan (1973)	32 Af. states 14,500 events	1964-1966	conflict & coop	ed/s, d	
McGowan & Shapiro (1973)	200 studies				ULO; PI; empirical survey
McGowan & Rood (1975)	101 alliances	1814-1914	allowance & time	ag/s	Poisson test
Melko (1973)	52 peace societies	recorded history	d: peace	ag/s	
de Mesquita (1975)	21 wars	1900-1960	d: war probability i: polarity	ag/s	
Midlarsky (1974, 1975)	41 wars	1815-1945	d: war; i: uncertainty, polarity & status	ag/s, r	Singer-Small data
Midlarsky (1975)	65 empires	recorded history	88 attr; d: wars	ag/r, d	
Michalka (1976)	264 mil conflicts	1816-1970	d: targets resistence, i: capability, alliance, location	ag/s, r	Singer-Small data
Milstein (1972)	Arab-Israel dyads	1948-1967	d: violence	ed, ag/s, r	
Modigliani (1972)	US surveys	Vietnam & Korean Wars	d: war attitudes	ss/s, d	
Mogdis (1969, 1970)	Sino-Soviet dyad	1950-1967	perceptual, beh, & attr var	ed, ag, co/r, d, c	applies Balance Theory, Rummel Model
Moore, D. (1974, 1974a)	116 states	1963	d: IR beh; i: pol syst, attr	ag/s, r, d	
Moore, J. (1970)	86 states	40m, 1966-1969	d: IR beh; i: attention	co, ed, ag/s, r, d	WEIS data
Moore, J. & Young (1969)	states	12m, 1968-1969	d: events, i: past events	ed/s, r	WEIS data; prediction study

TABLE III: Characteristics of Published Quantitative International Relations Studies (Cont)

AUTHOR (YEAR)[a]	SAMPLE[e]	DATA PERIODS[f]	VARIABLES[b]	METHODS[c]	COMMENTS[d]
Moore, J. et al. (1975)	72 crises	1946-1973	attr	ag/s	
Most & Starr (n.d. 1976)	wars	1946-1965	war, borders, time	ag/s	tests Poisson Dist.
Mueller (1971)	US surveys	Korean & Vietnam wars	public opinion	ss/s	
Munton (1973)	states	1963, 1967, 1968	events	ed/s, c	CREON data validity study
Naroll (n.d.)	58 societies	unrestricted	6 war attr.	fd/d	
Naroll (1966)	58 societies	unrestricted	d: war attr.	fd/s	
Naroll (1967)	28 empires	3,000 BC –	size & time	ag/s	cycle study
Naroll (1970)	primitive societies	unrestricted	attr	fd/d	ULO
Naroll, et al. (1974)	20 historical periods	unrestricted	d: war attr	fd/s	
Newcombe & Wert (1972)	states	1950-1968	d: wars; i: tension	ag/s	prediction study
North & Choucri (1971)	Sino-Soviet dyad	20 years	d: IR beh, i: population	ag/s, r	ULO
Northedge & Donelan (1971)	50 IR disputes	1945-1970	diverse	hi	
Nye (1971)	IOs	contemporary	conf & coop	ag/s	
Oliva & Rummel (1969)	all states	1963	24 conf var	ed/d, r	DON data; prediction study
Omen (1975)	1552 dyads	1950-1965	conf & coop	ed, ag/r, d	DON data; prediction study
Onate (1974)	all states	1950-1970	d: ext conf, i: int conf	ed/r	
Otterbein (1968, 1970)	50 societies	unrestricted	d: war	fd/s	

TABLE III: **Characteristics of Published Quantitative International Relations Studies (Cont)**

AUTHOR (YEAR)[a]	SAMPLE[e]	DATA PERIODS[f]	VARIABLES[b]	METHODS[c]	COMMENTS[d]
Park, T. (1969, 1969a)	342 A. dyads; 19 A. states	1955, 1963	d: conf & coop scale	ed, ag/r, d, c	DON data; test Rummel models
Park, T. (1970, 1973)	21 A. states	1949-1968	48 attr & IR beh.	ag/d	dynamic dimensions
Park, T. (1972)	342 A. dyads	1963	d: IR beh; i: distances	ed, ag/c	DON data; test of modified Rummel Model
Park & Ross (1971)	20 A. states	months, 1962-1968	15 conf. variables	ed/r, d	DON data; dynamic dimensions
Park, Y. (1975)	nation triads	1950, 1965	coop & conf var	ed, ag/d, c	DON data; applies Balance Theory
Peterson (1972)	US-USSR dyad	1955-1964	d: conf; i: attitudes	ed, ss/s	
Phillips (1969)	267 dyads	1963, 12 m	23 conf var.	ed/d, c	DON data; conf dynamics
Phillips (1970)	65 states	1963	23 conf var.	ed/d, c	DON data; conf dynamics
Phillips (1972)	182 dyads	1967	22 conf & coop var	ed/c	cf DON & WEIS data
Phillips (1973)	73 states	1963	23 conf var	ed/d, c, r	DON data
Phillips & Lorimore (n.d.)	21 crises; 50 dyads	1962-1968	22 conf var	ed/r, d	DON data; crisis dynamics
Phillips & Hainline (n.d.)	US, USSR, China dyads	72 mo, 1962-1968	21 conf. var	ed/d, c	DON data; dynamic dimensions
Phillips & Hainline (1972)	21 crises	1962-1968	22 conf var	ed/d, c	DON data
Phillips & Crain (1974)	states	1959-1968	d: reciprocity	ed/c	CREON data
Pool (1951)	19,553 editorials in 5 inter'l newspapers	1890-1950	hostility & friendship symbols	co/s	
Powel et al. (1974)	16,512 dyads; 13,520 events	1966-1969	d: coop & conf	ed, ag/s, r	WEIS data

TABLE III: Characteristics of Published Quantitative International Relations Studies (Cont)

AUTHOR (YEAR)[a]	SAMPLE[e]	DATA PERIODS[f]	VARIABLES[b]	METHODS[c]	COMMENTS[d]
Randle (1972)	500 wars	1500-1971	d: war outcomes	ag/s	
Ray (1974)	wars, 8 states	1816-1970	d: war; i: status	ag/r, s	Singer-Small data
Rhee (1971)	81 China dyads	1955; 1963	d: IR beh i: attr distance	co, ed, ag/d, c	DON data; tests Rummel Model
Rhee (1977)	456 China dyads	1950-1965	d: IR beh; i: attr distances	co, ed, ag/d, c	DON data; tests Rummel Model
Richardson, L. (1960b)	282 violent conflicts	1820-1949	d: war	ag/s	diverse studies; develops Richardson Model
Richardson, L. (1960a)	282 violent conflicts	1820-1949	d: war	ag/s	war statistics; diverse studies
Richardson, R. (1966)	380 conflicts	1946-1964	war attr	ag/s, r	conf statistics
Rosecrance (1963)	9 IR systems	1715-1955	diverse	hi	
Rosen (1972)	40 wars	1815-1945	d: victory	ag/s	Singer-Small data
Rosenau & Hoggard (1974)	16,512 dyads 13,520 events	1966-1969	d: conf & coop; i: size, wealth, politics	ed, ag/s	
Rubin (1973)	states	1968-1971	conf & coop	ed/s	
Rubin & Schainblatt (1969)	78 states	1964-1965	d: conf	ed, ag/r	
Rummel (1963)	77 states	1955-1957	9 int & 13 ext conf var	ed/d, r	DON data
Rummel (1963a)	77 states	1955-1957	d: int & ext conf	ed, ag/r	DON data
Rummel (1965)	41 dyads	1955-1957	d: conf; i: dist	ed, ag/r, d	test of Rummel Model
Rummel (1967)	779 dyads 211 wars	1820-1952	84 war attr	ag/d	Richardson data
Rummel (1967a, 1968)	340 dyads 2,139 events	1955	16 conf var	ed/d	DON data

TABLE III: Characteristics of Published Quantitative International Relations Studies (Cont)

AUTHOR (YEAR)[a]	SAMPLE[e]	DATA PERIODS[f]	VARIABLES[b]	METHODS[c]	COMMENTS[d]
Rummel (1969, 1969a)	346 dyads	1955	40 IR beh var	ed, ag/d	DON data
Rummel (1972)	82 states	1955	236 attr	ed, ag/d, r	DON data; applies Rummel Model
Rummel (1972a)	81 US dyads	1955	d: IR beh i: attr distances	ed, ag/d, c	DON data; tests Rummel models
Rummel (1977)	diverse	1950-1965	>500 attr & beh	diverse	development & tests of Rummel Model
Rummel (1978)	all states 182 dyads	1950-1965	150 attr & beh	ed, ag/d, c	dynamic dimensions
Russett (1963)	17 cases	1935-1961	d: deterence	ag/s	
Russett (1967)	all states	1946-	diverse	ag/s, r, d	diverse studies
Russett (1971, 1974)	137 alliances	1920-1957	44 attr	ag/d	
Russett & Monsen (1975)	>80 states	1965	d: war, growth, equality; i: pol syst	ag/s, r	
Salmore & Hermann (1970)	9,791 events 76 states	1966-1967	d: IR events	ed, ag/s	WEIS data
Salmore & Munton (1974)	73 states	1966-1969	22 conf & coop var	ed/d	WEIS data
Salmore, et al. (1974)	36 states	mid-1960s	< 26 conf & coop var	ed/d, c	cf. WEIS, CREON, & other data
Salmore & Salmore (1975)	36 states	1959-1968	d: foreign policy i: pol syst	ed/s	CREON data
Schubert (1975)	38 A dyads	1960-1971	d: coop & conf	ed, ag/s, c, d	DON data
Schwartz (1972)	US-USSR dyad 8 crises	1946-	perception, conf & coop	ag, co/s	

TABLE III: Characteristics of Published Quantitative International Relations Studies (Cont)

AUTHOR (YEAR)[a]	SAMPLE[e]	DATA PERIODS[f]	VARIABLES[b]	METHODS[c]	COMMENTS[d]
Schwerin (1977)	106 US dyads	1963	d: IR beh / i: attr distances	ed, ag/d, c	DON data; tests Rummel models
Sigler (1972)	states	May, 1967	conf & coop var	ed/s	tests WEIS data sources
Singer & Small (1966, 1966a, 1968)	wars	1815-1945	d; war; i: alliances	ag/r	Singer-Small data
Singer & Wallace (1970)	wars	1816-1964	d: war; i: IO	ag/r	Singer-Small data
Singer & Small (1972)	wars	1816-1965	d: war; i: attr	ag/s, r	Singer-Small data; war statistics
Singer, et al. (1972)	wars	1820-1965	d: war; i: power	ag/s	Singer-Small data
Singer & Small (1974)	93 wars	1816-1956	d: war; i: power, alliances IO	ag/s	Singer-Small data
Siverson (1970)		Suez crises	d: conf; i: perception		
Smith (1969)	Indian White Papers		coop & conf	ed/s	cf. ed sources
Smoker (1965)	US-USSR dyad	1948-1962	d: polarization / i: trade	ag/s	
Smoker (1969)	India-China dyad	1959-1965	d: conf	ed/s	conf dynamics
Sorokin (1937-1941; 1957)	historical wars	classical Greece-modern times	war var	ag/s	dynamic analysis
Starr (1972)	30 wars	1815-1967	d: participation & outcome	ag/s, r	
Starr & Most (n.d.)	all nations	1946-1965	d: war; i: borders	ag/s	

TABLE III: Characteristics of Published Quantitative International Relations Studies (Cont)

AUTHOR (YEAR)[a]	SAMPLE[e]	DATA PERIODS[f]	VARIABLES[b]	METHODS[c]	COMMENTS[d]
Stohl (1975)	US	1890-1970	d: int conf; i: ext conf	ed/s	dynamics
Sullivan, J. (1972)	300 dyads	1963-1967	d: alignment	ed, ag/s	DON data; ULO;
Sullivan, M. (1970)	29 dyads 16 conflicts	1945-	d: conf; i: polarity	ed/s	DON & Fitzsimmon's data
Sullivan, M. (1972)	US	Vietnam war	d: escalation i: symbolic usage	co, ag/s	conf dynamics
Sullivan, M. (1976)	diverse	diverse	diverse	diverse	ULO, PI
Swanson (1976)	12,038 events	1959-1968	d: IR beh; i: expectations	ed, ag/s	CREON data
Sybinsky (1975)	all states	1950-1965	d: conf; i: 59 att	ed, ag/d, o	DON data; Rummel Model
Tanter (1966)	83 states	1958-1960	int & ext conf	ed/d, r	DON data
Tanter (1974)	Berlin crises	1948-1949, 1961	scaled conf; time	ed/s, r	crises dynamics
Taylor & Hudson (1972)			conf	ed/s, d	tests of ed coder reliability
Terrell (1971)	75 states	1955	d: mil effort; i: stress, instability	ag/s, r	
Teune & Synnestvedt (1965)	East-West alignments	1946-	alignment & conf	ed, ag/s	
Triska & Finley (1968)	crises	1946-	d: USSR risk-taking	ag/s	
Tung (1975)	East-West system	1948-1967	conf & polarization	ag/s	
"United . . ." (1968)	90 states 351 conflicts	1945-1966	150 attr	ed, ag/d	
Van Atta & Robertson (1975)	USSR dyads	1955, 1963	12 beh var	ag/r	DON data; applies Rummel Model

TABLE III: Characteristics of Published Quantitative International Relations Studies (Cont)

AUTHOR (YEAR)[a]	SAMPLE[e]	DATA PERIODS[f]	VARIABLES[b]	METHODS[c]	COMMENTS[d]
Van Atta & Rummel (1977)	107 states, 348 dyads	1963	94 attr; 56 IR beh	ag, ed/d	DON data; tests of Rummel Model
Vasquez (1975, 1976)	research studies		d: IR	co/s	ULO; PI; reviews statistical results
Väyrynen (1973)	East-West system	1948-1968	d: US & USSR conf & coop	ed, ag/s, d	
Vincent (1968, 1971c)	UN delegates	1965	d: IR attitudes; i: attr	ss, ag/s, d	
Vincent (1971a, b)	UN votes	1968, 1969	d: UN votes; i: attr	ag/s, d, c	
Vincent, et al. (1973)	dyads	1962-1964	conf & coop scales; 67 attr	ed, ag/d, c	tests Rummel's models
Vincent (1976a)	16,256 dyads	1963-1967	144 attr distances	ed, ag/d	
Vincent (1976b)	16,256 dyads	1966-1968	d: conf & coop scales i: distance deviations	ed, ag/r	WEIS data
Vincent (1977a)	UN votes	1968-1969, 1971	d: pro & con US & USSR; i: attr	ag/c	
Vincent (1977, b-f)	16,256 dyads	1966-1968	d: conf & coop scales i: distances	ed, ag/d, c, r	WEIS data; diverse results & analyses
Voevodsky (1969)	wars	19 & 20th C.	d: process & ending	ag/s	war dynamics
Wallace (1970, 1971)	93 wars	1820-1964	d: war; i: power & status	ag/s, r	Singer-Small war data
Wallace (1972)	93 wars	1820-1964	d: war; i: capabilities & change	ag/s	Singer-Small war data
Wallace (1973)	IR systems	1815-1964	war, cross-cutting, & polarization	ag/r, d	Singer-Small data

TABLE III: Characteristics of Published Quantitative International Relations Studies (Cont)

AUTHOR (YEAR)[a]	SAMPLE[e]	DATA PERIODS[f]	VARIABLES[b]	METHODS[c]	COMMENTS[d]
Wallace (1975)	IOs	1865-1964	IO co-memberships	ag/d	
Wallensteen (1968)	economic sanctions	1932-1967	d: sanctions	ag/s	
Wallensteen (1973)	87 conflicts	1920-1968	d: conf; i: status	ag/s	applies Galtung Model
Weede (1970)	59 states	1955-1960	d: conf; i: attr & beh	ed, ag/s, d	DON data
Weede (1975)	3,321 dyads	1950-1969	d: violence, i: interests, i: polarity	ed, ag/s, d	
Weede (1977a)					ULO, PI
Weede (1977b)		1950s-1960s	IR position & mil allocation	ag/s	ULO
Weil (1975)	26 E states	1950-1970	12 variables	ed, ag/r	scaled WEIS data
Weiss (1963)	315 wars	1825-1952	d: duration & trend	ag/o	Richardson data; Marchov chain
Wesley (1969)	over 300 wars	1820-1940	d: war dead; i: geography	ag/s	Richardson data
Wilkenfeld (1972, 1973)	74 states	1955-1960	int & ext conf; political systems	ed, ag/o	Marchov chain
Wilkenfeld, et al. (1972)	6 ME states 7,958 events	217m, 1949-1967	int & ext conf	ed/r, d	dynamic dimensions
Wilkenfeld & Zinnes (1973)	77 states	1955-1960	int & ext conf	ed/o	
Wilkenfeld, et al. (1977)	56 states	1966-1970	conf & coop; 23 attr	ed, ag/d	Marchov chain
Wittkopf (1971)	71 states	1964	d: US aid	ag/s, r	dynamic dimensions
Wright (1942)	diverse historical wars	historical periods	diverse	diverse	ULO
Wright (1965)	45 IR conflicts	1918-	escalation var	ag/s	

TABLE III: Characteristics of Published Quantitative International Relations Studies (Cont)

AUTHOR (YEAR)[a]	SAMPLE[e]	DATA PERIODS[f]	VARIABLES[b]	METHODS[c]	COMMENTS[d]
Zinnes (1971)	wars	1815-1945	d: war; i: cross-pressures	ag/s	Singer-Small data
Zinnes (1972)	diverse	diverse	hostility & perception	co/s	ULO; Sprout Model
Zinnes (1976)	diverse	diverse	diverse	diverse	ULO; PI; Richardson Model
Zinnes, et al. (1972)	1914 crisis	1914	hostility & perception	co/s	

a. Year refers to year of publication listed in references

b. *Abbreviations*

attr:	attributes	ed:	event data
beh:	behavior	exp:	expenditure
conf:	conflict	ext:	external
coop:	cooperation	i:	independent
d:	dependent	int:	internal

IO:	international organization
IR:	international relations
mil:	military
pol:	political
syst:	system
var:	variables

Reference is made only to the major variables employed for the results used in this book.

c. *Data type/analysis method*

ag:	aggregate data	fd:	field (e.g., anthropological) data
co:	content analysis	hi:	historical analysis
cs:	case study	ss:	sample survey; public opinion; questionaire data
ed:	event data	c:	cannonical analysis

d:	factor, cluster, grouping, or dimensional analysis
o:	other
r:	regression
s:	descriptive statistics, cross-tabulation, and correlation
v:	analysis of variance

Reference is made only to the major methods underlying the results used in this book.

d. *Abbreviations*

cf:	compares
conf:	conflict
COPDAB:	Conflict and Peace Data Bank
CREON:	Comparative Research on the Events of Nations Project
DON:	Dimensionality of Nations Project
ed:	event data

E:	European
IO:	international organization
PI:	propositional inventory
ULO:	useful literature review given
WEIS:	World Event/Interaction System

e. *Abbreviations*

A:	Asia
AF:	Africa

ME:	Middle East
SA:	South America
SEA:	South East Asia

f. m = months

N O T E S

1. I also excluded results whose underlying methods were not made clear, unless through personal knowledge I had confidence in the researcher's capability. Also, a work may be mixed: some of the research may be skillfully done, while the remainder may involve methods over which the author obviously does not have command. In such cases, I utilized only the competent parts, if relevant. Therefore, the inclusion of a study in Table III *does not imply* a view that all its research is ably done.

REFERENCES

Abravanel, Martin and Barry Hughes. "The relationship between public opinion and governmental foreign policy: A cross national study," in Patrick J. McGowan (Ed.), *Sage International Yearbook of Foreign Policy Studies,* Vol. 1 Beverly Hills: Sage Publications, 1973, 107-133.

Addo, Herb. "Structural basis of international communications." The Papers of the Peace Science Society (International), Vol 23 (1974) 81-100.

Adelman, Murray L. "Crisis decision-making and cognitive balance," in John H. Sigler, John O. Field, and Murray L. Adelman, "Applications of Events Data Analysis: Cases, Issues, and Programs in International Interaction," *Sage Professional Papers in International Studies,* Vol 1, 02-002, Beverly Hills: Sage, 1972, 61-95.

Ahn, Chung-Si. "Conflict and Conflict Resolution in Asian Perspective – An Exploratory Macro-Analysis of Armed Conflicts in Asia During the Post-War Era (1945-1970)." Korea and World Affairs, Vol. 1 (Fall 1977), 258-284.

Alcock, Norman Z. "An Empirical Measure of Internation Threat: Some Preliminary Implications for the Middle East Conflict." Peace Research Society (International), Vol 15 (1970), 51-71.

Alcock, Norman Z. and Alan G. Newcombe. "The perception of national power." The Journal of Conflict Resolution, Vol 14 (September, 1970), 335-343.

Alger, Chadwick, F. " 'Foreign' policies of U.S. publics." International Studies Quarterly, Vol. 21 (June 1977), 277-318.

Allison, Graham T. "Conceptual models and the Cuban Missile Crisis." American Political Science Review, Vol. 63 (September 1969), 689-718.

Andriole, Stephen J. "Progress Reports on the Development of an Integrated Crisis Warning System." Technical Report 76-19, Decisions and Designs, Inc., Mclean, Virginia, December, 1976.

Angell, Robert C. *Peace on the March.* New York: Van Nostrand Reinhold Co., 1969.

Aron, Raymond. *Peace and War: A Theory of International Relations,* Translated by Richard Howard and Annette Baker Fox. New York: Doubleday Garden City, 1966.

–––. "What is a theory of international relations?" Journal of International Affairs, Vol. 21 (No. 2, 1967), 185-206.

Atkinson, Tom. "A Propositional Inventory of the Empirical Work Involving Foreign Affairs and National Security Attitudes, 1960-1966: A Non-Evaluative Review," Civil Defense Research Project, Oak Ridge National Laboratory, October 24, 1967.

Azar Edward, E. "Analysis of international events." Peace Research Reviews, Vol. 4 (November, 1970), 1-106.

–––. "Conflict escalation and conflict reduction in an international crisis: Suez, 1956." Journal of Conflict Resolution, Vol. 35 (June 1972), 183-201.

–––. "Behavioral forecasts and policymaking: An events data approach," Charles Kegley, Jr., Gregary A. Raymond, Robert M. Rood, and Richard Skinner, *International Events and the Comparative Analysis of Foreign Policy,* Columbia; University of South Carolina Press: 1975, 215-236.

Azar, Edward E., Richard A. Brody, and Charles A. McClelland. "International Events Interaction Analysis: Some Research Considerations," *Some Professional Papers*, Vol. 1, 02-001, Beverly Hills: Sage Publications, 1972.

Azar, Edward E., Stanely H. Cohen, Thomas O. Jukam, and James M. McCormick. "The problem of source coverage in the use of international events data." International Studies Quarterly, Vol. 16 (September, 1972a), 373-388.

Azar, Edward E., James P. Bernett, and Thomas J. Sloan. "Steps toward forecasting international interactions." The Papers of the Peace Science Society (International), Vol. 23 (1974), 27-67.

Babst, Dean V. "A force for peace." Industrial Research (April, 1972), 55-58.

–––. "Elective governments–a force for peace." The Wisconsin Sociologist. (n.d.) (This is largely reproduced in Babst, above.)

Banks, Arthur. *Cross-Polity Time-Series Data*. Cambridge, Mass: The MIT Press, 1971.

Barker, Ernest. *Social Contract: Essays by Locke, Hume, and Rousseau*. London: Oxford University Press, 1958.

Barringer, Richard E. *War: Patterns of Conflict*. Cambridge, Mass: MIT Press, 1972.

Bartos, Otomar J. "How predictable are negotiations?" Journal of Conflict Resolution, Vol. 11 (December, 1967), 481-496.

Beer, Francis. "How Much War in History: Definitions, Estimates, Extrapolations and Trends." *Sage Professional Papers in International Studies*, Vol. 3, 02-030, Beverly Hills: Sage, 1974.

Berle, Adolph A. *Power*. New York: Harcourt, Brace, and World, 1967.

Berry, Brian J.L. *Essays on Commodity Flows and the Spatial Structure of the Indian Economy*. Chicago: University of Chicago Press, 1966.

Blainey, Geoffrey. *The Causes of War*. New York: The Free Press, 1973.

Blechman, Barry M. "The impact of israel's reprisals on behavior of the bordering arab nations directed at israel." The Journal of Conflict Resolution, Vol. 16 (June, 1972), 155-181.

Bloom, Alfred H. "Cross-cultural investigations of the moral basis of political reasoning." The Papers of the Peace Science Society (International), Vol. 23, (1974), 101-111.

Bloomfield, Lincoln P. and Amelia C. Leiss. *The Control of Local Conflict: A Design Study on Arms Control and Limited War in the Developing Areas*, Vols, 1-3. Prepared for the U.S. Arms Control and Disarmament Agency (ACDA/WEC-98), Center for International Studies: Massachusetts Institute of Technology, 1967.

–––. *Controlling Small Wars: A Strategy For the 1970's*. New York: Alfred A. Knopf, 1969.

Bobrow, Davis B. "Ecology of international games: Requirement for a model of the international system." Papers, Peace Research Society (International) Vol. 11 (1969), 67-87.

Bobrow, Davis B. and Allen R. Wilcox. "Dimensions of defense opinion: The american public." Peace Research Society: Papers, Vol. VI (1966), 101-142.

Boulding, K.E. "National images and international systems." The Journal of Conflict Resolution, Vol. 3 (June, 1959), 120-132.

–––. *Conflict and Defense*. New York: Harper & Brothers, 1962.

Brady, Linda P. "The International Events Data Movement: A New Approach to the Identification of Foreign Policy Outputs." CREON Publication No. 6, Columbus, Ohio: Ohio State University, March 1971.

–––. *Threat, decision time, and awareness: The impact of situational variables on foreign policy behavior*, Ph.D. dissertation, Columbus: The Ohio State University, 1974.

–––. "Bureaucratic Determinants of Foreign Policy Behavior: An Events Data Test of the

Bureaucratic Politics Paradigm." Presented to the annual meeting of the International Studies Association, Washington, D.C., February 19-22, 1975.

Brecher, Michael. "Research findings and theory-building in foreign policy behavior." in Patrick J. McGowan (Ed.), *Sage International Yearbook of Foreign Policy Studies,* Vol. 2, Beverly Hills: Sage Publications, 1974, 49-122.

Brecht, Arnold. *Political Theory.* Princeton, N.J.: Princeton University Press, 1959.

Brodie, Bernard. *War and Politics.* New York: Macmillan, 1973.

Bremer, Stuart, J. David Singer, and Urs Luterbacher. "The population density and war proneness of european nations, 1876-1965." Comparative Political Studies, Vol. 6 (October 1973), 329-348.

Broch, Torn and Johan Galtung. "Belligerence among primitives." Journal of Peace Research, 1 (1966), 33-45.

Buchanan, William and Hadley Cantril. *How Nations See Each Other.* Urbana: University of Illinois Press, 1953.

Bull, Hedley. "Society and anarchy in international relations," in Herbert Butterfield and Martin Wright, *Diplomatic Investigations,* London: George Allen & Unwin Ltd., 1966, 40-48.

Bunge, Mario. *Causality: The Place of the Causal Principle in Modern Science.* New York: The World Publishing Co. (Meridian Books), 1963.

Burgess, Philip M. *Elite Images and Foreign Policy Outcomes: A Study of Norway.* A Publication of the Mershon Center for Education in National Security: The Ohio State University Press, 1967.

Burgess, Philip M. and Raymond W. Lawton. "Evaluating events data: problems of conception, reliability, and validity," in Charles W. Kegley, Jr., Gregory A. Raymond, Robert M. Rood, and Richard A. Skinner, *International Events and the Comparative Analysis of Foreign Policy.* Columbia, South Carolina: The University of South Carolina Press, 1975, 106-119.

Burrowes, Robert. "Mirror, mirror, on the wall . . . : A comparison of event data sources." in James N. Rosenau, *Comparing Foreign Policies: Theories, Findings, and Methods.* New York: Halsted Press, 1974, 383-405.

Burrowes, Robert and Bertram Spector. "The strength and direction of relationships between domestic and external conflict and cooperation: Syria, 1961-67." in Jonathan Wilkenfeld (Ed.), *Conflict Behavior and Linkage Politics.* New York: David McKay Company, 1973, 294-321.

Burrowes, Robert and Jose Garriga-Pico. "The Road to the Six Day War: Relational Analysis of Conflict and Cooperation." The Papers of the Peace Science Society (International), Vol. 22 (1974), 47-74.

Burton, J.W. *Systems, States, Diplomacy and Rules.* New York: Cambridge University Press, 1968.

Butterworth, Robert Lyle. *Managing Interstate Conflict, 1945-1974: Data with Synopsis.* Pittsburgh: University Center for International Studies, University of Pittsburgh, 1976.

Bwy, Douglas P. "Political instability in Latin America: The cross-cultural test of a causal model," in Ivo K. Feierabend, and Ted Robert Gurr, *Anger, Violence, and Politics.* Englewood Cliffs, N.J.: Prentice-Hall, 1972.

Cannizzo, Cynthia. "The Costs of Combat: Predicting Deaths, Duration and Defeat In Interstate War, 1816-1965." Paper Delivered to the annual meeting of the International Studies Association, Washington, D.C., 1975.

Carr, Edward Hallett. *The Twenty Years' Crisis, 1919-1939.* New York: Harper and Row, 1964.

Carroll, Berenice A. "How wars end: An analysis of some current hypotheses." Journal of

Peace Research, No. 4(1969), 295-321.

———. "War termination and conflict theory: Value premises, theories, and policies." Annals of the American Academy of Political and Social Science, Vol. 392 (November, 1970), 14-29.

Caspary, William R. "United States public-opinion during the onset of the cold war." Peace Research Society (International): Papers, Vol. 9 (1968), 25-46.

———. "Dimensions of attitudes on international conflict: Internationalism and military offensive action." Peace Research Society (International): Papers, Vol. 13 (1970), 1-10.

Cattell, Raymond B. "The dimensions of culture patterns by factorization of national characters." Journal of Abnormal and Social Psychology, Vol. 44 (October, 1949), 443-69.

———. "The principle culture patterns discoverable in the syntal dimensions of existing nations." Journal of Social Psychology, Vol. 32 (November, 1950), 215-53.

———. "A quantitative analysis of the changes in the culture pattern of Great Britain, 1837-1937, by p-technique." Acta Psychologica, Vol. 9 (1953), 99-121.

Cattell, Raymond B., H. Bruel, and H.P. Hartmen. "An attempt at more refined definitions of the cultural dimensions of syntality in modern nations." American Sociological Review, Vol. 17 (August, 1951), 408-421.

Cattell, Raymond B. and Marvin Adelson. "The dimensions of social change in the U.S.A. as determined by P-technique." Social Forces, Vol. 30 (1951), 190-201.

Cattell, Raymond B. and Richard Gorsuch. "The definition and measurement of national morale and morality." Journal of Social Psychology, Vol. 67 (1965), 77-96.

Chadwick, Richard W. "International Involvement: Steps Toward the Quantitative Measurement and Explanation of International Politics." Dimensionality of Nations Project Research Report No. 37, Honolulu: University of Hawaii, July, 1972.

Chan, Steve. "An Assessment of Interstate Conflict Coverage of Event Data Projects: The CREON Data." Sponsored by the Advanced Research Projects Agency, Contract No. N00014-75-C-0846: Department of Political Science, University of Maryland, n.d.

Choi, Chang-Yoon. "The contemporary foreign behavior of the United States and Soviet Union: An application of status field theory." Ph.D. dissertation, Honolulu: University of Hawaii, 1973. Also excerpted in Rummel (1977).

———. "Interactions among the East Asian actors and their impacts on the Korean peninsula." Unification Policy Quarterly, (Research Center for Peace and Unification, Seoul, Korea), Vol. 1, (1975), 96-121.

———. "Theoretical perspectives on the development of Soviet-Korean relations." Problems of Korean Unification, 1 (August, 1976), 91-111.

Choucri, Nazli. Population Dynamics and International Violence: Propositions, Insights, and Evidence. Lexington, Mass: D.C. Heath and Company, 1974.

Choucri, Nazli and Robert C. North. Nations in Conflict: National Growth and International Violence. San Francisco: W.H. Freeman and Co., 1974.

Churchill, Winston. The Gathering Storm. Boston: Houghton Mifflin Company, 1948.

Clausewitz, Karl von. On War. (Translated by O.J. Matthijs Jolles), New York: Modern Library, 1943.

Clemens, Walter C., Jr. "Underlying Factors in Soviet Arms Control Policy; Problems of the Systematic Analysis." Peace Research Society: Papers, Vol. 6 (1966), 51-70.

Cobb, Roger W. and Charles Elder. International Community: A Regional and Global Study. New York: Holt, Reinhart and Winston, 1970.

Cobb, Stephen. "The impact of defense spending on senatorial voting behavior: A study of foreign policy feedback," in Patrick J. McGowan (Ed.), Sage International Yearbook of Foreign Policy Studies, Vol. 1. Beverly Hills: Sage Publications, 1973, 135-159.

Coleman, James S. Introduction to Mathematical Sociology. Glencoe: The Free Press, 1964.

Collins, John N. "Foreign conflict behavior and domestic disorder in Africa," in Jonathon Wilkenfeld (Ed.), *Conflict Behavior and Linkage Politics.* New York: David McKay Co., 1973, 251-293.

Conquest, Robert. *The Great Terror.* New York: Macmillan, 1968.

Coplin, William D., Charles W. Kegley, Jr. (Eds.). *A Multi-Method Introduction to International Politics.* Chicago: Markham, 1971.

Coplin, William D. and J. Martin Rochester. "The permanent court of international justice, the International Court of Justice, the League of Nations, and the United Nations: A comparative empirical survey." American Political Science Review, Vol. 66 (June, 1972), 529-550.

Copson, Raymond W. "Foreign policy conflict among African states, 1964-1969," in Patrick J. McGowan (Ed.), *Sage International Yearbook of Foreign Policy Studies,* Vol. 1. Beverly Hills: Sage Publications, 1973, 189-217.

Coser, Lewis A. *The Functions of Social Conflict.* Glencoe, Ill.: The Free Press, 1956.

———. "The termination of conflict." Journal of Conflict Resolution, Vol. 5 (December, 1961), 347-353.

Cutler, Neal E. "Generational succession as a source of foreign policy attitudes: A cohort analysis of American opinion, 1946-66." Journal of Peace Research, 1 (1970), 33-47.

Dahl, Karl Nandrup. "The role of I.L.O. standards in the global integration process." Journal of Peace Research, 4 (1968), 309-351.

Dahl, Robert A. and Edward R. Tufte. *Size and Democracy.* Stanford: Stanford University Press, 1973.

Denton, F.H. "Some regularities in international conflict, 1820-1949." Journal of the International Studies Association, Vol. 9 (February, 1966), 283-296.

———. *Patterns in political violence and war: 1751-1960.* Ph.D. dissertation: University of Southern California, August, 1968.

———. *Factors in International System Violence—1750 to 1960.* Santa Monica, Calif. The RAND Corporation, October, 1969.

Denton, Frank H. and Warren Phillips. "Some patterns in the history of violence." The Journal of Conflict Resolution, Vol. 12 (June, 1968), 182-195.

Deutsch, Karl W. and Dieter Senghaas. "The steps to war: A survey of system levels, decision stages, and research results," in Patrick J. McGowan (Ed.), *Sage International Yearbook of Foreign Policy Studies,* Vol. 1. Beverly Hills: Sage Publications, 1973, 275-329.

Deutsch, Morton and Lois Biener. "Differences in Perceived Similarity of Nations." Technical Memorandum MM 69-1221-21, Bell Telephone Laboratories, November 28, 1969.

Dewey, E.R. "A new cycle in war discovered." Cycles, Vol. 13 (February, 1962), 33-40.

———. "The 17.7 year cycle in war 600 B.C. - A.D. 1957." Research Bulletin 1962-4, Pittsburgh, Penn.: Foundation for the Study of Cycles, 1964.

———. "A review of the research on the war index." Cycles, Vol. 17 (November, 1966), 248-256.

———. "More about cycles in war." Cycles, Vol. 20 (April, 1969), 91-95.

———. "Evidence of cyclic patterns in an index of international battles, 600 B.C. - A.D. 1957." Cycles, Volume 21 (June, 1970), 121-158.

———. "A study of possible cyclic patterns in human aggressiveness leading to National and International Conflicts." Journal of Interdisciplinary Cycle Research, Vol. 2 (March, 1971), 17-21.

Donelan, M.D. and M.J. Grieve. *International Disputes: Case Histories 1945-1970.* New York: St. Martin's Press, 1973.

Dowty, Alan. "Conflict in war-potential politics: An approach to historical macroanalysis." Peace Research Society (International): Papers, Vol. 13 (1970), 85-103.

———. "Foreign-linked factionalism as a historical pattern." The Journal of Conflict Resolution, Vol. 15 (December, 1971), 429-442.

———. "The application of international guarantees to the Egypt-Israel conflict." The Journal of Conflict Resolution, Vol. 14 (June, 1972), 253-267.

Duncan, George T. and Randolph M. Siverson. "Markov Chain Models for Conflict Analysis: Results from Sino-Indian Relations, 1959-1964." International Studies Quarterly, Vol. 19 (September, 1975), 344-374.

East, Maurice A. "Rank-dependent interaction and mobility: Two aspects of international stratification." Peace Research Society (International): Papers, Vol. 14 (1970), 113-28.

———. "Status discrepancy and violence in the international system: An empirical analysis." in James N. Rosenau, Vincent Davis, and Maurice A. East (Eds.), The Analysis of International Politics. New York: The Free Press, 1972, 299-319.

———. "Size and foreign policy behavior: A test of two models." World Politics, Vol. 25 (July, 1973), 556-576.

East, Maurice A. and Phillip M. Gregg. "Factors influencing cooperation and conflict in the international system" International Studies Quarterly, Vol. 2 (September, 1967), 244-269.

East, Maurice A. and Charles F. Hermann. "Do nation-types account for foreign policy behavior?" in James N. Rosenau (Ed.). Comparing Foreign Policies: Theories, Findings, and Methods. New York: Halsted Press, 1974, 269-303.

Eckhardt, William. "The factor of militarism." Journal of Peace Research, 2 (1969), 123-132.

———. "Primitive militarism." Journal of Peace Research, Vol. 12, 1 (1975), 55-62.

Erb, Eugene A., Jr. "Forecasting and factor analysis." Mission Identification Program: Phase I–Long Range Forecasting, Holloman Air Force Base, New Mexico: Office of Research Analysis, United States Air Force, December, 1968.

Etzioni, Amitai. "On self-encapsulating conflicts." The Journal of Conflict Resolution, Vol. 8 (September, 1964), 242-255.

Feierabend, Ivo K. and Rosalind L. Feierabend. "Aggressive behaviors within politics, 1948-1962: A cross-national Study." The Journal of Conflict Resolution, Vol. 10 (September, 1966), 249-271.

Feierabend, Ivo K., Rosalind L. Feierabend, and Ted Robert Gurr (Eds.). Anger, Violence, and Politics. Englewood Cliffs, N.J.: Prentice-Hall, 1972, 136-183.

Ferris, Wayne H. The Power Capabilities of Nation-States: International Conflict and War. Lexington, Mass.: Lexington Books, 1973.

Field, John Osgood. "The Sino-Indian border conflict: An exploratory analysis of action and perception," in J.H. Sigler, J.O. Field, and M.L. Adelman, Applications of Events Data Analysis. Beverly Hills: Sage, 1972.

Fitzsimmons, Barbara J. "The role of violence in international conflicts." Support Study #1, World Event/Interaction Survey Project, University of Southern California, March, 1969.

Galtung, Johan. "Foreign policy opinion as a function of social position." Peace Research Society (International): Papers, Vol. 2 (1965), 206-231.

———. "East-West interaction patterns." Journal of Peace Research, 2 (1966), 146-177.

———. "On the effects of international economic sanctions with examples from the case of Rhodesia." World Politics, Vol. 19 (April, 1967), 378-416.

Gamson, William A. and Andre Modigliani. "Soviet responses to Western foreign policy, 1946-53." Peace Research Society (International): Papers, Vol. 3 (1965), 47-78.

———. "Some aspects of Soviet-Western conflict." Peace Research Society (International): Papers, Vol. 9 (1968), 9-24.

———. *Untangling the Cold War: A Strategy for Testing Rival Theories.* Boston: Little, Brown, and Co., 1971.

Gibb, C.A. "Changes in the culture patterns of Australia, 1906-1946, as determined by P-technique." Journal of Social Psychology. Vol. 43 (1956), 225-238.

Gitelson, Susan Aurelia. "Why do small states break diplomatic relations with outside powers?" International Studies Quarterly, Vol. 18 (December, 1974), 451-484.

Gleditsch, Nils Petter. "Rank theory, field theory, attribute theory." Paper Presented to the Conference on Secondary Data Analysis, Institute for Vergleichende Sozialforschung, Cologne, West Germany, May 26-31, 1969.

———. "Rank Theory, Field Theory, Attribute Theory: Three Approaches to Interaction in the International System." Research Report No. 47, Honolulu: Dimensionality of Nations Project, University of Hawaii, 1970.

Goldman, Kjell. "East-West tension in Europe, 1946-1970: A conceptual analysis and a quantitative description." World Politics, Vol. 26 (October, 1973), 106-125.

Gough, J.W. *The Social Contract.* Oxford: Clarendon Press, 1957.

Greaves, Fielding L., "Peace in our time—Fact or fable." Military Review (December, 1962), 55-58.

Gregg, Phillip and Arthur S. Banks, "Dimensions of political systems: Factor analysis of a cross-polity survey." The American Political Science Review, Vol. 59 (September, 1965), 602-613.

Gross, Feliks. *Foreign Policy Analysis.* New York: Philosophical Library, Inc., 1954.

Gurr, Ted Robert. "A comparative study of civil strife," in Hugh Davis Graham and Ted Robert Gurr (Eds.), *Violence in America.* New York: Bantam Books, 1969, 572-632.

Haas, Ernst, Robert L. Butterworth, and Joseph S. Nye. *Conflict Management by International Organizations.* Morristown, N.J.: General Learning Press, 1972.

Haas, Michael. "Societal approaches to the study of war." Journal of Peace Research, 4 (1965), 307-323.

———. "International subsystems: stability and polarity." The American Political Science Review, Vol. 64 (March, 1970), 98-123.

———. *International Conflict.* New York: The Bobbs-Merrill Co., 1974.

Haendel, Dan, Gerald T. West, with Robert G. Meadow. *Overseas Investment and Political Risk.* Philadelphia: Foreign Policy Research Institute Monograph Series, No. 21, 1975.

Hall, Dennis and R.J. Rummel. "The Dynamics of Dyadic Foreign Conflict Behavior, 1955 to 1963." Research Report No. 16, Honolulu: Dimensionality of Nations Project, University of Hawaii, 1969.

———. "The patterns of dyadic foreign conflict for 1963." Multivariable Behavioral Research, Vol. 5 (July, 1970), 275-294.

Halle, Louis J. *The Cold War as History.* New York: Harper and Row, 1967.

Halle, Nils H. "Social position and foreign policy attitudes." Journal of Peace Research, 1 (1966), 46-74.

Halloran, James D., *et al. Demonstrations and Communications: A Case Study.* Harmondsworth: Penguin Books, 1970.

Hannah, Herbert. "Some Dimensions of International Conflict Settlement Procedures and Outcomes." Research Report No. 11, Dimensionality of Nations Project, Honolulu: University of Hawaii, 1968.

———. *Some dimensions of International Conflicts, 1914-1965: The Prediction of Outcomes.* Ph.D. dissertation, Honolulu: The University of Hawaii, 1972.

Harf, James E. "Internation conflict resolution and national attributes," in James N.

Rosenau (Ed.), *Comparing Foreign Policies: Theories, Findings, and Methods.* New York: Halsted Press, 1974, 305-325.

Harf, James E., David G. Hoovler, Thomas E. James, Jr. "Systemic and external attributes in foreign policy analysis," in James N. Rosenau (Ed.), *Comparing Foreign Policies: Theories, Findings, and Methods.* New York: Halsted Press, 1974, 235-249.

Hart, Hornell. "Depression, war, and logistic social trends." American Journal of Sociology, Vol. 52 (September, 1946), 112-122.

———. "The logistic growth of political areas." Social Forces, Vol. 26 (May, 1948), 398-405.

Hart, Jeffrey. "Symmetry and polarization in the European international system, 1870-1879: A methodological study." Journal of Peace Research, Vol. 11, No. 3 (1974), 229-244.

Hayek, F.A. *Law, Legislation and Liberty,* Vol. 1-2. Chicago: The University of Chicago Press, 1973-1976.

Hazlewood, Leo A. "Externalizing systematic stress: International conflict as adaptive Behavior," in Jonathan Wilkenfeld (Ed.), *Conflict Behavior and Linkage Politics.* New York: David McKay Company, 1973, 148-190.

———. "An appraisal of the methodology and statistical practices used in the dimensionality of nations project," in Francis W. Hoole and Dina A. Zinnes, *Quantitative International Politics.* New York: Praeger, 1976, 176-195.

Hazlewood, Leo A. and Gerald T. West. "Bivariate associations, factor structures, and substantive impact." International Studies Quarterly, Vol. 18 (September, 1974), 317-337.

Healy, Brian and Arthur Stein. "The balance of power in international history." The Journal of Conflict Resolution, Vol. 17 (March, 1973), 33-61.

Hefner, Robert, Sheldon G. Levy, and H. Lester Warner. "A survey of internationally relevant attitudes and behaviors," Peace Research Society (International): Papers, Vol. 7 (1967), 139-150.

Hermann, Charles F. "What is a foreign policy event?" in Wolfram F. Hanrieder, *Comparative Foreign Policy: Theoretical Essays.* New York: David McKay, 1971.

———. "Policy classification: A key to the study of foreign policy," in James N. Rosenau, *et al., The Analysis of International Politics.* New York: Free Press, 1972, 58-79.

———. "Comparing the Foreign Policy Events of Nations," in Charles Kegley, Jr., Gregary A. Raymond, Robert M. Rood, and Richard Skinner, *International Events and the Comparative Analysis of Foreign Policy.* Columbia, South Carolina: University of South Carolina Press, 1975, 145-158.

Hermann, Charles, Maurice East, Margaret G. Hermann, Barbara G. Salmore, and Stephen A. Salmore. "CREON: A foreign events data set." *Sage Professional Papers in International Studies,* 2, 02-024, Beverly Hills, Sage Publications, 1973.

Hermann, Margaret G. "Leader personality and foreign policy behavior," in James N. Rosenau (Ed.), *Comparing Foreign Policies: Theories, Findings, and Methods.* New York: Halsted Press, 1974, 201-234.

Herz, John H. *Political Realism and Political Idealism: A Study in Theories and Realities.* Chicago: The University of Chicago Press, 1959.

Hill, Kim Quaile. "Domestic politics, international linkages, and military expenditures: A cross-national analysis." Presented to the annual meeting of the International Studies Association, St. Louis, Missouri, March, 1977.

Hilsman, Roger. *To Move a Nation.* New York: Dell Publishing Co., 1964.

Hilton, Gordon. "The 1914 studies—A re-assessment of the evidence and some further thoughts." Peace Research Society (International): Papers, Vol. 13 (1970), 117-141.

———. "A review of the dimensionality of nations project." *Sage Professional Papers in International Studies* 02-015, Beverly Hills: Sage Publications, 1973.

———. "An appraisal of the philosophy of science and research design involved in the dimensionality of nations project," in Francis W. Hoole and Dina A. Zinnes, *Quantitative International Politics*. New York: Praeger, 1976, 155-175.

Hinsley, F.H. *Power and the Pursuit of Peace*. London: Cambridge University Press, 1963 (September, 1967).

Hobbes, Thomas. *Leviathan, Parts I and II*. New York: Bobbs-Merrill, 1958.

Hoffmann, Stanley (Ed.). *Contemporary Theory in International Relations*. Englewood Cliffs, N.J.: Prentice-Hall, Inc., 1960.

———. *The State of War*. New York: Praeger, 1965.

Hoggard, Gary. "Differential source coverage in foreign policy analysis," in James N. Rosenau, *Comparing Foreign Policies: Theories, Findings, and Methods*. New York: Halsted Press, 1974, 353-381.

Hollist, W. Ladd. "An analysis of arms processes in the United States and the Soviet Union." *International Studies Quarterly*, Vol. 21, (September, 1977), 503-528.

Holsti, K.J. "Resolving international conflicts: A taxonomy of behavior and some figures on procedures." The Journal of Conflict Resolution, Vol. 10 (September, 1966), 272-296.

———. "National role conceptions in the study of foreign policy." International studies Quarterly, Vol. 14 (September, 1970), 233-309.

———. *International Politics: A Framework for Analysis*, Englewood Cliffs, N.J.: Prentice-Hall, 1977.

Holsti, Ole R. "The belief system and national images: A case study." The Journal of Conflict Resolution, Vol. 6 (September, 1962), 244-52.

———. "East-West conflict and Sino-Soviet relations." The Journal of Applied Behavioral Science, Vol. 1 (April-May-June, 1965), 115-130.

———. *Crisis, Escalation, War*. Montreal, Canada: McGill-Queen's University Press, 1972.

Holsti, Ole R., Richard A. Brody, and Robert C. North. "The management of international crisis: Affect and action in American-Soviet relations," in Dean G. Pruitt and Richard C. Snyder (Eds.), *Theory and Research on the Causes of War*. Englewood Cliffs, N.J.: Prentice-Hall, (1969), 62-79.

Holsti, Ole R., P. Terrence Hopmann, and John D. Sullivan. *Unity and Disintegration in International Alliances: Comparative Studies*. New York: Wiley & Sons, 1973.

Hoole, Francis W. and Dina A. Zinnes (Eds.), *Quantitative International Politics: An Appraisal*. New York: Praeger, 1976.

Hopple, Gerald W., Jonathan Wilkenfeld, Paul J. Rossa and Robert N. McClauley. "Frameworks and analytic strategies in the study of foreign policy." Presented to the annual meeting of the Southern Political Science Association, Atlanta, Georgia, November 4-6, 1976.

Horvath, William J. "A statistical model for the duration of wars and strikes." Behavioral Science, Vol. 13 (January, 1968), 18-28.

Horvath, William J. and Caxton C. Foster. "Stochastic models of war alliances." The Journal of Conflict Resolution, Vol. 7 (June, 1963), 110-116.

Huntington, Samuel. "Arms races: Prerequisites and results." Public Policy, Vol. 8 (1958), 41-86.

Ikle, Fred C. *How Nations Negotiate*. New York: Harper and Row, 1964.

———. *Every War Must End*. New York: Columbia University Press, 1971.

Jarvad, Ib Martin. "Power versus equality," in *Proceedings of the International Peace Research Association Second Conference*, Vol. 1, Assen, Netherlands: Van Gorcum & Comp. N.V., 1968, 297-314.

Jensen, Lloyd. "American foreign policy elites and the prediction of international events." Peace Research Society (International): Papers, Vol. V (1966), 199-209.

Jervis, Robert. *The Logic of Images in International Relations*. Princeton: Princeton University Press, 1970.

Jones, Susan D. and J. David Singer. *Beyond Conjecture in International Politics*. Itasca, Ill.: F.E. Peacock Publishers, 1972.

Kahn, Herman. *On Escalation: Metaphors and Scenarios*. New York: Praeger, 1965.

———, *et al.* "War Termination Issues and Concepts." Harmon-on-Hudson, New York: Hudson Institute, 1968.

Kean, James G. and Patrick J. McGowan. "National attributes and foreign policy participation: A path analysis," in Patrick J. McGowan (Ed.), *Sage International Yearbook of Foreign Policy Studies*, Vol. 1. Beverly Hills: Sage Publications, 1973, 189-217.

Kegley, Charles W., Jr. "Chinese behavior in the context of the pattern of foreign policy interactions in Asia: A quantitative assessment," in Roger L. Dial (Ed.), *Advancing and Contending Approaches to the Study of Chinese Foreign Policy*. Halifax, Canada: Center for Foreign Policy Studies, Dalhousie University, 1974.

———. "Introduction: The Generation and Use of Events Data," in Charles Kegley, Jr., Gregory A. Raymond, Robert M. Rood, and Richard Skinner. *International Events and the Comparative Analysis of Foreign Policy*. Columbia, South Carolina: University of South Carolina Press, 1975, 91-105.

Kegley, Charles, Jr., Stephen A. Salmore, and David J. Rosen. Convergences in the measurement of interstate behavior," in Patrick J. McGowan (Ed.), *Sage International Yearbook of Foreign Policy Studies*, Vol. 2 Beverly Hills: Sage Publications, 1974, 309-339.

Kegley, Charles W., *et al*, (Eds.). *International Events and the Comparative Analysis of Foreign Policy*. Columbia, South Carolina: University of South Carolina Press, 1975.

Kegley, Charles W. Jr., and Llewellyn D. Howell, Jr. "The dimensionality of regional integration: Construct validation in the Southeast Asian context." Paper, n.d.

Keim, Willard D. "Nations and conflict individuality." Journal of Peace Research, 3-4 (1971), 287-292.

Keim, Willard and R.J. Rummel. "Dynamic Patterns of Nation Conflict 1955-1963." Research Report No. 27, Dimensionality of Nations Project, Honolulu: University of Hawaii, 1969.

Kende, Istvan. "Ninety-Seven local wars in twenty-five years: 1945-69." Budapest: Karl Marx University, International Peace Research Institute, Paper, n.d.

———. "Twenty-five years of local wars." Journal of Peace Research, 1 (1971), 5-22.

Kissinger, Henry. "Morai purposes and policy choices." Department of State Bulletin, Vol. 69 (October 29, 1973), 525-31.

Klingberg, Frank L. "Predicting the termination of war: Battle casualties and population losses." The Journal of Conflict Resolution, Vol. 10 (June, 1966), 129-171.

Köhler, Gernot. *Events Research and War/Peace Prediction*. Oakville-Dundas, Ontario, Canada: Canadian Peace Research Institute, 1973.

Kuhn, Thomas S. *The Structure of Scientific Revolutions*. Chicago: University of Chicago Press, 1962.

Lasswell, Harold D. " 'Inevitable' war: A problem in the control of long-range expectations." World Politics, Vol. 2 (October, 1949), 1-39.

Lasswell, Harold D. and Abraham Kaplan. *Power and Society: A Framework for Political Inquiry*. New Haven, Conn.: Yale University Press, 1950.

Laulicht, Jerome. "An analysis of canadian foreign policy attitudes." Peace Research Society (International): Papers, Vol. 3 (1965), 121-136.

———. "Public Opinion and Foreign Policy Decisions." Journal of Peace Research, 2 (1965a), 147-160.

Lauren, Paul Gordon. "Ultimata and coercive diplomacy." International Studies Quarterly, Vol. 16 (June, 1972), 131-165.

Leavitt, Michael Rohrlich. *Towards the Development of an Empirical Index of Hostility and Friendship Between States.* Master's thesis, Department of Political Science, Wayne State University, 1968.

Leng, Russel J. and Robert A. Goodsell. "Behavioral indicators of war proneness in bilateral conflicts," in Patrick J. McGowan (Ed.), *Sage International Yearbook of Foreign Policy Studies,* Vol. 2 Beverly Hills: Sage Publications, 1974, 191-226.

Lentner, Howard H. "The concept of crisis as viewed by the United States Department of State," in Charles F. Hermann (Ed.), *International Crises: Insights from Behavioral Research.* New York: The Free Press, 1972, 112-135.

Levine, Mark. "The characterization of alternative eras in the international system, 1880-1965: Varying patterns of attribute interdependency." Presented to the annual meeting of the American Political Science Association, New Orleans, September 4-8, 1973.

Lindsay, Franklin A. "Program planning: The missing element," in Bernard C. Cohen (ed.), *Foreign Policy in American Government.* Boston and Toronto: Little, Brown and Company, 1965.

Liska, George. "International equilibrium," in Stanley Hoffman, *Contemporary Theory in International Relations.* Englewood Cliffs, N.J.: Prentice-Hall, 1960, 137-149.

Locke, John. *Of Civil Government: Second Essay,* New York: Henry Regnery Company, 1955.

Luard, Evan. *Conflict and Peace in the Modern International System.* Boston: Little, Brown and Co., 1968.

Mahoney, Robert B., Jr. "American political-military operations and the structure of the international system, 1946-1975." Paper presented to the annual meeting of the section on Military Studies, International Studies Association, Ohio State University, October, 1976.

———. "European perceptions and East-West competition." Paper presented to the annual meeting of the International Studies Association, St. Louis, Mo., March, 1977.

Mangone, Gerald J. *A Short History of International Organization.* New York: McGraw-Hill, 1954.

Manheim, Henry L. "Intergroup interaction as related to status and leadership differences between groups." Sociometry, Vol. 23 (December, 1960), 415-427.

Mansbach, Richard W., Yale H. Ferguson, and Donald E. Lampert. *The Web of World Politics.* Englewood Cliffs, N.J.: Prentice Hall, 1976.

Martin, John L. and Harold L. Nelson. "The historical standard in analyzing press performance." Journalism Quarterly, Vol. 33 (1956), 456-466.

Martin, Leo. "The problem of war causation." American Catholic Sociological Review, Vol. 3 (1942), 231-243.

Masters, Roger D. "World politics as a primitive political system." World Politics, Vol. 16 (July, 1964), 595-619.

McClelland, Charles A. "Access to Berlin: The quantity and variety of events, 1948-1963," in J. David Singer (Ed.), *Quantitative International Politics: Insights and Evidence.* New York: The Free Press, 1968, 159-186.

———. "The beginning, duration, and abatement of international crises: Comparisons in two conflict areas," in Charles F. Hermann (Ed.), *International Crises: Insights from Behavioral Research.* New York: The Free Press, 1972, 83-105.

McClelland, Charles A., *et al.* "The Communist Chinese Performance in Crisis and Non-Crisis: Quantitative Studies of the Taiwan Straits Confrontation, 1950-1964." Final Report of Completed Research Under Contract for Behavioral Sciences Group, Naval

Ordnance Test Station, China Lake, California (N 60530-11207), 1965.

McClelland, Charles A. and Gary Hoggard. "Conflict patterns in the interactions among nations," in James N. Rosenau (Ed.), *International Politics and Foreign Policy,* Revised Edition, New York: The Free Press, 1969, 711-724.

McClelland, Charles A. and Anne Ancoli. "An interaction survey of the Middle East." Paper, Department of International Relations, University of Southern California, March, 1970.

McClelland, Charles A. and Robert A. Young. "The Flow of International Events." Interim Technical Report, Prepared in Support of Office of Naval Research Contract # N 0014-67-A-0269-0004, University of Southern California, January, 1970.

McClelland, Charles A., *et al. The Management and Analysis of International Event Data: A Computerized System for Monitoring and Projecting Event Flows.* School of International Relations, University of Southern California, September, 1971.

McCormick, David M. *Decisions, Events and Perceptions in International Crises,* Vol I. Final Report of a Project funded by ARPA, N00014-75-C-0328, Ann Arbor, Michigan: First Ann Arbor Corporation, 1975.

McCormick, James M. "Evaluating models of crisis behavior." International Studies Quarterly, Vol. 19 (March, 1975), 17-45.

McGowan, Patrick J. "Dimensions of African foreign policy behavior: In search of dependence." Presented to the annual meeting of the Canadian Association of Africa Studies, Ottawa, February 16-18, 1973.

McGowan, Patrick J. and Howard B. Shapiro. *The Comparative Study of Foreign Policy: A Survey of Scientific Findings.* Beverly Hills: Sage Publications, 1973.

McGowan, Patrick J. and Robert M. Rood. "Alliance behavior in balance of power systems: Applying a poisson model to nineteenth-century Europe." The American Political Science Review, Vol. 69 (September, 1975), 859-870.

McGowan, Patrick J. and Michael K. O'Leary. "Methods and data for the comparative analysis of foreign policy," in Charles Kegley, Jr., Gregary A. Raymond, Robert M. Rood, and Richard Skinner, *International Events and the Comparative Analysis of Foreign Policy.* Columbia, South Carolina: University of South Carolina Press, 1975, 243-279.

McKenna, Joseph C. *Diplomatic Protest in Foreign Policy: Analysis and Case Studies.* Chicago: Loyola University Press, 1962.

Melko, Matthew. *52 Peaceful Societies.* Oakville, Ontario: Canadian Peace Research Institute, 1973.

Merritt, Richard L. and Donald J. Puchala. *Western European Perspectives on International Affairs.* New York: Praeger, 1968.

Midlarsky, Manus I. "Power, uncertainty, and the onset of international violence." The Journal of Conflict Resolution, Vol. 18 (September, 1974), 395-431.

———. *On War: Political Violence in the International System.* New York: The Free Press, 1975.

Michalka, Michael. "Hostilities in the European state system, 1816-1970." Peace Research Society (International): Papers, Vol. 26 (1976), 100-116.

Milovidov, A.S. and Kozlov, V.G. (Eds.). *The Philosophical Heritage of V.I. Lenin and Problems of Contemporary War.* Moscow: 1972 (Translated and Published under the auspices of the United States Air Force, U.S. Government Office, Stock No. 0870-00343).

Milstein, Jeffrey S. "American and Soviet influence, balance of power, and Arab-Israeli violence," in Bruce Russett (Ed.), *Peace, War, and Numbers.* Beverly Hills: Sage Publications, 1972, 139-166.

Modigliani, Andre. "Hawks and doves, isolationism and political distrust: An analysis of public opinion on military policy." The American Political Science Review, Vol. 56 (September, 1972), 960-978.

Mogdis, Franz. "Project Triad," Bendix Aerospace Systems Division, Contract F44620-68-C-0083 for AFXDOC, USAF, circa 1969.

———. "The verbal dimension in Sino-Soviet relations: A time-series analysis." Presented to the annual meeting of the American Political Science Association, Los Angeles, California, September 8-12, 1970.

Moore, David W. Governmental and societal influences on foreign policy in open and closed systems," in James N. Rosenau (Ed.), *Comparing Foreign Policies: Theories, Findings, and Methods*. New York: Halsted Press, 1974, 171-199.

———. "National attributes and nation typologies: A look at the Rosenau genotypes," in James N. Rosenau (Ed.), *Comparing Foreign Policies: Theories, Findings, and Methods*. New York: Halsted Press, 1974a, 251-267.

Moore, James A. "Attention and Interaction in the International System: A Case Study." Support Study No. 3, World Event/Interaction Survey Project: Department of International Relations, University of Southern California, June, 1970.

Moore, James A. and Robert A. Young. "Some Preliminary Short-Term Predictions of International Interactions." Working Paper # 1, World Event/Interaction Survey Project: University of Southern California, September, 1969.

Moore, James A., Rachel Comperi, Anne Gilar, Jeffrey Krend, Vivian Moore, and Theodore Rubin. *Crisis Inventory*. Final Report Prepared for the Defense Advanced Research Projects Agency, Arlington, Va., Consolidated Analysis Centers, Inc., August, 1975.

Morgenthau, Hans J. "The mainsprings of American foreign policy: The national interest vs. moral abstractions." The American Political Science Review, Vol. 44 (December, 1950), 833-854.

———. *Politics Among Nations*. New York: Knopf, 1962.

Morse, Edward L. "The transformation of foreign policies: Modernization, interdependence, and externalization." World Politics, Vol. 22 (April, 1970), 371-392.

Most, Benjamin A. and Harvey Starr. "Techniques for the detection of diffusion: Geo-political considerations in the spread of war." Paper presented to the annual meeting of the International Studies Association, Toronto, February 25-29, 1976.

———. "The Spread of War: An Empirical Critique of the Poisson/Modified Poisson Approach to the Study of Diffusion." Reports and Research Studies, Bloomington, Indiana: Center for International Policy Studies, Indiana University, n.d.

Mueller, John E. "Trends in popular support for the wars in Korea and Vietnam." The American Political Science Review, Vol. 65 (June, 1971), 358-375.

Munton, Don. "Multiple source coverage and international events analysis: Patterns versus frequencies in assessing validity." Paper presented to the annual meeting of the International Studies Association, New York, March, 1973.

Naroll, Raoul. "Does military deterence deter?" Trans-Action, Vol. 3 (January-February, 1966), 14-20.

———. "Imperial cycles and world order." Peace Research Society (International): Paper, Vol. 7 (1967), 83-101.

———. "What have we learned from cross-cultural surveys?" American Anthropologist, Vol. 72 (December, 1970), 1227-1288.

———. "Warfare, peaceful intercourse and territorial change: A cross-cultural survey." Evanston, Ill. Institute for Cross-Cultural Studies, Northwestern University, paper, n.d.

Naroll, Raoul, Vern L. Bullough, and Frada Naroll. *Military Deterrence in History*. Albany, New York: State University of New York Press, 1974.

Newcombe, Alan and James Wert. *An Inter-Nation Tensionmeter for the Prediction of War*. Oakville, Ontario: Canadian Peace Research Institute, 1972.

North, Robert C., and Choucri, Nazli. "Population and the international system: Some implications for United States policy and planning." Paper submitted to the Commission on Population Growth and the American Future, 726 Jackson Place, N.W., Washington, D.C., August 15, 1971.

Northedge, F.S. and M.D. Donelan. *International Disputes: The Political Aspects.* New York: St. Martin's Press, 1971.

Nye, J.S. *Peace in Parts: Integration and Conflict in Regional Organization.* Boston: Little, Brown and Company, 1971.

Oliva, Gary and R.J. Rummel. "Foreign Conflict Patterns and Types for 1963." Research Report No. 22, Dimensionality of Nations Project, Honolulu: University of Hawaii, 1969.

Omen, George E. Jr. *A Forecasting Model of International Conflict.* Ph.D. dissertation, Honolulu, Hawaii: University of Hawaii, 1975.

Onate, Andres D. "The conflict interactions of the People's Republic of China 1950-1970." The Journal of Conflict Resolution, Vol. 18 (December, 1974), 578-594.

Organski, A.F.K. *World Politics.* New York: Alfred A. Knopf, 1958.

Osgood, Charles E. *An Alternative to War or Surrender.* Urbana: University of Illinois Press, 1962.

Otterbein, Keith F. "Cross-cultural studies of armed combat," in Glenn H. Snyder (Ed.), *Studies in International Conflict.* Research Monograph No. 1, Buffalo, New York: Center for International Security and Conflict Studies, State University of New York at Buffalo, 1968.

–––. *The Evolution of War: A Cross-Cultural Study.* Human Relations Area Files Press, 1970.

Park, Tong-Whan. *Asian Conflict in Systematic Perspective: Applications of Field Theory (1955 and 1963).* Ph.D. dissertation, Honolulu, University of Hawaii, 1969.

–––. "Peaceful Interactions in Asia: The Delineation of Nation Groups." Research Report No. 32, The Dimensionality of Nations Project, Honolulu: University of Hawaii, 1969a.

–––. "Measuring dynamic patterns of development: The case of Asia, 1949-1968." Presented to the American Political Science Association Annual Meeting, Los Angeles, September 7-12, 1970.

–––. "The role of distance in international relations: A new look at the social field theory." Behavioral Science, Vol. 17 (July, 1972), 337-348.

–––. "Measuring the dynamic patterns of development: The case of Asia 1949-1968." Multivariate Behavioral Research Vol. 8, (April, 1973), 227-251.

Park, Tong-Whan and D. Scott Ross. "Asia as a conflict arena in global perspective: Dynamics of intra-and inter-regional confrontation." Paper, Evanston, Illinois: Northwestern University, October 1971.

Park, Yong-Ok. *The Structural Balance of the International System–1950-1965.* Ph.D. dissertation, Honolulu, Hawaii: University of Hawaii, 1975.

Parsons, Talcott and E.A. Shills (Eds.). *Toward a General Theory of Action.* Cambridge: Harvard University Press, 1951.

Parsons, Talcott. *Structure of Social Action.* Glencoe: Free Press, 1958.

Payne, James L. *The American Threat: The Fear of War as an Instrument of Foreign Policy.* Chicago: Markham Publishing Company, 1970.

Peterson, Sophia. "Events, mass opinion, and elite attitudes," in Richard Merritt (ed.), *Communication in International Politics.* Urbana: University of Illinois Press, 1972.

Phillips, Warren R. *Dynamic Patterns of International Conflict.* Ph.D. dissertation, Honolulu: University of Hawaii, 1969.

––. "The Dynamics of Behavioral Action and Reaction in International Conflict." Research Report No. 49, Dimensionality of Nations Project, Honolulu: University of Hawaii, 1970.

–––. "Two views of foreign policy interaction: Substantially the same or different?" Paper Presented to Midwest Regional Meeting of the International Studies Association, Toronto, Canada, May 11-13, 1972.

–––. "The conflict environment of nations: A study of conflict inputs to nations in 1963," in Jonathan Wilkenfeld (Ed.), *Conflict Behavior and Linkage Politics*. New York: David McKay Company, 1973, 107-147.

Phillips, Warren and Robert C. Crain. "Dynamic Foreign Policy Interactions: Reciprocity and Uncertainty in Foreign Policy," in Patrick J. McGowan (Ed.), *Sage International Yearbook of Foreign Policy Studies*, Vol. 2, Beverly Hills: Sage Publications, 1974, 227-266.

Phillips, Warren and Michael Hainline. "Crisis typologies: Perspectives from the systems and decision-making approaches." Paper, Columbus, Ohio: Department of Political Science, Ohio State University, 1972.

–––. "Major power conflict exchanges in the sixties: A triadic analysis of the U.S., Soviet, and Chinese sub-system from a comparative foreign policy view." Paper, Columbus, Ohio: Department of Political Science, The Ohio State University, n.d.

Phillips, Warren and Theron Lorimore. "The effect of crises upon the stability of the international system" Paper, Columbus, Ohio: Department of Political Science, Ohio State University, n.d.

Phillipson, Coleman. *Termination of War and Treaties of Peace*. New York: Dunton, 1916.

Pool, Ithiel de Sola. *Symbols of Internatalism*. Stanford: Stanford University Press, 1951.

Powel, Charles A., David Andrus, William A. Fowler, and Kathleen Knight. "Determinants of foreign policy behavior: A causal modeling approach," in James N. Rosenau (Ed.), *Comparing Foreign Policies: Theories, Findings, and Methods* New York: Halsted Press, 1974, pp. 151-170.

Rajan, Vithal. "Variations on a theme by Richardson," in Patrick J. McGowan (Ed.), *Sage International Yearbook of Foreign Policy Studies*, Vol. 2. Beverly Hills: Sage Publications, 1974, 15-45.

Randle, Robert F. *The Origins of Peace: A Study of Peacemaking and the Structure of Peace Settlements*. New York: The Free Press, 1972.

Rashevsky, N. *Mathematical Theory and Human Relations, An Approach to a Mathematical Biology of Social Phenomena*. Bloomington, Indiana: Principia Press, 1947.

–––. *Mathematical Biology of Social Behavior*. Chicago: University of Chicago Press, 1951.

Rawls, John. *A Theory of Justice*. Cambridge, Mass.: The Belknap Press of Harvard University, 1971.

Ray, James Lee. "Status inconsistency and war involvement in Europe, 1816-1970." The Peace Research Society (International): Papers, Vol. 23 (1974), 69-80.

Rhee, Sang Woo. *Communist China's Foreign Behavior: An Application of Field Theory Model II*. Ph.D. dissertation, Honolulu: University of Hawaii, 1971. Also excerpted in Rummel (1977).

–––. "China's Cooperation, Conflict and Interaction Behavior Viewed from Rummel's Field Theory Perspective." in R.J. Rummel, *Field Theory Evolving*. Beverly Hills: Sage Publications, 1977, 371-401.

Richardson, Lewis F. *Arms and Insecurity*. Pittsburg: The Boxwood Press, 1960a.

–––. *Statistics of Deadly Quarrels*. Pittsburg: The Boxwood Press, 1960b.

Richardson, R.P., *et al. An Analysis of Recent Conflicts*. Research Contribution No. 144, Washington, D.C.: Institute for Naval Studies, Center for Naval Analysis, 1966.

Rosecrance, Richard N. *Action and Reaction in World Politics*. Boston: Little Brown & Co, 1963.

Rosen, Steven. "War, Power and the Willingness to Suffer," in Bruce Russett (Ed.), *Peace, War, and Numbers*. Beverly Hills: Sage Publications, 1972, 167-183.

Rosenau, James N. "Private preferences and political responsibilities: The relative potency of individual and role variables in the behavior of U.S. senators," in J. David Singer (Ed.), *Quantitative International Politics: Insights and Evidence.* New York: The Free Press, 1968, 17-50.

Rosenau, James N. and Gary D. Hoggard. "Foreign policy behavior in dyadic relationships: Testing a pre-theoretical extension," in James N. Rosenau (Ed.), *Comparing Foreign Policies: Theories, Findings, and Methods.* New York: Halsted Press, 1974, 117-149.

Rosengren, Karl Erik. "International news: Intra- and extra-media data." Action Sociologica, Vol. 13 (1970), 96-109.

———. "International news: Methods, data and theory." Journal of Peace Research, Vol. 11 (1974), 145-156.

Rubin, Theodore J. and A.H. Schainblatt. "Empirical Development of the Prototype Environmental Information System, Phase I." Interim Research Report, Vol. 1-2, for research sponsored by Directorate of Doctrine, Concepts and Objectives, United States Air Force, Contract No. F44620-68-C-0077. Santa Barbara, California: General Electric TEMPO, 1969.

Rubin, Theodore J. "International Affairs Indicators for Defence Decision-Making." Research Report RM 305, Sponsored by the Advanced Research Projects Agency, Department of Defence, Washington, D.C.: Consolidated Analysis Centers, Inc., 1973.

Ruggie, John Gerard. "The structure of international organization: Contingency, complexity and post-modern form" Peace Research Society (International): Papers, Vol. 18 (1972), 73-91.

Rummel, R.J. "Dimensions of conflict behavior within and between nations." General Systems Yearbook of the Society for General Systems Research, Vol. 8, (1963), 1-50.

———. "Testing some possible predictors of conflict behavior within and between nations." Peace Research Society (International): Papers, Vol. I (1963a), 79-111.

———. "A field theory of social action with application to conflict within nations." General Systems Yearbook of the Society for General Systems Research, Vol. 10 (1965), 183-211. Also excerpted in Rummel (1977).

———. "A Foreign Conflict Code Sheet." World Politics. Vol. 18 (No. 2, 1966), 283-296.

———. "Dimensions of conflict behavior within nations, 1946-1959." The Journal of Conflict Resolution, Vol. 10 (March, 1966a), 65-73.

———. "Dimensions of dyadic war, 1820-1952." The Journal of Conflict Resolution, Vol. 11 (June, 1967), 176-183.

———. "Research communication: Some attributes and behavioral patterns of nations." Journal of Peace Research, vol. 4 (no. 2, 1967a), 196-206.

———. "International pattern and nation profile delineation," in Davis. B. Bobrow and Judah L. Schwartz. *Computers and the Policy-Making Community: Applications to International Relations.* Englewood Cliffs, N.J.: Prentice-Hall, 1968, 154-202.

———. "Field theory and indicators of international behavior." Paper Presented to the Sixty-Fifth Annual Meeting of the American Political Science Association, New York, September 2-6, 1969. Also excerpted in Rummel (1977).

———. "Indicators of cross-national and international patterns." The American Political Science Review, Vol. 63 (March, 1969a), 127-147.

———. *Applied Factor Analysis.* Evanston, Ill.: Northwestern University Press, 1970.

———. *Dimensions of Nations.* Beverly Hills: Sage Publications, 1972.

———. "U.S. foreign relations: Conflict, cooperation, and attribute distances," in Bruce Russett. *Peace, War, and Numbers.* Beverly Hills: Sage, 1972a, 71-113. Also excerpted in Rummel (1977).

———. *Understanding Conflict and War,* Vols. 1-3. Beverly Hills: Sage Publications, 1975-1977.

–––. "The dimensionality of nations project," in Francis W. Hoole and Dina A. Zinnes, *Quantitative International Politics*. New York: Praeger, 1976, 149-154.

–––. *Peace Endangered: The Reality of Détente*. Beverly Hills: Sage Publications, 1976a.

–––. "Roots of faith," in James N. Rosenau (Ed.), *In Search of Global Patterns*. New York: The Free Press, 1976b, 10-30.

–––. "Will the Soviet Union Soon Have a First-Strike Capability?" Orbis, Vol. 20 (Fall, 1976c), 579-594.

–––. *Field Theory Evolving*. Beverly Hills: Sage Publications, 1977.

–––. "The statistical dynamics of the U.S./U.S.S.R. military balance." Paper Presented to the International Studies Association Convention, St. Louis, Missouri, March 16-20, 1977a.

–––. *National Attributes and Behavior*. Beverly Hills: Sage Publications, 1978.

–––. "A warning on Michael Haas's *International Conflict.*" The Journal of Conflict Resolution, Vol. 22 (March, 1978a), 157-162.

Russett, Bruce M. "The calculus of deterrence." The Journal of Conflict Resolution, Vol. 7 (June, 1963), 97-109.

–––. *International Regions and the International System*. Chicago: Rand McNally, 1967.

–––. "Delineating international regions," in J. David Singer (Ed.), *Quantitative International Politics: Insights and Evidence*. New York: Free Press, 1968, 317-352.

–––. "An empirical typology of international military alliances." Midwest Journal of Political Science. Vol. 15 (May, 1971), 262-289.

––– (Ed.). *Peace, War and Numbers*. Beverly Hills: Sage Publications, 1972.

–––. *Power and Community in World Politics*. San Francisco: W.H. Freeman and Co., 1974.

Russett, Bruce M. and R. Joseph Monsen. "Bureaucracy and polyarchy as predictors of performance: A cross-national examination." Comparative Political Studies, Vol. 8 (April, 1975), 5-31.

Salmore, Stephen A. and Charles Hermann. "The effect of size, development and accountability on foreign policy." Peace Research Society (International): Papers, Vol. 14 (1970), 15-30.

Salmore, Stephen A. and Donald Munton. "An empirically based typology of foreign policy behaviors," in James N. Rosenau (Ed.), *Comparing Foreign Policies: Theories, Findings, and Methods*. New York: Halsted Press, 1974, 329-352.

Salmore, Stephen A., Fred Butler, Barbara G. Salmore, and Scott Taylor. "The limits of factor analysis: Some findings and explanations." Presented to the Events Data Approaches Workshop on Foreign Policy Behavior, Convention of the Southern Political Science Association, New Orleans, Louisiana, November 7-9. 1974.

Salmore, Barbara and Stephen A. Salmore. "Regime constraints and foreign policy behavior." Paper presented to the annual meeting of the American Political Science Association, San Francisco, California, Sept. 2-6, 1975.

Sande, Oystein. "The perception of foreign news." Journal of Peace Research, 3-4 (1971), 221-237.

Schubert, James Neal. *The Functional Approach to Peace in Asia*. Ph.D. dissertation, Honolulu: University of Hawaii, 1975.

Schwartz, D.C. "Decision theories and crises behavior: An empirical study of nuclear deterrence in international political crises." Orbis 11, 1967, 459-490.

–––. "Decision-making in historical and simulated crises," in Charles F. Hermann (Ed.), *International Crises: Insights from Behavioral Research*. New York: The Free Press, 1972, 167-184.

Schwerin, Edward W. "U.S. foreign relations for 1963," in R.J. Rummel, *Field Theory Evolving*. Beverly Hills: Sage Publications, 1977, 301-314.

Seidelmann, Reimund. "Systemic Interaction and the Determination of National Factors which Condition it: A Model Critique of Rudolph J. Rummel's Studies Within The Framework of the Dimensionality of Nation's Project." *Politische Vierteljahresschrift,* Sanderheft 5/1973: Internationale Beziehungen als System.

Sigler, J.H. "Reliability Problems in the measurement of international events in the elite press," in J.H. Sigler, J.O. Field, and M.L. Adelman, "Applications of Events Data Analysis," *Sage Professional Papers,* Vol. 1, 02-002, Beverly Hills: Sage Publications, 1972, 9-29.

Sigler, John H., John O. Field, and Murray L. Adelman. "Applications of events data analysis: Cases, issues, and programs in international interaction." *Sage Professional Papers,* Vol. 1, 02-002, Beverly Hills: Sage Publications, 1972.

Simmel, George. *Conflict and the Web of Group-Affiliations.* (Translated by Kurt H. Wolff and Reinhard Bendix), Free Press: Glencoe, 1955.

Simon, Herbert A. *Models of Man.* New York: Wiley and Sons, 1957.

Singer, David and Michael Wallace. "Intergovernmental organizations and the preservation of peace, 1816-1964: Some bivariate relationships." International Organization, Vol. 24 (Summer, 1970), 520-547.

Singer, J. David and Melvin Small. "National alliance commitments and war involvement, 1815-1945." Peace Research Society (International): Papers, Vol. 5 (1966a), 109-140.

———. "Formal alliances, 1815-1939: A quantitative description" Journal of Peace Research, Vol. 3 (No. 1, 1966), 1-32.

———. "Alliance aggregation and the onset of war, 1815-1945," in J. David Singer (Ed.), *Quantitative International Politics: Insights and Evidence,* New York: The Free Press, 1968, 247-286.

———. *The Wages of War 1816-1965: A Statistical Handbook.* New York: John Wiley and Sons, 1972.

Singer, J. David, Stuart Bremer and John Stuckey. "Capability distributions, uncertainty, and major power war, 1820-1965." in Bruce Russett (Ed.), *Peace, War, and Numbers.* Beverly Hills: Sage Publications, 1972, 19-48.

Singer, J. David and Melvin Small. "War in history and in the state of the world message." Policy Sciences, Vol. 5 (1974), 271-296.

Siverson, R.M. "International conflict and perceptions of injury: The case of the Suez crises." International Studies Quarterly, Vol. 14 (1970), 157-165.

Small, Melvin and J. David Singer. "Patterns in international warfare, 1816-1965." The Annals of the American Academy of Political and Social Science, Vol. 391 (September, 1970), 145-155.

Smith, Raymond F. "On the structure of foreign news: A comparison of the New York Times and the Indian White Papers." Journal of Peace Research, No. 1 (1969), 23-36.

Smoker, Paul. "Trade, defense and the Richardson theory of arms races: A seven nation study." Journal of Peace Research, No. 2 (1965), 161-176.

———. "A Time-Series analysis of Sino-Indian relations." Journal of Conflict Resolution, Vol. 13 (June, 1969), 172-191.

Snyder, Glenn H. " 'Prisoner's dilemma' and 'chicken' models in international politics." *International Studies Quarterly,* Vol. 15 (March, 1971), 66-103.

Solzhenitsyn, Aleksandr I. *The Gulag Archipelago 1918-1956,* I-II, (Translated by Thomas P. Whitney), New York: Harper and Row, 1973-1975.

Sorokin, Pitirim. *Social Mobility.* New York: Harper, 1927.

———. *Social and Cultural Dynamics,* Vol. 1-4. Boston: Porter Sargent, 1937-1941.

———. *Social and Cultural Dynamics,* Revised and Abridged Edition. Boston: Porter Sargent, 1957.

———. *Sociological Theories of Today.* New York: Harper and Row, 1966.

Sprout, Harold and Margaret Sprout. *Foundations of International Politics.* Princeton, New Jersey: D. Van Nostrand Company, 1962.

–––. *The Ecological Perspective on Human Affairs with Special Reference to International Politics.* Princeton: Princeton University Press, 1965.

Starr, Harvey. *War Coalitions: The Distributions of Payoffs and Losses.* Lexington, Mass.: D.C. Heath and Co., 1972.

Starr, Harvey and Benjamin A. Most. "A Return Journey: Richardson, 'Frontiers' and Wars in the 1946-1965 Era." Reports and Research Studies, Bloomington, Indiana: Center for International Policy Studies, Indiana University, n.d.

Stohl, Michael. "War and domestic political violence: the case of the United States 1890-1970." Journal of Conflict Resolution, Vol. 19 (September, 1975), 379-416.

Strausz-Hupé, Robert and Stefen T. Possony. *International Relations in the Age of the Conflict Between Democracy and Dictatorships.* New York: McGraw-Hill, 1950.

Sullivan, John D. "Cooperating to conflict: Sources of informal alignments," Paper prepared for delivery at the Sixty-Sixth Annual Meeting of the American Political Science Association, Los Angeles, California, 1970.

–––. "Cooperating to conflict: Sources of informal alignments," in Bruce Russett (ed.), *Peace, War, and Numbers.* Beverly Hills: Sage Publications, 1972, 115-138.

Sullivan Michael P. "Levels of international violence: The empirical differentiation of conflict systems." Paper presented to the annual meeting of the Western Political Science Association, Sacramento, California, April 2-4, 1970.

–––. "Symbolic involvement as a correlate of escalation: The Vietnam case," in Bruce Russett (Ed.), *Peace, War, and Numbers.* Beverly Hills: Sage Publications, 1972, 185-212.

–––. *International Relations: Theories and Evidence.* Englewood Cliffs, N.J.: Prentice-Hall, 1976.

Swanson, Dean. *Degree of Specificity: Actor Expectations in Foreign Policy Behavior.* Ph.D. dissertation, Columbus, Ohio: The Ohio State University, 1976.

Sybinsky, Peter A. *Integration and Conflict: Theory, Application, and Test.* Ph.D. dissertation, Honolulu: University of Hawaii, 1975.

Tanter, Raymond. "Dimensions of conflict behavior within and between nations, 1958-1960." The Journal of Conflict Resolution, Vol. 10 (March, 1966), 41-64.

–––. *Modelling and Managing International Conflicts: The Berlin Crises.* Beverly Hills: Sage Publications, 1974.

Taylor, Charles Lewis and Michael C. Hudson. *World Handbook of Political and Social Indicators,* Second Edition. New Haven: Yale University Press, 1972.

Taylor, Robert Martin. *International Mail Flows: A Geographic Analysis Relating Volume of Mail to Certain Characteristics of Postal Countries.* Ph.D. dissertation, Seattle: University of Washington, 1956.

Terhune, Kenneth W. "From national character to national behavior: A reformulation." The Journal of Conflict Resolution, Vol. 14 (June, 1970), 203-263.

Terrell, Louis M. "Societal stress, political instability, and levels of military effort." The Journal of Conflict Resolution, Vol. 15 (September, 1971), 329-346.

Teune, Henry and Sig Sunnestvedt. "Measuring international alignment." Orbis, Vol. 9 (Spring, 1965), 171-189.

Triska, Jan F. and David D. Finley. *Soviet Foreign Policy.* New York: Macmillan, 1968.

Tung, R. Ko-Chih. "International structure, inter-and intra-state violence, a causal model analysis of change." Proceedings of the International Peace Research Association, Fifth Conference, Oslo, 1975, 229-257.

United States Naval Operations in Low Level Warfare. Final Report (BSR 2453) of Research Sponsored by the Office of Naval Research under Contract N00014-66-C0262, Ann Arbor, Michigan: Bendix Aerospace Systems Division, December, 1968.

"The Utilization of ARPA-Supported Research For International Security Planning." Interim Technical Report No. 2, Arlington, Virginia: Consolidated Analysis Center Inc., October, 1972.

Van Atta, Richard and Dale B. Robertson. "An analysis of Soviet foreign economic behavior from the perspective of social field theory." Paper presented at the annual meeting of the Midwest Political Science Association, Chicago, 1975.

———. "An appraisal of the substantive findings of the dimensionality of nations project," in Francis W. Hoole and Dina A. Zinnes, *Quantitative International Politics.* New York: Praeger, 1976, 196-218.

Van Atta, Richard and R.J. Rummel. "Testing field theory on the 1963 behavior of nations," in R.J. Rummel, *Field Theory Evolving.* Beverly Hills: Sage, 1972, 133-152.

Vasquez, John A. "Statistical Findings in international politics: A data-based assessment." Paper presented to the annual meeting of the American Political Science Association, San Francisco, California, September 2-5, 1975.

———. "Statistical findings in international politics: A data-based assessment." International Studies Quarterly, Vol. 20 (June, 1976), 171-218.

Väyrynen, Raimo. "Militarization, Conflict Behavior and Interaction. Three Ways of Analyzing the Cold War." Research Report, No. 3, Tampere, Finland: Tampere Peace Research Institute, 1973.

Vincent, Jack E. "National attributes as predictors of delegate attitudes at the United Nations." The American Political Science Review, Vol. 62 (September, 1968), 916-951.

———. "A Examination of Voting Patterns in the 23rd and 24th Sessions of the General Assembly." Research Report No. 54, Dimensionality of Nations Project, Honolulu: University of Hawaii, 1971a.

———. "Predicting voting patterns in the General Assembly." American Political Science Review, Vol. 65 (June, 1971b), 471-498.

———. "Testing Some Hypotheses About Delegate Attitudes at the United Nations and Some Implications for Theory Building." Research Report No. 52, Dimensionality of Nations Project, Honolulu: University of Hawaii, April, 1971c.

———. "Distance theory: A comparison of various regional groupings in 1966-69 conflict data." Unpublished research monograph, 1976a.

———. "Explorations in D-space: An application of deviance theory." Comparative Political Studies, Vol. 9 (April, 1976B), 107-135.

———. "Analyzing U.S.-U.S.S.R. support patterns in the general assembly." *Attributes and National Behavior: Part I.* Unpublished Research Monograph, 1977a.

———. "Comparing of various regional groupings in 1966-69 conflict data, using distance theory." *Attributes and National Behavior: Research Monograph No. 6.* Unpublished Research Monograph, 1977b.

———. "Distance theory: An inventory of significant findings for conflict." *Attributes and National Behavior: Research Monograph No. 27.* Unpublished Research Monograph, 1977c.

———. "Project theory: An overview and selected results." Paper delivered to the Canadian School of Peace Research, Carleton University, Ottawa, August, 1977d.

———. "Project theory: An inventory of results for conflict and cooperation, 1966-69." paper, 1977e.

———. "Testing new attribute-based models of international conflict and cooperation on selected dimensions." paper, 1977f.

References   [435]

Vincent, Jack E., Roger Baker, Susan Gagnon, Keith Hamm, and Scott Reilly. "Empirical tests of attribute, social field, and status field theories on international relations data." International Studies Quarterly, Vol. 17 (December, 1973), 405-443.

Voevodsky, John. "Quantitative behavior of warring nations." Journal of Psychology, Vol. 72 (1969), 269-292.

Wall, Charles and R.J. Rummel. "Estimating Missing Data." Research Report No. 20, Dimensionality of Nations Project, Honolulu: University of Hawaii, 1969.

Wallace, Michael D. "Status, formal organization, and arms levels as factors leading to the onset of war, 1820-1964." Paper prepared for delivery at the annual meetings of the American Political Science Association, Los Angeles, September, 1970.

–––. "Power, status, and international war." Journal of Peace Research, 1 (1971), 23-35.

–––. "Status, formal organization, and arms levels as factors leading to the onset of war, 1820-1964," in Bruce Russett (Ed.), Peace, War, and Numbers. Beverly Hills: Sage Publications, 1972, 49-69.

–––. "Alliance polarization, cross-cutting, and international war, 1815-1964: A measurement procedure and some preliminary evidence." The Journal of Conflict Resolution, Vol. 17 (December, 1973), 575-604.

–––. "Clusters of nations in the global system, 1865-1964: Some preliminary evidence." International Studies Quarterly, Vol. 19 (March, 1975), 67-110.

Wallensteen, Peter. "Characteristics of economic sanctions," Journal of Peace Research, 3 (1968), 248-267.

–––. Structure and War: An International Relations 1920-1968. Stockholm: Roben and Sjogren, 1973.

Waltz, Kenneth N. Man, the State and War: A Theoretical Analysis. New York: Columbia University Press, 1959.

Weede, Erich. "Research communication: Conflict behavior of nation-states." Journal of Peace Research, 3 (1970), 229-235.

–––. "World order in the fifties and sixties: Dependence, deterrence, and limited peace." The Papers of the Peace Science Society (International), Vol. 24 (1975), 49-80.

–––. "National position in world politics and military allocation ratios in the 1950's and 1960's." The Jerusalem Journal of International Relations, Vol. 2 (Spring, 1977a), 63-80.

–––. "Threats to Détente: Intuitive hopes and counterintuitive realities." European Journal of Political Research, Vol. 5 (1977b), 407-432.

Weil, Herman. "Forecasting conflict: A multimodel-multimethod approach." Paper presented to the annual meeting of the International Studies Association, Washington, D.C., February 18-23, 1975.

Weiss, Herbert K. "The ending of war considered as a markoff process." Proceedings of the Military Operations Research Symposium, Vol. I (Fall, 1961), 57-69.

–––. "Stochastic models for the duration and magnitude of a 'deadly Quarrel'." Operation Research, Vol. 11 (January-February, 1963), 101-21.

Weis, Thomas G. "The tradition of philosophical anarchism and future directions in world policy." Journal of Peace Research, Vol. 12 (No. 1, 1975), 1-17.

Wesley, James Paul. "Frequency of war and geographical opportunity." in Dean G. Pruitt and Richard C. Snyder (Eds.), Theory and Research on the Causes of War. Englewood Cliffs, N.J.: Prentice-Hall, 1969, 229-231.

White, David M. "The 'gate keeper': A case study in the selection of news." Journalism Quarterly, Vol. 27 (1950), 383-390.

Wilkenfeld, Jonathan. "Models for the analysis of foreign conflict behavior of states." in

Bruce Russett (Ed.), *Peace, War, and Numbers.* Beverly Hills: Sage Publications, 1972, 275-298.

———. "Domestic and foreign conflict." in Jonathan Wilkenfeld (Ed.), *Conflict Behavior and Linkage Politics.* New York: David McKay Co., 1973, 107-123.

Wilkenfeld, Jonathan, Gerald W. Hopple, and Paul J. Rossa. "Action-reaction, societal, and economic explanations: Testing a partial model of interstate behavior." Paper prepared for delivery at the annual meeting of the International Studies Association, St. Louis, March 1977.

Wilkenfeld, Jonathan, Virginia Lee Lussier, and Dale Tahtinen. "Conflict interactions in the Middle East, 1949-1967." Journal of Conflict Resolution, Vol. 16 (June, 1972), 135-154.

Wilkenfeld, Jonathan and Dina A. Zinnes. "A linkage model of domestic conflict behavior," in Jonathan Wilkenfeld (Ed.), *Conflict Behavior and Linkage Politics.* New York: David McKay Company, 1973, 325-356.

Wittkopf, Eugene. "Containment versus underdevelopment in the distribution of United States foreign aid: An introduction to the use of cross-national aggregate data analysis in the study of foreign policy," in William D. Coplin and Charles W. Kegley, Jr., (Eds.) *A Multi-Method Introduction to International Politics: Observations, Explanation, and Prescription.* Chicago: Markham Publishing Company, 1971, 174-188.

Wright, Quincy. *A Study of War,* Vol. 1-2 Chicago: University of Chicago Press, 1942.

———. *The Study of International Relations.* New York: Appleton-Century-Crofts, 1955.

———. *A Study of War,* Abridged Edition. Chicago: University of Chicago Press, 1964.

———. *A Study of War,* Second Edition With a Commentary on War Since 1942. Chicago: University of Chicago Press, 1965a.

———. "The escalation of international conflict." The Journal of Conflict Resolution, Vol. 9 (December, 1965), 434-449.

Wynn, Mark. "The Event Data Approach to Political Research." Arlington, Virginia: Consolidated Analysis Centers, Inc., March, 1973.

Yee, Herbert. "Decisions to establish diplomatic relations with China: A cross-national analysis." Paper presented to the annual meeting of the International Studies Association, St. Louis, March 16-20, 1977.

Zinnes, Dina A. "An analytical study of the balance of power theories," in Clagett G. Smith (Ed.), *Conflict Resolution: Contributions of the Behavioral Sciences.* Notre Dame: University of Notre Dame Press, 1971, 364-379.

Zinnes, Dina A. "Some evidence relevant to the man-milieu hypothesis," in James N. Rosenau, Vincent Davis, and Maurice A. East (Eds.), *The Analysis of International Politics.* New York: Free Press, 1972, 209-251.

Zinnes, Dina A. *Contemporary Research in International Relations: A Perspective and a Critical Appraisal.* New York: Free Press, 1976.

Zinnes, Dina A., Joseph L. Zinnes, and Robert D. McClure. "Hostility in diplomatic communications: A study of the 1914 crises," in Charles F. Hermann (Ed.), *International Crises: Insights from Behavioral Research.* New York: Free Press, 1972, 139-162.

NAME INDEX

Abravanel, M. 269
Adler, A. 14
Ahmavaara, Y. 14
Alger, C. 66
Allison, G. 65
Andriole, S. 390
Angell, R. 51
Aron, R. 20, 43, 51, 129
Azar, E. 205, 236-7, 339, 391-3
Babst, D. 279
Banks, A. 391
Barker, E. 53
Barringer, R. 30, 201, 205-6, 283-4, 288, 291, 324, 325
Beer, F. 34
Bentham, J. 66
Berle, A. 56, 64
Bierce, A. 353
Blainey, G. 268, 275, 276
Blechman, B. 391
Bloomfield, L. 205
Bockelman, B. 378, 382
Boulding, K. 21, 119
Brady, L. 293, 391
Brecht, A. 49
Bruel, H. 112
Buchanan, W. 221, 269
Bullough, V. 304
Bunge, M. 261
Burgess, P. 119, 391, 393
Burrowes, R. 228, 391-2
Burton, J. 55, 64, 87, 95, 119
Butterfield, H. 52
Bwy, D. 391

Cantril, H. 221, 269
Carr, E. 64
Carroll, B. 187, 206
Cattell, R. 14, 110, 112, 118
Chan, S. 393
Choi, C. 54, 86, 137, 391

Churchill, C. 69
Churchill, W. 175
Clausewitz, K. 181
Coleman, J. 21
Collins, J. 391
Conquest, R. 51
Copson, R. 391
Coser, L. 49, 187

Dahl, K. 85
Dahrendorf, R. 14
Denton, F. 53, 288, 347
Dewey, E. 348
Donelan, M. 30, 46, 48, 201, 205-6, 282-3, 291
Durant, W. 14

Etzioni

Feieraband, I. 391
Feieraband, R. 391
Ferguson, Y. 66
Field, J. 205
Fitzsimmons, B. 205, 228

Galtung, J. 51
Gamson, W. 392-3
Garriga-Pico, J. 228, 391
Gilbert, W. 159
Goodsell, R. 205
Gough, J. 53
Grieve, M. 205
Gross, F. 109
Gurr, T. 391

Haas, M. 290, 304, 315
Haendel, D. 391
Hainline, M. 223, 226, 234-6, 293, 305, 390
Hall, D. 50, 173, 221, 226, 235, 380, 390
Halle, L. 187
Hannah, H. 187, 319

SUBJECT INDEX

accommodations, 30, 184-5, 191, 218; component of, 230; propositions of, 229-234
actions, 71-3, 75, 83n6, 91-2
acts, 71-73, 75, 83n6, 91-2, 121, 130
aggression, 44, 133n5
alignment, 155n18, 173n5; component of, 79, 86n29, 140
alliances. See alignment
Angola, 65n13
antagonistic behavior, 73, 81-3
antifield, 57-8, 60, 63n3, 65n15, 134n9
antiforeign behavior, 79, 235; component of, 140, 218-9, 234-5
approach, 211-2
Armaments 173n5, 239n7. See also preparations; warning and defensive actions.
attitude, 27, 63n2, 115, 117, 121, 130, 160, 162-4, 164n2
attributes, 129, 382-5; components of, 384; data on, 389; proposition on, 389
authoritarian; component of, 114-115; political system, 114-5, 130-1, 137, 247, 250, 250, 292; state, 60, 146-154, 277-8
authoritarian society, 373; proposition of 359-60
awards, 184
awareness, 162-3, 164n3, 193, 247, 251, 270-1

balance of powers, 40-1, 49n7, 55, 64n5, 78-9, 85n21, 157, 185, 201, 217, 255-6, 267, 361, 374-5; change in, 247-8, 252; propositions of, 268-70, 321-3
balancing of powers, 29, 30, 78, 130, 159, 189, 191, 218, 227, 246; principle of, 371; propositions of 229-35
behavior 97; common, 27, 91, 123; flows, 389; meaning of, 71-3; principle of, 370; social 71, 83n1; space, 71; structures, 389; theoretical components of, 26, 73-4. See also actions; act; antagonistic;

compulsory; contractual; familistic; international; moral; practices; reflexes; situation; solidary
behavioral components, 26, 75-80; measurement of, 96n9
behavioral dispositions, 87-9, 99-100, 117, 123, 129, 169; common 27, 91; and expectations, 89-94; and situation, 100-101. See also contractual; dispositions
behavioral equation, 90-4, 123-7; proposition of, 359
behavioral space-time, 91, 103, 105n7, 135; measurement of, 95-6n9
behavioralism, 18-19
bias, 210, 312-5, 392-3. See also events
Big Powers, 131-2, 145-7; intervention of, 248, 253; proposition of, 284
bureaucracy, 84n7

Cambodia, 52n22
canonical analysis, 135-7; model of, 154n1
capability, 27, 55, 63n4, 115, 117-8, 130, 159-60, 163-4, 165n10, 169, 184, 255, 283, 318, 371-2; change in, 269; component of, 110; empirical, 131-2, 141-54; equation of, 121-3; proposition of, 321-3. See also balance of powers.
case, 213
casualties; proposition of, 325-6
Catholic culture, 140; component of, 114
cause, 122; principle of, 371. See also conditions; conflict behavior; termination; violence; war.
change, 129, 133n2, 159, 319, 372; and conflict helix, 331-3; propositions of, 268-70, 324-5, 347-8, 359-60, 362. See also balance of powers; dynamics.
China, 44, 52n23, 54n33, 86n35, 87-9, 117, 137, 144-54, 226, 235, 385-6
choice. See intentions.